Handbook of
Strategic Planning

HANDBOOK OF STRATEGIC PLANNING

JAMES R. GARDNER
ROBERT RACHLIN
H. W. ALLEN SWEENY

Editors

A WILEY-INTERSCIENCE PUBLICATION

JOHN WILEY & SONS

New York . Chichester . Brisbane . Toronto . Singapore

90566

Preface

Corporate strategic planning groups in a number of major multinational corporations have recently "felt the axe." Reductions in staffing range from extensive to total. The shock value of these events is increased by the fact that some occurred in corporations long seen as being at the "cutting edge" of strategic planning—General Electric and International Paper, for instance. Rumors of the death of strategic planning may be inaccurate and exaggerated, but it cannot be denied that a fundamental transformation is under way: a new era in managing strategic planning.

Rapidly disappearing is the highly centralized "ivory tower" approach to corporate strategic planning. A clear disillusionment has set in with highly analytical models and matrices, tools that were embraced during the 1970s with an almost evangelical fervor. Also eroding is a prior preoccupation with highly elaborate (and, in practice, often irrelevant) planning systems and techniques.

On the upsurge is a "back to basics" emphasis on "lean and mean" corporate planning, closely linked to and supportive of key decision makers. Under the banner of "decentralization," strategic planning is being increasingly touted as a responsibility of line management at all levels, not just the domain of "corporate intellectuals."

Concern seems to be shifting from methods for "number crunching" to the quality of fundamental business insights and the effectiveness with which plans are executed. The objective is not just planning strategically but managing strategically, characterized by an integration of planning activities between levels and functions. The sought-after result is a capability to "create the future"—not just anticipate or respond to it.

This book addresses current needs and has been developed in response to this "back to basics" phenomenon. As such, it is distinctively different from other ostensibly similar "handbooks." This is *not* a collection of consultant-generated reports, taken off the shelf and bound together. Nor is it an assemblage of academic papers, each striving to be more arcane than the others. Instead, it is a hands-on handbook for action-oriented "thinkers and doers," written by those who have done both with success, recognized leaders in their respective areas of expertise. Thirty-three authors share their practical experiences and present the latest thinking on the subject of strategic planning.

Included are twenty-six chapters, arranged into five parts.

The *Introduction* outlines the evolution of "strategic management" and the changing nature of the planning process, highlighting where it has been and where it is going.

Planning discusses key components of "thinking strategically," such as organizing, the role of consultants, assessing the competition, portfolio analysis, formulating strategies and contingency plans, and "a view from Japan."

Implementation reviews critical aspects of "implementing strategically," that is, making plans work through administering, controlling, and implementing reward systems, while avoiding strategic failure.

Functional Plans provides detailed "how to do it" coverage of planning in various functions, including acquisitions and divestitures, marketing, manufacturing, research and development, human resources, public affairs, and venture capital.

Special Cases describes the application of strategic planning in special situations and environments—high technology, international, voluntary, small business, the military, and others.

The book's format is as deliberately pragmatic as are the contents. Each chapter is written to "stand on its own," allowing the reader to probe specific topics in detail, if so desired. Alternatively, the book can be read either by section or fully, in chapter sequence. A comprehensive index is provided and extensive use is made of charts and diagrams for easy-to-follow concepts and approaches to a multifaceted subject. This is a most comprehensive and practical work on the subject of strategic planning.

In creating a comprehensive and useful handbook, the indispensable contributions are those of the chapter authors, whose time, effort, and knowledge constitute the basis for this book. Without their willingness to share both time and thoughts, this project would have remained only an idea. To them, we extend our deepest appreciation.

Sincere thanks are also due Michael J. Hamilton, our editor at John Wiley & Sons, for his guidance and forbearance, and to the Wiley production staff. Finally, very special thanks to Ines Botero H., whose dedication and administrative assistance were vital in keeping our "team" coordinated and moving ahead.

JAMES R. GARDNER
ROBERT RACHLIN
H.W. ALLEN SWEENEY

New York, New York
Plainview, New York
New York, New York
January 1986

Contents

1

INTRODUCTION

CHAPTER *1*

Strategic Management: An Overview

FREDERICK W. GLUCK

FREDERICK W. GLUCK is a director for McKinsey & Company. He is a member of the Executive Committee, Directors Committee, and Shareholders Committee. He also chairs the Practice Committee, which is responsible for the company's research and development in management approaches and techniques and the continuing development of the consulting process. Mr. Gluck has served a wide variety of clients in such industries as telecommunications, glass, electronics, railroads, electrical machinery, broadcasting, and international trade. Before joining McKinsey & Company, he spent 10 years with Bell Telephone Laboratories, working in the areas of program management, systems analysis, and engineering and hardware design. He was also program manager for the Spartan anti-missile program. Mr. Gluck holds a bachelors degree in electrical engineering from Manhattan College and a masters degree in electrical engineering from New York University. He has also completed graduate studies in operations research at Columbia University. Mr. Gluck speaks frequently on the subject of strategic management and has published articles on managing technological change in *Harvard Business Review* and *Research Management* as well as articles on strategic planning/strategic management in *Harvard Business Review*.

The author gratefully acknowledges the invaluable assistance of Ellen Nenner in the research for and preparation of this chapter.

OUTLINE

Not long ago, I sat listening to a senior executive of a ten-billion-dollar corporation describe what he believed it took to bring about significant change in a rapidly evolving industry. He based his comments on his own recent experience in pulling off a major strategic redirection in one of the corporation's core businesses—with very impressive results.

His objective for the business was clear: market leadership. His strategy was simple and direct: manage the business's products and markets in a focused, customer-oriented, profit-conscious way. As he went on to describe the specifics of his strategy, he punctuated his remarks with two recurrent themes. First, change must be looked at as an opportunity to find new ways to beat your competition. Second, it is important to be flexible enough to execute fast and get to the market early; otherwise you risk losing the opportunity to gain competitive superiority. He spoke about innovative product design, market-focused distribution systems, and building internal commitment by explaining the strategy and "marketing the hell out of early strategic successes." "To ensure implementation," he said, "make sure the line managers are deeply involved in tactical planning." Above all, the CEO must lead the change effort; he has to be the strategic planner. Asked what he considered to be the key to the successful management of change, the speaker replied, "Well-thought-out strategies, bold implementation actions, and management drive."

Why does this incident stick in my mind? For one thing, it was an exciting case study of a manager turning a loser into a winner. What really engaged me, however, was the setting for all this. It was not, as you might imagine, the bloodied fields of Silicon Valley. Rather, the setting was the retail business of a large regional bank holding company.

These remarks really drove home the fact that you don't have to be a high-tech company to be vulnerable to rapidly changing technology, unexpected competition, and saturated markets. And—given the major environmental disruptions that many industries are facing—planning that relies on past experience, extrapolation, and incremental moves to meet such challenges is the riskiest path of all. His words made it clearer than ever that corporate America's love affair with 1970s-style strategic planning was certainly on the rocks if not over.

There are many signs that planning as it developed and prospered in the 1960s and 1970s is in trouble. General Electric (GE), the pioneer in the introduction of strategic planning in the 1960s and the classic model of the strategically managed company in the 1970s, has recently cut its corporate planning staff from 58 to 33 and has cut the size of planning staffs throughout the company substantially.[1] Dozens of other companies have made similar cuts. Much of planning theory is being attacked as well. Methodologies once held in esteem are now being challenged and even ridiculed.

Planning—and planners—are being squeezed by several forces. *Business Week's* recent cover story "The New Breed of Strategic Planner" reports: "In a fundamental shift of corporate power line managers in one company after another are successfully challenging the hordes of professional planners and are forcing them from positions of influence."[2]

Commenting on the growing obsolescence of middle management, a recent *Fortune* article argues that "computerized systems lessen the need for information gathering, a principal task of corporate bureaucrats."[3] More important, hopscotching the middle manager is a reflection of "the new corporate fashion [which] calls for fewer levels of authority, with each manager controlling more people, and for participative management, with decisions pushed to lower levels of the company, and out into the field."[4]

Finally, a recent study of the planning function in a cross section of American corporations indicates that "CEOs are reassuming their leadership responsibility . . . as the originators or focal points of the corporate strategic planning process. The CEOs interviewed believe future economic success will depend to a large extent . . . on a stronger, more proactive planning role for the CEO—one of chief strategic thinker and corporate culture leader, rather than simply the apex of a multi-layered organizational structure."[5]

What does all this restructuring and role changing mean? Is it a passing fad—part of the antirational, antianalytical thinking now in vogue—or is it in fact a new era for management? I would suggest that these changes are here to stay and that they indicate that chief executives are taking the steps necessary to make their planning more relevant and more effective.

ENVIRONMENTAL CHANGE AND MANAGEMENT RESPONSE

Consider the disruptions that we have seen over the last decade or so: slower growth, intense global competition, burgeoning automation, obsolescence caused by technological change, deregulation, an explosion in information availability, rapid shifts in raw material prices, chaotic money markets, and major changes in macroeconomic and sociopolitical systems. The impact of these discontinuities on industry after industry runs broad and deep (Exhibit 1-1). Destabilization and fluidity have become the norm in world business.

As a result, there are many more strategic alternatives for all types of industries. From switching device and check cashing technologies to food

EXHIBIT 1-1 *Discontinuities Impact Broad and Deep*

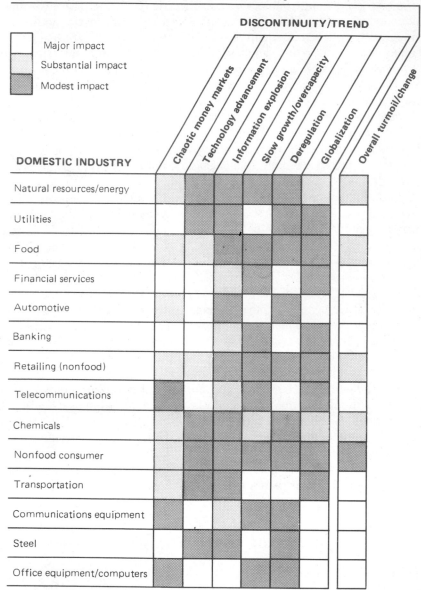

Source: McKinsey analysis.

and service outlet and steel mill configurations, people are constantly coming up with new ways of making products and getting them to market. Those comfortable oligopolies and monopolies—in banking, telecommunications, airlines, and automobiles, to name a few—are disappearing. Barriers to entry are much more difficult to maintain. Markets are open, and new competitors are coming from unexpected directions. Small enterprises are overcoming barriers through automation and new technology or by unique sourcing or partnering arrangements. Hardware businesses are becoming software or systems businesses. Big companies are crossing industry lines with new products and processes. Competitors seem to come from everywhere, including across the oceans, and, as Third World skills improve, this trend is likely to accelerate. Competition, in consequence, is not only palpably more intense but unpredictable.

In almost every industry, many corporations that were dominant in the 1960s ran into trouble in the 1970s and are scrambling in the 1980s. Fifteen or twenty years ago, the CEOs of these companies spent most of their time operating their businesses and planning for growth. Change was the enemy. "No surprises" was the watchword. Strategic planners had two main tasks: analysis and implementation, which boiled down to capital allocation. Resources were distributed and businesses bought and sold on the basis of financial analysis and creative accounting. If the analysis was right, the correct strategy would pop out automatically.

In contrast, the companies that capitalized on the discontinuities of the 1970s viewed the world differently. The CEOs of these companies saw instability as an opportunity, not a threat. New ideas, new technologies, new ways to meet customer needs, new distribution and sourcing strategies, and new modes of motivation were the ingredients of their competitive success. They accelerated change in their industries much faster than the more traditional companies would have done. And, to a large extent, much of the planning of these companies was inextricably entwined with execution. They were devotees of the "do it, try it, fix it" approach.

Their success proved that analyzing and allocating isn't enough when things are changing fast. The effective planner in today's world cannot simply answer the question of *what* to do, leaving the *how* to the line manager. He or she must be able to work closely with line management, synthesizing new ways to compete and building the organization's capability and confidence to see them implemented. The manager of strategic planning for GE's Aerospace Business Group provides a case in point. Commenting that the time he spends "pestering divisions and departments for information ordered by corporate and sector offices has dropped about 90%," Keller goes on to explain that "people mired in their markets are asking us how we can bring a broader perspective to them in assessing their new opportunities. . . . For example, [we are] helping managers of GE's simulation and training business assess a possible move into the graphics market."[6]

Most corporations recognize the need for change—at least intellectually. We hear plenty of rhetoric about the need for innovation, vision, and leadership. But, too often, real response has been inadequate. Very few of our largest and most successful corporations are able to rethink the way they do business—to renew themselves—when the fundamental nature of competition in their industries changes or new market opportunities open up.

The New York Times, writing on the current spate of American entrepreneurial activity, describes it as "second only to the period. . .when the

United States shifted from an agrarian to an industrial society.'' This was the era of the entrepreneurial giants: Rockefeller, Ford, Carnegie. ''Between the two world wars,'' the article continues, ''entrepreneurial activities shifted to large corporations—DuPont, Westinghouse, RCA and General Electric— which provided an umbrella for the development of such dazzling innovations as radio, television and nylon.''[7]

Today, however, many, if not most, large corporations are so mired in bureaucratic red tape and often unconscious prejudices about how things ought to be done that they find it almost impossible to induce the kind of entrepreneurial spirit required to develop the new businesses and products they need for self-renewal. Furthermore, the changes that so many of our large corporations need in order to compete successfully are threatening and potentially disruptive. Few like to contemplate them except as a last resort, and often that's simply too late.

Compounding these problems is the fact that many companies misread the nature of the challenges confronting them. They don't look at their situation and the kind of change required in the proper context. Often this is because those in a position to make things happen—the general managers— aren't getting the raw information they need, or top management is simply not investing the time to grapple with the implications of how their customers, competitors, markets, and technologies are changing. The result may be a response that is inadequate or inappropriate.

Take the steel companies, for example. They failed to see the need for reinvestment in more modern equipment until late in the day, keeping inefficient, outdated capacity open too long. They didn't recognize the threat of European and Japanese imports until response was difficult, and they failed to anticipate the impact of minimills. Granted, the U.S. steel industry has come a long way up since its reckoning with these problems at the end of the 1970s. But this is a classic case of ''too little, too late.'' What these companies needed was a fundamental change in the way they both thought about and conducted their business, not adaptation after the fact.

What does all this mean for top management? In simple but realistic terms, it means that business success in the 1980s and 1990s requires a new kind of management thinking and behavior. Management by remoteness, management by the numbers, and management by exception are dead. Management by involvement is in. Commenting on the kind of management style that breeds top performers, *Business Week* wrote recently of the ''passion for competitive excellence'' and the ''fire that makes things happen at companies such as the new-style GE under John F. Welch, Jr., and at IBM under John R. Opel.''[8]

Many top managers either haven't quite realized that a new type of management is now called for or are immobilized by the frightening implications of that fact. The truth is, if our major corporations are to develop the flexibility to compete, they are going to have to make some major changes in the way they go about planning and managing, both at the top and in their operating units.

To start with, top management will have to assume a more explicit strategic decision-making role, dedicating a large amount of time to deciding how things ought to be instead of listening to analyses of how they are. Second, the nature of planning must undergo a fundamental change from an exercise in forecasting to an exercise in creativity. Third, planning processes and tools that assume a future much like the past must be replaced by a mind-set that is obsessed with being first to recognize change and turn it into competitive advantage. Fourth, the role of the planner must change from that of a purveyor of incrementalism to that of a crusader for action and an alter ego to line management. And, finally, strategic planning must be restored to the core of line management responsibilities.

STRATEGIC PLANNING IN THE SEVENTIES

Perhaps if we look more closely at strategic planning in the 1970s, it will become clear why I believe that management that relies on 1970s-style planning to win in the 1980s and 1990s is doomed to failure. This planning style is by and large retrospective in nature. When things are stable, experience is an acceptable basis for decision making and action. But we are in a period of dramatic change. The extent and duration of competitive advantage depend on the vagaries of a constantly shifting economic order. Companies that continue to rely on the past as the best guide to the future get caught in the experience trap—they become rigid in their thinking, set in their ways, and lose the flexibility that is crucial to turning change into opportunity or even effectively responding to it. Reliance on experience becomes the ultimate handicap in an environment that is turning that very experience topsy-turvy.

The three key planning concepts in the 1970s were the experience curve, the strategic business unit, and portfolio planning.

The Experience Curve

The experience curve was a derivative of the learning curve theory that arose from the observations of the commander of Wright-Patterson Air Force Base in Dayton, Ohio, in 1925. He observed that production worker hours for airplanes appeared to decline as cumulative production volume increased. In the mid-1960s, Bruce Henderson and The Boston Consulting Group (BCG), which he founded, renamed the learning curve the "experience curve" and elaborated on the curve's relationship to market share and competitive dynamics.

Simply stated, experience curve theory is the hypothesis that the relative costs of two competitors are a function of their relative accumulated production volumes. It follows, then, that a market-share leader would enjoy an inherent cost advantage over smaller competitors—an advantage it could exploit by setting industry price levels to provide itself, but not its higher-cost competitors, with a satisfactory return on investment. Faced with either accepting an inadequate return or losing market share, the competitors would eventually withdraw from the market.[9]

The de facto message of this theory was that management's strategic objective was to make the company the market leader by gaining market share early in a product's life and holding it. However, as Walter Kiechel observed in a *Fortune* article, "The Decline of the Experience Curve," the real world did not prove to be so simple. "[If the company was already a significant player in the market,] probably the easiest first step was to cut price in the hope of gaining share. The not infrequent result . . . was a kick-'em, pound-'em, wrestle-'em to the ground price war [with no real winners]."[10]

Then again, the market-share-based strategies that were inherent in the experience curve concept ignored some very fundamental facts. For example, William K. Hall in a *Harvard Business Review* article, "Survival Strategies in a Hostile Environment," provides several examples of companies in mature industries that have enjoyed high profitability in spite of low market share. Hall writes: "High market share and accumulated experience are not essential for cost leadership in a mature market, as indicated by proponents of the experience curve. . . . Four of the eight low-cost producers in this study— Inland Steel, Whirlpool, Miller and Philip Morris—have achieved their lowest cost positions without the benefit of high relative market shares."[11]

Another major difficulty is that experience curves don't just happen; cost decreases have to be "managed." As Kiechel comments in his article, "getting Amalgamated Widget's costs to proceed down the curve was no easy matter. . . . It required constant managerial attention—meeting productivity goals, pushing new technology, pruning superfluities."[12] The concept also presented mammoth problems when it came to shared experience: just how does one go about breaking out and allocating costs shared by different product lines?

Although the experience curve concept was successful in getting management to focus on costs and relative competitive position, which was all to the good, its usefulness has proved limited. For one thing, it is most appropriately applied when products are sold on the basis of price alone, which reflects a rather narrow industry band. Furthermore, the curve is most valid in high-growth eras when there's a good chance the market will eat up all you can produce and economies of scale constitute a real, sustainable competitive advantage.

Alan Zakon, who now heads BCG, concedes that the experience curve slipped into disfavor when the world changed from a high-growth, "big is beautiful" situation to a low-growth, "big bust" situation.[13] And that's exactly the point I want to get across. In today's business environment, competitive advantages that rely too heavily on economies of scale—in manufacturing or distribution—may no longer be sustainable.

Moreover, competitive advantage cannot be achieved by attempting to defend a *static* technological position. The status quo is under continual stress from the forces of change. What leads to competitive success is *dynamic,* or continual, technological leadership—the ongoing ability to design, manufacture, sell, and service any product better than the competition. Competitive advantage in the 1980s and 1990s will have to be continually earned and renewed as change becomes the norm. Top management will have to ensure that the organizational flexibility to develop new, critical skills is an ever-present corporate characteristic.

The Strategic Business Unit

The notion behind the strategic business unit (SBU) concept, which Mc-Kinsey & Company developed in its work with GE in the late 1960s, was that a company's activities in the marketplace ought to be understood and segmented "strategically" so that key resources could then be best allocated for competitive advantage. That is, a company ought to be able to answer three questions: What business am I in? Who's my competition? What's my position relative to that competition? Getting the "right" answer to the first question was the hard part; once you got that, it was a lot easier to establish who your competition was and how you stacked up against it.

To be designated an SBU, businesses had to meet specific criteria. They had to:

Have a unique business mission, independent of other SBUs

Have a clearly definable set of competitors

Compete in external markets

Be able to carry out integrative planning relatively independent of other SBUs

Be able to manage resources in key areas

Be large enough to justify senior management attention and small enough to serve as a useful focus for resource allocation

In simplest terms, an SBU had to look and act like a freestanding business.

The great strength of the SBU concept lay in its focus on a management style that stressed the strategic position of businesses and the selective allocation of key resources for competitive advantage. It sought to do this through deep understanding of each of the company's businesses and the placement of these businesses into the most relevant "strategic" units for purposes of top-down objective setting, strategy review, and resource allocation.

In actual practice, however, SBU definition was enormously difficult, particularly in complex organizations that shared such crucial resources as R & D or sales.[14] There was (and still is) no simple, definitive methodology for isolating SBUs. Although the criteria for designating SBUs are clear-cut, the selection is highly judgmental and problematic. For example, in certain situations, real advantages could accrue from businesses sharing resources at the R & D, manufacturing, or distribution level. If autonomy and accountability are being pursued as ends in themselves, these advantages may be overlooked or unnecessarily sacrificed. To complicate matters further, if management designated SBUs around each product/market segment in order to develop a highly focused strategy, the resulting number of SBUs would likely be unmanageable from the corporate perspective. If, on the other hand, SBU designation were restricted to a manageable number, it would be difficult to arrive at a strategic mission appropriate to all the businesses that then made up any one SBU.

Portfolio Planning

The logical extension of the SBU concept was its implementation as the basis of the corporate planning process known as portfolio planning. A variety of portfolio planning matrices were developed in the late 1960s and 1970s to help evaluate the strategic position of a company's individual businesses. All were based on the very plausible postulate that if top management understood the relative attractiveness of the markets the company was in and its competitive strength in each of them, it would have a sound basis for making decisions on where to invest its resources.

Regardless of which portfolio matrix was used, the process of portfolio planning was the same. The firm's businesses (or products) were divided into SBUs, which were then evaluated on a grid or matrix that essentially measured the strength of the SBU relative to its competitors and the prospects for growth in the market for that product (or business). Once that evaluation was made, an appropriate "strategic mission" was assigned to each SBU and strategies developed to achieve it. These strategic plans were, in turn, reviewed by corporate management to ensure that they accurately reflected both the strategic mission assigned and the appropriate balance of cash and resource flows.

The major difference among the various portfolio matrices was the approach taken to determine market attractiveness and competitive position. McKinsey took the position that the factors determining market attractiveness and competitive position varied by market and so had to be factually developed for each market. The resulting multicriteria, nine-box matrix was criticized by some as overly complicated and cheered by others as realistic and practical (Exhibit 1-2).

Another version was the 2 × 2 growth/share portfolio matrix developed by BCG. This matrix was based on BCG's assumption that two factors— growth and relative share—outweighed all others and that a company's success depended on a portfolio of businesses or products representing mixed growth rates and market share. Fundamental to the growth/share concept was BCG's experience curve–based contention that margins were a function of market share; that is, high market share produced high margins.

Another matrix, developed by Arthur D. Little, focused on market position

EXHIBIT 1-2   McKinsey's Nine-Box Matrix

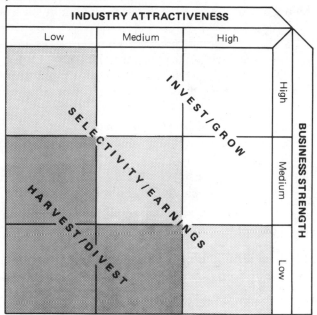

Factors affecting industry attractiveness and business strength
Market size (domestic/global)
  Market growth (domestic/global)
    Price trend
      Captive market
        Cyclicality
          SOM change/new entry
            Concentration
              Competitive characteristics
                Top group strength
                  Replacement threats possibility
                    Market leader's profit trend
                      KFS for profitability
                        Position in life cycle
                          Socio - political and economic environment
                            Labor situation
                              Legal issues

Source: McKinsey & Company, Inc.

and industry maturity as the two best indicators of profit performance. Finally, PIMS (Profit Impact of Market Strategies), a multiple regression model originally developed by GE and now a part of the Strategic Planning Institute, related profitability to some 37 business variables.

The fast-growth economy of the late 1960s and early 1970s found management ripe for a planning approach that would help deal with the prospects and problems of diversity. The portfolio approaches described above represented a real advance in strategic thinking in several ways:

1. Portfolio planning encouraged top management to evaluate the prospects of each of the company's businesses individually, to set tailored objectives for each business based on the contribution it could realistically make to corporate goals, and to allocate resources accordingly.
2. It stimulated the use of externally focused, empirical data to supplement managerial judgment in evaluating the potential of particular businesses.
3. It explicitly raised the issue of cash flow balances as management planned for expansion and growth.
4. The verbal and graphic language of portfolio planning facilitated communication across all levels of the organization.

Portfolio approaches also have very serious limitations, however, which are exacerbated by the serious challenges presented by the economic disruptions of the last decade:

1. It is not easy to define the business or product/market units appropriately before you begin to analyze them, especially when changing market conditions are blurring the boundaries.
2. Most portfolio approaches are retrospective and overly dependent on conventional wisdom in the way they treat both market attractiveness and competitive position. For example, despite evidence to the contrary, conventional wisdom suggests that:
    a. Dominant market share endows companies with sufficient power to maintain price above a competitive level or to obtain massive cost advantage through scale economies and the experience curve. However, the returns for such companies as Goodyear and Maytag show that this is not always the case (Exhibit 1-3).
    b. High market growth means that rivals can expand output and show profits without having to take demand out of each other's plants and provoke price warfare. But the experiences of industries as different as the European tungsten carbide industry and the U.S. airline industry suggest this is not always true (Exhibit 1-3).
    c. High barriers to entry allow existing competitors to keep prices high and earn high profits. But the U.S. brewing industry seems to contradict that conventional wisdom (Exhibit 1-3).
3. Most portfolio approaches suggest standard or generic strategies based on the portfolio position of the individual SBUs. But these kinds of responses can often result in lost opportunities, turn out to be impractical or unrealistic, and stifle creativity. For example:

EXHIBIT 1-3   Determinants of Market Attractiveness

Market situation	Conventional wisdom	Case examples	Return on total capital employed 1975–79
1. Dominant market share	Market leader gains: Premium prices Cost advantages due to scale and experience curve	Goodyear: 40% of U.S. tire market market leader	7.0%
		Maytag: 5% of U.S. appliance industry niche competitor	26.7%
2. High market growth	High market growth allows companies to expand output without provoking price competition leading to higher profits	European tungsten carbide industry: 1% annual growth	15.0%
		U.S. airline industry: 13.6% annual growth	5.7%
3. High barriers to entry	High barriers prevent new entrants from competing away previously excess profits	U.S. brewing industry is highly concentrated with very high barriers to entry	8.6%

Source: McKinsey analysis.

    a.   The standard strategy for managing "Dogs," that is, SBUs that have a low share of a mature market, is to consider them candidates for divestment or liquidation. New evidence demonstrates, however, that with proper management Dogs can be assets to a diversified corporation. Hambrick and MacMillan, in a study of the performance of over 1000 industrial-product businesses classified into the four cells of the BCG matrix, found that the average Dog had a positive cash flow, even greater than the cash needs of the average Wildcat.[15] Moreover, in a slow-growth economy, a majority of businesses might qualify as Dogs. Disposing of them all would be neither feasible nor desirable. Yet the portfolio ap-

proach provides no suggestions for improving the performance
of such businesses.

This problem has been recognized by even some of portfolio
planning's most ardent supporters. An article in the *Financial
Times* quoted a vice president of BCG as follows: "The theme
that should run through these [dog business] strategies is realism;
an acceptance that dogs . . . present problems, and will need to
be managed differently from more strongly placed businesses.
Given this realism there is no reason why results from the dog
quadrant should not make a worthwhile contribution within the
corporate portfolio."[16]

b. Even GE, long a proponent of the portfolio approach, finds that
    generic strategies have stifled creativity, so much so that chairman
    Jack Welch is leading the charge to put less analysis and more
    strategic thinking about innovation into GE's planning approach.
    In contrast to the past, strategic planners at GE headquarters will
    be focusing on issues of interest to more than one SBU. William
    Rothschild, formerly a staff executive of corporate business de-
    velopment and strategy at GE, commented, "[GE's] effort will
    be built more around specific issues—the impact of new tech-
    nologies, say—and less on specific businesses."[17]

4. Like most sophisticated models, the portfolio, if it is used uncritically,
    can give users the illusion that they are being rigorous and scientific
    when in fact they may have fallen prey to the old "garbage-in, garbage-
    out" syndrome. For example, a recent *Harvard Business Review* ar-
    ticle indicates that the nature of a business unit's relationship to head-
    quarters can have as much effect on its performance as its competitive
    position and the industry's environment. Specifically, in studying the
    relationships that 12 organization headquarters have with their divi-
    sions (a total of 69 business units), Hamermesh and White found that
    "the administrative arrangements concerning the degree of autonomy
    a business unit has, how line responsibilities are structured, and how
    the unit's incentive compensation program is designed have as much
    effect on its performance as market share and cash flow considera-
    tions."[18] Strategies derived from portfolio analysis rarely consider such
    relationships with respect to expected or desired business perform-
    ance.

Notwithstanding the contributions that portfolio planning has made to
management practice, the fact is that the portfolio approach works best when
conditions are stable, when the alternatives are known and relatively constrained, and when the future is a confirmation of the past. In and of itself,
the portfolio approach is virtually useless for identifying new opportunities
and/or setting new directions for businesses or corporations.

Granted, portfolio techniques facilitate top-management decision making, but somewhere along the line management mistakenly got the impression that portfolio planning *is* strategy. If overused or used exclusively as the strategic planning framework in a company, portfolio planning can easily cause management to lose touch with the dynamics of the markets in which the company competes. In periods of dramatic change, this is tantamount to corporate suicide.

POST-SEVENTIES PLANNING

Earlier I suggested that if American businesses are to develop the flexibility they need to compete in the decade ahead, management will have to make some major changes in the way it goes about planning and managing. I also said that events had demonstrated that staff-dominated, paper-based, deterministic planning approaches were not only an anachronism but a serious obstacle to strategic thinking. Can we then identify new trends in planning that focus on ideas rather than processes and that sharpen management's ability to understand the marketplace and achieve the quantum leaps in performance that will be required to compete successfully? What does the current "state of the art" look like?

Portfolio Planning

Portfolio planning, it appears, is still very much with us. In a *Harvard Business Review* article, Philippe Haspeslagh reported the results of a survey on the use and impact of portfolio planning on the *Fortune* 1000 companies: as of 1979, 36 percent of the *Fortune* 1000 and 45 percent of the *Fortune* 500 industrial companies used the portfolio to some extent. "Each year during the last five years," Haspeslagh reports, "another 25 to 30 organizations have joined the ranks."[19]

What seems to be emerging is a second generation of portfolio planning matrices. Although admirably more sensitive to customers, competition, and industry dynamics than their predecessors, these new matrices still hold out the promise of a strategic "quick fix" in the guise of generic strategies or prescriptive game plans that derive from the various matrix positions.

For example, the "strategic environment matrix" reflects BCG's current portfolio approach. In contrast to its earlier growth/share matrix, the determinants of profitability represented by the axes of BCG's new matrix are the potential sources of advantage a business has relative to its competition (i.e., many/few) and the magnitude of the advantage (i.e., small/large). The matrix also divides the competitive environment into four industry types: stalemate, fragmented, specialization, and volume. The theory is that businesses migrate around the matrix as they mature, with earnings and returns on investment varying significantly depending on position. Once management locates its business in the proper quadrant, its industry type and the generic strategies that conform to it are revealed.

Let's say, for example, you have a business in the lower left-hand quadrant; that means you're in a stalemate industry where there are few ways to beat your competition and those few ways don't provide much payoff. The suggested game plan in such a situation is to control costs, limit the importance of the business within the portfolio, look for ways to transform the business, *and* be ready to exit fast if you get the chance.[20]

The fact is that a lot of companies in "stalemate" industries are doing just fine. Companies like Haagen-Dazs in ice cream, Vanderbilt in jeans, Celestial Seasonings in teas, GE in radios, and Sony in consumer electronics were able to change the basis of competition and win big. And they are strong evidence that it's time we started fixing businesses rather than selling them.

Another 1980s-style portfolio planning approach, introduced by Strategic Planning Associates (SPA), recognizes that competitive advantage manifests itself in lower costs or higher value for customers. SPA goes on to suggest that management's fundamental business decision is whether to compete on the basis of cost or value to the customer. This cost/value tradeoff is captured in a 2×2 portfolio matrix with the vertical dimension being "customer price sensitivity" and the horizontal dimension "product mystique," that is, the degree to which customers perceive a difference among competitors' products (Exhibit 1-4).

Once you position your business on the matrix, the theory seems to say, you will know whether you should be following a commodity, transitional, hybrid, or specialty strategy to gain and sustain a competitive edge. An article in *Fortune* elaborates on two of SPA's generic strategies: "Selling to a market that is price-sensitive but not conscious of difference—buyers of flat steel

EXHIBIT 1-4   SPA Cost/Value Matrix

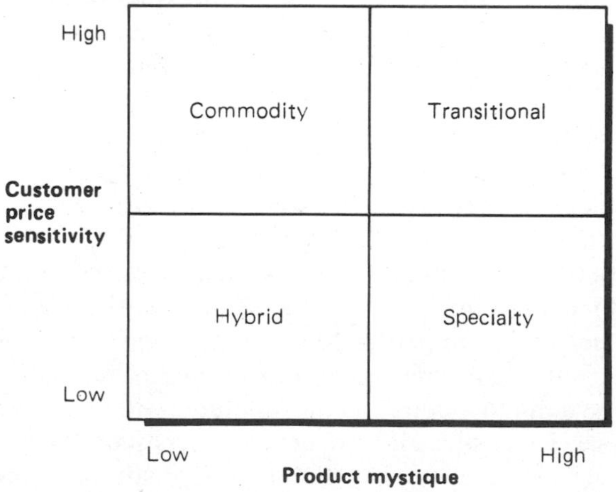

Source: Strategic Planning Associates, 1982.

or gasoline—calls for a 'commodity' strategy: back to the old experience curve and the market-share wars. Customers who don't worry much about cost but care a lot about some other quality—buyers of vintage champagne or narrow-isle lift trucks—require a 'specialty' strategy: continue to add the special value that sets your product apart from the rest. . . ."[21]

The unspoken, but very important, truth behind the SPA model is that management needs to do a much better job of understanding who their customers are and what drives their decisions. The same kind of diligent information gathering some managers reserve for their competition should be applied to getting "closer" to their customers. Focus groups and field surveys are two simple and useful ways of doing this. In addition, recent developments in information technology provide a myriad of ways managers can respond more effectively to their customers.

An article in *Sloan Management Review* describes how information technology has brought GE closer to its customers:

> In 1980, the company found that consumers did not feel that GE was adequately responsive to their inquiries. They wanted more product information before their purchase and additional information after the purchase. The GE Answer Center, utilizing an "800" line for toll-free calling was opened. . .to better meet customer needs. The system covers all GE products and handles over one-and-a-half million calls per year. Computers are used to retrieve 500,000 pieces of information about GE's 8,500 products. Some 94% of the customers who use the system express satisfaction with the result.[22]

Industry Structure Model

Professor Michael E. Porter of Harvard Business School is another advocate of generic strategies. Earlier I discussed the inability of the experience curve concept to explain the competitor with low market share who was making high profits or who performed brilliantly even when the rest of the economy was going sour. Porter, whose industry structure model has contributed significantly to our understanding of the interrelationship between competitive strategy and industry structure, has developed a theory of competition that goes a long way toward explaining why certain firms outperform others in the same industry.

What Porter has done so well in his work is to dispense with the concept of competition as a unidimensional conflict. Competition is not simply the rivalry of firms doing business in the same industry arena. The state of competition in an industry depends on *five* basic competitive forces, Porter contends. They are, in addition to rivalry of existing competitors; the bargaining power of suppliers, the bargaining power of buyers, the threat of new entrants, and the threat of substitute products or services (Exhibit 1-5). The ultimate profit potential in an industry depends on the collective strength of these five forces.

How can management manipulate these competitive forces to ensure that

EXHIBIT 1-5　Industry Structure Model

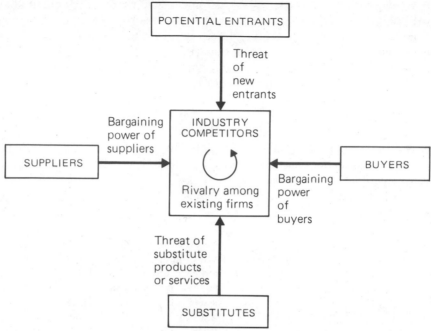

Source: Michael E. Porter, *Competitive Strategy,* Free Press, New York, 1980.

its business gets the lion's share of potential industry profits? Porter suggests that "in coping with the five competitive forces, there are three potentially successful generic approaches to outperforming other firms in an industry; 1) overall cost leadership, 2) differentiation, i.e., creating something—a product or service—that is perceived industry-wide as being unique, and, 3) focus, i.e., concentrating on a particular buyer group, segment of the product line, or geographic market."[23]

On the surface this doesn't sound so very different from some of the other approaches we've looked at. However, Porter's model is far more complex and demanding. Management must select its generic strategy, not simply in response to rival companies, but to the other four forces driving industry competition as well: substitutes, customers, suppliers, and potential entrants. Porter goes on to say, "Certain characteristics of the industry not only must be considered in choosing a generic strategy, they in fact dictate the proper choice."[24]

The breadth of information and knowledge required to lay out such an industry panorama is daunting; executing the generic strategy cannot be less than a formidable undertaking. Yet, by forcing managers to deepen their understanding of the totality of forces driving industry competition, Porter's model also forces management to consider the kinds of strategic issues that ultimately determine competitive success: What will each competitor's probable reaction be to the range of strategic moves other firms could initiate? Why are some firms competing in the same industry persistently more profitable? What are the driving forces at the root of industry change and how can management recognize change before its competition? What are the skills and resources required to pursue a particular strategy? What are the organizational requirements? What are the risks?

Value-Based Planning

Value-based planning emerged in the early 1980s as a way to look at a company's portfolio of businesses that integrates modern financial theory and strategy. Its basic premise is that the principal purpose of a corporation (or a business) is to create wealth (i.e., economic value) for its shareholders. The corporation does this by increasing its market value (stock price) and by paying dividends. Specifically, if a company's market value exceeds the replacement cost of its equity assets—which represent the equity that shareholders have invested in the company through direct investment or retained earnings—the company has created wealth over time for its shareholders. On the other hand, if its market value is less than replacement costs, the company has eroded shareholder wealth.[25]

The power of the economic value concept is that it provides management with a better way to think about the relationship of business performance to stock price. By using wealth creation as a measure of business performance (i.e., the quality of business strategies), management can invest in or withhold resources from businesses based on their ability to create economic value. The kicker in all of this is that the key to economic value creation is the ability to achieve sustainable competitive advantage. And that leads us right back to managers who know their customers, competition, and markets. And with customers, competition, and markets characterized by rapid changes—as they are today—managers must supplement current planning techniques with the one necessary thing that tools and techniques alone cannot provide—innovative ideas. They must broaden strategic planning to such an extent that it becomes strategic management.

A FRAMEWORK FOR MANAGEMENT: McKINSEY'S BASIC BELIEFS

McKinsey's approach to strategic management rests on a number of basic beliefs about what managing a business involves and what it takes to build an innovative and self-renewing organization. These principles of management reflect the way we feel top management should think about its institution. They are predicated on the assertion that management's fundamental task is to create an institution that is responsive to—or, better yet, creates—change and, as such, becomes self-renewing. Implicit in this assertion are three assumptions: that management is concerned with the institution's long-term survival; that good people doing good things are essential to the "survivability" of the institution; and that management can design an organization and fashion systems that encourage people to provide for institutional survival. These basic beliefs fall into one of four general categories.

Managing a Business for Competitive Advantage

Whenever I'm asked to assess whether a business has a strategy, I ask management just one question: What are you doing in this business that will lead you to a sustainable competitive advantage?

Organizations in a market economy are concerned with delivering a service or product in the most profitable way. The key to that profitability in most market situations is achieving a sustainable competitive advantage, which, in turn, is a function only of superior performance relative to competition. In other words, competitive success hinges on building a cost or value edge into whatever product or service you're selling and then getting to the marketplace ahead of your competition. There's simply no other way I know of to gain competitive advantage.

Fortune magazine recently ran an article describing the extraordinary performance of a group of 13 companies over the last 10 years, a period the author dubs "the dark decade." The measure of performance used was average return on equity of at least 20 percent, and never less than 15 percent, for the 10-year period 1974–1983.

The article's author, Carol Loomis, writes, "The stars come from a spread of industries, but tend to share certain characteristics. Most are leaders in at least one product market; many are tight with a dollar; and many believe in sticking to businesses they clearly understand."[26] She later comments, "The generalization that goes a long way to explain the whole list [of 13 companies] is that they have established a special standing in their markets."[27]

While three of the companies clearly dominate their markets, leadership in these companies takes other forms as well. For example, Nalco's edge is its expertise in the use of the chemicals it sells—it is a counselor and problem solver to its customers. In steel, Worthington has a reputation for quality workmanship that allows it to obtain premium prices. American Home Products thinks of itself as having specialty products and as marketing these with particular skill. And Dow Jones's traditionally high margins clearly flow in great part from the unique product they offer—the *Wall Street Journal,* a product their customers want and need, and for which they are willing to pay a premium.

Managements of these companies do three things much better than their competition. First, they excel at product/market definition. They are keen observers of the marketplace and have a true understanding of their own strengths and weaknesses. They use both these attributes to select what they want to produce and for whom. Second, they have a better-designed business system (i.e., the operating concepts, system, or structure that enables them to outperform competitors in producing and delivering the product or service). Third, they manage the overall business system better. This is a complex and demanding task that includes managing not only the interrelationships within the corporation, but also the critical external interrelationships with suppliers, customers, and competitors.

When managers in these companies think about improving performance, they either push for better functional execution *within* the business system (e.g., better purchasing, better sales force management, better manufacturing) or tinker at the interfaces of functional areas to "balance" the business system better—for example, helping marketing and manufacturing work together to improve customer service. Or, if need be, they redesign the entire business system (or individual operating concepts) to come up with a new and better way to get the product/service to the marketplace.

Viewing Change as an Opportunity

In addition to managing for competitive advantage, "stars" are skilled at adapting their business systems to continuously changing conditions. Roberto Goizueta, chairman of Coca-Cola, one of the group of 13, comments in the Loomis article, "The next ten years are going to be. . .an age of uncertainty. Managements are going to have to be very flexible and action-oriented. They won't have the luxury of crossing all the 'Ts'. . . . The world is going to pass you by if you try to do that."[28]

Goizueta's remark underscores an essential point about management's ability to compete successfully. Too often, management is preoccupied with the here and now: the will to change is simply not there. Change is looked on as a problem—unsettling, risky, annoying. But change can also be seen as a source of opportunity, providing the potential for creativity and innovation. This is the perception of change that top management must embrace and work toward inculcating within their organization.

In *Fortune's* recent article on innovation in large companies, the author put his finger on a number of the important aspects of creating an innovative company: the notion of controlled experimentation; the obsession with meeting customers' needs; the importance of a strong culture; the looseness in the idea generation stage; and the disciplined assessment of these ideas in terms of commercial viability. He also observed that the management of each of the eight "big masters of innovation" was thoroughly convinced of the *need* to innovate. "Resting on the status quo is perceived as a sure way to corporate disaster," he writes.[29]

All companies large and small need to pursue some degree of innovation and find new business opportunities. Past practices cannot accommodate the demanding business environment that social and economic changes have brought about.

Managing through People

After Jack Welch had been CEO of GE for three weeks, he was invited to speak to a group of Harvard Business School students about his plans for the company. One of the students asked him what he considered his most important task as CEO. Welch answered without hesitation, "choosing and developing good people." [30]

Management has a number of important tasks to perform. The first is to create a vision of where the organization should be going, which involves a clear assessment of the corporation's strengths and weaknesses, what markets it should compete in, how it will compete, and the major action programs required. The second is to take the leadership actions necessary to convert vision to reality—to develop the capabilities of the organization, to expedite change and remove obstacles, and to shape the environment. Central to both the establishment and execution of a corporate vision is the effective acquisition, development, and deployment of human resources.

John W. Gardner writes in *Self-Renewal,* "Institutions are renewed by individuals who refuse to be satisfied with the outer husks of things."[31] In the end, management is measured by the skill and sensitivity with which it manages and develops people, for it is only through the quality of their people that organizations can change effectively.

Shaping the Strategically Managed Organization

McKinsey's Bob Waterman, who wrote *In Search of Excellence* with Tom Peters, commented that executives he spoke with were concerned with how they could build the kind of innovative, self-renewing organizations that the 1980s and 1990s demand.

McKinsey's 7-S model holds that organizational effectiveness is not just a product of structure or strategy but stems from multiple factors (Exhibit 1-6). Organizational change comes about through the interrelationship and orchestration of seven factors: structure, strategy, systems, style, skills, staff, and shared values (i.e., the guiding concepts of the organization). Organizations that design these seven *S*s from an externally focused and forward-looking perspective have a much better chance at self-renewal than those that take a predominantly internal and historical orientation. This does not imply that line management shouldn't strive to get their products or services to the market efficiently or to understand past experience. Nor does it imply that the source of strategic success may not lie in improved execution of an already-developed skill. It is simply that most large organizations we have studied are satisfied with pursuing incremental improvements, rather than searching for quantum leaps that involve major change.

People resist change. Overcoming this natural resistance, and then *using* it to one's own advantage, is the primary opportunity for institutions continually to improve their effectiveness and revitalize themselves. Chief ex-

EXHIBIT 1-6   McKinsey's 7S Model

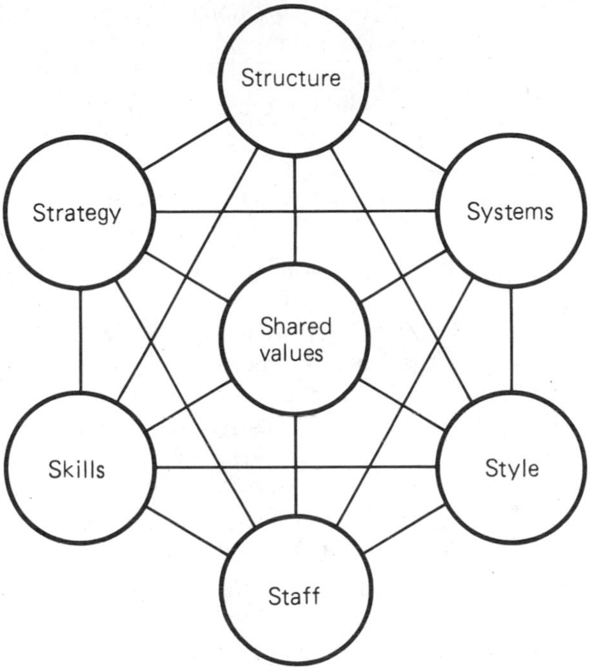

Source: McKinsey & Company, Inc., 1982

ecutives can take the lead in moving their institutions toward strategic management by designing organizations and developing management systems that look forward and look out. For example, top management may require functional managers to submit periodic competitive/market reports or to focus on a project/issue-oriented approach to strategy development, rather than a formalized process. The approach ought to ensure strong linkages between human resource management systems and strategic planning so that skills required for the future are continually being developed or acquired, as the company moves from a culture that perpetuates the status quo to one that continually searches for the next step. Management must approach information acquisition and dissemination in a way that puts a great deal of raw information in the hands of many people—planners, market researchers, designers—but, most important, line managers, because they're the ones who are most likely to make things happen. The company must have management systems that will attract, encourage, and reward people who have the ability to combine, order, or connect this raw information in novel and better ways.

McKinsey's continuing research into companies with reputations for innovation and sustained financial performance has convinced us that tomorrow's excellent companies will be those that have built organizations that value self-renewal. These organizations will have the capabilities to pursue successfully both the incremental small wins and the big, bold innovations. They will also have the ability to switch emphasis as the competitive situation demands. They will be led by managements that understand and effectively use the forces at work in the external environment to their own advantage. Such companies will truly be able to create their own futures.

EVOLUTION TOWARD STRATEGIC MANAGEMENT

Consultants, corporate planners, the business press, and academia inundate us with new buzzwords, new organizational theories, and new planning techniques, all aimed at helping top management deal with the residue of the past decade and the challenges of the next. No one underestimates the importance of building awareness of and sensitivity to the human dimension of corporate enterprise. No one would deny the value of understanding past success and failure as we pursue the future. It is difficult to argue that long-term corporate survival does not depend on the ability of the corporation to grow profitably over time. My concern is with the single-minded espousal of *any* analytic technique or formal planning process or management system as a surrogate for the continuing search for, and generation of, innovative, good ideas.

In *Self-Renewal,* Gardner writes eloquently about the inescapable reality of change and the great task of renewal facing us. He cautions, "It is not enough for a society to recognize the need for renewal. It must have the institutional arrangements that make orderly change a possibility . . . institutional arrangements that make for adaptiveness and flexibility." Gardner also writes that the virtue of the institutional arrangements of a free society is that "they nourish the kind of people who contribute most [to renewal]— the innovators."[32]

Can top management fashion the "institutional arrangements" necessary for corporate renewal? Can it balance creativity and control? Can it encourage and nurture innovation without causing fragmentation? Can management walk the fine line between executional agility and executional efficiency that an unstable business world demands? Can it, in essence, manage strategically?

A few years ago, in the *Harvard Business Review,* two McKinsey colleagues and I asserted that companies go through four stages in developing an effective capability for strategic management.[33] They start with simple financial planning (Stage I); move through forecast-based planning (Stage II) and externally oriented, or strategic, planning (Stage III); and finally arrive at Stage IV, strategic management (Exhibit 1-7).

In Stage I, budgets and financial objectives dominate the planning process, and line managers and planners are concerned with getting an accurate budget and then managing to meet it. Stage I companies manage by remoteness. Their senior executives are frequently so married to the way things used to be that they are unable to recognize and understand the changes that have

EXHIBIT 1-7   Evolution of Strategic Management

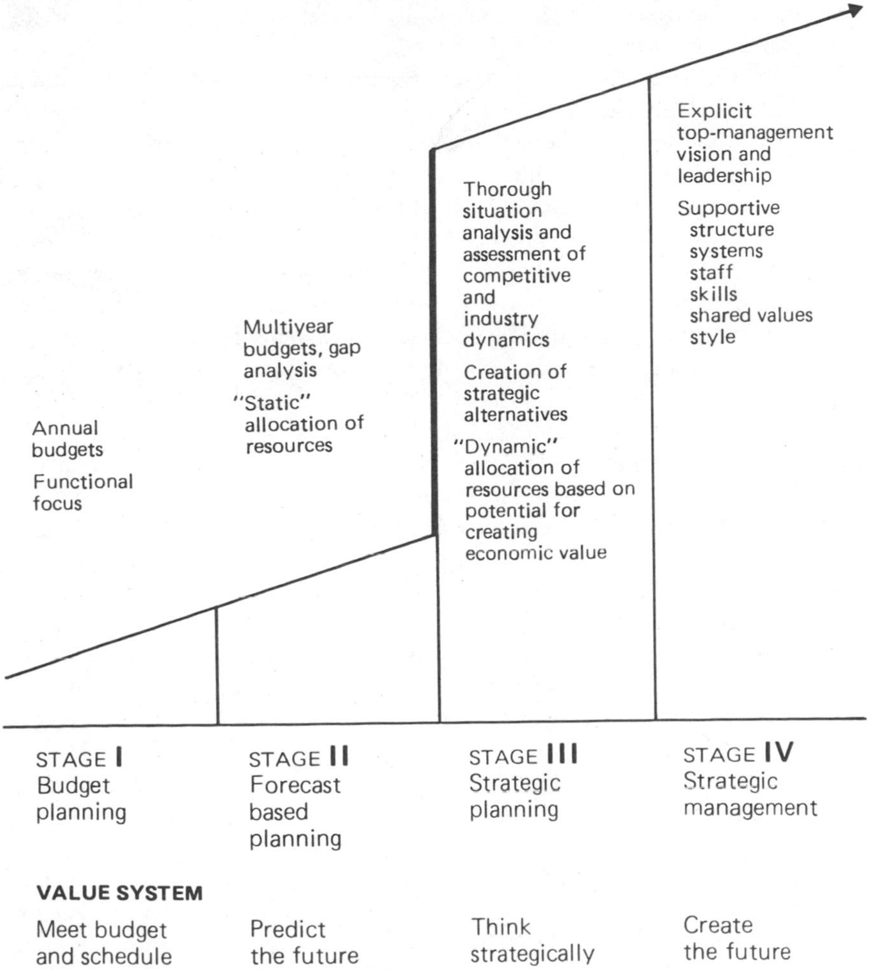

Annual
budgets
Functional
focus

Multiyear
budgets, gap
analysis

"Static"
allocation of
resources

Thorough
situation
analysis and
assessment of
competitive
and
industry
dynamics

Creation of
strategic
alternatives

"Dynamic"
allocation of
resources based on
potential for
creating
economic value

Explicit
top-management
vision and
leadership

Supportive
structure
systems
staff
skills
shared values
style

STAGE I	STAGE II	STAGE III	STAGE IV
Budget planning	Forecast based planning	Strategic planning	Strategic management

VALUE SYSTEM

Meet budget and schedule	Predict the future	Think strategically	Create the future

Source: McKinsey & Company, Inc.

taken place in their industries and, as such, are incapable of proactive leadership. The question of "corporate direction" is seldom raised, and strategy resides only in the hearts and minds of a few key executives. Management is internally focused and execution-oriented.

A company's movement from Stage I to Stage II—forecast-based planning—reflects management's ability to extend its horizon beyond the one-year financial plan and to consider the future. It also reflects a growing concern with the marketplace and the company's position in the marketplace. The Stage II company, however, is basically *reactive* as opposed to *proactive,* static as opposed to dynamic. Management's perspective on how to run a business is still internally oriented and history-based. Planning in Stage II is a staff responsibility; line management rarely participates in the strategic decisions on operating policies, focusing instead on how to avoid or fill a profit gap.

Because the strategies, businesses, management systems, and organizational culture of the Stage II company are all forecast-driven, management tends to become too confident that it understands the industries in which it is competing, too sure about how the company is likely to develop. Although management may perceive clouds on the horizon, nothing in the nature of the organizations it has developed encourages it to take the next step: pushing to understand the forces at work, the possible implications of changing circumstances, and what to do about these implications. Much of the strategic planning methodology described earlier serves to reinforce the forecast-based approaches to management and obsolete assumptions of stability that characterize Stage II companies.

A big jump in the effectiveness of strategic planning usually occurs between Stages II and III, when a company is well on its way to becoming truly externally oriented. At this point, the planning focus has turned away from forecasting volume and revenues, fine tuning estimates of future financial performance, and shuffling resources toward understanding changing customer needs, technological developments, competitive position, and competitor initiatives. The responsiveness of the company improves noticeably, and decisions seem better attuned to the external world. The transition to Stage III is clearly signaled when line managers and top management routinely discuss and debate the changes currently under way in the competitive marketplace.

The Stage III company equips itself both analytically and conceptually to create new sources of sustainable competitive advantage. It is, in essence, deciding how to make changes in the way in which it competes and determining specifically what to do. This is a lot more complicated than simply analyzing the patterns in the marketplace. It calls for a blend of analysis, judgment, experience, synthesis, and gut feeling. Business unit general managers should be at the forefront of this effort. In truth, capable chief executives and general managers would not allow staff planners or analysts to make this kind of decision for them: they would want to control the design of it because they alone would be held responsible for its success or failure. Furthermore, bringing about a major change requires capability building, confidence transfer, and culture shifting skills that only general managers can bring to the task. Though he or she may delegate key preparation tasks to others, the business unit general manager must *own* the strategy.

But are all general managers ready (or able) to assume the full implications of this responsibility? In many cases, the answer is no. Managements are a lot more willing to accept new information into their decision-making processes than they are to change the perspective from which they approach their decisions. In other words, whereas they're prepared to use new information, many still regard change as a problem, not as an opportunity.

Several years ago, McKinsey conducted an internal study to try to characterize the patterns of behavior that precede the decline of a company's leadership position. We studied a number of "losing situations" and, although each case was unique in some respect, there was enough commonality in corporate behavior to suggest that leading companies that lose do so because they fall into one or more of these fundamental traps: (1) they use unrealistic or obsolete criteria to assess company strengths and/or weaknesses (for example, depending on the competitive advantage that no longer provides any advantage); (2) they become complacent about their leadership position—an attitude that breeds inflexibility and a conventional-wisdom mentality, both of which leave the company prey to the smart competitor waiting in the wings; and (3) they fail to acknowledge industry change or to take action to make the results of that change work to their advantage.

I remember thinking as we reviewed our analyses that not one of the executives in the organizations we studied could satisfactorily explain away the company's decline in performance. To my mind, these were classic studies of management by remoteness and management by the numbers, and therein lay the crux of the problem. No one was looking anywhere but *inside* the company; no one was focusing on tomorrow, only on today. And no one thought to challenge the basic assumptions and corporate mind-set that had brought the company to its leadership position to see if they were still valid and appropriate. The result was that competitive vigor simply died away and the leaders became losers.

Other leading companies, however, are willing to reshape themselves to deal with the new realities. The willingness of Procter & Gamble (P & G) to take new and radical steps to become more cost-efficient and aggressive stands in sharp contrast to the losers' head-in-the-sand attitude. *Business Week* writes, "[CEO] Smale apparently has decided that a tougher competitive environment and changing consumer and retailing trends warrant a fresh look at P & G's methods of waging war. . . . Brand managers . . . who have traditionally been judged on their success in increasing unit volume and market share, are now also being measured on their success in controlling costs. . . . In a departure from P & G's paternalistic past, Smale is combing out mediocre performers from management ranks."[34] A recent article in the *Wall Street Journal* comments, "Procter & Gamble's decision to start selling its *Always* brand sanitary napkins nationwide [after it had been tested for only one year in one area] illustrates the new, faster pace at the company that wrote the book on painstaking market research."[35]

The point I want to stress is that even companies that have embraced strategic or externally driven planning frequently retain the conservative mind-set—or a defensive perspective on change—that limits their ability to consider creative, revolutionary solutions, the kinds of solutions that characterize the true Stage III company. In such cases, top management and its corporate planning staff must work to dismantle the barriers to strategic thinking and focus the attention of business unit general managers on generating the kinds of options that will upset the equilibrium of the marketplace and reestablish it in their favor.

STRATEGIC MANAGEMENT: COPING WITH THE WORLD OF CHANGE

Let's now hypothesize that you're a general manager in a company that prides itself on being strategically managed—that is, a Stage IV company. What exactly does this mean? What are the distinctive characteristics of such a company?

The Norms of Strategic Management

Top management in a strategically managed company accepts change as a permanent condition and recognizes that a company unwilling or unable to change will end up a loser. In responding to change, management is not afraid to think big or, as a colleague of mine puts it, "tamper with the mainspring." Finally, top management is supported by an organization that has both the willingness to "act big" (i.e., institutional courage) and the ability to "think big" (i.e., institutionalized strategic thinking). Although only a handful of today's companies are strategically managed, we can identify certain characteristics that set them apart organizationally, culturally, and managerially, that allow them not only to accommodate change but also to create it.

Despite highly sophisticated planning systems, it is not planning technique that distinguishes an IBM or a Citicorp—rather, it is a CEO who has a vision of future industry development, who can anticipate contemporary events, and who can act to turn those expected events to the organization's advantage. Walter Wriston, commenting on the impetus behind Citibank's enormous investment in building a proprietary global communications system, stated: "At the beginning of 1970, I said our competitors at the end of the Seventies would be Sears and Merrill Lynch. . . . In the 80s it is going to be IBM and the telephone companies, Reuters and Dow Jones, because information about money . . . is now more important than money itself."[36]

The strategically managed company is superb at continually adjusting its competitive strategy as the marketplace demands it. But it is also dedicated to the proposition of winning by changing the rules of the game and making quantum leaps beyond the competition—the sort of spectacular competitive advance that is exemplified by the successes of companies like Club Mediterranee in packaged holidays and Perrier in bottled water.

We also know that such companies are managed by what Alvin Toffler calls "adhocracy" rather than bureaucracy. Reward and motivation systems are developed that create an "ownership mentality" among business managers and make them responsible for strategic thinking. Planning is streamlined, the primary focus is on operating plans, and the resolution of externally driven issues is left to small task forces of high-talent line managers—much as Jack Welch has recently done at GE. Welch has scrapped GE's former system of annual, highly formalized presentations and has substituted a system of operating plans that may be changed without formal meetings if circumstances change, as well as a system of running reviews (monthly financial reporting remains untouched in order to prevent any unexpected adversities from developing).[37]

The CEO is the ultimate strategic planner in Stage IV companies. As my colleague Quincy Hunsicker has so aptly observed, "For the CEO's involvement to have greatest effect, he should enter the arena at an early stage, deciding objectives, challenging assumptions, forcing options, and generally orchestrating the diverse human elements of the planning process so as to steer it on a course between advocacy and consensus toward the best possible strategy for the corporation as a whole."[38]

However, he expects his key operating lieutenants to be strategic thinkers as well. In the short time he has been CEO, Welch has made "freeing GE's managers to take advantage of GE's own strength" a top priority. He is consciously changing a management style that he felt stifled enterprise and cooled innovation to make GE "not simply more high-spirited, but more adaptable, more agile than companies that are a twentieth or even a fiftieth of our size."[39] "To prove what he says," *Forbes* writes, "Welch has been loudly rewarding some near misses. When a $20 million project was scrapped because of a change in market, Welch promoted the manager and gave him a bonus. The 70-man project team got VCRs instead of exile; the result: things move faster at GE today."[40]

Strategically managed companies are expert at creating the "institutional arrangements" self-renewal demands. They do not, however, simply establish systems and procedures and then retreat into them. Instead, they constantly reevaluate and reassess the requirements for competitive success and refine their management approach appropriately—as we've seen IBM, P & G, and GE do in the several examples used earlier. What distinguishes these companies is the care and thoroughness with which management links strategic planning to operational decision making and then executes its plans in the marketplace. This skill draws its strength from a culture uncompromising in its commitment to competitive success and a management style and system that have been fashioned explicitly to support that commitment. Lawrence Small, group chief of Citibank's North American Banking Group, speaking to an audience of analysts, said, "Our clear-cut objective is to blow the opposition out of the surveys." In describing Citibank's technological edge he said, "We are spending our competitors into the ground."[41]

Strategically managed companies are masters of the balancing act: making incremental changes when reason dictates; pursuing the quantum leap that their vision and gut feeling tells them is there. Witness some of IBM's recent moves. They run the gamut from "small experiments"—the possibility of using mass-merchandising channels (K-Mart) to market the PCjr and preempt the competition—to such big, bold moves as acquiring Rolm in order to obtain additional expertise in telecommunications.

The leaders of such companies not only think big, they have the courage to act big as well. When IBM made its initial 250-million-dollar purchase of 12 percent of Intel to ensure the supply of the microprocessor that gives IBM's personal computer its intelligence, *Fortune* described the move as "previously unimaginable" and commented, "To its old motto, 'Think,' IBM seems to appended the word 'differently.' "[42]

Corporate planners in strategically managed companies are expected to provide insights, not descriptions, and to be knowledgeable about key issues that cut across businesses or do not specifically relate to any business. When they deal with a specific business, they do so from a corporate perspective.

The New Role of Corporate Planners

McKinsey's Ken Ohmae, in an address to the North American Society for Corporate Planning, spoke about the new planning requirements of our increasingly complex and changing world: "It may be time for us to think of a more accurate word for corporate planning. A better expression may be corporate development, or corporate pathfinding."[43]

His point was that doing better in what you're already doing is not likely to be enough to win competitively: "Status quo seekers have problems, because nothing stays still."[44] Consequently, new business opportunities must continually be found. Corporate planners must hone their skills to this end. Brainstorming and scanning are very important; sensitivity to new possibilities and imagination are essential. In short, planners should be catalysts for action.

The role of the planner has changed because the context of planning has changed. We used to have a very clear product concept to which we could affix our business planning. Today, it is often unclear what product or service we are talking about. For example, until quite recently, typewriters, telephones, mainframe computers, and copying machines were all discrete products and, in general, were made by different manufacturers and sold in different ways. Now, a glance around your office will show that data and word processing, storage, retrieval, and communication combine elements of all these products and services and are rapidly obliterating the old distinctions.

Demand forecasts used to be relatively simple. For example, demographics, existing car populations and purchase patterns, and the general state of the economy gave us a good picture of the number of prospective new automobile owners. Today, with product concepts becoming more amorphous, we can only estimate the demand for things like word processors and personal computers.

Not too long ago, you could quickly count off who your competitors were.

Today, with industry lines blurring and the Third World awakening, you are wise to recognize that you can't always be sure who the competition is.

The old planning was essentially product market strategy; you had a product or service, and you developed a product market strategy for it. The new planning is all about finding new products, new niches, and new businesses. Planning has become synonymous with creating change.

Environmental change has made the new planning contest not only different but far more complex. Flexibility is crucial as uncertainty plays havoc with systematized and forecast-based planning. In the VCR business, for example, where more and better features—the competitive edge—are constantly being redefined by changing technology and consumer preference, how do you plan?

The rapid rate of new technology has compressed time to the extent that the traditional notion of product life cycles might not survive. In stereo and audio equipment, for example, the showcase for new products is the Consumer Electronics Show in Chicago—an event that takes place every six months.

Increasing numbers of industries are evolving toward globalization, whereby markets and competition cross national and continental boundaries, and coordination of businesses across countries is required to gain a sustainable competitive advantage. This trend is reflected in the increasing incidence of companies from the United States, Japan, and Europe entering into a wide range of cooperative ventures with their competitors. The computer industry is a prime example (see Exhibit 1-8, in which the consortia illustrated were formed to compete with IBM). This movement toward collaboration among competitors means, among other things, that the company that may at first glance appear to be weak is a formidable adversary six months later as a result of a partnering agreement. How does a planner anticipate this?

Commenting in *Business Week*'s recent special report, "New Alliances Reshape the Computer Industry," My colleague, Bob Conrads asserts that the formation of such alliances, a phenomenon he calls "strategic partnering," is becoming a critical element in almost any successful strategy. "[Alliances] are central to a company's direction and to its way of achieving future competitive advantages."[45] It is essential either to get to the best potential partner(s) first as teammates or to prevent competitors from teaming up with them. However, most companies and top managers are geared either to going it alone or to engaging in formal joint ventures, and will resist the idea of competing through partners because the resulting competitive advantage will seem, and indeed may be, more slippery than sustainable. How does the corporate planner help change a bias toward autonomy to accommodate collaboration? What guidelines can he identify for establishing successful cooperative ventures—ventures that are appropriate to both the institution's current and future objectives?

Whereas ultimate responsibility for competitive success rests with those

EXHIBIT 1-8   Facing Up to the IBM Challenge

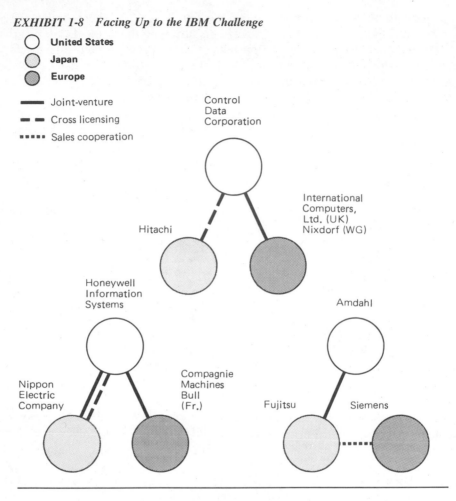

Source: McKinsey analysis

managers closest to the market, there can be no strategic success without
an understanding of the forces at work in the industry, fundamental insight
into competition and the marketplace, and quick and effective execution. It
is the corporate planner's role to provide line management with timely feedback on new developments in the marketplace, to alert business managers
to the "weak signals" that invariably precede important industry shifts, to
study the organizational implications of new strategic alternatives, and to
work with top management to help discover major new businesses and to
revitalize existing ones.

Design of the Strategically Managed Company

Strategic management is not merely a collection of methodologies or tools, nor is it a collection of systems and procedures. It is a frame of mind and a set of behavioral patterns that can be reinforced and enhanced—although not created—by tools, methodologies, systems, and procedures. The test of the strategically managed company is its ability to adjust organically to gain competitive advantage in periods of discontinuity and change—to renew itself.

Organizational change comes about through the interrelationship and orchestration of the factors that determine organizational effectiveness: structure, strategy, systems, style, skills, staff, and shared values. CEOs can play a leading role in strengthening their institutions' response to change by "designing" these seven organizational effectiveness factors to reflect strategic management attributes.

For example, in the strategically managed company, no compromises are made in staffing pivotal, basic positions—a policy Hewlett-Packard (H-P) followed when it decided to enter the personal computer business. Management determined that, in order to succeed, H-P had to manage the marketing dimension of the business superbly. It also recognized that it did not have the necessary in-house talent. Ed McCracken, formerly general manager of Hewlett-Packard's Business Development Group and the individual responsible for leading the company into the commercial computer business comments, "In an unconventional move for H-P, we hired six executives in key marketing positions. They came from General Mills, Heublein, Lego and others. We brought them in to manage market research, advertising, and brand management—techniques unfamiliar to Hewlett-Packard."[46] (It remains to be seen whether acquiring marketing talent alone is sufficient for H-P to be successful in the personal computer business.)

An organization's management style clearly defines where it is focusing its attention. Senior executives in strategically managed companies send out strong signals about what counts by the way in which they spend their time. Simply "touching bases" is not adequate; results-oriented initiatives are what they focus on. For example, Jack Welch's determination to free up GE's business managers to "make mistakes" culminated in the board's approval of a multimillion-dollar discretionary fund to reward "risk-takers."[47]

Stage IV management systems are designed to encourage proactive response to change. Meetings between corporate and business units are informal, substantive, and direct. Jack Welch has made a point of managing meetings for greater productivity: "One of the things we have put in place to achieve more candor, more constructive conflict is CEO[48] meetings where the three of us will have meetings with SBU managers, one on three, two on three, in a small room."[49] Strategy reviews focus on key issues for each business, not comprehensive strategic documentation. One issue raised repeatedly is what each SBU will be doing to benefit GE in 1990.[50]

Strategically managed companies also recognize the power of information technology as a competitive weapon. Citibank is a case in point. Its reputation for quality service and ability to serve customers worldwide are built on information technology capabilities. A large medical supply company provides on-line order entry terminals and inventory management software for customers. As the customers' systems are integrated with the supplier's, it becomes much more difficult for customers to order from a competitor. The more sophisticated the systems, the greater the switching costs and the less likely buyers will be to switch indiscriminately to a competitor.[51]

Finally, as companies evolve toward strategic management, there is an increasing need for "strategic intelligence systems" to help management understand the entire panorama of its business environment: competition, customers, sociopolitical dynamics, and regulatory and economic factors.[52] Stage IV companies develop rapid and precise communication systems to disseminate and exchange valuable information; communication channels are open and as direct as possible. Ed McCracken, commenting on H-P's strategy for facilitating change, stated: "In order to make decisions to get a product out in three months or six months, or to enter a new business in nine months, you need information [systems]. . . . Hewlett-Packard has 70,000 people. . . . We have 17,000 work stations tied to an electronic mail network that provides a way to communicate data [almost instantly] throughout our organization . . . on an international basis."[53]

The environmental changes that characterize the 1980s are rapid, frequent, and complex. This means that a company's skill at simply responding strategically to change does not automatically lead to competitive success or even survival. The constancy and complexity of change have placed a premium on two corporate attributes: the ability to think strategically and the flexibility to bring good ideas to the marketplace ahead of the competition. Strategists must, in a sense, unlearn the art of adaptation and begin instead to "think big": to ask smart questions early, and to listen wisely. Top executives must consciously move their institutions toward strategic management.

L. C. Knight, writing on the nature of the Fool in Shakespeare's *King Lear,* observes that the fool "speaks to (and out of) a quite different order of apprehension."[54] Companies need to look at their environments from a "different order of apprehension"; they need to nurture individuals who will dare to try the "unimaginable." To do this, chief executives must build organizations that value the innovative spirit and are led by a forward-looking, externally oriented management group.

Change is the one thing we know to be constant. Organizations must aggressively anticipate, seize, and exploit it to prosper and survive. And, although this may require a dramatic transformation in terms of management thinking and behavior, it is not at all at odds with the fundamental drive people have to succeed and renew themselves. Without the uncertainty brought about by constant change, the potential for innovation might not exist. To quote Jeremy Campbell, a British writer, as he describes Norbert Wiener, the father of cybernetics: "As his mathematical horizons expanded, he came to realize that the power to create the new out of the old cannot exist in any proper sense in a world where everything is necessary and nothing is uncertain."[55]

NOTES

1. "The New Breed of Strategic Planner," *Business Week,* September 17, 1984, pp. 62–68.
2. Ibid.
3. "The Recovery Skips Middle Managers," *Fortune,* February 6, 1984, p. 112.
4. Ibid.
5. Yankelovich, Skelly and White, Inc., "Business Planning in the Eighties: The New Competitiveness of American Corporations," Coopers & Lybrand, 1983.
6. "The New Breed of Strategic Planner."
7. "A Pioneer Spirit Sweeps Business," *New York Times,* March 25, 1984.
8. "RCA: Will It Ever Be a Top Performer?," *Business Week,* April 2, 1984, p. 52.
9. R. DeNeui, "The Experience Curve as a Strategy Tool," *McKinsey Staff Paper,* August 1980.
10. W. Kiechel III, "The Decline of the Experience Curve," *Fortune,* October 5, 1981, pp. 139–146.
11. W. K. Hall, "Survival Strategies in a Hostile Environment," *Harvard Business Review,* September/October 1980, p. 75.
12. W. Kiechel III, "The Decline of the Experience Curve," *Fortune,* October 5, 1981, pp. 139–146.
13. Ibid.
14. See R. A. Bettis and W. K. Hall, "The Business Portfolio Approach—Where It Falls Down in Practice," *Long Range Planning,* vol. 16, no. 2, April 1983, pp. 95–104, for a discussion of the difficulties of identifying independent SBUs in a diversified company and the ramifications of this for SBU-based planning systems.
15. D. Hambrick and I. MacMillan, "The Product Portfolio and Man's Best Friend," *California Management Review,* Fall 1982, vol. 25, no. 1, pp. 84–95.
16. "How Dogs Can Be Given More Bite," *Financial Times,* November 13, 1981, p. 10.
17. W. Kiechel III, "Corporate Strategists Under Fire," *Fortune,* December 27, 1982, pp. 34–39.
18. R. Hamermesh and R. White, "Management Beyond Portfolio Analysis," *Harvard Business Review,* January/February 1984, pp. 103–109.
19. P. Haspeslagh, "Portfolio Planning: Uses and Limits," *Harvard Business Review,* January/February 1982, pp. 58–73.
20. "Conference for Chief Executives," The Boston Consulting Group, October 1981.
21. W. Kiechel III, "Three (or Four, or More) Ways to Win," *Fortune,* October 19, 1981, pp. 181–188.
22. R. I. Benjamin, J. F. Rockart, M. S. Scott Morton, and J. Wyman, "Information Technology: A Strategic Opportunity," *Sloan Management Review,* Spring 1984, pp. 3–10.
23. M. E. Porter, *Competitive Strategy,* Free Press, New York, 1980, p. 396.
24. W. Kiechel, "Three (or Four, or More) Ways to Win."
25. See W. E. Fruhan, *Financial Strategy: Studies in the Creation, Transfer and Destruction of Shareholder Value* (Richard D. Irwin, Homewood, Ill., 1979) for a discussion of the relationship between economic value and stock price.

26. C. J. Loomis, "Corporate Stars That Brightened a Dark Decade," *Fortune*, April 30, 1984, pp. 224–322.

27. Ibid.

28. Ibid.

29. S. P. Sherman, "Eight Big Masters of Innovation," *Fortune*, October 15, 1984, pp. 66–84.

30. "General Electric: Business Development," Harvard Business School Case Study #9-382-092, Rev. 6/82.

31. J. W. Gardner, *Self-Renewal*, W. W. Norton & Co., New York, 1981, p. 144.

32. Ibid.

33. F. W. Gluck, S. P. Kaufman, and A. S. Walleck, "Strategic Management for Competitive Advantage," *Harvard Business Review*, July/August 1980, pp. 154–164; also *The McKinsey Quarterly*, Autumn 1980.

34. "Why Procter & Gamble Is Playing It Even Tougher," *Business Week*, July 18, 1983, pp. 176–186.

35. *Wall Street Journal*, May 11, 1984, p. 33.

36. *Euromoney*, October 1983, p. 299.

37. H. Banks, "General Electric—Going with the Winners," *Forbes*, March 26, 1984, pp. 97–106.

38. J. Q. Hunsicker, "Can Top Managers Be Strategists?," *Strategic Management Journal*, vol. I, 1980, pp. 77–83.

39. J. F. Welch, "Growing Fast in a Slow-Growth Economy," Executive Speech Reprint, 1981.

40. H. Banks, "General Electric—Going with the Winners."

41. *Institutional Investor*, July 1983, p. 92.

42. P. D. Petri, "Meet the Mean New IBM," *Fortune*, June 13, 1983, pp. 68–82. (Note: IBM has since increased its equity position in Intel to 20%.)

43. K. Ohmae, "Key Factors for Survival in the Microelectronics Industry," Annual Conference, North American Society for Corporate Planning, May 1984.

44. Ibid.

45. "New Alliances Reshape the Computer Industry," *Business Week* Special Report, July 16, 1984, pp. 84–106.

46. Address by E. McCracken at the Annual Conference of the North American Society for Corporate Planning, San Francisco, May 1984.

47. H. Banks, "General Electric—Going with the Winners."

48. Corporate Executive Office: Chairman J. Welch, Vice Chairman J. Burlingham, Vice Chairman E. Hood.

49. "General Electric: Business Development," Harvard Business School Case Study #9-382-092, Rev. 6/82.

50. Ibid.

51. G. L. Parsons, "Information Technology: A New Competitive Weapon," *Sloan Management Review*, Fall 1983; also *The McKinsey Quarterly*, Spring 1984, pp. 3–13.

52. D. B. Montgomery and C. E. Weinberg, "Toward Strategic Intelligence Systems," *Journal of Marketing*, Fall 1979, pp. 41–52; also *The McKinsey Quarterly*, Spring 1981.

53. Address by E. McCracken at the Annual Conference of the North American Society for Corporate Planning, San Francisco, May 1984.

54. L. C. Knight, "Some Shakespearean Themes," Stanford University Press and Chatto & Windus, Ltd., Stanford and London, 1959.

55. J. Campbell, *Grammatical Man*, Simon & Schuster, New York, 1982, p. 319.

2

PLANNING

CHAPTER 2

Organizing for Planning

WALTER P. BLASS

WALTER P. BLASS recently retired as director of strategic planning at the AT&T Company. In that capacity, he was responsible for the strategic positioning of AT&T in the global market for information transport and management. He was also responsible for the scanning of the social, political, workplace, and international environments. He was part of a team responsible to the corporate vice president for the statement of mission, formulation of a strategic plan, contingency plans, and special studies for the Office of the Chairman. He is currently president of a consulting company. Mr. Blass is widely published and is a speaker in such institutions as Wells and Meredith colleges, Columbia, City University of New York, Grenoble University in France, and Fudan and Peking universities in the People's Republic of China. He is currently teaching the strategic planning course at the Fordham University Graduate School of Business and is also a Senior Fellow for the Woodrow Wilson Foundation in Princeton, New Jersey.

OUTLINE

Many students in prestigious business schools despise courses in organizational development or design. They are "soft" or "mushy," and are certainly not quantifiable as courses in accounting, econometrics, statistics, or even manufacturing. Such courses mainly revolve around the endless variety of human beings that populate businesses in this country or abroad. At 27, the median age of business school students, it's hard to get one's intellectual arms around this degree of dispersion, the ambiguity of motives and language, and the conflicts between line and staff, craft and management, and field and headquarters.

Unfortunately for the graduate students, and even for those of us with more gray hair, these complexities lie at the heart of organizing for strategic planning. Organizing for anything requires an explicit or implicit understanding of what is required, who wants it, who doesn't want it, what came before, and what kind of an enterprise this process is to be grafted onto. It is not merely a matter of defining terms, but of being clear about the whole thing. Too often chief executives run for the nearest fad—which currently happens to be strategic planning—without asking themselves if they would similarly buy a four-million-dollar machine, or tell the accountants to go back to FIFO.

This chapter suggests some answers to these questions, some ways of going into and through the forest. But caution is recommended. More *huge* errors have been committed in the name of strategic planning than in nearly any other discipline, in far less time. If the Bendix–Martin Marietta fight is any indication, CEOs are justly suspicious of strategic planning. One false assumption, one scenario not examined, one gaming strategy insufficiently thought through, and the croupier rakes up the chips and it's all over. Can proper organizing help?

WHAT ARE THE OBJECTIVES?

Starting with one's objectives is never wrong. Why do we want to set up a strategic planning organization? What is it anyway? Why not just hire the best consultant around and skip the overhead? What happens if you defy fashion and just do without? One of my CEOs posed that very question to me a month after he had taken over the reins. At the time, the company was owned by a *Fortune* 100 conglomerate, although we alone had up to 35 percent of the U. S. market for certain services.

"Well," I replied, throwing caution to the winds, "you really don't have to, provided two conditions obtain:

1.   The parent company is correct in every forecast they make—interest rates, regulatory policy in Washington, the course of the GNP, and so on.
2.   Even if they aren't right, they'll blame themselves and not you if something goes wrong and "eat" the resulting shortfall in earnings.

If these conditions, however, do not hold for your tenure as CEO, you'r
better served by having an independent hand to read the sextant and th
weather, and compare the course with the charts.''

What, then, is strategic planning? It is, briefly, a process of making expli
the goals of the enterprise, the environment in which it operates, the strateg
to be employed to reach those goals, the programs subsumed by the st
egies, and finally the feedback loops that tell the firm whether each of th
steps has been identified correctly. In small firms, this can be done la
from the intuitive insights of the owners or managers, especially give
scale of the operation. In larger firms with more resources at stake
more exposure to a shifting environment, and with much greater o
tional complexity, it is necessary to be more explicit about this   and
possibly to devote skilled resources to making sure that one hasn'
a factor of major importance. As suggested in the colloquy w
above, strategic planning comprises a deliberate attempt to c   course
of the enterprise against known and unknown factors and
of the actual progress against the desired path. Strategi
cannot be grafted onto an existing enterprise like a   or legal department. The "setting" for such planning is almost
itself, and it is to this that we now turn.

The Setting

It has been a part of the received wis   n ot psychologists that al
to the content of human interaction
Whether the setting is an open fiel
draws you outward or, conversel , into yoursen,
a great deal of difference. So it is
the descriptors are not of a phy
there such an effort in the past? Did it
Was it actually dealing with s
Was it used solely as a mear
a desperate gamble against foreo   nine"
operation, far removed fror   other principal
officers?

These questions almost answ   et often they are not asked,
and the results are judged   much attention being paid to them. I have
seen dozens of questionn res that ask if the planning function reports to
the CEO, but none has asked if the planning office was physically colocated
with the executive suite or accessible within a two-minute interval. Yet that
"setting" may in fact make the difference between actual eye-to-eye interaction and none at all. Of course the inevitable bias that reporting relationships bring to the planning function cannot be wished away. The operations
group is not likely to impale itself on questions that have no current answers.
If planning reports through the financial officer, it will not have a marketing

or implementation cast to it. If the corporation has a culture in which the line officers bear total responsibility for results, the planning function has to be melded in without getting between the line officers and the CEO, yet positioned so that the line officers will want to consult and interact with it. If the culture of the corporation is one of financial controls, with responsibility for strategic business unit (SBU) operations left strictly to the SBU heads, it is clear that a planning function separate from the financial function will be seen as either redundant or threatening.

The Turf

The turf covered by strategic planning organizations differs greatly from enterprise to enterprise. In the Pentagon, Joint Plans has responsibility for an overall strategic posture for the defense of the United States, but no tactical or operational accountability. By contrast, it is clear that Bendix used the strategic planning function both before and during the Martin Marietta episode not only for the conceptualizing but also for the analytic and operational function of divestiture and acquisitions. Exhibit 2-1 shows a recent survey

EXHIBIT 2-1   Strategic Planning Involvement

Task	Primary	Secondary
Formulating corporate objectives	56%	36%
Formulating corporate strategy	58	34
Functioning of planning system	55	32
Idea man for CEO	39	39
Aid line management strategy	31	43
Communicate business plan	39	33
Monitoring progress vs. plan	38	39
Educating management about planning	33	34
Evaluating operating management's plans	29	41
Identify new development opportunities	25	32
Monitor development of new business	20	39
Consolidate operating management plans	32	25
Interpret information about company markets	18	35
Interpret information about social climate	13	23
Interpret information about economic trends	20	39
Interpret information about government actions	12	24
Interpret information about international markets	6	20
Mergers and acquisitions—analysis	33	30
Mergers and acquisitions—integration	20	26

Source: Coopers and Lybrand; Yankelovich, Skelly and White: "1983 Survey of Planning in 250 Firms."

Note: Percentages denote corporations, with or without formal planning departments, answering yes to each question of total sample. Totals add up to 100 percent on each line with "indirectly or not involved."

of the functions carried out by planning organizations in private sector organizations. As stakeholder theory has become practice, many corporations have learned to analyze their primary stakeholders much as politicians view their constituencies.[1] Inasmuch as business leaders understand their primary customers, large stockholders, and powerful union bosses, so should the strategic planner understand his or her constituents.

Mary Cunningham, former vice president of strategic planning for the Bendix Corporation, was quite explicit in her book, *Powerplay: What Really Happened at Bendix:*

> It was exactly as Agee had predicted: He had no one at the top he could rely upon and so became increasingly dependent on me.

> Did you mean all those glowing things you said about me, that one of the decisions you're proudest of is hiring me?'' I said. For by now I realized how awful my dilemma was. I was utterly alone. There was only one person with any clout in this company whose complete support I had and I wanted to make sure I still had that.[2]

The problems that beset Bendix are illustrative of the dangers of seeing the CEO as the only constituency for the planner. Since the planner should have the future of the entire organization as his or her focus, *all* the constituencies should be considered. Given his or her vulnerability to actions by consumers, regulatory agencies, environmental activists, unions, minority groups, suppliers, customers, and so on, why would a CEO—and therefore a planner—deliberately neglect a potential threat or opportunity?

Too few CEOs and planners, however, have given adequate thought to including these constituencies deliberately in the planning charter, explicitly or implicitly. For example, how often does a planning group choose to consult outsiders who are among these groups? A CEO frequently takes advantage of an invitation to speak at their annual convention, but what about the planner? How many planners have taken it upon themselves to go out with a salesman and call on a representative group of customers? Some planners have spent their own funds in visiting Japan or the People's Republic of China just to get a personal sense of "what the competition is doing." A few planners have had union experience and, unlike most college graduate managers, have some understanding of the dilemma of the craft employee down at the bottom of the chain of command—feeling vulnerable and impotent, and almost always ignorant of the waves of new technology, competition, and ideology sweeping through the industry. A truly competent planner will seek to defuse potential opposition to change, as well as to understand and get insight into the issues, by explicitly including contacts with constituencies in the mission of the planning group.

STRUCTURING THE STAFF

Imagine an ideal firm, which is now considering its planning options. What choices would be available for structuring a strategic planning staff? They can be listed as follows:

No strategic planning staff at all

A very small staff reporting to the CEO

An integrated strategic and business planning group

A strong headquarters adversarial staff reporting to a very senior officer who would critique (openly) the line divisional plans

The use of outside consultants

No Strategic Planning Staff

Contrary to the current trend, there is a case to be made for having no strategic planning group at all. If the firm is a small one in which the CEO is capable of grasping and executing a vision of where the firm should be going, a strategic staff is unnecessary. If the firm is in a turnaround situation in which the reduction of costs is paramount and the indications of what is required are equally clear to CEO, board of directors, and administration alike, strategic planners might well get underfoot.

In the latter situation, if there is even the slightest doubt whether the firm should remain in the "business as defined" there may be a good reason to consider an alternative strategy. Many U.S. shipbuilders, steelmakers, and textile mill owners might have profited 10 or more years ago from having a strategic planning group question their implicit assumption that they need only reinvest in more modern equipment to become profitable. U.S. Steel's purchase of Marathon Oil may be seen as having resulted from the technique of strategic positioning, given the comparative disadvantage to producers of basic steel in low-wage economies such as Korea or Brazil. Where there is a choice to be made of investment of resources outside the industry or of deliberate disinvestment for the purpose of benefiting one or more of the constituencies, it would behoove senior management to consider the use of a strategic planning group.

Small Staff Reporting to CEO

If the null option has been rejected—and it does seem to be rejected in most *Fortune* 200 companies, if only because of their diversity and size—how might one go about choosing among the options shown above? Clearly, small is better than large. In one multibillion-dollar electronics company the strategic planning staff—domestic as well as international—is composed of only three individuals. All three have been with the company in a number of other roles, and all are considered by the line division officers to be worthy of consulting because of their personal knowledge and experience as well as their proximity to the CEO and the CEO's thinking. The latter point is worth considering carefully. Unlike an accounting staff, which may number in the thousands, a planning staff cannot conceive, communicate, or implement strategy if it is too large. By its nature, the strategic staff must be privy to the most closely held options of the CEO, the doubts and fears that he or she may have about the firm's future, and the most delicate negotiations that may be underway. The larger the planning staff, the more artificial the plan.

The option of a small staff reporting to the CEO has some attractive aspects. Presumably staff members are chosen from the most knowledgeable executives in the firm or from a consulting firm that has worked with it. The latter approach was the route taken by Sears, Roebuck when it asked Philip Purcell, formerly of McKinsey & Co., to head their planning.

Attractive as that approach may be, it does have some drawbacks. Small headquarters staffs have a hard time turning a large company around. The culture of a large company that has been operating in a given fashion for decades does not change easily. A small headquarters staff may not prove equal to the challenge. Another reason against the staff's reporting to the CEO lies in the excesses typified by the Mary Cunningham episode at Bendix. Line officers should not feel cut off from their chief by a planning staff. Also, one must consider the possibility of error in the staff's conclusions and how best to spot the mistake and counteract it. This problem may have less to do with positioning than with the way in which the CEO listens and examines evidence, but this possibility is worth keeping in mind if this approach is chosen.

Integrated Strategic and Business Planning

A common approach is to merge the strategic and business planning functions. This amalgamation has the merit of avoiding the duplication of expertise and consequent review of plans that would otherwise be necessary. On the other hand, it carries considerable disadvantages.

Business plans are by necessity extrapolations of today's budget and operational plans. They need to be in sync with strategic plans, but their sheer number and volume may result in a displacement of the strategic questions and thrusts. One company, which had merged strategic and business planning for five years, found itself with 33 volumes of plans for a 10-billion-dollar business. It was impossible to find the strategic needle in the planning details haystack. It may be a great deal more informative to utilize a separate staff to deal with the strategic dimension in a large company. Likewise, since business plans have to be reasonably detailed and numerical, they require a fairly sizable staff to examine and critique them. This point is also of importance when a major change of direction in the business is required. The preliminary thinking should be done by the strategic staff, and business plans should be made to conform only after the decision and its ancillary steps, such as divestiture and acquisition, have been made.

Strong Headquarters Staff

A variant of this latter approach is characterized by IBM's planning approach, which entails a close examination at the corporate staff level into the divisional plans. Other companies have attempted this technique with less success than IBM. It takes both considerable familiarity with the divisional operations and a certainty that some day the tables will be turned on the planner to make that system effective. Even then the process may lead to a degree of overhead that is unacceptable. For example, Jack Welch, upon becoming CEO of General Electric, systematically cut back the planning staff of over a hundred with a curt mandate that SBUs that were not likely to be number one or two in their markets be closed down. By contrast, where SBUs are not separated by unique markets, production facilities, or design processes, Welch's approach may prove unusable. Large integrated operations such as the Japanese trading companies (Mitsui, Mitsubishi, Matsushita) require a grasp of all the interrelations to maximize their utility. Michael Porter's comment that planning at the group, sector and corporate levels should be *qualitatively different* is well taken at this juncture.[3] He makes the point that, whereas the SBU should plan for costs, profits, and markets, the group level should be concerned with efficiency of R & D and other common costs, the sector level should take an overview of common distribution channels or common regulatory problems, and the corporate level should constantly be asking, Why are we in this line of business at all? A unified planning staff only at the corporate level may lose the benefits that a more disaggregated approach carries for each level of the firm.

Use of Outside Consultants

One quite different approach is to rely largely on outside consultants for the major strategic reorganization of the business, and leave the execution to an internal group, whether designated as strategic planning or not. This approach has been widely followed. Sears, Roebuck uses it, as did AT&T in its approach to moving the company from an engineering and utility outlook to a more marketing-oriented outlook in the middle 1970s.

The virtue of such an approach is that, depending on who the consultants are, the company may get excellent advisors that it would otherwise take the firm years to accumulate. Major consulting firms hire the best and the brightest from the business schools in this country, winnowing out those in an elimination process until the partners are skilled and experienced. If one is fortunate or perspicacious enough to select a consulting firm whose partners include individuals knowledgeable in the pertinent industry, and to get that partner assigned to one's account, one may indeed have the best consultant possible.

Unfortunately, consultants vary a great deal and some are dominated by a "master program" approach to consulting that entails picking one or more standard answers from the "bookshelf" of their experience. Fifteen years ago I had such an experience with a firm whose product was so well-known that a business school professor whom I met at a conference casually identified all four of their major recommendations and—smiling like a Cheshire cat—added that they had probably charged a seven-digit fee to boot! In addition, most of the consultants in large firms are themselves rather young people fresh out of school and with very little working experience, particularly in specific industries or firms. Although there may be an advantage to a fresh outlook, it may also be a serious disadvantage if it blocks recognition of the complexities of a specific enterprise and distinction between those things that are doable and those that are technologically or humanly impossible.

Consultants do what they are asked to do, and if a CEO knows what he or she wants, they can be most useful. Consultants can make inquires into the firm that are awkward for a new CEO to make personally. They can serve as lightning rods for criticisms and changes that are badly needed. They can propose a solution that can then be discussed freely within management without the complications that could be present if the CEO's own planning group or the CEO had recommended it. The implementation phase, however, may not proceed smoothly. Consultants are often hired by one CEO, work for a year to two, and then see their recommendations tossed into limbo by a successor to the CEO. Another problem may come from a lack of planning expertise inside the firm to implement skillfully the approved recommendations. This facet is critical and deserves consideration.

As long as one is using a consultant, perhaps the optimal planning situation is one in which there is a clear understanding of what the consultant is expected to do, and a small staff that has the confidence of the CEO to monitor and work with the consultant, and to ultimately carry out the implementation of the plan. Not all consulting firms want such continuity with a planning staff at a lower level of activity over a period of years. Some firms are geared up to do large, costly, one-time projects. My own experience as a new planner, however, was that the "continuity" approach gave the firm the external as well as internal push it needed while allowing the CEO an independent view of how well the internal planner was doing his or her job.

This discussion of structure cannot have a simple, resolute conclusion. The objectives of planning, the historical setting of a planning organization, the turf and constituencies covered, and the corporate culture all enter into the equation. Furthermore, the choices of actual individuals to run such an organization may in fact force the choice of structure. It is this activity to which we now turn.

CHOOSING THE CHIEF PLANNER AND STAFF

Of all the steps involved in organizing strategic planning, probably the most critical lies in the appointment of its chief. Much has been made of the desirability of the CEO's being the chief planner for the firm, and, indeed, nothing that follows should take away from that truth. Nonetheless, even the best CEO has responsibilities that keep him or her from paying full attention to long-range planning, and it will be necessary, if the CEO is the firm's chief planner, to select a head planner. Too often, this position goes to a court favorite, whether it be an up-and-coming line executive, a divisional chief too important to be savaged for a disaster in his division, or an outsider who happens to strike the CEO's fancy. Other firms choose attorneys because they are assumed to have the capability to make peace among warring factions in the firm. Finally, some firms pick a person with a scientific or economics background for the expertise that this may bring to the task.

Requirements for the Head Strategist

Error in terms of selection of the head planner is equaled only by the board's poor selection of a CEO. Planners are inherently trusted with the long-range welfare of the firm. Selection of an individual who is not trusted by his or her colleagues for personal reasons, whose grasp of the concepts of planning may be weak or absent, or whose vision may not extend past the next promotion is paralytic to the firm. Background seems to matter far less than it would appear. The personal qualities of the head planner—the abilities to bring insight into the task, maintain good relationships with critical constituents, and articulate clearly the desired course—seem to matter a great deal more.

A Person of Integrity

If these traps can be avoided, what qualities or qualifying signs should be looked for? First, seek an individual who has a record of maintaining integrity even when strained by circumstances. The chief planner will be tempted or threatened by many circumstances. In all likelihood the best path will naturally cause some powerful persons to come out against it. The story of Honda's move into large motorcycles related by Richard Pascale is instructive.[4] It seems that Mr. Honda was known for his temperamental outbursts early in the history of his company. He had been known to throw geishas out of windows when displeased. Yet his chief engineer persisted in pointing the boss toward the larger horsepower market despite great resistance. Indeed, only the prospect that Mr. Honda might win the Isle of Man race proved significant enough an inducement to get the resources devoted to such a project. Surely a less redoubtable officer would long before have given up at the CEO's public expression of his disagreement. Similarly, other issues will sorely try the judgment and wisdom of the planner.

As a Conceptualizer

Another critical facility of the head planner should be an ability to conceptualize courses of action, directions, and reconstitutions of the firm beyond the normal extrapolations of this or that product line. True strategic planning requires a leap of imagination; not all individuals can make such a leap. In an assessment program in which I have served for several years as an assessor, we saw considerable evidence that some personality makeups and prior scientific or engineering experience militate against that required leap. The psychologists David Keirsey and Marilyn Bates single out the type of leader who thinks intuitively as one who "has to be conceptualizing something to feel good about himself within the organization. He must design, and so is called the Visionary leader. . . . The Visionary leader is the architect of change. He is interested in the principles on which the organization is built or to be built. . . . He is able to see the dimensions and axes of systems as if he had x-ray vision and so can plan and construct capably."[5] Their results are based on the well-known Myers-Briggs psychological test, which, however, has been rarely used in the selection of managers in large firms. The test itself is based on a set of dichotomies that the Swiss psychologist Carl Jung proposed 60 years ago. Certainly those of us who have seen a large number of managers at work on a standardized set of tasks have seen the usefulness of these typologies in selecting individuals for certain tasks.

As a Communicator

The ideal planner should also be a communicator. In large firms this quality, not easily found in the individual who is as visionary as Keirsey and Bates would have him be, is an absolute must. No CEO will take on the task of "socializing" the vision of his planner; more often he is likely to adopt it only after the latter has gained "respectability" and adherents to his or her views. If there is a lesson to be learned from Franklin Roosevelt's style of leadership, it lies partly in his brilliance in finding a means of communication so commanding as the fireside chats on raido, which enabled him to reach over the heads of Congress into most households in the country. Would that most planners were equally gifted!

As a Fallible Person

Finally, the chief planner should have the extraordinary quality of being able to admit error or ignorance. Most individuals in a corporation get ahead by some degree of bluffing their presumed knowledge or skill at facing the unknown. Woe to the company whose planner has similar pretensions. Precisely because he or she is dealing with daunting complexity and uncertainty, the head planner should be able to follow the counsel of Oliver Cromwell, who enjoined: "I beseech you, in the bowels of Christ, think it possible that you may be mistaken." This statement should not be read as suggesting that the planner give way to every adverse wind and change course. On the contrary, she or he should attempt to make the best possible case for the proposed plan; at the same time, the planner should be very sensitive to the critical fact or scenario that may upset the underlying assumptions for its success. Just as the planner should be frank and open at pointing out fallacies or inconsistencies in operating plans, he or she should be equally sensitive at the beginning to contradictory evidence or better alternatives even if "not invented here."

Rotating Promising Managers as Head Planner

This is a limited but formidable list; one would be hard pressed to find such an exemplar of all these virtues. One way some companies have found around this problem is to rotate a promising senior manager through the position of chief planner. Robert Frederick, now Chairman and CEO of RCA, for example, became vice president of planning at General Electric after having headed one of the SBUs. After a successful tour in that position, he was promoted to a group vice presidency where he supervised several SBUs. The "permanent undersecretary," as he is known in the British Civil Service, for the department was Bill Rothschild, a well-known planner who had been in the department for 20 years prior to Frederick's arrival. This rotation approach coupled with the retention of a "permanent" planner allows a CEO or designated headquarters officer to vary the leadership of the planning function without losing valuable information and experience every time the incumbent is changed. The permanent planner enables the department to retain its continuity, its history, and, one hopes its accumulated wisdom while preserving the necessary flexibility to change with new management or new requirements. It also allows the firm to groom its most promising future officers through a function that they will greatly need at top management levels.

The disadvantages of this approach are obvious. No promising "star" will risk alienating his chief or even some of his more powerful peers with hard critiques of current trends or with revolutionary proposals. The possibility of obtaining a truly "alternative" scenario or plan to that of the CEO is commensurately reduced by appointment of someone whose tenure is based on something other than the best possible planning. I can recall one such individual who was in fact told upon his appointment: "Stay out of trouble for two years, and you're guaranteed promotion to the job you really want!" Subsequently the opportunities lost in those two years became all too obvious.

Wisdom versus Power: The Constitutional Limits

Another potentially destructive planning situation concerns the wise use of the power inherent in the function of the strategist. Some head planners get so inflated in their positions that they begin to encroach on the powers of the chief executive in promulgating policy and pursuing independent courses of action without higher blessing, or in undermining their superiors' authority over fellow officers. A "constitutional set of limits" needs to be adhered to by the chief planner in his or her playing out of the assigned role, regardless of the apparent vacuum that may be left by a weak CEO. Many is the planner who feels that he or she could run the corporation better than the CEO. But feeling that you could do better is far from carrying it out successfully. A well-known example may be found in the apparently successful progression from chief planner to CEO by W. Richard Goodwin at Johns Manville in 1970, who was removed by the board six years later. As planners we should always maintain our standards of the best that could be done for the corporation, but retain during our tenure as planners the humility of Voltaire's injuction to "cultivate one's own garden."

Ensuring Sufficient Diversity

Another major task is to assure sufficient diversity among the planning staff. Too many corporations with strong internal cultures maintain a narrow "insider's view" of the world by failing to reach outside that culture for their planning staff. Pierre Wack, recently retired chief strategist of Royal Dutch Shell, insisted that the planning staff be supplemented by nationals of countries other than Holland and the United Kingdom, in which Shell had operations. As a result, Shell had the benefit of insights into how specific corporate actions would be perceived in a given country, as well as a far richer base of ideas and critiques than it could have obtained with its usual "Dutch engineers and Scottish accountants."

A similar plea should be made for gender and age diversity. A form of disciplined brainstorming called synectics requires the selection of individuals who differ considerably by management level, age, and gender in order to maximize the creative potential of the group. In my experience, the results fully justify this practice.[6] One individual whose ignorance of the laws of physics was egregious was the suggester of outrageous ideas that set off in others implementable (and physically correct) ideas. Someone with experience in government, in areas outside industry, or in businesses with smaller or much larger competitors, may likewise bring in fresh ideas that would otherwise be missed.

Gaining Acceptance through Choosing Staff

The process of staffing a planning group may have a great deal to do with its ultimate success in gaining acceptance for its plans. It is tempting always to look for "the best and the brightest" inside and outside the corporation without considering what the consequences are for those who are "planned for." They may be more than a little curious about what is happening in the seemingly elite planning group. Why not enlist their help in staffing the group, thereby removing the aura of mysterious silence, in return for a far greater likelihood of plan implementation? Some planning groups deliberately reserve a "divisional seat," much as a presidential candidate may choose a running mate from another part of the country. Control may be given up to some degree, but the information and commitment gained are likely to offset greatly the ensuing disadvantages. Besides, total secrecy is seldom an asset in strategic planning for much the same reason as the propensity for error mentioned earlier. "Leaky secrets," when properly managed, can be good insurance policies against error. Some of the constituencies affected by the "secret plan" when drawn into the process quietly and informally may bring considerable critical intelligence to the task.

PLANNING PITFALLS

It would be delightful to predict that by following some set of rules or guidelines a perfect planning organization would produce a perfect plan. It is not possible to come up with a cookbook set of rules to guide the novice planner or the CEO who wants to strengthen this aspect of the company. Too many variable factors get in the way of a resolution with a simple pattern. As with so many human activities, planning is strewn with problems and pitfalls. This section will deal with these pitfalls, and will be followed by a discussion of the hallmarks of success. An organization chart alone will not tell us whether a successful plan will emerge, but we go forewarned if we look at these pitfalls and hallmarks in advance.

Only Paper Plans

Consider the issue of the utility of the product. Many corporations issue fancy five- or ten-year plans and put them into bound numbered binders that reside on the shelves of a dozen executives, never pulled out for reference until the next time a planning "exercise" is called for. How does that happen? Is it preventable?

Such paper plans happen frequently in organizations in which the passion for elegance and plans that can be "shown to be good" prevail over the will to "make it happen." Ironically, there seems to be a rule similar to Albert Hirschman's Principle of the Hidden Hand with respect to planning: if you knew how difficult it was going to be, you would never start it in the first place.[7] In planning, to succeed you must relinquish control to those who will have to implement the plan. Logically, that would seem to be a major error. After all, if they knew what to do, why bother with a planning staff at all? If the latter's views are not to be promulgated, why go through all the effort? That conundrum is at the root of sound planning. If the results of planning are to have any lasting effect, those who initiate the plans must give way to those who will execute the plans—not at the end of the process but close to the beginning. It is comparable to the process by which young medical students are encouraged and permitted to practice on live human beings. Surely they are not as capable as their teachers, yet without the actual experience of having the responsibility and making the decisions, they never would develop the skills required for medical practice. So it is with planning.

However skillful the planner may be, the passing of the torch to the line executives is imperative. Without that act of faith, real planning is not merely unlikely but impossible. All that will result are fancy paper plans, pleasing to read but of no consequence to the firm, its customers, employees, or stockholders. Does that passing of the torch weaken the rigor and originality of the planner's plan? Of course if does, and it would be naive to think not. But precisely because *some* parts of the original conception will in fact be implemented, it is a better plan than if it had remained pristine but neglected.

Internally Acceptable, but Ultimately Failed, Strategies

Another possible outcome is the inverse of the one just outlined. The planning effort may result in a set of strategies that is internally acceptable to all constituencies but fails in the marketplace, vis-à-vis government or some other external environment. Such an outcome usually results because a planner is more concerned with internal politics than with what is happening in the outside world, not an unusual occurrence in very large firms with an assured market (defense contractors, utilities, "chosen instrument airlines," etc.). The dominant culture allows corporate staff to be essentially inwardly turned, concerned with their own interpretation of outside events, filled with managers who have "grown up in the business" and have an almost immunologic reaction to outsiders.

Several examples of this come to mind. The American auto industry in the post-1973 period of sharply higher fuel costs was caught totally unprepared for a shift in the market toward smaller cars with higher mileage per gallon. By contrast, both the European and the Japanese automakers were already sensitive to the price elasticity of fuel due in large measure to the sumptuary taxes on gasoline that their governments imposed as a means of restricting car ownership. Once OPEC had succeeded in making the initial quadrupling of the price of oil stick, the small car manufacturers instantly made the most of their capabilities while Detroit suffered with outdated plants and designs. Yet the information was there to be heeded. Some petroleum authorities like Walter Levy and Morris Adelman were speaking out well before 1973 on the vulnerability of the West to price increases.

Another example may be drawn from the service crisis that Bell Telephone companies experienced in the late 1960s. Massive changes had penetrated the environment within which they operated; the work force had deteriorated badly as hard bargaining by the companies with unions had forced wages down to the 60th percentile of the Bureau of Labor Standards entry wage level; new immigrants were streaming into the franchised territory but holding off telephone service because of old-country habits; the Johnson Great Society program had started in 1965 but did not affect demand for service until three to four years later; the Vietnam War had been "a small war just exciting enough to be interesting" (W. W. Rostow's prophetic phrase in his book *The Stages of Economic Growth*) until 1968 when it unseated a President and exploded into the U.S. economy. The result of all this was not perceived by telephone companies who largely relied on *their own internal statistics* of demand. Since many of them had considerable overcapacity in the early 1960s stemming from the slowdown in the U.S. economy during the Eisenhower years, this inertial change was not noticed. Plans were based on the average of three prior years' growth. Many moves of customers, while capable of being interpreted as major trends in socioeconomic mobility (e.g., Puerto Rican moves into Rockland and Westchester counties out of New York City), were just assumed away as "churn" and no one bothered to notice the directionality of the moves. The results were a massive scrapping of corporate plans as well as drastic remedial measures far more costly than they would have been if the external environment had been sufficiently understood.

A third example may be drawn from a bank that wanted to move quickly into the international business market. Demand was clearly there; many other banks were already capitalizing on the burgeoning market. Equipment was available to computerize transactions for instantaneous availability around the clock. All that was missing was an awareness that the internal culture of the bank was geared to a middle-income-residence customer. No one had bothered with articulating procedures for customers that were taken for granted with the Park Avenue trade, with customer service standards that were considered de rigeur for major international firms, or with employee attitudes toward customers who now could switch to another bank with massive profit consequences on the basis of one disastrous transaction. The consultant who had been called in by the bank ruefully informed management that their strategy was foundering on a factor that could only slowly be changed, too slowly to make the shift they had anticipated; only with a massive and long-term human resource change could they hope to succeed.

What is the *organizational moral* to be drawn from these episodes? Clearly it lies in cultivating a "third ear," as Theodore Reich called it, for the sensitivity to factors not *normally* considered. The tendency to please successive layers of management with news that is not too upsetting, with "evolutionary" rather than revolutionary change as some perceive it, must be curbed. General Motors, for example, had a group of external consultants who were themselves not bound by the GM employees' practice of buying only GM cars; many had imported cars and were articulate in explaining why. But management's ears were not listening. It may in fact take some strong words at the highest levels to convince senior managment that only grief lies ahead with internally comfortable plans. The CEO of a subsidiary of one of the firms just mentioned offered his resignation when the chairman of the board insisted on conformance to existing plans; his successor learned only several years later how prescient his colleague had been. Seeding the organization with people from other perspectives, young people and foreigners, and then heeding their warnings, may be the only way to prevent such happenings.

Tactics Masquerading as Strategies

The line between strategy and tactics is always a debatable issue. As some wit noted, "what you see depends on where you stand." At the platoon leader's level, movement over several miles is the strategy, and it may take him weeks to accomplish it; at the level of the general, this is a mere tactical push and the strategy may be measured in years and hundreds of thousands of soldiers. So it is with business. When strategies are conceived by lower-level employees they typically lack the breadth required for success at the level of the firm as a whole. This is not their fault, but that of the CEO and his lieutenants, who frequently are much too busy with current operations to be concerned with long-range strategy. One consultant boldly informed his client that such was the case and that the CEO needed to take strong measures to have his officers delegate operational tasks and assume the strategic hats they should have been wearing all along.

Highly quantified plans can appear strategic while masking their lack of critical operational assumptions behind a screen of nicely interlocking mathematical formulae. Such gaps can be spotted by asking a knowledgeable field manager if he would be willing to assume responsibility for such plans over a three to five-year period. The experienced manager can quickly spot the gaps in such a document, however sophisticated the financials and the econometric modelling. Financial ratios are but refracting mirrors through which reality can be viewed. They seldom allow adequate perception of the richness, diversity, and ambiguity of the "real world" in which the field manager must operate. Why else would a CEO like Donald Kendall spend the 60 percent of his time in the field that assures his Pepsi Cola company a place among Waterman and Peters' *In Search of Excellence: Lessons from America's Best-Run Companies?* A constant testing of proposed plans by a selected group of "outsiders," "cynics," or company "naysayers" may be the only way to surface the weaknesses that are easily missed in an otherwise excellent-looking document.

When the Organization Lacks the Will to Implement

In organizations, as in individuals, there comes a point at which the diagnosis of a problem has been made and accepted, a proposed solution has been discussed and agreed to, but the client—in this case the corporation—lacks the will to implement the recommendations. As in the case of individual psychotherapy, to which many of the aspects of planning can be compared, the phenomenon has its roots in the state of mind of the decision makers with regard to the existing state of affairs.[8] Clearly, if the present, although uncomfortable, is not perceived as life-threatening, or at least worse than any proposed change of action, it is doubtful that the client will demonstrate the will or energy to change. In psychiatry this state of an individual is called neurosis, a condition of dysfunctional behavior that nevertheless allows a certain predictability and "proof" that the client is the perpetual victim. Such a condition was shown by the railroads and certain telephone companies who were complaining during much of the era of detailed regulation that all the blame for their condition lay on the regulators: the lack of pricing flexibility, the cross-subsidization resulting in uneconomic investments, the inability to serve emerging market segments with new technology, and so on. In reality, as we have found out since deregulation, many of these carriers were unable to handle themselves in a high-change environment, did not understand their own roles in their situations, and lacked the drive to adapt which some of their competitors had.

This phenomenon is easily perceived in the client corporation that seems comfortable with its bureaucratic neurosis. As the recommendations fall into place and gain acceptance among the younger, lower-level management, they encounter increasing resistance at the top. Established executives see their turf as invaded, if not completely removed. Conservatives exaggerate the risk involved, unwilling to admit the risks of continuing on the present course. After the planning effort, by insiders or outside consultants, is over, the recommendations are quietly left to shrivel in a corner of the bureaucracy. Only the competitor who has sensed the need for change and tried to make the adaptation benefits from their failure.

Can better structuring of the planning effort help? Some planners have deliberately sought a "planning board" or "strategy council" composed of, among others, those very conservatives who might be most likely to object to change, in order to engage them in the process of change at the beginning and thus ensure the necessary implementation.

No Follow-Through to Accountable Organizations

It is no great achievement to fashion criteria of accomplishment and lines of responsibility for ongoing operations. All well-run organizations have a published set of criteria specifying who is responsible for what, and many have embodied these criteria in compensation plans for key executives. It is considerably more difficult to specify in advance what an existing organization is expected to accomplish under a new set of strategies. The temptation frequently is to copy President Franklin D. Roosevelt's approach: create a new "alphabet soup" agency to replace the function of the established line agency but let the latter continue its make-believe work until Congress will see the results and abolish it. Unfortunately, corporations today do not function in the decades in which Roosevelt successfully implemented his solution. Overhead cuts into profits and the more rapidly the environment changes, the worse the squeeze on profits becomes. Thus corporations cannot afford the luxury of duplicate staffs, overlapping jurisdiction, and sinecures for aging executives.

The solution is to designate *within the strategic recommendations* the accountable organizations, preferably established ones, whose mission will change and whose criteria of accomplishment will reflect the new mandate. One consultant, recognizing that the client would find it hard to understand what was involved in the concept, meticulously prepared charts showing a typical day's in-basket and the disposition of every item that the executive would be responsible for. Another approach includes a comparison to other firms in which the proposed accountability is an established fact. Whichever method is used, the principle that "what does not get measured does not get done" should be noted. Together with a careful pinning of the measurement tail to the right donkey, this will assure that the CEO will know whom to hold responsible for a finite accomplishment of the objective under the new strategy.

HALLMARKS OF SUCCESSFUL ORGANIZATION

We have now reviewed most of the pitfalls and errors that planning efforts can fall prey to. By contrast, what are the hallmarks of successful efforts? Is there a set of *organizational* criteria that can be used to tell the likely successes from the failures?

Small Size

There seems to be a pattern in bureaucracies of internal growth regardless of external circumstances. C. Northcote Parkinson enshrined that rule in his "law." The inverse must apply to strategic planning. Size of the planning organization cannot simply be proportional to the size of the firm. It is quite possible that a handful of people suffice in a 100-million-dollar company, but not more than 20 may be required for the 50-billion-dollar company. Clearly, the tasks must be delegated and decentralized beyond the planning staff as the temptation to grow gets stronger. "Graduates" of the planning department do not lose their capabilities when they become influential in their new organizations, and can be used by strategic planning to help out on an ad hoc basis. In any case, the CEO knows from experience that a small group of individuals he or she can relate to personally is a far more valuable resource than a huge department, where nameless individuals with no known experience, track records, or intimate knowledge of what is wanted by the CEO are the source of a given strategy.

CEO Support

If smallness is desirable, then the support of the CEO is mandatory. It may be taken as a dictum that there is no strategic planning worth the name without the CEO's involvement from the start. There are still some CEOs who believe that they can safely leave such an esoteric topic to a delegate with more specialized skills, but that number is shrinking daily. Industries that collapse because of external technological change (e.g., electronic tubes), localized distribution channels that are invaded by the entry of an international conglomerate with a far more appealing set of products to display (e.g., L'Eggs stockings, the boutique movement in retailing), sources of financing that the company has traditionally been dependent on that dry up under high interest rates—all these should convince CEOs of how vulnerable their firms are to displacement. If this is the environment that is changing so rapidly, can the CEO afford to leave the adaptation of the firm to others and to receive their report only as a finished product? The CEO must give active recognition that she or he is responsible to the Board for the future of the company. Mere delegation of that task will not be acceptable to a sensitive Board that recognizes the CEO's unfamiliarity with what options there are for strategic responses to industry changes, competitive positioning, or the imperatives of political changes. If the CEO neglects the strategic planning effort until a final product is available, the whole organization will take its cues from that neglect and hinder considerably the tasks of assembling the critical information, testing the alternative strategies, and ensuring commitment to the ultimate strategy chosen.

A Strategy Worth Hiding from Competitors

Many strategic plans unfortunately say so little of consequence that they might just as well be part of the pabulum that is usually offered to public inquiries with respect to company policies. If the strategy is worth something, it is worth safeguarding from the competitor. Eventually the astute competitor will get the message from actions in the market, be it technological, distribution, or pricing strategy. Yet every month that can be garnered from such a disclosure is another month gained for the strategically run firm. This is not to overlook the possibility of using strategies to signal competitors—witness Kodak's behavior in 1979 with regard to instant film cameras vis-à-vis Polaroid. Nor should the passion for secrecy extend to such extremes as failure to inform the managers who need to understand the strategies to contribute most to their success. Yet, in the final analysis, one question should be asked as the strategy is defined and refined: Is it meaningful and important to our competitors? If not, if it contains mere assertions of prowess, promises of miracles to be wrought in the marketplace, and commitment of resources that are not realistically within the firm's command, it isn't really a strategy.

Line Organization Plans That Implement the Strategy

Some planning organizations feel their job is done when a 15-page document containing the essence of the corporation's plans has been approved by the

CEO. Others go into excruciating detail of operational plans that have no place at the corporate level.

A proper balance needs to be struck, and it is best accomplished by assuring that line operations plans conform to corporate strategy within a reasonable amount of time. Once a process is worked out, the CEO should be able to call on the appropriate line executive and ask him or her for fairly detailed implications of the corporate strategy for the particular SBU or group. If the line executive has been brought in at the conceptual stage, involving early analysis and the consideration of alternative strategies, none of this will come as any surprise. On the contrary, the strategic planner will have reflected the problems or risks inherent in that strategy's impact on the SBU in the corporate overview. A strategic plan is not complete, however, until the line people have done their work to conform their plans to it. That is part of their accountability. It is also a test of the viability of the strategies for, if upon due consideration of the corporate strategy's impact on the SBU, a satisfactory line operations plan cannot be constructed, it will speak volumes about the original corporate view.

Clear, Auditable Environmental Assumptions

Some strategic plans are written as though they were unchangeable holy writ. In fact any plan is based on a set of environmental circumstances that are likely to change or, worse, are already outdated. The sound strategic plan has a set of assumptions spelled out in such a manner that the critical reader as well as implementer can readily recognize if, and more important when, these assumptions need to be changed. Such assumptions must include not only the more obvious economic aspects (interest rates, GNP growth, foreign currency equivalencies, demographics, etc.) but must have due regard to technology changes, market maturity, number and positioning of competitors, governmental influences, social ideology changes, and so on. Had electric utility plans included a specific assumption on fuel costs, it would have become a great deal more obvious that they were overbuilding central generating capacity at a time when the basic cost of fuel was rising exponentially and alternative technologies based on high fuel costs (co-generation, for example) would become highly viable. Such assumptions cannot be copied from some textbook or consultant's manual. One of the characteristics of a successful planning organization is the presence of one or more individuals directly responsible for the gathering and examination of environmental assumptions.

Strategic, Auditable Mileposts

Some businesses have readily auditable measures of success. Broadcasters rely on Nielsen ratings, newspapers depend on ABC readership surveys, and automobile companies intimately know the cars they sell, and those sold by their domestic and foreign competitors. In many cases, however, a new measure synthesized from others will have to be developed to measure the foreseen stages of strategic success. Market share, as economists and trust busters have found, is a trickier concept than most businessmen assume. Costs, although easily understood in terms of accounting concepts, are much less definite when the life cycle of the product is variable, depending on market obsolescence or technological retrofits. New markets are particularly prone to exaggerated claims of size and time frames. Susceptibility to disappearing market boundaries (computers vis-à-vis communication, print media vis-à-vis electronic displays and memory) are seldom mentioned in documents of grand strategy, unless the corporation is the one to benefit by their disappearance. In all cases, strategies must be organized with a set of factual, measurable benchmarks or mileposts that may be tested for timeliness or actuality. Anything less is wishful thinking.

Willingness to Tolerate Change and Uncertainty

One of the hallmarks of good strategies is the willingness of the drafters to encompass the likelihood of change and consequent uncertainties. Too often one finds strategic documents that are written like France's World War II Maginot Line: A 200-kilometer barrier to tank warfare and invasion that was designed with an eye firmly fixed on World War I technology and political realities. When Belgium fell before the German air force assault and rapidity of parachute landings which outflanked the Maginot Line, the French general staff tried vainly to use its vaunted guns, but to no avail, since their perimeter did not allow either elevation to anti-aircraft use or horizontal azimuth to shoot back into France itself.

Many a strategy is open to the same questions. What will you change if a well-heeled competitor enters the market; what would you do if our assumption about the physics of solar cells undergoes a massive discovery of higher yields; how does unemployment in Europe or South America affect political restrictions on foreign-based firms? Such eventualities need to be considered not only as contingencies but as part of the strategic planning process. If an organization has as its goal a fixed strategy that it will reexamine once every year or two, it will surely founder on the rocks and shoals of change. If, on the other hand, an organization sets out a strategy that is *designed to encompass change,* it will surely be more likely to be master of that change rather than have to react to it. Sometimes we planners seem to forget our own injunctions: we want to remain fixed lighthouses on the shifting sands of the harbor. Not only will "they" change, but so do we need to change our methods and our sense of ourselves to remain useful adjuncts to our organizations rather than reminders, like Ozymandias, of a great but almost-forgotten past.

NOTES

1. J. R. Emshoff and R. E. Freedman, "Who's Butting into Your Business," *Wharton Magazine,* Fall 1979, p. 16.
2. M. Cunningham and F. Schumer, *Powerplay: What Really Happened at Bendix,* Linden Press, New York, 1984, pp. 98, 159.
3. M. Porter, *Competitive Strategy,* Free Press, New York, 1980.
4. R. T. Pascale, "Perspectives on Strategy," Strategic Management Society Conference, Montreal, Quebec, October 1982.
5. D. Keirsey and M. Bates, *Please Understand Me,* Prometheus Nemesis Books, Delmar, Calif., 1978.
6. G. M. Prince, *The Practice of Creativity,* Collier Books, New York, 1970.
7. A. Hirschman, *Journeys Towards Progress,* Norton, New York, 1973.
8. W. P. Blass, "Corporate Planning as Psycho-Therapy: Guiding Your Company to Self-Knowledge," *Managerial Planning,* July/August 1980, pp. 11–15.

CHAPTER **3**

The Role of Consultants

THOMAS C. BARRON

THOMAS C. BARRON is a director and founding partner of Ayers, Whitmore & Company. He leads the firm's strategy development practice and over the years has had particular experience in industrial companies. He has also been extensively involved in international projects in Europe, the Far East, Africa, and Latin America. Prior to the founding of the firm in 1974, Mr. Barron was a consultant with McKinsey & Company and with Theodore Barry and Associates. He is an engineering graduate of the United States Military Academy at West Point and of the Harvard Business School. He is a member of The Planning Forum, the American Marketing Association, and the American Institute of Mining Engineers. He is also on the advisory board for the Management of Organizations faculty at Columbia Graduate School of Business.

OUTLINE

Acknowledgment is given to Frank Cook and Katherine Mullin for their participation in preparing this chapter.

Strategic planning—development of a framework for strategic decision making—is widely recognized as critical to company performance and essential in today's rapidly changing business environment. It is, however, probably one of the more difficult activities to conduct consistently well within the corporate environment. At its best, planning is issue-oriented and directly linked to ongoing operating decisions; at its worst, it is simply an exercise that is routine, superficial, and without management commitment.

The difficulty in planning effectively within companies is that it runs contrary to the dynamics of running a business from day to day. To keep a business profitable, management must devote critical time and energy to operating issues—making immediate marketing, sales, production, and financial decisions. Strategic planning, however, requires stepping back from the immediate—reviewing long-term trends in markets, governmental regulations, and competitive actions; analyzing "what if" possibilities; and identifying alternative routes to future objectives. These activities do not fit easily into daily operations. As one chief executive said, "You can't underestimate how little time I actually spend on strategic issues, but I'd be embarrassed to admit it publicly."

So whereas line management's knowledge and input are critical to effective strategic decision making, asking managers to step back and think strategically is difficult. Even institutions with the best, most professional planning departments often cannot bridge these two dramatically different requirements. In fact, many companies are deemphasizing planning as a formal ongoing effort and are cutting back on planning staffs to save overhead. At the same time, top managers in all industries are more convinced than ever that thinking and managing strategically are vital to long-term profitability, if not survival.

Because virtually all companies face this dilemma, strategic planning is probably one of the activities that most benefits from the judicious use of consultants. All companies—large or small, single-product–oriented or highly diversified—can benefit from the expertise of professionals who have intimate knowledge of the companies' requirements and challenges and can spend concentrated amounts of time focusing on analyses and issues outside the daily demands of operations. Time and again, company successes have proved the value of the effectively combined efforts of management and consultants.

Effective use of consultants in developing strategic decisions, however, requires management skill and commitment to guiding, shaping, and directing the consulting effort. Management must view consultants as extensions of their teams, valuable members whose roles and contributions will be directly influenced by the quality of direction and feedback they receive from the top.

This chapter will focus on two important considerations in the use of consultants in strategic decision making: one, determining when and how to obtain the greatest value from consulting expertise; and two, ensuring the effectiveness of the combined company/consulting effort. Let's first concentrate on obtaining value from consultants in the strategic decision making process.

Consultants—either individuals with expertise in specific fields or teams trained in analysis and counseling—are ideally suited to assist companies in strategic planning. Their skills and services can be selected to augment a company's current strategic resources, whether basic or highly sophisticated. Management can seek their expert help at any time to respond to events requiring strategic change.

AREAS OF CONSULTING PLANNING EXPERTISE

As Exhibit 3-1 shows, the planning services that consultants provide can generally be grouped into four broad categories: market/industry analysis, internal company analysis, strategy formulation, and strategy implementation. Depending on a company's requirements, management can seek outside ser-

EXHIBIT 3-1   Strategic Planning Activities

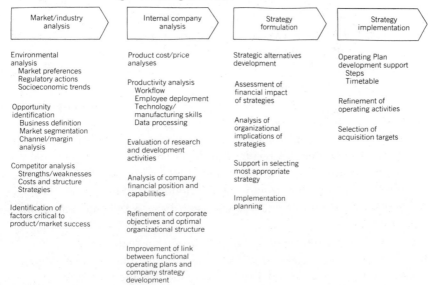

vices in any one area, or in a combination of several. Briefly, consulting services involve the following:

1. *Market/Industry Analysis.*   Analytical services directed outside the company to provide the underpinning for strategy formulation and involving, for example, customer and competitor field interviews, supply and demand forecasts, and market share analyses in order to:

    Assess a wide range of trends (e.g., market, legislative, political) that could affect the company over the long term.

    Identify opportunities for competitive advantage by developing product, customer, market, and supplier profiles.

    Identify competitors' strengths and weaknesses in product lines, market positions, financial condition, and organizations.

    Agree on the three or four factors, both external and internal to the company, that are critical to its business success or failure.

2. *Internal Company Analysis.*   Analytical services directed internally to assess the company's strengths and weaknesses within its external environment. Most depend on company data and internal interviews, including review of planning processes in place and the ultimate objectives of management, in order to:

    Assess profitability and competitive position of company products through product cost/price analyses by customer group.

    Evaluate research and development activities.

    Assess financial position and capabilities (e.g., asset management, cash flow, and capital resource availability).

    Assist in defining corporate objectives and determining optimal corporate structure for achieving those objectives.

    Strengthen links between capital and operating budgets, functional operating plans, and company strategy development.

3. *Strategy Formulation.*   Analytical services to facilitate strategy development and resource allocation:

    Develop strategic alternatives through study of market opportunities and internal capabilities and resources.

    Analyze the financial and competitive impact of asset redeployment within the company's business portfolio.

    Assess organizational implications of alternative strategies (i.e., necessary restructuring or additional resources required).

    Work with corporate and line managers to select the most appropriate strategy.

    Plan implementation of strategy within the organization.

4. *Strategy Implementation.*   On-site services to assist management in making changes essential to carrying out selected strategy:

Assist management in developing operating plans, action steps, and timetables for integrating strategy into operating unit.

Work with line managers to modify, augment, or streamline specific operating activities.

Assist top management in diversification planning and targeting potential acquisition candidates.

All companies do not have the same need for services in each of these categories. The amount of consulting expertise required varies with the level of management sophistication in planning and the urgency to act.

TAILORING CONSULTING EXPERTISE TO THE COMPANY'S STATE OF PLANNING DEVELOPMENT

Knowing how far advanced an organization is in planning for strategic change helps target consulting services to gain the greatest value. It also adds perspective to the length of time it may take to strengthen the organization's capabilities and planning sophistication and thus sharpens the focus of the consultant's role in the organization.

The recognition that all companies pass through similar phases in developing strategic management capabilities has gained wide currency only in the past several years. As Fred Gluck maintains in his article, "Strategic Management for Competitive Advantage,"[1] there are four basic phases of evolution ranging from the first, in which companies depend on one-year budgets and simple financial performance measures to guide operations, to the fourth, in which strategic management is a way of life at all levels within the corporation. Briefly, the four phases of development are:

I. Basic financial planning
II. Forecast-based planning
III. Externally oriented planning
IV. Strategic management (see Exhibit 3-2)

In Phase I companies, planning is essentially an outgrowth of the annual budgeting process. Processes exist to provide basic planning information such as forecasts of revenues, costs, and capital needs. However, development of business strategy is generally limited to one-year projected earnings growth and other explicit financial objectives. Although companies in Phase I may have rudimentary product/market and competitive strategies, they often exist only in the minds of the CEO or management team and are not clearly articulated or formally outlined for line managers.

Increasing organizational complexity and market dynamics tend to propel companies into Phase II of the planning evolution. In this phase basic financial

EXHIBIT 3-2   *Four Phases in the Evolution of Formal Strategic Planning*

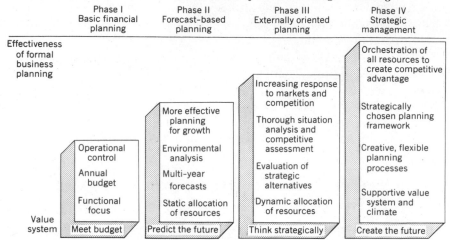

Source: Frederick W. Gluck, Stephen P. Kaufman, and A. Steven Walleck, "Strategic Management for Competitive Advantage," *Harvard Business Review,* July–August, 1980, p. 157. Reproduced by permission.

objectives mature into formal, forecast-based plans addressing the long-term impact of political, economic, and market trends. At first this planning differs from annual budgeting only in the length of its time frame. Later, however, advanced forecasting tools, such as regression and computer simulation models, assist in predicting the future. Phase II planning improves the effectiveness of the basic financial planning process by forcing managers to assess the potential impact of discernible trends and long-term implications of their decisions. Most large American companies moved into this stage of planning by the early 1970s.

Phase III, externally oriented planning, allows companies to identify product/market opportunities and allocate resources to take advantage of attractive market sectors in rapidly changing environments. In Phase III companies line managers or planners present top-level executives with a number of strategic alternatives for resource allocation rather than with simple projections of current business requirements. Such externally oriented planning requires in-depth understanding of multiple markets and businesses acquired through ongoing assessment of customer needs, supplier capabilities, distributors' requirements, possible regulatory changes, and competitive forces.

As an organization's planning sophistication grows at all levels so do its strategic opportunities. Consequently, planners and line managers in large, widely diversified companies are able to make explicit choices that may affect the entire company's future without top management participation. High-level concern over this phenomenon, therefore, thrusts managers into Phase

IV of strategic planning evolution, strategic management. Strategic management embodies the concept that successful performance must ultimately encompass not only planning processes but also a shared corporate value system and market orientation, plus an organization that supports planning as an integral part of strategic decision making. It is generally agreed that only a few of the world's great corporations can claim to have reached the fourth phase, and a number of them are Japanese. Matsushita, Sony, and IBM are often placed in this select group. Most of the rest of America's next 5000 companies are still striving along the path from the first through the third phases of development.

Progress through these planning phases is a long learning process during which management accumulates knowledge about the company itself, its markets, and its competitors. A company or unit cannot leap from Phase I to Phase III; in fact, only concerted effort over time will change anything at all.

Consultants can make valuable contributions to a company's development in strategic decision making. Of course, what they contribute differs among companies depending on the existing levels of planning development. Exhibit 3-3 gives an idea of consulting services companies usually find valuable as they improve performance and add to their capabilities.

A few examples illustrate ways in which consultants have assisted companies in different stages of development:

1. The head of a small, family-owned machinery manufacturing company needed assistance in planning for future growth. Annual revenues had stagnated at 30 million dollars and the company was run in the same entrepreneurial manner as it had been for 20 years. As is typical in Phase I companies, planning was limited to preparing the annual budget and information for decision making was limited to sales data. The consultants worked with the chief executive to assess the company's strengths and potential for growth in its market sector and devised a program for expanding the product line and changing distribution that increased market share and doubled profitability. Crucial to achieving these results was a top-management reorganization to allow more delegation and a simple system designed to provide regular market information and analysis.

2. A 3-billion-dollar natural resource company suffering loss of share and declining profits as a result of shifting customer demands asked a consulting team to design a corporate and division planning process oriented to the marketplace. Although quite large, the company had only a rudimentary Phase II planning process in place (i.e., detailed annual budgets and financial projections but no contingency or multiscenario plans for its commodity products and markets). The consultants helped corporate management to: (1) appoint a respected line executive to head a revitalized planning department responsible for

EXHIBIT 3-3 Typical Needs in Planning by Phase of Company's Evolution

	Phase of Planning Evolution			
Type of Strategic Planning Activities	Phase I Basic Financial Planning	Phase II Forecast-Based Planning	Phase III Externally Oriented Planning	Phase IV Strategic Management
Market/Industry Analysis	In-depth assessments of markets and competitors—first time	Systematic provision of quality information Segmentation Competitors	Competitor-driven analysis and information Understanding of critical factors necessary for market leadership	Fast, in-depth assessment of new areas and potential threats
Internal Company Analysis	Establishment of a formal planning process, linked with budgeting	Rigorous understanding of strengths and weaknesses	Periodic, fresh assessments	Periodic, fresh assessments
Strategy Formulation		Market-driven strategy	Sophisticated resource allocation	Organizational strategy melded into strategy formulation process
Strategy Implementation	Additional resources to complement existing staff and experience	Ad hoc support where gaps exist	Ad hoc support, especially new markets/businesses	Ad hoc support, especially organizational aspects of strategic action

3.8

product–market-segment analysis; (2) begin top-down/bottom-up long-term planning linking corporate objectives and divisional goals; and (3) redeploy assets—including divestiture of 30 percent—to position the company for long-run profitability. The company is now moving steadily toward Phase III in its evolution as it becomes more market-driven and responsive in its strategic planning efforts.

3. A large conglomerate in Phase III of its strategic planning evolution was looking for ways to build upon its strength in distribution. Although the company had long had a formal planning process and ongoing programs for watching important external trends, management retained a consulting firm to identify growth opportunities in industries requiring distribution expertise. The consultants recommended strategic alternatives to take advantage of the company's strengths, outlined the required organizational changes and resource allocations, and recommended a course of action. Following board approval of the recommendation, the consultants assisted in implementing the plan, which resulted in the acquisition of a small health care products firm and its integration into the company's business.

4. A large high-technology firm in Phase IV of the strategic decision making evolution has a highly sophisticated and integrated planning process driven by strategic issues understood by all of its top managers. Management carefully monitors the external environment and takes action to reshape it whenever possible. The company, however, continues to use consultants frequently but selectively to refine strategy in rapidly changing parts of its business, particularly in obtaining competitive information. Through consultants, top management receives objective assessments of its own organization, technology, and manufacturing processes that it adds to information generated internally.

As these examples show, consultants can be extremely valuable in assisting management develop more sophisticated planning techniques for whatever reason—to expand, to respond to competitive pressures, to achieve industry leadership, or simply to strengthen internal planning resources. Even the most effectively managed companies regularly use consultants on strategy-related issues—in good times as well as bad. In short, they view consulting services as one of several essential investments for maintaining competitive advantage in the marketplace.

CRITICAL EVENTS THAT TYPICALLY CREATE NEEDS FOR CONSULTING EXPERTISE

Just as companies use consulting expertise to augment ongoing strategy development, management frequently seeks expert help to respond to specific, often unforeseen, events. Such events may be external to the company or internal. In either case, the ability of consultants to help develop appropriate strategic responses can be extremely valuable.

Some typical "external triggers" are:

1. *New entrants to a marketplace,* particularly those that achieve an element of surprise and appear with sizable resources, such as IBM when it entered the semiconductor and telecommunications business through major investments and working arrangements with Intel and Mitel. Consultants can help companies expedite competitive strategies and provide insights into the future market developments as a result of the new entry.

2. *New legislation or regulatory changes* restricting, enlarging, or altering the direction of a business—airline deregulation, tax law changes, and acid rain legislation, for example. Consultants can help anticipate these changes, but more important, they can aid in developing strategy to deal with the new reality.

3. *New technology that radically changes skills required for competitive success*—for instance, the introduction of microprocessor technology to the industrial process control industry, long dependent on electrical and pneumatic technologies. Companies able to acquire new skills, change product offerings, and build credibility with their risk-averse customers made rapid market share increases. Management often uses consultants to develop strategic responses to such situations because an objective, in-depth view of the competitive environment and the company's skills helps build momentum for change.

4. *Bleak economic outlook for a company's "core" business*—such as declining demand, declining margins, and product line obsolescence. When a company has relied heavily on a product or market that is declining, often management is reluctant to accept and act on the need for change. In such companies, consultants can be particularly valuable in identifying and evaluating diversification alternatives, developing successful new strategies, and building internal momentum to redeploy assets.

There are also several typical "internal triggers" that lead to valuable use of consultants in the strategic planning area:

1. *Declining Market Share.* Market position can deteriorate even though profitability remains satisfactory, but the causes and effects may not be clear for a long time. Management gets many mixed signals in such situations and agreement on causes or actions may be hard to reach. Although this happens more frequently to medium-sized or small companies with limited market research capability, even large companies have had this experience; for example, Xerox lost the entire low-volume copier market to Japanese manufacturers in only five years in the 1970s. Once again, the objectivity consultants can bring to man-

agement in assessing the competitive environment and capitalizing on strengths can help stem such a decline.

2. *Acquisition or Merger.*   Whether a company is on one side of an acquisition or the other, a new merger usually raises many strategy issues relating to business definition and capital allocation to the new operations. Because organizational change is inevitable during acquisitions or mergers, strategic planning is complicated by internal power struggles. Outside consultants are in an ideal position to help the CEO put in place the elements to maintain his or her strategic direction: new or modified planning and resource allocation processes; new organization structure and business boundaries; and key managers to lead the merged organization's units.

3. *Excess Cash but Only Limited Investment Opportunities in the Base Business.*   When excess cash is a new experience for management, rigorous diversification planning efforts can guide the company to logical acquisitions or investments. Consultants experienced in diversification can add skills and efficiency to this process, even for companies in which diversification is an ongoing, integral part of their planning.

The second consideration that must be discussed is the lasting effectiveness of the company/consulting joint effort. The expertise, objectivity, and flexibility consultants bring to strategic planning can be extremely valuable. However, the way in which the consultants and client organization work together has a major impact on the success of the planning effort. The responsibility for ensuring the success of the strategic planning project lies with the head of the business unit involved (i.e., the chief executive officer, the chief operating officer, group president, division president, or general manager).

Because the role of the consultant is to act as an extension of this key executive's staff, the executive must carefully prepare for the success of the effort. Just as the executive prepares carefully and judiciously to engage any other professional—doctor, lawyer, or accountant—the same care is critical in working with consulting experts. Specifically, the executive must:

Determine how the company can make the best use of outside expertise.
Select the consultant most appropriate for the project.
Be prepared to participate actively in the project.

The steps involved in each process are described below.

HOW THE ORGANIZATION CAN BEST USE OUTSIDE EXPERTS

The organization's effective use of consulting expertise depends on two basic factors:

1. The magnitude of the problem or opportunity at hand in terms of its potential dollar impact on the bottom line over time
2. The information and planning resources already available internally and the level of sophistication in strategic decision making the organization has attained

Assessing the dollar magnitude of the project helps determine the stakes involved and whether it is necessary to invest in outside assistance and, if so, to what degree. For example, if an external event—say deregulation of industry standards or government action—has made traditional pricing, distribution, and organization structures obsolete, the magnitude of the problem over the long term can be substantial. Witness AT&T and other telecommunication companies, airlines, and banks—all of which face tremendous strategic decisions as a result of recent governmental decrees. In most cases even the most sophisticated of these organizations are choosing to augment their internal staffs to deal with their new strategic options—and the long-term implications warrant significant investment in such planning.

Strategic decisions of lesser immediacy, but possibly equal long-term importance, face companies in many nonregulated industries. Many organizations whose traditional businesses are sound seek outside experts to help frame strategic options for expanding product lines, modifying distribution/ pricing practices, and/or entering new markets. Examples from a range of industries include:

1. Insurance companies investigating direct sales distribution avenues, acquiring other financial institutions, modifying traditional products
2. Entertainment companies investing in new audio/video product lines, establishing footholds in cable TV distribution networks, exploring new technologies for information transmission
3. Oil drilling and related machinery/services companies experiencing continued declines in demand and facing further erosion in crude oil prices for the foreseeable future

In each case, key executives of such organizations can assess the potential bottom-line impact of strategic change and, accordingly, the value of obtaining consulting expertise to assist in the effort. Part of the assessment involves knowing the resources of professional staffs already in-house—for example, market research information on current customer groups, products, prices, and changes in distribution channels; contingency plans in place for considering alternative courses of action; information on major competitors; and cost data by product line. If the information bases and planning already available is significant, the need for consulting expertise may focus more on creative analysis—resegmenting the business, portfolio techniques, and financial implications.

Whatever the key executive's assessment of the problem or opportunity, successful use of consulting expertise requires the support and agreement of key reporting executives as well. It is therefore essential that the key executive gain support from the next level of management on the benefits the organization can achieve by engaging outside help. Even though a group of leading executives rarely see eye to eye on all aspects of a key issue or its ultimate impact on the organization, their support for studying the problem with consulting help is essential to the project's success.

SELECTION OF THE MOST APPROPRIATE CONSULTANT

After an assessment of the magnitude of the problem, the availability of internal resources, and the potential investment appropriate in consulting expertise, it is possible to select either an individual consultant or a team of consultants from a firm to assist in the project. Selecting the most appropriate consultant involves three steps: finding candidates, evaluating candidates, and evaluating proposals.

Finding Candidates

Matching consultants' functional skills, industry knowledge, or relevant project experience to the company's situation is certainly critical in selection; but equally important to success is finding consultants with whom a trust relationship can be established over time. There are approximately 100 U.S. management consulting firms with five or more full-time professionals and 40 with more than 100 professionals. Since no two firms have precisely the same combination of skills, services, and industry experience, finding the few that fit a specific company's requirements may take time.

To engage an appropriate consulting firm for a large project, key executives often assign one or two high-level executives to screen potential candidates. Since trust in the team is essential for success, the management team often relies on sources with direct knowledge of firms—their partners, functional skills, and reputations. These include firms the company has used before, business associates in consulting firms, or executives in other companies.

Other search activities may include consulting directories or associations, such as the Association of Consulting Management Engineers (ACME) in New York City, to identify firms in the right size range and to scope the fee ranges in small versus large firms. (However, only a final proposal based on the agreed scope of work can give an accurate range of total project costs.) The need for international consulting capabilities, multiple domestic locations to be covered, and the breadth of skills the project requires may also figure in the selection process.

The advantages of engaging individual consultants rather than a firm may be flexibility, specific expertise, or relatively low cost. Since independent consultants typically charge less than even the smallest management consulting firm, they are often highly suitable when cost is a critical issue or when the project may have a relatively low payout for the company. In some cases management teams choose to engage individual consultants over long periods to lend special expertise to their existing staffs. Such relationships often exist between companies and academicians—for example, professors at university business schools.

Evaluating Candidates

After the three or four most suitable candidates are identified, two time-tested steps are critical to selection: personal interviews by the key executive, leading to detailed proposals tailored to the project requirements. At its best this process is an interactive one, in which company management and the consultants together shape the project.

To start, it is essential that candidate firms have enough information and background about the project to respond with detail and insight. The executives responsible for screening candidates should invite the consultants to the company for detailed discussions and description of the issues, available internal resources, and expected results. If time permits, other executives who will be key to the effort should also be available to meet with the candidates. Such additional perspective provides insight into special areas to be explored during the study—internal barriers within the company, and key staffs and individuals who should be involved, for instance.

The key executive's interview with the consultants is the principal way by which he or she assesses their skills and "the chemistry"—how comfortable their working relationship will be. The executive could expect to meet with one partner and at least one other senior person from each firm who would lead and actively work on the project. In turn, the consultant should expect the executive's candid assessment of the project and hoped-for results. The dialogue that ensues typically uncovers new issues and areas for investigation and often redirects the focus of the study before the proposal is even written.

Evaluating Proposals

Following these executive meetings, consultants submit written proposals outlining their understanding of the project, key issues and background, their proposed steps, a timetable, and fees for addressing the project. Often, a proposal's value to the client is enhanced by an oral presentation to the management team.

In general, companies evaluating the proposals should look for specificity, articulation of the issues, and a logical approach to solutions; specifically:

1. Consultant's understanding of the assignment.

   Key success factors in the business, background to the problem or opportunities, and potential implications.

   Company/industry culture and political forces at work.

   Issues or potential barriers critical to solutions.

2. Proposed approach, including specific tasks, working relationships, timing, reviews, and expected results. Questions to ask are:

   Does it ensure that all critical issues are examined in sufficient detail? Is the approach specific to your situation and not just a general description of "canned" techniques or models?

   How does the team propose to work with and capitalize on the staff and resources already at hand?

   Are the end products clearly identified? Do the deliverables directly relate to the issues and the consultant's understanding of the issues as outlined in the proposal?

   Is the timetable acceptable? Is there a clearly stated completion date?

   Does it provide for frequent reviews and discussions to ensure company input and direction and to build consensus as the project proceeds?

3. Commitment of the right people for the right amount of time.

   Do the qualifications of the consultant's project manager fulfill the requirements of the task (e.g., technical qualifications and industry experience)?

   Who will be the primary contact on the assignment and what portion of the work will the person be responsible for and directly involved in?

   What are the qualifications of the junior staff members? Will there be any substitution of less-qualified staff once the project is underway?

   What is the time split between senior and junior consulting staff on the project? What tasks will be handled by each?

4. Proposed project costs. Cost relates directly to project scope and approach. If a cost estimate is out of line with other proposals, it usually means the consultant does not understand the assignment or has an inappropriate approach. Naturally there are also cost differences caused by differing fee schedules among firms. However, accepting a clearly mediocre proposal or consulting team simply on the basis of cost does little to insure project success. It's far better to accept the best team and try to renegotiate the scope of work to fit the budgetary constraints.

Exhibit 3-4 provides a checklist of the factors that should be considered in evaluating consultants.

In general, when reviewing consultants' proposals, look for specificity, good understanding and articulation of the issues, and clearly defined end products that resolve the issues raised. The following checklist will assist you in identifying the consultant(s) that can best serve your organization.

EVALUATION CRITERIA

Check
(as
appropriate)

Yes   No

☐   ☐   Do the consultants demonstrate complete understanding of the
☐   ☐   situation—business operations, critical success factors, and the
unique issues you confront?

☐   ☐   Is the problem fully and accurately articulated?

☐   ☐   Will the proposed approach lead to the collection of all data
critical to analysis of the problem?

Will the consultants utilize available company resources that can
☐   ☐   effect project cost savings?

Are the interim and end products clearly defined? Do they fulfill
☐   ☐   your assessment of what is required?

☐   ☐   Are frequent progress reviews and discussions with corporate
management planned?

Do the qualifications (e.g., technical and industry specific) of the
☐   ☐   proposed project consultant(s) meet the requirements of the
assignment?

☐   ☐   Will senior consulting staff perform the bulk of the analysis?

Is the style of the proposed consultant(s) compatible with your
☐   ☐   corporate culture?

Is the time frame of the assignment suitable to company needs?
☐   ☐   Is the time sufficient in light of the resources allocated to
accomplish the outlined goals?

☐   ☐   Does the firm have adequate experience in this type of study
☐   ☐   and/or industry?

Is the cost of the project commensurate with your estimates of
the requirements of the task?

Does the quality of the proposed study justify the expense?

☐   ☐   Do the consultant's references and general reputation confirm
their quality?

If the answer to all of the above questions is yes, then you have identified the consultant(s) that best meet your needs.

COMMIT AND GIVE DIRECTION

After having selected the consulting team, it is critical that the key executive commit time and give personal direction to the study effort. Key executive involvement throughout is crucial to achieving the results expected. Without it, contending views can paralyze ultimate actions. Involvement is a signal for the organization to join in and push hard on the project. Moreover, the key executive benefits from the interaction, gaining new ideas, insights, and impressions on issues and implementation suggestions.

Involvement takes a number of forms, from launching the project to pushing implementation:

1. Prepare the organization to comprehend the project's objectives and support the actual work program of the team. Set up and participate in an initial meeting of the consultants, internal team members, and key managers to communicate formally that the effort is underway and the chief executive is behind it. Communicate to the broader organization by letter or memo, and in some instances distribute the consultants' proposal to a wider internal audience.
2. Agree on dates for formal reviews and request a joint consultant/internal work plan.
3. Stay in touch with line managers informally to anticipate serious issues.
4. Require that practical implementation planning be part of the project results. Ask the consultants to develop an overall implementation approach that has been agreed with key staff people *before* a final presentation is made. Ask management members to prepare their own implementation programs as a result of the project, and follow up.

Throughout, the key executive's ability to participate in the team's efforts while at the same time remaining responsive to management's reactions and concerns will in the end determine the ultimate success of the combined effort.

In conclusion, the role of consultants in strategic planning can be extremely valuable. Their objectivity, flexibility, and varying areas of expertise make them ideal assets in developing plans for strategic decisions. Their analytical skills, exposure to numerous organizations and industries, and experience in problem solving can greatly assist line managers in assessing strategic options outside their immediate operations.

Effective use of consulting expertise, however, requires close partnership with top management, who must ultimately direct and shape the outcome of the joint company/consulting effort. Together a committed management/ consulting team can keep strategy sound and strengthen company performance.

NOTE

1. F. Gluck, S. Kaufman, and A. Walleck, "Strategic Management for Competitive Advantage," *Harvard Business Review,* July–August 1980, pp. 154–164.

CHAPTER *4*

Assessing the Competition: Business Intelligence for Strategic Management

WILLIAM L. SAMMON

WILLIAM L. SAMMON is a senior analyst in the Corporate Strategic Planning Department of Pfizer Inc. From 1979 to 1982 he was on the corporate staff at International Paper Co., where his last position was manager of corporate competitive analysis. Mr. Sammon served on active duty in the U.S. Army from 1968 to 1979. As a specialist in strategic intelligence and counterintelligence he served in a number of field and staff assignments as a military intelligence officer. A Major in the Army Reserve, he holds a post as Visiting Professor of International Politics at the United States Military Academy at West Point. Mr. Sammon is the coauthor of *Business Competitor Intelligence* (John Wiley & Sons, New York, 1984). He earned his B.A. in Political Science at Boston College, an M.A. in Political Science at the University of Chicago, and an M.B.A. in Finance at the University of Long Island.

OUTLINE

COMPETITORS: THE CRITICAL VARIABLE

Companies compete against each other in a complex struggle for customers, capital, and organizational resources. The ultimate objective is to achieve and maintain the coveted status of "industry leader." The basic goal is survival. In this continual contest, a host of environmental forces interact to influence the competitive outcome—technological innovation, social change, political regulation, economic goals, and financial markets, to name the more prominent. But none of these affects a company's standing more directly than the actions and inactions of competitors—its organizational rivals. Today the competition is getting leaner, hungrier, and tougher; moreover, an increasing number are powerful, foreign-based firms driven by unusual strategic assumptions.

In a global economy of increasing uncertainty, the term "competitive edge" has become synonymous with strategic success. Implicitly this suggests a comparative knowledge of competitors and the strategic bases of competition within a firm's industry. But knowing *who* the firm's competitors are isn't enough. To achieve and, more important, sustain a "competitive edge," that is, a strategic position based on a comparative advantage, a company must have a thorough understanding of its competitors—direct and indirect, foreign and domestic. Yet few do. Consequently, the corporate battlefield is littered with the failed strategies of wounded companies whose management kept their eye on all the critical variables save the most dangerous—competitors.

The continuously successful firms—IBM, Coca-Cola, Matsushita, General Electric, Nestlé, Shell, and Boeing, for instance—outperform corporate rivals by an embarrassingly large margin. Their unusual track records highlight the harsh truth that, although many firms pursue business strategies based on a competitive edge, few succeed. To outperform business competitors over the long term, it is necessary to outthink them. To outthink them, you must first understand them. Herein lies the practical value of systematic competitor intelligence—one of the most overlooked and underutilized managerial resources available to business executives.

Whereas most firms devote significant assets to understanding their markets, monitoring internal operations, and forecasting environmental trends, the systematic analysis of competitors is rarely a priority on management's agenda. William Bain, a leading management consultant, noted the scope of this imbalance in a recent speech to business executives:

You can remember the four "C's": Customer, Competitors, Costeffectiveness, and Culture. They're all important, and the truly outstanding companies have an excellent balance among them. My second point, though, is that the vast majority of us in this country—or even in the Western World—don't have a balance. My observation after looking at a lot of companies over the years is that only about 15 percent of the focus is on customers and not more than 5 percent is on competitors, and the other 80 percent is on internal matters which only indirectly deal with customers and competitors.[1]

Driving this indifference is the often unchallenged assumption that what needs to be known about a competitor is known and intuitively incorporated into management's plans and decisions. Such an attitude fosters conventional thinking, strategic myopia, and lackluster performance.

Every business organization routinely collects information about competitors from published and field sources, from external and internal contacts, and from staff and line functions. But more often than not, these useful nuggets of competitor data are neither mined nor managed. Consequently, their potential value to the company's strategic planning process is not realized. The result is that managements' understanding of competitors continues to be casual, cursory, and frequently wrong, *for information is not intelligence*.

Information is data that has been selectively collected, integrated, and organized for specific analytical purposes. Intelligence is the end product of that analysis. Intelligence is also an organizational process and an analytical filter by which raw data about competitors is first upgraded to "information" and then converted into focused intelligence that adds value to managements' tactical moves, operational plans, and strategic decisions.

INTELLIGENCE FOR COMPETITIVE ANALYSIS

As the concept of "comparative advantage" increasingly becomes the focal point of business strategy, more companies have begun to address the "competitor intelligence gaps" that frequently undermine strategic planning. As noted by a number of leading commentators, the objective of a "competitive strategy" is to marshall a firm's resources and employ them in a timely fashion to leverage the changing "sources or factors of comparative advantage in a business"—manufacturing technology, product mix, R&D focus, sales coverage, raw materials, distribution channels—more effectively than one's rivals.[2]

Understanding the operational details and strategic implications of these "factors of comparative advantage" is crucial, for they define the most significant axis of competition in an industry and the comparative strategic positions rival firms hold. The interrelationships a company's management creates among these factors underlies its current profitability and competitive ranking. This is the focus of strategic competitor intelligence.

In the ethical pharmaceutical industry, for example, a short list of the core factors of comparative advantage would probably include the following:

Productive, large-scale research
Strategic management
Product development and licensing
Flow of commercially significant, innovative products
Effective governmental/regulatory relations
Physician-focused marketing competence
Global market reach
Pricing leverage
Therapeutic breadth of product mix
Strong financial resources
Rationalized global manufacturing
Synergies with nondrug businesses

By contrast, companies in the generic pharmaceutical industry, a low-margin non-asset–intensive business with comparatively high "service" requirements, face quite a different competitive environment. The "factors of comparative advantage" in generic drugs reflect the distinctive features of a price-sensitive, commodity healthcare business:

Low-cost manufacturing
Ability to rapidly shift product mix
Timely regulatory approvals
Distribution access
Low marketing costs
Quality of operational management
High service capability
Lean organization/low overhead
Forward integration into distribution
Broad product line
Technological, manufacturing, or marketing differentials

Although factors of comparative advantage are industry-specific, they must not be viewed as static. Business competition is an ever-shifting struggle in which both the players and the bases of strategic success change in response to environmental forces and the internal dynamics of industry competition. For example, current trends in the U.S. pharmaceutical industry suggest that the following factors of comparative advantage may be emerging to supplement and/or replace some of the established factors listed above for the ethical pharmaceutical industry:

Therapeutically efficient and *cost effective* products

Marketing/R&D *joint ventures*

Specialized therapeutic focus

Shortened research and regulatory review periods

Consumer/third-party promotional programs

Limited *generic exposure*

By using detailed business intelligence keyed to specific factors of comparative advantage, the relative abilities of competitors to both understand and leverage these strategic factors can be analyzed in a more cogent manner. With this strategic intelligence a company's management is better prepared to make the crucial executive decisions necessary to carve out, defend, and enhance its firm's strategic position vis-à-vis the competition.

Ideally the objective is to obtain a strategic position that minimizes the threat posed by competitors and maximizes the opportunity to exploit a rival's lapses. For example, Hospital Corporation of America (HCA), the preeminent company in the rapidly growing hospital management industry, has developed an enviable strategic position based on a clear understanding of the factors of comparative advantage in its business and a shrewd grasp of its competitors' strategic shortfalls. At HCA strategic intelligence precedes strategic actions—both defensive and offensive.

With 4.3 billion dollars in sales (1983), HCA is the world's largest hospital manager. It operates or owns 405 hospitals and is far ahead of the competition in expanding its position in the strategically significant hospital teaching facility market. The company's strategy is based on three key factors of comparative advantage: broad geographic distribution, cost-saving hospital designs, and a favorable image within the medical profession. State and local regulatory authorities (many of whom are medical doctors) play a crucial role in licensing new hospitals and in the more controversial decision to convert a voluntary or nonprofit hospital to a for-profit status. Many of the administrators and medical professionals who staff these regulatory boards view the organizational priorities of the new hospital management companies with a jaundiced eye. HCA's "blue chip" image, underscored by an advisory board of governors made up of leading physicians and the company's highly visible share of the teaching hospital market, helps to moderate these concerns. HCA's carefully cultivated "blue chip" image provides a significant competitive edge in the sharply contested bidding for local hospital contracts and the growing diversification into outpatient, alternative delivery healthcare services. HCA is quick to use this advantage to pick up business at the expense of more "hard-nosed" competitors who underestimate both the importance of their "image" with skeptical regulators and the quality of HCA's intelligence on that strategic lapse.

Planning programs that don't place a high priority on analyzing the relative strategic position and changing competitive potential of business rivals—direct and indirect—are more than vacuous. They constitute a positive danger to the long-term health of a corporation. They foster a dangerously egocentric view of the competitive environment, give unwarranted emphasis to internal organizational concerns, and encourage operating managements' natural bias toward excessive optimism.

As anyone who has had the pleasure of enduring the conventional strategic plan review knows, all things are possible in a business world without rivals. And when these strategic plans based on navel gazing and great expectations fall apart in the face of "unexpectedly stiff competition," rarely is the failure attributed to its proper cause—a business intelligence gap of embarrassing proportions.

While it is increasingly fashionable to attribute the extensive shortcomings of strategic planning to poor implementation, the so-called paralysis by analysis syndrome, those reform-minded critics whose rallying cry is "action not reflection" ought to consider the trenchant observations of G.E.'s current chairman, Jack Welch, an "action-oriented" executive of the first order who views strategic planning as an intellectual discipline for operating managers, not a form-filling routine for planning administrators:

> I make the argument that 80 to 90 percent of the things that fail are not because people don't execute or implement—it's because they don't read how fast our competition is moving or how fast the market is changing. Too many times in a company with a lot of processes to go through, a lot of implementation reviews, the competitive analysis may not get enough time. . . .
>
> It's better for us to look back over the last three years and clearly analyze how we performed against our competitive world. The degree to which we outperform industry will be the measure of our success.[3]

LEVELS OF INTELLIGENCE—A QUESTION OF FOCUS

In developing the business intelligence required for the kinds of competitive analyses that foster more effective business strategies information is rarely the problem. A modern corporation has within it a veritable storehouse of data on competitors and some of the most valuable sources of additional knowledge—its own employees. Supplementing these in-house intelligence resources is an ever-expanding array of external, readily available categories of competitor data. They range across a broad spectrum of detail and coverage, from expensive multiclient market research reports to inexpensive trade press clippings. There are also, of course, a host of outside agencies such as consulting firms, brokerage houses, and data base vendors that can provide useful "intelligence services" in the form of raw information (e.g., a foreign competitor's financial statements); general analytical data (e.g., stock reports or technology surveys); and specialized research (e.g., a customized evaluation of a small division buried in a large corporation, or a series of field interviews with competitors' customers, suppliers, and distributors). However, if a company's intelligence effort is not to be overwhelmed by the cornucopia of competitor information readily available, an *appropriate analytical focus* and a *minimal organizational network* is required.

The analytical focus of business intelligence, that is, what competitor issues, facts, and questions it addresses, should be oriented to the specific kinds of decisions different management groups face. As outlined in Exhibit 4-1, this suggests three distinct but overlapping levels of business intelligence—tactical, operational, and strategic. These categories of intelligence roughly correspond to the three key management levels within a corporation—product line, business division, and corporate. Both the scope of interest in competitor activity and the kinds of functional business intelligence (e.g., marketing, manufacturing, R&D, financial) emphasized by different levels reflect this structural dimension. In short, management's organizational responsibilities drive their perceived intelligence requirements. Unfortunately, this often results in an excessively narrow focus on competitor intelligence—particularly below the corporate level. A pharmaceutical product manager, for example, is probably indifferent to information that comes his or her way about a key competitor's investment plans for an unrelated market; an operational vice president running a consumer packaged goods business is unlikely to be concerned with the financial setback a competitor is experiencing in its hospital products business segment; a specialty chemical plant manager is probably not following the investment community's approval of his or her suppliers' plans to integrate forward into production; credit managers in treasury may have valuable information about a key competitor's working capital that could influence an operating division's new business plan, but the information is never asked for or passed on.

Management surveys and other research on companies' business intelligence efforts strongly suggest that in most firms tactical and operational types of competitor intelligence are given priority over the more complex competitor issues that are the focus or target of strategic intelligence. These targets are as follows:

Industry leadership
Corporate reputation
Financial strength/performance
Shareholder value
Organizational growth
Functional synergies
Business mix
Business development
Strategic position

As suggested by the following list, the typical competitor intelligence targets at the tactical and operational levels usually have a strongly quantitative character and a narrow functional orientation.[4]

EXHIBIT 4-1 Levels of Business Intelligence

Management Level	Key Actors	Driving Functions	Core Resources	Time Horizon	Competitive Constraints	Intelligence Level
Product line	Sales force Market research Product manager	Sales and marketing	Marketing plan Product characteristics Sales management Customer loyalty	Short: 6–18 months	Market growth Price elasticity Product substitution Number of competitors Share of leading rival	Tactical

Business division	General management
	Manufacturing managers
	Divisional staff:
	  Planning
	  Finance
	  Marketing
	  Technical
		Marketing and manufacturing
		Finance
		Technical
			Business strategy
			Divisional plan:
			  Operating Capital
			  Production capability
			  Product development
			  Product mix
				Intermediate: 1–5 years	Product line breadth
					Competitors' customer base
					Demand cyclicality
					Manufacturing costs and processes
					Raw material supply
					Corporate commitment
						Operational

Corporate	Board of directors
	Senior management
	Coordinating committees
	Functional staff:
	  Finance/treasury
	  Planning
	  R&D
	  Licensing
	  Human resources
	  Purchasing
	Specialized staff:
	  Legal/tax
	  Public affairs
		Corporate management
		Finance
		Planning
		R&D
			Corporate strategy
			Capital
			Management
			Organization
			R&D
			Business mix
				Long: 3 + years	Environmental forces
					Industry trends
					Global competition
					Strategic peers
					Investor valuation
						Strategic

Tactical Intelligence Targets	Operational Intelligence Targets
Sales budgets	Revenues/costs
Market share	Asset management
Account mix	Product mix
Distribution channels	Market segments
	Geographic coverage
	Business plan objectives

It is the particular piece of data, an isolated element of a competitor's operations or plans, that usually piques management's interest, (e.g., the introduction date of a new competitive product, unexpected price discounts to a major distributor, the annual growth in a competitive product's advertising budget, a competitor's energy costs in the Southeast, capital investments in a competitor's mill, the financial details of a competitor's joint venture with a foreign firm, or the market fallout when a competitor is forced to recall a key product).

An intelligence analysis of the competitor as a whole, as a rival commercial organization with a distinctive history, development, management style, corporate performance, and strategic ambition, has less appeal at the operational level and often no audience in the tactical trenches where the competition is products, not companies. As management's appetite for the business insights afforded by strategic competitor intelligence is limited at the product line and sometimes even at the business level so also is the inclination to search out and communicate competitor data that can add depth and perspective to the firm's strategic planning efforts.

Compounding this nonstrategic view of business intelligence is the all-too-common tendency to approach the targeting, collection, and use of competitor information in an ad hoc, diffused, and frequently uncoordinated manner. As an ancillary element, competitor data is regularly generated in marketing analyses, business development proposals, licensing negotiations, country management reports, corporate litigation, purchasing contracts, labor relations, personnel recruitment, lobbying activities, and research studies. This inexpensive but valuable competitor information is easily lost to others in the company who may need it but are often ignorant of its existence and thus unable to access it. Moreover, there is usually no incentive to identify, collate, and aggregate the nuggets of competitor data that constantly flow through the firm's staff and line operations. Functional competitor intelligence is not routinely communicated to operating divisions; business units competing in diverse industries against the same firm fail to share their intelligence insights; domestic divisions derive little benefit from the extensive competitor data available to their international counterparts, and vice versa. In short, the often extensive competitor intelligence gained is rarely communicated beyond the acquiring element. Moreover, the strategic significance of this tactical and operational intelligence is too often ignored. The usual result is a wasteful duplication of effort, a dangerous lack of perspective, excessive use of costly vendors, and inevitably business and corporate strategies flawed by unnecessary competitor intelligence gaps.

Such an overly compartmentalized, subcorporate approach to competitor intelligence is a consequence of the typical functional barriers and organizational dynamics found in most corporations. It lowers the quality of tactical and operational intelligence efforts and seriously handicaps the development of the intelligence needed for strategic competitive analyses.

The lack of adequate strategic intelligence in most corporations is more of an organizational than an informational problem; the remedy therefore requires an organizational component. Competitor intelligence needs to be identified as a high priority that requires broad management support of an "intelligence network" that can:

Bridge internal operational and organizational boundaries.

Tap various functional sources of competitor information.

Integrate disparate insights about competitors into a coherent and comparative strategic analysis.

Although there are a number of ways to structure such a program, it is essential that the intelligence network devised place a premium on the *process,* and not the administration, of intelligence.

THE INTELLIGENCE PROCESS

Competitor information is the raw material of the intelligence process. It is useful but unevaluated data about the competitor derived from every possible *legal* source—customers, former employees, union newsletters, security analyst reports, the business press, sales-call reports, business peers, executive speeches, government offices, product brochures, consultant studies, and court records, to name a few. Intelligence is the analytical process whereby the disaggregated bits of competitive data flowing into the company are transformed into relevant and actionable knowledge about competitors' strategic positions, competitive performance, functional capabilities, and corporate values. The vital importance of competitor intelligence to business planning is reflected in the following definition of intelligence used by the military services:

Intelligence—The product resulting from the collection, evaluation, integration and interpretation of all available information which concerns one or more aspects of foreign nations or of areas of operations and which is immediately or potentially significant to planning.[5]

Like planning and strategy, the concept of "intelligence" has strong political and military connotations. In most national governments, planning is an extensively developed staff activity that draws heavily on the state's intelligence resources. Formal intelligence produced on other nations is continually updated and fed into the government's planning process. The evidence suggests that systematic intelligence improves the capabilities of the political planning process and gives key decision makers more timely and realistic strategic options.[6] Nowhere is the interrelationship between the *planning* function and the *intelligence* process more developed than in the military—a professional group that has a long-standing obsession with the concept of strategy.[7]

While the risks they incur and the objectives they seek are radically different, both the business manager and the military leader face a common intellectual and organizational task—to achieve the maximum strategic gain with the most efficient use of resources against adversaries trying to do the same. Over the past 40 years the military (and other agencies in the governmental intelligence community) has developed a systematic approach to the incorporation of competitive information into planning procedures and decision-making routines. The proven analytical techniques, organizational forms, and operational methodology that constitute this body of intelligence doctrine in the governmental sphere can, with certain modifications, be adapted to the planning requirements and decision-making needs of corporate managers. In fact, the more developed a company's planning system and the greater its executives' orientation to the analytical requirements implied by "strategic management," the easier it is to make this translation.[8]

The Intelligence Cycle

One of the most simple but useful analytical concepts business organizations can borrow from the intelligence community is the notion of the "intelligence cycle." It is both a blueprint for building an intelligence network and an analytical picture of the way in which the discrete phases of the intelligence process are integrated. As depicted in Exhibit 4-2, the mission, that is, the purpose or objective, of the organization intelligence serves is the focal point. This is not a decorative matter. Intelligence production can become an end in itself. Divorced from the executive decision-making process, intelligence quickly becomes a reactive librarylike service or an obscure, distant research function filling up files that are rarely used. The most vital element in the management of intelligence—planning and supervision—is keeping the process and the network focused on the big picture: management's strategic tasks. The purpose of intelligence is to increase senior management's understanding of the competitive environment and thereby assist them in making the best strategic decisions. As the father of military strategy, Clausewitz, reminds us, all else is secondary: "Most battles are won or lost before they are ever engaged, not by those who will fight them—but by their strategists."

EXHIBIT 4-2   Intelligence Cycle

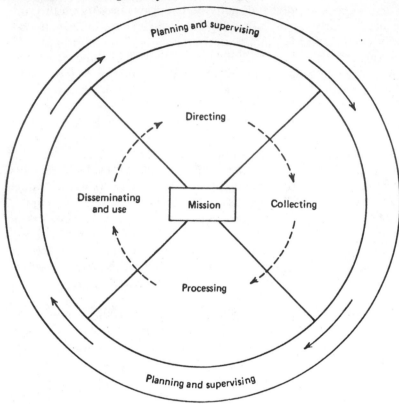

Direction

To keep intelligence focused on management's decision-making needs it is necessary to have executives involved in the process as well as the output of the intelligence cycle. In the first phase of the cycle, senior executives have the opportunity and obligation to provide substantive and organizational guidance to those managers and analysts who accomplish the subordinate intelligence tasks. Those who will use the competitor intelligence developed need to address the following issues:

1. *Defining Intelligence Requirements*

    For the core industries, businesses, and markets we are in, what are the key factors of comparative advantage that determine strategic success?

    What do we need to know about our competitors to enhance our understanding of the competitive environment?

    How will this competitor intelligence be integrated into the company's planning and decision-making procedures?

2. *Setting Intelligence Priorities (Essential Elements of Information)*

   What competitors should be tracked, at what level in the company, in what detail?

   Who are our *corporate strategic peers?* Based on what criteria—industry, markets, size, technology?

   For each major business unit, who are the key competitors that constitute that *division's strategic peers?*

   How much effort should be made at the corporate and divisional level to go beyond direct competitors (i.e., strategic peers) in order to provide intelligence coverage of a broader competitive spectrum (see Exhibits 4-3 and 4-4).

   In light of the above and given time and cost constraints, what are the *essential elements of information* (EEIs) that need to be covered at the tactical, operational, and strategic levels? What are they now? How can they be improved? (See Exhibits 4-5 through 4-7, which suggest how the scope of EEIs can be broadened over time.)

3. *Determining Indicators to be Monitored*

   What are the specific ongoing activities of competitors (i.e., indicators) that should be monitored closely because they provide valuable data about the EEIs, which define core intelligence requirements? (Indi-

EXHIBIT 4-3 Competitive Spectrum

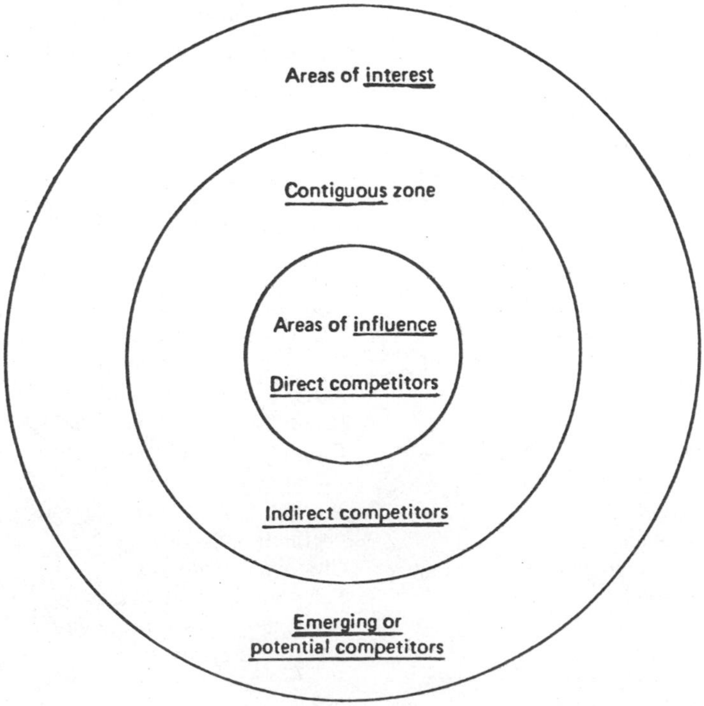

Areas of <u>interest</u>

Contiguous zone

Areas of <u>influence</u>

Direct competitors

Indirect competitors

Emerging or potential competitors

EXHIBIT 4-4   Intelligence Coverage

Intelligence Zone	Strategic Significance	Illustration
Areas of influence	Core industry and/or market segments	Ethical pharmaceuticals Professional hospital products
Contiguous	Close or indirect competitors	Generic pharmaceuticals OTC medicines Diagnostic medical products Biotechnology
Areas of interest	Longer-term competitive threats and opportunities	Hospital management industry Health maintenance organizations Commodity and specialty chemical companies Drug wholesalers Drugstore chains

cators are essentially factual data that require contextual interpretation, e.g., new plant additions, earnings reports, product announcements, management statements, regulatory filings, major customers, institutional ownership, acquisitions, divestments, and licensing activities. Indicators are collated and evaluated in terms of the EEIs they address.)

4.   *Allocating Resources and Setting Deadlines*

How much effort, in terms of budgets and personnel, should be devoted to the competitor intelligence program?

EXHIBIT 4-5   Tactical Competitor Intelligence Priorities

Established EEIs	Emerging EEIs
Pricing trends/behavior	Market segmentation approach
Product characteristics	Product life cycle trend
Product innovations	Product sales forecast
New products: timing and location	Relative market share trend
Product sales	Market share valuation
Terms of trade	Product contribution estimate
Marketing communications	Promotional budgets, plans, responses
Advertising agencies/costs	
Distribution channels	Marketing costs: pattern and effectiveness
Customer loyalty	
Sales-force coverage and organization	Customer evaluation
	Sales-force capabilities
Account structure	Analysis of marketing tactics
Customer service	Substitute products

EXHIBIT 4-6   *Operational Competitor Intelligence*

Established EEIs	Emerging EEIs
Product line relationships	Product line marketing strategy
Product mix and sales	Product line sales and profit
Industry segmentation	contribution
Production costs:	Business division strategy and
Fixed	goals
Variable	Financial performance
Manufacturing processes	Asset management
Plant/capacity change	Financial contribution to parent
Labor/unionization situation	company
Raw material costs	Organizational status in parent
Patents, infringements, licenses	company
Inventory practices	Role in corporate strategy
Technical service	Business peer comparisons:
Geographic concentration	Independent Firms
Organizational structure	Units of Larger Corporations
	Private Firms
	Nature of comparative advantage
	Perception of comparative
	advantage
	Functional capabilities
	Supplier relationships
	New product development
	Reverse engineering of products
	Dominant management style/
	functions

What costs should be borne by what groups? Given the scope and kinds of intelligence required, what is the most cost-effective approach? How much reliance should be placed on external agents, consultants, and information vendors?

How often do we need this intelligence? In what form? Should intelligence deadlines coincide with other ongoing corporate and business controls such as the planning cycle or periodic budget reviews? What tradeoffs are we willing to accept between shorter deadlines and increased costs? What kinds of intelligence should be exempt from deadlines? How often should it be updated?

Collection

Like the legendary pack rat, neophytes at the intelligence game are usually obsessed with the collection of information. The temptation to collect every shred of data available about a competitor must be resisted. In no other phase of the intelligence process is it more true that less is often more. Quality

EXHIBIT 4-7 *Operational Competitor Intelligence*

Established EEIs	Emerging EEIs	Future EEIs

Industry/Business Issue Analyses
Industry segment comparison
Mergers, acquisitions, divestments
Financial/economic
Functional strategy studies:
  e.g., R & D, manufacturing
Regulatory/political
	Comparative Monitoring of Industry Peers
	Financial performance
	Global strategic position
	Business mix and development
	Investment patterns
	R & D capabilities
	Core products: mix and contribution
	Industry standing/reputation
	Functional strengths/weaknesses
	Geographic focus
	Strategic planning capability
	Sources and scope of comparative
	  advantage
	Strategy and goals
		Industry Strategic Group Analyses
		Number, mix, trend
		Bases:
		  Corporate function vs. industry segment
		Strategic priorities
		Management background
		Operating style
		Base of comparative advantage
		Intragroup competition
		Intergroup competition and alliances

Internal Support Digests of corporate intelligence Intelligence resources development Training/source referrals Assistance to operational intelligence Special line and staff projects	*Net Strategic Assessment of Industry Peers* Past record and potential Business capabilities and resources Organizational character Management style Strategic assumptions Core objectives Probable reactions	*Net Strategic Assessment of Nonindustry Peers* Potential entrance to industry Major suppliers Major customers Strategic leaders Strategic failures

4.16

of data and focus of effort should be the operating principles. In collecting information, the traditional *80/20 rule* should be paramount: 20 percent of the indicators monitored provide 80 percent of the information needed; 20 percent of the collectors used can access 80 percent of the commander's EEIs; and only 20 percent of the EEIs are strategically significant. The trick, of course, is to identify the 20 percent. But that skill is what makes intelligence an art, not a science.

In line with the policy guidance established by senior management's intelligence direction, a collection plan should be developed. Depending on the level of effort, time constraints, and coordination involved, the plan can range from a mental note to a formal presentation. At a minimum, the collection plan should cover the following points:

Statement of management's *intelligence requirements*

Conversion into *essential elements of information* and definable *indicators*

Identification of relevant, accessible, balanced, and cost-effective *collection agencies*

Evaluation of *data* and *sources*

Organization of information for transmission

The useful distinction between information collectors and data sources is often overlooked. A source is a person (e.g., a competitor's ex-employee), a thing (e.g., financial statement), or a system (e.g., distribution channels) from which information is gathered. A collector or agent is an individual (e.g., a sales representative) or organization (e.g., market research firm) that can obtain specific kinds of information. Of course, some sources are also collectors (e.g., security analysts). The kinds of sources targeted should determine the type of collector used. The key criteria in selecting collectors are their cost, their access to the source, and their knowledge of the source. Tradeoffs are inevitable, and thus a balanced mix of collectors is advisable. Excessive reliance on one type—say sales representatives or consultants—is particularly dangerous.

Most sources of competitor information are public or at least semipublic; that is, there are no legal or ethical restrictions in accessing them. There are, of course, some sources of competitor information that are highly secret or confidential, such as trade secrets and customer lists. Other sources may be regarded as proprietary or off limits to outsiders, for example, marketing plans and employees. While these kinds of sources will always be targeted by unscrupulous and rash collectors, they should be studiously avoided because of the grave legal risks involved.[9]

The more detailed the information required on competitors' manufacturing costs, intercompany relationships, and foreign businesses, the more dependent will the collection plan be on field research sources. Moreover, compared to other components of the strategic environment, the amount of

EXHIBIT 4-8   Types of Sources by Data Category

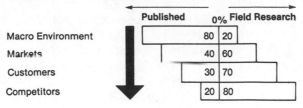

	Published		Field Research
		0%	
Macro Environment	80	20	
Markets	40	60	
Customers	30	70	
Competitors	20	80	

EXHIBIT 4-9   Strategic Intelligence—Corporate Files

Competitors' corporate publications
  Focus on major multibusiness competitors (corporate peers)
  Financial statements/press releases
  Employee communications
  Executive presentations
  Technical papers
  Government regulatory filings (e.g., tax, health)
Press clippings
  General (e.g., *New York Times, Financial Times, Wall Street Journal*)
  Business (e.g., *Fortune*)
  Specialized trade and industry newsletters and magazines
  Regional and local media
Financial
  Security analyst reports
  Press (e.g., *Wall Street Transcript*)
  Credit reports (e.g., *D & B,* internal)
  Subscription services (e.g., *Value Line, Moody's, S & P Financial Dynamics*)
  Electronic data services (e.g., *Disclosure, Compuserve*)
  Standard reference directories (e.g., *Moody's* Robert Morris Associates, *Annual
    Statement Studies*)
  Economic (e.g., *Data Resources Inc., Control Data's (EIS)*)
Industry
  Government reports
  Consultant studies and subscription reports (e.g., ADL, SRI, Kline)
  Trade/industry association materials
  Standard reference directories (e.g., *Predicast F & S Index, Findex, Ayers*)
Other
  Debriefing reports (own employees, competitors' former employees)
  Specialized field research reports
  Key court cases (excerpts)
  Operational, tactical, and functional intelligence reports (selective extracts or
    executive summaries)
  Contact reports (e.g., investment bankers, security analysts, business
    journalists, executive recruiters, lobbyists, senior executives)
  Electronic data bases (e.g., Dialog, Nexus) (hard copy extracts filed by subject)
  Information and investigative services
  Academic reports (e.g., case studies, Ph.D. theses)

---

relevant published information available on competitors is small and that which exists is extremely diffused (see Exhibit 4-8).

As they are first developed and then used over time, information sources need to be evaluated and organized. Exhibits 4-9 and 4-10 list the kinds of competitor information source files that could be developed at the corporate and divisional (or functional staff) levels in most companies with a minimal amount of effort. Note that these files constitute a mixture of published and field sources.

Time and circumstances will show which sources are more valuable. As an aid in that learning curve, an evaluation rating is a useful part of the collection plan. This alphanumeric rating is a practical shorthand device for profiling the *reliability of the source* and the probable *accuracy of the information*.

Source Reliability	Data Accuracy
A—Completely reliable	1—Confirmed by other sources
B—Usually reliable	2—Probably true
C—Fairly reliable	3—Possible true
D—Not usually reliable	4—Doubtfully true
E—Unreliable	5—Impossible
F—Cannot be judged	6—Cannot be judged

The latter bit of evaluative data is particularly useful to the analyst who must put the jigsaw puzzle of competitor information together to draw out the intelligence pattern.

As shown in Exhibit 4-11, a simple collection plan matches EEIs and indicators, lists and distinguishes potential sources and collectors, sets deadlines, and notes relevant references. Besides organizing the collection effort, it's an historical record that will be useful in redirecting collection agencies, adding new intelligence requirements triggered by the information obtained, and identifying new or more detailed indicators. Like the intelligence process it supports, collection should be managed as a continuous, logical, integrated, and sequential activity. The more valuable competitor information comes only to those who collect it in an organized and continuous manner.

Processing

Processing is an intellectual art form in which experienced analysts upgrade competitor information into business intelligence. It is driven by two key variables: the quality of the data and the capabilities of the analysts. The latter is more important as the great English scientist (and part-time intelligence operative) Sir Francis Bacon tells us:

> Those who have handled sciences have been either men of experiment or men of dogmas. The men of experiment are like the ant, they only collect and use;

EXHIBIT 4-10   *Operational Intelligence—Divisional Files*

Strategic business unit competitors—corporate/business segments
  Focus on divisional peers
  Divisions of firms covered by corporate staff
  Single business competitors
  Multibusiness competitors not covered by corporate staff

Marketing
  Subscription services (e.g., SAMI, IMS, Nielsen)
  Customer and public opinion surveys (e.g., SRI's *VALS*)
  Market research reports (external and in-house)
  Product substitute files (by exception)
  Product managers' analyses
  Sales managers' reports
  Price lists
  Sales reps call reports (by exception)
  Legal (e.g., antitrust, product liability)
  Product/trade show reports
  Advertisements/sales promotion literature
  Distributor reports/interviews

R&D/technical
  Competitor regulatory filings (e.g., FDA, EPA)
  Specialized media (e.g., scientific, professional, technical)
  Competitor product evaluation (e.g., reverse engineering analyses)
  Convention trip reports
  Licensing staff memos and contact reports
  Litigation and patent filings
  Scientific meetings, abstracts, trip reports
  Venture capital proposals

Human resourses
  Labor relations files and union newsletters
  Consultant reports/contacts
  University recruitment contacts
  Identification of competitors' ex-employees
  Competitor directories and organizational charts
  Employment interviews
  Help wanted ads

Manufacturing/engineering
  Engineering/construction consultants and companies
  Facility observations (reports and photographs)
  Plant tour trip reports
  Purchasing department memos on supplier contacts
  Standard cost accounting comparisons
  Plant and product cost profile

Other
  Telephone directories (Yellow Pages)
  Governmental data (filed by function)
  Commercial loan filings (state office of corporations departments)

EXHIBIT 4-11 Intelligence Collection Plan
(Period Covered: July 1 to October 1, 1984)

Requestor	EEIs	Indicators	Collection Resources	Deadlines	References	Remarks
President #A84-Z9/5	Competitor Z's S.E. strategy update	Distribution change / Plant X capacity investment / Management switch	B Division management / S.E. public affairs / Purchasing / S & T department — Consultant X / Consultant N	Aug. 1, 19__ (1 Month)	Oplan #5 / Mkt. Report #8 / File #4	Review Wigwam project / Contact JV partner / Priority
Corporate planning Mr. ___ #N84-X7/4	Competitor analysis of industry segment	Passage of new legislation / New trade association / Competitor A's Zulu acquisition	Washington office / F Division planning / X Division mfg. / R & D — Security Analyst C / Information research firm L	Sept. 15, 19__ (3 Months)	Strategic issues file / F Div. operations plan / Consultant X files	Review strategic profiles of competitors: / A-1, B-17, A-24, F-8 / Secondary
Division O Mr. ___ #D84-Y10/6	Competitor M's strategy for its Zonan Div. (1984–86)	Severe price decline in X product / Influx of resumes from engineers M involved in two LBOs (1983)	Industry L & P files / Financial data base L / D & B current — Executive Recruiter Z / LBO Consultant M / Suppliers 4 and 6 (purchasing)	Ongoing	Division X new business plan / R & D Product 2 presentation / File #12	Contact Board Member Z / Contact Investment Banker N / Secondary

the reasoners resemble spiders, who make cobwebs out of their own substance. But the bee takes a middle course; it gathers its material from the flowers of the garden and of the field, but transforms and digests it by a power of its own.

Like a good journalist the intelligence analyst must record essential data, summarize it in a way that adds perspective, and evaluate it for underlying meaning. From disparate details the analyst seeks to discern the tactical characteristics, the functional priorities, the operational patterns, and the strategic thinking that distinguish one competitor from another. Having done this, he or she must then assess the developed picture and state what the probable implications of this competitor intelligence are for his or her firm's current operation and strategic goals. In essence, intelligence analysis is an interpretive task of reducing complex, confusing, and frequently contradictory information about business rivals to its most basic element—intelligence that addresses the core questions:

What are the key factors of strategic success in this industry, business, or market?
What business rivals are creating a competitive advantage harmful to our strategic interests?
What vulnerabilities of business rivals can we exploit?
Are we operating our business as well as we should in light of what we know about competitors?

The main elements of the processing phase of the intelligence cycle are listed below:

1. **Efficient and economical recording**
2. **Interpretation**
   Collation, categorization, integration
   Sifting, screening
   Pattern analysis
3. **Evaluation**
   Assessment
   Significance
   Projection
   Perspective
4. **Personnel**
   Seasoned analysts
   Team approach

Each organizational level or functional group that has a staff of intelligence analysts should recruit individuals with:

The ability to produce both quantitative and qualitative analyses (a skill that sensitizes one to the inherent limitations of both).

A passion for knowledge and understanding but not authorship (intelligence analysis is best when it's a team effort).

An inquisitive but skeptical intellect, comfortable with ambiguity but not inaction.

The ability to ask the salient questions and to ignore the distracting and irrelevant clutter.

The skill to extract intelligence from people and paper by observation, induction, and deduction.

An understanding of the techniques of competitive analysis and the dynamics of business planning.

To facilitate the processing of information, data should be recorded and organized in an economical routine that aids interpretation. For example, while competitors' financial details must be scrutinized and translated into comparable categories, the analytical focus should be on *strategic direction* not *decimal points*. Exhibits 4-12 and 4-13 show 14 competitors' corporate financial performances (operating profitability and sales growth rate) in a relational, graphic dimension. Where believable business segment data is available, it can also be portrayed in a recorded form that favors comparative strategic insights (see Exhibits 4-14 and 4-15).

The proliferation of personal computers and sophisticated graphic software

EXHIBIT 4-12   U.S. Pharmaceutical Industry 1979–1983: Profitability and Sales Growth

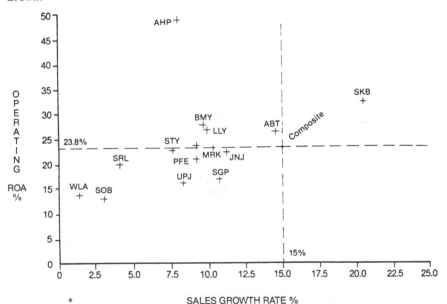

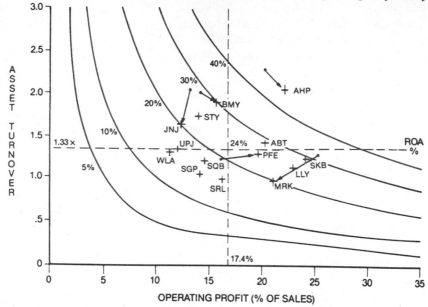

EXHIBIT 4-13 U.S. Pharmaceutical Industry 1979–1983: Operating Profitability

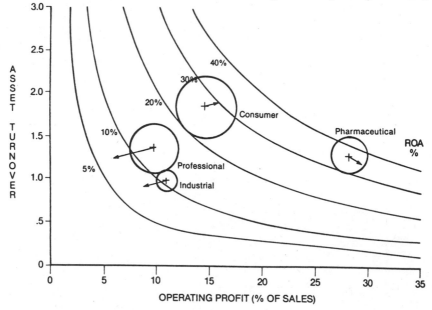

EXHIBIT 4-14 Johnson & Johnson—Business Segments' Profitability 1979–1983

EXHIBIT 4-15   *Bristol-Myers—Business Segments' Profitability 1979–1983*

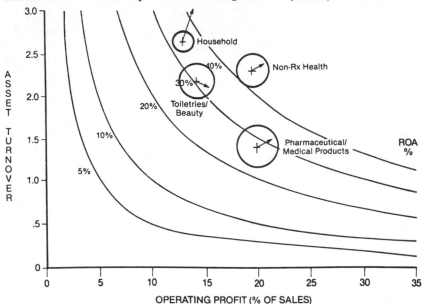

available today give the intelligence analyst a broad choice of innovative tools with which to manipulate, display, and see into the voluminous competitor data collected. Whatever electronic files, matrices, charts, or graphs are used to improve the data record, they should be selected because they help the analyst to:

Provide a comparative basis for competitor assessment.

Identify trends.

Facilitate insights.

Suggest issues for deeper exploration.[10]

Dissemination

Intelligence that isn't communicated can't be used. In the final phase of the intelligence cycle the critical communication and feedback dialogue between analysts and decision makers begins. The classic tradeoff is that between the analyst's passion for *thoroughness* and the decision maker's need for *timeliness*. Usually the former will and should give way, particularly in light of the 80/20 Rule mentioned earlier. When a decision can't be delayed and action is required, a limited amount of timely intelligence is preferable to an exhaustive report read only after the competitor has launched a new product, sold an old business, or captured a key account. Besides senior decision makers, others in the company have an operational use for different aspects of competitor intelligence. The form the finished intelligence takes (e.g., a formal company report, electronic mail, a strategic profiling session, chapter in a market research study, group briefing, or telephone call) will vary. So will the scope of the dissemination (e.g., senior executives only, planning staffs, marketing managers, project scientists, or sales directors). However, both should be tailored to the classic intelligence principle of "need to know." Prudential security, not obsessive secrecy, should be the watchword.

At the dissemination phase, competitor intelligence becomes a product. Whatever its specific format and content it probably will fall into one of four general product categories.

As shown in Exhibit 4-16, these intelligence products cover the full spectrum of research and analysis from the quick answer to a specific question, to the full strategic assessment of a corporate competitor. Together they constitute an *integrated* series of finished intelligence packaged to suit user needs. While brevity and clarity are always prized in the corporate paper jungle, Professor Sherman Kent, a dean of the American intelligence community, wisely cautions us that the two are not always synonymous:

> There is such a thing as a complicated idea; there is such a thing as so complicated an idea that it cannot be expounded in 250 words, or in two pie-charts, an assemblage of little men, little engines, and three-quarters of a little cotton bale. The consumer who insists that no idea is too complicated for the 300-word summary is doing himself no favor. He is requiring the impossible and is paying heavily for it. He is paying in two ways: he is kidding himself in his belief that he really knows, and he is contributing to the demoralization of his intelligence outfit. The intelligence people who spend weeks of back-breaking work on a substantive problem and come up with an answer whose meaning lies in its refinements are injured at the distortion that may occur in a glib summary from which all real meaning has been squeezed."

EXHIBIT 4-16   *Competitor Intelligence Products*

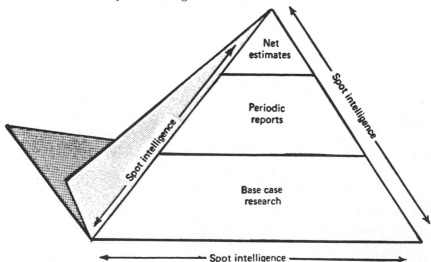

Rank ordered by their strategic value, the four generic types of dissemination products are defined as follows:

1. Net estimates: competitor strategic evaluation
2. Period report: current activity monitor
3. Base case file: background research
4. Spot report: narrow, topical-focus query

They serve complementary but different intelligence purposes and each has distinct characteristics.

Strategic Net Estimate

As the ultimate focal point is better strategic decisions, no competitor intelligence product has greater potential value than a net estimate of a competitor's strategy. It should provide senior management with the essential strategic intelligence about selected corporate or business unit competitors who:

1. Have the capabilities to disrupt or retard the company's strategy.
2. Are undergoing a fundamental change in their competitive position and that potentially represent a new strategic threat or opportunity for the firm.
3. Are members of a target strategy group, industry, or industry segment that figures prominently in a major strategic issue or decision facing the company.

Competitors in the first category constitute, by definition, a company's or business group's strategic peers. Given the ongoing importance of direct business competitors, it is worth the effort to insure that a strategic net estimate of each key rival is updated at least annually, if not every six months.

A net estimate is a shrewd guess about the overall strategic significance of a competitor. It is, however, a *reasoned* guess based on a systematic evaluation of the best intelligence available. Clear, concise, and brief, it should communicate its intelligence in a comparative format that explains the competitor's strategic direction (see Exhibit 4-17) and assesses that strategy in terms of the key factors of comparative advantage operative in the industry and/or businesses of concern to senior management. The strategic net estimate is an overall summary that follows a highly analytical structure, as shown in the following list:

1. Description of competitor's strategy:
   Current/projected
   Stated/inferred

EXHIBIT 4-17   Competitor's Strategic Direction

2. Evaluation of competitor's strategy in terms of:
    Key factors of comparative advantage
    Changing factors of comparative advantage
3. Capabilities/limitations:
    Corporate
    Key business units
    Core business functions
4. Response profile:
    Staying power
    Adaptability
5. Implications to the company:
    Threats
    Opportunities
    Issues
6. Key intelligence gaps

Often overlooked is the important use of a net estimate to identify key *strategic intelligence gaps*. When senior managers jointly consider and then critique the best strategic assessment available on a target competitor, it is often disquieting to learn what fundamental gaps exist in a firm's knowledge of the strategic thinking and direction of business rivals. The purpose of a net estimate is to gain a critical understanding of competitor's strategy vis-à-vis your firm, other competitors, and the industry's key factors of comparative advantage. It can be a daunting analytical exercise, particularly on the first round. A useful "warm-up" that enables analysts to quickly run through a related number of competitors from a comparative strategic perspective, and thereby "test" the relevancy of the perceived factors of comparative advantage and the common functional characteristics and financial performance of the firms involved, is the brief competitor strategic profile. Exhibit 4-18 is a sample outline useful for this preliminary exercise.

EXHIBIT 4-18   Corporate Strategic Profiles

Purpose: These brief profiles are the *initial steps* in a comparative analysis of key competitors' strategies. In this strategic overview, readily available data are compiled to develop a *broad understanding* of a competitor's strategy with respect to fundamental issues such as its criteria for selecting and funding businesses and the influence of company culture and management structure on strategic goals and competitive behavior.

I. Competitive Position/Company Background:
    A. Business/product mix
    B. Major qualitative characteristics/competitive reputation
    C. Corporate financial performance (last five years) and expected performance (next five years)
    D. Corporate culture
    E. Management/organizational structure
    F. Historical milestones

II. Corporate Goals:
    A. Strategic objectives
    B. Management style and priorities
    C. Planning and implementation capabilities
    D. Past strategies

III. Investment Focus/Business Segments' Analysis:
    A. Existing product mix, financial performance, market structure
    B. Geographic balance/joint ventures
    C. Diversification/concentration
    D. New initiatives—products and markets

IV. R & D Focus and Issues

V. Initial Strategic Assessment:
    A. Capabilities and intentions
    B. Match between company resources and strategic goals
    C. Match between factors of comparative advantage and company strategy:
        1. Coherence and consistency
        2. Management perceptions
        3. Financial issues
        4. Timing and implementation
        5. Probable competitor reactions
        6. Expected performance (probability of success)
    D. Implications:
        1. Threats and opportunities
        2. Key issues
        3. Critical EEIs (essential elements of information)

Another analytical technique that facilitates the production of useful strategic net estimates is the effort to identify and define competitors by their respective strategic groups.

Strategic Group Analysis

Strategic group or industry segmentation analysis focuses on the core economic, marketing, and technological variables that divide an industry into key business areas and distinguish one group of competitors from another.[12] Companies within an industry can be classified into specific strategic groups on the basis of their relative size, predominant business function (e.g., manufacturers, raw material suppliers, distributors), market focus, or some other variable that seems to be particularly significant because it strategically links one set of companies into a definable competitor segment of the industry. For example, in Exhibit 4-19 selected health-care industry competitors are divided into four distinct groups based on their most important business segment: hospital products, pharmaceuticals (prescription), proprietaries (OTC medicines), and personal care. Using available business segment results, the groups are plotted on a matrix that highlights strategically important financial data.

A smaller set of competitors—large U.S. pharmaceutical manufacturers—are screened in Exhibit 4-20. Here the strategic issues are R&D intensity and business mix. Quantitative data (health-care sales contribution percentage and ethical drug sales contribution percentage) are used to subdivide 14 ethical pharmaceutical companies into four competitor groups. Ongoing shifts in

EXHIBIT 4-19   Health Care Industry Segments (5 year average)

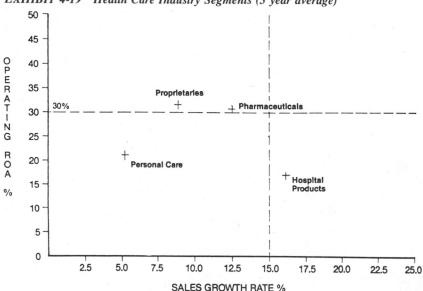

EXHIBIT 4-20   U.S. Pharmaceutical Industry: Strategic Group Map

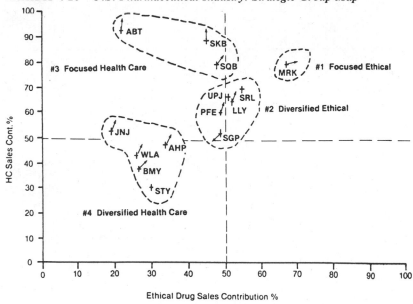

Ethical Drug Sales Contribution %

business mix and general strategic direction are suggested by the directional arrows.

In the delineation and analysis of strategic or competitor groups, the strategic variables selected to screen the data and the definitions of those variables is crucial. To the extent that competitors classified into a specific group share common operational and functional characteristics, the analytical utility of that group's designation increases. Ideally, firms in a particular competitive group:

Have similar buyers and suppliers.

Share common mobility barriers and switching costs.

Have comparable asset investments.

Have similar operating costs.

Emphasize similar business functions.

Develop similar product and business mixes.

Target the same market segments.

Have common development patterns.

Share common strategic assumptions and goals.

Consequently, their corporate and business division strategies tend to be very close in design and direction.

In contrast, the strategies pursued by companies within disparate competitor groups reflect substantially different *factors of comparative advantage*

EXHIBIT 4-21 U.S. Generic Pharmaceutical Industry: Competitor Groups

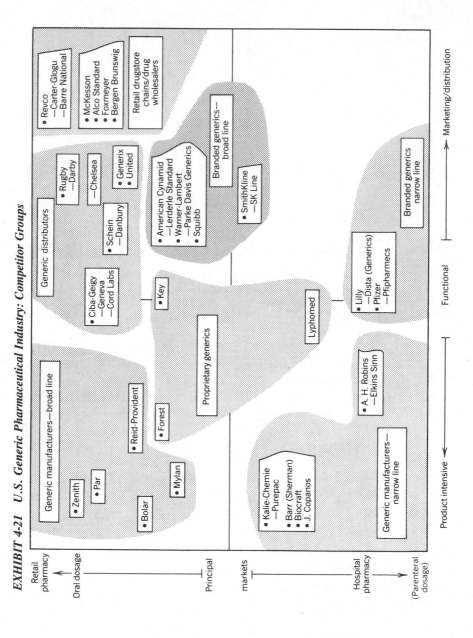

and corporate sources of *competitive strength*. As Exhibit 4-21 shows, preliminary intelligence is useful in the initial effort to identify and compare major competitor groups within an industry. After the estimated strategic positions of key competitor groups have been mapped out, more detailed intelligence is then developed in order to evaluate the characteristics and future potential of the competitive advantages each enjoys. In Exhibit 4-22, a variation of the Boston Consulting Group's Industry Matrix is used to depict the strategic relationship between different competitive groups in the generic pharmaceutical industry and the bases of their competitive advantage.

Companies and competitor groups that share a common basis of competitive advantage are usually closely attuned to each other's strategies and tend to compete against each other in operational and tactical terms. They are cognizant of, but far less attuned to, the character of the strategic threat

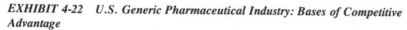

EXHIBIT 4-22 U.S. Generic Pharmaceutical Industry: Bases of Competitive Advantage

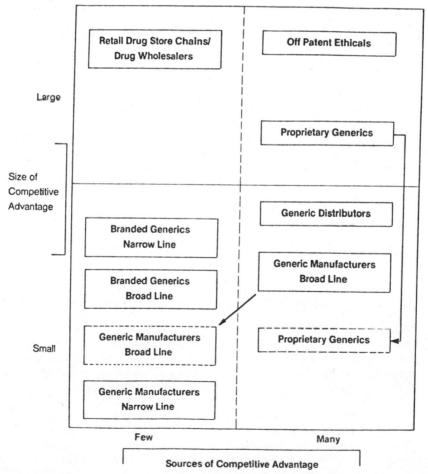

posed by firms in competitor groups whose strategies are based on a different mix of corporate resources and factors of comparative advantage.

Periodic Intelligence

Periodic intelligence is heavy on facts and comparatively light on analysis. Combining elements of an intelligence newsletter and a data-filled scorecard on competitor indicators, activities, and trends, it is a succinct report useful for organizing the routine stream of data flowing into the company. Regularly

EXHIBIT 4-23 *Periodic Competitor Intelligence*

Division: FOREST PRODUCTS   Period: THIRD QUARTER 19__
Subject: MANUFACTURING INVESTMENTS

NBIP LTD. has received federal and provincial grants totaling $12.5 million for the expansion and modernization of its Dalhousie, New Brunswick, mill which will raise capacity to produce offset and standard newsprint by one-third to 100 metric tpd when completed in early fall. The project, now estimated at C$60 million, is the largest ever undertaken by parent *CIP LTD.* Included in the project are rebuilds of Nos. 1 and 2 machines with addition of twin-wire formers, Tri-Nip presses and improvement of dryer, calendar and reel sections. Other major components include a new sulfonated chemimechanical pulping plant developed by CIP Research and a woodwaste boiler which is expected to save the equivalent of 108,000 barrels per year of fuel oil.

CIP INC.'s 230 tpd corrugated medium mill in Natane, Quebec, will undergo C$12.5 million in improvements over the next three and a half years. Provincial and federal governments are contributing about $2 million between them for the program which recently began with the installation of a $2 million clarifier needed to comply with provincial discharge regulations.

THE CHESAPEAKE CORP. OF VIRGINIA announced that it has purchased the hardwood lumber manufacturing facilities and 40-acre site of the West Point Log Co. Inc. in West Point, Virginia. The sawmill is about a year old and was built to process hardwood. Start-up of the mill is indefinite at this time pending an improvement in the lumber market. The mill, which includes planing facilities, is capable of producing eight MMBF of lumber per year on a one shift basis.

CONTAINER CORP. OF AMERICA announced plans to sell its Composite Can Division. The division comprises eight manufacturing plants, a research facility and general office. The division's plants are in Atlanta, Georgia; Jamesburg, New Jersey; Los Angeles, California; New Orleans, Louisiana; Piqua, Ohio; Portland, Oregon; Willow Springs, Illinois; and Maplewood, Missouri.

DOMTAR LTD. reports that its Carlaw Avenue corrugated combiner plant in Toronto—one of four facilities in the area—will be permanently closed September 1 because it is no longer economically sound. Domtar's Corrugated Containers Division currently operates 15 combiner plants in six nationwide provinces.

---

produced and widely disseminated, it helps to keep the subject of competitor intelligence visible as an ongoing activity.

Short in length and highly descriptive in content, periodic intelligence is also a convenient way to update base case intelligence files and to communicate new EEIs, indicators, and intelligence requirements to those staff and line groups actively involved in the ongoing competitor intelligence effort. With an emphasis on current competitor intelligence occurring within a limited time frame (usually three to six months), periodic intelligence reports or briefings should make maximum use of summary, bulletinlike formats and graphical/tabular data to communicate relevant competitor intelligence throughout the company (for examples, see Exhibits 4-23 and 4-24). Used in this manner, it can be a limited but very low-cost competitor intelligence product that bridges the past and the future and thus overcomes a major limitation in most corporate intelligence programs—a lack of continuity.

Base Case Intelligence

This is the one intelligence product that is never finished and probably should not be disseminated outside the analytical section. It is basically a set of working intelligence files or notebooks. Based on either a manual or computerized file structure, base case intelligence is the raw material of competitor information that has been organized into a coherent whole to facilitate further research and analysis. It's a compendium of selected tactical, operational, and strategic intelligence that details the past competitor record, outlines the present knowledge level, and suggests the probable scope of future intelligence requirements. The following list outlines a limited workbook structure that integrates core documentary material and semifinished analyses into a base case file:

1. Key documentation
    Company reports
    Security analyst reports
    Executive presentations
    Consultant studies
    Major media articles
    Public files
    Field summaries
2. Financial comparisons
    Industry
    Segments
    Product line
3. Background
    Competitive position/markets

EXHIBIT 4-24   Periodic Intelligence By Category (January to March 1984)

Competitor	Organizational–1	Manufacturing–2	R & D–3	Products–4
X	Joint Venture with KMP for Evs Market on M-4 product line. F3	Annual capacity of Rock Hill S.C. plant (8/8) to expand by 600M bbs by close 1985. D4	Product Kale hit with major recall in U.K.: spillover to U.S. expected; aborts key product line extensions. A3	Minn. test market of OTC version of product reported as strong success. B2 Calif. follow-up expected. C3
Y	Zale subsidiary will be sold to Fr. mfr. within 6 mos. A2 Major reorganization of Ag. Div. in works (after 2 years of losses). C1	500 acre industrial site optioned in So. Houston: possible warehouse/ distribution center. A1	Successful Phase II clinicals on product X12384 reported in Japan: 2 mos. behind schedule. B3	Severe market share loss in product line Zelman reported: primarily premium accounts. D2
Z	Nothing significant.	Linden, NJ Alona plant permanently closed; production shifted to Rollin plant in Dothan, Ala. B1	Announced formation of seed genetics bio tech project with Univ. of Wash. A1	New veterinary line of animal vaccines launched nationwide: major promotional support ($6–10MM). B2

Note: Each "block" of information is given an intelligence evaluation. The more significant items are effect on business and corporate strategies. Follow-on EEIs and indicators are identified where

       Historical development
       Investment strategy
       Geographic balance
       Corporate culture
4. Current strategy/goals
       Corporate
       Segments
       Geographic
       Functional
5. Joint ventures/licensing
6. Functional areas
7. Management
8. Net estimate

As this is the analyst's research core, base case intelligence should be tailored to his or her operational needs. On rare occasions, such as an acquisition

LEVEL: Divisional

Marketing–5	Financial–6	Assessment
Northeast hospital sales force cut by 20% B2 Will license Nemo-type line from Belgium mfrs. C3	K-P puts out a nega-tive sell report; stock down 20% in period. A1	① Major impact on Group A: possible share loss for P-1 line; EEI: timing.
New media campaign rumored for divi-sion Tango con-sumer line (print, TV, POS, up to $100MM). B2	Arranged Eur. debt through H&D ($200MM to $300MM). C2 LBO of Donner Div. ($60MM est.) C3	⑥ Minor impact on Group B's SE markets. ③ Major impact on T-4 product if Phase III success-ful. Close track.
Oran's OTC analgesic line switched to DDB from JWT advertising. B3 E.R. Hams recruit-ed as new VP-Consumer Market-ing from ABT. A1	Ups stake in Laker Drugs by 40% (TV for marketing expected). C3	③ Minor impact on Ag. Div.'s 4-L market. EEI's: R & D Focus; Personnel.

also given a quick assessment to highlight their potential near-term
appropriate to facilitate the development of new collection plans.

of a competitor or a radical change in the competitive status of a strategic
peer, a full base case written intelligence analysis may be warranted. But
as these voluminous reports are referenced but rarely read by busy executives, they should be prepared on an exception basis by request of senior
management only.

Spot Intelligence

To the user, spot intelligence is a helpful product; to the analyst it is a necessary evil. Spot intelligence is a limited, narrowly focused query concerning
a tactical or operational subject such as:

In the German pharmaceutical market, what has been the effect of competitor X's generic line on our brand name products?

Is competitor Z negotiating a leveraged buy-out of its specialty plastics
business?

What is the production capacity of competitor Y's Covington, Virginia,
paperboard mill? What are the key bottlenecks in the plant?

Outline the organizational structure of competitor T's Central Research Division.

Estimate the direct manufacturing cost per unit of Z production at competitor B's Fresno chemical plant.

What are the sales and profit contribution of competitor D's parenteral nutritional products?

Depending on the frequency of the queries, the quality of the competitor data base, and the obscurity of the topics, spot intelligence can be a minor task or a major headache. As the "fast food" of intelligence, these queries have a high factual content, a short deadline, provide (at best) a quick insight into competitor strategies, and basically satisfy managers' ad hoc intelligence needs. Analytically, the danger is that the useful snippet of spot intelligence will be taken out of context. The greater danger, however, is organizational: the volume of spot intelligence queries and/or the priority given them by top management will simply overwhelm the resources (particularly time) of the intelligence analysts. Should this occur, the concept of integrated intelligence products covering a full analytical spectrum will be cratered. Intelligence will degenerate into a reactive data base management exercise. To avoid this an aggressive effort should be made to constantly screen spot intelligence queries and filter out those that can be answered by cheaper means or that are of secondary value.

A CORPORATE INTELLIGENCE NETWORK—AN ORGANIZATIONAL APPROACH

A companywide program modeled on the elements of the intelligence cycle can knit together a firm's scattered information resources, integrate different levels of intelligence, and promote the strategic utilization of the competitor intelligence produced.

However, unless the intelligence program is carefully tailored to the organizational structure and the management culture of the company, it is likely to be ignored as irrelevant or viewed as a threat to existing departmental or managerial interests. Competitor intelligence is a novel concept in most firms, and its subject matter—the status, performance, and direction of business rivals—is controversial. Better understood and packaged for top management review it may invite invidious comparisons.

Business intelligence programs tend to take one of two general forms in those companies that acknowledge their importance (see Exhibit 4-25). The less-common form is the small, centralized staff section (often attached to corporate planning) that produces financially oriented, strategic intelligence on corporate peers or acquisition candidates for a select group of senior executives.

In the other version, competitor intelligence activities are carried out in a highly diffused manner by marketing groups, divisional business planners, and some functional staffs (e.g., R&D or manufacturing). Corporate competitors tend to be evaluated in a disaggregated, nonstrategic fashion, and little of this intelligence is collated for senior management use.

One way to minimize the internal political concerns, organizational barriers, and informational black holes that lessen the effectiveness of competitor intelligence programs is to develop a companywide intelligence network designed as an *integrated* but *decentralized* system with the following features:

Wide but coordinated use of employee "collectors"

Part-time activity to organize available competitor information in each department

Minimum amount of administration; maximum amount of intelligence communication and management feedback

Small number of full-time intelligence analysts at corporate, business division, and selected staff groups

Coordinated mid-level management of the intelligence program

Linkage of tactical, operational and strategic intelligence

Strong orientation toward strategic intelligence

For example, a corporate intelligence system could be developed along the following lines (see Exhibit 4-26) at a relatively modest cost because it utilizes personnel and resources that are, in large measure, already in place.

Competitor Information Channels

Internal and external information channels are first identified and then used to access a broad spectrum of competitor data. This requires a one-time companywide intelligence audit that:

Outlines existing competitor information resources.

Identifies the most valuable internal data sources.

Profiles managers' competitor intelligence priorities.

Tracks existing competitor information flows.

Defines information and source biases.

Delineates major and minor competitor intelligence gaps.

The competitor intelligence audit is a crucial first step, although it will generate resistance from those managers and departments reluctant to identify and catalog their data bases and key sources of competitor information. However, the overall value to the company of mobilizing its internal intelligence resources justifies the costs of an extensive and well-coordinated audit.[13]

EXHIBIT 4-25 *Usual Forms of Competitor Intelligence Programs*

Type	Key Departments	Focus	Core Information Sources	Collectors	Key Products	Remarks
Centralized	Corporate planning	Strategic: Corporate peers, Core industry, Acquisition targets	Financial statements, Electronic data bases, Security analyst reports, Industry studies	Staff analysts	Industry overviews, Strategic group studies, Competitor strategic profiles, Acquisition analyses, Sr. executive briefings, Intelligence annex to corporate plan	*Positive* — Minimal cost, Little coordination with internal groups required, Quick response to executive requests, Strong strategic focus. *Negative* — Heavy financial orientation, Little or no use of field research, Slow update of competitor profiles, Lacks operational and functional intelligence inputs, Very restricted sources.

4.40

Functional and/or divisional	Selected corporate staffs:	Functional issues	Nonfinancial	Departmental analysts	Functional studies	
	Manufacturing	Operational:	Marketing	Field employees	Divisional plans	*Positive*
	R&D	Divisional	research	Product	Market	No direct costs
	Marketing	competitors	Manufacturing	managers	research re-	attributable
	Operational	Country risk	cost profiles	Divisional	ports	Ancillary, "low profile"
	groups:	analysis	Process and	planners		intelligence effort
	Business units	Tactical:	product data	Country		No "turf" concerns
	International	Marketing seg-		directors		Rapid updates of
	Product/	mentation				intelligence
	markets	Product				
		studies				*Negative*
						Lack of strategic focus
						Lateral coordination
						difficult
						Relevant competitor intel-
						ligence gets to the top
						slowly, if at all
						Duplication of coverage
						Peripheral or emerging
						competitors ignored
						Disparate competitor intel-
						ligence not integrated

EXHIBIT 4-26   Corporate Intelligence Network

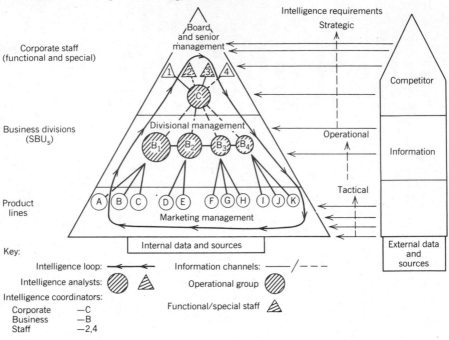

Key:

Intelligence loop: ←———←   Information channels: ———/————

Intelligence analysts: ⊘ ◮   Operational group ⊘

Intelligence coordinators:

    Functional/special staff ◮

Corporate   —C
Business   —B
Staff   —2,4

Maintenance of information channels is assigned to those personnel who have the *organizational access* and *functional expertise* to monitor and screen the available competitor data; for example, corporate or divisional purchasing agents would be responsible for eliciting data from supplier salesmen while country divisional managers would forward information about competitor activities in their region.

Intelligence Contacts

Each organizational level (product line, operating division, corporate) and all major staff functions (R&D, human resources, manufacturing, legal) have at least a limited collection program designed to cull, collate, and organize for quick access the competitor data reported through their information channels. At each of these corporate collection points a current intelligence working file is kept. It identifies the principal sources of competitor data monitored and the key industries, competitors, and markets covered. In each department a mid-level staffer manages the collection effort as a part-time task. This individual is designated as the group's intelligence contact. All agents or collectors used (internal and external) receive intelligence guidance from the departmental contact who is also responsible for the evaluation ratings of collected data.

Intelligence Producers (Analysts)

Specialized and periodic intelligence products, tailored to the planning and operational needs of the company's key divisional and corporate executives, are the responsibility of a small group of intelligence analysts.

They are located within the corporate planning department, the marketing, technical, or planning staffs of each operating division, and selected corporate functional staffs that have an exceptionally high interest in competitor activities (e.g., R&D, manufacturing, finance). These professionals constitute the analytical core of the company's intelligence network. Their primary task is to research, prepare, and disseminate specific competitor intelligence products, such as company background reports, competitor analyses for corporate or business unit strategic plans, industry or market segment briefings, specialized reviews of selected competitor functions or divisions, business development critiques, and evaluations of the quality of competitor intelligence in external reports and studies.

Intelligence Coordinators

The planning, marketing, or other managers to whom the intelligence analyst reports have the key supervisory and coordinating role in the intelligence network. They manage the vertical and lateral communication of intelligence requests, review and disseminate finished intelligence, monitor the performance of the intelligence contacts scattered throughout the corporation, and create systems to upgrade and expand critical information channels. They also develop and sponsor information and training sessions that enhance the visibility and effectiveness of the intelligence network. But their most critical task is to advise corporate and divisional executives on the progress and requirements of the company's total competitor intelligence program. The intelligence coordinators should meet periodically as a semiformal committee to exchange ideas, develop closer personal ties, review key intelligence operational problems, and critique the quality and coverage of the intelligence their analysts produce. As required, they would jointly develop interdepartmental analysis teams to prepare and present special intelligence assessments of key corporate peers and critical competitor issues to executive management.

As a safety precaution against potentially unethical or illegal intelligence activities that can creep in (e.g., such as bribery of competitor's suppliers, the use of bogus employment interviews to acquire proprietary information, or the intentional acquisition of a competitor's confidential property), corporate legal counsel should have a formal advisory role on this intelligence coordinating committee. Nothing can destroy the utility of a company's intelligence program more quickly than the foolish action of overly aggressive collectors (employees or outside agents) who cross the ill-defined boundary into industrial espionage. The information gained is rarely—if ever—worth the serious legal risk involved or the potential public relations fallout.[14]

Intelligence Loop

The intelligence loop is the central dissemination/feedback element of the competitor intelligence network. Without it, the network will not sustain itself. As shown in Exhibit 4-26, via the intelligence loop finished intelligence in its various formats circulates widely throughout the company. Unless the flow of competitor intelligence is visible, inclusive, and accessible, it will dry up. Managers and analysts will become dependent on fewer and more costly information channels. The integration of tactical, operational, and strategic competitor intelligence will cease. More importantly, the rich intelligence resource potential inherent in the knowledge, experience, and contacts of the firm's employees will not be mobilized.

While the primary purpose of a business intelligence program is to serve the decision-making needs of key executives, many other managers and professionals in the company can benefit from improved competitor intelligence. For both substantive and psychological reasons, selective elements of the intelligence produced should be disseminated down and across the company to mid- and low-level personnel who have an operational need for it, for example, product managers, buyers, business analysts, country directors, project researchers, plant managers, auditors, and sales representatives.

Timely, informative, and succinctly packaged intelligence about business rivals is inherently interesting. Most people have a natural curiosity to know how their group and their company stacks up against the competition. Carefully used, business intelligence can heighten employees' competitive instincts, sharpen their ability to work smarter, and increase their awareness of the strategic situation facing the firm. But more importantly, periodic intelligence feedback in the form of bulletins, briefings, and summaries specifically designed for those who select sources, collect data, monitor channels or indicators, and analyze information, keeps them alert to new competitive threats and opportunities. It also involves them in emerging intelligence requirements and commits them to the maintenance of the intelligence network. Feedback carried on the intelligence loop is a vital and visible demonstration that the company's management places a high priority on systematically collecting and *using* competitor intelligence at all levels. It is a continuous reminder to those who make the network run that their intelligence contribution has a practical payoff—to their company, their department, and their careers.

An ancillary benefit of the intelligence loop is that it can be used by senior executives and the intelligence coordinators to overcome one of the core obstacles to effective competitive strategy—the tendency of the corporate bureaucracy to lose or ignore negative information. In the best of companies, data about key competitors and the strategic environment is rarely regarded as neutral information. The future of products, businesses, and careers often depends on the interpretation of the data and its strategic implication for the corporation. Good news has a chorus. But bad news is frequently handled with such care and discretion that its strategic significance is obfuscated—

sometimes by intent, more often by default. Seasoned executives are usually alert to this information syndrome. It is a common feature of all complex organizations, whether they be business, government, or military. The more successful leaders take various actions to minimize this information syndrome, as a recent article on IBM's top management noted:

> But both Mr. Opel and Mr. Akers [IBM's new CEO] apparently share some common approaches to the company's management. Both, for example, are known for a habit of seeking information by calling employees far down in IBM's bureaucracy, circumventing levels of executives.[15]

The intelligence loop and the network that supports it are designed to surface competitor information however negative or controversial. As it gives senior managers both broad and quick access to those personnel closest to the competitor data and the intelligence analyses, it can make the task of "calling down" for sensitive information easier and the opportunity to camouflage or ignore it more difficult.

Intelligence Focus

A strong bias toward strategic intelligence should become an integral aspect of the intelligence network. Personnel involved in collecting, sifting, and processing the diverse strands of competitor information flowing into the company will have a natural inclination to focus on specific kinds of data and intelligence most relevant to their departments' tasks. Consequently, valuable bits of information and analytical insights that do not directly relate to near-term tactical, operational, or functional matters, but may have an important bearing on emerging strategic issues such as rumors of new distribution channels, obscure investments in foreign markets, unexpected management changes, or the technical evaluation of a competitor's innovative manufacturing procedure, may be easily overlooked or lost in the communications shuffle.

The development of strategic competitor intelligence is the primary responsibility of the intelligence analysts, particularly those on the corporate planning staff. Yet all who have a hand in the company's intelligence network must be sensitive to the critical value of competitor information that may have a strategic implication. Once identified and confirmed, these data and analyses can and should move rapidly up through the system. To foster such an orientation an understanding of the competitive analyses that drive strategic intelligence should be a core element of the company's intelligence program, and the training that supports it.

CONCLUSION

As noted at the outset, the organizing principle of strategic competitive analyses is the assessment or evaluation of competitors in terms of the key factors of comparative advantage. The definition of these factors of comparative advantage at the corporate or divisional level is broad and general: global market reach, shared distribution channels, business synergies, or manufacturing economies of scale, for instance. But behind each are numerous concrete details against which a specific competitor must be continuously measured, compared, and monitored. Within this mosaic of business details—tactical, operational, and functional—is a strategic pattern that can be identified and evaluated by seasoned analysts. Used in this way the factors of comparative advantage help managers orient the competitor intelligence network to its most vital function—the collection, analysis, and dissemination of strategic intelligence.

In addition, if personnel have a coherent understanding of the key factors of comparative advantage around which the business strategies of their firm and its competitors revolve, there is a much greater probability that intelligence resources will be efficiently employed and that the accepted factors of comparative advantage will be based on a current and accurate view of the competitive environment. Given the sharp discontinuities and increasing volatility of the contemporary business world, it is painfully evident that the objective realities that underlie established economic relationships, proven business practices, and key factors of comparative advantage change more rapidly than analysts and executives alike realize. Ideas and assumptions one learns are not easily unlearned. However, a business strategy anchored in an obsolete understanding of the competitive situation and the key factors that drive it is a ticket to stagnation and slow decline.

When and if the competitor data and intelligence reveal a new source of comparative advantage or indicate that the established factors may have become less important—or worse, irrelevant—to strategic success, it is likely to be realized first, if only dimly, by those employees closest to the competition—the sales representatives, the research scientist, or the distribution manager. These are the personnel best positioned to pick up the gradual or sudden shift in the tactical, operational, and functional details that foreshadow strategic change. Without the active input and feedback of these experienced collectors, analysts who draft strategic intelligence and the executives who act on it lose an important window on competitors. Even the shrewdest executive is occasionally trapped in a cerebral world of policy papers, planning reviews, and committee meetings, in which strategic perspective can be distorted by the rigorous analysis of outdated facts and false assumptions. It is an occupational hazard of the first order. For as the first principle of intelligence reminds us, "It isn't the things you don't know that hurt you, it's the things you do know that aren't so."

There are few better antidotes to the strategic myopia caused by an outburst of conventional thinking in the executive suite than a well-organized companywide competitor intelligence network. Given the narrow margin for corporate mistakes in an increasingly complex and competitive business environment, an efficient and economical support system that provides senior management with a reliable, steady flow of fact-oriented competitor data and actionable intelligence is rapidly becoming a functional necessity. In the harsh new world of strategic management, companies slow to upgrade their *competitor information assets* to the status of *competitor intelligence resources* will be competing with one eye closed. Lacking the strategic perspective and the peripheral vision integrated competitor intelligence affords, they will be forced, as some already are, to react to the unforeseen initiatives of business competitors and driven to the hapless defense of deteriorating strategies.

NOTES

1. W. W. Bain, "Competitors and Profits: Staying Close to Customer's Needs," *Vital Speeches of the Day*, July 15, 1984, p. 583.
2. See M. E. Porter, *Competitive Strategy*, Free Press, New York, 1980; P. Carroll, "Marketing Strategy: Competitive Analysis," in C. Heyel, Ed., *The Encyclopedia of Management*, 3rd ed., Van Nostrand Reinhold, New York, 1982, pp. 676–679; and W. E. Rothschild, *How to Gain and Maintain the Competitive Advantage in Business*, McGraw-Hill, New York, 1984.
3. M. Potts, "GE Makes Strategic Planning More Than a Numbers Game," *The Washington Post;* reprinted in *The Reporter Dispatch*, White Plains, N.Y., October 17, 1984, p. C12.
4. See F. T. Pearee, "Business Intelligence Systems—The Need for Development and Integration," *Industrial Marketing Management*, June 1976, pp. 115–138; and D.I. Cleland and W. R. King, "Competitive Business Intelligence Systems," *Business Horizons*, December 1975, pp. 19–28.
5. *Dictionary of United States Military Terms for Joint Usage*, Departments of the Army, Navy, and Air Force, Washington, D.C., May 1955, p. 53.
6. W. L. Sammon, "Strategic Intelligence: An Analytical Resource for Decision Makers," in Sammon, *Business Competitor Intelligence*, pp. 21–37; H. H. Ransom, *The Intelligence Establishment*, Harvard University Press, Cambridge, Mass., 1970.
7. R. E. Dupuy and T. W. Dupuy, *The Encyclopedia of Military History*, Harper & Row, New York, 1970, p. 343; E. M. Earle, Ed., *Makers of Modern Strategy*, Princeton University Press, Princeton, 1941; B. H. L. Hart, *Strategy*, Praeger, New York, 1967; M. Howard, *Studies in War and Peace*, Viking, New York, 1971.
8. J. R. Gardner, "Corporate Intelligence: The Sine Qua Non of Corporate Strategic Planning," in Sammon, *Business Competitor Intelligence*, pp. 3–20; and F. W. Gluck, S. P. Kaufman, and A. S. Walleck, "The Evolution of Strategic Management," Staff Paper, McKinsey & Co., October 1978, p. 3; reprinted as "Strategic Management for Competitive Advantage," *Harvard Business Review*, July–August 1980.
9. S. Flax, "How to Snoop on your Competitors," *Fortune*, May 14, 1984, pp. 30–33; K. McManus, "Who Owns Your Brains?," *Forbes*, June 6, 1983, pp. 168–178; and "How to Protect Corporate Secrets," *Dun's Review*, August 1977, pp. 49–50, 76–77.
10. In the burgeoning strategic planning and business intelligence literature, there is a wealth of data on useful recording and display formats to draw on. See Porter, *Competitive Strategy;* Sammon, *Business Competitor Intelligence;* and particularly Michael M. Kaiser Associates Inc.'s two excellent workbooks, *Understanding the Competition: A Practical Guide to Competitive Analysis* and *Developing Industry Strategies: A Practical Guide to Industry Analysis*, Arlington, Va., 1983 and 1984, respectively.

11. S. Kent, *Strategic Intelligence for American World Policy,* Princeton University Press, Princeton, 1971, pp. 176–177. Sherman Kent was a senior professor of history at Yale University when he was recruited in 1941 to serve in an important post in the Research and Analysis Branch of the federal government's new intelligence arm—the Office of Strategic Services (OSS). He later served in the State Department and retired in 1968 as director of the CIA's Office of National Estimates. In 1948, after his World War II service, he published *Strategic Intelligence for American World Policy,* which drew on his intelligence experience in the OSS's analytical and policy divisions. The book was one of the first systematic analyses of the organizational, substantive, and methodological elements of strategic political intelligence. It is a classic in its field.

12. Porter, *Competitive Strategy,* pp. 126–155.

13. See W. L. Sammon, "Competitor Intelligence: An Organizational Framework for Business," in *Business Competitor Intelligence,* pp. 61–72; E. B. Delson and E. Izakson, "Assessing Your Worldwide Competitors," Business International Research Report, Business International Corp., New York, 1983.

14. R. Eells and P. Nehemkis, *Corporate Intelligence and Espionage,* Macmillan, New York, 1984; S. Lieberstein, *Who Owns What Is in Your Head?,* Wyndham, New York, 1979; D. Parker, "Legal Implications of Competitor Intelligence," and W. L. Sammon, "Competitor Intelligence or Industrial Espionage?," *Business Competitor Intelligence.*

15. D. Sanger, "New Old-Hand at I.B.M. Helm: Akers Ready to be New Chief," *New York Times,* January 29, 1985.

CHAPTER 5

Corporate Portfolio Analysis

FRED G. WEISS

ELIZABETH E. TALLETT

FRED G. WEISS is Vice President, Planning, Investment and Development of the Warner-Lambert Company. Prior to that he was Vice President and Treasurer of Warner-Lambert and Assistant Treasurer, International. Before joining Warner-Lambert Mr. Weiss spent 12 years with Exxon worldwide subsidiaries. Mr. Weiss holds a B.S. degree from the University of Pennsylvania, Wharton School and an M.B.A. from the University of Chicago; he also studied at the London School of Economics.

ELIZABETH E. TALLETT is now the Director of Marketing Operations for the Parke-Davis subsidary of Warner Lambert Co. Prior to that she was the Corporate Director of Strategic Planning at Warner-Lambert. In that position she was responsible for the coordination of the strategic planning activities throughout the corporation and has played an active role in the development and implementation of Warner-Lambert's strategy. Mrs. Tallett has been with Warner-Lambert since 1973, first with the U.K. affiliate, then as the International Director of Strategic Planning. Mrs. Tallett holds an honors degree in Mathematics and Economics from Nottingham University in the United Kingdom.

OUTLINE

5.1

Portfolio analysis has been developing as a powerful business planning tool since the early 1960s. Like any tool, it can play an indispensable role in helping its user achieve a goal. In many cases, it would be impossible to do the job without the tool. It is equally true that the same tool in the hands of two different users will yield totally different results. As with any tool, design improvements are always possible even though may of the "improvements" prove to be no more than surface changes and add no real value.

Before we provide a short history of the evolution of portfolio analysis, it is essential to emphasize our strong bias. We believe the object of strategic planning is to support strategic management. A planning department can discover new tools and assist management in understanding how they work and how to get the most out of a given tool. However, the planning department is not the primary user of the tool. Line management must understand and accept the planning tool as a part of its efforts to manage the business. The chief planner of any business must be its chief executive officer. Without this commitment to planning, no tool will be productive. The construction of neat, well-bound volumes of analyses is not enough. Reports, graphs, and associated paraphernalia are only means to an end, not ends in themselves. When a firm takes on the complex and time-consuming efforts associated with portfolio analysis, it is important that senior management view this as their tool.

Setting the correct example and establishing the necessary corporate attitudes are more important to success in strategic management than is the choice of the specific planning tool. The key is to involve the responsible doers in planning so that there is understanding and support for the resulting conclusions. This is the only way we know of to implement the changes flowing from the use of portfolio analysis. We are not against the use of consultants; however, consultants have very limited long-term use. They can introduce you to a tool and help you use it, especially the first time, but unless you take responsibility for the results, the tool will prove to be useless or destructive.

What follows is a short history and description of several types of portfolio analysis. This is followed by a description of how these tools were used by Warner-Lambert's management to complete a major redirection of the company. As with any tool, watching it in use is often a very valuable way of learning.

BACKGROUND

Most major corporations and the majority of small companies have more than one business. Each of these businesses is a potentially freestanding, separate financial proposition. Warner-Lambert, for example, is a major supplier of pharmaceuticals, medical devices, and consumer products such as mouthwashes and chewing gum. Each of these businesses is unique in terms of its competitive challenges, its customers, and its internal management. Corporate portfolio analysis attempts to take a logical systematic approach to the collective management of these various businesses, which is required because of three main factors: (1) individual businesses are moving through unique life cycles and are thus contributing differently to corporate performance at any one point in time, particularly with regard to sales, profits, and cash flow; (2) short- and long-term contributions of these diverse businesses must be balanced with corporate goals; and (3) top management needs some guidelines and priorities for allocating resources among these businesses.

A variety of tools and techniques have been developed to assist top management in assessing these three criteria. In order to understand the tools and techniques it is important to start out with a basic understanding of exactly what a business is. At Warner-Lambert, businesses are defined as "the income stream from a group of products and/or services being sold to a group of customers." Warner-Lambert's equation for a business looks like this: $\$ = P \times M$. There are products looking for markets and markets looking for products. Unless there is a match, there is no income stream and hence no business. In order to "portfolioize" a collection of businesses, one must be sure that the businesses are organized into strategic business units (SBUs). For our purposes, we have defined an SBU as a set of product/market combinations that meet the following four requirements: (1) a unique business mission within the company; (2) clearly identifiable competitors; (3) an external market focus (clearly defined customers); and (4) all major business functions (marketing, manufacturing, R&D, finance) under the directon of an SBU Manager.

BUSINESS LIFE CYCLE

The simple $\$ = P \times M$ equation represents some interesting facts. To change the stream of income, changes must occur either in the products or services

EXHIBIT 5-1   Business Life Cycle—Overview

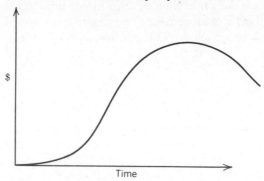

and/or in the markets. If we look at this stream of income from any particular business over time, we end up with the product life cycle (see Exhibit 5-1). This curve would be better named the *market life cycle* or even more appropriately the *business life cycle*.

   The time axis on business life cycles can range from months to many years. Also, the shape of the curve in Exhibit 5-1 is generalized for purposes of illustrating the concept. There are many different variations of these business life cycles (see Exhibit 5-2). One of the major functions of managing businesses is to attempt to extend the business life cycle—that is, keep it from maturing by either making changes to the products or entering new markets. If we plot the income stream of sales and the income stream of profits for all competitors in a particular business arena over time, we end up with the two curves shown in Exhibit 5-3. You will notice that the total profits from

EXHIBIT 5-2   Variations on Business Life Cycle

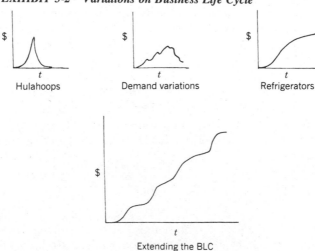

EXHIBIT 5-3   Business Life Cycle—Sales and Profits

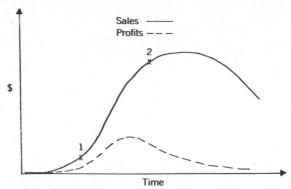

competitors in a particular business arena peak before the market peaks. If these business life cycles are indeed correct, then clearly the most desirable situation would be to enter into a business at point 1 on the curve and exit the business on point 2. Looking at the income stream during that period of time, we would have a business with rapid growth in both sales and earnings. We would exit the business as it starts to mature or decline not only in sales revenue but also in potential profit. This is a nice theoretical concept. Can it be made to have practical value in managing a collection of businesses?

Exhibit 5-4 represents a business life cycle for a typical company. You will notice that at any one point in time there are nine different businesses

EXHIBIT 5-4   *Products in Business Life Cycle—Warner-Lambert Company*

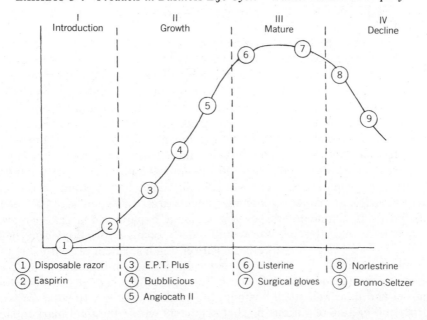

EXHIBIT 5-5   Business Life Cycle—Nature of Competition

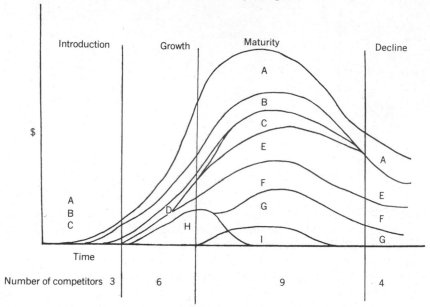

at different points in their unique life cycles. This means that at any one point in time a company is likely to have businesses that are just beginning, businesses that are experiencing rapid growth, businesses that are mature, and businesses that are declining. As top management, your function is to allocate capital investment across these nine businesses. Knowing their positions on the business life cycle begins to give you some guidelines for the allocation of your limited capital.

It is important to look at a typical business life cycle in terms of the number of competitors entering the marketplace, as in Exhibit 5-5. While companies enter and exit a marketplace in all stages of these cycles, the number of competitors clearly increases until the market matures and starts to decline. This is typically followed by a reduction or classic shakeout for survivors.

The composite business life cycle is made up of different market segments, as shown in Exhibit 5-6. Consider the business of breath fresheners and consider that you are segmenting your market for teenagers and people in their twenties, thirties, and forties. If you enter the business by concentrating on the teenage market segment, you will obviously have certain advertising, promotional, and market positioning systems geared to your targeted teenage customers. If as time progresses you decide to expand and target the market of people in their thirties, you would clearly change your copy and media strategy as well as your marketing position. Each segment of customers represents a different size of market and will saturate and mature at different points in time. Understanding the different market segments in your total market and their individual business life cycles is the key to successful entering and exiting of various market segments within the total marketplace.

EXHIBIT 5-6   *Market Segments in Business Life Cycle*

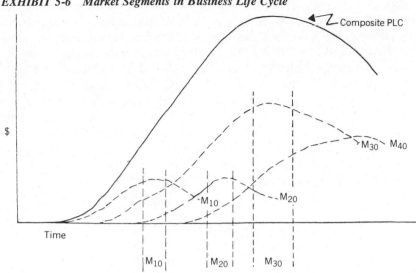

PORTFOLIO ANALYSIS

Corporate portfolio analysis began with the business life cycle. Management scientists began to study these business life cycles. They started by characterizing the nature of the marketplace in each of these four phases. From these characteristics, they then proceeded to predict certain theories about competition, performance, and strategy. Finally, there emerged a series of guidelines for managing a business depending on its position in its own unique business life cycle. In essence, the introductory phase was characterized as one of *market establishment*—that is, persuading early adapters to buy the product or service. The growth phase was mainly one of *market penetration,* in which most efforts were dedicated toward persuading the bulk of the market to prefer your brand. As the markets matured, primary emphasis was on *defense of the brand position,* and most efforts were directed at checking the inroads of competitors. As the market began to decline, management began to focus on preparation for *market removal*—that is, milking the brand dry of all possible benefits.

Trying to bring these theoretical concepts down to the actual management of a firm resulted in a series of guidelines for each element of the business system. During the growth phase, product line managers should be working toward ensuring the fullest and broadest product line available to maximize sales and share. When the markets begin to decline, the product line managers should not add new products but should trim back the existing line to its "heart." During the growth phase, manufacturing should drive for economies of scale to minimize "stock-out risk" and ensure supplies adequate for customer requirements. During the declining phase, manufacturing should try to "variable-ize" by cost cutting and consolidation. Further, it is important to minimize working capital by increasing order lead time, producing to order where possible, and increasing the order size requirements. During the growth phase, R&D should emphasize the development of new products and technologies. During the maturity phase, R&D should defend the brand against competition, while, in the declining phase, R&D efforts, if any, should be directed toward major cost-reduction potentials. These early planning principles for managing business by stages of their life cycles remain useful even though many advancements have been introduced. They help top management set direction among the various components of the firm. They allow functional department managers to allocate people, dollars, facilities, and so on, appropriately across each particular business.

CORPORATE PORTFOLIO MATRIX—THE BCG APPROACH

Approximately 15 years ago the Boston Consulting Group, founded by Bruce D. Henderson, constructed a corporate portfolio matrix that eventually had a dramatic effect on the corporate world. What Bruce Henderson and his firm did for corporate portfolio analysis involved two rather commonplace concepts. The first of these, the experience curve, differed radically from the previously known learning curve in which employees' productivity rose to a threshold level the more times a task was performed. The experience curve had no thresholds and basically operated on the principle that any time the number of tasks performed doubles, the cost of performing those tasks should decline by approximately 20 percent. This means that every time the sales force doubles the number of sales, the cost of selling to one customer should decline by 20 percent. Every time the order processing department doubles the number of orders it cuts, the cost of cutting these orders should decline by 20 percent. Texas Instruments used the experience curve in setting prices for many of its products. By anticipating their future position on the experience curve, they were able to introduce a new product at prices below current market prices and effectively preempted their competition.

The second concept BCG brought forth was one of *relative* market share. BCG began to evaluate the competitors in a particular business in relation to one another and all in relation to the largest competitor. They put these two concepts together in a four-box matrix that came to be known as the BCG growth/share matrix (Exhibit 5-7). BCG would plot relative market share and market growth rates for each of the businesses a company owned. The size of the circles shown in Exhibit 5-8 are relative sales amounts. There was then an attempt to anticipate what would happen to these businesses in a 3 to 5-year time frame. For example, business A would go from its present state to one in which its sales would triple in 3 to 5 years. The market growth rate would decline somewhat, and business A would lose some market share. Business E, on the other hand, was expected to lose volume in sales while

EXHIBIT 5-7 BCG "Zoo"—Growth Share Matrix

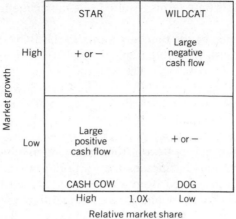

EXHIBIT 5-8 BCG Business Portfolio Matrix

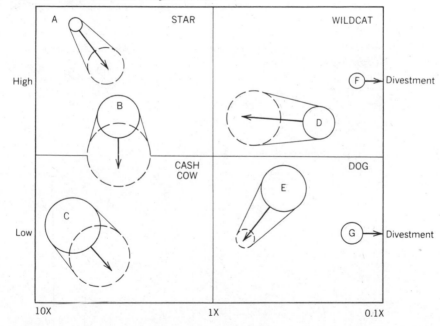

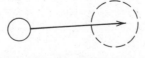

Present position   Future position

increasing its market share in a declining market. Each of these boxes was given a name. They were the Wildcat or Problem Child, the Star, the Cash Cow, and the Dog. (These terms resulted in a nickname for the matrix—the "BCG Zoo.")

If you look at each of the four quadrants in the BCG Zoo and try to anticipate what the cash flow requirements will be in the next 3 to 5 years certain patterns begin to emerge. The Star or the Dog should have relatively *minimal* positive or negative cash flows. The Cash Cow, on the other hand, should have a large *positive* cash flow. The Wildcat should have a large *negative* cash flow. In effect the BCG Zoo was a very clear and simple way of expressing the concepts developed in the earlier business cycle principles.

The beginnings of corporate portfolio analysis involved balancing cash flows among the various businesses the corporation held. The theory was that the cash being generated from a Cash Cow should be invested in the Wildcat to build market share and hence competitive position. This in turn would drive that business into the Star box. However, all markets eventually slow down in growth and that Star business would eventually drop down into the Cash Flow box. Because of its dominant market share and relatively strong competitive position, it should be able to generate lots of cash. This

EXHIBIT 5-9   *Boston Consulting Group-Cash Flow Implications—Growth-Share Matrix*

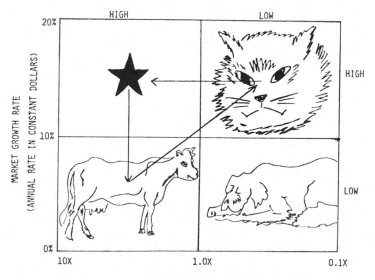

BOSTON CONSULTING GROUP

CASH FLOW IMPLICATIONS
GROWTH-SHARE MATRIX

RELATIVE MARKET SHARE
(RATIO OF COMPANY SHARE TO SHARE OF LARGEST COMPETITOR)

cash should then be reinvested in a new Wildcat business. The cycle would then continue (see Exhibit 5-9).

The rationale behind the BCG matrix is that the most desirable strategy was to strive for dominant market share when the market matured. The logic is as follows: (1) maximum profits are gleaned when the market matures; (2) dominant market share enjoys the largest volume; (3) the largest volume competitor should have the lowest cost (because of the experience curve); and (4) the lowest cost competitor would have the highest margins. BCG's fame as a corporate portfolio balancer as well as corporate strategist quickly rose. Within a few years most of the Fortune 1000 corporations had either been "BCG'd" or were looking at their businesses in this way. Corporate strategists began to compare the slope of their experience curves against their competitors. Competition began to focus on who could travel down the experience curve the fastest. Speed was important because the markets would soon mature.

BCG's competitors were not about to step away from this growing market without a major challenge. McKinsey & Co. raised questions about the BCG portfolio concept and then developed their own matrix. McKinsey reasoned that it was more than market growth rate and market share that determined a good portfolio. The size of the markets, the margins, diversity, competitive structure, and the profitability were also very important. McKinsey put all these market factors together, weighted them appropriately, and came up with the consolidated term "Market Attractiveness."

MARKET ATTRACTIVENESS MATRIX—THE McKINSEY APPROACH

McKinsey's analysis rightly argued that there were factors apart from market share in a comapny's relative competitive position. It was necessary to examine the product technology, current quality level, defensibility, share trends, sales-force strengths, and manufacturing efficiencies. All these factors, appropriately weighted, became known as "company qualifications"—a company's ability to compete relative to its competitors.

Rather than describe their businesses as a zoo, McKinsey differentiated themselves from BCG by using such well-known labels as "Invest Grow" for the Star, "Maintenance" for the Cash Cow, "Limit Investment" for the Dog, and "Selectively Invest" for the Wildcat. With this matrix McKinsey sought to perform corporate portfolio analyses with a broader scope of relevance for their clients.

TECHNOLOGY PORTFOLIO TECHNIQUE—BOOZ-ALLEN & HAMILTON APPROACH

Booz-Allen & Hamilton were not to be outdone in this competitive race to examine corporations' portfolios. They attacked BCG on its experience curve philosophy. Basically, they said the experience curve does not hold in high technology businesses. Their argument was that, whenever technology changes high-tech businesses start down a different experience curve and then shift when new technologies emerge. They reasoned that, in order to analyze a portfolio correctly, there had to be some mechanism to incorporate the likely changes in technology. This was achieved by contrasting the technological position of a business relative to its competitors with the degree to which its technology could be leveraged across all the company's businesses. Booz-Allen began to do two types of portfolios: their version of market attractiveness versus company qualifications, which they called the market/product portfolio, and the technology portfolio. The technology portfolio contrasted the relative competitive technology position with technology leverage. They combined these two matrices into one. This allowed for the contrasting of business positions with relative technology positions. If your business was a Wildcat, for example, in the upper right quadrant, you had only two choices for that business: either invest in increasing your relative technology position or withdraw from the business. That would move the business to the Star position or to the Dog position. If your business was located in the lower left-hand corner, it meant that you had very strong relative technology position but a very weak business position. If this was the case, you then had two choices: build your business position to preempt your competitors or sell the technology. In either case, one of these moves would change the position to a Star or a Dog.

OTHER MATRIX TECHNIQUES

Many other firms developed portfolio models. They include such terms as the "Strategic Environment Matrix," the "Arthur D. Little Business Profile

EXHIBIT 5-10   Today's Zoo—Combined BLC/Growth Share Matrix—Cash Flow Implicatons

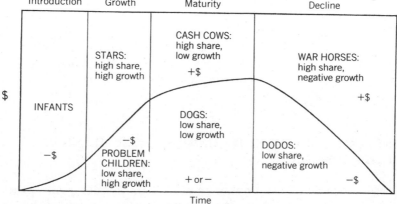

Matrix,'' and the ''Shell International Directional Policy Matrix.'' The basic concepts of these grids for multibusiness companies are not radically different. The key is that every one of these grids provides a systematic way of evaluating and communicating the competitive strategic options resulting from the business cycle stage, as shown in what is called Today's Zoo, (Exhibit 5-10). Today's Zoo has basically seven positions: the Infants, the Wildcats, the Stars, the Cash Cows, the Dogs, the War Horses and the Dodos.

MISUSES OF MATRICES

A word of caution is necessary in using these matrices. Misinterpretations abound with regard to reason for classifying a business. Many individuals and firms have considered that a portfolio position label dictates a strategy. Informing a profit center manager that his or her business is a Cash Cow is neither informative nor strategic. It does not assist in managing. At Warner-Lambert strategy requires specific illustration of *''how* you will *compete* in the *marketplace.''* Knowing that you have a Cash Cow or a Wildcat does not answer the question. These portfolio positions all require investment. If you have a maintenance business, you need to invest in that maintenance business. You must also continue investments, albeit on a lesser scale, on Dogs and Wildcats.

An additional misuse of these matrices is the widely held belief that any business can become a Star. Rationalizing your analysis and biasing your market and environmental perceptions can be a dangerous game. The reason so many firms use consultants to develop these matrices is to eliminate the in-house biases. Another danger is not revalidating your assumptions. Not only must your assumptions be monitored, but changes in the competitive environment as well as the external environment often indicate a complete review of your anticipated portfolio positions.

HOW PORTFOLIO POSITIONS ASSIST FAVORABLE RESULTS

A very useful aspect of portfolio positions is the expected financial parameters. Each classification on the matrix implies a different pattern for sales, earnings, and cash flow over time (see Exhibit 5-11). There is no requirement that portfolios be perfectly balanced at any point in time, but over time significant imbalances are not viable. For example, a company with four businesses all in the Star category and no other businesses in the remaining three quadrants would sound extremely attractive; however, most companies cannot support this portfolio over the near term. The amount of investment to keep pace with the growth of these four different Star businesses is beyond the means of many companies. Managing four Star businesses requires considerable investment not only in capital but in plant, equipment, people, and time. Companies in this fortunate situation usually end up being acquired at

EXHIBIT 5-11   Different Patterns for Sales, Earnings, and Cash Flow

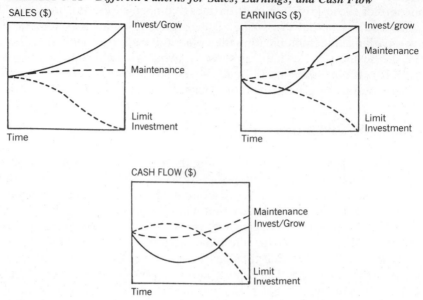

large multiples of current earnings by larger firms that have the resources via their Cash Cows to maintain these Star categories.

In a similar way, the company portfolio with three Dog businesses and one small Cash Cow indicates a near-term demise. Companies must ensure that they have a new stream of Wildcats to drive into Star categories to keep the portfolio in relative balance. High-technology firms have particular problems in this area in that the life cycles for these businesses are getting shorter and shorter and market windows are getting narrower and narrower while the cost of entering new businesses keeps mounting.

The key concept in corporate portfolio analysis is the ability to classify each business into opportunity categories based on product/market attractiveness and planning unit competitive strengths. The matrices reveal a company's current financial condition and provide a basis for identifying alternative strategic options. The attractiveness of each product/market business is clearly defined in factors such as market size, growth, profitability, and opportunity to segment. Each business is also evaluated in relation to the competition in terms of relative product technology, marketing strength, manufacturing skills, and the like. The corporate portfolio approach to strategic planning has practical value. It provides a uniform measurement system to evaluate all product lines. It assists in identifying key issues and needs both for individual businesses and for the company as a whole. It identifies the need for new products in businesses, and it helps focus planning and operational groups to address key issues and to allocate resources according to matrix classification.

These portfolios are not limited to sales. Portfolios can be developed for the profit stream, cash flow, and technology in each business, and for industries as a whole. The sales portfolio is by far the most commonly used. The profit portfolio can provide a means for assessing current and future income streams, tax requirements, future capital leveraging, and so forth. A technology portfolio can give insight into the appropriateness of shifting investments into new technologies from existing technologies, while an industrywide portfolio allows you to assess the desirability of entering a particular industry, the relative risk/reward ratios of entrance, and the requirements for success.

Corporate portfolios can also be developed for competitors. This is particularly useful in determining a competitor's most vulnerable businesses and can also provide a key to their anticipated future strategies. You can also overlap competitor portfolios to anticipate merger or acquisition possibilities, to strengthen your own portfolio, or to analyze the combined competitiveness of two merging competitors.

When developing these corporate portfolios, it is extremely important to understand fully the current strategy (i.e., how the business will compete in the marketplace) of each business. Furthermore, you need to make sure that the assumptions, both explicit and implicit, about the business's relative positions, strengths and weaknesses, competitors, and industry trends will be valid in the 3 to 5-year time frame.

You need to be clearly focused on what is happening in the marketplace environment. The industry analysis must address the key factors for competitive success and the important industrywide opportunities and threats. The competitive analysis should address the capabilities and limitations of existing and potential competitors and their probable future moves. The external environment must be taken into account to address what important governmental, social, and political factors might present opportunities or threats to the future of the business. You need to test the assumptions embodied in the current business strategy and compare that to what is happening in the environment. Is the future strategy of the business consistent with company resources? Can it be understood? Can it be implemented? You should look at the feasible strategic alternatives available to each business and decide which of these alternatives is best for the company. Ultimately, you need to test a portfolio analysis against the reality of the business environment. Are the anticipated goals for each business achievable? Do your existing key operating policies address these goals? Do the policies reinforce the goals? Does the future portfolio fit the environment; that is, does it exploit industry opportunities? Does the timing of the goals and policies reflect the ability of the environment to absorb your anticipated actions? In many cases, the future portfolio positions require understanding ability of the business to change. It is important that the objectives for these businesses be understood by the key implementers. Is there enough congruence between the goals and policies of the new portfolio positions and the values of the key implementers to ensure commitment? Finally, is there sufficient managerial capability to allow for effective implementaton?

WARNER-LAMBERT CASE HISTORY

Having gone through a short review of the theory of corporate portfolio analysis, it may be instructive to consider an actual case history by looking at one specific company, Warner-Lambert. Warner-Lambert operates in more than 130 countries, employs approximately 42,000 people, and manages more than 100 manufacturing facilities and four major research centers.

Forty-six percent of Warner-Lambert's 3.5-billion-dollar sales in 1982 was generated outside the United States. Health-care sales represent about 70 percent of the company's business. Warner-Lambert's product lines include prescription pharmaceuticals from the Parke-Davis drug division; diagnostic products and devices for hospitals and laboratories; surgical products such as surgeons' gloves and instruments; intravenous infusion devices and catheters; scientific instruments, including microscopes; and empty gelatin capsules for use by drug manufacturers. Warner-Lambert's consumer health-care business includes a wide range of over-the-counter medications and personal care products, from vitamins and cold remedies to mouthwashes. In addition, Warner-Lambert is a major worldwide marketer of chewing gums, breath mints, and shaving products.

Through the 1960s the strategic history of Warner-Lambert was largely one of growth through acquisition—American Chicle for gums and mints, American Optical for vision care, Schick for shaving products, Parke-Davis for pharmaceuticals, and many other smaller additions both in the United States and overseas. In the 1970s Warner-Lambert shifted to a strategy of business consolidation and international expansion to meet the challenge of increasing competition and to protect its widespread market positions. By 1978 top management had grown concerned about the future direction of the company, realizing that unless strong action was taken, the company would be facing major problems.

There were many recognizable signs of these problems: several of the company's major plants were outdated and inefficient; others duplicated function; many were underutilized. And the company was hanging on to problem businesses despite their lack of growth and earnings shortfall. Warner-Lambert's financial mode of management, like that of so many other companies, was short-term and was burdened with all the negatives that such a course involves. The development of new products stagnated, innovation diminished, and venture projects with good potential for return were rare.

The company's portfolio at that time, using the standard McKinsey matrix, was as shown in Exhibit 5-12. Warner-Lambert had many businesses that were in the latter stages of their life cycles and without any real prospects

EXHIBIT 5-12   Matrix of Warner-Lambert

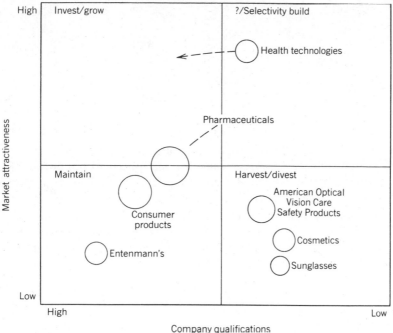

for growth. In order to take the necessary action a strategic redirection had to be instigated by a strong CEO with a clear vision for the future of the business. Fortunately in Ward Hagan and Joe Williams the company had such a CEO/COO team who were committed to taking the necessary action.

In the latter part of 1970 major strategic initiatives were presented to Warner-Lambert's board of directors and to all key management personnel. The highest priority was given to harvesting or divesting areas with low potential. Next, it was necessary to strengthen the company's core activities with an investment program designed to arrest the weaknesses identified in its pharmaceutical and consumer businesses. Third, over the long term it was important to boost the company's growth by developing a position in emerging health-care markets driven by high technology.

By mid-1982 Warner-Lambert's divestment program was virtually complete (see Exhibit 5-13)—the company had sold or closed out more than a dozen businesses. The biggest was the vision care and safety business of American Optical. All together these divestitures represented annual sales of approximately 450 million dollars—but they also accounted for annual losses of more than 30 million dollars. The company had thus eliminated the poorest elements in its business portfolio. However, along with these divestitures it obviously had two further tasks: the strengthening of existing core businesses—pharmaceutical and consumer—and the developing of new

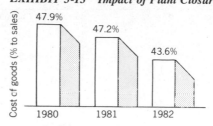

EXHIBIT 5-13   *Impact of Plant Closures*

growth opportunities. In carrying out its portfolio analysis the company had identified that both of its core businesses had potential for improved performance and pharmaceuticals offered the greatest opportunity for growth.

With businesses in the mid-phase of their life cycle you need to concentrate on becoming more cost-competitive and productive. In order to improve its cost of goods Warner-Lambert closed two major antiquated manufacturing facilities, one for consumer goods and one for pharmaceuticals. In addition another 20 plants worldwide were closed or consolidated. Alongside these rationalizations, a companywide productivity program that continues to this day was instigated. The focus of this program is improving both the quality and cost of products and includes consideration of just-in-time inventory systems and quality enhancement programs. As a result of these activities, the company's cost of goods has been reduced by four percentage points over a three-year period.

The improvement in cost of goods also helped Warner-Lambert fund increased advertising and promotion for its core businesses. In the past years the company had undersupported some of its major consumer franchises. To correct this, ad spending was boosted about 20 percent, and the company plans to keep it at these higher levels. As a result, the decline in unit sales has been halted and market shares of Warner-Lambert's major brands are growing.

These plant closings, business divestitures, and reallocations of resources were only the problem-solving phase of the company's strategic plan—a necessary "clean-up" operation. The vital issue was to build on this more efficient base to achieve real and profitable growth—the third part of the company's strategy. Warner-Lambert recognized the need for growth opportunities in its existing businesses and in new and faster growing markets as well. Faced with this challenge, it was clear that the only reasonable starting point was to establish a sound and fundamental understanding of the potential of the company's existing businesses in terms of the external environment, market forces, the competition, and its own ability to compete in the long term (see Exhibit 5-14). It meant identifying the requirements for success, technology demands, and distribution needs in each of the company's markets and taking a look at organization requirements as well as products and manufacturing.

EXHIBIT 5-14 *Existing Business Analysis*

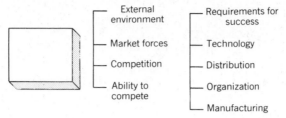

Warner-Lambert used a number of different techniques to perform the analysis and found that no one method was superior to the others. Initially, the standard portfolio matrix analysis, plotting market attractiveness versus relative company qualifications, was used. This was found to be a simple but useful tool when applied with common business sense.

The company began with an assessment of its external operating environments, identifying the key market forces for each business segment, then matched itself against its competition to see if any competitive advantages could be discovered. Then the company's internal capabilities were analyzed—its strengths and weaknesses relative to competition—in technology, products, distribution, and organization.

It was found that Michael Porter's model of competitive analysis (see Exhibit 5-15) was particularly useful for identifying the strategic characteristics of different markets and the relative power of the different market players. Warner-Lambert considered the threat of new entrants as well as possible substitute technologies, then analyzed how the current participants in a particular marketplace compete and used this information in its strategic mappings with two key competitive dimensions (in this example, technological leadership and specialization—see Exhibit 5-16). Another accepted form of portfolio analysis—growth versus return on assets (see Exhibit 5-17)—is a primary measure of performance for Warner-Lambert. Not only does the company track its own portfolio, but it also tracks those of major competitors.

EXHIBIT 5-15 *Model of Competitive Analysis*

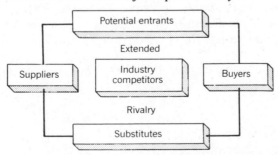

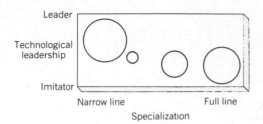

EXHIBIT 5-16   Company/Group
Strategic Mapping

The company also analyzed each element of the competitive business system. For example, it identified measures of performance within each key department and evaluated the effectiveness of that department against its major competitors. The company then studied the relationship and contributions of the functional departments within the business system. Three priorities emerged from these studies:

Investment in technology
Keep abreast of technology developments in key parts of the business system
Grow by entering new markets

Investment in technology is now the very essence of Warner-Lambert strategy. Since 1979 it has doubled its R&D funding, now up to 175 million dollars a year. In 1982 the company increased the budget by 26 percent. In 1983 it will go up another 20 percent. Warner-Lambert is spending an additional 100 million dollars in capital expansion for new R&D facilities in California, Utah, Michigan, New Jersey, the United Kingdom, and Germany. More than two-thirds of the company's research dollars are allocated to ethical pharmaceuticals, and Warner-Lambert is applying the new technology strategy to its consumer products business as well. For example, it has also opened a laboratory in New Jersey for the development of new consumer products.

Some of the new R&D programs promise unique and exciting therapies. The new field of pharmaceutical cognition activators to improve human memory is one example. On the consumer side, more new products are on the way to market than at any time since 1975, and Warner-Lambert is investigating a new line of diagnostic kits that can be purchased in the pharmacy and used in th home to test for symptoms previously detectable only in the

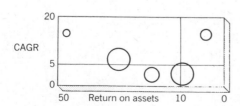

EXHIBIT 5-17   Business Analysis

laboratory. To supplement this internal effort, Warner-Lambert has an active program of acquisition and licensing to acquire technology. Its antibiotic ERYC, recently licensed from Australia, is a good example.

The company's second identified need was to keep abreast of technology developments within the business system. It has established a modern distribution network using advanced computer systems for material handling that has significantly reduced the number of distribution centers. Most of its manufacturing facilities in the United States, including quality control, computer-assisted manufacturing, and automation techniques have been upgraded. Warner-Lambert is also working on improved management information systems throughout the company, making microcomputers available whenever needed.

While studying the company's core pharmaceutical and consumer businesses, analysts recognized quite clearly that these markets offered relatively slow growth because of their maturity. This forced the company to prepare to implement the third part of its overall strategy—growth through entry into new markets, a much more difficult challenge than analyzing long-familiar businesses. First, it was necessary to establish decisive criteria for new market areas. The company decided to stay close to familiar business areas— high-technology health care. Second, Warner-Lambert has to add its own internal expertise to any new venture. A third guideline was that any new market had to offer fast growth and a good business environment.

Lastly, there was the recognition that a crucial requirement for success in high-tech areas is the need to nurture an entrepreneurial spirit—not always easy in a large corporation. Nevertheless, rapidly changing technology calls for a work culture and business organization different from more mature operations.

After resolving these underlying concepts, the predominant question still remained—where and how to generate real growth in the high-technology health-care market. Analysts studied the technology, the competition, and the external market forces. The objective was to expand from the company's existing portfolio; leverage its product, marketing, and distribution strengths; and take advantage of available synergies within the Health Tech Group. The methodology used in selecting new invest/grow markets was straightforward. First, the growth market segments within the high-technology health-care field were identified and analyzed. For example, drug-delivery systems, which had links with the company's existing catheter capability, were of special interest to Warner-Lambert.

Then the keys to success within each growth market were identified. Present and future competition, as well as present and future technology, were analyzed. Analysts looked at distribution requirements and screened for possible fit with existing Warner-Lambert capabilities. The company studied apparent gaps in technology and capabilities that could affect its success in entering a new market. Planners developed risk/reward ratios and listed and considered strategic alternatives, then began to develop action plans, along with options and alternatives to be held in reserve.

Warner-Lambert used the best expertise available, both internally and externally, to accomplish these analyses. Consultants carried out such tasks as specific technology assessments, competitive analyses, and acquisition searches. Throughout the process, executive and top-level management were deeply involved. Senior operating management was responsible for selecting the potential new market areas as well as the candidates for acquisition. The role of corporate strategic planning was limited to assistance and guidance. Planners offered advice and specific planning expertise, such as econometric modeling. It was felt that this carefully defined relationship, coupled with the total involvement of the operating people was essential for success.

Warner-Lambert has made a significant number of changes in the manner in which it does business. With the advent of strategic planning each of the company's divisions has become more focused on individual strategic business units and the growth potentials therein. Each year the company reanalyzes its portfolio to identify areas of opportunity and/or weakness. It continues to invest heavily behind research and development in order to develop sound businesses for the future. At the same time, Warner-Lambert is managing its more mature businesses in a manner appropriate to that maturity. Warner-Lambert is well placed to be an exciting company in the late 1980s.

CONCLUSIONS

In this chapter we have tried not only to identify the historical development of the theory of portfolio analysis, but also to give a review of its practical applications. As with all theories, the benefits gained are in large measure due to the ability and wisdom of the people using these tools. Portfolio analysis in all its varied forms is just another tool on the businessperson's desk, but we believe that it can lead to great insights into both the marketplace, competition, and your own business. When applied with common business sense, and allied to some prudent risk taking, we believe it is a powerful part of any strategic planning effort.

CHAPTER **6**

Formulating Strategies and Contingency Plans

WILLIAM C. KING

WILLIAM C. KING was Vice President, Corporate Planning, for Gulf Oil Corporation in Pittsburgh, Pennsylvania, with primary responsibility for the corporation's strategic planning program and for activities related to developing future business activities. He held prior positions within the company such as Director—Corporate Policy Analysis, Director—Market Research and Economic Planning for the Chemicals Department, and Vice President for chemical activities in Europe and the Middle East. He is currently retired. William C. King holds an M.S. degree in Chemical Engineering from M.I.T. and a B.S. degree in Chemical Engineering from Carnegie-Mellon University. He was Vice Chairman of the Council of Planning Executives of The Conference Board, a member of the North American Society for Corporate Planning, a director of the Pittsburgh Chapter of the NASCP, and a member of the Strategic Management Institute. He was a member of the American Petroleum Institute, the Energy Committee of The Atlantic Council, and the American Institute of Chemical Engineers.

This chapter is based, in large part, on the work done over the past several years by members of the Corporate Planning Department of the Gulf Oil Corporation, who have done an outstanding job in developing an effective and practical strategic planning process. In particular, I want to express appreciation to P. A. Michelon, senior director of the department; W. B. Davis, former Chief Economist; F. E. Martin, director; and R. S. MacDonald, director, who provided invaluable editorial support for this chapter. Exhibits 6-1, 6-2, and 6-4 to 6-9 were developed within the Gulf Corporate Planning Group and are reproduced by permission.

6.1

OUTLINE

This chapter reviews procedures for formulating corporate strategies and contingency plans. Both the planning process and product are covered; each is an essential and inseparable part of any effective planning program. The role of strategic planning in the overall management process also is treated, since this provides the context for strategic planning. The approach is primarily generic, since no two corporations are alike, and planning programs should be customized to specific conditions within each corporation and its business environment.

Boiled down to its essence, strategic planning is simply the means by which a corporation organizes its resources and actions to achieve its objectives. The better the strategic planning effort, the more readily the corporation will realize its goals. To the extent that a corporation carries out this activity more effectively than its competitors, it will gain advantage over those competitors. Maintaining competitive advantage over an extended period of time is the surest way of rewarding the shareholders, employees, customers, and the supporting economy.

Conversely, without sound strategic planning, a corporation will have to rely on continuing good luck to maintain adequate performance. It is far better, and more certain, for a corporation to take more direct control of its own future.

There has been adverse comment periodically about the effectiveness of strategic planning.[1] This does not reflect on strategic planning's importance— it is vitally important. Rather, the criticism relates to the failure of strategic planning to live up to expectations. This is due in part to the unrealistic expectation that strategic planning provides a quick-fix solution for complex corporate problems and a means of avoiding sound analysis, hard work, and tough decisions. This is exacerbated by those who, in their enthusiasm to use new sophisticated technical approaches to planning problems, overstress the theoretical aspects, causing doubting Thomases within the organization to see strategic planning as just another passing business school fad.

Despite the criticism, there is growing recognition that strategic planning is essential in the modern business world. The rate and extent of change throughout the world continues to accelerate rapidly. Technical innovation and obsolescence, government regulation and deregulation, growing consumer sophistication and political power, environmental concerns, shifting demographics, and international competition are all in a state of flux and directly impact every business. As Emerson so aptly observed, "This time, like all others, is a good one, if we but know what to do with it."

Amid all this uncertainty good strategic planning will not substitute for good decisions, but it will make it possible to systematically identify and examine issues, trends, and options and to evaluate alternative courses of action so that prudent decisions can be made. Equally important, strategic planning provides an understanding of the assumptions and limitations supporting those decisions so that, as conditions change during plan implementation, adjustments can be made quickly and accurately.

WHAT IS STRATEGIC PLANNING?

Walter Kiechel observed recently that today most corporations have corporate strategies, but fewer than 10 percent of American corporations effectively execute the strategies.[2] This observation strikes directly at a major weakness in the management practices of companies today. But it also poses a dichotomy, since a good strategic plan should include not only clear implementation steps but also performance measures, feedback systems, and corrective actions.

To be effective strategic planning must encompass all of the aspects of initiating and carrying out major company programs. Exhibit 6-1 presents an outline of the key elements of strategic planning.

The mission is a statement of the broad business purpose of the corporation or corporate element. The objectives and goals are more specific targets that must be achieved if the business purpose is to be accomplished. Each should be achievable and all should improve the competitive position. The strategy is a set of programs designed to enable the corporation to achieve the goals and objectives. These programs include three essential components:

1. Action plans and resource commitments
2. Specific implementation steps
3. Performance measures against which to monitor actions and results, providing management feedback as the basis for ongoing adjustments

Strategic planning is dynamic. Adjustments are periodically required for changes in external factors or for over- or underperformance in carrying out the plans. Adjustments in the goals and objectives should be made less frequently, and only rarely in the missions. This iterative process is termed the "planning loop" and is shown in Exhibit 6-2.

EXHIBIT 6-1   Elements of Strategic Planning

Mission: Defines the present business and its future boundaries.

Objectives: Qualitative statements of what the business is to accomplish over a period of years.

Goals: Selected short- and long-term quantitative results that directly support the objectives. They should be achievable, related to the key factors for success in the business, and congruent with the objectives.

Strategy: A number of separate but related and reinforcing programs for accomplishing the selected business objectives and goals.

Strategic Planning includes three phases:

1. Scoping the strategy
    What are the factors critical to success in this business?
    Who are our competitors, their strengths and weaknesses?
    What are our strengths and weaknesses?
    What are our options?
    What major assumptions have we made?
2. Detailing the strategic programs
    What specific programs do we choose to achieve our goals and why?
    What resources will these require?
    What are the risks/rewards for each program?
    Who will do it—what, when, how?
3. Ensuring implementation of the strategic programs
    What intermediate checkpoints are there to tell if we are on track?
    Have performance and accountability measures been set?
    Do we have an early-warning system?
    Is there an adequate and visible reward/penalty system in place?

Actually there are two loops—a shorter-term planning and implementation loop within the longer-term strategy development loop. The short-term loop cycles annually or biannually, carries out the basic strategy and, together with environmental monitoring, provides feedback (the dotted lines) to monitor the continuing suitability of the basic strategy.

The basic strategy should change infrequently, and then only in response to fundamental, unanticipated environmental or competitive changes or major over- or underperformance in strategy implementation. Lacking such events, frequent strategy changes jeopardize the continuity needed to refine planning and implementation efforts.

Integrating these strategic planning loops into the actual running of the corporation leads to strategic management. This integration normally evolves over a period of time in a series of steps requiring increasing understanding and participation by both line and staff management. This evolution is ef-

EXHIBIT 6-2   The Strategic Planning Loop

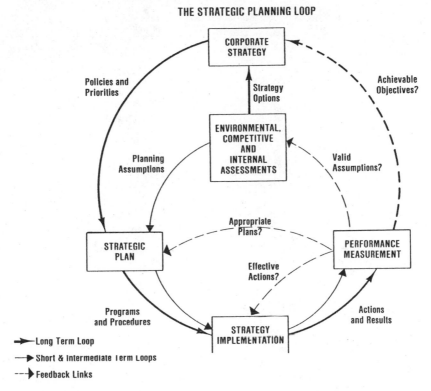

fectively illustrated in Exhibit 6-3, developed by McKinsey & Co.[3,4] The transition from Stage II to Stage III represents a clear transition from mechanistic budgeting and forecast-based planning to conceptual planning of how best to use available resources to gain competitive advantage. The transition from Stage III to Stage IV can only be made when the entire management team makes these strategic disciplines a vital part of its daily and ongoing activities.

This corporate strategic process has been effectively summarized by Arthur D. Little:[5]

> The corporate strategy system consists of four elements: (1) strategy development; (2) strategy planning—which is the translation of strategies into detailed and costed plans; (3) strategy implementation; and (4) strategic performance measurement. Managing by strategy means, therefore, that the strategy system, as we have just defined it, becomes the core of the whole corporate management process. This implies that the resource allocation process of the corporation, its organization, budgeting, reporting and control, performance measurement and reward and management information systems, internal communications and management development processes, are all linked to, and shaped by, the corporate strategy system. This has far-reaching implications on the day-to-day management of the corporation.[5]

EXHIBIT 6-3   *The Evolution of Strategic Decision Making*

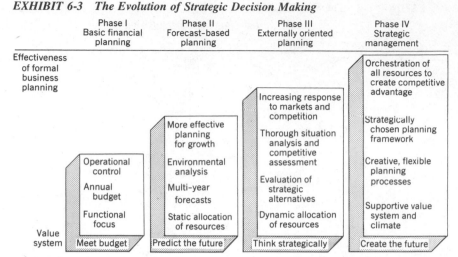

Source: F.W. Gluck, S.P. Kaufman, and A.S. Walleck, "Strategic Management for Competitive Advantage," *Harvard Business Review*, July–August, 1980, p. 157. Reproduced by permission.

FORMULATING CORPORATE STRATEGY

Basically, corporate strategy is determined by a melding of the chief executive officer's appraisal of the present state of the corporation with what he or she wants it to be in the future. This requires a candid appraisal of the corporation's present strengths and weaknesses; a clear and confident—but not necessarily correct—view of the future business environment; and a vision of the place that he or she wants the corporation to fill in that environment. The CEO may either create or adopt the corporate strategy, but he or she is its only parent. If the strategy is to be effective, he or she must have a hands-on role in developing it in order to have full insight into what it is and why it suits the corporation. In short, it must be "his or her" strategy, and he or she must "own" it. Only with such strong, personal support from this person can the strategy be clearly and continually communicated throughout the organization and be implemented effectively.

Based on this insight, the CEO provides guidance on which corporate activities he or she wants to develop further and indicates the speed and priority of development; the CEO also indicates those activities that are to be run for cash, streamlined, or divested. This requires an assessment of corporate strengths and weaknesses to estimate what is doable: which gaps can be filled and which gaps are too costly to fill. In arriving at preliminary judgments the CEO almost invariably blends intuitive feeling with perceptive analysis.

The corporate strategy cannot be arrived at solely by adding together the strategies of the subsidiary or operating companies as individual businesses.

While the corporate strategy is built on those businesses, and forms the context for them, it is necessarily separate. The corporate strategy must explicitly recognize the shareholders' needs and relationships with the financial community. It must include the overall human resources and public affairs policies, and it is charged with continually upgrading the corporate portfolio either through internal improvement and growth or through acquisition and divestiture.

In effect, the CEO is the leader of the corporate strategy development task force. Its members are the top corporate executive and operating company officers. Its staff is the planning department, which acts as a facilitator, monitors the task-force schedule, and carries out analyses and information gathering. This frees up the executive and operating heads so that their time can be utilized in sharpening their own thinking, in discussions, and in developing a consensus.

In developing the corporate strategy, it is essential to know where the corporation is in regard to its competitors, and where it has recently been. An effective tool for this evaluation is shown in Exhibit 6-4. This indicates the relationship between (1) the corporation's return on equity (ROE) and (2) the ratio of the corporation's aggregate value on the stock market to its book value.

EXHIBIT 6-4   *Return on Equity Versus Ratio of Market Value to Book Value, 16 Integrated Oils*

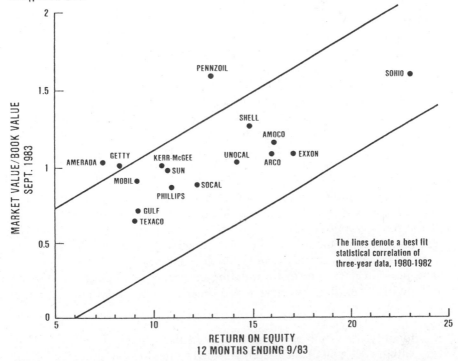

EXHIBIT 6-5   *Market Value Versus Book Value, Industry and Company X*

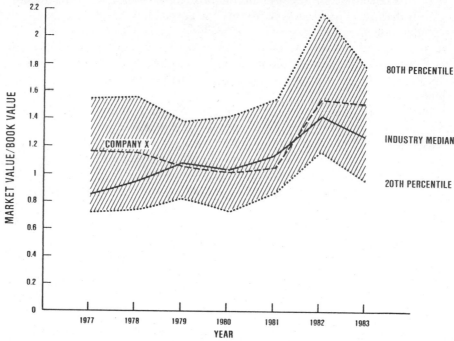

For any industry there is invariably a scattering of companies as plotted on this chart. Rapid growth, perceived appreciation potential, and a strong management reputation will tend to attract investors, pushing those companies to a higher level on the chart for a given ROE. The corporate strategy must be designed so as to move the corporation more rapidly toward the upper right corner of the chart than the competition can be expected to move.

While data for several years can be shown on such a chart, this makes the chart difficult to use. An alternate way of showing this trend is indicated in Exhibit 6-5, which plots the market value/book value ratio over a period of years and indicates the performance of a given company and the range of performance within that industry. This shows clearly whether or not a corporation is improving its position relative to its competitors.

Yet all this is merely descriptive. Whether the corporation is over- or underperforming its competitors, it is critical to determine the reasons why. These then become the focal points for strategy, the key business aspects that strategic programs must exploit, avoid, or repair.

The point of departure in formulating corporate strategy is the current condition of the existing businesses. To determine this, the following steps are needed:

1.   Identify the major operating units and the specific lines of business within each unit. This is comparable to the identification of strategic

business units. These should be discrete activities that are or can be identified on a stand-alone basis and have an explicit market orientation.

2. Determine the key success factors of the business (which account for different levels of competitive performance) and assess the business' strengths and weaknesses with regard to each.

3. Identify business activities not now in the corporation but which would strengthen the corporation, and current activities which are not essential to the main mission of the corporation.

4. Identify the chief risks and potentials for these activities and the resources required to achieve those potentials.

5. Categorize the activities based on their importance to the corporation in the short range and long range.

A convenient way to do this categorization is shown in Exhibit 6-6. This is analogous to the Arthur D. Little strategic condition matrix,[6] which is useful in developing this categorization. It identifies the core businesses as well as growth areas and the chief sources of cash flow.

Based on this, a series of corporate strategic priorities can be developed and from them a set of roles for the various businesses to play in making their individual contributions to the overall corporate strategy. These should be designed to provide the strongest possible competitive position to the highest priority lines of activities in the corporation. It is essential that corporate resources be adequate for those activities to achieve that competitive position. These resources include not only money, but people, technology, know-how, organization capabilities, and raw materials.

Selected strategies must also be compatible with the corporate culture. If not, either the strategy or the culture will have to be modified. In making this appraisal and resource allocation, it may be necessary to recategorize various activities until a balanced program is achieved.

Once the business roles are set and responsibilities are assigned, specific implementation programs and targets are outlined and an effective reward/penalty system is established to insure that the desired performance is achieved.

In developing the business assignments, priorities, and accountability programs, all corporate executives should play an active, direct, personal role, as should the key operating and staff department heads. The input of these individuals will result in a better strategy, aid in communicating that strategy throughout the corporation, and provide operating management with the strategic insights necessary for effective strategy implementaton.

All of the above should be done in a limited amount of time—perhaps three to six months. One way to initiate this process is to conduct a strategy audit—a candid review of current actions and intentions to determine the strategy they imply for the corporation. The effort here is to determine what objective outsiders would infer the strategy to be if they had access to inside

EXHIBIT 6-6   Business Roles Assigned to Each Operation

Business Roles	Cash Flow MM$	%	Capital Employed MM$	%	ROCE %
A. Priority Businesses—having first call on corporate discretionary resources to improve long-range competitive positions.					
1. Business A					
2. Business B					
B. Self-Funding Growth Businesses—based on strengths and ample attractive investment opportunity					
1. Business C					
2. Business D					
3. Business E					
C. Cash Generation Businesses— holding basic competitive positions					
1. Business F					
2. Business G					
3. Business H					
D. Maintain Future Option Businesses—but at minimal current costs					
1. Business I					
E. Withdraw Businesses					
1. Business J					
Total		100		100	

information. The result may well be at variance with what many in the corporation believe the strategy to be, and this can provide a useful basis for senior management to make judgments on the appropriateness or inappropriateness of various business activities in an overall corporate strategic context.

There is little point in trying to perfect the strategy at this point, since it will be modified when the strategic plans of the operating companies are developed and measured against the corporate strategy. Once this initial strategy is set, several iterations of the planning loop will likely be required—from corporate objectives, through strategy development and implementation, to performance measurement—to insure that the strategies of the operating subsidiaries are fully consistent with the corporate strategy and, of course, to keep them in tune with dynamic changes in the business environment.

There is no right or best strategy within a given industry. There are excellent to poor strategies for each company within an industry, and these will vary for individual companies. There is no magic formula for developing a winning corporate strategy. If there were, every corporation woud have such a strategy. In fact, as was so ably brought out in the book *In Search of Excellence*,[7] outstanding companies achieve that position through a pattern of action, rather than through a set of stated goals and objectives. An integral part of that pattern of action is the ability within a corporation to continually and openly challenge itself to more demanding levels of competitive performance. As Quinn incisively observed; "Successful strategies require commitment, not just acceptance."[8]

THE PLANNING CYCLE

The strategy system is described above as an iterative process or strategic loop involving a repetitious process of strategic development, strategic planning, strategic implementation, and strategic performance measurement. This planning cycle generally is repeated on an annual basis, but the frequency can vary from a few months to two or more years. Also, all corporate units can utilize identical planning schedules or schedules that are phased throughout the planning cycle.

Of more importance are the general steps within the planning cycle (see Exhibit 6-7), although these too will vary among companies.

1. *Executive Briefing.* The planning process formally commences with senior management review (and modification) of at least three items:

EXHIBIT 6-7   *Annual Planning Cycle*

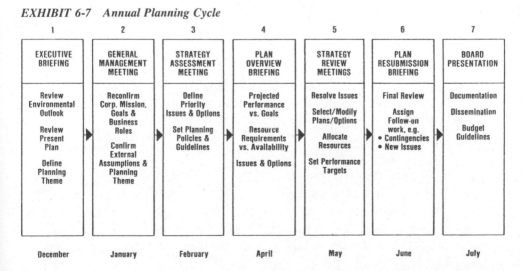

1	2	3	4	5	6	7
EXECUTIVE BRIEFING	GENERAL MANAGEMENT MEETING	STRATEGY ASSESSMENT MEETING	PLAN OVERVIEW BRIEFING	STRATEGY REVIEW MEETINGS	PLAN RESUBMISSION BRIEFING	BOARD PRESENTATION
Review Environmental Outlook	Reconfirm Corp. Mission, Goals & Business Roles	Define Priority Issues & Options	Projected Performance vs. Goals	Resolve Issues	Final Review	Documentation
Review Present Plan	Confirm External Assumptions & Planning Theme	Set Planning Policies & Guidelines	Resource Requirements vs. Availability	Select/Modify Plans/Options	Assign Follow-on work, e.g. • Contingencies • New Issues	Dissemination
Define Planning Theme			Issues & Options	Allocate Resources		Budget Guidelines
				Set Performance Targets		
December	January	February	April	May	June	July

Environmental Outlook.   The external planning assumptions; changes from the previous outlook and implications, if any; alternative sets of assumptions (scenarios) that could also be considered.

Plan Review.   The current status of the existing plan with respect to key program implementation and performance against goals. This may require a top-down update of existing plan projections if conditions have changed sufficiently to alter fundamental expectations.

Planning Theme.   Recommended emphasis for the upcoming planning cycle; for instance, generation of alternatives (options) in specific business areas, development of contingency plans, improvement of performance measures, addressing specific issues.

2.   *General Management Meeting.*   The mission, goals and objectives of the corporation and their priorities are reconfirmed, and the decisions reached in the executive briefing (external assumptions, planning theme) are communicated broadly to the operating management ranks.

3.   *Strategy Assessment Meeting.*   Corporate and senior operation managements follow up on the general management meeting with informal, intensive, and candid discussions of:

Issues and Options.   The substantive focus for the planning effort, specific matters to be dealt with.

Policies and Guidelines.   Directives to be followed in meeting corporate management's expectations for the plan submission.

4.   *Plan Overview.*   The plan submissions of the operating components (under development since Step 2) are consolidated and reviewed with corporate management, focusing on:

Performance projections relative to goals and objectives.

Resource requirements relative to resource availability.

Issues and options review, setting the substantive agenda for upcoming strategy review meetings.

5.   *Strategy Review Meetings.*   Corporate management meets individually with operating company managements to review their plan submission, issues, and options (if any). Emphasis is placed on developing a strong, shared perception of the business unit's strategy and how it contributes to corporate strategy. From this:

Options are selected.

Plans are accepted or modified.

Issues are resolved.

Resource allocation guidelines are set.

Performance targets are established.

6.   *Plan Resubmission.*   Operating companies adjust their plan submissions to reflect decisions taken in the strategy review meetings. These

are then consolidated with any corporate-level adjustments and given final review by corporate management. This is also an appropriate point for corporate management to assign any follow-on work they feel is required, such as contingency plans or new issue analysis.

7. *Board Presentation.* This "final" plan is then summarized in corporate strategy terms and formally documented for review by the board of directors. This document results from the blending of specific business opportunities with overall corporate directions and priorities worked out during the previous six steps. It should effectively integrate the basic strategic business concepts, the major action programs, and the key performance targets that comprise the corporate plan.

The plan, of course, is not final and can never be final. It must be continually updated to reflect ever-changing conditions in the corporation, its competition, and its environment, yet the planning cycle affords an opportunity to periodically reassess and reconfirm (or modify) the direction of the corporation from the top. Periodically "finalizing" the results of this process simply ensures clear, consistent, and explicit statements of management's assumptions, aspirations, and intentions at successive points in time. And these provide useful, even necessary, references against which to manage the evolution and implementation of corporate strategy over time.

An additional major consideration is the relationship of the annual budget schedule to the planning cycle. Two variations are most commonly used:

1. The planning and budget schedules are concurrent, usually ending just prior to the coming year. This helps make each as timely as possible, but the detail-oriented budget process frequently diverts time and attention from the more conceptually focused planning process.

2. The planning and budget schedules are sequential, with the first year of the plan forming the basis for the budget. This means that the plan will be about six months older than the budget, but it is more likely that the resulting budget will provide a more effective implementation of the corporate strategic plan.

There are, of course, many possible variations of the planning schedule and its components. For example, one major company that uses a portfolio management approach uses a 24-month planning cycle, with the cycle for each subsidiary starting on a different month. If subsidiary businesses differ greatly in their characteristics and operations, it may be best to modify the planning cycle to fit their individual needs, resulting in multiple or complex cycles. In short, the planning cycle must be adapted to best fit the needs of the corporation, the characteristics of its businesses, and the preferences of management.

PLANNING SCENARIOS

As shown in the preceding section, the first step in the planning cycle is the development of external assumptions, or the plan scenario, which describes the outside world in which it is judged the corporation will be doing business during the planning period. The time frame for the scenario should cover the plan period and extend sufficiently beyond it to provide the context for activities that will be initiated toward the end of the plan. Plan periods typically are for five years, but may be longer for long lead-time industries such as mineral extraction, oil and gas exploration, and utilities, or research-intensive businesses such as ethical pharmaceuticals and agricultural chemicals.

For each plan year the scenario must explicitly provide the key environmental factors that most significantly impact the corporation. Key environmental factors frequently used are:

Macroeconomic—GNP; inflation rates; interest rates

Political/regulatory—taxes; environmental; health and safety regulations; land access; liability exposure

Industry—Supply and demand; prices; import/export balances; plant operating rates

Multiple scenarios should be constructed. These should be plausible, internally consistent, pertinent to the business, and sufficiently different from one another to cover a wide range of possible outcomes. Some of the scenarios should stretch the extremes of possible developments. Little purpose is served if they differ only moderately from each other. The scenario the senior management feels most comfortable with (because, say, they view it as the most relevant or likely) is used as the base case in the planning cycle.

Perhaps the most important requirement in using scenarios is that they be described in prose clearly and in a way that will be fully understood by the operating managers. In short, the business environment for each scenario must be so described that the operating personnel can directly relate to it and different personnel will see in it the same business conditions. If this is done, the many plan decisions will tie together and will result in a plan that can be implemented advantageously in the projected business climate. Without such a description, different individuals will have different perceptions of the projected environment and their plan premises may then be inconsistent or even incompatible.

The techniques for developing scenarios will have to be tailored for each industry and corporate situation. Exhibit 6-8 outlines a process that was used successfully in the Gulf Oil Corporation.

Six steps are involved in this process:

1. The scenarios are developed by a group of planners and economists from the corporate and operating company planning staffs. These in-

EXHIBIT 6-8   Energy Scenario Development Process

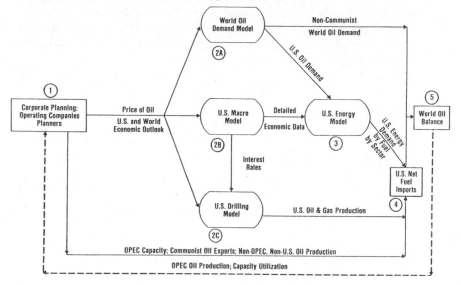

dividuals continually survey and analyze a range of information, data, and projections on the general economy and on the oil markets and form their individual views on where the economy and the oil markets are headed. Those individuals then meet to compare and discuss their views. Based on those discussions, and taking into account the views of corporate management, a consensus is reached on the number and general characteristics of the scenarios. Each involves three sets of key variables: real GNP, inflation rates, and the price of oil (usually in constant dollars). For each scenario, and consistent with its three key variables, the participants from Corproate Planning construct the following:

The price of deregulated, new contract natural gas

OPEC capacity

Non-OPEC, non-U.S. oil production

Communist oil exports

2. Three models are then used to construct a set of oil demand, macroeconomic, and U.S. oil and gas production projections for each scenario:

The World Oil Demand Model.   This model uses oil prices, GNP and inflation as inputs and provides oil demand projections for the U.S., OECD, non-OPEC LDCs, and OPEC.

The U.S. Macroeconomic Model.   This also uses oil prices, GNP, and inflation as inputs and projects the detailed economic data needed for subsequent steps by the corporate and operating company planning groups.

The U.S. Drilling Model.   This uses oil prices, interest rates, and inflation as inputs and calculates exploration costs and exploration expenditures at the level that maximizes the present value of exploration activities. The output is oil and natural gas production in the United States.

3.   Next, the U.S. Energy Model is used. Inputs, which have been developed in the preceding steps, are GNP, inflation rates, interest rates, car sales, housing starts, industrial production and personal income. The output consists of detailed U.S. energy demands by fuel, by sector. This model's U.S. oil demand is set equal to that which is determined by the World Oil Demand Model.

4.   Based on the data derived above, the net imports/exports of oil, natural gas, and coal are determined.

5.   In this step the world oil balance is determined, including OPEC production—which is treated as the residual supply—and OPEC capacity utilization. The oil price is then reviewed for compatibility with the level of OPEC capacity utilization. If the two are not compatible (e.g., stable prices at high capacity utilization rates), then the price is adjusted and the entire scenario construction process is repeated.

6.   Finally, a description of the scenario is carefully written, clearly describing the economic and industry situation that has resulted in the projected prices, production and demand patterns, GNP, inflation, and interest rates. This description provides the context against which the many planning decisions are made. This means that it must be internally consistent and plausible, even though it could well be viewed as being highly unlikely to occur. Such a description is needed for each scenario developed.

FORMULATING OPERATING COMPANY STRATEGIES

Environmental assumptions are the frame of reference for developing operating company and corporate strategies. It is, accordingly, desirable to review the base scenario (and any alternative scenarios) with corporate and operating company managements to be sure they are comfortable with them.

The strategic plans may be formulated in relation to the base scenario only. While it is technically feasible to work out plans for alternative scenarios as well, the resulting workload is generally too great to justify the effort. Also, there are other effective ways of using these scenarios, as we shall see in our discussion of contingency planning. However, the plan options chosen for the basic scenario should be those that will be the most durable or that can be easily modified to adapt to alternative scenarios should they occur.

While the corporate management can use the annual general management meeting to set the stage for the planning cycle and to get valuable input from the attendees, such a meeting is usually too large and too general in scope to provide a clear policy basis for each operating company's planning effort. This can be accomplished more effectively in small strategy assessment meetings in which the corporate management and the operating company head discuss openly and candidly current performance, shortcomings to be corrected, opportunities and successes to be stressed, potential problems or limitations, approximate allocation levels, and any modification of objectives or goals. The purpose of these meetings is to ensure that the basis on which the operating company plan is to be developed is shared by both managements. Otherwise, the plan, when submitted, may not meet the requirements of the corporate management, requiring last-minute revisions that will too often impair the ability to implement the plan effectively.

In developing its plan, the operating company reviews the fundamentals of its business and changes in competitive position and business environment and develops specific action programs to improve that competitive position. This is a top-down management process, and must involve operating company management on a significant and continuing basis. The plan finally approved for their company must be theirs, and they must "own" it. This is true for two reasons:

Only the management level is in a position to consider bold or drastic new actions.

The management must implement the plan. This requires full insight into the plan's essential elements and how the plan should be modified should the environment vary from the assumptions, as it usually will.

In the introduction to Chapter 7, it was noted that many companies plan well but implement the plan poorly. A contributing factor to poor implementation is lack of, or perfunctory, involvement in the planning process by senior operating management. Strategic planning and management if it is to be effective, must be an integral part of the way the entire management team runs its business.

A bottom-up, numbers-crunching approach to planning has basic weaknesses:

It substitutes data for judgment. Comfort blankets are no help in a tough, competitive world.

It precludes consideraton of widely differing options, resulting in a planning straitjacket.

It invariably disenchants operating management, causing them to ignore or disown the plan.

In developing its plan, an operating company must:

1.   Objectively identify and analyze its shortcomings and successes in the past year, new threats and opportunities which may be developing, and the availability of resources.

2. Make a similar analysis of its competitors.

3. Devise specific action programs to improve its competitive position. This, in turn, may lead to some modification of goals and, infrequently, to modification of objectives.

In carrying this out, realism and objectivity are essential, and the action programs should include specific milestones for measuring performance.

Another important planning tool is the use of key factors for success (KFS). These are the few elements that are critical to success in a given business or those factors that help explain the difference between superior and poor performance among competitors.

The KFS depend, in particular, on:

1. The type of industry (e.g., whether the cost structure is mainly fixed or variable, whether there are many or few competitors, and their strength).

2. The degree of maturity of the industry (i.e., embryonic vs. growth vs. mature vs. declining).

3. The actions taken by the current and potential competitors themselves (e.g., whether competitors are changing their own strategies, modifying the services they supply to the market).

The KFS are hard to identify because the tendency is to feel that everything is important. And everything is. But some aspects of the business are *more* important than others. KFS analysis looks for these leverage points—how a competitor can most distinguish itself in terms of values provided or costs incurred, or possibly both—and these can prove useful in concentrating strategic planning attention.

In developing a plan many options will be considered. Until recently it was practical to evaluate only a few of the most likely options. Today, however, it is quite feasible to examine a large number of quite different plan options. This involves the use of top-down business models for each line of business (i.e., each strategic business unit). These models should involved the key factors for success as well as a limited number of important external variables. They should not be permitted to get too complex, for that makes them hard to maintain and understand.

By developing a number of plan options for each strategic business unit in the operating company and by selectively aggregating these options, the operating company can consider and evaluate a large number of alternative plans. The key to doing this successfully is careful selection of the options so that they represent meaningful alternative action programs, requiring different levels of allocation of corporate resources and different risk/reward profiles.

Such an approach has been used by the management of one corporation to develop a very effective hands-on planning procedure. In this case, the chief executives of the operating companies meet weekly with the corporate executives during the planning period to consider a number of operating company options and the resulting corporate plan. These are discussed in detail and adjustments or alternatives are agreed on. These changes or options are then run through the operating company planning models to quantify the results, which are then consolidated at the corporate level. At the following week's meeting, the revised plan projections are discussed by the operating company and corporate executives. This process is repeated through the planning period until a suitable range of internal programs and external factors can be matched so that a final plan can be developed that provides a high capability for taking advantage of opportunities and a minimum exposure to potential adverse developments.

With computer business models such a procedure can be made to work effectively and is applicable at both operating company and corporate levels. It provides a powerful tool for reviewing a range of plan options and for quantifying them on a consistent basis. It also provides an excellent vehicle to ensure that the appropriate management personnel become intimately involved in developing the plan.

This procedure is readily applicable to businesses that are well-established, and particularly to mature businesses. At best, it has only limited application to very fast-moving industries, such as some high-technology industries in which the entire planning cycle covers only a few months. This would be insufficient time to update business models and review various options in an iterative program. In such cases, a corresponding selection and analysis of options should be made and the most desirable combination selected, but this will be done primarily through company review meetings based on operating experience and intuitive judgment. Even in these cases, however, some models may be applicable and should be developed as soon as they are warranted, for they do provide an effective means of examining alternatives.

The financial data required at the corporate level should be limited to those data that are absolutely necessary to provide the desired corporate consolidation and any standard cross-business comparisons that management requires. In addition, the quantitative aspects of the plan should include those items that in operating management's judgment best serve to display the effects of their strategy on their business' results.

With the financial modeling capabilities available in business computer systems today, there may be a problem in providing plan projections in formats that clearly focus on the key issues of concern to management. The danger of having detailed financial projections is the tendency to use them. Care must be taken to use them in their proper context—top-down projections of management's judgments about a business' future. The numbers are necessary as a relatively unambiguous language to communicate the assumptions, aspirations, and intentions embodied in a given plan, but care must be taken not to let plan reviews degenerate into number-juggling exercises. The judgments behind them are what is important. The numbers themselves are useful only as a means for expressing those judgments.

These consolidated data provide the basis for setting corporate guidelines for allocation of capital and other resources and provide projected plan performance of the operating companies so that the corporate executives can make preliminary judgments as to any plan adjustments they may wish to have made. These are then discussed in detail at the strategy review meetings, as are the various options that the operating companies have chosen to present.

Discussion of plan options should be made a routine part of any plan presentation and review. Otherwise the corporate executive is limited to either fine-tuning the plan presented or requesting major changes, but with limited insight as to the impact that these changes may have. This puts the corporate executive in a difficult and tenuous position and generally results in frustration, questionable decisions, or both.

Following the strategy review meetings, the operating companies finalize their plans based on the options selected and decisions made by the corporate executive. These are reconsolidated with corporate-level items to form the overall plan that is presented to the board of directors and used for future reference in tracking actual performance against plan projections.

CONTINGENCY PLANNING

The basic business plan outlined above is keyed to its scenario, yet the one thing certain about any scenario is that events will unfold differently from the way they are projected. If these differences are small, implementation of the plan can be adjusted readily by the operating units. But all too frequently, conditions change so drastically that the plan can no longer be modified; it must be overhauled or even jettisoned. In such situations, the corporation may be caught largely by surprise with little time to develop a plan for the new conditions. The result is that actions are usually taken on a reactive and hit-or-miss basis.

Such a drastic turn of events can be handled more effectively if a similar situation can be postulated in advance and contingency plans prepared. This involves using the alternative scenarios discussed earlier.These scenarios should represent plausible, if unlikely, situations and should be developed in the same detail and with the same clear description as the base scenario.

It is important that these alternative scenarios differ significantly, even radically, from the base scenario. They should represent a major change in the future course of events. This makes the contingency planning process more useful and effective and avoids the problem of modifying plans frequently because of nominal environmental changes. Too frequent changes in the plan impair the ability to achieve the plan goals.

Examples of such dramatic changes in the conditions affecting an industry are legion: the impact of oil on coal in the 1930s; the impact of nuclear power on coal in the 1960s; Three Mile Island; the Santa Barbara oil spill in 1968; the fall from power of the Shah of Iran; the impact of jet airplanes and the interstate highway system on the railroads; foreign steel and car imports; and deregulation of the airline industry and of the banking system. Most of these events have led to corporate upheavals or to industry restructuring. Contingency planning should be used by a corporation to prepare itself, at least partially, for such events. More importantly, it can be used to help a corporation gain competitive position at such a time.

Tying the contingency plan to such a scenario helps reduce the risk that employees may perceive this activity as an indication that management believes the contingent events will actually occur. The Conference Board reports that one company, to guard against such a reaction, "issues broad guidelines for its managers to observe in developing contingency plans. They are: (1) protect the financial capability of the company (i.e., maintain the company's AA rating); (2) protect earnings; and (3) do no long-term damage to the company."[9] The analysis of a possible future emergency should not become a self-fulfilling exercise.

Contingency planning can and should be less comprehensive than that undertaken in the regular planning cycle. To be that comprehensive would involve more work than is justified and would place an undue added burden on the operating managers and planners.

A more practical approach is to determine what changes should be made in the basic plan to best meet the new conditions. The operating managers should think through and list the early-warning signals for the scenario, the preparatory steps to take, the trigger points for major corrective or aggressive actions, and what those actions would be. This analysis will frequently identify actions or conditions which, if initiated under the base scenario, would inhibit or restrict attractive responsive actions in the alternative scenarios. To the extent feasible, such actions and conditions should be modified in the basic plan to reduce or eliminate this problem.

The changes to be made in the basic plan to meet the contingency scenario should be quantified. Since the contingency is itself quite speculative, detailed quantification is not justified. It should involve reasonable approximations using a top-down approach. The various actions proposed and the quantified result should be reviewed for internal consistency.

When these quantifications are completed these data are transmitted to corporate planners for consolidation. Also transmitted are the individual major actions and the financial and operating impact of each action. A summary of such actions and of the resulting corporate financial and operating outlook is then reviewed with the corporate executive. They may request changes in specific actions of individual operating companies to achieve a better-balanced corporate result. A reconsolidation and action summary based on these changes will then be made.

Contingency planning is basically a discipline that leads operating and corporate management to think through such a situation resourcefully and carefully. The warning signals, trigger points, and action steps should be listed in enough detail so that they can quickly be checked for applicability and used efficiently should such a situation occur. In such events, timing of the corporate actions is often critical—particularly in regard to competitors. Contingency planning should enable management to recognize and evaluate the devlopments sooner and to act faster and more accurately.

Contingency planning provides valuable insight into the corporation's ability to make adjustments in bad times to maintain a strong financial and competitive position, and into actions to take in good times to maximize opportunities. If contingency planning is done well and consistently, credibility will be developed. This could make management less defensive under adverse conditions and more alert in good times. Such an attitude could lead, for example, to countercyclical investment policies for the corporation, which is a much more efficient way of investing capital and generally results in better timing in bringing new production capacity into operation.

PLAN IMPLEMENTATION

A brilliant plan poorly implemented will be of little value; a reasonable plan well implemented will result in improved corporate performance. Too frequently, once a plan is developed and agreed on it is assumed that implementation will take care of itself and the strategic management effort subsides until the next planning cycle. Actually at that time the job is only half done. The discipline and techniques for plan implementation are just as vital and demanding as the program for plan development.

The plan, and each of its components, is directed toward improving the competitive corporate position. Each plan component includes goals to be achieved, specific action programs, and intermediate targets against which interim performance can be measured. If a significant number of plan goals are achieved, corporate performance will improve and its competitive position should improve. These goals should all lead toward improving the corporation's market value to book value ratio, which requires both solid growth and sound returns—a difficult combination to achieve.

To measure performance and progress a set of performance measures is used, including key factors for success and other important variables. Such performance measures should:

1. Be measurable at reasonable expense
2. Be controllable either directly (e.g., unit operating costs) or indirectly (e.g., market share)
3. Be accounted for by a single identified executive or manager
4. Be readily understood

5. Cover the key elements or challenges in a given business

6. Indicate operating results as well as financial results (This is highly important since operating results are frequently available on a current basis, permitting fast control response. Financial results are generally not available until well into the following month.)

7. Include key comparisons with competitors

8. Be combined in groupings of not less than about four or five, not more than about eight to ten, so they can be comprehended as a group and provide an effective overview of the business

9. Be reappraised or adjusted periodically to ensure that they continue to represent the key elements or challenges in a given business

10. Be supported by additional performance measures required down through the lower working levels.

Of course, it is one thing to set a variety of desirable measures and another thing entirely to achieve them. Beyond the question of setting challenging but achievable levels for individual measures is the question of mix and relative priority among these measures. It is difficult—often impossible—to pursue all desirable measures simultaneously. There are often tradeoffs to be made, and these can have major consequences for business strategy.

As a simple example, assume two identical single-product companies. One believes that lower costs through greater volumes is the key to financial success and therefore sets market share as its primary objective. This can be achieved through price reductions and capacity investments, but the company also wishes to remain solvent so it sets a minimum profitability (ROE) level to be maintained. The second company believes higher returns are key to improved market value and therefore sets ROE as its principal objective. This could be achieved (in the short term) by higher prices and restricted reinvestment, but the company also desires to stay in business long term, so it sets a minimum market share requirement. These two identical companies now both have the same two prime objectives—ROE and market share— but different priorities between them. It will not be very long before they are two very different companies. Which is ultimately more successful will depend on the evolving characteristcs of the market they serve and the dynamics of the competition they will face—in short, the critical success factors in their industry.

The strategic plan should provide guidance as to the relative importance of potentially conflicting business aims. One approach to dealing with this is simply to sort measures into two camps: objectives and constraints. The constraints are to be *satisfied,* not necessarily exceeded, particularly if doing so would affect the performance against objectives. Objectives are to be *maximized, subject to* satisfying the constraints. This approach can considerably sharpen management's thinking about what they really want from a business (for a specified period) and what they are prepared to give up in terms of minimum constraint levels to get it.

An almost limitless number of performance measures can be identified in an operation. To do so and to report these periodically tends to swamp the management with data and starve it of information. This does not provide an effective implementation system. Performance measures should be carefully identified, and used in limited numbers and as a package that reasonably defines the operation being measured.

The performance measures will vary with corporate level and by type of activity, as indicated in Exhibit 6-9. The areas of all sections in the pyramid are approximately equal, indicating that any given management group can efficiently handle only so many individual performance measures and their implications. The appropriate performance measures to use will vary with management level and operating sector. At each successively lower level in the organization the performance measures will cover a narrower scope of operations but will relate to increasingly specific activities. Each executive or manager is accountable for the performance measures at his or her own level and responsible for those at the next lower level—he or she must intimately understand both.

Establishing a system of performance measures requires extensive thought, a deep understanding of the business, and a lot of hard work. Once they are chosen, recognizing the 10 characteristics listed above, they need to be organized in a standardized reporting format and reviewed at every reporting period. No significant cost or management level should be left out of the system.

There are many formats and many combinations of performance reports that can be used. Any such report should include the current reading of the performance measure, recent trends, plan targets, intermediate milestones, the performance of the top competitor(s), and the major action programs being implemented. This report should become the basis for performance

EXHIBIT 6-9   *Conceptual Structure of Performance Measurement System*

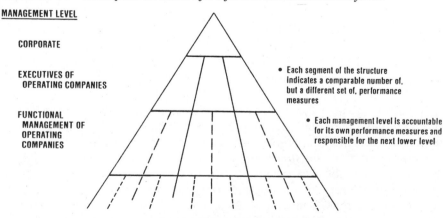

MANAGEMENT LEVEL

CORPORATE

EXECUTIVES OF
OPERATING COMPANIES

FUNCTIONAL
MANAGEMENT OF
OPERATING
COMPANIES

- Each segment of the structure indicates a comparable number of, but a different set of, performance measures

- Each management level is accountable for its own performance measures and responsible for the next lower level

◄────────── OPERATING ELEMENTS ──────────►

review sessions to determine whether performance is on target, or if not, why, and what corrective actions are needed.

As the performance measurement system moves upward through the organization, it must ultimately lead to the return on equity and the corporation's ratio of market value to book value. Accordingly, at the earliest level performance measures should include profits and the composition of investments.

As internal problems are solved and as external issues arise, there will be changes in both key factors for success and critical performance measures. Periodically the package of performace measures will have to be improved and modified to accommodate such changes. This may be difficult to do since operating personnel have a strong tendency to set a system firmly in place and to run it ever more efficiently. That, of course, is an essential competitive practice—as long as the system is suited to the current business conditions. However, these conditions continually change, and when the changes are significant enough a given performance measurement system must be updated.

Use and maintenance of performance measurement systems have been simplified by the advent of the computer. All of the basic operating and financial data are normally collected in the company's data base. If they are stored so that they can be individually retrieved, they can then be utilized in any useful performance measure format.

A successful performance measurement system requires the understanding and unflagging support of the corporation's chief executive officer—almost to the point of religious zeal. While the detail work will generally be done by corporate and operating company staffs, the use of performance measures as a vital strategic management tool must be a top priority for management at all levels.

When a performance measurement system is initiated the organization will study the actions of the corporate executives as much as their words. If it is observed that individuals who are indifferent in setting challenging performance targets and in meeting them are rewarded, the system will not be a meaningful one. If a system of performance targets, measures, and action programs is to be effective, those managers who establish and utilize such a system successfully must be rewarded. Conversely, lack of performance should result in special attention to the specific problem since it may not be a result of factors under the manager's control. However, if the manager's performance is below standard and persists, he must be replaced.

At least part of the corporation's incentive or bonus system should be tied to an individual's performance in developing and implementing the strategic plan. All managers tend to look relatively good in boom times, during which organizations tend to become smug and complacent. Conversely, all managers tend to have poor performance during a recession, and the organization typically attributes its problems to outside factors. In each case, the factors exerting the major impact on their business are beyond their control. However, if a corporation does not gain on the competition during the bad times, it is likely to be further outstripped by the competition in the good times. Therefore an important factor in any performance measurement system is the measurement of the corporation's performance against that of its leading competitors, and this measurement must be maintained during economic recessions and recoveries.

Since external factors can have a major or even overwhelming impact on the corporation, it is essential that the environmental conditions be continually scanned and evolving issues be identified and analyzed at an early date. When warranted, these factors and issues may result in modifications of the business plans. Generally this can be done at the operating company and headquarters levels by making top-down adjustments to the current plan. Again, the use of computers enables this to be done with facility and within a matter of days if need be.

The plan update should generally be reviewed with the corporate and operating company managements so they can be informed of the projected impact of the environmental changes. If these changes are significant enough, a reappraisal of the corporate strategy may be required. This continual monitoring of performance and of the outside environment is fed back both into the annual planning cycle and into the corporate strategic development cycle, completing the planning loop discussed earlier.

In today's environment static strategy cannot survive. Without ongoing feedback and renewal, any strategy will quickly degenerate. Performance measures to provide feedback are absolutely fundamental to an effective planning system, but performance measures also pose great challenges. Because they are associated with forecasts, they are suspect. Because they involve choice, they contain conflicts. Because they are tied to appraisal and reward systems, they are emotionally charged. Yet with these problems comes opportunity. Because feedback links are so important to successful strategy, and yet difficult to effectively establish, the management team that overcomes these difficulties will have secured—by that effort alone—a substantial competitive advantage. With an effective system for setting performance measures they will have a firmer consensus abou their objectives and priorities—a better sense of strategy. With an effective system for using performance measures they will be able to take informed actions with speed and conviction, exploiting changes while competitors struggle with doubts about what is happening and what to do. With these advantages, the competitive gap can become very wide.

THE INTERNAL VERSUS THE EXTERNAL STRATEGIES

For strategy formulation to be effective, it must be championed by the corporate executives, and in particular by the chief executive officer. In practice this is not always the case. Numerous surveys have been made of the attitudes and opinions of the chief executive officer, the chief planning officer, and top operating officers regarding the role of planning, the role of planners, and their effectiveness. Such surveys indicate that a reasonable number of companies develop fairly good strategic plans, a limited number implement these plans effectively, and even fewer integrate the system into an effective strategic management process.

The transition from bottom-up, forecast-based planning to an effective strategic management system takes time; it cannot be accomplished all at once. The desired final program should be reviewed with and subscribed to by the corporate executive but shoud be implemented in stages. A phased approach could evolve as follows:

1. During the first phase, the system to be ultimately achieved is reviewed, transitions are made from forecast-based planning to active planning participation by managers at all levels, the use of plan options is established, and business models for each operating company and for the corporation are developed.
2. In the second phase, contingency plans and performance measures may be introduced, and the new planning capability is refined.
3. In the third phase, incentive programs are linked to the planning process, prior development stages are refined, and stress is placed on closing the planning loop.

Three to five years may be required for a strategic management system to become an integral and effective part of the corporate culture.

Any strategic management system must be pragmatically oriented. The academic and philosophical tools that have been developed to aid in planning are only aids and should be used only when they serve a specific purpose. Planning staffs should be kept very small and should include primarily individuals with excellent line experience and with the ability to quickly assimilate planning techniques and systems. Ideally, high-performing line personnel are periodically transferred to the planning group for periods of three to five years and then reassigned to a line position. This provides an excellent opportunity to broaden the business expertise and corporate exposure of those individuals. By using able line people in planning functions the planning groups will be able to communicate with and relate to the line operations effectively. Planning groups will generally also include a few specialists such as economists and management service experts.

The head of the corporate planning group should report to the chief executive officer, and his or her chief allegiance is to that person. In effect the planning group becomes the business staff for the CEO, but in addition the corporate planning group must act as a partner, not an opponent, of the operating companies. For the corporate planning group to be effective it is essential that it build a strong level of credibility and trust with the operating elements. This means that the corporate planning group must maintain its own independence in evaluating major programs and strategies but must discuss any differences openly with the line management before they are discussed with others in the corporation. A cardinal rule is that the planning group can never unpleasantly surprise an operating manager in front of his or her peers or superiors.

In essence the planner's role is to coordinate the annual planning program, to be a facilitator on issues and strategic developments, to see that internal challenges are maintained on an open and objective basis, to stay abreast of any planning developments, and to do special studies. Together with the financial departments the planners should check action plans and goals, track performance, and highlight deviations from goals and objectives.

The corporate and operating company planning staffs can be the stewards of the planning efforts, but they cannot do the planning! Planning will be effective only if it is done by the corporate executive and by operating company line management. They are the ones who must make the decisions and bear the responsibility for those decisions, and who have the hands-on feel for their business and for the environment in which that business works. They cannot do their job well unless planning becomes an integral part of their ongoing activities, and no surrogate can do their planning for them.

The Conference Board, in surveying 18 chief executive officers,[10] found that:

> Virtually all of the CEO's also point out that it is the company's line operating executives who will be implementing the necessary strategic changes. They believe their line executives are much more likely to accept and to translate strategic plans into effective practice if they have been involved in formulating the requisite changes. As one CEO put it: "Strategic change has now become essential for corporate survival. But it is what a company does, not what it plans, that is its real strategy." . . . "Group ownership" of the decision apparently carries with it the need to demonstrate its correctness by "making it happen."

Given such involvement, if it is done enthusiastically, a strategic management system will develop as a powerful means of improving performance and of improving competitive position.

SUMMARY

Formulation and implementation of corporate strategy is a complex process by which all of the corporate assets are focused to take advantage of the ever-changing environment. This comprehensive process has been skillfully summarized by Kenichi Ohmae.[11] He suggests there are five conditions met by "winning" competitors:

1. The business domain is clearly defined.
2. The forces at work in the business environment are extrapolated into the future on the basis of cause and effect.
3. Of the many strategic options open to the business, only a few are chosen. Once the choice is made, people, technology, and money are deployed aggressively. By concentrating more resources in support of fewer options, the company gains a bigger edge over its competitors in those businesses and thereby improves its success rate. This is why successful and unsuccessful companies diverge so greatly over time.
4. The company paces its strategy according to its resources, rather than going all out to achieve too much too soon.
5. Management adheres to the basic assumptions underlying its original strategic choice as long as those assumptions hold. But if changed conditions demand it, they are prepared to change even the basic direction of the business.

The system of strategy formulation, of preparing for contingencies, and of implementation must become an integral part of the corporate culture and a permanent part of corporate procedures.

Planning is done by the corporate executive, line managers, and line employees. Planners and planning staffs are an important catalyst in this system, but they can never be the planning surrogate for the corporate executive and line personnel.

The strategic management system is like a wheel; it will only provide a smooth journey if it is complete. Its components are the development of corporate strategy, strategic planning, performance measures, implementation (including rewards and penalties), environmental and issue scanning, and a constant upgrading of the process. The system must always be focused on gaining position against competitors. This is fundamental, since business in a free economy is a form of commercial warfare—often with survival of the fittest directly at stake. Strategic management can be a powerful process for achieving success on the commercial battlefield.

NOTES

1. W. Kiechel III, "Corporate Strategists under Fire," *Fortune,* Vol. 106, no. 13, December 27, 1982, p. 34.
2. W. Kiechel III, "Sniping at Strategic Planning," *Planning Review,* North American Society for Corporate Planning, vol. 12, no. 3, May 1984, p. 8.
3. F. W. Gluck, S. P. Kaufman, and A. S. Walleck, *The Evolution of Strategic Managements,* McKinsey Staff Paper, October 1978, p. 4.
4. F. W. Gluck, S. P. Kaufman, and A. S. Walleck, "Strategic Management for Competitive Advantage," *Harvard Business Review,* July 1980, p. 157.

5. Arthur D. Little, Inc., *A Management System for the 1980s,* Arthur D. Little, Inc., New York, 1980, p. 40.

6. Ibid., p. 27.

7. T. J. Peters and R. H. Waterman, Jr., *In Search of Excellence,* Harper & Row, New York, 1982, p. 154.

8. J. B. Quinn, *Strategies for Change,* Richard D. Irwin, Homewood, Ill., 1980, p. 167.

9. R. O'Connor, *Planning under Uncertainty: Multiple Scenarios and Contingency Planning,* Conference Board Report No. 741, The Conference Board, Inc., New York, 1981, p. 23.

10. R. Gilbert Shaeffer, *Developing Strategic Leadership,* Conference Board Report No. 847, The Conference Board, Inc., New York, 1984, pp. 9, 11.

11. K. Ohmae, *The Mind of the Strategist,* McGraw-Hill, New York, 1982, pp. 242–243.

CHAPTER *7*

Strategic Planning: A View From Japan

WARREN D. CHINN

YOSHIHISA MURASAWA

JOHN D. VANDENBRINK

WARREN D. CHINN is a senior vice president of Booz, Allen & Hamilton and manages the firm's office in Tokyo. Prior to relocating to Japan he was based in San Francisco where he managed the firm's operations in the western United States. During his career of 23 years with Booz-Allen he has directed over 300 assignments for more than 75 clients in a broad spectrum of industries. In recent years his focus has been in aerospace, banking and financial services, consumer products, consumer services, electronics, energy, and transportation. He is one of the firm's leading experts in the integration of business and organization strategies. His extensive experience in the past includes evaluating and assisting clients in implementing mergers, acquisitions, divestitures, and joint ventures. Mr. Chinn received his B.S. degree in Electrical Engineering with honors from the University of Kansas. Prior to joining Booz-Allen he spent several years with Allis-Chalmers Manufacturing Co. in engineering, marketing, and personnel management. Mr. Chinn has served on the board of directors of Booz-Allen and is a member of the firm's operating council.

YOSHIHISA MURASAWA is a vice president with Booz, Allen & Hamilton Inc. based in Tokyo. His areas of experience include corporate strategy, industrial and consumer marketing, and technology evaluation. He has consulted extensively for Japanese, American, and European clients. He has played a major role in a number of complex business strategy assignments in such industries as financial services, electronics, automobiles, chemicals, and electronic materials. Prior to joining Booz-Allen Mr. Murasawa was a senior staff member with a consulting firm specializing in business strategy. He also was a member of the professional staff of the Japanese affiliate of Arthur D. Little, Inc. Mr. Murasawa has an M.B.A. degree from the Graduate School of Business at Stanford University with emphasis in business policy, marketing, and international economics. He also has a B.E. degree in Marine Engineering and an M.E. degree in Information Engineering from the University of Tokyo.

JOHN D. VANDENBRINK is a research associate in the Chicago office of Booz, Allen & Hamilton, where he provides support for both client work and internal projects. One of his chief responsibilities is assisting a managing director of the firm in developing and marketing new practices. In recent client assignments he has helped develop a long-range market strategy for a telecommunication company and has worked with a team evaluating merger candidates in the food industry. Mr. Vandenbrink holds a B.A. in History from Williams College and an M.A. in East Asian Studies from the University of Michigan. He is presently a doctoral candidate in History at the University of Chicago. He speaks Japanese and has conducted research at the Faculty of Law, University of Tokyo. He has taught social science at the University of Chicago. In 1983 he edited the book *Corporate Strategy and Structure: Japan and the USA* for the Chicago Council on Foreign Relations.

OUTLINE

The prowess of Japan's large international corporations is well known; Western business people face it abroad and in their home markets, and to compete effectively they must understand and anticipate the moves of these tough competitors. This is a difficult task today, not only because of differences in culture but also because the strategic objectives of many Japanese corporations are changing in response to low economic growth and the maturing of their businesses. Often these changes are subtle, but the magnitude of Japanese competition is such that their impact on world markets will be significant.

Few Western executives know Japan well enough to predict what the impact of Japanese competition will be. For the sake of their own corporations they have to become good judges of Japanese corporate moves. One way to do this is to study how Japanese corporations develop their strategies. When Western business executives do this they will discover that the context of strategic planning in Japan is very different from what it is in the West.

STRATEGIC PLANNING IN JAPAN: AN OVERVIEW

What is strategic planning in Japan? It is not a formal discipline with an acknowledged set of techniques and body of literature, as it is in the United States. Nor is it practiced by professional strategic planners, as in many U.S. corporations. While a number of the tools of American-style planning (like portfolio analysis, for example) are known in Japan, they are usually not employed with the rigor and purposefulness with which they are employed in the United States.

Large Japanese firms typically do have formal planning departments, but most of these are relatively recent in origin. Many were established in the early and mid-1970s. In part they were created in response to the onset of lower rates of growth in Japan, and partly they were a response to the uncertainties of the period, especially uncertainties about energy supplies. But the power of example was also an important factor: formal planning departments worked in the West, and they seemed to answer a new need of Japanese corporations.

Formal planning departments take various forms within different Japanese corporations. Most often they are organized as regular staff departments, like personnel or finance. In these cases they usually report to the board of directors of the firm or, in the case of large firms with large boards of directors, to an operating committee (*jomu-kai*) made up of the managing directors of the firm. However, in small and mid-sized firms, and in some large firms with traditions of strong executive leadership, often they are organized as "offices of the president" (*shacho-shitsu*) that report directly to the top executive.

The employees who staff the planning positions in Japanese companies rarely have undergone special training in the planning function; they are assigned as part of the regular, constant rotation of managers within the company. They may come to the planning assignment directly from the plant, from a sales position, or from any other managerial post within the company. Occasionally a company may have one or two employees who specialize in planning, but this is definitely uncommon.

While planners in Japan are generalists who come to their assignments with a variety of backgrounds, they do share one trait—they are usually competent employees who are well regarded within their companies. Duty in the planning department is widely considered to be fine training for future leaders, so personnel departments frequently assign the best people there. This tendency is not so strong that it raises planning to the level of an elite function, but certainly most employees are pleased to receive an assignment in the planning department.

The acknowledged responsibility of planners in Japan is to create long-term visions for their organizations, but this task is not as clear-cut as it might be in a typical U.S. corporation. Short-range planning and medium-range planning are generally considered to be the province of the operating divisions, so the realm of strategic planners is circumscribed from the start.

In practice, this means that planners in Japan must work closely with other managers within their companies. While they may initiate proposals, more often they serve as counselors and coordinators. They provide research assistance to divisions, departments, and the president, simultaneously seeking to integrate the diverse planning activities of the company. Often they are cast in the role of mediator between warring divisions. Sometimes their chief function is to provide long-term forecasts for the divisions, not necessarily long-term plans for the corporation.

In sum, strategic planning in Japan is not as sharply defined as the strategic planning that we know in the West. Strategic issues have to be dealt with, of course, but generally they are not isolated and given the special, professional treatment that they often receive in the West.

JAPANESE CORPORATE PRACTICES AND STRATEGIC DECISION MAKING

The Japanese Conception of a Corporation

In the United States and Western Europe strategic planning has developed around a conception of the corporation as a financial entity. It presumes that the foremost objective of the corporation is to enhance shareholder value by generating dividends and increasing the market value of the corporation's stock. In this scheme of things, managers are the agents of the shareholders and labor is an input, just like any other input in the production process.

In Japan, however, the conception of a corporation is fundamentally different, and strategic planning there has developed with subtly different objectives. In the Japanese view a corporation is a social entity above all else. It is a community with responsibilities to its members. Financial goals are by no means ignored, but their importance stems from their relationship to the ultimate goal of the corporation in Japan: the well-being and perpetuation of the corporate community.

In Japan a company's managers and workers alike are members of its corporate community, but the shareholders are not. (Managers and workers may own stock, and frequently do, but that is not what makes them members of the community.) Shareholders supply capital and legally they have about the same powers as shareholders in the West. In practice, however, their influence is considerably less. Basically, in Japan corporate managers and employees tend to absorb the effects of business cycles and supply a stable stream of dividends, and in exchange they are left alone by the shareholders. This arrangement leaves the corporate community free to pursue its own interests.

Of course, these interests are not necessarily discordant with the interests of shareholders, and in practice the objectives of strategic planning end up being much the same in Japan as they are in the West. Nevertheless, the conception of a corporation in Japan does influence strategic planning in important ways. It encourages corporations to place a premium on maintaining employment, for example. It also shapes the process that corporations follow to reach strategic decisions.

The Impact of Lifetime Employment and the Seniority System on Strategic Planning

In many Japanese organizations lifetime employment is regarded as a matter of course by both employers and employees. It is part and parcel of the concept of corporate community. In Japan guarantees of permanent employment are not written formally into employment contracts, but they are understood to exist and all major Japanese corporations must honor them. For this reason the responsibility of providing secure employment is a major factor in strategic planning in Japan. To appreciate the significance of this responsibility, it is necessary to understand the nature of employment in Japanese corporations.

Lifetime employment is not universal in Japan. Smaller firms often do not provide this benefit; female employees are usually expected to work only a few years and then leave the firm to get married; many firms have part-timers whose employment can be relatively easily terminated when business is slow. Indeed, statistics show that lifetime employment extends to only about 30 to 40 percent of the Japanese labor force. However, it is the rule in government and in virtually all of Japan's large, leading corporations, including all whose names are well known in the West.

The origin of the Japanese system of lifetime employment is a subject of much serious scholarly debate, but certainly it flowered in the postwar period mainly in response to perennial shortages of skilled and highly educated labor. Employers fostered the system as a way to secure the loyalty of their employees. It has enabled them to invest considerable amounts of time and money in job rotation and training without fear of losing the benefits of their investment. The system also benefits employees, most obviously through job security, which is highly valued in Japanese society. Indeed, many talented young people reject careers in start-up companies and foreign-affiliated firms, even in fields in which they have strong interests, because these firms offer less security than Japan's prestigious, established firms.

Closely tied to the system of lifetime employment is the system of paying and promoting by seniority. It is a system that treats employees not according to what they do—not according to merit or skill—but according to their identities as members of the corporate community. Male college graduates, for example, enter the firm at the age of 22, move up over the course of their careers, and leave the firm at the age of mandatory retirement, which is usually somewhere between 55 and 60. While they are new to the firm— and single—their pay is low; but as their careers advance—and as they marry and have children—their salaries increase to meet their personal responsibilities.

All the while they move up in rank in the corporation in virtual lockstep with colleagues who entered in the same year. Not until age 40 or so do differences in performance begin to be reflected in differences in rank. Similarly, differences in salary are typically modest in the early years—approximately plus or minus 7 percent within individual firms for employees 30 years of age according to a recent survey by the Japan Institute of Personnel Administration. This fosters a feeling of fairness and equity within the company, and therefore also a sense of community. Thus the seniority system in Japan, like permanent employment, is part of a set of assumptions and obligations that ties employees and their companies very closely together.

In terms of corporate performance this closeness undoubtedly has many virtues. However, it does place severe constraints on strategic planning. For example, Japanese corporations often hesitate to enter attractive new fields of business because the personnel problems involved are considerable. Securing workers for new projects can be troublesome. Because permanent employment is widespread, and because Japanese employees are expected to remain loyal to their companies, it is difficult to attract people from other companies. Those who can be hired away tend to be lower-quality employees who have been shunted aside within their own companies. They carry the stigma of tainted goods, and this can hinder their assimilation into the company that hires them away.

On the other side of the coin, however, it is relatively easy for a company to retrain its own workers. Most labor unions in Japan are company unions with only loose ties to other unions in their industries, so the interests of the unions lie close to the interests of the company. Therefore, when a Japanese company enters a new market and needs to expand its sales force, for example, it can train machine operators to become salesmen. Nevertheless, when requirements for new workers are large, or when special expertise is called for, Japanese employment practices constitute a serious obstacle.

Another limitation on strategic planning is the Japanese taboo against buying and selling businesses. Given the communal conception of a corporation in Japan, it is not surprising that acquiring another firm is considered unfair—reaping where one has not sown. Moreover, being acquired is dishonorable. Giving up the responsibility of maintaining the corporate community is considered almost as bad as selling one's family. This makes rationalization through divestitures and mergers very difficult.

Let us look, for example, at the Japanese polyvinyl chloride (PVC) industry. This industry, like other petroleum-based chemical industries, developed rapidly in the 1960s and early 1970s thanks to a stable supply of inexpensive oil. However, two oil shocks in the 1970s brought prosperity to an end. Since the late 1970s the industry has not grown. In 1981, total production dropped more than 20 percent from the previous year and almost all of the 17 competitors recorded heavy losses. Since that time, at least, it has been clear that the industry is structurally depressed. Its problems are not going to disappear.

Despite this gloomy situation, none of the competitors has withdrawn from the market. Instead, the industry has tried to save all 17 participants by forming an antidepression cartel under Japanese law. Indeed, there was no shakeout until two Mitsubishi-group companies consolidated recently. Despite prolonged poor performance, managers in the industry have been unwilling to liquidate, merge, or sell their businesses because doing so would be considered giving up managerial responsibility.

Reducing the scale of business can also be very difficult because it usually involves labor reductions, and with the guarantee of lifetime employment and the commitment to the corporate community these are very hard to accomplish. Japanese companies will go to extreme lengths to avoid layoffs. It is not unusual to see a troubled firm begin formally and substantively to reduce labor only after it is in or near bankruptcy. An example is Riccar, a leading manufacturer of sewing machines. Only after the financial situation became hopeless and the main banks had stopped extending new loans did the firm begin to reduce labor.

Nippon Steel presents an example of how less urgent labor reductions are accomplished. The steel industry in Japan is no longer growing, and Nippon Steel reduced its work force from 82,000 in 1970 to 73,000 in 1980. It took the firm 10 years to cut back 11 percent because it depended on "natural decrease," a euphemism for mandatory retirement. As of March 1983 the firm employed approximately 69,000 people. It has announced further reduction of 6000 employees over three years; this it will also carry out through a natural process. Because virtually all its employees stay with the firm until they reach the mandatory retirement age of 60, Nippon Steel knows exactly how much—or rather, how little—it can reduce its labor force every year.

"Natural reduction" is fairly standard in structurally depressed industries in Japan. Unless a firm is desperate, drastic actions like layoffs are not taken. When layoffs do occur they are regarded as evidence of a social failure as well as business failure on the part of management. The managers of the firm are branded inept and irresponsible.

The unavailability of layoffs as an option limits the scope of strategic planning in Japan to a great extent. During the recessions of the 1970s Japanese industry in general endured losses and squeezed profitability in order to maintain employment.

More than being merely a limitation on strategic moves, the employment imperative in Japan may actually impel them. According to a survey conducted by MITI (Ministry of International Trade and Industry), more and more Japanese corporations plan to diversify their business lines, and their chief motivation is to utilize currently available resources, that is, human resources, facilities, and capital. Of these three, the one most on the minds of managers in Japan today is definitely human resources—finding new ways to keep existing employees working productively.

For example, Kubota, a large machinery manufacturer, experienced a sharp decline in profits in 1980. By 1983 the firm realized that its difficulties were structural and that more than 10 percent of its employees were superfluous. In order to cut jobs in its main operations yet uphold its practice of permanent employment, the firm established a number of subsidiaries.

Kubota did not diversify because it saw new business opportunities. It diversified because subsidiaries would absorb excess labor. Like Kubota, many Japanese companies are now looking at new fields of business. Sometimes these fields are ones in which the companies have little direct experience. Brother Industries, Riccar's competitor in the sewing machine business, foresaw the decline of its main line of business and is moving successfully into office products. Whether other Japanese companies will be successful in their diversification moves is still an open question.

A Case Study: Seiko Instruments & Electronics ·

Seiko Instruments & Electronics, one of two watch manufacturing firms within the Seiko group, has undertaken an aggressive diversification strategy. The essence of the project is to quadruple the nominal revenue of the firm in 10 years—from approximately 400 million dollars in 1980 to over 1.6 billion dollars in 1990. The firm plans for half of 1990 revenue to come from products other than watches, although such products accounted for less than 10 percent of the firm's total revenue as recently as 1980. New business development is being pursued in three major areas: industrial electronics, scientific instruments, and precision machine tools. If the project is successful Seiko Instruments & Electronics (formerly known as Daini Seikosha) will become an electronics firm with strength in precision mechanics.

The declared purpose of the project is to chart a path for growth. While this is accurate, the planning process itself reveals that more was involved. The project team determined that the watch business could at most double by 1990 and that this would not be large enough to maintain employment at the 1980 level. They calculated that the firm would need revenues of approximately 1.3 billion dollars in order to maintain employment. They called this revenue the "survival line." Allowing some minimum employment growth in order to maintain the "health of the organization," they came up with the target revenue level of 1.6 billion dollars.

As this project proceeds, personnel must shift from the watch business to new businesses, from mechanics to electronics, and, most important, from engineering and manufacturing to sales and marketing. These shifts are being facilitated by various forms of educational programs and internal publicity.

The Seiko diversification project is indicative of strategic planning in Japan in several ways. First, the ultimate objective is survival of the firm without reducing employment. The revenue growth target is a means to achieve the objective rather than the objective itself.

Second, despite very aggressive goals for revenue and diversity of business mix, no acquisitions or mergers are planned. This would violate the conception of corporate community and its contribution to employment would be minimal.

Third, Seiko's plan sacrifices short-term profitability for a long-term goal. Ichiro Hattori, the president of the firm, admits that the new businesses are not profitable yet. It is his opinion, and he is undoubtedly correct, that Japanese firms have more flexibility than American firms in formulating long-term strategy because they are less subject to pressure from shareholders.

Participative Decision Making

One of the most important characteristics of corporate planning in Japan is the depth and breadth of involvement by employees in the decision-making process. Various adjectives have been used to explain the process—participative, collective, bottom-up, and so on—but each refers simply to the fact that all members who are influenced by a decision actively participate in making the decision. As will be described later, top management's role in decision making is increasing in Japan, especially in key strategic issues. However, for routine matters, including fairly important issues, a standard participative decision-making process is followed in most firms.

This process involves two stages: first, building a consensus through informal discussion, negotiation, and consultation, and second, circulating a

EXHIBIT 7-1   Typical Japanese Consensus-Building Process

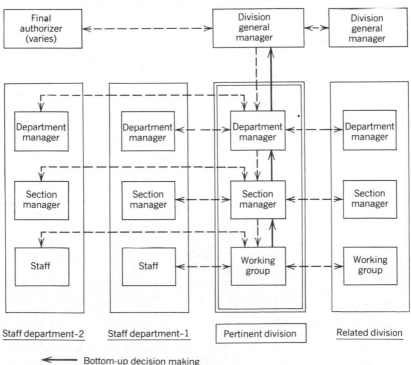

document for stamps of formal approval. The process of building consensus is highly complex, as Exhibit 7-1 suggests. Usually in this process the task of generating alternatives is given to a working group of young members, sometimes with the guidance of a section manager (*kacho*). Discussions, negotiations, and consultations take place informally among all the members related to the decision, including the department manager (*bucho*), division general manager (*jigyo-bucho* or *hon-bucho*), staff departments, and sometimes other business line departments.

Once consensus has been achieved, the so-called *ringi* procedure begins. It substitutes for a formal discussion meeting. Each participant in the process puts the seal (equivalent of signature) on a form to confirm the agreement (see Exhibit 7-2). It is not unusual to see 20 or 30 seals on a completed *ringi* form. Since great effort has been devoted to developing a consensus, decisions are rarely changed during or after the formal *ringi* procedure.

This decision-making process, from informal consensus building to formal approval, can consume a great deal of time. It is not well-suited to strategic issues, in which time may be of the essence. Organizations may miss opportunities to enter new markets, form promising joint ventures, or make other strategic moves. Moreover, a decision reached by consensus may not be the right one because it requires the agreement of middle managers who are caught up in routine tasks and may not possess the broad view necessary to make proper strategic judgments.

EXHIBIT 7-2   Typical Ringi Approval Procedure

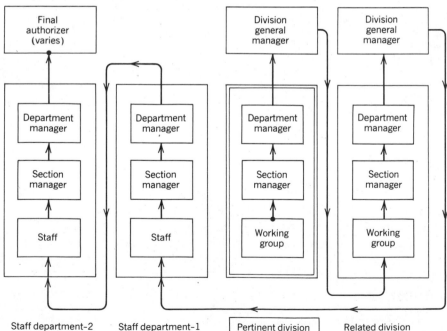

However, the participative process does have one overriding virtue. Because the process involves all the members concerned, and because a deep-level agreement is obtained, at the end of the decision-making process the entire organization is prepared to implement full speed ahead. This has brought about many successes, and successes have bred legitimacy for the process. In Japan it must be honored, even in the breach.

HOW STRATEGIC PLANNING IN JAPAN IS CHANGING

From the end of World War II until about the time of the first oil shock in 1973, Japan was a late-developing country trying to catch up to the advanced industrial economies in the West. During that time Japanese corporations could plan with the advantage of the latecomer. By studying industries in the advanced West, they could gain insight into the future structure of their own economy, the shape of future demand, and the costs and efficiencies of various technologies. Also, a hodgepodge of quotas, tariffs, and restrictions on foreign investment protected them against the vagaries of foreign competition. In this environment, the uncertainties of planning in Japan were fewer than those faced by contemporary planners in the West, or by corporate planners in Japan today. Implementation, however, was crucial, and the participative style of planning served Japanese corporations very well.

But the 1970s brought great change. Japan's corporations advanced to the front ranks of world competition, leaving their follower status behind. The Japanese government opened domestic markets. Oil shocks sent the economy reeling. And real economic growth, which had averaged over 10 percent per annum throughout the 1960s, dipped to 5.2 percent in the seventies. Now, in the decade of the 1980s, it is running at 3 to 4 percent.

Changes in Employment

The new environment is forcing changes and hard hit, it appears, will be Japanese employment practices. While high growth was the rule, Japanese corporations were able to maintain a pyramid structure of employment with large numbers of new recruits at the base and increasingly fewer numbers of older employees up through the levels of authority within the organization. So long as corporations were growing, they needed to increase the employee base and could not afford to lose any existing employees. Quantity was important, and they secured it by fostering employee loyalty through permanent employment and the seniority system. This meant that occasionally they had to pay the cost of not having the right people in the right positions, but the cost was seldom severe and growth masked the problem.

Now, however, many large firms have cut back hiring because they project low growth. The reductions in hiring mean that these corporations are unable to maintain the pyramid. This, in turn, means that many middle-aged employees have no one to manage and hence are left waiting for promotion. This is happening in many corporations and it will surely erode employee loyalty in Japan.

Also, many firms are finding that they have trained generalists but that they need specialists in today's business environment. As a result, for the first time some are hiring to obtain specific skills in fields like international business, bioengineering, microelectronics, software, and finance, to name but a few. The companies most in need of these skills are Japan's new venture businesses, like Sord in microcomputers. But even some of Japan's most conservative companies are beginning to source skills externally. Moreover, there are examples of employers today who believe that bringing in outside people can "revitalize" their organizations.

There are other signs of change on Japan's employment scene. Executive recruiting, a most un-Japanese practice recently introduced to Japan by U.S. firms, has thrived, and Japanese companies themselves are belatedly entering the field. Also, with increasing frequency employees are rejecting their companies' requests for relocation, especially overseas.

In essence, then, employees in Japan are beginning to pay less heed to their assumed obligation to work for a single company for life, and so too are companies beginning to pay less heed to the elaborate expectations that have surrounded employment in Japan. This suggests that worker productivity may become a problem in the future, and it suggests that options for Japan's strategic planners may increase.

Changing Attitudes toward Buying and Selling Businesses

There are ample signs that the taboo in Japan against mergers and acquisitions is beginning to weaken. In July, 1984, Nomura Securities, Japan's largest securities firm, sent a ripple of concern through the world of Japanese business when it announced the formation of a department to provide assistance in mergers and acquisitions. Although Nomura stated that it was "not looking at major short-term business opportunities," it was clear that Nomura did expect an increase in business combination activities among Japanese corporations in the long run.

Another sign of change is the appearance of strategically inspired merger and acquisition activity in Japan. Kyocera Corporation, for example, has been active in this area. It made its first major domestic acquisition in 1979 when it acquired Cybernet Electronics, a leading CB radio manufacturer. Then, in October 1983, Kyocera caused a sensation by merging with Yashica Camera. These actions were made possible by troubles at Cybernet and Yashica, but in neither case was the strong partner (Kyocera) a firm with historical ties to the troubled firms, as is usually the case in corporate rescues in Japan. Kyocera's actions were calculated, opportunistic moves designed to broaden its technical expertise in electronics and precision manufacturing.

This style of merger and acquisition is relatively new in Japan, but it appears to be becoming more common.

Japanese companies are gaining experience in acquisitions through their operations overseas. For example, in recent years Fuji Bank has acquired several American financial firms and Mitsubishi Bank has purchased the Bank of California. Sumitomo Rubber purchased four of Dunlop's tire plants in Europe in September 1984. Kyocera has also been active in international merger and acquisition activities.

At the same time, several Japanese industries are ripe for acquisition, especially by foreign firms. The Japanese pharmaceutical industry, for example, is volatile and vulnerable as a result of sweeping changes in the government's medical reimbursement system. Already Merck has absorbed Banyu, and it is an open secret that other foreign pharmaceutical firms are seeking to match Merck's access to the Japanese marketplace through acquisitions of their own. Another industry ripe for change is banking and financial services, in which projected liberalization is expected to increase the attractiveness of the Japanese marketplace to foreign firms. Several attempts have already been made by American banks to acquire Japanese financial institutions, though none has yet succeeded. Another potential target is the Japanese automobile industry. Major U.S. auto makers already own large shares of Isuzu, Suzuki, Mazda, and Mitsubishi Motors.

In sum, the Japanese taboo against mergers and acquisitions is beginning to break down. Although few observers believe that firms will ever be bought and sold as readily in Japan as in the United States, it seems clear that in the future Japanese corporate planners will have increasingly more room to maneuver.

Changes in Decision Making

The new environment is also militating changes in corporate decision making. It is said in Japan that the present is the age of uncertainty: uncertainty about the future of the corporation, uncertainty about one's career opportunity, and uncertainty about social values. In business this mood has led to many calls for leadership. Men like Akio Morita of Sony, Konosuke Matsushita of Matsushita Electric, and Seiemon Inaba of Fanuc are frequently held up as examples of the kinds of business leaders Japan needs today. In a late-1984 world survey of senior executives conducted by Booz, Allen & Hamilton, the management consulting firm, and the *Nihon Keizai Shimbun,* Japan's leading business daily, 62 percent of Japanese respondents indicated that the successful corporate executive of the future will be a top-down manager, not one who seeks the participation of lower-level employees.

Japanese firms do not always depend on bottom-up decision making. There are so-called top matters that are decided by a single leader or small number of senior leaders. Top matters are typically the big issues that require secrecy at the planning stage, or potentially decisive issues that call for strong leadership. They include organizational changes, senior personnel transfers, and sometimes new business development.

The balance of top-down versus bottom-up decision making varies from firm to firm. Some companies that are noted for strong top management leadership include Sony, Matsushita Electric, Kyocera, Fanuc, Casio Computer, Toyota Motors, Sumitomo Bank, Suntory, Ohtsuka Pharmaceutical, and Computer Services Corporation (CSK), to mention a few. These firms are also known as very high performers. On the other hand, firms like the Mitsui and Mitsubishi companies, which have roots in the financial cartels of prewar Japan, usually depend more on bottom-up decision making.

MITI has traced the relative frequency of top management styles in Japan for over a decade. For their surveys they defined three categories of decision-making style:

1. President makes decisions, with the approval of key board members
2. Extensive participation by board members, but final decisions made by the president
3. Board members reach decisions collectively, with the president co-ordinating the process

According to the survey, the second category has long been the most prevalent style in Japan and has been increasing its percentage (see Exhibit 7-3). On the other hand, the firms with strong leadership from their presidents have been performing better than other firms (see Exhibit 7-4).

EXHIBIT 7-3   Top Management Decision-Making Style

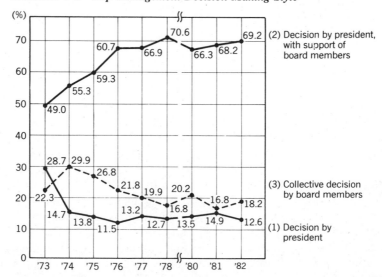

Source: Sōgō Keieiryoku Shihyō (Corporate Management Capabilities), Ministry of International Trade and Industry. Note that no data are available for 1979.

EXHIBIT 7-4   Relative Performance by Decision-Making Style

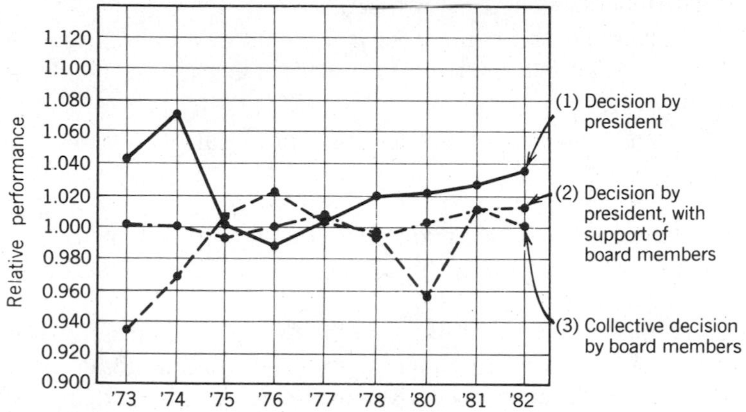

Source: *Sōgō Keieiryoku Shihyō* (Corporate Management Capabilities), Ministry of International Trade and Industry. Note that no data are available for 1979. Performance = growth + profitability. MITI constructed the performance index by assigning points for growth in revenue and improvement in return on assets relative to the results of other companies.

The reasons behind the current interest in leadership in Japanese business are relatively easily understood. In the face of rapid environmental changes, especially in technological fields, quick response is vital. There are many occasions in which firms cannot afford to wait for a consensus to develop before taking action. Moreover, the slowdown in the growth of base businesses in many firms is forcing them to try new approaches: new products, new markets, new partners, new organizations, and so forth. While the Japanese participative approach can work effectively to eliminate problems and reach solutions with which a majority of the members can feel comfortable, it is usually not effective for generating creative solutions. Even if a creative idea is proposed by one member, it is very likely to be either rejected or "corrected" by members who consider it drastic or eccentric. Japanese businessmen are coming to recognize this, hence the calls for stronger top-management leadership.

But even though the need for strong leadership is widely perceived, the ethic of participative decision making persists and resistance to strong leadership runs deep. A forceful leader in Japan runs considerable risk of being considered autocratic and domineering. Even when the need to take firm action is readily apparent to all in the organization, a direct top-down order will not be welcomed at the lower levels. Therefore top management has to respect the forms of the traditional decision-making process in order to lead effectively. Usually this is accomplished in the following manner:

1. A senior manager communicates with the group (department or division) that he considers most closely related to the decision to be made and he lets the group generate basic ideas as if those ideas were

   initiated by the group itself. At this stage, the top manager gives only
   directional guidance, not details.

2. The group takes the initiative in developing a consensus, sometimes
    among senior management only, sometimes among middle and lower
    management as well.

3. The senior manager approves the "proposal" that comes out of the
    consensus process.

In this procedure, the senior manager actually approves his own decision,
although it comes back to him in concrete form, usually accompanied by
detailed plans.

To carry this off successfully, it helps to enjoy the trust of lower-level
employees, and one way to generate trust is informal contact. More and
more in recent years senior executives in Japan are striving to open channels
of informal communication. Yoshio Yokoyama, president of Calpis Food
Industry, has regular luncheon and breakfast meetings with lower-level employees. Keizo Saji, president of Suntory, takes employees to bars for informal conversation. Isao Ohkawa of CSK is famous for fostering close relationships with employees by drinking and singing with them. According
to the MITI survey cited earlier, 60.5 percent of the firms responding have
some kind of regular informal meetings between the president and managers,
and the performance of these firms tends to be better than that of firms
without the meetings.

The Seiko example cited previously illustrates how Japanese executives
carry out top-down management in the Japanese context. Company president
Hattori initiated the diversification project in the spring of 1978 by contacting
the corporate planning office. He refers to this as "triggering" the planning,
and he considers triggering an important part of his role as president. Once
the planning staff had completed its basic analysis the main ideas were communicated to the senior executives group in the summer of 1979. Another
year was spent at this level discussing realistic approaches to the goal generated by the planning office. In the summer of 1980, upon Hattori's approval,
the project was "kicked off" and communicated to middle management.

In this case, despite strong presidential leadership, it took the firm two
years to move from inception of planning to announcement of the project.
Hattori believes, however, that it would have taken much longer to start
such a major program had he not "triggered" it.

The role of top management in Japan is becoming increasingly important.
Top management leadership can work effectively in Japanese firms, provided
the ethic of participative decision making is respected and provided the proper
supportive culture exists.

CONCLUSION

In Japan strategic issues are usually not singled out as such for special treatment but are handled within the context of the overall participative decision-making process. Planners are involved in this process, but they are regular managers assigned to planning departments, not the trained, professional strategic planners who often work in these departments in the West.

The Japanese style of planning is closely linked to implementation. It is also strongly influenced by the values embedded in the Japanese conception of a corporation, in the system of lifetime employment, and in the seniority system. These values make maintenance of employment an important strategic objective. They also limit strategic moves such as diversification, merger, acquisition, reduction in capacity, liquidation, and divestiture.

However, the advance of many Japanese industries and the onset of lower economic growth are altering the context of strategic planning in Japan. They are beginning to erode the values that surround the employment system, and this will increase the ability of corporations to make strategic moves. They are also placing a premium on strong leadership. In the future, Japanese corporations will become quicker in actions, more capable of embarking on new courses, more profit-conscious, and less growth-oriented.

Japanese corporations have finished the first round of international competition, and some of them did very well. But in the second round they will have to compete in a different environment. No longer will the future be laid out for them in the modern economies of the West. Strategic planning and leadership will take on much greater importance. Japanese corporations have already started the adjustment, but how successful they will be remains to be seen.

3

IMPLEMENTATION

CHAPTER 8

Making Plans Work: Administering and Controlling Strategic Plans

GEORGE C. SAWYER

GEORGE C. SAWYER is president of Management Technology & Resources, consultants in business growth, planning, and corporate strategy, and a professor in the Administration and Management area, Economics Department, City College of New York. Formerly Director of Corporate Planning and also of Commercial Technology Management for Hoffmann-La Roche, he is president of the Foundation for Administrative Research and a past president of the New York chapter of the North American Society for Corporate Planning. Dr. Sawyer is a member of the Society for Long Range Planning, Planning Executives Institute, senior editor of *Planning Review,* and a licensed Professional Engineer. Dr. Sawyer's bachelor's and master's degrees in chemical engineering are from the University of Wisconsin; his M.B.A. and Ph.D. in management are from the New York University Graduate School of Business Administration. He has written a variety of journal articles drawn from experience including venture analysis, commercial development, acquisition, and line management assignments with various corporations. His book *Business and Society: Managing Corporate Social Impact* was published in 1979, *The Quiet Crisis of Public Pensions* in 1980, and *Corporate Planning as a Creative Process* in 1982; *Business and Its Environment* and *Designing Strategy* are his most recent books.

OUTLINE

In order to help you appreciate the problems that can be created in the administering and controlling of strategic plans, this chapter begins with a simple scenario that actually occurs frequently. It's late Friday afternoon and the phone rings. It's your boss. He congratulates you because the plan your group spent four hard hours explaining to top management just got final approval. You had put your best efforts into getting that plan approved, and the staff involved had worked hard putting it together. You call them to pass on the good news and then lock your desk, sweeping the remaining papers into your briefcase. During the drive home you enjoy a warm feeling of accomplishment.

Monday morning you pick up the plan, but the glow is gone. Now it is a performance contract with top management, accepted only after your own strong endorsement. You realize, "And now we—*I*—have to deliver. . . ."

The issue is simple. You need to watch over the action as this plan turns into reality, to be sure that nothing goes astray. How to do it? This chapter addresses that question, and is directed toward those individuals engaged in bringing a plan to life. This includes the executive who is responsible for the manager and group who must deliver the results promised in the plan, the planning or other staff person who is assigned to aid in following plan progress, and the leader and the various members of the planning team.

TAKING CONTROL

Nobody would make a bad plan on purpose; it happens only by mistake. But there are many bad plans, and in each case the mistakes would have been corrected if any of the key people had noticed them. Strategic blindness is a major problem; preoccupation with immediate problems obscures strategic factors and blunders result.[1] At the moment of completion every plan is, according to the group that just finished it, the best plan that ever was. Yet many plans are flawed, and if they fail in execution, this is bad for companies and for the careers of the responsible executives.

An obvious cure is to make plans better in the first place; the earlier chapters of this handbook deal with that process.[2] But here we are dealing with a later stage; in one way or another a plan has been made and approved, and you are responsible or share responsibility for the outcome as the group begins to push buttons and levers and to try to achieve what that plan promised. How can you keep control over this process? How can you make sure that the Plan succeeds?

Rather than worry, act. The following is a checklist to guide that action:

Checklist 1

1. Establish a plan control framework and fill any gaps.
2. Reevaluate from where you are; be sure the plan makes sense.
3. Act as necessary to keep the plan on schedule.
4. If budgets or schedules must be allowed to slip, review the strategy.
5. Rebuild the plan if that is the only way to make it work.
6. Keep the plan pointed at its intended targets even as they move; avoid strategic blindness.

The first step in the checklist is to establish a plan control framework. This step has a checklist of its own, as follows:

Checklist 2

1. Detail the action and fill gaps.
2. Make a control chart (PERT).
3. Polish up the logic.
4. List dependencies.
5. Establish routine reporting.

Once again, the first step of this checklist, detailing the action and filling gaps, has a checklist of its own:

Checklist 3

1. With the help of those who must make them work, list the mission, goals, and strategies.

   Establish the intended domain of action (by area and by timetable).

   List the goals in clear and tangible terms.

   List statements of the strategy and specific substrategies, functional strategies, and unit strategies. In case of omissions note them and add a statement of the strategy implied or required by the plan.

2. List the plan control structure and checkpoints, the projected time and cost for achieving each, and the name of the person undertaking this responsibility.

3. Fill any gaps in the control structure.

   Add checkpoints as necessary.

   Ask those responsible for the action how they would prefer to have their performance measured.

MISSION, GOALS, AND STRATEGY

The first step is to find the plan's mission, goals, and strategy.

Mission

The mission defines the social role the business seeks to fill, but a business may not attempt complete fulfillment of its mission immediately. To follow the progress of the plan the key element is an understanding of the desired *domain* of that business; within the territory suggested by its mission, in what specific business areas will the business become active during the span of this plan, and when will activity begin in each?[3]

Goals

What are the specific achievements being attempted in this plan? How will we know that they are achieved? How clear-cut and measureable are the end results? What subgoals and contributing functional goals can be defined to aid in obtaining and measuring progress?

Strategy

The plan should be based on an explicit strategy; this strategy should be detailed in its different aspects and supported by functional strategies as appropriate. List the relevant strategies; in case of omissions, add the implicit strategy required by the action sequence, preferably with the help of those who must make it work. The purpose is a sharpened concept of the required action as a basis for the required plan oversight.

LIST THE PLAN CONTROL STRUCTURE

Find the subdivisions of the plan's action requirements. Most plans have several separate programs of action that move independently. Each should have checkpoints for its progress—find them.

From the detailing of the mission, goals, and strategy a framework should be quite clear and should be used for control structure based on the series of action programs. Each program needs checkpoints that are frequent enough so that it can be tracked effectively.

FILL ANY GAPS IN THE CONTROL STRUCTURE

If the plan was built without a control structure, add it. Or, if there were gaps in the control structure, fill them in. The objective is to develop a clear and comprehensive set of action steps and checkpoints. Every checkpoint should be specific as to time, cost to that point, and achievement expected. Every significant action should be the assigned responsibility of a specific person.

This is an opportunity for participation of all of the managers and others who have specific responsibilities to fulfill. Everyone should be measured by the checkpoints and should have an opportunity to suggest the appropriate measures. This is much like management by objectives, by which each sets his or her own goals, but includes an added interaction with the others who share the task of making the plan work and who want everyone to contribute fully and be measured fairly.

When the control structure is completed, this will also complete checklist 3. As Exhibit 8-1 shows, checklist 3 aids in detailing the action and filling

EXHIBIT 8-1   Checklist 3 Feeds Checklists 2 and 1

Checklist 1	Checklist 2	Checklist 3
Plan control framework	Detail action	Mission, goals, strategy
Reevaluate	Make control chart	List control structure
Act as necessary	Polish logic	Fill gaps
Review strategy	List dependencies	
Rebuild if necessary	Routine reporting	
Keep on target		

gaps, the first point from checklist 2, moving discussion to the making of a control chart, the second point on that checklist.

MAKE A CONTROL CHART

Once a plan has a clear control structure, this can be used to make a control chart. A suitable control chart will greatly aid in following the plan's progress. A simple CPM (critical path method) chart will be adequate for many plans; this may be expanded into PERT (project evaluation and review technique) to give a more detailed control perspective. Steiner gives a good summary of CPM and PERT techniques, as well as a summary of the incorporation of multiple cost estimates and other related information.[4]

Most plans have more than one program. That is, more than one activity must be carried out simultaneously in order for the plan to succeed in the allotted time. In defining the plan control structure, each of these programs has been detailed into a sequence of checkpoints. The idea is to lay out this pattern of checkpoints and responsibilities in a network and use it for control. Exhibit 8-2 shows a simple CPM chart of this type.

Exhibit 8-2 is based on a plan requiring that development of a new product first be completed. Then, while government approval to market the product is being sought, a plant to produce it is to be designed and built, a marketing organization created, and a sales force hired and trained. When the product

EXHIBIT 8-2   A Simple CPM Chart for a New Product Plan

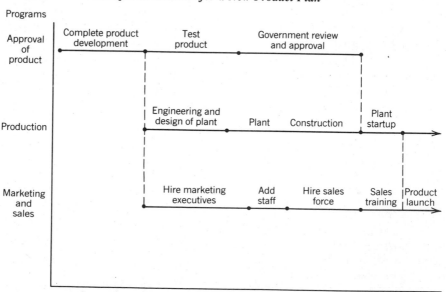

is approved, the plant will start up; when sufficient stocks have been accumulated, the product will be launched into the market. Exhibit 8-2 shows three parallel programs of activity—one for approval of the product, one for its production, and one for the marketing and sales effort. It also shows that the company is planning to gamble capital and expense money by building a plant and a marketing force before the product is approved but is not planning to risk the additional investment of actually manufacturing inventory for sale prior to that approval.

The value of the chart is in showing the parallel paths and the interrelationships they have. For instance, the plant design is not planned to start until development of the product is complete, in case of changes in the necessary production process.

In the PERT expansion of the CPM network, three time estimates are made for each step—a normal estimate, an optimistic one ("if everything goes right"), and a pessimistic one ("if everything goes wrong"). Then, aided by a widely available computer program, the network can be analyzed to determine the critical path, the expected time to completion, the standard deviation of the time estimates, and alternatives for speeding up the process. The example in Exhibit 8-2 is simple and would hardly require computer analysis, but actual networks usually get more complex after all of the interrelationships between the programs are defined.

Cost estimates can be built into the PERT system for more detailed control, and this is often useful. However, the level of detail suitable for control over any specific plan depends on its nature and the circumstances. The purpose is to maintain an adequate knowledge of what is going on, with minimum extra effort and expense, as the plan is brought to life. This includes a full understanding of the linkage between the accomplishments or delays in the different program streams.

A good control chart can assist the manager in getting and keeping this degree of control. Along with reports that will keep him or her fully informed on progress or problems in meeting the time and cost objectives established for each checkpoint, a CPM or PERT chart can be used as the basis for following the plan progress.

POLISH THE LOGIC

If a plan was put together and approved without a complete analysis of the components of the required action, including target date, cost at each checkpoint, and responsibility for each step, this detail when developed afterward will likely bring surprises. Plans assembled casually often have flaws in their schedules, such as actions dependent on information not yet available or actions not possible within the allotted time.

Flaws that come to light require prompt correction. Either (a) find a way to get back on schedule and/or budget, or (b) tell your management that the plan schedules cannot be met. Management does not like to receive this sort of report, but it is worse to report a disaster or major slippage a year later.

LIST DEPENDENCIES

All plans contain a series of assumptions, and these may control the possibility of achieving any specific plan. A start on making a plan work includes a full understanding of the sorts of assumptions on which it is dependent. These range from the assumption that top management will approve the capital appropriations on which an approved plan is based, to the expected interest costs and rate of market growth the next year. These dependencies are summarized in the following list:

1. **Internal approvals needed**
   Capital appropriations?
   Approvals to hire people?
2. **Shared resources**
   Sales Time?
   Key staff services?
   Production facilities?
   Shared distribution?
   Time on key equipment?
3. **Outside approvals needed**
   Regulatory?
   Environmental?
   Import licenses?
4. **Key assumptions/states of nature**
   Interest rates?
   Inflation?
   Exchange rates?
   Competition?
   Prosperity/recession?

Internal Approvals

What resources are required and where will they come from? Are there potential barriers, such as a watchdog vice president who feels obliged to veto all new hiring plans? Are there additional internal approvals (e.g., necessary capital appropriations) to be gained? Are there potential problems or delays? Who is responsible for gaining each approval?

In many firms the approval of a plan is just that: a serious, considered top-management approval of a *document*. A document is only paper; but the action commitment of a plan requires use of resources. If the approval of a plan does not in itself give that firm's approval of the needed resources, then the responsible managers must follow the routine capital, expense, and personnel budgeting procedures, requesting the necessary elements through the channel appropriate for each, and attempting to gain such approvals in a timely fashion so that the program and performance commitments in the plan can be fulfilled.

To approve a plan and accept it as an action commitment from the responsible managers without giving approval of necessary resources is a serious violation of unity of command. It puts these managers in the position of responsibility for actions they have not been given sufficient authority to execute. Nonetheless, this is a frequent situation. A key element in the control structure for a plan is surveillance over requests for key resources; intervention by higher levels of management is often required in order to obtain resource approvals consistent with fulfillment of plan commitments.

Plan commitments should not be used as a means of bypassing the internal rationing and control over use of resources. However, representatives of the financial function almost invariably participate in plan drafting and review. No doubtful resource requests should be included in a plan in the first place, and opportunities to seek their modification or to protest their inclusion in a plan should be more than adequate to prevent abuses of the system.

Shared Resource Control

Does your plan require any use of shared resources? If so, how is the allocation controlled, and by whom? Is there any potential jeopardy to the plan?

Many companies find it economical to share key resources between different business elements. Just as one oil refinery produces products for many markets, a key press machine or other large piece of capital equipment may serve several processes, and a research group may carry out projects with potential in several different markets. This sharing is often necessary, but it puts the sharing businesses in a position of dependency on resources they may not control.

In one company top management turned down a proposal that a particular business organize its own sales force, suggesting instead that it obtain sales time from a much larger sister division that contacted the same customers. However, just as the smaller division launched the major new effort on which its future depended, the larger division ran into sudden trouble with the company's most profitable product. Solving this problem became everyone's priority for several months. The smaller division's product launch failed dramatically because of the total absence of sales support.

Of course, no one planned on such a disaster in the marketplace, but every dependence on resources controlled by someone else carries the risk of some event's interfering with the resource allocation. A proper and logical part of a plan control structure includes recognition of such dependencies, together with an analysis of the way in which this resource control could be affected by unexpected events.

Outside Approvals

Special attention is required where the schedule of the plan assumes control over semicontrollable or noncontrollable elements (e.g., approvals by government agencies). The only degree of control is in knowing the approval process and in timely and effective application, but the ultimate timing and fact of approval is often based partly on factors internal to the agency or growing out of the public and political processes of the time. Such approvals and their schedules should be noted in the plan.

However, this qualification should not itself become an excuse for delay because innovative approaches to fulfilling regulatory requirements are often possible. Large differences in the regulatory approval experience of different companies are at least partly due to differences in the effectiveness and skill of their staffs; there is a premium on approaching the problem correctly. A regulatory or other external approval becomes a special challenge and often requires special effort in order to be obtained on the necessary time schedule.

The Economy and Other State-of-Nature Problems

Every plan is based on certain assumptions; some list them as premises. In the case of a specific plan what are those assumptions? Are they wise? How much shift in external variables would put the plan in trouble?

A manager planning the introduction of new products bases the sales and profit forecasts on some estimate of the overall market. Is the estimate reasonable? Is it vulnerable to upset? Many rubber industry suppliers were taken by surprise when the U.S. tire industry effectively shrank to half its former sales volume in the shift to longer-lasting radial tires. Several industries that had correctly anticipated a business downturn in 1980 were caught by surprise by the briefness of the recovery and found themselves in difficulty when the recession of 1982 followed so quickly.

Any plan is built on a series of state-of-nature assumptions about the economy, the markets, the actions of competitors, development of new technologies, and other important but essentially noncontrollable variables. In establishing a control pattern for a plan, and in attempting to guide its managers to success, it is important to recognize the extent and sensitivity of the assumptions about external variables that are built into the plan.

ESTABLISH ROUTINE REPORTING

A detailed control structure, and a control chart presenting the relationships contained in the structure, will lay the groundwork for careful, routine fol-

EXHIBIT 8-3   Checklist 2 Feeds 1

Checklist 1	Checklist 2
Plan control framework	Detail action
Reevaluate	Make control chart
Act as necessary	Polish logic
Review strategy	List dependencies
Rebuild if neessary	Routine reporting
Keep on target	

lowing of plan progress. Still missing is the routine flow of information required as the business operates and as progress on the plan occurs from day to day.

Some managers will already have an adequate flow of accurate and timely information, but an ambitious plan or one that must overcome significant obstacles usually faces problems not covered in the daily information flow. In any case, a part of establishing control over a plan is to survey the information needs, to determine where that information can be obtained, and to establish the necessary pattern of reporting.

One approach is to ask the subordinates responsible for each plan step how they would prefer to keep you up-to-date with their progress. Giving them a chance to make suggestions could add to the efficiency of the control process and will increase their awareness of your need to be kept fully informed. In any case, decide on the information you need, arrange for its reporting, and start the process in motion. The plan is moving to action, and your control process should be moving also.

This discussion of information flows is the final step in checklist 2. As Exhibit 8-3 shows, this brings the discussion to a reevaluation of the plan and its schedule, the second point on checklist 1.

REEVALUATE: BE SURE THE PLAN MAKES SENSE

Second Thoughts on Strategy and Plan Quality

By this point the quality of the plan and of the thinking that went into it should be much clearer. An additional searching analysis will usually turn up a point or two that needed more attention initially, but the real concern is with larger problems. As mentioned earlier, strategic blindness often causes busy managers to overlook external factors completely obvious to an outside observer. Sometimes such an omission underlies a plan strategy; the earlier in the action process that such a problem can be brought to light the less likely that the oversight will prove fatal.

Therefore at this point in the analysis of a plan it is wise to stop and review its construction, to judge its quality, and to see if there are signs of strategic blindness or of the sort of preoccupation with the routine and the familiar that usually accompanies it.

Risks of Accident or Misfortune

What if a key person were killed in a traffic accident or some other unfortunate event were to occur? Few companies had any rule about how many executives could fly together until Texas Gulf lost a planeload of its top management. Often the dependence of a program on any one person can be reduced somewhat by a little forethought.

Define Your Default Options

What could you do if the progress toward the goals of the plan begins to lag; or if the cost of maintaining an acceptable rate of progress begins to rise unreasonably? Actual decisions should wait on specific events, but a general survey of the available choices is a part of sound plan-control philosophy. The programming analogy is that of default options, where certain sorts of failures bring a preselected response unless someone intervenes and redirects the action. A degree of the same sort of preprogramming is a wise addition to plan control.

Define Time/Cost Tradeoff Boundaries

The plight of several utilities grew worse in relatively small increments as nuclear plant construction lagged behind schedule and costs overran budget after budget. Had the executives controlling the flow of those plans preselected default options, it seems likely that they might have triggered a basic review of the strategy and its financing many billions of dollars and several years earlier in the expense overrun.

Instead several of these companies seem to have struck doggedly to the initial construction plan until every possibility of further financing was exhausted. The result was a major waste of construction resources followed by a public policy dilemma between allowing bankruptcy to wipe out the stockholdings and bondholdings (the traditional reward of mismanagement) and creating public subsidies for private business mistakes.

Summary: Define the Limits of the Strategy

To avoid the trap of holding doggedly to a strategy for too long, you should define review-of-strategy thresholds in advance. Look over your plan, analyze its likely pattern of progress, and define a series of default options, which are things you could do to overcome specific problems and regain the schedule.

Drive hard to keep the plan on schedule, but think also about the management options available in case of trouble and about ways of reducing the vulnerability of the program to accidental events. Also consider the risk that the operating concentration on plan control will recreate the hazard of strategic blindness; success may require a sensitive redirection of effort as external conditions shift.

ACT TO KEEP THE PLAN ON SCHEDULE

Show a continuing interest; everyone involved should know that the plan is important, that its timely accomplishment is an urgent priority, and that you are giving this your personal attention.

Meeting Checkpoints

When a checkpoint is missed in terms of time or cost find out why, ask questions until you understand the significance of the miss for the total schedule, and take appropriate action. In any CPM or PERT chart some sequences control and others have slack. Often a failure at one point can be regained at another point.

Overall the plan should stay on cost and on schedule. If it cannot, the slippages may require incremental strategy changes. Any strategy is based on certain costs and payoffs achieved within a certain time, and a slippage is a challenge to its viability. A strategy also depends on outside conditions that may shift with time. Within reason, prompt corrective action should be taken to bring the plan back to budget and schedule.

Repair

The first group of alternatives for an off-schedule plan includes assignment of additional resources and replacement of the managers responsible for the slippage. More fundamental action is necessary when the cause of the slippage is more basic to the project—if a flaw in an assumption comes to light or if a new product or service loses its promise as development continues.

Retreat

If you can't keep the plan on schedule, or if a program can no longer reach the desired targets, notify the boss. No one wants to retreat, but at the point where the frank and honest outlook is for failure, the quicker the higher-ups are faced with the bitter news the less severe the ultimate repercussions are likely to be. But don't be too quick to give up; first consider rebuilding the plan.

Rebuilding

Modify the plan so it will work. Why give up, just because the initial plan and its action sequence won't play through the way they were written? Assuming that the basic concept is still sound, why not make it work anyway? Techniques for rebuilding a faltering plan are discussed in the next section.

REBUILDING A TROUBLED PLAN

If a plan won't work because of an omission or breakdown in the original schedules or assumptions, and if it still seems basically sound in concept, rebuild it into a plan that *will* work.

Alternate Schedules and Equipment

A frequent cause of plan failure is bad scheduling or schedules lost by troubles at some earlier stage. Why not gain back the time? Can the plan goals be achieved in some other way? The PERT or CPM chart can aid in discovering alternatives. How about more and different equipment, other vendors, subcontracting, use of overtime, and so on?

Replace Lost People or Opportunities

Plans often get into trouble when key people are lost to the project for any reason or when specific opportunities fail to materialize. A plan for a new business may have been based on acquisition of a small company, and then it turned out that the candidate had toxic waste troubles or a balance sheet with massive continent liabilities. What other candidates are there, and what would the schedule look like if you had to turn aside and find another company to acquire?

In the same way, meet any threat to the schedule as a challenge; the result is still the same if reached by another route. Plan changes only bring extra hazard if made in too much haste, but present no more difficulty than any other management decision if approached in an orderly manner.

Replace Lost/Discredited Products and Ideas

The managers handling the action programs also have options to replace lost and discredited products and ideas with other, better ones. The replacement process may represent a scheduling disadvantage because time is usually lost when a product must be abandoned. Sometimes there are alternative products in sight, or perhaps they can be licensed from another company or another country.

Invent New Solutions to Problems

When a failure threatens the completion of a program consider inventing a better solution to the problem and going ahead full steam. This sounds ambitious, and it is. But it has been done before. Human creative processes are only partially understood, but the catalysis of a pressure situation can, with good leadership, bring surprisingly good ideas out of a group.

This is the domain of programmed innovation—an art more managers need to practice. Brainstorming is a familiar beginning, but this is only one of a large family of techniques a skilled group leader can invoke to help a group tap its own creative resources. Buggie discusses a long list of these techniques.[5]

Buggie also describes techniques for tapping the creativity of outside experts, although a consultant can often handle this process better. While the consultant is unlikely to know as much about the challenges underlying a specific business as the firm's own technical people, a skillful creativity specialist can provide a remarkably effective bridge to an outside world of experts and creative thinkers not directly accessible to a client company, and the success rate is very impressive.

The process is expensive and may take six to nine months, but where a client can define reasonable, testable criteria for a feasible creative solution, the record shows that a skilled consultant can provide several approaches meeting the criteria; if the chosen criteria lead directly to new products then the client can have the desired new products in the time it takes to complete the development cycle. When a plan is in need of a key innovation, the concepts necessary for the innovation can usually be developed in six to nine months or less.

TRADEOFFS

Many of the schedule-saving devices cost money. Overtime, extra machinery, special transportation—all come at a premium price. The initial objective always is to meet both time and cost targets, but where one or the other must be sacrificed, tradeoffs are necessary. In many cases the carrying costs and opportunity costs facing an ongoing commercial program are such that delays in getting to the desired performance levels are very expensive. Frequently the decision will be to keep the project on schedule at almost any cost, up to the point at which the cost increments force total abandonment or a major strategy change.

SPECIFIC PROBLEMS

Some of the above could seem to make the management or oversight of plan progress sound as if it were only a matter of following a formula. There is a formula, or at least a pattern to the necessary action, but also there are a number of issues that must be left to judgment. We will treat some of those here.

Logical Flaws

What do you do when close analysis of a plan shows a logical flaw in its construction? One plan was based on a market introduction schedule for a new veterinary product. A reasonable time allowance for the normal Food and Drug Administration regulatory approval was included. However, the group later discovered that for this specific use the product also required Department of Agriculture approval based on tissue residue data that had not been collected. Embarrassment and a schedule revision followed. The revised schedule began with the time necessary to collect the missing data.

As in this case, when a flaw or oversight in the plan or schedule structure is discovered, the oversight must be corrected immediately and the schedule and budget reconstructed to reflect the impact of the change. Hopefully some alternative later in the action sequence can allow recapture of the time, if not the money, but that hope is secondary to the need to restore realism to the schedule and budget whenever any significant flaw is found.

Nonenforceable Performance Commitments

Plans often build in performance assumptions based on promises from vendors, foreign governments, and others whose behavior cannot be controlled. A common problem occurs with equipment deliveries when the vendor offers estimates based on typical experience for planning purposes but may not stand behind these estimates when committing to delivery on a firm order. Worse still is the case in which the vendor or construction contractor makes a commitment and then does not fulfill it; in some cases performance penalties in the contract discourage such delays, but they are rarely large enough to offset the impact of delay on the development of a business.

A failure of some outside party to fulfill a commitment has the same impact as a mistake in the original schedule. If the performance guarantee cannot be enforced, then the default becomes a fact and the schedule must be rebuilt to accommodate it.

Some companies and some managers are unnecessarily passive when confronted with defaults and delays. Such a failure cancels or at least weakens the obligation to continue dealing with that vendor or contractor, and any strong manager will review the possibility of getting someone else to do the job on time before simply pushing back the schedule and blaming the vendor.

Inadequate Delegation of Authority

Any manager must have authority equal to his or her responsibility in order to have a fair chance of completing the assigned tasks. Clearly this applies in the case of a manager with the task of turning a plan with cumbersome application problems into reality. Because of the conceptual breadth of a business plan, it crosses many organizational boundaries, and most top managements are reluctant to erase these boundaries even though they abridge the authority needed to carry out a plan.

Discussed above was the need to obtain separate capital appropriations and budget approvals for resources necessary to implement a plan and the problems of dependence on shared resources not controlled by that business manager. Other such abridgements include organizational controls over the addition of new employees to the payroll, special oversight authority held by a particular senior executive (i.e., the right to review all R&D spending), or inadequacies in delegation of authority to the responsible manager in the first place.

The manager who implements the plan must have responsible oversight and control; it is essential that others recognize the need of the manager for an adequate delegation of authority. A superior can often assist in repair of gaps in this authority, and can aid the manager in dealings with capital review committees and other parts of the organizational framework that abridge needed authority. The manager needs authority that matches the plan responsibility, or assistance in bridging any gaps, in order to have a fair chance at success in making the plan work.

SUMMARY

The checklist below brings together the three checklists developed earlier into a final summary checklist. This list presents a pattern of action intended to aid control over a plan, to make it easier for the responsible managers to make that plan work, and to yield the results that were visualized by the planning team and promised to top management when the plan was approved.

    1.   Establish a plan control framework and fill any gaps.

          Detail the action and fill gaps.

              With the help of those who must make them work list the mission, goals, and strategies.

                  Establish the intended domain of action (by area and by timetable).

                  List the goals in clear and tangible terms.

                  List statements of the strategy and specific substrategies, functional strategies, and unit strategies. In case of omissions note them and add a statement of the strategy implied or required by the plan.

                  List the plan control structure and checkpoints, the projected time and cost for achieving each, and the name of the person undertaking this responsibility.

Fill any gaps in the control structure.

Add checkpoints as necessary.

Ask those responsible for the action how they would prefer to have their performance measured.

Make a control chart (CPM/PERT).

Polish the logic.

List dependencies.

Establish routine reporting.

2. Reevaluate from where you are; be sure the plan makes sense.
3. Act as necessary to keep the plan on schedule.
4. If budgets or schedules must be allowed to slip review the strategy.
5. Rebuild the plan if that is the only way to make it work.
6. Keep the plan pointed at its intended targets even as they move; avoid strategic blindness.

In reviewing the basics of how a plan can be brought to life successfully and a business made to deliver the sales and profits that the plan promised, an obvious conclusion is that good planning helps. When the original plan is thought out well, with the necessary internal and external constraints properly considered, the implementation job is far easier. Planning is action laid out in advance. Plan well, and the action will flow much more smoothly.

Making plans work is a management action process. The late Harold Koontz summarized the functions of management as planning, organizing, staffing, directing, and controlling. These are all action verbs. In their book *In Search of Excellence,* Peters and Waterman report that "a bias for action" is a characteristic of the managers in the excellent companies.[6] To make a plan work, *act* as is necessary.

And to make a plan work let all the workers help. The dynamics and payoffs from a genuinely participative team effort are clearly established. There is no inconsistency between strong and dynamic leadership by a manager and a genuinely participative management process; the best managers achieve both roles honestly and effectively.

Systems and programs must not be made too complicated or they will not perform dependably. Simple, direct action will often reach the heart of a problem best. Problems are best eliminated the first time they appear. And when all else fails use common sense.

Bringing a plan to life is a common-sense managerial process. Too much could be made of paperwork and form in constructing a control system, yet some system is needed to keep the oversight process organized, constructive, and effective.

The basic process is that of planning, but in a managerial dimension separate from that of the plan that is being made to work. A pattern of action must be found; by careful analysis of the commitments and action elements in the plan this pattern must be laid out in advance, tracked through action sequences and checkpoints, and used as the basis for additional managerial action whenever the plan action sequence needs to be reinforced or redirected.

Remember this approach summary as you set about making your plans work:

1. Good planning helps.
2. Manage the action.
3. Let your people help.
4. Use common sense.

NOTES

1. For more on strategic blindness and its prevention see G. C. Sawyer, *Corporate Planning as a Creative Process,* Planning Executives Institute, Oxford, Ohio, 1983.

2. For more on getting the planning system working see P. Lorange, *Implementation of Strategic Planning,* Prentice-Hall, Englewood Cliffs, N.J., 1982. See also P. J. Stonich, Ed., *Implementing Strategy: Making Strategy Happen,* Ballinger, Cambridge, Mass., 1982, and Sawyer, 1983 on building a plan that will hold together.

3. For more on development of mission, goals, and strategy see Sawyer, *Corporate Planning;* domain is discussed in B. Yavitz and W. H. Newman, *Strategy in Action,* Free Press, New York, 1982.

4. G. A. Steiner, *Top Management Planning,* Macmillan, New York, 1969, pp. 462–471.

5. F. D. Buggie, *New Product Development Strategies,* Amacom, New York, 1981.

6. T. J. Peters and R. H. Waterman, *In Search of Excellence,* Harper & Row, New York, 1982, pp. 119–155.

CHAPTER *9*

The Role of Company Culture and Internal Politics

WILLIAM H. NEWMAN

WILLIAM H. NEWMAN is currently Chairman, Strategy Research Center, Graduate School of Business, Columbia University and is also a Bronfman Management Scholar. He has held the position of Samuel Bronfman Professor of Democratic Business Enterprise and is currently a visiting professor at Claremont Graduate School, Claremont, California. He has served in many management capacities on the staffs of McKinsey & Company and Marshall Field Company. Mr. Newman served as faculty leader at many company and university executive training programs in the United States and abroad. Mr. Newman holds a Ph.D degree from the University of Chicago and an A.B. from Friends University. He is a member of the Academy of Management (past president; Dean of Fellows Group), International Academy of Management (Fellow); American Economic Association; American Management Associations; American Society for Public Administration; European Foundation for Management Development, and is a Beta Gamma Sigma Distinguished Scholar. His publications include *The Building Industry and Business Cycles, Management of Expanding Enterprises* (with J.P. Logan), *Administrative Action,* 2nd ed., *Constructive Control: Design and Use of Control Systems, Managers for the Year 2000* (ed.), *The Process*

The research of M. L. Tushman and E. Romanelli has contributed substantially to the ideas presented in this chapter, namely, "Organizational Evolution: A Metamorphosis Model of Convergence and Reorientation," in B. Staw and L. Cummings, *Research in Organization Behavior,* vol. 7, Greenwich, Conn., JAI Press, 1985.
The author also wishes to acknowledge the research of R. J. Hermon-Taylor as a contributing factor.

of Management, 5th ed. (with E. K. Warren and J. E. Schnee), and *Strategy in Action* (with B. Yavitz). His most recent book is *Strategy, Policy, and Central Management,* 9th ed. (with J. P. Logan and W. H. Hegarty).

OUTLINE

To move from strategic planning to concrete results, strategy must permeate the behavior of many people. Results emerge only if and when people in the company do act, and we are naive to assume that their actions will always conform neatly to the plans we write down on a piece of paper.

The frameworks outlined in this chapter can be used by strategic managers to predict internal support or opposition to strategic moves. They help spot sources of potential conflict and indicate the nature of the hurdles to be crossed.

Two aspects of building a good fit between actual behavior and strategy are company culture and internal politics. The first, company culture, is a crucial part of the setting in which strategic action takes place; it is both unavoidable and influential—and more difficult to manipulate than, say, product design or capital allocation. The second, internal politics, can be friend or foe; since it is also unavoidable we had better harness it in support of our new strategy.

COMPANY CULTURE

"Company culture" has become a popular summary term referring to the customs, attitudes, values, and beliefs widely held by the people who work in a company. Such a culture includes:

1. *Personal values* that are desirable and important to the person. In a company these values often relate to concern for customer service, equity among workers, regular dividends, good citizenship in the community, bribing politicians, reliability, promoting blacks and women, and so forth. Widely held values are typically endorsed by, even promoted by, senior executives—but this is not always so.

2. *Attitudes and beliefs* about how and why events happen. For example, "a computer printout is always correct," "our R & D effort will give us the best product," or "high tariffs protect union jobs."

3. *Expected roles* for many positions. The accountant ferrets out padding in expense accounts; a supervisor battles for his/her subordinates; a sales manager's estimates are 20 percent to 35 percent high; the company attorney will never give you a clear answer—and many more subtle expectations about how people in particular positions will act.

4. *Rewards and punishments* within the company. Taking big risks, or never make a mistake? Be a "yes man"? Innovate? Both what really happens and what people believe happens are important.

5. *Informal information flows.* How to find out the real score; informal clearance; advance warning; what not to discuss.

6. *How decisions are made.* What gets attention and who controls the agenda; who has power and who has influence over what; what kind of evidence and support carries weight.

Every company has a culture—a normal way of dealing with the points just outlined. Part of this culture is formally recognized in manuals and policy statements. However, a large part is informal custom, often unwritten, but nonetheless "the way we do things around here." And it is this latter *real* behavior that matters most.

In a conservative company the culture is rigidly enforced by social pressure. By contrast, other organizations permit—even encourage—small deviations in some areas. Such flexibility adds to the subtlety of culture because you have to sense how much variation on what topics may be acceptable. For example, is whistle blowing ever OK?

Culture does change, usually slowly and in one area at a time. Through external pressure, for instance, women in managerial roles are becoming commonplace. Perhaps competition will force a revised attitude toward government subsidies. A new CEO may stress unswerving loyalty to the company. At the start an exception to the old norm is made; then another exception and another; before long the new pattern rather than the old becomes socially accepted behavior. Nevertheless, for purposes of strategic management company culture must be treated as a force with great inertia.

Company culture is a valuable asset. Without it the day's work would never be finished. We don't have time to discuss personal values every time they arise. I have to know quickly where to check the reliability of rumors that a supplier is close to bankruptcy and I have to know how the plant superintendent is likely to react. Every organization depends on its numerous informal assumptions and customs to keep afloat.

To run smoothly an organization must have predictability and reliability, at least internally. We depend on each other as we transact hundreds of steps each day—when we accept a customer's order, hire a truck driver, make a bank loan, and perform the many other specialized business tasks. The existence of a corporate culture tells us how our company—our social machine—will work. We depend on it.

If we don't like the way the organization behaves, we can *try* to change it. But we can't operate without patterned behavior. Without culture, chaos would reign.

Converging versus Frame-Breaking Change

Typically, strategic change is imposed on an existing company culture. The success of the strategy depends in part on how skillfully that culture can be adapted to support the new strategy. A good fit of the strategy and culture is vital.

Recent research shows that there are two distinct types of marriages of new strategy and company culture: converging change and frame-breaking change. Converging change involves refinements of the culture so that there is closer harmony between a new strategic direction and the elements of culture listed above. Typically, achieving this fit involves (1) fine-tuning structures, behavior patterns, controls, and the like; (2) small adjustments in the culture to make it compatible with the revised strategy and/or shifts in the environment; and (3) a cumulative building of momentum, or inertia. Such converging changes carefully build on past success.

Frame-breaking change, in contrast, involves much more disruption and reorientation. Typically, there is (1) a sharp change in direction—in markets, competitive threats, products, technology, or the like; (2) *concurrent* revision in mission, behavior patterns, key people, and power; and (3) resistance because many of these concurrent changes upset the patterns, beliefs, amd values that were built up over the past years. Here, parts of the social inertia become obstacles rather than aids.

When introducing a new strategy, the manager should decide whether the change requires convergence or frame-breaking. The following paragraphs suggest how to proceed based on this identification of the type of change.

Converging Change: Fine-Tuning

Successful companies wisely tend to stick to what works well. Their strategy focuses primarily on finding better ways of exploiting (and defending) their present mission. In this setting, insofar as any effort is directed toward modification of company culture, it typically deals with one or more of the following:

1. Improving policies, methods, and procedures.
2. Utilizing increased volume to create more specialized subunits, to refine coordination among subunits, and to exercise closer control.
3. Developing personnel especially suited to the present strategy through improved selection and training, and tailoring reward systems to match strategic thrusts.

4. Fostering individual and group commitments to the company mission and to the excellence of one's own department.
5. Promoting confidence in the accepted norms, beliefs, and myths.
6. Maintaining established roles, power, status, dependencies, and allocation mechanisms.

This fine-tuning suits an existing strategy that is effective; it leads to a refined and stable structure. It fits the happy situations romanticized by Peters and Waterman in their book *In Search of Excellence*.

Converging Change: Compatible Adjustments to Shifts in Environment

Of course no company—or culture—stays completely still. In addition to refinements initiated in the fine-tuning just outlined, shifts in the environment will call for some modifications. Even conservative organizations expect, perhaps welcome, small changes that don't rock the boat too much.

A popular expression is that almost any organization can tolerate a "10 percent change." At any one time only a few changes are being made and these changes are compatible with the prevailing culture. Examples of such adjustments are an expansion in sales territory, a shift in emphasis among products in the line, or improved processing technology in a plant.

The usual process of making changes of this sort is well-known: wide acceptance of the need for change, openness to possible alternatives, objective examination of the pros and cons of each plausible alternative, participation of those directly affected in preceding analysis, a market test or pilot operation where feasible, time to learn the new activities, established role models, known rewards for positive success, and evaluation and refinement.

Note that the uncertainty created for people affected by such changes is well within tolerable limits. Opportunity is provided to anticipate and learn what is new, while most features of the culture remain unchanged. The overall system adapts, but it is not restructured.

Forces Leading to Frame-Breaking Change

Strategic change of the sort just described relies on existing company culture. Values are already established; managers know what is expected of them and what they can count on from others; decisions are made in a predictable fashion. In these and other ways there is a momentum upon which new thrusts can be built.

Conversely, the repeated use of old ways and attention to their refinement tends to reinforce and solidify the culture. The beliefs and patterns of behavior become more ingrained through continuing use. And, especially when they are associated with successful operations, a conviction arises that current practice is "correct" and "sound." What, then, leads to frame-breaking change? Why defy tradition?

First, sooner or later *major shifts* occur in the environment—shifts that require more than small adjustments. Perhaps a new technology such as quartz crystals and tiny batteries for wristwatches, or satellites for long-distance communication, will revolutionize the nature of the industry. Also common is a basic change in consumer preferences—such as a decline in the demand for corsets, bowling alleys, and spittoons. Government deregulation has fundamentally altered our concept of a rural bank. Compounding these forces may be powerful new competitors from the Far East or the back yard. Changes such as these often call for a sharp redirection in company strategy.

Second, the evidence is strong that many companies in an industry make a *tardy response* to these more drastic shifts in their environment. Often it is the leading firms that are slow to read the handwriting on the wall. This sluggish recognition often reflects (a) a short-run focus on present operations, (b) a blindness to new threats and opportunities because of a conviction that a revolution is not possible, and/or (c) a reluctance to upset a revered culture. The longer an adjustment to a major change is delayed, the more hurried the reorientation will have to be when it is undertaken.

Third, with only occasional exceptions, frame-breaking change is postponed until a company gets into a *financial crisis,* or at least a major and continuing loss in market share. We rarely have sufficient confidence in predictions of doom to forestall that doom. Typically, a "hold that line" CEO stands resolutely until red ink and outside pressures force his resignation.

Resistance to Frame-Breaking Change

Even when the need for a frame-breaking change is recognized resistance to such action is very likely. If we understand why opposition arises we can deal with it more effectively. Three factors are usually involved:

1.   A feeling of *uncertainty* will be widespread. The comfort and confidence of working in a known culture is gone. No one is sure just what the new world will be like. Of course, many features will be the same and several new ones may be better than in the past, but at first this is far from clear. Most of us don't like high uncertainty.

2.   Old habits and attitudes have to be *unlearned.* Survival of the values, the systems, the roles that we learned to rely on will now be inappropriate—wrong. They have to be erased, and that's not easy. The old dog has trouble with new tricks partly because he has to unlearn his old tricks.

3.   Loss of personal assets will be inevitable. Each person is likely to lose something—perhaps power, status, the importance of a specialized skill, of accumulated knowledge, or of friendships among dis-

carded customers and suppliers. Often an individual will have worked hard to build up these personal strengths, and now the new strategy threatens to make them obsolete. Even self-respect is at stake.

Converging change does not stir up resistance of this magnitude. Frame-breaking change, in contrast, does clash with many features of the prevailing culture.

Scope of Frame-Breaking Change

Many features of a company's formal management design and its informal structure are modified in a frame-breaking change. The following are normally involved:

1. *Mission and Core Values.*   The strategy shift involves a new definition of company mission. Entering or withdrawing from an industry may be involved; at least the way in which the company expect to be outstanding is altered. The revamped AT&T is a conspicuous example. Success on the new course calls for new dedication; some of the core values about what is important must be modified.

2. *Reorganization.*   The new direction calls for added activity in some areas and less emphasis in others. Organization changes are a typical means to assure that this reallocation of effort is made. The reassignments deliberately break business-as-usual behavior. New jobs become new challenges.

3. *New Brooms.*   Almost always different people are placed in several of the key managerial positions. Commitment to the new mission, energy to overcome prevailing inertia, freedom from past obligations, a symbol of change—all are needed to refocus the work of the organization. A few exceptional members of the old guard can personally make this sort of shift, but their previous roles linger in their own habits and in the expectations of their associates. New executives (perhaps promoted from elsewhere in the corporation) are more likely to provide the necessary drive.

4. *Revised Interaction Patterns.*   The way many people in the organization work together has to change. Because of the difference in the work to be done, we will set up new procedures, altered information flows, and revised data processing and reports. From this inevitably comes new friends, different dependencies, informal bypasses, reshaped trust or the absence of trust, and redefined "own turf" boundaries. However, as emphasized earlier in this chapter, for an organization to be effective these interaction patterns must restabilize and be predictable. So, soon after the reorientation we hope to start a fresh period of convergence.

5. *Altered Power and Status.* Power is necessary to break inertia. The individuals who bring about frame-breaking change in organizations need the capability to reward or punish and to control allocation of resources. The use of such power may be constrained and gentle. Nevertheless, in the new ballgame different people have clout, and members throughout the organization quickly observe who makes the influential decisions in the new regime. We back up the new mission, organization, key appointments, and revised procedures with power. (In some situations, it is the persons with power who shape the other features; but whatever the sequence we still have and need a merging of power and direction of major change.) Closely related to modifications of power and influence are shifts in status. The new culture alters the prestige of key positions.

Clearly, frame-breaking change has a profound effect on company culture. The mission, organization, key managers, interaction patterns, and power/status relationships are all altered. A pressing question is what parts of the former culture to retain. For example, when Singer Sewing Machine Company decided to diversify and deemphasize its worldwide sewing machine business, it had a distribution network and manufacturing facilities as well as thousands of loyal workers—all potential assets that might be fitted into a revamped organization. Uncertainty prevails until the new mission and structure are clarified enough to incorporate those parts of the former organization that will become vital elements in the new setup. As in the metamorphosis of a caterpillar to a butterfly, this transition is a period of danger. Usually the sooner the uncertainty is removed, the better the chances of survival.

Why All at Once?

Executives who are thinking of a frame-breaking change must decide whether to make all the adjustments just described concurrently, or at least in a short space of time. The reasons for doing so include:

1. *Synergy* within the new structure can be a powerful aid. Recently selected executives with a fresh mission, working with a redesigned organization and revamped relationships and backed up with power and status, provide strong reinforcement. The pieces are pulling together, not apart.
2. Typically there is a *pent-up need for change*. During the converging period, basic adjustments were postponed. What worked well has been continued. Boat rocking has been discouraged. Then, once the constraints are relaxed, a variety of desirable improvements press for attention.

3. *Pockets of resistance* may have to be removed. The new mission, the shifts in organization, and other frame-breaking changes will upset the roles of some managers. Their resistance to such an upset is natural, and if executives in these positions are left alone they may deliberately try to undermine the entire new thrust.

4. The exhilaration and momentum of a fresh effort may make difficult moves more acceptable. Change is in fashion. This is the time to *sweep away the cobwebs*.

How to Make Frame Breaking Less Costly

Several costs are associated with frame-breaking change. The action is likely to be tardy. Indigestion may occur; there may be too much planning, learning, and uncertainty swirling around at the same time. The transition can be bloody, especially when power alone is used to gain acceptance.

Six possible ways to reduce these costs are:

1. Build *recognition of the need* for a frame-breaking change. A severe financial crisis is one way to obtain this recognition, as noted above, but that is hazardous, costly, and sharply restricts bail-out options. Much smarter is early recognition by key executives at a time when diagnosis of trends and competitors' behavior indicates that continuing convergence offers a dismal future. However, recognizing such a need to upset a familiar and successful past structure is bitter medicine. Furthermore, achieving credibility for such an early diagnosis is a major undertaking. This planning task of developing a consensus is discussed in other chapters of this handbook.

2. Possibly a consensus about the need for change will be clear and some powerful and influential person will insist that the question, what do we do next? be addressed. Then participation in finding good alternatives is wise. If the key executives have the mental and emotional capacity to take such a challenge seriously, their participation in plotting a new course will help build a *commitment* to frame-breaking action. Note that we may be asking some executives to make themselves obsolete!

3. If the two preceding steps—early recognition and committed participation—can be achieved by the key executives of a company, then perhaps time and resources will be found for a *pilot* trial of a proposed new strategy. Lacking the consensus and commitment of the reigning executives, it is unlikely that a pilot trial of a frame-breaking nature will receive a fair test. The old company culture will continue to dominate.

4. Again assuming consensus and commitment of key executives has been obtained, perhaps a *phased transition* to the new strategy will

be possible. Instead of pockets of resistance and delayed action, the social pressure at least from the top will give support to the early transition steps.

5. For this sort of group backing of a movement into a frame-breaking strategy to stay in tune with competitive pressures, the executive group will need unusual *learning skills*. A fixed program will be too rigid. Unexpected hurdles will surely arise. Then the executive group will need skill in profiting from past mistakes, or what Argyris and Schon call "learning to learn." This calls for an openness and candor in confronting problems. So in addition to consensus and commitment the executives should learn as they run.

6. Finally, when all five of the preceding steps (or their equivalent) have been achieved, a movement toward a revised company culture will be underway. At this stage the executives can begin to live and preach about their new *focused climate*.[1]

The foregoing steps are very difficult. They run counter to inertia pressures that we noted in discussing converging strategy. Only a few companies have the leadership and the flexible personnel necessary to follow them. Consequently, our prediction is that most frame-breaking change will come only when severe pressures force an upheaval in the prevailing culture.

INTERNAL POLITICS

A fact of life is that internal politics affect both strategy formulation and strategy execution. Such an influence can be either good or bad. Therefore, wise managers take time to channel these political forces into support for the optimum company strategy. They use politics constructively.

Because "politics" is often considered a dirty word, and because idealistic rational managers often deny the existence of internal politics in their companies, we will consider the nature of internal politics separately. Then the interaction between politics and strategic management will be discussed.

Politics Based on Exchange of Favors[2]

Since pioneer days neighbors have helped each other. That help is freely given. Nevertheless, an expectation is created that the favor will be returned when an opportunity arises. Similar exchanges take place in any normal organization. Indeed, most voluntary coordination relies on a lot of give-and-take.

Politics are based on an exchange of favors. The politician is a helpful person. He or she also recognizes that it is convenient to have friends—outside the chain of command—in times of need.

The danger in this process is that we become so busy helping each other that the goals of the organization get lost in the shuffle. I can occasionally help the sales manager meet rush orders of new customers, but if done too often the whole production schedule falls apart. Also, what if the sales manager puts my niece in a sales trainee job when better candidates are available? Note that the dividing line of desirable and undesirable cooperation is likely to be fuzzy.

Here we are using "politics" to cover any building of influence through the exchange of favors. Whether the practice is done in a desirable manner—to support a new strategy, for example—is a separate and important issue.

Power Builds Political Potential

Persons in powerful positions clearly have many opportunities to take actions that have political overtones. By power we mean the ability to grant or withhold something that other people want. For example, ability to give a key endorsement on a capital expenditure request, or assigning scarce engineers to a particular project, are sources of power. If a person uses such power in exchange for favors, he or she can generate support for his or her favored move. The exchange may be implicit rather than explicit, and the move sponsored by the powerful person may be consistent with company goals. Nevertheless the political dimension is present.

Since power and politics are intertwined, we should be very sensitive to powerful spots in organizations. Typical powerful locations include:

1. Senior positions in line management. Here the incumbents may have authority to add or drop products, grant discounts, appoint other executives, select plant locations, pay bonuses, and the like. A serious issue is what sorts of constraints should be placed on the exercise of this authority.
2. Approval or clearance points. For example, often a controller can hold up capital allocations, a chief counsel can withhold legal approval of a contract, or an EEOC officer can challenge a personnel move.
3. Direct supervision of an essential resource. The managers of a centralized computing service or of purchasing, for instance, sometimes can vary the speed and quality of their services. If so, their friendship becomes a valuable asset.
4. Influential access to busy people in powerful positions. Such advisers, or "powers behind the scene" may be able to influence what does or does not happen. Even if they are only believed to have such influence, they have potential power.

When a person in such a spot chooses to take care of friends and punish enemies, he or she can muster a lot of backing for a favored program—maybe the *old* strategy! Typically, the political use of such power is not exercised explicitly; instead, rationalizations are provided for speed-ups or delays. For people working within the organization, however, the message is usually clear. Ways to confine and channel the use of such organizational power are outlined in a later section.

Political Backing of a Cause

Few employees pursue political activities within their company solely for their own advancement. Instead, most political effort is tied to a "cause." For example, the individuals who are trading favors typically are protecting their own department, supporting women's liberation, encouraging trade with Russia, opposing a plant shutdown in Topeka, backing the sale of unbranded products, or building a strong base for some other objective. They are still using their power in a manipulative way, but now the criterion for whom to help and whom to hurt is tied to the cause.

The linking of political activity to a cause has several profound effects. Psychologically, people develop an emotional commitment and a sense of righteousness when working for a cause. Promoting a cause tends to remove doubts, to provide an inward rationalization, and even to justify hurting other people and other causes. With this underpinning, political maneuvering becomes a justifiable means to a worthy end.

Personal advancement may be helped or hurt by promoting a cause. The safety director, for instance, who reduces the accident rate probably promotes the cause and his or her personal reputation at the same time. The champion of a successful new product line is likely to be promoted. So it is very difficult to distinguish selfish motives from the serving of external objectives. Consequently, we cannot brand all political efforts merely selfish and self-seeking.

Finally, since linking internal politics to causes generates strong emotional drive as well as mobilizing indirect support, a general manager must give close attention to *what causes* are being promoted. A further issue is whether even worthy causes are being pushed to such a degree or in a way that *other objectives are unduly sacrificed*. The compatibility between such politically backed causes and a new company strategy is critical.

Coalitions: A Form of Politics

Promoting a cause may require joint action of several people in the organization; they pool their political power. Such a coalition might be formed, say, to support (or block) the appointment of a particular person to a vacant position, or a coalition in a bank might strongly advocate nationwide branches.

Coalitions of this sort are usually single-purpose. That is, on most other matters the members proceed along independent paths. To be effective, however, the members need to support a single, consistent plan, and to hold the coalition together, modifications or concessions to particular members may have to be agreed upon. A coalition does not necessarily have an explicit campaign, especially in a company in which patterns of conduct are well-established. The essential elements are a consensus about particular actions related to the cause and a willingness of coalition members to use their political clout to promote those actions.

To summarize, internal politics are based on exchanging favors, using power, serving a cause, and, often, forming coalitions.

Politics: Inevitability, Desirability, and the Need for Channeling

The preceding terse analysis of internal politics leads to three basic guidelines for managers:

1. *Recognize that Political Behavior is Inevitable.* Normal sociability leads people to exchange favors, and in this process informal obligations and pressures arise. Then when such give-and-take is mixed with power and with commitment to causes, political behavior is sure to arise. Indeed, politics in this sense will be found in all large organizations—church, government, armies, and pretzel factories. Because internal politics are a fact of life, managers should try to understand how politics influence the decisions and actions within their own organization.

2. *Internal Politics Have Desirable Features that Should Be Utilized.* The give-and-take contributes to informal coordination. It helps meld the activities of specialized individuals who otherwise tend to pursue their particular tasks according to their own priorities. The deviant person is pressured into considering the goals of other persons. Moreover, joining in promoting a cause—playing on the team—can build enthusiastic commitment. A political achievement can be an uplifting experience. Managers should try to harness these influences. They help define directions, and they may stir up strong motivation.

3. *Internal Politics Should Be Channeled toward Company Objectives.* Like fire, internal politics can be either destructive or a useful source of harnessed energy. The dangers are real. Individuals who are obsessed by personal power can use politics for self-gratification. Politics can be used to promote causes that are incompatible with company goals or values. More subtly, politics can place so much emphasis on a particular kind of action that values are distorted; other desirable results get pushed aside. Finally, there is the possibility that political maneuvering can escalate into internecine war in which more effort is devoted to winning internal battles than to serving stakeholders. To reduce these dangers, central managers should keep track of political behavior in their organization and take steps to channel it—as outlined below.

Guides for Harnessing Internal Politics

Controls on internal politics have two primary aims: to minimize the opportunities for petty politics and to link the remaining political behavior to company goals and values. The following measures help achieve these aims:

1. *Clarify the Objectives, Strategy, and Values of the Company.* Then insist that all political behavior be compatible with these guidelines. In practice, there will be gray areas where the company position is vague or does not exist; that leaves room for political action that is not "out of bounds." As the company culture and strategy are being reshaped former standards will be open to challenge. Nevertheless, every company does have some consensus on desired direction. Political action that runs counter to this endorsed direction is bad.

   One of the benefits of a clear-cut strategy is providing a permeating guide for behavior throughout the organization. The clearer the strategy and the wider its acceptance, the more useful it will be in constraining internal politics.

2. *Make the Criteria for Rewards and for Allocation of Resources Explicit and Public.* This should be done insofar as it is practical. Most activities in any organization can be easily linked to a recognized objective; what contributes to those objectives can be rather easily distinguished from what does not. These activities should not be cluttered up with political payoffs.

   For standard, repetitive situations the steps to be taken to obtain resources and rewards and the criteria that will be used in allocating them should be known in advance. Then individual discretion—aside from judging the facts in each case—is reduced to a minimum. And there is little room for intramural politics.

   For nonrepetitive situations in which resource allocations or rewards do not fit into a standard pattern insist on joint and open decisions. Budget allocations, personnel quotas, R & D support, and promotions are in this nonrepetitive category. In such decisions several executives should participate, and opinions should be secured from an even wider group. Final approval should be given by a senior executive after he or she has had opportunity to check any disagreements for selfish political bias.

   For more subtle withholding or for providing intangible support—for example, promptly providing key information or being willing to adjust operations to unexpected needs—procedural control is impractical. Here the primary check on abuse is selecting the right persons for influential posts. Positions of subtle power should be filled by individuals who can be trusted to use that power to support identified company goals—including a new strategy (see 1 above).

3. *Punish Deviant Power Seekers.*   The primary ways to channel internal politics are the positive steps of defining goals and coupling them with allocation procedures that support those goals, as just recommended. If in spite of these efforts individuals are discovered who are resorting to politics that run contrary to company interests they should be promptly and openly reprimanded. Perhaps transfer or dismissal will be necessary.

   Part of a company culture is the way politics are tolerated. The reason for taking a firm stand against individuals advancing private interests that conflict with company aims is to establish a cultural norm: "private empire building does not pay." To avoid becoming infested with petty power players, consistent discipline is necessary.

4. *Separate Resource Mobilization from Its Allocation.*   In some companies the executive who is responsible for acquiring a resource— money, employees, raw materials, computer service, or the like— also regulates who within the company gets the resource to use. Such an arrangement creates power centers. And power can be abused politically.

   The simplest way to avoid this risk is to separate allocation from mobilization or creation of a service. The treasurer, for instance, should not determine who can spend the cash in the till, nor should the manager of a central computer decide who has priority for its use. The separation cannot be complete. Cost of mobilizing does bear on allocation, and vice versa. So we want inputs about costs and availability from the mobilizer. However, we *don't* want that expert to be the one who doles out the resource.

The foregoing measures will not eliminate politics in an organization. They will reduce political maneuvering and channel it.

Politics and Strategy Formulation

Strategic management has an unusual linkage with internal politics in two respects. First, strategy creates many of the goals that become the criteria for acceptable or unacceptable political behavior. For a company, approved strategy becomes the top guideline. It is established through judgment and negotiation. But with strategy located at the top of the company's means– end hierarchy there are no higher well-defined goals that can be used to judge the politicizing involved in selecting the strategy itself as there are for subordinates' behavior. Second, because strategy deals with the longer-run, dynamic future, it is permeated with a lot of uncertainty. In uncertain situations we have more difficulty stipulating what is acceptable behavior. These two considerations affect both strategy formulation and strategy execution.

Room for Debate—and Politics

The process of strategy formulation provides many opportunities for rewarding your friends and punishing your enemies. For instance, all strategies have a variety of results—on people, on costs and profits, on market position, on risks, on the timing of payoffs, etc. In selecting a particular strategy, which of these results should receive the greater weights? Political pressure often has a strong influence on how much importance we attach to, say, reducing employment in the home town of the CEO or taking a high risk on solar energy.

Because the values attached to multiple goals are subjective, and therefore debatable, political tradeoffs are almost irresistible. Repeated efforts are necessary to keep final choices focused on what is good for the company as a whole.

The debate may also arise at several different stages in the strategy formulation process. Early screening of proposals for change may simply rule out some kinds of suggestions and encourage others. Your bright idea gets shot down in the first review (or you have learned never to mention such an idea). The projected outcomes of various proposals are sufficiently debatable so that one or two proposals may be favored while others are dropped from further consideration. Expressions of support, or of grave doubt, may be voiced by any of the several departments affected by a strategic proposal. In the review committee a bit of trading may take place to get a "balanced plan" that has widespread backing.

At each of these stages opinions may differ as to the importance of various outcomes and to the degree of uncertainty. These are normal spots for political influences to be strong. If politics have been permitted to be dominantly self-serving, the best proposals never get to the top. In contrast, if a commitment to a company mission has been established, then the winnowing at each stage can reflect company values.

Political Support of Converging Strategies

When changes in strategy are converging (as that term was explained earlier in this chapter) the existing management structure remains in place. In most respects, the prevailing criteria and behavior norms will be continued. The power structure is not threatened. The criteria for acceptable internal politics will be known and power to discipline deviants will continue.

Under these circumstances the refinement or adaptation of company strategy should not stir up unusual political activity. Rather, the screening and analysis of proposed changes is likely to be conservative. The political activity that has been condoned in the past will tend to foster hesitancy to change. Indeed, the political constraints on change may be too narrow and the emerging strategy not bold enough. What we need here is greater tolerance for thoughtful change without a thirst for individual permissiveness.

Coalitions Promoting Frame-Breaking Strategies

The politics of frame breaking are very different. Here the established order will probably feel threatened and will resist, so new and unorthodox political strength will have to be mustered. Frame-breaking strategies typically originate with some internal missionary who has a vision of what might or must be done. This vision may be an original creation or a variation of what competitors are already doing, but it does involve a sharp change in direction for the company. Because the proposal runs counter to prevailing norms, a lot of persuading is needed. This usually takes persistence, time, and tact. Of course, if the CEO can be persuaded early (unlikely in most companies) the process is speeded up. Nevertheless, considerable foot dragging via political pressures should be anticipated.

A potent ally for frame-breaking change is financial crisis. The crisis drives home the argument that change of some sort is necessary.

Fine-tuning the strategy, which generally is politically acceptable, is inadequate in such situations. Instead, the company mission has to be revised; a new lineup of players with realignment of their powers is probably necessary, and considerable modification of criteria, procedures, and other ground rules will have to be worked out.

No single missionary, not even a CEO, can bring about such a reorientation alone. He or she needs allies. This means that a coalition of managers and influential staff people must be formed. This group combines its energies— and reputations— to work out and gain acceptance for a new strategy. To win the necessary commitment up and down the line, this coalition rewards friends of the new strategy. Also, after a reasonable opportunity for those involved to learn the implications of the new strategy and become converts to it, the coalition punishes resisters.

In other words, formulation of a frame-breaking strategy by its very nature is partly a political process. At first political hindrance is to be expected. But once the new strategy has been adopted then political measures, among others, backing up the new goals probably will be necessary. Use coalitions to muster the backing needed to break with tradition.

Politics and Strategy Execution

The execution of a new strategy requires thoughtful interpretation and elaboration of what that strategy implies for each segment of the company. For instance, a shirt manufacturer's strategy to cater to small- and medium-sized retailers has been interpreted into a policy of uniform prices for the branded line and a policy of no special advertising allowances for big chains. The advertising allowance policy in turn leads to standardized criteria for deciding who is eligible for regular advertising allowances.

In this elaboration process wide variation can arise in the way a strategy is actually applied. Internal politics help shape these interpretations. In fact, a series of interpretations by unsympathetic managers can twist the original intent. Consequently, periodic audits should be made of the application of a strategy. Perhaps the strategy should be revised to better fit actual competitive conditions. However, the point here is that the administration should not be so lax that local political forces can construe strategy almost as they wish. Insist on a clear means–end chain back to the strategy.

As in strategy formulation, internal politics can be channeled more easily when executing converging changes rather than frame-breaking changes. For converging change only small modifications are needed in existing norms and procedures. For frame-breaking change a revamping of company culture and top personnel is often required, and this means that the internal political patterns have to be reshaped and refocused. While the company culture is still in a state of flux, make clear what kind of political activity for what causes will be tolerated.

Creeping changes in the actual strategy also complicate execution. From time to time adjustments are made in response to external forces or to internal political pressures. Such flexibility may be wise. The danger lies in a growing belief among company managers that the official strategy can be easily bent by political influence. Such an attitude invites the creation of political power to circumvent strategy. Then freewheel politicking takes over. The preventive measure, of course, is to make clear that strategy is indeed adapted to new situations, *but* local power centers are not free to make new interpretations to suit their short-run convenience. Instead, central endorsement of a desired change is required. And then consistent action in line with the updated strategy is expected. New ground rules do not mean no ground rules.

Internal politics are inevitable and potentially useful, but they need to be channeled.

NOTES

1. For further discussion of creating a focused climate see B. Yavitz and W. H. Newman, *Strategy in Action,* Free Press, New York, 1982, pp. 136ff.

2. The following description of internal politics draws on ideas in W. H. Newman, E. K. Warren, and J. E. Schnee, *The Process of Management,* 5th ed., Prentice-Hall, Englewood Cliffs, NJ, 1982, Chapter 21.

CHAPTER *10*

Reward Systems and Strategy

EDWARD E. LAWLER III

EDWARD E. LAWLER III is Director, Center for Effective Organizations and Professor of Research at the University of Southern California. Professor Lawler has held positions as Professor of Psychology and Program Director in the Institute for Social Research, and at the University of Michigan. He has also served on the faculty of Yale University. Dr. Lawler is a member of many professional organizations in his field and is on the editorial board of five major journals. He is the author and coauthor of over 100 articles and 12 books. His most recent books include *Organizational Assessment,* and *Managing Creation,* both published by Wiley-Interscience and *High Involvement Management* published by Jossey-Bass in 1986.

OUTLINE

Based upon Edward Lawler, "Reward Systems in Organizations," a chapter in J. Lorsch, Ed., *Handbook of Organizational Behavior,* Prentice-Hall, Englewood Cliffs, in press. Partial financial support was provided by the Office of Naval Research under Contract N00014-81-K-0048; NR 170-923.

Reward systems are one of the most prominent and frequently discussed features of organizations. Indeed, the organizational behavior literature is replete with the examples of their functional as well as their dysfunctional role in organizations.[1] All too often, however, a thorough discussion of how they relate to strategic planning is missing. The underlying assumption in this chapter is that, when properly designed, the reward systems of an organization can be a key contributor to the effectiveness of organizations. However, for this to occur careful analysis needs to be made of the role that reward systems can and should play in the strategic plan of the organization.

OBJECTIVES OF REWARD SYSTEMS

The first step in discussing the strategic role of reward systems is to consider what behavioral impact they can have in organizations. The research on reward systems suggests that they can influence five important types of behavior and that these in turn influence organizational effectiveness. A brief discussion of how rewards affect them follows.

1. *Attraction and Retention.*   Research on job choice, career choice, and turnover clearly shows that the kind and level of rewards an organization offers influences who is attracted to work for an organization and who will continue to work for it.[2] Overall, those organizations which give the most rewards that individuals value tend to attract and retain the most people. Research also shows that better performers need to be rewarded more highly than poorer performers if they are to be attracted and retained. They expect more and can obtain more in the marketplace. Finally, the way rewards are administered and distributed influences who is attracted and retained. For example, better performing individuals are often attracted by merit-based reward systems.

2. *Motivation.*   Those rewards that are important to individuals can impact their motivation to perform in particular ways. People in work organizations tend to behave in whatever way they perceive leads to rewards they value.[3] For a reward to be motivating three conditions must exist: it must be valued, it must be perceived as depending on performance, and the rewarded performance must be perceived as

achievable. Thus, an organization that is able to tie valued rewards to the behaviors it needs to succeed is likely to find that the reward system is a positive contributor to its effectiveness.

3. *Skill Development.*   Just as a reward system can motivate performance it can motivate skill development. When valued rewards are offered for mastering a particular skill, motivation will be present to master it among those individuals who feel they can learn it. Thus, in organizations in which strategy depends on the presence of particular skills, reward systems can be particularly important. Most reward systems primarily encourage the development of management skills because they deliver rewards according to level in the management hierarchy.

4. *Culture and Structure.*   Reward systems contribute to the overall culture or climate of organizations. Depending on how reward systems are developed, administered, and managed, they can cause the culture of an organization to vary quite widely. For example, they can influence the degree to which it is seen as a human-resources–oriented culture, an entrepreneurial culture, an innovative culture, a competence-based culture, or a participative culture.

    The reward system of an organization can also reinforce and define the organization's structure.[4] Often this feature of reward systems is not fully considered in the design of reward systems; as a result their impact on the structure of an organization is unintentional. This does not mean, however, that the impact of the reward system on structure is usually minimal. Indeed, it can help define the status hierarchy, the degree to which people in technical positions can influence people in line management positions, and it can strongly influence the kind of decision structure that exists. The key features here seem to be the degree to which the reward system is strongly hierarchical and the degree to which it allocates rewards on the basis of movements up the hierarchy.

5. *Cost.*   Reward systems are often a significant cost factor. Indeed, the pay system alone may represent over 50 percent of the organization's operating cost. Thus it is important in strategically designing the reward system to focus on how high these costs should be and how they will vary as a function of the organization's ability to pay. For example, a reasonable outcome of a well-designed pay system might be an increased cost when the organization has the money to spend and a decreased cost when the organization does not have the money. An additional objective might be to have lower overall reward-system cost than business competitors.

In summary, reward systems in organizations should be looked at from a cost-benefit perspective. The cost can be managed and controlled and the benefits planned for. The key is to identify the outcomes needed in order for the organization to be successful and then to design the reward system in such a way that these outcomes will in fact be realized.

RELATIONSHIP TO STRATEGIC PLANNING

Exhibit 10-1 suggests the first way in which the reward system needs to be taken into consideration in the area of strategic planning. It suggests that when the strategic plan is developed it is important to assess a number of things including the human resource management systems and to determine what kind of behavior, climate, and structure they are supportive of. This step is needed so that when the strategic plan is developed it is based on a realistic assessment of the current condition of the organization and the changes that are likely to be needed to implement the new strategic plan. This point is particularly pertinent to organizations that are considering going into new lines of business, developing new strategic plans, and acquiring new divisions.

   Often, new lines of business require a different behavior and therefore a different reward system. Simply putting the old reward system in place in the new business is often not good enough and, indeed, can lead to failure in the new business. On the other hand, developing a new reward system for the new business can cause problems in the old business because of the type of comparisons that are made between different parts of the same organization. This is not to say that organizations should avoid venturing into new businesses; it is merely to say that a careful assessment of the kinds of

EXHIBIT 10-1   Relationship to Strategic Planning—Step 1

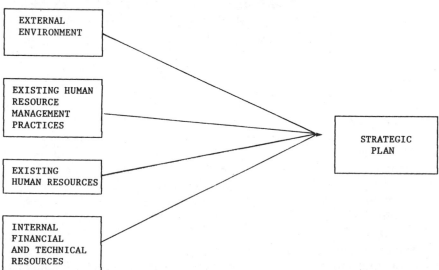

EXHIBIT 10-2   Relationship to Strategic Planning—Step 2

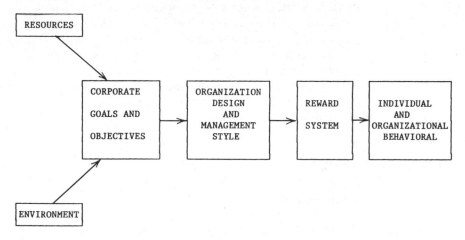

reward system changes that are needed should take place before organizations enter into new strategic plans that call for different behaviors.

Exhibit 10-2 presents the second step in viewing the relationship between strategic planning and reward systems. It suggests that once the strategic plan is developed, the organization needs to focus on the kind of human resources, culture, behavior, and management practices that are needed in order to make it effective. The next step is to design reward systems that will motivate the right kind of performance, attract the right kind of people, and create a supportive culture and structure.

DESIGN OPTIONS

There are almost an infinite number of ways to design and manage reward systems in organizations. This is because there are a host of rewards that can be given, and of course a large number of ways that they can be distributed. The focus in the remainder of this chapter will be on the visible extrinsic rewards that an organization controls and that can as a matter of policy and practice be allocated to members on a targeted basis. Included will be pay, promotion, status symbols, and perquisites. Little attention will be given to such intrinsic rewards as feelings of responsibility, competence, and personal growth and development.

A useful dichotomy in thinking about options in the design of reward systems is the process/content one. All organizational systems have a content or structural dimension as well as a process dimension. The structural or content dimension of a reward system refers to its formal mechanisms, procedures, and practices (e.g., the salary structures, the promotion policies, the performance appraisal forms)—in short, the nuts and bolts of the system.

The process side refers to the communication and decision-process parts of the system. A key issue here involves the degree of openness with respect to information about how the reward system operates and how people are rewarded. A second issue is the degree of participation that is allowed in the design of the reward system and the ongoing administration of it. Many organizations, without ever analyzing whether it is best, choose to administer rewards in a top-down, secretive way. As will be discussed further, this is not the only way that rewards can be administered. The discussion of design choices will begin by looking at the key structural choices and then turn to a consideration of the key process choices.

STRUCTURAL DECISIONS

Performance-Based Reward Systems

Perhaps the key strategic decision that needs to be made in the design of any reward system is whether or not it will be based on performance. Once this decision is made, a number of other features of the reward system tend to fall into place. The major alternative to basing pay on performance is to base it on seniority or on the job performed. Many government agencies, for example, base their rates on the job the person does and on how long they have been in that job. In Japan individual pay is also based on seniority, although individuals receive bonuses based on corporate performance.

Most business organizations in the United States say that they reward individual performance, and they call their pay and promotion systems merit-based. Having a true merit pay or promotion system is often easier said than done, however. Indeed, it has been observed that many organizations would be better off if they didn't try to relate pay and promotion to performance and relied on other bases for motivating performance.[5] The logic for this statement stems from the difficulty of specifying what kind of performance is desired, and then determining whether in fact it has been demonstrated. There is ample evidence that a poorly designed and administered reward system can do more harm than good.[6] On the other hand, there is evidence that when pay is effectively related to the desired performance it can help to motivate, attract, and retain outstanding performers. It can also help to create a culture of competence and excellence. Thus, when it is feasible, it is usually desirable to relate pay to performance.

There are numerous ways to relate pay to performance, and often it is the most important decision that organizations make when they decide how to implement the strategic plan. The options open to organizations are enormous. The kind of pay reward that is given can vary widely and include such things as stock and cash. In addition, the frequency with which rewards are given can vary tremendously from time periods of a few minutes to many years. Performance can be measured at the individual level so that each individual gets a reward based on his or her performance. Rewards also can be given to groups based on the performance of the group, and rewards can be given based on the performance of total organizations so that the same reward is given to everyone in an organization. Finally, there are many different kinds of performance that can be rewarded. For example, managers can be rewarded for sales increases, productivity volumes, their ability to develop their subordinates, their cost reduction ideas, their implementation of a strategic plan, and so on.

Rewarding some behaviors and not others has clear implications for performance, and thus, decisions about what is to be rewarded need to be made carefully and with attention to the overall strategic plan of the business.[7] Consideration needs to be given to such issues as short- versus long-term performance, risk taking versus risk aversion, division performance versus total corporate performance, ROI maximization versus sales growth, and so on. Once the strategic plan has been developed to the point where key performance objectives have been defined, the reward system needs to be designed to motivate the appropriate performance. Decisions about such issues as whether to use stock options (a long-term incentive) or cash bonuses, for example, should be made only after careful consideration of whether they are supportive of the kinds of behavior that is desired.[8]

It is beyond the scope of this chapter to go into any great detail about the pros and cons of the many approaches to relating pay to performance. Exhibit 10-3 gives an idea of some of the design features that are possible in a pay system and some of the pluses and minuses associated with them.[9]

First, each plan is evaluated in terms of its effectiveness in creating the perception that pay is tied to performance. In general, this indicates the degree to which the approach ties pay to performance in a way that leads employees to believe that higher pay will follow good performance. Second, each plan is evaluated in terms of whether or not it results in the negative side effects that often are produced by performance-based pay plans (e.g., social ostracism of good performers, defensive behavior, and giving false data about performance). Third, each plan is evaluated in terms of the degree to which it encourages cooperation among employees. Finally, employee acceptance of the plan is rated.

The ratings range from 1 to 5; a 5 indicates that the plan is generally high on the factor, and a 1 indicates it is low. The ratings were developed based on a review of the literature and on my experience with the different types of plans.[10]

A number of trends appear in the ratings. Looking first at tying pay to performance, we see that the individual plans tend to be rated highest; group plans are rated next; and organizational plans are rated lowest. This occurs because in group plans, to some extent, and in organizational plans, to a great extent, an individual's pay is not directly a function of his or her behavior. An individual's pay in these situations is influenced by the behavior of many others. In addition, when some types of performance measures (e.g., profits) are used pay is influenced by external conditions that employees cannot control.

Bonus plans are generally rated higher than pay-raise and salary-increase

EXHIBIT 10-3 *Ratings of Various Pay Incentive Plans*

		Tie Pay to Performance	Negative Side	Encourage Cooperation	Employee Acceptance
Salary Reward	*Measurement*				
Individual plan	Productivity	4	1	1	4
	Cost effectiveness	3	1	1	4
	Superiors' rating	3	1	1	3
Group plan	Productivity	3	1	2	4
	Cost effectiveness	3	1	2	4
	Superiors' rating	2	1	2	3
Organizational plan	Productivity	2	1	3	4
	Cost effectiveness	2	1	2	4
Bonus Reward					
Individual plan	Productivity	5	3	1	2
	Cost effectiveness	4	2	1	2
	Superiors' rating	4	2	1	2
Group plan	Productivity	4	1	3	3
	Cost effectiveness	3	1	3	3
	Superiors' rating	3	1	3	3
Organizational plan	Productivity	3	1	3	4
	Cost effectiveness	3	1	3	4
	Profit	2			

Note: On a scale of 1 to 5, 1 = low and 5 = high.

plans. This is due to the fact that with bonus plans it is possible to substantially vary an individual's pay from time period to time period. With salary increase plans this is very difficult, since past raises tend to become an annuity.

Finally, note that approaches that use objective measures of performance are rated higher than those that use subjective measures. In general, objective measures enjoy higher credibility; that is, employees will often accept the validity of an objective measure, such as sales volume or units produced, when they will not accept a superior's rating. When pay is tied to objective measures, therefore, it is usually clearer to employees that pay is determined by performance. Objective measures are also often publicly measurable. When pay is tied to them, the relationship between performance and pay is much more visible than when it is tied to a subjective, nonverifiable measure such as a supervisor's rating. Overall, the suggestion is that individually based bonus plans that rely on objective measures produce the strongest perceived connection between pay and performance.

The ratings of the degree to which plans contribute to negative side effects reveal that most plans have little tendency to produce such effects. The notable exceptions here are individual bonus and incentive plans at the nonmanagement level. These plans often lead to situations in which social rejection and ostracism are tied to good performance, and in which employees present false performance data and restrict their production. These side effects are particularly likely to appear where trust is low and subjective productivity standards are used.

In terms of the third criterion, encouraging cooperation, the ratings are generally higher for group and organizational plans than for individual plans. Under group and organizational plans, it is generally to everyone's advantage that an individual work effectively, because all share in the financial fruits of higher performance. This is not true under an individual plan. As a result, good performance is much more likely to be supported and encouraged by others when group and organizational plans are used. If people feel they can benefit from another's good performance, they are much more likely to encourage and help other workers to perform well than if they cannot benefit and may be harmed.

The final criterion, employee acceptance, shows that, as noted earlier, most performance-based pay plans have moderate acceptance. The least acceptable seems to be individual bonus plans. Their low acceptance, particularly among nonmanagement employees, stems from their tendency to encourage competitive relationships between employees and from the difficulty in administering such plans fairly.

It should be clear that no one performance-based pay plan represents a panacea. It is therefore unlikely that any organization will ever be completely satisfied with the approach it chooses.

Many organizations choose to put individuals on multiple or combination reward systems. For example, they may put individuals on a salary increase system that rewards them for their individual performance, while at the same time giving everybody in the division or plant a bonus based on divisional performance. Some plans measure group or company performance and then divide up the bonus pool among individuals on the basis of their individual performance. This has the effect of causing individuals to be rewarded for both individual and group performance in the hope that this will motivate individuals to perform all needed behaviors.

A common error in the design of many pay-for-performance systems is the tendency to focus on measurable short-term operating results because they are quantifiable and regularly obtained anyway. Many organizations reward their top-level managers in particular, on the basis of quarterly or annual profitability. This can have the obvious dysfunctional consequence of causing managers to be very short-sighted in their behavior and to ignore strategic objectives that are important to the long-term profitability of the organization.

A similarly grievous error can be the tendency to depend on completely subjective performance appraisals for the allocation of pay rewards. Considerable evidence exists to show that these performance appraisals are often biased and invalid, and instead of contributing to positive motivation and a good work climate that improves superior subordinate relationships, they lead to just the opposite.[11] These are just two of the most common errors that can develop in the administration of performance-based reward systems. Other common errors include the giving of rewards that are too small, failure to explain systems clearly, and poor administrative practices.

The discussion so far has a clear message about the relationship between the pay system and the strategic planning process: the two must be closely tied together. Organizations get the behaviors they reward; thus if the behaviors called for in the strategic plan are to be present, they must be rewarded. One implication of this point is that whenever there is a change in the strategic plan the reward system needs to be changed to reward the desired behavior. A second implication is that divisions of companies that have different strategic plans need to reward different behaviors, and that usually means they must have different reward systems. Although these points seem obvious, they are often ignored and as a result many strategic plans are never implemented.

In summary, the decision of whether and how to relate pay to performance is a crucial one in any organization. The error of automatically assuming that they should be related can be a serious one. Admittedly, the advantages of doing it effectively are significant and can greatly contribute to the organizational effectiveness. What is often overlooked is that doing it poorly can have more negative consequences than positive ones. Specifically, if performance is difficult to measure and/or rewards are difficult to distribute based on performance, the effect of the pay-for-performance system can be the motivation of counterproductive behaviors, lawsuits charging discrimination, and the creation of a climate of mistrust, low credibility, and managerial incompetence. On the other hand, total abandonment of pay for performance means that the organization gives up a potentially important motivator of performance and as a result may condemn itself to a reduced level of performance. The ideal, of course, is to create conditions in which pay can be effectively related to performance and as a result can be an important contributor to the effectiveness of the organization. Doing this requires a careful articulation between the reward system and the strategic plan so that the strategically correct behaviors are perceived to be rewarded.

Basis for Pay Structure

Traditionally, in organizations such rewards as pay and perquisites are based on the type of jobs that people do. Indeed, with the exception of bonuses and merit salary increases, the standard policy in most organizations is to evaluate the job, not the person, and then to set the reward level. This approach is based on the assumption that job worth can be measured and that the person doing the job is worth only as much to the organization as the job itself is worth. This assumption is in many cases valid, since through such techniques as job evaluation programs it is possible to determine what other organizations are paying people to do the same or similar jobs. Among the advantages of this system is that it assures an organization that its compensation costs are not dramatically out of line with those of its competitors, it gives a somewhat objective basis to compensation practices, and it provides a basis for controlling and predicting the attraction and retention of people.

An alternative to job-based pay is to pay individuals for the skills that they possess. In many cases this will not produce dramatically different pay rates than are produced by paying for the nature of the job. The skills people have usually match reasonably well with the jobs they are doing. It can, however, produce some different results in several respects. Often people have more skills than the job uses and in such cases these individuals are paid more than they would be paid under a job-based system. In other cases individuals don't have the skills when they first enter a job and do not deserve the kind of pay that goes with the job. In these cases individuals have to earn the right to be paid whatever it is the job-related skills are worth.

The most important changes that are introduced when skill-based or competence-based pay is used occur in the kind of climate and motivation it produces. Instead of being rewarded for moving up the hierarchy, people are rewarded for increasing their skills and developing themselves. This can create a climate or culture of concern for personal growth and development, and of course it can produce a highly talented work force. In the case of factories where this system has been used, it typically means that many people in the organization can perform multiple tasks, and thus the work force is highly knowledgeable and flexible.

In most cases where skill-based pay has been tried it tends to produce an interesting mix of positive and negative features as far as the organization is concerned.[12] Typically it tends to produce somewhat higher pay levels for individuals, but this is usally offset by having a more knowledgeable and flexible work force. This in turn leads to lower staffing levels, better decision making, fewer problems when absenteeism or turnover occur, and, indeed, it often leads to lower absenteeism and turnover itself because people like the opportunity to utilize and be paid for a wide range of skills. On the other hand, skill-based pay can be rather challenging to administer because it is not clear how one goes to the outside marketplace and decides, for example, how much a skill is worth. Skill assessment can also often be difficult to accomplish. There are a number of well-developed systems for evaluating jobs and comparing them to the marketplace, but there are none that really do this with respect to the skills an individual has.

There are no well-established rules to determine which organizational situations fit job-based pay and which fit skill- or competence-based pay. In general, skill-based pay seems to fit those organizations that want to have a flexible, relatively permanent work force that is oriented toward learning, growth, and development (e.g., high-tech firms, knowledge work firms, process production manufacturing). It also seems to fit particularly well with new plant start-ups and other situations in which the greatest need is for skill development. Despite the newness and the potential operational problems with skill-based pay it does seem to be a system that more and more organizations will be using.

Market Position

The reward structure of an organization influences behavior partially as a function of how the amount of rewards given compare to what other organizations give. Organizations frequently have well-developed policies about how their pay levels should compare with the pay levels in other companies. For example, some companies (e.g., IBM) feel it is important to be a leading payer, and they consciously set their pay rates at a high level. Other companies are much less concerned about being in the leadership position with respect to pay, and as a result are content to target their pay levels at or below the market. This structural issue in the design of pay systems is a critical one because it can strongly influence the kind and number of people that are attracted and retained. Simply stated, those organizations that adopt a more aggressive stance with respect to the marketplace end up attracting and retaining more individuals. From a business point of view this may pay off for them, particularly if turnover is a costly factor in the organization and if a key part of the business strategy demands attracting and retaining highly talented individuals.

On the other hand, if many of the jobs in the organizations are low-skilled and people are readily available in the labor market to do them, then a corporate strategy of high pay may not be effective. It can increase labor costs and produce a minimum number of benefits. Of course, organizations don't have to be high payers for all the jobs. Indeed, some organizations identify certain key skills they need and adopt the stance of being a high payer for them and an average or below-average payer for other skills. This has some obvious business advantages in terms of allowing organizations to attract the critical skills that are needed to succeed and at the same time to control costs.

The kind of market position that a company adopts with respect to rewards can have a noticeable impact on organization culture. For example, a policy that calls for above-market pay can contribute to the belief that the organization is elite, that people must be competent to be there, and that they are indeed fortunate to be there. A policy that puts certain skill groups into a high market position and leaves the rest of the organization at a lower level can, on the other hand, contribute to a set of elite groups within the organization and cause some divisive social pressures.

Finally, it is interesting to note that some organizations try to be above average in noncash compensation as a way of competing for the talent they need. They talk in terms of producing an above-average quality of work life, and stress not only hygiene factors but interesting and challenging work. This stance potentially can be an effective one because it puts organizations in the position of attracting people who value these things, and could give them a competitive edge at least with these people.

In summary, the kind of market position that an organization has with respect to its total reward package is crucial in determining the behavior of the members as well as the culture of the organization. It needs to be carefully related to the general business strategy of the organization and, in particular, to the kind of human resources and organization culture that are called for by the strategic plan.

Internal/External Equity

Organizations differ in the degree to which they strive toward internal equity in their pay and reward systems. Those organizations that are highly internal-equity–oriented work very hard to see that individuals doing similar work will be rewarded the same, even though they are in very different parts of the country and in different businesses. Some corporations (e.g., IBM) set a national pay structure for their organization based on the highest pay that a job receives anywhere in the country. They are also careful to prescribe the kinds of benefits and perquisites that are given so that people in similar positions throughout the organization receive the same. Those organizations that do not stress internal equity typically focus on the labor market as the key determinant of what somebody should be paid, and although this does not necessarily produce different pay for people doing the same job, it may. For example, the same job in different industries (e.g., electronics and auto) may be paid quite differently.

There are a number of advantages and disadvantages to the strategy of focusing on internal pay comparisons and paying all people in similar jobs the same, regardless of where they are in the organization. It can make the transfer of people from one location to another easier since there aren't any pay differences to contend with. In addition, it can produce an organizational climate of homogeneity, the feeling that everyone working for the same company is treated well and fairly. It also can reduce or eliminate the tendency of people to want to move to a higher-paying division or location. Finally, there is little tendency for rivalry and dissatisfaction to develop within the organization because of poor internal pay comparisons.

On the other hand, a focus on internal equity can be very expensive, particularly if the organization is diversified and, as usually happens, pay rates across the corporation get set at the highest level that the market demands anywhere in the corporation.[13] The disadvantage of this is obvious. It causes organizations to pay a lot more money than is necessary in order to attract and retain good people. Indeed, in some situations it can get so severe that organizations become noncompetitive in certain businesses and find they have to limit themselves to those businesses in which their pay structures make labor costs competitive. Overly high labor costs, for example, often have made it difficult for auto and energy companies to compete in new business areas. It is particularly important to consider this point in the strategic planning process. Before organizations commit themselves to new plans, they need to consider whether it will require a major change in orientation toward market position and how possible/desirable such a change is. Realistic consideration of this point along with some others might have stopped the unwise business diversification that has gone on in some companies.

In summary, the difference between focusing on external equity and internal equity is a crucial one in the design of pay systems. It can determine the costs structure as well as the culture and behavior of organizations. The general rule is that highly diversified companies find themselves pulled more strongly toward an external market orientation, while organizations that are single-industry– or single-technology–based typically find themselves more comfortable with an internal equity emphasis.

Centralized/Decentralized Reward Strategy

Closely related to the issue of internal versus external equity is the issue of a centralized versus decentralized reward system strategy. Those organizations that adopt a centralized strategy typically assign to corporate staff groups the responsibility for seeing that pay practices are similar throughout the organization. They typically develop standard pay grades and pay ranges, standardized job evaluation systems, and, perhaps, standardized promotion systems. In decentralized organizations policy and practice in the areas of pay, promotion, perquisites, and recognition are left to local option. Sometimes decentralized organizations have broad guidelines or principles they wish to stand for, but the day-to-day administration and design of the systems is left up to the local entity.

The advantages of a centralized structure rest primarily in the expertise that can be accumulated at the central level and the degree of homogeneity that is produced in the organization. This homogeneity can lead to a clear image of the corporate culture, feelings of internal equity, and the belief that the organization stands for something. It also eases the job of communicating and understanding what is going on in different parts of the organization. The decentralized strategy allows for local innovation and, of course, close fitting of the practices to the particular business.

Just as is true with many other critical choices, there is no choice between a centralized and decentralized approach that is right for all organizations. Overall, the decentralized system tends to make the most sense when the organization is involved in businesses that face different markets, have different strategic plans, and, perhaps, are at different points in their maturity.[14] It allows those unique practices to surface that can give a competitive advantage to one part of the business but may prove to be a real hindrance or handicap to another. For example, such perquisites as cars are often standard operating procedure in one business while they are not in another. Similarly, hiring bonuses may be needed to attract one group of people (e.g., software engineers), but make little sense in attracting other groups (e.g., research scientists). Management bonuses based on profits may make sense in an established Cash-Cow–type business but not in a start-up business going for market share. Overall, an organization needs to examine carefully its mix of businesses and the degree to which it wants to stand for a certain set of principles or policies across all its operating divisions. Then it can decide whether a centralized or decentralized reward strategy is likely to be most effective.

Degree of Hierarchy

Closely related to the issue of job-based versus competence-based pay is the strategic decision concerning the hierarchical nature of the reward systems in an organization. Often organizations don't make a strategic decision to have a relatively hierarchical or a relatively egalitarian approach to rewards. A hierarchical approach simply happens because it is so consistent with the general way organizations are run. Hierarchical systems usually pay people greater amounts of money as they move higher up the organization ladder, and give people greater perquisites and symbols of office as they move up. The effects of this are many, including strongly reinforcing the traditional hierarchical power relationships in the organization, motivating individuals to seek higher-level jobs, and creating a culture of different status and power levels. In steeply hierarchical reward systems, the reward system may have more levels (e.g., pay grades) in it than the formal organizaion chart and, as a result, create additional status differences in the organization.

The alternative to a hierarchical system is one in which few differences in rewards and perquisites are based on hierarchical level. For example, in those large corporations (e.g., Digital Equipment Corporation) that adopt an egalitarian stance to rewards, such things as private parking spaces, executive restrooms, and special entrances are eliminated. People from all levels in the organization eat together, work together, and travel together. Further, individuals can be relatively highly paid by working their way up a technical ladder and do not have to go into a management ladder in order to gain high levels of pay. This less hierarchical approach to pay and other rewards produces a quite different climate in an organization than does the hierarchical one. It tends to encourage decision making by expertise rather than by hierarchical position, and draws fewer status differences in the organization.

As with all reward system strategic choices, there is no right or wrong answer as to how hierarchical a system should be. In general, a steeply hierarchical system makes the most sense when an organization needs relatively rigid bureaucratic behavior, strong top-down authority, and a strong motivation for people to move up the organizational hierarchy. A more egalitarian approach fits with a more participative management style and with the desire to retain technical specialists and experts in nonmanagement or lower-level management roles. It is not surprising, therefore, that many of the organizations that have emphasized egalitarian perquisites are in high-technology and knowledge-based industries.

Reward Mix

The kind of rewards that organizations give to individuals can vary widely. For example, the money that is given can come in forms varying all the way from stock to medical insurance. Organizations can choose to reward people almost exclusively with cash, downplaying fringe benefits, perquisites, and status symbols. The major advantage of paying cash is that the value of cash in the eyes of most recipients is high. When the cash is translated into fringe benefits, perquisites, and other trappings of office, it may lose its value for some people and as a result be a poor investment.[15] On the other hand, certain benefits can best be obtained through mass purchase, and therefore many individuals want the organization to buy them. In addition, certain status symbols or perquisites may be valued by some individuals beyond their actual dollar cost to the organization and, thus, represent good buys. Finally, as was mentioned earlier, there often are some culture and organizational structure reasons for paying people in the form of perquisites and status symbols.

One interesting development in the area of compensation is the flexible or cafeteria-style benefit program.[16] Here individuals are allowed to make up their own reward package to fit their needs and desires. The theory is that this will lead to organizations' getting the best value for their money because they will give people only those things they desire. It also has the advantage of treating individuals as mature adults rather than as dependent people who need their welfare looked after in a structured way. At the moment this approach has been tried in relatively few organizations. The results have been favorable; thus there is reason to believe that others may be adopting it in the near future because it can offer a strategic cost-benefit advantage in attracting and retaining certain types of employees.

Overall, the choice of what form of rewards to give individuals needs to be driven by a clear feeling of what type of culture the organization wishes to have. For example, the idea of a flexible compensation package is highly congruent with a participative, open-organization climate that treats individuals as talented, mature adults, and wants to attract such people. A status-symbol, noncash-oriented approach may appeal to people who are status-oriented and need a high level of visible reinforcement for their position. This would seem to fit best in a relatively bureaucratic organization that relies on position power and authority in order to carry out its actions.

Summary and Conclusions

The relationship between the key structural features of reward systems and organizational behaviors is summarized in Exhibit 10-4. It shows that the

EXHIBIT 10-4   *Impact of Structure on Key Behaviors*

	Membership	Performance Motivation	Skill Motivation	Culture	Cost
Performance	2	3	1	3	1
Job/competence	2	1	3	2	2
Hierarchy	2	1	2	2	2
External/internal	2	1	1	2	3
Market position	3	1	1	2	3
Innovative	1	1	1	3	2
Centralization	2	2	1	2	1
Cash/benefits	2	1	1	2	2

Note: 0 = no impact; 3 = high impact.

structural dimensions are differentially powerful in affecting the five organizational behaviors. In all cases one or two design features are the most important in determining a particular kind of behavior. For example, performance motivation is primarily determined by the degree to which rewards are based upon performance. The discussion so far clearly indicates that rewards systems can be designed to produce those behaviors that are called for by the strategic plan. The challenge is to match the strategic plan to the design features shown.

PROCESS ISSUES AND REWARD ADMINISTRATION

A number of process issues with respect to reward system design and administration could be discussed here. In some respects process issues come up more often than do structure and content issues because organizations are constantly having to make reward system management, implementation, and communication decisions, while structures tend to be relatively firmly fixed in place. Specific process issues will not be discussed here; rather, the focus will be on two broad process themes that can be used to characterize the way reward systems are designed and administered.

Communication Policy

Organizations differ widely in how much information they communicate about their reward systems. At one extreme, some organizations are extremely secretive, particularly in the area of pay. They forbid people from talking about their individual rewards, give minimal information to individuals about how rewards are decided upon and allocated, and have no publicly disseminated policies about such things as market position, their approach to gathering market data, and the rewards individuals can and do receive. At the other extreme, some organizations are so open that everyone's pay is a matter of public record, as is the overall organization pay philosophy (many new high-involvement plants operate this way).[17] In addition, all promotions are subject to open job postings, and in some instances peer groups discuss the eligibility of people for promotion.

The difference between an open and a closed communication policy in the area of rewards is enormous. Like all the other choices that must be made in designing a reward system, there is no clear right or wrong approach. Rather, it is a matter of picking a position on the continuum from open to secret that is supportive of the overall culture and types of behavior needed for organizational effectiveness. An open system tends to encourage people to ask questions, share data, and ultimately be involved in decisions. On the other hand, a secret system tends to put people in a more dependent position to keep power concentrated at the top and to allow an organization to keep its options open with respect to commitments to individuals. Some negative side effects of secret systems are the existence of considerable distortion about the actual rewards that people get and creation of a low-trust environment in which people have trouble understanding the relationship between pay and performance.[18] Thus a structurally sound pay system may end up being rather ineffective because it is misperceived if strong secrecy policies are kept in place.

Open systems put considerable pressure on organizations to do an effective job of administering rewards. Thus if such difficult-to-defend policies as merit pay are to be implemented, considerable time and effort need to be invested in pay administration. If they are done poorly, strong pressures usually develop to eliminate the policies and pay everyone the same.[19] Ironically, therefore, if an organization wants to spend little time administrating rewards, but still wants to have merit pay, secrecy may be the best policy, although secrecy in turn may limit the effectiveness of the merit pay plan. As far as strategic planning is concerned, communication policy may be crucial if the plan calls for a high-involvement work culture. As will be discussed later, open communication fits well with a high-involvement culture.

Decision-Making Practices

Closely related to the issue of communication is the issue of decision making. Open communication makes possible the involvement of a wide range of people in the decision-making process concerning rewards. Further, if individuals are to be actively involved in decisions concerning reward systems, they need to have information about policy and actual practice.

In discussing the type of decision-making processes that are used in organizations with respect to reward systems, it is important to distinguish between decisions concerning the design of reward systems and decisions concerning the ongoing administration of reward systems. It is possible to have different decision-making styles with respect to each of these two types of decisions. Traditionally, of course, organizations have made both design and ongoing administration decisions in a top-down manner.

Systems typically have been designed by top management with the aid of staff support and administered by strict reliance on the chain of command. The assumption has been that this provides the proper checks and balances in the system and in addition locates decision making where the expertise rests. In many cases this is a valid assumption and certainly fits well with an organizational management style that emphasizes hierarchy, bureaucracy, and control through the use of extrinsic rewards. It does not fit, however, with an organization that believes in more open communication, higher levels of involvement on the part of people, and control through individual commitment to policies. It also doesn't fit when expertise is broadly spread throughout the organization. This is often true in organizations that rely heavily on knowledge workers, or that spend a great deal of effort training their people to become expert in technical functions.

There have been some reports in the research literature of organizations experimenting with having employees involved in the design of pay systems.[20] For example, employees have been involved in designing their own bonus systems and the results have been generally favorable. When employees are involved, it leads them to raise important issues and to provide expertise that is not normally available to the designers of the system. And perhaps more importantly, once the system is designed the acceptance level of it and the understanding of it tends to be very high. This often leads to a rapid start-up of the system and to a commitment to see it survive long-term. In other cases, systems have been designed by line managers rather than by staff support people because of the need to have them support it, maintain it, and be committed to it. In the absence of significant design input from line people, it often is unrealistic to expect them to have the same level of commitment to the system as the staff people.

There also has been some experimentation with having peer groups and low-level supervisory people handle the day-to-day decision making about who should receive pay increases and how jobs should be evaluated and placed in pay structures. The most visible examples of this are in the new participative plants that use skill-based pay.[21] In these, typically, the work group reviews the performance of the individual and decides whether he or she has acquired the new skills. Interestingly, what evidence there is suggests that this has gone very well. In many respects this is not surprising, since the peers often have the best information about performance and thus are in a good position to make a performance assessment. The problem in traditional organizations is that they lack the motivation to give valid feedback and to respond responsibly; thus their expertise is of no use. In more participative open systems this motivational problem seems to be less severe, and as a result involvement in decision making seems to be more effective. There also have been isolated instances of executives assessing each other in a peer group (e.g., in Graphic Controls Corporation). Again, there is evidence that this can work effectively when combined in a history of open and effective communication. Deciding on rewards is clearly not an easy task for groups to do and thus should be taken on only when there is comfort

EXHIBIT 10-5   *Impact of Process on Key Behaviors*

	Membership	Performance Motivation	Skill Motivation	Culture	Cost
Participative:					
Design	2	1	1	3	1
Administration	2	1	1	3	1
Open/Closed:					
Design	2	2	0	3	1
Administration	2	2	0	3	1

Note: Rating = 0 (no impact) to 3 (high impact).

with the confrontation skills of the group and trust in their ability to talk openly and directly about each other's performance.

Overall, there is evidence that some participative approaches to reward-system design and administration can be effective. The key seems to be articulating the practices in the area of reward systems with the general management style of the organization. In more participative settings there is good reason to believe that participative approaches to reward systems can be effective because of their congruence with the overall style, and because the skills and norms to make them effective are already in place. In more traditional organizations the typical top-down approach to reward-system design and administration probably remains the best. From a strategic point of view the decision about how much participation should exist in the reward-system design and administration must rest upon whether a participative high-involvement–type organization is best in order to accomplish the strategic objectives of the business. If so, then participation in pay decisions and reward system decisions should be considered.

Summary and Conclusions

The relationship between process and behavior is summarized in Exhibit 10-5. It shows that the major impact of process is on culture. There also is an impact on membership that is very much related to culture. Individuals differ in the kinds of process they want, and as a result, not everyone likes an open participative culture. Still it is seen as attractive by many and usually leads to low absenteeism and turnover. Finally, performance is likely to be impacted only to the degree that it is perceived to be rewarded, something that can be made clearer with an open information system.

REWARD-SYSTEM CONGRUENCE

So far each reward-system design feature has been treated as an independent factor. This was done for exposition of the concepts only; it fails to emphasize the importance of overall reward-system congruence. Reward-system design features are not stand-alone items. There is considerable evidence that they effect each other and need to be supportive of the same types of behavior, reflect the same overall managerial philosophy, and be generated by the same business strategy.

Exhibit 10-6 illustrates one effort to define congruent sets of reward-system practices.[22] Here the effort is to show how two different management philosophies call for two very different reward-system practices. The two management philosophies portrayed here are a traditional bureaucratic management style and a participative employee involvement strategy. Every reward-system practice needs to be different in these two cases. The reward-system practices that go with traditional bureaucratic models tend to be more secretive, more top-down, and oriented toward producing regularity in behavior. On the other hand, the participative practices encourage self-development, openness, employee involvement in reward-system allocation decisions, and, ultimately, more innovation and commitment to the organization. Whether these are desirable or not is a function of the strategic plan

EXHIBIT 10-6   *Appropriate Reward System Practices*

	Traditional	Participative
Noncash Rewards		
Fringe benefits	Vary according to organization level	Cafeteria—same for all levels
Promotion	All decisions made by top management	Opening posting for all jobs; peer group involvement in decision process
Status symbols	A great many; carefully allocated on the basis of job position	Few present, low emphasis on organization level
Pay System		
Type of System	Hourly and Salary	All Salary
Base rate	Based on job performed; high enough to attract job applicants	Based on skills; high enough to provide security and attract applicants
Incentive plan	Piece rate	Group and organizationwide bonus, lump sum increase
Communication policy	Very restricted distribution of information	Individual rates, salary survey data, all other information made public
Decision-making focus	Top management	Close to location of person whose pay is being set

of the organizations; thus reward-system congruence is good only if it fits the strategic plan.

The importance of congruence is not limited to just the reward system in an organization. The reward system needs to fit the other features of the organization in order for the total human resource management system to be effective. This means the reward system needs to fit such things as the way jobs are designed, the leadership style of the supervisors, and the types of career tracks that are available in the organization, to mention just a few. Unless this kind of fit exists, the organization will be replete with conflicts, and, to a degree, the reward system practices will potentially be cancelled out by the practices in other areas. To mention just one example, an organization can have a very well-developed performance appraisal system, but in the absence of well designed jobs and effective supervisory behavior it will be ineffective. Performance appraisal demands interpersonally competent supervisory behavior and jobs that allow for good performance measures.

REWARD SYSTEMS AND CHANGE

The implementation of a new strategic plan frequently calls for major behavior changes in the organization. New behaviors are often needed both to install the plan and to adhere to it over a period of years. As has been stressed throughout this chapter, behavior change in turn requires changes in such important features of an organization as its structure, information systems, membership, and, of course, its reward systems. So far so good, but reward systems often can be difficult to change themselves and can be an obstacle to change in other areas as well.

The reasons why reward systems are difficult to change are many, but one stands out: concern about the negative impact of change on the rewards people receive. Even though individuals may complain about their existing reward system, the prospects of a new one may be more negative. This is particularly likely to be true in an older organization when the reward system has been in place for a number of years. Over time, those people who strongly object to the system usually leave, and the remaining employees are ones who feel the existing system treats them favorably. The fact that new members of the organization often come because they like the reward system further contributes to maintenance of the status quo. In short, most existing members of an organization typically have a vested interest in maintaining the present system.

The reward system often is an obstacle to other kinds of change because of its connection to the other features of an organization. Changes in almost any other area have implications for the reward system; thus other changes are often resisted by those who prefer to maintain the existing reward system. A clear example of this point involves changes in organization structure, a common consequence of a new business strategy. Changes in structure usually call for the reallocation of resources (e.g., budgets, subordinates, etc.). This, in turn, calls for the reevalutation of jobs and in many cases changes in pay rates. Those individuals who stand to lose by this reevaluation may be expected to resist the restructuring and the strategic plan.

Unfortunately, there is no simple formula for overcoming resistance to change in the reward system. As has been discussed elsewhere in considerable detail, sometimes process innovation can help.[23] In particular, openness and participation can facilitate change by reducing fear of the unknown and by allowing individuals to influence the changes in ways that will make them acceptable.

There also are some structural things that can be done to overcome resistance to change. One obvious thing is to guarantee that no one's pay and benefits will be reduced as a result of the change. This can slow the effect of the change in some cases, but it will reduce the resistance. A second approach is to offer one-shot bonuses or incentives for successfully implementing the change. Few organizations have done this, but it fits with the idea that major strategic change involves moving through a period of transition before the new steady state is reached. During this transition period special reward systems may be needed to encourage people to perform effectively and move toward the new steady state.

CONCLUSION

Overall, the design of an effective reward system demands a close articulation between the business strategy of an organization and the reward system. It also depends on a close fit between the reward system and other design features of the organization. Thus, there is no one right set of reward-system practices and it is impossible to design an effective reward system in the absence of knowing how other design features of the organization are arrayed. This suggests that the key strategic decisions about the reward system need to be made in a fashion in which tentative reward system design decisions are driven by the business strategy and then are tested against how other features of the organization are being designed. The key, of course, is ultimately to come up with an integrated human resource management strategy that is consistent in the way it encourages people to behave, that attracts the kind of people that can support the business strategy, and that encourages them to behave appropriately.

NOTES

1. See, for example, W. F. Whyte, Ed., *Money and Motivation: An Analysis of Incentives in Industry,* Harper, New York, 1955.
2. See, for example, E. E. Lawler, *Motivation in Work Organizations,* Brooks/Cole, Monterey, Calif., 1973; W. H. Mobley, *Employee Turnover: Causes, Consequences, and Control,* Addison-Wesley, Reading, Mass., 1982.

3. See, for example, V. H. Vroom, *Work and Motivation,* Wiley, New York, 1964; Lawler, *Motivation in Work Organizations.*

4. See E. E. Lawler, *Pay and Organization Development,* Addison-Wesley, Reading, Mass., 1981.

5. S. Kerr, "On the Folly of Rewarding A, While Hoping for B." *Academy of Management Journal,* vol. 18, 1975, pp. 769–783.

6. See, for example, Whyte, *Money and Motivation;* E. E. Lawler, *Pay and Organizational Effectiveness: A Psychological View,* McGraw-Hill, New York, 1971.

7. See, for example, J. R. Galbraith and D. A. Nathanson, *Strategy Implementation: The Role of Structure and Process,* West, St. Paul, 1978; J. Salscheider, "Devising Pay Strategies for Diversified Companies," *Compensation Review,* 1981, pp. 15–24.

8. See, for example, G. S. Crystal, *Executive Compensation,* 2nd ed., AMACOM, New York, 1978; B. R. Ellig, *Executive Compensation—A Total Pay Perspective,* McGraw-Hill, New York, 1982.

9. See Lawler, *Pay and Organizational Effectiveness.*

10. Ibid.

11. See, for example, D. L. DeVries, A. M. Morrison, S. L. Shullman, and M. L. Gerlach, *Performance Appraisal on the Line,* Wiley-Interscience, New York, 1981; G. P. Latham and K. N. Wexley, *Increasing Productivity through Performance Appraisal,* Addison-Wesley, Reading, Mass., 1981; E. E. Lawler, A. Mohrman, and S. Resnick, "Performance Appraisal Revisited," *Organizational Dynamics,* 1984.

12. See Lawler, *Pay and Organization Development.*

13. See Salscheider, "Devising Pay Strategies."

14. L. Greiner, "Evolution and Revolution as Organizations Grow," *Harvard Business Review,* vol. 50, no. 4, 1972, pp. 37–46; see also Galbraith and Nathanson, *Strategy Implementation.*

15. See, for example, S. Nealy, "Pay and Benefit Preferences," *Industrial Relations,* vol. 3, 1963, pp. 17–28; Lawler, *Pay and Organizational Effectiveness.*

16. See, for example, Lawler, *Pay and Organization Development.*

17. See, for example, E. E. Lawler, "The New Plant Revolution," *Organizational Dynamics,* vol. 6, no. 3, pp. 2–12; R. E. Walton, "Establishing and Maintaining High Commitment Work Systems," in J. R. Kimberly and R. H. Miles and Associates, *The Organizational Life Cycle,* Jossey-Bass, San Francisco, 1980.

18. See, for example, Lawler, *Pay and Organizational Effectiveness;* F. Steele, *The Open Organization,* Addison-Wesley, Reading, Mass., 1975.

19. See, for example, J. D. Burroughs, "Pay Secrecy and Performance; The Psychological Research," *Compensation Review,* vol. 14, no. 3, 1982, pp. 44–54.

20. See Lawler, *Pay and Organization Development,* where these are reviewed.

21. See, for example, Walton, "Establishing and Maintaining High Commitment Work Systems."

22. E. E. Lawler, "Reward Systems," in J. R. Hackman and J. L. Suttle, Eds., *Improving Life at Work,* Goodyear, Santa Monica, Calif., 1977.

23. See Lawler, *Pay and Organization Development.*

CHAPTER *11*

Failures in Strategic Planning

PETER A. MICHEL

PETER A. MICHEL is President of the Penn Central Technical Security Co. an electronic security services subsidiary of the Penn Central Corporation. He was previously Vice President for Business Development of Penn Central's Electronics, Defense and Telecommunications Group, responsible for identifying and developing new business opportunities with special emphasis on U.S. government customers and overseas business relationships. These activities involved him in acquisitions, joint ventures, and product-line expansions. He has had planning responsibilities in the White House, where he served on the Domestic Council Staff, and in three U.S.-based multinational corporations. Mr. Michel holds a B.A. in Political Science from Colgate University and a Master's Degree in Public Administration from the University of Virginia.

OUTLINE

THE STRATEGIC PLANNER'S ENVIRONMENT

Within U.S.-based multinational corporations, corporate strategic planning has frequently failed to be an effective contributor to the strategic management process. As a practitioner of the art and science of strategic planning, I conducted an heuristic review of strategic planning experiences in the federal government and in three Fortune 200 corporations to highlight the nature of some of these failures.

First, some definitions:

Strategic management: Strategic management is the discipline employed by top corporate decision makers to assure the survival and prosperity of the enterprise as a wealth-creating institution.

Strategic Planning: Strategic planning is a staff support activity with the task of assisting the strategic managers.

The strategic planners are not decision makers, but they must raise issues and they must provide solutions. The analytical skills on which the profession has put such focus are only relevant to the extent that they are brought to bear on issues that are important and for which real action choices are available.

Conscious Decisions

The objective of strategic planners is to do everything they can to make sure that designated decision makers are making conscious decisions. Most business decisions are made in the context of inadequate, misleading, and inconsistent information. Therefore a great deal of judgment is required. Strategic planners have the responsibility to see that the decision makers have whatever helps them to make those judgments in as informed a fashion as possible and that they are conscious of the potential consequences.

Large U.S. Multinational Corporations

The types of business enterprises discussed here are those that are made up of thousands of people and have financial resources measured in the hundreds of millions of dollars. Such enterprises will likely have annual sales of at least one billion dollars. The distinction of size is crucially important because communication within such giant institutions is qualitatively different from that within smaller entities.

The political, social, and economic contexts within which giant institutions exist are also different from those experienced by smaller entities. Increasingly, all corporations, but particularly the largest ones, are being pressured by outside forces to take on roles that are far removed from their fundamental wealth-creation imperative. They are being pushed to be providers of employment, trainers of the overall labor force, educators of marginal workers, providers of financial resources for cultural and educational institutions, providers of social services for their own employees and for members of their communities, etc.

Given their own complexity and the external pressures giant enterprises face, they must focus on only a limited number of fundamental objectives in order to be effective.

Wealth Creation

The wealth-creating profit that corporations are responsible for making is a real excess of cash beyond that required to meet expenses necessary to maintain the corporations' ability to generate future real profits. It is not the after-tax net income reported in financial statements. This latter accounting construct is a useful measurement tool but, by definition, it is not necessarily available in cash form.

The cash profit is essential to provide a return on the capital invested in the enterprise to owners. If this return is not forthcoming, the capital invested will either be withdrawn or will be diminished in reduced valuations.

Achieving Real Cash Profits

Profit is not an automatic consequence of conducting business activities. It is essential, however, if an enterprise is to continue conducting business. The competitive environments in which all corporations function are essentially unstable. There are, of course, periods of apparent stability when one corporation will appear to have such a secure position as to be unassailable. However, it has been repeatedly shown that once such a corporation actually behaves in accordance with the perception that its prosperity is guaranteed, its decline has likely already begun.

Frequently, the corporation that appears to be in a secure position of dominance is very slow to recognize its decline and consequently is slow in altering its behavior. The American railroads and their regulators did not recognize the implications of the growth of commercial aviation and increased automobile use until many of those giant corporations were weakened beyond the point where they could be returned to financial health.

More recently, the decline of the American steel industry, perhaps best exemplified by United States Steel's desperate takeover of Marathon Oil Corporation, which was motivated by the unprofitability of steel, has followed the same pattern.

THE PLANNING PROFESSION AND TACTICAL DECISIONS

Strategic management involves both tactical and strategic decisions, those relating to operational and to directional matters, respectively. Most decisions are tactical in the sense that they are consistent with past assumptions and present directions and are designed to improve the results of an ongoing business activity. Important decisions in this category involve incremental changes in such areas as:

Research and development
Advertising
Pricing (including payment terms)
Product enhancement
Overhead burdens
Plant expansion and modernization
Personnel policies

Individuals at several levels have critical roles in such decision making. Successively higher levels of management tend to act in a testing and review capacity, while operating managers directly responsible for results are generally the initiators of specific proposals. Such initiation is frequently encouraged, sometimes strongly, by higher management.

The systemic failures in planning have generally not been in the tactical arena or in the analytical techniques employed by planners to support tactical decision-making processes. This support system has generally been effective.

From time to time, different analytical methods and conceptual frameworks are in vogue. Environment scanning, share-of-market analyses, price-point positioning, and numerous other tools for tactical decision support have been honed to great precision over the last decade. Practicing planners have made important contributions to the improved operation of strategic business units through the application of such tools.

THE PLANNING PROFESSION AND STRATEGIC DECISIONS

In contrast, strategic decisions, which result in changes in business direction, are the unique province of top management. It is in this area that corporate strategic planners have failed repeatedly to support effectively the strategic decision making of top management.

Strategic decisions are formulated at some distance from the activities of the particular business. They require the objectivity that comes from distance and the perspective that allows for tradeoffs between totally unrelated businesses. Planners have frequently failed to provide that perspective.

Strategic Issues

In any particular period, each industry and/or company faces, at the most, only a few directional issues relating to its fundamental ability to create wealth. These issues are the ones that have long been recognized as needing careful monitoring and are the topics of almost continual discussion.

At any given time in the life of the institution, there are lots of questions or items requiring resolution, clarification, or change, but the major ones, the ones that really affect the fundamental health of the institution, are very few in number—perhaps three or four. A good way to distinguish major issues from minor ones is the relationship of these issues to the continuation of the enterprise or to an important part of it.

Examples of such major issues include:

1. The effect of the emergence of solid-state electronic devices on the vacuum tube industry.
2. The impact of superior smaller automobiles from overseas on the U.S. automotive industry.
3. The aging of the U.S. steel industry relative to its worldwide competition.
4. The impacts of overseas expropriation, the loss of federal tax preference, and the alternating shortages and surpluses of crude oil on the U.S.-based multinational oil companies.
6. When and how to get out of a particular business activity or country:
   Real estate development where it appears to be incompatible with the operating culture and accounting methods
   Country X in a situation where political and economic climates are unfavorable
   A failed joint venture in which the objectives and capabilities of the partners are incompatible
   Technology, such as synthetic fuels, that may never pay off commercially in a reasonable time frame

If these types of issues are not promptly resolved, the entire organization deteriorates, good people leave, customers lose confidence, market share erodes, product quality deteriorates, and earnings go down. These effects in turn reduce the company's ability to respond creatively.

"The People Problem" Masking a Strategic Issue

Frequently such strategic issues are perceived and stated in terms of people, a perspective that diverts attention from the root issue. Such formulations have the added effect of reducing the likelihood of early action of any variety.

When a strategic issue is masked by an actual, or at least a perceived, people problem, it probably will not be addressed squarely. Why aren't the people generously provided for and directed to future career paths that would be more personally appropriate? When it is evident to everyone that the current unit head is not the man to lead the unit in the future, why don't top managers act?

Top managers are in most cases possessed by the most exemplary motives. They do not want to disrupt the operation. They want to give the unit head as much of a chance as they can. They do not know where they can get a better person.

These good motives, however, tend to divert attention from the strategic dilemma that frequently exists. If there is a real sense among top management that a discontinuous change in direction is needed, it may turn out that the current unit head, with his undeniable knowledge of the industry, may be just the individual to implement the new direction. What is missing is (1) the recognition of the strategic dilemma in addition to a people problem, if there is one, (2) the thorough analysis of new strategic options, and (3) a firm action-forcing decision.

The Bad Fit Division

Every large corporation has one or more units that really do not fit its long-term strategy. Why don't the decision makers "bite the bullet" and sell off or shut down such units? Sometimes they are waiting for the market, hoping conditions for the sale of such a unit will improve. Sometimes they intend to package it for sale, use it as a Cash Cow, or find more promising businesses and then sell it.

These are not bad concepts, but they frequently result in the same catastrophe. The market conditions are never quite right. People inside and outside of the company sense that the unit is targeted for disposition and act accordingly. Therefore things get worse. Many companies run the scenario out to the extent that, by the time that they are finally ready to act, the asset can only be disposed of at a write-down that is so colossal that the management group puts off action indefinitely.

The New Product or Acquisition

In most large corporations, discussions will go on for months or even years concerning the need to enter a new market, provide a different product, or do something to reposition a particular business significantly. However, somehow the more visible the requirement is, the less likely it is that anything meaningful will be done—the market is never right. Several false starts will be made involving token efforts to "test the water." Management becomes convinced that redirection is no longer an issue because they have made a decision and are simply awaiting the right circumstances to implement it. Those circumstances seldom materialize as hoped.

THE FAILURE PATTERNS

There are a number of patterns that underlie the failures of strategic management and the supporting strategic planning. Recognition of these and conscious avoidance of such behavior modes can enhance the strategic planner's contribution to good strategic management. The patterns that are symptomatic of serious corporate problems and that should generate quick action by strategic planners are:

1. Tolerance for major unresolved issues.
2. Inaction on emerging major issues.
3. The general's doing the colonel's job.
4. Making key decisions outside of the normal process.
5. Redesigning the process for each decision.
6. Incomplete decision communication.
7. Poorly designed strategic mission statements.

Tolerance for Major Unresolved Issues

Most of the major strategic failures in large institutions, both public and private, stem from an excessive tolerance of major unresolved issues. The problem is not a lack of information or analyses. It is a paralysis similar to that of a pilot, a ship's captain, or a racing-car driver who sees an accident about to happen and becomes mesmerized by the evolving catastrophe rather than stimulated into action to prevent it.

In most large strategic failures, when action is finally taken it is too small in magnitude and too late. The problem has usually been observed, analyzed, consulted on, and discussed repeatedly at the highest levels of the institution, including the board of directors. Frequently a "decision" has even been made. However, it is often a decision without an implementation schedule.

What distinguishes great management from average management is the speed with which it does the obvious. The resolution of strategic issues require a force of will and a commitment of management resources in addition to financial resources. Such issues also require the elimination of options, a rejection of alternatives, and a dedicated effort that is both public and pervasive. The action taken must be obvious and its consequences must be rapidly evident. Thus action of the proper magnitude cannot be hidden; the consequences of a wrong decision are obvious. This reality tends to encourage caution.

It is probably of this, the failure to facilitate action-forcing decisions on crucial issues, that the strategic planning fraternity is the most guilty. While the problem may be recognized, the need to act on it decisively is not.

In response to corporate management's concerns about such issues, the planners often produce in-depth analyses, ultimately trying to know more about the particular area than the designated line managers know. While this is academically fascinating, it generally does not move the resolution of the issue ahead.

A key responsibility of the planning community is to alert management as early as possible to the fact that decisive action needs to be taken. This is a difficult marketing job.

In the case of weak or faltering divisions, there is a tremendous amount of investment in the form of time, money, and commitment behind these activities, and there is a great hesitancy to take the literal or figurative write-off associated with the decision to terminate an activity or to redirect an activity fundamentally. It is the responsibility of the planners to alert managers as soon as possible that the time for change has arrived. The decision to make a major strategic change, to add an important new activity, or to terminate an important present activity is traumatic because it represents a discontinuous change rather than an evolutionary change.

The recent demise of Gulf Oil Corporation, at one point one of America's great companies, was not caused by the recent takeover battle. Rather, it was caused by strategic drift that went on for more than a decade, during which time Gulf Oil considered buying circuses, and a variety of other bizarre activities, in order to employ its "excess" cash. When Jimmy Lee became Chairman and began to address Gulf's fundamental strategic issues—its diminishing oil and gas reserves and its unprofitable "downstream" operations—he was too late. He had too few options. Obviously, for many years, the planners had failed to convince top management that decisive action on getting more oil and cutting "downstream" costs was needed.

During the middle 1970s, Gulf's research-and-development focus shifted from emphasizing oil detection techniques and enhancing recovery methodologies to turning coal into synthetic fuel. While the latter activity may have had some long-term potential, it sapped the R & D efforts that were directly related to the corporation's number one issue.

The situation at Gulf in the 1970s that resulted in its demise in the 1980s is akin to the breakdowns in diplomacy that began a decade before World War I. The assassination of the Austrian Archduke in Sarajevo might have been the spark that ignited the conflagration, but incendiary conditions had been present for a long time.

The responsibility rests with the planners to identify key issues requiring resolution and to present thoroughly planned options for action to persuade senior management that the time for a decision has arrived. The persuasion is by far the more difficult task.

A strategic failure in a large company has a certain macabre quality. What is wrong is evident and is intensively studied and debated, but the action needed to fix the problem is not taken.

Inaction on Emerging Major Issues

The corollary to the problem of an excessive tolerance for major unresolved issues is failure to address emerging issues adequately. These are the tactical questions that can ultimately become major issues if left unaddressed. Success for strategic planners can be defined as keeping the number of major issues as low as possible. This can be done by defining the minor problems that need resolution, determining the proper level in the organization to address them, persuading the appropriate individuals that action is needed, and doing the work that will clearly present the options. Such minor issues are not survival issues, but are incipient survival issues.

Major capital decisions, new factories, new manufacturing processes, and major R&D expense choices all have long-term impacts and need to be focused on by strategic planners so that the implicit decisions are consciously made. If these questions are not addressed as they arise, the available options for the business narrow quickly.

Singer's U.S. sewing machine business was plagued by minor problems many years before it nearly took the whole company down with it. Increasing overseas competition, deteriorating quality, and antiquated production facilities, among other problems, were well-known to the Singer decision makers. Yet they were not effectively addressed. If these problems had been considered in a strategic context and squarely dealt with, many of the later problems could have been avoided. The strategic planners failed to convince the decision makers that, if left unresolved, these issues would become major survival questions.

A similar situation was present in Gulf Oil during the 1970s. The Canadian government was proposing a greater percentage of Canadian ownership of the Canadian affiliates of U.S. oil companies. Gulf Oil owned two-thirds of Gulf Canada and recognized that it would have to reduce its stake. Studies were done, recommendations for partial sale were made, and no action was taken. By waiting for the ideal time to sell, Gulf management failed to take advantage of a window of opportunity that was open before such ownership reductions were mandated. Thus the value potential was allowed to diminish due to inaction.

The General's Doing the Colonel's Job

Strategic planning as a profession has also failed its clients by either not recognizing or not alerting the clients to the breakdown of the strategic management process itself. In military parlance, if the General is doing the Colonel's job, then the General's job is not being done adequately. They have different responsibilities.

When there is a problem, senior levels of an organizational hierarchy frequently get deeper and deeper into the day-to-day operations; several unintended consequences result from this. Nobody has any perspective. The accountability of line operating management is heightened and its responsibility is diminished. Discontinuous changes are not considered because all interested parties are taking a limited view of the situation.

The organizational sicknesses that result from such situations include the loss of key middle managers, the reduction of productivity, people spending their time reporting on what they are doing rather than doing what they are reporting, etc. Under the most favorable circumstances, this inappropriate allocation of managerial resources results in highlighting some of the less significant operational matters while the strategic direction of the business is increasingly neglected. The battles are won and the war lost.

The most obvious example of this syndrome occurs when corporate management usurps the pricing authority of the business unit. In planning meetings, the operating executive will explain his or her pricing plans relative to maintaining market share. Corporate management, while agreeing with the market share goals, will emphasize margins that can be achieved only by giving up share. If the business unit gives in to this sort of directed pricing pressure, serious dislocations frequently follow. Corporate strategic planners, who are often eager to make operating decisions, easily fall into the trap of helping the corporate decision makers second-guess field managers. They can become infatuated with complex price calculations while remaining ignorant of the many intangible elements of the business relationships of which pricing is only one part.

Making Key Decisions Outside the Normal Process

A fourth failure of strategic planners is allowing the normal strategic decision-making process to be circumvented. The governmental crisis that resulted in the resignation of President Richard M. Nixon was finally precipitated by a progression of events in which strategic decisions were made outside the established channels.

The Nixon White House had a very effective decision-making process in place. Presidential decisions were preceded by the collection of options, recommendations, and opinions from all relevant elements within the government. This information was then thoroughly reviewed within the major affected agencies and departments and then was again reviewed and analyzed by the White House staff. The final analysis by the White House staff itself did not eliminate any of the information, but rather provided recommendations and provided a variety of pro and con arguments associated with each of the major options.

Had the response to the Watergate break-in been handled by this well-oiled system, errors would have been identified, publicly acknowledged, and corrected. As it was, because lots of different organizations and individuals were involved in various aspects, the enormity of the problems was not evident to anyone until the situation had become terminal for the Administration.

Donald Rumsfeld, Secretary of Defense under President Ford and an unusually astute decision maker, has observed that "process is substance." While this comment was made in a different context from Watergate, it certainly applies to it.

Many major business acquisitions are made exactly the same way: The planning and analysis systems in place to support strategic decision-making processes are completely circumvented. A classic apocryphal story is that of the CEOs of two companies reaching an agreement to merge on a golf course, with no meaningful prior analysis. In retrospect, many of these decisions turn out to be great mistakes. This is because the thorough analysis that should have preceded such decisions was never done. What then happens is that the implementation process becomes a catch-as-catch-can effort resulting in confusion, reversed strategic directions, and so forth.

A strategic planning system has great value only if it is employed properly. The responsibility for the failure of top decision makers to utilize strategic planners at such critical junctures in most cases lies with the planners themselves. They have not anticipated the need or the opportunity for major acquisitions, or in any case have not provided valuable support to the decision maker as he or she searches for acquisitions. When the moment comes, the decision maker concludes that the planners would not be very helpful anyway, so they are not brought in until after the fact.

Redesigning the Process for Each Decision

W. Edwards Demming observes that 94 percent of quality problems are systemic or common, while the remaining 6 percent are random. Statistical quality control à la Demming cannot reasonably be applied to strategic decisions due to the judgment factors involved, but a similar perspective can be fruitfully applied to the process itself. If a unique decision-making process is used for each separate major decision, the results are likely to be disappointing at best.

If the same basic process is used each time, two important opportunities are presented. First, the decision makers are more likely to learn from past mistakes. Second, the decision support process itself can be improved through exercise. Decision makers will get a better sense of what they need and planners will improve their decision support skills.

The process is truly a team effort. The different styles, perceptions, and perspectives of individual CEOs and other top decision makers require a customized decision support system. What works well for one, say voluminous notebooks, will be inappropriate for another, who may want to be briefed orally by industry experts, etc. It takes time and practice for the team to become truly effective.

In other words, don't redesign for each decision, but do redesign for each decision-maker.

Having a well-exercised system is crucial when a major issue must be dealt with. That is not a good time to be figuring out how to address an issue.

Incomplete Decision Communication

Another failure of planners is in decision communication—the facilitating, orchestrating, and coordinating of communication within a corporation concerning its strategic decisions. It is a task that few strategic planners are willing to take on. It is time-consuming, it is frustrating, and it inevitably results in conflicts. This function, however, is probably as important as the decision support function itself, because implementation of strategic decisions requires first and foremost that the people affected by the decisions understand what they are. Therefore if the strategic planners take the responsibility of communicating strategic decisions, they will have an added incentive to insure that the steps necessary to implement a strategic decision have been defined as part of the decision process.

Where the communication of a strategic decision is informal, from the corporate decision maker to the division head, key elements of the decision can be glossed over. By their very nature strategic decisions involve changes in direction and therefore should influence many of the operations of the affected business unit. If the intended consequences are not spelled out, implementation will be plagued by confusion and reinterpretation.

Effective communication and subsequent monitoring of progress must be intergral parts of the process or implementation will break down. If the planners can get themselves a charter to be communicators, the quality of the decisions will improve in tandem with implementation experience.

Poorly Designed Strategic Mission Statements

A final failure of planners is as editors of "mission statements." All institutions need to have a clear sense of where they are trying to go in order for the diverse elements that make them up to pull in a uniform direction. This is particularly true for large, complex multinational corporations.

Strategic planners need to serve as editors or critics of the corporation's internal and external statements of strategy. To be meaningful, strategic mission statements need to be limiting. They need to state implicitly or explicitly what is not, as well as what is, intended, and, further, they have to identify how the planned result is going to be achieved.

The greatest flaw of most mission statements is that the implicit message is that "we" are smarter, will work harder, and will do a better job. In the competitive marketplace of goods, serivices, and ideas, to assume that you are smarter, faster, or meaner than the competition inevitably leads to surprises and the realization that you and your colleagues are just about on par with the quality of the people with whom you are competing. This is a matter of statistical averages. If all competitors think they are superior, some must be wrong.

To be meaningful and operative, the strategies and implementation programs must be discrete, measurable, and finite. Most importantly, these must be precisely articulated if they are to have any real potential for success.

4

FUNCTIONAL PLANS

CHAPTER 12

Acquisition Planning

PETER L. GARTMAN

PETER L. GARTMAN is Vice President, Development for Emerson Electric Company. He has over 16 years of experience with major corporations in such areas as acquisitions, divestitures, security analysis, portfolio management, foreign exchange exposure management, financial analysis, and control and strategic planning. Mr. Gartman held numerous positions with Black & Decker Manufacturing including Vice President, Corporate Planning and Acquisitions. He was a security analyst for U.S. Fidelity & Guaranty. He earned an M.B.A. from Loyola College and a B.S. in Chemical Engineering from Lehigh University.

OUTLINE

Strategic acquisition planning has as an ultimate objective the maximization of the owner's value given some level of acceptable risk. The process of creating value through acquisition is particularly troublesome. First, the presence, or feared presence, of other bidders in the active market affects the purchase price. Second, the level of risk that other bidders are willing to accept may be higher than that which the company is willing to accept. Finally, for its value to be realized, the acquired company must be well-managed. To increase the likelihood of creating value through acquisition, a well-structured acquisition program must include five processes:

1. Obtaining senior management commitment
2. Organizing for success
3. Identifying target industries and companies
4. Managing the acquisition process
5. Integrating the acquired entity

Acquisition is one of many tools available to management to assist in the achievement of the overall strategic plan and must be understood in the context of the overall strategic plan. The rationale for making acquisitions must be clearly identified within the strategic plan. The reasons for acquisition can be many, but typically include the following:

The industries served by the existing portfolio businesses will not generate the desired levels of growth and profitability due to the economic environment, demographics, or competitive position.

A significant repositioning of the company cannot be achieved solely through internal means.

The company has strategic strengths that can be positively leveraged through acquisitions.

OBTAINING SENIOR MANAGEMENT COMMITMENT

Corporate management should be prepared to assume the risks associated with acquisitions. The availability of acquisition targets, at reasonable prices, that match or can achieve the company's forecasted profitability and growth prospects may be limited. The existing operating culture may be alienated or confused by a change in acquisition policies. If the acquisition policy involves diversification, the depth or skills of the existing organization may not be sufficient to manage beyond the existing businesses.

Because mistakes sometimes are made with acquisitions, it is necessary to prepare a subjective analysis of the impact of a mistake for each major acquisition. This exercise is useful in determining the upper size limit of acquisitions to be considered. Furthermore, the definition of success and failure after the acquisition needs to be identified with measurable checkpoints. More important, the actions to be taken in case of an unsuccessful acquisition should be delineated; a link with the divestiture plan becomes mandatory. While it is important to be aware of the risks associated with acquisitions, managers implementing the acquisition plan must feel that mistakes, while obviously not desired, are permitted and are an unfortunate reality of an active acquisition plan. The manager's objective is to be right more often than not.

Resources allocation is critical to an acquisition plan. The most important allocation is the amount of time senior management, particularly the chief executive officer, will commit to the acquisition plan. If the CEO cannot spare a great deal of time, the success of an active acquisition plan is in jeopardy. Allocation of financial resources is also important. The amount of debt that can be prudently added to the balance sheet to support acquisitions, as well as the maximum amount of new equity that could be added without materially impacting the current shareholders, must be considered. Finally, management must decide how much near-term dilution (in terms of earnings per share, return on capital, return on equity, etc.) is acceptable.

The achievement of any strategic plan is dependent on the motivation of the executives implementing it. Clearly, linkage between an executive's compensation and the strategic plan is crucial. If operating executives are charged with the responsibility of developing and executing an acquisition plan, this linkage can be achieved in many ways. A portion of an executive's annual bonus can depend on the development of an active acquisition plan that includes the identification of target companies and the establishment of a systematic contacting program. An executive's annual bonus can also be increased by a certain percentage for every acquisition that his or her operating unit has actively identified and evaluated.

ORGANIZING FOR SUCCESS

Organizing for success is the process of allocating responsibility and authority so that the probability of making successful acquisitions is enhanced. There are many conflicting goals that need to be resolved to implement a successful acquisition plan:

In the process of evaluating a target company, vested interest in its success must be created; involvement is vital in that process.

In many acquisitions, secrecy is demanded by one or both parties; limited involvement is necessary for high secrecy.

A decisive yes/no decision is the ultimate outcome of every acquisition idea; this calls for concentrated authority.

In many acquisitions speed is required/desired by one or both parties; this is another argument for concentrated authority.

Given the risk involved in making acquisitions, a thorough investigation is desirable; a high level of involvement of the various experts is required.

EXHIBIT 12-1   Acquisition Responsibility

	Strategic	Product Line	Technology
Generate ideas	Development	Operations	Technology
Identify candidates	Development	Development	Development
Evaluate product/market	Development	Operations	Technology
Perform financial due diligence	Finance	Finance	Finance
Authorize transaction	CEO	CEO	CEO
Price/negotiate transaction	Development	Development	Development
Develop business plan	Development	Operations	Technology
Close transaction	Legal	Legal	Legal
Operate unit	Operations	Operations	Operations

Exhibit 12-1 displays one approach to allocating acquisition responsibility by types of acquisition.

Allocation of responsibility and authority is dependent on the types of acquisition. Exhibit 12-2 highlights the differences between three categories of acquisition: strategic, product line, and technology.

Strategic acquisitions are large entities in an unrelated business whose organization will be retained intact. Typically such acquisitions are well-known public companies and are therefore evaluated in a highly secret fashion. Such acquisitions are made because they are in an attractive industry segment and may become the "flagship" for future product-line acquisitions or internal growth opportunities.

Product-line acquisitions are related to an existing business and can be of various sizes. Value is maximized by keeping the entity separate, by partial integration with existing businesses, or by total merger. The level of secrecy required during evaluation is typically much less than that required for strategic acquisitions, and accordingly the evaluation process can be expanded to include greater numbers of people. These acquisitions are made for positive synergistic effects.

Technology acquisitions are small, sometimes start-up, ventures that possess technology that is not available to an existing business. These acquisitions are made because the technology either has long-term value to the existing business or is attractive in and of itself. The evaluation requires

EXHIBIT 12-2   Types of Acquisitions

	Strategic	Product Line	Technology
Size	Large	Varied	Small
Relationship	Unrelated	Related	Unrelated
Organization	Stand alone	Varied	Varied
Secrecy	High	Varied	Low
Why	Diversification	Synergy	Long range

technically competent people and does not usually involve high levels of secrecy.

Development is a corporate department of generalists capable of managing the acquisition process. The department should report directly to the chief executive officer. The size of the department is a function of the number of acquisitions pursued. Because the development department generates work demands on many other functions, it is doubtful that most organizations can support more than three or four corporate development professionals.

Operations assists in the acquisition process by making available senior line management, marketing, manufacturing, and technology personnel.

Technology is a corporate department charged with supporting the organization in maintaining its technological expertise.

Finance refers to the various corporate functions including financial analysis, accounting, auditing, tax, treasury, insurance, and planning departments that play a role in the evaluation of acquisitions.

Legal support can be obtained from an in-house legal department, external law firms, or a combination.

Generate Ideas

In an organization committed to acquisitions, ideas are generated from many sources. The corporate development department generates them by attending trade shows, reading technical magazines and journals, interacting with other corporate development departments, and commissioning specific investigations by consultants. Also, there is generally a constant flow of ideas from finders, brokers, bankers, and investment bankers. In dealing with the latter, it is necessary to have a widely communicated policy regarding third parties and associated fee arrangements.

Policy Regarding Third Parties

The following is an example of a policy distributed within an organization. In order to avoid the generation of needless fees, it is necessary to maintain a certain control over third-party–generated ideas through this policy and the maintenance of accurate internal acquisition records (logbook).

> The company is pleased to work with third party intermediaries. In those instances in which the intermediary has not been retained to represent the interest of sellers, corporate development will authorize the intermediary, by specific written direction signed by the Senior Vice President Corporate Development, to represent the company if it has sufficient interest in the acquisition opportunity.

> The company prefers to have the selling interests pay any fees associated with an acquisition. However, in those instances in which the intermediary represents the sellers, but has no agreement with the sellers to pay the fee, or where corporate development has retained the intermediary to represent the company, corporate development will negotiate a suitable fee arrangement.

A suitable fee arrangement will be based on the specific acquisition opportunity under consideration and will take into account such factors as the size of the proposed transaction, our degree of interest, the specific services to be performed by the intermediary, etc. The company prefers to conduct dicussions and negotiations with an acquisition candidate independently of intermediaries. As a result, the intermediary's role will normally be limited to providing assistance in the initial contact with, and introduction to, the acquisition candidate.

In submitting an acquisition candidate for initial review, the company would prefer that the candidate not be identified. Corporate development will make a preliminary determination of the company's interest based on the product, market, and financial information submitted and will advise the intermediary of our conclusions. When the identity of a candidate is disclosed, corporate development will review our internal acquisition records to insure that there is no conflict. In the event that an intermediary happens to identify a candidiate that has previously had discussions with the company concerning possible acquisition, corporate development will notify the intermediary of the fact, and the payment of any fee will be precluded.

Operations are an excellent source of high-quality, product-line acquisition ideas. These ideas are generated by the marketing, manufacturing, and R&D departments and should be reinforced by making an active acquisition plan part of the operating-units plan. Furthermore, a portion of the operating executive's annual bonus should be tied to the existence of a good acquisition plan.

The remainder of the organization should be encouraged to submit ideas. Typically, the corporate departments of technology, planning, and financial analysis can generate quality ideas.

Identify Candidates

In a company with an active acquisition plan with high levels of involvement it is important that the corporate development department have control over selected events. An important event is the decision to make contact with the target company. The actual contact should be made as the logic of the particular situation dictates and is often a function of whoever within or without the company has the best contact.

Evaluate Product/Market

The evaluation of the markets, products, manufacturing, etc., for strategic acquisitions is typically the responsibility of corporate development. By the nature of their jobs, operations personnel are typically unfamiliar with the target and its business. Often it is desirable to use consultants to assist in the various phases of the evaluation. For product-line acquisitions, it is imperative that operating personnel be involved in the evaluation. They are in the best position to apply their day-to-day knowledge, and their participation will aid in the process of creating vesting interests in success. For technology acquisitions, either the technology department or consultants should be used in the evaluation.

Perform Financial Due Diligence

The areas of financial analysis, accounting, auditing, taxes, treasury, and insurance are best analyzed by the respective experts. In any given deal, one or more of the areas may not have enough significance to deserve a detailed review, and the corporate development department should identify the areas that require focus. A strong internal audit department is often quite useful in performing both operational and financial due diligence. The audit department's follow-up is often a good second opinion and can provide the comfort necessary to continue with the acquisition. Personnel should also be involved in reviewing fringe benefit packages, labor relations, incentive compensation schemes, etc.

Authorize Transaction

At some point in the evaluation, corporate development and operations will feel comfortable enough with the target company to recommend making an offer. The responsibility, subject to board approval, for making this decision rests with the chief executive officer. On acquisitions of sufficient size and importance, the CEO should visit the target company and meet key management before giving his approval. This first round of approval should address the maximum price that the company is willing to pay and, in general, the nonprice terms to be offered.

Price/Negotiate Transactions

Negotiations of all transactions must be closely controlled and should be the exclusive responsibility of corporate development. Operating executives should not have any direct responsibilities because this might interfere with successful integration after the negotiations are complete. Neither should the process be fully delegated to the legal department, because in many cases it lacks the business insights to make or propose the various compromises required to close a transaction.

Develop the Business Plan

Prior to closing a transaction, it is exceedingly important that the company commit to writing the proposed business plan for managing the target company after the acquisition. The business plan should be detailed with regard to the next 12 months, and specific reference should be made to manufacturing, marketing, development, financial systems, employee compensation and benefits, and announcements.

Close the Transaction

The actual closing of a transaction is a bureaucratic necessity to insure that all legal documents have been correctly completed, the cash has been transferred, and insurance is in place; the closing should be the responsibility of the legal department. If the sellers are going to continue with the business, it is often desirable to make the closing an "event" and have a closing dinner or other similar ceremony.

Operate the Unit

Upon closing, the appropriate operational unit should take responsibility for the day-to-day management. Corporate development should brief the operating executive on its findings and commitments to the acquired company (assuming this has not taken place already).

IDENTIFYING TARGET INDUSTRIES AND COMPANIES

The company must have a method of analyzing industries and companies to determine the desirability of making an acquisition. The approach to be outlined can be used to determine attractive industries and companies to contact or, alternatively, to screen ideas that are presented to corporate development from operating units or finders. The method should be systematic (to ensure all pertinent areas are examined in an unbiased fashion) and flexible (because every acquisition is unique). By studying the following categories, the company will ensure that each idea generated or screened has been properly reviewed:

> General
> Industry
> Management and organization
> Marketing
> Manufacturing
> Technology
> Finance
> Administration
> Summary

General

Prior to launching a search, or when screening ideas, the company should attempt, in a general fashion, to limit its scope. Factors to be considered include:

Industries with a favorable outlook (good fundamentals, good fit, or a combination)
Industries with an unfavorable outlook
Size of target company (significance versus risk)
Friendly versus unfriendly acquisitions
Acquisition versus internal development
Turnaround and start-up situations

Industry

The evaluation of the industry to be targeted for acquisition is critical. A company must identify its own particular strengths and match them with industries by which those strengths can be leveraged. Additionally, the industry must possess characteristics that permit the achievement of the acquisition objectives if the target company is successfully managed. Factors to be considered include:

Size, growth, and concentration of industry
Consumer, industrial, or government
Service versus manufacturing
Component parts versus complete products
Barriers to entry (capital, technology, reputation)
Offshore competition
Technology trends
Critical mass to compete within industry
Cyclicality
Seasonality
Domestic/international

Management and Organization

In most acquisitions, a company is acquired for the skills and talents of its people. Determining their desire to create a growing stream of profit for the company becomes one the most important determinants of whether to make the acquisition. This evaluation process is by nature very subjective. Factors to be considered include:

Principal shareholders
Outside business interest of principals
Why the principals want to sell
What the principals' plans are after the sale
Brief company history and general business description

Who founded the target company
Where the founders are today
Officers and directors of the target company
Biographies of key management
Continuity of management after the acquisition
Reporting relationship of target to company after the acquisition
Management style/fit with company
Acceptance of management to be acquired
Quality of management
Management turnover
Strengths and weaknesses
Management compensation/incentive plans
Management fringes versus typical fringes
Total management compensation versus typical compensation
Trends in management compensation
Total number of employees
Organization chart

Marketing

In evaluating a target's product or service offering, the key question to answer is, why will this product or service be successful under the company's management? Factors to be considered include:

Industry market trends
Target company market share trends
Competition (reputation, market share trends, estimated cost position, location of facilities, financial condition, distribution method, pricing philosophy)
Technology trends
Product life cycle
New product opportunities
Penetration today/potential
Price of product/(10 cents per part versus 50-million-dollar contract)
Integration opportunities with other divisions
Impact on other relationships (will existing customers feel threatened by acquisition?)
Geographical areas served/leverage opportunities
Seasonal sales patterns
Unique characteristics of product

Reputation
Trademarks/trade names
Advertising strategy/expenditures
Product literature
Pricing versus competition
Pricing trends
Concentration of customers
Twenty largest customers
Contractual arrangements with key customers
Channels
Distribution/Selling organization (method, numbers, compensation, turn-over, contractual arrangements)
Market plan

Manufacturing

In evaluating the manufacturing base, these are key questions to be answered: Does the target company have a competitive cost position? What investments are required to maintain the competitive cost position? Are there any trends (e.g., technology/offshore competition) that will result in its cost position's being noncompetitive? Factors to be considered include:

Low-cost producer
Cost reduction opportunities
Capital expenditures history
Investment requirements
Amount of vertical integration
Level of automation
Cyclicality of demand
Technology threats and opportunities
Location of factories
Age of buildings and equipment
Layout/floor plan
Condition of equipment
Replacement value versus book value
Expansion potential
Control systems
Labor force (labor relations, union activity [history/threats/existence], wage levels, fringe benefits, trends for total compensation, turnover, absenteeism, availability, special skills, productivity)

Purchasing (key suppliers, contractual agreements, availability of alternate suppliers, opportunities for improvement)

Technology

In valuing acquisitions, it is important to position a company on a technology curve correctly. Are there any significant technology threats that will make the target's products or processes obsolete? Does the target possess a technology that can be leveraged into new products and applications? Factors to be considered include:

High/medium/low technology content
Amount of R&D expenditure
Size of R&D department
Background of R&D department
Patent position
Critical mass to compete/talent required
Trends for technology
Rate of change of technology in this industry
Threats/risks from different technologies
Continuity of key people

Finance

Given the uncertainties of making a forecast for an acquisition target, the focus should be on developing an understandable, consistent yardstick for measuring the value of a potential target versus that of other acquisition opportunities, rather than on a quest for the theoretically correct methodology. Yardsticks like return on capital employed and earnings per share contribution (assuming 100% cash transactions) are easily understood by management and provide a basis for making decisions. Factors to be considered include:

Five years of audited financial statements (income, balance sheet, and funds flow)
Eight most recent quarters of financial statements
Tax returns for past five years
Accounts receivable aging
Inventory analysis (turns, quality, difference between physical and book at last audit)
Terms of indebtedness
Capital expenditures for past five years

Accounting policies and procedures

Five years of product-line sales and profitability

Forecasted product-line sales and profitability (five years)

Forecasted financial statements (five years)

Tax impacts of acquisition terms

Analysis of acquisition price (return on capital, return on equity, discounted cash flow, E.P.S. contribution, pooling versus purchase)

Financial alternatives (lease versus buy, deferred payments, notes)

Comparison of target to existing company (returns, growth rates, investment rates)

Administration

There are many opportunities for acquisition targets to provide surprises. The due diligence process is designed to uncover as many as possible. Factors to be considered include:

1. Insurance

   Listing of insurance policies

   Current premium and history

   Claims

   Cost of duplicating coverage

   Opportunities for savings

2. Taxes

   Review of prior years' tax returns

   Level of reserves

   Consistency with company's tax policies

   Areas of aggressive tax planning

3. Audit

   Review of control systems

   Review and discussion of external audit workpapers

   Asset quality

   Potential unreported liabilities

4. Pension/profit sharing/savings plan

   Review of plan documentation

   Determination of plan liabilities

   Current assumptions and changes in assumptions

   Actuarial reports

   Number of participants

   Management of pension assets

5. Legal
   Review of all major contracts
   Review of all major leases
   Compliance with laws
   Antitrust implications
   Suits threatened and outstanding
   Tradename/trademarks outstanding
   License required to do business
   Title search
   Transferability of major contractual commitments
6. Patents
   Number
   Relationship to the business
   Age
   Quality

Summary

Prior to making an acquisition there should be a clear, precise reason for acquiring a target and a plan showing how it will be managed for success. Factors to be considered include:

Critical success factor
Why the target is being purchased
Strengths/weaknesses of target company
Management continuity and transition
Terms and conditions (compensation to be paid, obligation to be assumed, fees to be paid [e.g., finder's fee])
Financial impact

MANAGING THE ACQUISITION PROCESS

The end product of an acquisition plan is the acquisition of good companies, not an endless contract program. This requires both flexibility and defined points of authority. Throughout the process there should be decision points to eliminate situations in which the likelihood of success is remote or to remove undesirable target companies from consideration. This is important because an uncontrolled and unfocused acquisition plan can consume vast amounts of time and monetary resources.

Flexibility is required because a good acquisition idea can be generated anywhere in the company, and the flow of ideas must be stimulated and reinforced. Similarly, in evaluating target companies, the company will require one set of expertise on one target and may require a completely different set of expertise on the next. Additionally, if a target is acquired, it is important that there be many vested interests in its success. These interests are created through involvement.

High levels of involvement conflict with the desire for secrecy. This challenge can frequently be overcome by controlling and restricting involvement in a few key elements of the process: authorization of initial contact, authorization to conduct negotiations, and negotiations. In this fashion, most members of the organization know merely that large numbers of targets are being considered, while only a selected few know which are being actively pursued.

Finally, it is mandatory that there be a focal point that documents the process, from logging the original idea through a signed contract and receipt of an approved business plan. The focal point needs to be current on all targets and their precise status. If this disciplined approach is not followed, the company runs the risk of squandering resources and being unable to bid in timely fashion for a key attractive target. Exhibit 12-3 illustrates a means for managing the acquisition process. "Screen" identifies points where corporate development ensures that the process is working for this particular acquisition.

The generation of ideas at all levels of the company should be encouraged. One approach is to provide incentives through a bonus arrangement to key operating managers with active acquisition plans. The distribution of acquisition criteria is to be discouraged, because the criteria will be counterproductive to generating ideas. The recipient of the criteria will interpret them and screen his or her thinking. Any criteria distributed should therefore be general.

The first screen, to determine whether to make initial contact and who should make contact, should be made by corporate development. This initial contact does not commit large amounts of resources or require large amounts of time.

Initial contact should be made by corporate development and by representatives of the operating unit that likely will have ultimate responsibility for managing the acquisition. The levels of the people making the initial contact should be directly proportional to the potential impact the target will have on the company.

After the initial visit, another screen is conducted, with corporate development and the operating executive deciding the course of action. The possible outcomes include:

No further contact will be made.

There is insufficient data to launch a detailed evaluation and more background work is required.

A detailed evaluation is launched.

EXHIBIT 12-3   Managing the Acquisition Process

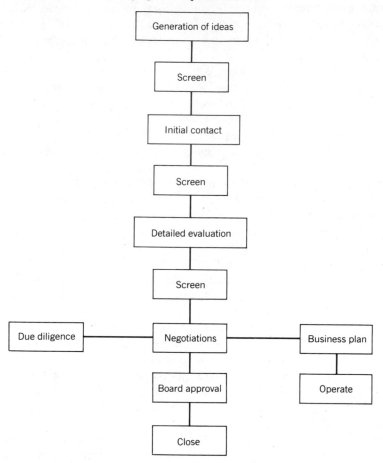

Typically, the decision to launch a detailed evaluation of a major acquisition target is done with the concurrence of the chief executive officer. It is also important that the number of acquisitions in the second category (insufficient data to make a decision) be limited. It is also possible that the seller is not ready to sell, and follow-up is required to convince the seller of the benefits of sale before a detailed evaluation can be launched.

In launching a detailed evaluation, corporate development and the senior operating executive must decide what the critical success factor is. This is necessary in order to allocate sufficient resources to gain the required information to make a decision. The critical success factor obviously varies by acquisition, but could be patent protection, product quality, growth potential for the product and market, low-cost manufacturing position, etc. It must be determined whether, and what, outside consultants should be used, who should be involved internally, what the timetable is, who else might be bidding, and what level of security is required. The purposes of the evaluation are to determine whether the target should be bought, what an appropriate purchase price is, if the sellers are willing to sell, and whether the target can be managed successfully after acquisition. The importance of objectivity, thoroughness, and speed—which often prove to be conflicting goals—cannot be overemphasized.

Upon completion of the detailed evaluation, corporate development must inform the chief executive officer of the outcome, which is either a decision not to proceed or a request to authorize negotiations. It is useful that the request to authorize negotiations be in a standard form (with modification if necessary to highlight unique features of the acquisition). This summary of the proposed deal should include:

Short history of the company (date founded, headquarters location, plant location and size)

Ownership and management (list of major owners and relationship to company, list of management, titles, and tenure)

Brief description of product of service offered (major product line, distribution channels, major competition)

Critical success factor (why the deal should be made, how and why the target can succeed)

Key financial data (historical figures, projected figures)

Deal summary (earnings and book multiple, EPS impact, potential returns)

Supporting this brief summary should be a fact book that details (including any consultant's reports):

The marketplace

The target company's product line (including product literature)

Organization chart and biographies

Evaluation of manufacturing (including floor plan)

Evaluation of technology

Detailed financials and financial analysis

Trip reports (notes of all trips made)

Preliminary business plan

The outcome of this meeting is either the authorization, subject to board approval, of a maximum price and terms to be offered or rejection of the idea.

After this meeting, assuming the CEO has approved, parallel processes are launched: negotiations, due diligence, and business plan preparation. The corporate development department, supported by legal counsel, should have the charter to negotiate the contract.

The conduct of the negotiations is an important element that is often overlooked in the acquisition plan. The corporate development department must have responsibility for negotiations and must invest in developing negotiating skills. The negotiator has the following roles:

Determines the significance of the issues raised

Uses the issues raised to gain insights into the business

Develops insights into the prime motivations of the sellers

Balances the goal of closing the transaction with the goals of buying a business with a certain risk-adjusted return

Insulates operating executives from the emotional upheaval of negotiations (especially when the seller plans to remain with the company)

Proposes compromises that move the negotiations forward without harming the basic position

Manages his emotions and the seller's emotions to reach the best deal

Identifies deals that should not be closed and breaks off negotiations

Conducts the negotiations in a professional manner that enhances the company's long-term reputation of being a tough, but good-faith, bargainer

Simultaneously with negotiations a due diligence process is launched that typically centers on the auditing, tax, accounting, and legal departments, but also involves personnel and operations. The discoveries of this process should be quickly transmitted back to corporate development to be incorporated into the negotiations or to kill the deal if required. Operations during this time period develops a final business plan. Corporate development ensures that the discoveries of negotiations and due diligence are communicated to operations.

Assuming the negotiations are successful, the transaction must be presented to the board for approval. Depending on the size of the transaction, the form of the request for approval typically is a summary and updated version of the request for authorization to negotiate what was presented to the chief executive officer, and should include:

Short history of the company

Brief description of products (including product literature)

Ownership and management

Critical success factor

Key financial data

Deal summary

Assuming the board of directors approves the transaction, closing occurs. The legal department should take prime responsibility for closing to ensure that the contract and closing documents are legally correct, all necessary approvals and consents have been obtained, and all necessary signatures have been made. Corporate development assumes the coordinating role of disseminating the required information to all other departments to ensure that:

The treasury deparment funds the transaction

The insurance department maintains coverage

The accounting department makes the opening entries

The public relations department releases an approved press release

The accounting department makes all required disclosures

INTEGRATING THE ACQUIRED ENTITY

The key to successfully integrating the acquired entity is a well-structured business plan. The plan serves two purposes. First, it is a roadmap for operating executives to follow. Second, it is a tool for corporate management to use to determine that the integration process is on target. The goal, then, of the business plan is to develop a list of specific actions required to achieve the desired results. The list should be accompanied by target dates and "milestone" events in order to ensure that prompt attention is paid if the plan moves off schedule. The business plan, prepared by operating management and reviewed by corporate development, addresses the following issues:

Executive summary

Organization

Marketing

New products

Served market

Manufacturing

Finance

The executive summary clearly defines the five-year objectives of the newly acquired company. These goals ultimately are expressed in financial terms of sales growth, profitability, and return objectives. From a strategic point of view, the organizational resources required to achieve those objectives are clearly developed, including the number of people, talents they should possess, compensation plans to motivate employees to achieve the goals, vacancies that will occur as a result of the acquisition, weak spots that need to be strengthened, potential problems that may arise in the integration process, and so on. Resources required to support the plan in new product development and manufacturing are addressed. The executive summary also addresses the key operational strategies to be followed. The overall manufacturing plan should be discussed, with its impact on capital expenditures, asset utilization, and manpower clearly identified. Finally, any particular problems that were uncovered during the acquisition review are addressed, together with an action plan to solve them.

The current organization chart, with key employees noted, is discussed. Known vacancies and planned changes in personnel are identified and discussed. The impact of the acquisition on all employees, but especially on the key people, is evaluated. The total compensation system (salary, bonus, perquisites, and fringe benefits) is compared to those of other divisions in the company and local levels. Any anomalies are discussed. Any planned changes are reviewed. The reporting relationship of the target company to the acquiring company is determined. If an interim approach is proposed, the future alternatives are discussed, as well as dates for making the decision.

The marketing section should give an overview of the industry, segmenting it by product line, distribution channels, and end-user categories. The target's position in each segment versus competition is noted with reference to any planned actions that might change its position. Key product features of the target are discussed, as well as key product features of the competition. The impact of all planned changes to the product offering are mentioned. Historic pricing trends versus competition, costs, and features are identified. Future pricing strategies versus competition, costs, and features are evaluated. Past industry growth trends by market segment are reviewed, as are projected trends. Specific factors that cause changes in growth rates should be identified. Sales, promotion, and distribution profiles versus competition are identified, as is the planned mix. Specific references are made to the numbers of employees, compensation plans, the amount and type of advertising, and expected competitive reaction. The results of any marketing research are discussed and the plans to implement the findings are addressed. Finally, the marketing plan at the target is compared to that of the existing company. A coordinated effort for addressing common customers is addressed. Any possible synergies are evaluated and specific plans identified for capitalizing on them.

New product efforts are specifically identified. A timetable should clearly state expected new product introduction dates. The necessary resources— in terms of manpower, equipment, and money—to achieve these introduction dates are identified and compared to the resources currently on hand. The need and availability of special talents and skills are addressed. Finally, the plan should state clearly why the new product proposals are being pursued and what positive and negative effects (e.g., cannibalization) they will have on the target.

The served market is accurately described and segmented by end user. The requirements and application trends of each end user, along with their likely impact on the target, are identified. The target's planned reaction to these events is determined. The characteristics of each segment (size, distribution patterns, and growth rates) are clearly identified.

The manufacturing plan lists the acquired facilities and includes data such as square footage, equipment used, and products produced. The type of labor force (union, nonunion) and the total compensation paid is identified. Any cost savings that could result by transferring production (to new locations or existing locations elsewhere in the company) are addressed. Any expansion plans and the impact these could have on the existing company are identified. The general pay scale and labor conditions are compared to those of the existing company and the local market.

The finance plan identifies the current capabilities of the acquired company. The reporting requirements of the corporation are related to the current output. A transition plan to gain the required consistency is developed. To the extent possible, the proceeding goals and objectives are quantified and a plan with key financial targets is prepared.

SUMMARY

An acquisition plan has been broken into the following parts:

Obtaining senior management's commitment
Organizing for success
Identifying target industries and companies
Managing the acquisition process
Integrating the acquired entity

In obtaining senior management's commitment there should be a clear understanding of why acquisitions are to be made. This is linked to the chief executive officer's commitment and desire to allocate sufficient time to the process. Additionally, the executive compensation plan is structured to motivate involvement of the key employees in the process.

When organizing for success, the importance is in creating vested interests in the success of the acquired company. These vested interests are created through involvement. This means that the acquisition process is too important to be delegated to a cadre of specialists, but must involve the entire organization. The process is controlled centrally through the key points of initial contact, pricing the transaction, and negotiating the deal.

The identifying of target industries and companies is not a process of comparing the universe of available companies to a preconceived list of criteria. Rather, it is a subjective process of identifying critical success factors and deciding if these factors are reinforced by the business combination. Additionally, it is the process of evaluating the people to be acquired to determine if they have the desire to create a growing stream of profits under new management.

In managing the acquisition process, the end product is to acquire good companies, not to make endless contracts. This requires an active screening process and central control over the key aspects of the process.

Finally, integrating the acquired entity successfully is a major component of making a good acquisition. A good acquisition plan does not stop at the closing, but goes beyond it and identifies a clear path for managing the new company.

CHAPTER *13*

Divestiture Planning

PETER N. WALMSLEY

PETER N. WALMSLEY is Manager, Acquisitions and Divestitures, E.I. du Pont de Nemours and Company. He joined du Pont in 1960 and held positions in research management and new ventures, and in 1975 he joined the Corporate Plans Department, He has been responsible for acquisitions and divestitures since 1979. Mr. Walmsley earned his B.Sc. Tech and Ph.D. in Chemical Engineering from Manchester University.

OUTLINE

For the purposes of this chapter, a corporate divestiture is broadly considered to be the elimination of a business from the company's portfolio. This may include selling the business or subsidiary in its entirety as a going concern, selling some of the assets of the business to another operator and liquidating others, or abandoning the business completely and liquidating all possible assets.

Ideally these options should always be included among the alternatives that are evaluated when business plans are formulated. If a primary objective is to devise the course of action that will most enhance the wealth of the shareholders, then the possibility that one of these options will have the greatest value should not be overlooked. This means that not only poorly performing businesses are considered for divestiture, but that any business believed to have a potentially greater value in other hands could be a candidate. However, it does not mean that a decision to divest can be made after a trivial exercise in net present-value computations. Many other factors have to be weighed, some of which may not be quantifiable for calculation, but judgmentally can be overwhelming.

REASONS FOR DIVESTITURE

Sometimes divestitures are enforced, and management has no other option. This may be the result of court or regulatory agency actions, as in cases in which an acquiring company is forced to divest certain operations of an acquired company for antitrust reasons. A company that is financially *in extremis* may be forced by its investors and creditors or by an agreeement in bankruptcy proceedings to divest some pieces. These special situations are outside the normal scope of strategic planning.

Planning divestitures is part of the process of intelligently utilizing the resources available to the company to improve performance. Financial resources consumed by a business in the wrong corporate environment are often less important than the time and talents of people that are diverted from other endeavors that could be more productive. Identifying these businesses is the first step toward an effective divestiture program. The second step is to engender the attitude that selling or closing down such businesses is good management, not failure.

Although in theory any business may become a divestiture candidate, in practice the most probable ones are those that have less-than-average performance; these are the ones most likely to have some missing requirement that another owner may be able to provide. It seems self-evident to state that a business should be divested if it is worth more liquidated or sold, but in fact it requires a thorough understanding of the operating characteristics to be able to explain what is required to increase the value of the business and where it can best be provided.

Problem businesses tend to consume a disproportionate amount of management attention. Technical, marketing, and manufacturing talent are applied to what is not always, but often, a losing battle. If the business is operated in a no-growth or low-growth mode in the hope of generating cash, management is often frustrated to find that only inconsequential amounts are returned to the corporation, or that cash continues to be consumed. The reasons for these outcomes are that margins tend to be low and that earnings get little tax shelter from depreciation if facilities are not being expanded or modernized. Working capital grows with inflation even when volume is constant, and some expenditures are required to keep manufacturing facilities operable, safe, and in compliance with regulatory requirements. In these cases the company would frequently be wiser to sell or liquidate the business for assured cash in hand and thereby free the management and functional expertise for more rewarding enterprises.

Other businesses that should be seriously considered for sale are those that do not fit the areas the corporation has chosen to be its primary interests for future growth and development. These may or may not be performing well at the time, but if they remain in the company, they will probably not realize their full potential. Such businesses exist in most large companies with diverse product lines. A business might have been part of a previous acquisition that came along with the part that was the real reason for the purchase. It might have been an internal development that did not live up to early expectations, so that what was hoped to be a major new diversification matured into an insignificant misfit. An industrial marketing company might develop a consumer product with related technology but not be able to justify an adequate consumer marketing effort for that single product. A unit that was once a mainstay of the company can become a historical anachronism; if the company has developed in other directions that are viewed as being far more important for the future, that unit is likely to be more valuable in the hands of a company that still regards that area of business as attractive.

Good performers with exciting prospects are rarely selected for divestiture on internal initiative. However, they are likely to be the ones that are targets for other acquiring companies and might have to be seriously considered, particularly if the suitor submits a written offer with a high enough price to force management's hand with respect to fiduciary responsibilities to the stockholders. In most cases such businesses are not divested, but there can be exceptions, such as when a company decides it does not have the necessary resources to compete long-range or has a less optimistic view of the future than the market does. If the business is performing very well, there is less opportunity for the buyer to improve results sufficiently to justify a premium over the seller's indifference price. Also, such businesses are usually given favorable prominence in the company and are a source of justified pride and confidence. They are good for morale, and the luster they add to the corporate image helps to attract and keep the high-caliber people essential to maintaining any company's edge in a competitive world. These intangible factors are not ground into a net present-value calculation, but a sensitive management will intuitively weigh them heavily. Divestitures have to be explicable, not only to the stockholders but also to the employees, and to sell a business that was previously a favorite can make management appear to be inconsistent and overly opportunistic.

IDENTIFICATION OF CANDIDATES

There are three ways in which candidates are identified: by corporate staff, by an operating division, and by outside approach. Corporate planners should periodically review the company's portfolio of businesses with the specific purpose of finding the ones that are potential divestiture candidates. If the usual practice in the planning organization is to monitor only the major businesses, leaving smaller businesses to the operating divisions, then for this audit the horizon should be extended to include the smaller businesses.

The first step is to categorize the units into those that fit the directions the company is following for its long-term development and those that do not. They can then be further subdivided into those with satisfactory performance and those with problems. To do this requires a thorough understanding of the corporate strategies as a framework within which the fit can be judged. It also requires a fairly detailed understanding of each business.

The second step is to value the businesses roughly as ongoing concerns, liquidated or sold. Valuation techniques are discussed in more detail later in this chapter. At this stage the valuations should be reasonable approximations and should use readily available data. In most cases the answers are clear, and more detailed work should be necessary only in a few borderline situations.

The third step is to assemble information on matters that could be barriers to divesting the businesses. Examples of such things include:

1. *Physical Entanglement.*   The plant is located in a shared complex in such a way that it cannot be fenced off or the equipment cannot be relocated.
2. *Key Personnel.*   People with skills critical to the business also serve other businesses and cannot be released.
3. *Contractual Relationships.*   Contracts with suppliers, customers, or distributors may not be assignable and could not be negotiated by a new owner on equally favorable terms. Military or government contracts in sensitive areas can also be a barrier.
4. *Economic Entanglement.*   Business has transfer relationships with other businesses that would suffer adverse effects. This problem might suggest reconsideration of business unit definition or transfer pricing practices.

5. *Employee Considerations.* Several divestitures from a company or division can have an adverse effect on morale, and it might be decided to have a moratorium in that area for a while. Particularly in liquidations in some foreign countries, the severance costs might be prohibitive and adverse reactions from governments might affect the environment for other businesses.

6. *Business Is in a State of Flux.* Changes have recently been made in the business or a major facility is still under construction and the effectiveness is not yet known, so it is impossible to judge the value.

With this information in hand, the candidates should emerge, and it will then be possible for the corporate staff to discuss the outcome with corporate management to reach conclusions on the stance toward each business. Some will be ruled out as divestiture candidates, some will become immediate candidates on corporate initiative, and some will be set aside as possible future candidates, particularly if there is an initiative from the operating division or an outside approach. At this stage there should be some prioritization of the candidates and a reasonable timetable should be set for actions. Implementing divestitures consumes a lot of time in the affected operating divisions and in the involved staff departments; realistic goals should take into account the capacity to handle the workload.

If the corporate survey has been done and kept current, it is much easier to respond to proposals to divest from operating divisions or from outside. Operating people usually propose divesting only fairly hopeless cases, and these should have been identified in the corporate search unless there has been a sudden adverse change. If the corporation has not forced the issue, it is probably because the priority was low or the management was being given a chance to turn the business around. When the operating management proposes the divestiture, the corporate response can be immediately encouraging. One situation that might be different is when the operating management proposes to purchase the business in a management buyout. Caution is needed to ensure that the business forecasts have not been tainted by self-interest. Corporate management also has to face the issue of what it will do with the managers in the buyout group if the decision is made not to sell and if it is felt likely that the group will be disappointed and resentful.

Similarly, outside approaches that name a specific business or clearly describe the types of business that would be of interest are easy to handle when the company has gone through the exercise of corporate search. When it is known that the business is not for sale, a refusal can be given rapidly without distracting the operating people and without leaving a time period while a response is considered, during which rumors may start that can be damaging to customer and employee relations. If the business is one the corporation favors selling, a positive response can be given quickly after a brief reaffirmation. Some precautions to be observed in dealing with outside approaches are covered in the section on finding buyers.

ORGANIZATION

A company that is contemplating undertaking a number of divestitures over a period of time should establish an organizational procedure for handling them. There seem to be basically three ways that corporations do this. A decision has to be made as to where the primary responsibility is going to rest for implementing a divestiture and leading the negotiations.

One way is to decide that primary responsibility will remain at the corporate level. A small group is created that has its own dedicated financial and legal experts and is led by someone who will usually be the chief negotiator. Personnel from the operating divisions are co-opted into the group temporarily as needed. The second way is to hand over the primary responsibility to the operating division management when serious negotiations begin and to leave the legal and financial experts in their respective functional departments. The corporate group in this case can be very small (one or two people) and will usually withdraw from active negotiations at an early stage. The third way is to assign the task to investment bankers.

In practice there are more similarities than differences between the first two approaches. In both cases the corporate group will be responsible for surveying the company for potential divestiture candidates and will be the group that is aware of the corporate posture toward divestiture of any business. The group will be the point of early activity when any divestiture is proposed by the corporation, an operating division, or an outside approach. All outside enquiries should be directed to this group for initial response. This avoids disruption of the operating units, and the response carries more weight if it originates at the corporate level. Once a company is known to be an active divestor, the flow of enquiries from brokers, investment bankers, private investment groups, and other companies can be substantial, and it is much easier to keep track of the many contacts and to be consistent in the responses if they are all handled in the same place.

When it is decided to enter serious discussions, the corporate divestiture group will then enlist the necessary legal, financial, and operating personnel. The roles of the legal and financial professionals are the same in both cases; the only difference is in where the key man in each case is administratively located in the organization. A negotiating team, preferably small (three or four people), should be designated. The negotiating team should include the chief negotiator, a lawyer, and a finance specialist. The negotiating team can be backed up internally by a larger advisory committee that provides information, advice, and ideas. In the first approach the chief negotiator will be the leader of the corporate divestiture group, or one of his or her assistants. This has the advantages that the negotiations can continue with the same person with whom the early exploratory conversations were held and that the chief negotiator will usually be experienced in this type of negotiation. The disadvantage is that the chief negotiator will not be personally familiar with all the nuances of the business. In the second approach the chief negotiator will be from the operating division. That person should be familiar with the business and at a level high enough in the organization that he or she can speak with authority and will not be included among those who would go with the business if it is sold. The advantage is that the person will know the business and its competitive climate better and can probably deal with the buyer's questions and concerns with more credibility. The disadvantage is the person is probably inexperienced in the peculiarities and process of divestiture negotiations and will have to be educated and coached. This second approach leaves the corporate group free to play two other roles that are not possible when it is directly negotiating. It can act as a second channel for communication if friction or a stalemate develops between the negotiating teams. At the point where the group hands the deal over to the negotiating team, there is always a positive relationship between the group and the buyer, since they are in agreement that serious discussions should begin. This relationship can be maintained and both sides can use the group to complain or explain indirectly if the direct confrontations become too adversarial. The fact that the group is not responsible for the negotiation permits it to take an objective view of the deal, and it can give corporate management an independent assessment.

FINDING BUYERS

Finding the right group of potential buyers is a very important step in the process and is one in which the corporate group usually plays a major role. To obtain the best price for the business it is necessary to identify the companies or investors who would find it most valuable. However, it is also necessary to be selective, since dealing with a large number of moderately interested purchasers can waste a lot of effort.

If the company has no experience and has only one or two divestitures in mind, it might prefer to use an investment banker or business broker to find buyers, rather than to organize an internal effort. Such a company will probably prefer to have the same intermediary guide it through the whole process to a closing. A company that is organized for continuing consideration of divestiture options will probably choose to seek its own buyers.

Finding buyers is partly a process of logical screening and elimination and partly a matter of unanticipated contacts. The first step is to understand the strengths and weaknesses of the business. Strengths can be valuable to someone with a need to bolster a complementary weakness, and weaknesses can present an opportunity for someone with a complementary strength to add value. Frequently candidates can be found among competitors or near-competitors, suppliers, and customers. These also happen to be the groups with which a horizontal or vertical antitrust problem is most likely to arise. The corporate and business management usually have extensive knowledge of these companies. It can be supplemented by consultants who specialize in the business field, computerized data bases, security analysts' reports, and literature searches of company reports and public speeches.

What is sought are logical fits between complementary features and fits with apparent strategies. Typical things to consider include:

1. *Market Shares.*   Are there companies with similar businesses that would find it valuable to add market share, assuming there are not any antitrust problems? These companies are usually competitors who, either by stated intent or by behavior, have shown that they have an affinity for the business and intend to be increasingly strong competitors.

2. *Product-Line Extensions.*   If the business has several product lines, are there companies who compete in some product lines but not others and could add value by having a more complete line to offer to customers?

3. *Forward and Backward Integration.*   Are there suppliers to the business or its competitors who might logically want to integrate forward? Similarly, are there customers who might want to integrate backward to a captive supply? If the industry has both integrated and nonintegrated competitors, and the integrated competitors seem to be in the best position, these are likely sources of potential buyers.

4. *Distribution Channels.*   Are there companies that distribute a larger volume or variety of products through the same channels and could handle your products more efficiently? Alternatively, are there companies who distribute similar products through other channels and would find it valuable to have access to your channels?

5. *Geographic Extension.*   If a domestic business is regional, are there operators in other regions who would find it attractive to extend their areas? Are there foreign companies that would like to enter the domestic market or have a local manufacturing facility? Does the business have foreign markets or manufacturing in regions that could be attractive to anyone else in the world?

6. *Manufacturing Capacity.*   Are there companies that make the same products or other products that can be made in the same facilities and that seem to be growing and will soon face an expansion decision? Purchasing an existing plant in good condition can be economically attractive if construction costs have escalated significantly. If regulatory permits are needed and can be difficult or time-consuming to obtain, an operating unit with permits granted can be valuable. Similarly, if personnel with particular skills that are in short supply are necessary, the fact that you have a functioning, experienced team can be a persuasive feature. Are there companies with facilities that are obsolete, facing environmental or zoning restrictions, or located in areas with uncompetitive labor rates that would prefer to move to a new site? Are there ancillary features such as land, utilities,

services, or waste disposal that would provide benefits to someone considering an expansion in a business that could use them? Are there companies with excess capacity that could consolidate manufacturing and gain cost benefits?

7. *Process Technology.* Does the business have process technology, either patented or trade secrets, that would be valuable to other identifiable companies? Are there companies with better process technolgy that could be applied to improve the business?

8. *Patents.* Does the business have an estate of patents for products, process, or use, and which companies would find it most beneficial to have the freedom to operate under those patents? Are there patents owned by others that create a problem for the business that would disappear if the others owned it?

9. *Marketing Efficiencies.* Are there companies with marketing forces that serve the same customers and could carry the products of the business to be divested with little incremental cost?

10. *Trademarks or Brand Recognition.* Are there companies that would benefit from use of your trademarks or brand recognition in marketing similar products or could extend the use of the names to enhance related products? Alternatively, would the business have more value if the products were sold under another company's labels?

11. *R&D Capability.* Is there someone who has a weakness in R&D and would find the R&D function in the business to be complementary? Are there new products, modifications, or process technology under development that would fit a need in another company? In health-care businesses a closely related function is the ability to take new products through the clinical development and approval processes that apply to different kinds of products in different countries.

12. *Services.* Is after-sale service for the products or technical service to guide the customer an important factor in the business? Your organization in these areas could be useful to a buyer, or a buyer might have an organization that could benefit the business.

13. *Complementary Products.* Are there companies making other products that could find the business to be a useful adjunct? Manufacturers of products that are used in conjunction with the business' products are prime candidates. For instance, an equipment manufacturer might find it attractive to buy a consumable product that is used by the equipment purchaser. These situations can be most promising when there is a need for compatibility that requires co-development of matching products.

With a good understanding of the business' characteristics, its competitive environment, and the industry structure, it is usually possible to identify a few prime candidates to approach. None of them is likely to be a perfect match, but one or more candidates with strong positive factors, no impassable negative factors, and with a variety of neutral factors can be sufficient. The search for buyers has some side benefits. For instance, ways to improve and modify the business prior to sale can emerge from the search process. Also, since the considerations and factors that lead to selecting the potential purchasers are known, reasonably persuasive arguments can be made to capture their interest in the initial contacts. It is important to convince purchasers that they have been selected for good reasons and to provide an explanation of why the business is sufficiently more valuable to them to allow both sides to gain from the transaction. Otherwise they will tend to assume that the seller is trying to unload a problem and will approach the whole process with deep suspicion.

The logical process described is not perfect, and potential buyers will be overlooked. Sometimes they identify themselves if they decide to take the initiative or hear rumors that the business is for sale. Sometimes they emerge after the public announcement of a letter of intent or sale agreement and complain that they were ignored. There is nothing to be done at this stage except to apologize and to contact them if the deal is not consummated.

Once a list of potential purchasers has been created, the next step is to decide who should make the first contact and with whom. If there are established relationships between people in appropiate positions in the two companies, it might be best to use those channels. A more common route is to have the head of the corporate group responsible for divestiture and acquisition activities contact his or her counterpart or the chief executive officer of the other company. This way the contact is most likely to be made with people who know the corporate attitude toward the business area in question. The objective of the initial contacts is to get discussions launched; both sides should have clear support and receptive attitudes at the corporate levels where the final decision will be made, although neither is yet committed. Starting at the corporate level on both sides is a good way to ensure this, even though negotiating responsibility may be assigned elsewhere.

An entirely different approach to finding purchasers is to publicly announce that the business is for sale. Before this is done it would probably be wise to forewarn employees, customers, and suppliers. Candidates may emerge that would not have been uncovered by internal studies. On the other hand, some people may miss the announcement and others may not be familiar enough with the business to recognize that they should be interested. The disadvantages of this method are the lack of confidentiality and lack of control over the number and quality of contacts.

Unsolicited outside inquiries are another frequent means by which buyers are identified. There tend to be three major groups of inquirers that can be further subdivided:

1. **Companies**
    Corporate level
    Operating level

2. **Intermediaries**
   Representing another company that will pay their fees
   Representing another company that will not pay their fees
   Wanting to represent the seller
3. **Investors**
   Wealthy individuals or groups
   Leveraged buyout organizers

The types of inquiries also tend to be of three kinds; specific, defined, and vague.

Provided the companywide survey has been made and the corporate stance toward the businesses is known, a large number of queries can and should be terminated on the first contact. These are inquiries from any source that specifically name a business that the company has no intention of selling, that descriptively define businesses in the same category, or that describe businesses that are not in the company's portfolio. An immediate and unequivocal negative response avoids wasting time and prevents rumors. It is worthwhile to retain a file of these inquiries because the company's attitude toward divesting a business might change in the future, and the file would be a useful source of potential buyers at that time.

Vague inquiries that ask for information about anything that the company wants to sell have to be treated with caution. If the inquirer is an intermediary, he or she is probably hoping to get a list of all available businesses that can then be used to find buyers who will pay him or her a fee. The best way to deal with these situations is to have a policy of never giving such a list to any intermediary or to anyone else and never to deviate from the policy; otherwise, control will be lost. Reputable companies or investors usually have a genuine interest in acquiring businesses, but in making a vague inquiry they are asking for information that will give more insight into the company's broad intentions than it is reasonable to give. Many companies have a public product bulletin that lists every product the company sells. One way to answer is to send a copy of the bulletin and to tell the inquirer that if he or she can name specific businesses it will be possible to give definite responses, either positive or negative.

The remaining approaches name or describe businesses that the company is willing to consider selling under the right circumstances. First of all it is necessary to establish the suitability and bona fides of the potential purchaser. If the approach comes from a public company, it is easy to check its reputation and financial resources. If the approach comes from operating-level people, it is wise to get early confirmation of corporate support. Private companies are more difficult to research, and it cannot be assumed that the financial resources available to the owners can be judged from the reported company information. If there is doubt, the inquirer should be asked how the purchase would be financed. An intermediary representing another company or investor group should be willing to name the party and offer proof that he or she has been retained. Intermediaries representing a buyer, but expecting a fee from the seller, are very rare. In such cases it is even more important to check the bona fides of the company, the intermediary, and the relationship between the two. An intermediary who has not been retained by anyone, but who wants to know if a business is for sale because he has clients he believes would be interested, has to be brought under control immediately. He or she should be told that the question will not be considered unless there is has a suitable client who has expressed interest, and in no way may the intermediary claim that the business might be on the market or claim to be representing the seller.

Investor groups have to be checked in a similar way to private companies. Leveraged buyout (LBO) organizers have different criteria from most other purchasers. They usually want mature, mundane, low-growth businesses that have little reliance on R&D and will not require plant expansions in the near future. Reliable free cash flow is essential. They also like to have assets in working capital and physical facilities that can be used as collateral for loans. Specialized single-purpose facilities and foreign sites are poor in this respect. The maximum price they can pay will be set by the required interest and principal payments of the loans rather than on a discounted cash flow valuation at normal capital costs. This frequently means that the business would have to be sold at a bargain price by normal corporate standards, and there is no incentive to sell. However, experienced LBO organizers are experts at revitalizing businesses by rigorous cost control and high incentives for successful management through equity participation. There are situations in which the best value can be found in an LBO structure.

Before agreeing to open serious discussions with any outside inquirer there should be some preliminary exploration of why they want the business, the intended treatment of employees, and what facilities and functions they want or need to acquire. If it is decided to open discussions, a decision has to be made whether to restrict negotiations to that potential purchaser or to approach other logical buyers at the same time. This is a trade-off between the prospects for getting a better price or more attractive deal structure from others versus the additional work, time consumed, and exposure risk from widening the circle.

EMPLOYEE CONSIDERATIONS

There are four groups of employees to be considered when a divestiture occurs:

1. Those who go with the business
2. Those who remain with the seller but have to be reassigned and perhaps retrained

3. Those who are not hired by the buyer and as a result have no employment
4. The employees in the rest of the company who are not directly affected

It is assumed for the purposes of this discussion that the selling company is a fair and ethical employer, genuinely concerned for the welfare of its employees and in maintaining good employee relations. A divestiture is initially a traumatic event in varying degrees for all of the four groups described, engendering feelings of shock, concern, and insecurity. Management should be sensitive to this for both humanitarian and business reasons.

The effect on the employees not directly involved will depend on their perceptions of how the other three groups fared. There will be some concerns about whether they themselves could be part of the next divestiture. If they believe the involved employees were not treated fairly, the company's image as a good employer will be tarnished and employee relations will become more adversarial. Also, when the next business is being sold the employees involved are likely to be suspicious and hostile. This can be sufficient reason to cause a wary buyer to walk away. In that case the seller is left with both the business and an employee relations problem.

The employees who go with the business will resign or be terminated and then rehired by the buyer, unless an incorporated entity is being sold. The assistance of employee relations and labor law experts should be sought to clarify the legal obligations of the seller toward various kinds of employees and collective bargaining units. However, beyond the bare legal requirements, the seller should try to insure that the employees get comparable compensation and benefits with the new employer. In some cases this may not be possible. For instance, if a business is chronically unprofitable, the alternative to selling the business with some reductions in benefits might be liquidation with widespread layoffs. If this is so, the employees should be made aware that the company has sought the better alternative. Even with fair treatment many employees will be disturbed by the change, but this will disappear with time if fair treatment continues. In fact many employees will eventually realize that they are better off working for a corporation that has a higher regard and more aggressive intentions for the business. The seller has to have employee considerations in mind from the beginning. There is little reason for initial concern if the potential buyer is a similar company with a good reputation for employee relations to protect. If the potential buyer is a private investment group, a professional leveraged buyout group, or a company with an unknown reputation in this area, then the seller should make inquiries about the buyer's intentions and track record. If the answers are unsatisfactory it is probably better to close the discussions at the exploratory stage.

Employees who remain with the seller but need to be reassigned or retrained will need reassurance. They should be usefully employed as soon as possible for reasons of both morale and economics. Many of these people are likely to be in staff or supervisory positions. In a large company the problem should be attacked on a corporate basis, not left to the division that divested the business. If it is handled at the division level, there are fewer potential opportunities, and other businesses in the division are likely to be overloaded with the excess personnel. This can result in generally reduced productivity in those businesses, resentment if promotional opportunities are preempted, and a deterioration in profitability from the additional cost burden.

In some cases layoffs are unavoidable. If the buyer does not take all the people and the seller no longer has a need for their skills, or will no longer operate in that geographic region, some people will become unemployed. This is always unfortunate, but the seller should follow the usual practices under company policies for retirement, severance compensation, and seniority. If the seller is aware in advance of the intention to sell, and that layoffs are probable, the seller may be able to ameliorate the situation by allowing normal attrition to reduce the roll and transferring people in advance. Under some circumstances it may be preferable to offer voluntary termination incentives rather than have no-work layoffs. This is a decision that is in the realm of the employee relations professionals.

When a business is identified as a potential divestiture candidate, it is well worth giving some consideration to how the business could be improved by eliminating excess staff or deleterious operations and product lines before offering it for sale. This way the seller has maximum control over the personnel questions and has a more profitable and attractive operation to present to the buyer.

Employee relations professionals and, where appropriate, labor law experts should be consulted early enough in the process for them to have time to consider all the personnel ramifications and to be able to provide some useful guidance.

LEGAL CONSIDERATIONS

Qualified legal assistance should be recruited as soon as the decision has been made to take action on a divestiture that involves sale of the business or any of its assets. Some corporations have internal legal resources adequate to handle divestiture and use outside counsel only for advice on especially difficult questions, whereas others rely largely on external law firms. It is immaterial to corporate planners which way the company has chosen to operate, but planners do need to be familiar with the broad legal aspects of divestitures so that they know when to involve the lawyers, and for what purpose.

As soon as potential buyers are identified, the lawyers should be asked to give an opinion on whether any of them is likely to represent a problem from an antitrust point of view. To do this the lawyers will need information on the market shares of the various competitors and information on the differences between competitors' offerings and the uses and customers for their products so that the appropriate segmentation of the industry can be judged and defended.

An opinion on whether a filing will be necessary to comply with the Hart-Scott-Rodino Act should be obtained early, since this will affect the timetable. All personnel involved in the process who are likely to prepare memoranda, letters, or presentations relating to the divestiture should be given advice by the lawyers on the nature of documents that must be retained to be volunteered to federal authorities at the time of filing a notification of the sale. Ideally all such documents should be reviewed by legal advisors before being presented to a corporate officer. Also, all personnel involved should be advised on the appropriate response in the event that further documents are requested or subpoenaed by federal agencies or courts. The legal documents prepared in the course of implementing a divestiture are the milestones in the process, and everyone, particularly those in the face-to-face negotiations, should be familiar with their names and purposes even though they will actually be prepared by the lawyers in most cases.

The milestone documents prepared during a divestiture are as follows:

1. *Prospectus.*   This is the document that describes the business and assets for sale to permit potential buyers to understand and evaluate what is offered. It is the exception in that it is usually prepared by the businesspersons and financial people and reviewed and approved by the legal advisors, rather than being prepared by the lawyers.

2. *Secrecy Agreement.*   This is the agreement between the seller and potential buyers that allows the buyers to see the information in the prospectus and any other confidential information given to them under terms that protect the seller from disclosure or use for purposes other than reaching a decision on the purchase.

3. *Letter of Intent.*   This is not a legally binding document and may be omitted if the parties choose to execute a definitive sales agreement immediately. A letter of intent is usually written after the process has narrowed down to the seller and one buyer, both of whom believe they wish to consummate a deal. The letter generally describes the business and assets, states the agreed price and other key terms, indicates the intent of the parties to reach a definitive agreement, and sets deadlines for negotiation. It will usually prevent the seller from negotiating with others during the specified negotiation period. The seller also agrees not to make extraordinary transactions outside the normal course of business that could strip value from it. The buyer will normally make a nonrefundable down payment toward the purchase at this point.

4. *Definitive Sales Agreement.*   This is the legally binding document that specifies in detail the property being sold and the obligations of both parties. The terms of payment will be specified. Real estate will

be described together with related easements, encumbrances, and rights of access. Other property such as machinery, equipment, inventories, receivables (if included), patents, copyrights, trademarks, technical and marketing information, and goodwill are specified. Any related assets or liabilities that are excluded should also be specified. Matters regarding compliance with government regulations, litigation related to the business, either in process or arising after the sale, indemnification of the buyer for liabilities arising after the sale, and warranties from the seller are addressed. Any ongoing agreements to supply materials or provide services or assistance after the sale should also be included.

5. *Closing Documents*.   Deeds to transfer title to real property, bills of sale for physical assets, and assignments and licenses to convey rights to other property are provided at the closing.

If the business being sold is only partially owned, has a publicly traded stock or foreign assets, or is a joint venture there can be other legal considerations in addition to those discussed for the sale of a wholly owned domestic division. Tax aspects of the transaction may require specialized legal expertise as well as accountants. Specialists in labor law may be needed to advise on personnel aspects.

It is worth reemphasizing the importance of having good legal advice throughout the process. As soon as serious discussions begin, the seller should have a legal advisor present at the meetings. The lawyers representing the two sides will have the responsibility for preparing the documents in legal language that truly reflect the intent of the parties and the agreements reached. The lawyer will be at a disadvantage if he or she is not present to hear it firsthand. If the chief negotiator is from operating management and is not a veteran of many divestiture negotiations, the guidance of experienced legal and financial advisors will be indispensable.

CONFIDENTIALITY

Confidentiality is frequently important in divestiture discussions to avoid premature disruption of business relationships with customers, suppliers, and distributors. Competitors are often quick to take advantage by suggesting that consideration of divestiture indicates a lack of commitment to the business. Employees can be disturbed before the picture of what is likely to happen is clear enough to permit any definitive answers to the questions they will naturally raise. In a divestiture virtually all the risk is carried by the seller until the deal is closed.

Throughout the process the seller is heavily reliant on trust to maintain security. Under a confidentiality agreement there will usually be some requirement to avoid premature disclosure of the discussions in addition to protection against unauthorized use of the confidential information. However, when leaks about discussions do occur, legal recourse is rare unless there has been insider trading in a public security or there is provable damage.

The best protection is to confine the circle of insiders to as small a group as possible and to make it clear that security is important and that they are being trusted to maintain it. This applies to involved employees of the seller as well as people on the buyer's side. It is sometimes useful to request a fee or deposit at the time the first confidential information is released. This serves three purposes. Information that has been purchased is treated with more respect than free information. Payment of such a sum is an unusual expenditure in most organizations, and people who can authorize it are usually in positions where acquisition decisions are ultimately considered; this insures their early involvement. Finally, casual browsers are eliminated.

Although precautions are taken to maintain security, it is necessary to be prepared for premature disclosure. Appropriate statements for release to the press, employees, and other inquirers should be prepared and updated as necessary and should be kept in the hands of those designated to respond. Confidentiality is helpful in preventing unnecessary problems for the seller and in maintaining a controlled environment for negotiations, but leaks are not fatal and the situation can be ameliorated if management is prepared and avoids making conflicting responses from uncoordinated sources.

FINANCIAL CONSIDERATIONS AND VALUATION

The financial objective of divestiture is to identify the course of action that will create the most value. This requires making several sets of valuations. For example, the value of the business as an ongoing operation and the liquidation value of the business must be determined. The greater of these two is the minimum value that must be netted from a sale. In addition, the indifference price for a sale must be calculated. This is the price for which the business must be sold to net the minimum value after all taxes and costs resulting from the transaction have been taken into account. Also, the value to the buyer after estimating the effects of any operating advantages and financial effects, such as redepreciation of the assets, must be determined. The difference between the indifference selling price and the estimated value to the buyer, assuming the latter is greater, is the calculated range for negotiation.

This section is not intended to be a treatise on financial analysis techniques. The whole array of methods used to value or assess the desirability of investments of all kinds are equally applicable to disinvestments. The purpose is to illustrate the various cases that need to be studied and indicate the items that should be considered.

Exhibit 13-1 illustrates an evaluation of the ongoing business in the seller's hands. The crucial part of this exercise is making the forecast assumptions.

13.18

EXHIBIT 13-1 Seller's Forecast

	1 Year:	0	1	2	3	4	5
2							
3	Sales ($millions)	100.0	105.2	112.3	117.9	123.8	130.0
4	Operating margin		12.0%	13.0%	14.0%	14.0%	14.0%
5							
6	Operating income		12.6	14.6	16.5	17.3	18.2
7	Tax depreciation		5.0	5.2	6.2	5.3	5.3
8							
9	Pretax income		7.6	9.4	10.4	12.0	12.9
10	Income tax		3.5	4.3	4.8	5.5	5.9
11	ITC		0.5	0.8	0.2	0.4	0.4
12							
13	Net income		4.6	5.9	5.8	6.9	7.4
14	Tax depreciation		5.0	5.2	6.2	5.3	5.3
15							
16	Cash inflow		9.6	11.1	11.9	12.2	12.7
17							
18	Capital expenditures		6.1	9.9	2.1	5.3	5.6
19	Increase in net working capital		1.5	2.1	1.7	1.8	1.9
20							
21	Cash outflow		7.6	12.0	3.8	7.1	7.4
22							
23	Annual cash flow		2.0	-1.0	8.1	5.2	5.3
24	Terminal value						40.8
25							
26	Total cash flow		2.0	-1.0	8.1	5.2	46.1
27							
28	PRESENT VALUE @ 13%		34.8				
29							

30 Interest @ 11%	1.8	1.9	2.1	2.0	2.1
31 Tax relief	0.8	0.9	1.0	0.9	1.0
32 Net interest	1.0	1.0	1.1	1.1	1.1
33 Increase in debt	0.8	2.0	-0.7	0.5	0.6
34					
35 Equity cash flow	1.8	0.1	6.3	4.6	4.8
36 Terminal value					29.9
37 Total equity flow	1.8	0.1	6.3	4.6	34.7
38					
39 Present value equity @ 16%	24.7				
40 Initial debt	16.5				
41 TOTAL VALUE	41.2				
42					
43 Net plant and equipment	26.1	30.8	26.7	26.7	26.9
44 Net working capital	31.5	33.6	35.3	37.1	38.9
45 Capital employed	57.6	64.4	62.0	63.8	65.9
46 Debt/capital	30%				
47 Debt	16.5	19.3	18.6	19.1	19.8
48 Equity	38.5	45.1	43.4	44.6	46.1
49					
50 Return on capital	8.2%	9.6%	9.1%	11.0%	11.4%
51 Return on equity	9.2%	11.3%	10.4%	13.2%	13.8%
52 Capital growth	4.7%	11.8%	-3.7%	2.8%	3.3%
53 Equity growth	4.7%	11.8%	-3.7%	2.8%	3.3%
54 Interest coverage	7.0	7.7	7.8	8.5	8.6

The objective is to predict a stream of cash flows and terminal value that can be used to calculate a reasonable and credible value for the business. The normal business forecast can rarely be used as it stands, and a separate forecast has to be made. The business forecast may include allocated overhead expenses and assets that will be unaffected if the business is sold or liquidated. These should be eliminated from the history and the forecast. Overheads that would be eliminated, either immediately or over time, if the business were divested should be included in the forecast.

Lines 3 and 4 (sales and operating margins) in Exhibit 13-1 summarize the most important and difficult assumptions to be made. All available information sources, internal and external, historical and forecast, should be used and cross-checked in an objective manner to ensure that the future sales and profitability are reasonable. It is not important to forecast the details of prices, volumes, and individual expense items accurately because the forecast is not going to be used for implementation of actions related to those details. In pursuing a business plan there are many opportunities to make corrections and change course as the years unfold, but once a business has been sold the decision cannot be revoked. The emphasis should be on developing values for items 3 and 4 that can be shown to be compatible with the economic, industry, and competitive environments that the business faces.

Tax basis depreciation is used because real cash flows, not bookkept earnings, are important. If bookkept depreciation were used, deferred tax effects would have to be included. No assumptions are necessary; the tax history of the existing plant and future capital expenditures lead automatically to the depreciation.

In capital expenditures, line 18, it is important to have actual intended expenditures in the early years because discounting will have little effect and capital expenditure patterns are usually cyclic. In the later years it is more important to have a good number in each year to reflect average expenditures required to offset obsolescence and support growth. This is especially the case in the final year used to establish a terminal value. Similar statements can be made about net working capital requirements (line 19).

The assignment of a terminal value in item 24 is the last step in this part of the process. In this case the discounted terminal value is more than half of the present value, which is usually the case with fairly short time horizons. The terminal value represents the value of the ongoing business beyond the forecast period. It can be estimated by capitalizing the final year's cash flow at the cost of capital with an estimated allowance for future growth or shrinkage of the flow. Caution is needed to make sure that the final-year cash flow does reflect sustainable relationships between cash outflow elements and sales growth and between depreciation and capital expenditures. If the final year contains an unsustainable relationship, such as depreciation being high and capital expenditures low because a plant was completed in the previous year, it may be necessary to create a dummy final year with average values to obtain a typical cash flow for capitalization. Other approaches are the applications of typical industry price/earnings ratios or market value/capital employed ratios. Care has to be taken to use the right ratios. Stock market P/E ratios and market/book ratios apply only to the equity captial, and so far a financing structure has not been provided for the business. To have usable ratios, the combined market values of debt and equity have to be related to earnings plus after-tax interest charges or to total capital employed. Line 28 calculates the present value at an estimated cost of capital of 13 percent.

The next three sections of Exhibit 13-1 look at the business from the stockholders' perspective. A capital structure is assigned so that operating cash flows can be adjusted to equity cash flows by allowing for after-tax interest charges and changes in debt. A terminal value for the equity piece is estimated and the cash flows discounted at the cost of equity capital, assumed to be 16 percent in this example. Assuming the interest rate used is current, the initial debt can be taken at face value and added to the equity value to give the total value of the business. There are several reasons to take the trouble to make the extra calculations from an equity viewpoint. The public financial information on companies in similar businesses can provide guidance on suitable debt ratios, costs of equity, interest rates, P/E ratios, and market-to-book ratios, all of which can be used to improve the quality of the evaluation. The factors used should be specific to the business, not to the overall selling corporation. Correct calculation of the value using an average cost of capital to discount the operating cash flows requires using a market-weighted average, not a book-weighted average, and it is difficult to know the market-weighted average a priori. In the example a book-weighted average of 13 percent was used to discount the operating cash flows and to estimate the terminal value, and the value is significantly lower than the total value calculated by the equity route. If a market-weighted average of 12 percent, computed from the values in lines 39 to 41, had been used to estimate the terminal value in line 25 and to discount the operating cash flows, the answer would not have been lower. Any time the present value is less than the book value, using a book-weighted average will undervalue the business; this is not an uncommon situation in divestiture cases.

Having focused on the effects on the stockholders in this case, the same approach will be used in the following examples.

Exhibit 13-2 looks at the liquidation case. The thirty million dollars of net working capital is assumed to be made up of twenty million dollars each of receivables and inventories offset by ten million dollars of current operating liabilities. The first section estimates the cash that can be received from buyers by selling miscellaneous tangible and intangible assets and by selling the inventories under distressed conditions. The second section allows for recovery of receivables, payment of payables, and taxes. Taxes on gains (in this case losses) are calculated in the bottom section. Some recapture of investment tax credits is assumed, and in this case it is assumed that the

EXHIBIT 13-2 Liquidation

1 Year:	0	1	2	3	4	5
2 Prices for assets sold				(Patents, technology, customer lists, trademarks, land, etc.)		
3 Miscellaneous	3.0	2.0				
4 Inventories	10.0	5.0				
5						
6 Cash from sales	13.0	7.0				
7						
8 Current asset recovery +		16.0				
9 Current liabilities −		10.0				
10 Taxes on gains −		−0.3			0.0	
11 ITC recapture −		0.6				
12 Depreciation tax shield +		3.0	2.3	1.8	1.4	0.6
13						
14 Other cash flows	0.0	10.7	2.3	1.8	1.4	0.6
15						
16 Severance costs	12.5					
17 Shutdown costs	3.6					
18 Contract penalties	0.3					
19 Retraining costs		1.7				
20 Residual costs		3.1	1.4	0.7		
21 Transaction costs	0.0					
22 Gross expenses	16.4	4.8	1.4	0.7	0.0	0.0
23 Tax relief	7.5	2.2	0.6	0.3	0.0	0.0
24						
25 Net expenses	8.9	2.6	0.8	0.4	0.0	0.0
26						
27 Salvage values		1.9	1.4			
28 Debt repayment		16.5				
29						

30 Equity cash flow	4.1	0.5	2.9	1.4	1.4	0.6
31						
32 Present value @ 16%	8.7					
33 Operating equity value	24.7					
34 NET PRESENT VALUE	−16.0					
35						
36 Operating equity cash flow	0.0	1.8	0.1	6.3	4.6	34.7
37 Differential cash flow	−4.1	1.3	−2.8	4.9	3.2	34.1
38 EQUITY IRR RUN VERSUS	64.2%					
LIQUIDATE						
39						

40 Tax calculation	Tax Basis	Price Allocation	Gain	Tax Rate	Tax Year 1	Tax Year 4
41						
42						
43						
44 Inventories	13.0	15.0	2.0	46%	0.9	
45 Receivables, etc.	20.0	18.0	−2.0	46%	−0.9	
46 Land	2.0	2.0	0.0	28%	0.0	
47 Buildings	4.0	0.0	−4.0	28%	−1.1	
48 Equipment predate	12.0	0.0	0.0	46%	0.0	0.0
49 Equipment postdate	7.0	0.0	0.0	46%	0.0	
50 Other	0.0	3.0	3.0	28%	0.8	
51						
52				Total taxes	−0.3	0.0

tax depreciation continues on schedule rather than being taken immediately. The correct treatment in each case should be provided by tax experts. The next section covers expense items that would occur. Severance costs cover severance pay and any other unemployment costs of employees who are dismissed. Shutdown costs to close and clean up facilities and contract penalties are self-explanatory. Retraining costs are for employees who are not dismissed, but who will have to be retrained. Residual costs are overheads associated with the business that will take time to eliminate. Nonreducible allocated corporate overheads have been eliminated from all cases. Assuming the company has other profitable businesses, these expenses can be netted for income tax effects. The case is credited with the net value of facilities that can be sold for use or scrap or utilized in other company operations. Since the objective is to compare on an equity basis, the allocated debt is paid off when the cash is available. This is solely to put the comparisons on an equivalent basis, and does not imply that the debt must actually be paid off. There is now a series of equity cash flows that can be discounted to get a comparable present value, which in this case is much less than the operating value. The correct discount rate to use for a liquidation case can be debated, since the risks are much different from those involved in the operating case, but in practice it is unimportant because the cash flows are all in the early years. The difference between the operating and liquidating cash flows is used to calculate an internal rate of return for the stockholders from running rather than liquidating the business, sometimes called the foregone IRR from liquidation. In this case the IRR is far greater than any reasonable cost of equity and reconfirms the preferability of continuing to operate. The last section is the tax calculation table, which requires that the tax basis, price allocated, appropriate tax rates, and payment timing be known for each asset.

Exhibit 13-3 presents a case in which the business is sold. The price is 30 million dollars for all the assets purchased, excluding working capital. Inventories are also purchased by the buyer for current value. Receivables and payables remain with the seller. This is a convenient arrangement when a division is sold from a corporation. If the business were a subsidiary with receivables and payables in its own name, it would be simpler to include everything in the package sold. Exhibit 13-3 is identical to Exhibit 13-2 in structure, so there is no need to repeat the description. The outcome in this example is that there is a significant gain from a sale at this price and the foregone IRR is well below the cost of equity. The possibility that the business has valuable assets that do not produce cash flow should not be overlooked. Examples can range from idle real estate to art collections. The value of these assets should be treated separately, according to whether they will be sold with the business or not, but the value should not be ignored.

The allocation of the price paid across the assets is an important matter to be negotiated with the buyer. The buyer prefers to allocate first to items that can be expensed against income as quickly as possible (inventories, for example), then to items that can be depreciated as quickly as possible, and finally to items that cannot be depreciated. The seller prefers to take gains on items to which capital gains rates will be applied and minimize gains at ordinary income rates. An agreed allocation between buyer and seller will usually be accepted by the IRS as an arm's-length transaction. If agreement cannot be reached, each partner to the transaction has the option of applying its own preferred allocation and defending it against the IRS if challenged.

Exhibit 13-4 is the seller's estimate of a buyer's case at the 30 million dollar price. It is very similar to the seller's operating case, and only the differences need be indicated. The initial prices for the business and inventories are shown as negative cash flows, and the receivables and payables left with the seller have to be recreated in the first year as a large increase in working capital. The buyer is given the benefit of redepreciating the assets from the new basis—not a large effect in this example, but a very significant one if the price is much higher than the seller's basis. The seller's estimates of the improvements in growth and profitability are the parts that require the most work and judgment and deserve the most care. All the knowledge that can be mustered about the business, the business environment, the buyer, and the buyer's strengths, weaknesses, mode of operation, and strategic intentions should be brought to bear on producing the critical assumptions.

Since the initial payments are included, net present values and IRRs can be calculated. In this example the equity NPV is positive and the IRR is moderately attractive. Note that, since the value is greater than the capital employed, calculating the value based on a book-weighted cost of capital produced a higher value. In this example both seller and buyer were given the same debt/capital ratio, since both have comfortable interest coverage and would have the freedom to choose higher or lower debt ratios. If, for instance, the business performed so poorly in the seller's hands that it could not support any debt, but in the buyer's hands would perform well enough to enjoy the benefits of leverage, this difference can be taken into account in calculating the value to the buyer.

Only one example of each case has been shown, but in fact several variations on each case would probably be run to test sensitivities to the various assumptions and highlight those that are most critical. When the most reasonable cases have been selected, it is then possible to construct a table similar to Exhibit 13-5. In this table the NPVs and IRRs for seller and buyer are shown against a range of prices for the business. The seller's indifference price is 17 million dollars and the buyer's is 41.5 million dollars. This puts the outside limits on the calculated negotiating range. The actual negotiating range will be from a point sufficiently above the seller's indifference point to give an adequate incentive to proceed to the seller's first asking price. The seller will never get more than his first asking price unless a third party intervenes with a higher offer or there are several interested buyers and the seller runs a bidding contest. In setting an asking price it should be remembered that the seller has run the estimated buyer's cases for its own guidance, not for the buyer's.

EXHIBIT 13-3 Sale

1 Year	0	1	2	3	4	5
2 Prices for assets sold						
3 Business	30.0					
4 Inventories	20.0					
5						
6 Cash from buyer	50.0					
7						
8 Current asset recovery +		18.0				
9 Current liabilities −		10.0				
10 Taxes on gains +		7.7			4.8	
11 ITC recapture −		0.6				
12 Depreciation tax shield +		3.0	2.3	1.8	1.4	0.6
13						
14 Other cash flows	0.0	2.7	2.3	1.8	−3.5	0.6
15						
16 Severance costs	2.5					
17 Shutdown costs	0.6					
18 Contract penalties	0.3					
19 Retraining costs		0.5				
20 Residual costs		3.1	1.4	0.7		
21 Transaction costs	0.5					
22 Gross expenses	3.9	3.6	1.4	0.7	0.0	0.0
23 Tax relief	1.8	1.7	0.6	0.3	0.0	0.0
24						
25 Net expenses	2.1	1.9	0.8	0.4	0.0	0.0
26						
27 Salvage values			1.6	0.4		
28 Debt repayment	16.5					
29						

13.26

30	Equity cash flow	31.4	0.8	3.1	1.8	−3.5	0.6
31							
32	Present value @ 16%	34.0					
33	Operating equity value	24.7					
34	NET PRESENT VALUE	9.3					
35							
36	Operating equity cash flow	0.0	1.8	0.1	6.3	4.6	34.7
37	Differential cash flow	−31.4	1.0	−3.0	4.5	8.1	34.1
38	EQUITY IRR RUN VERSUS SELL	7.7%					
39							

	40 Tax calculation	Tax Basis	Price Allocation	Gain	Tax Rate	Tax Year 1	Tax Year 4
43							
44	Inventories	13.0	20.0	7.0	46%	3.2	
45	Receivables, etc.	20.0	18.0	−2.0	46%	−0.9	
46	Land	2.0	3.0	1.0	28%	0.3	
47	Buildings	4.0	4.5	0.5	28%	0.1	
48	Equipment predate	12.0	10.5	10.5	46%	0.0	4.8
49	Equipment postdate	7.0	9.0	9.0	46%	4.1	
50	Other	0.0	3.0	3.0	28%	0.8	
51							
52					Total taxes	7.7	4.8

13.27

EXHIBIT 13-4 Buyer's Case

1 Year	0	1	2	3	4	5
2 Price for business	30.0					
3 Price for inventory	20.0					
4 Sales ($millions)		105.2	115.3	126.8	139.5	153.5
5 Operating margin		12.0%	15.0%	17.0%	19.0%	19.0%
6						
7 Operating income		12.6	17.3	21.6	26.5	29.2
8 Tax depreciation		6.0	6.0	6.8	5.9	7.0
9						
10 Pretax income		6.6	11.3	14.8	20.7	22.2
11 Income tax		3.0	5.2	6.8	9.5	10.2
12 ITC		0.6	1.0	0.2	1.1	1.3
13						
14 Net income		4.2	7.1	8.2	12.3	13.2
15 Tax depreciation		6.0	6.0	6.8	5.9	7.0
16						
17 Cash inflow		10.2	13.1	15.0	18.1	20.2
18						
19 Capital expenditures		6.1	9.9	2.1	11.4	12.6
20 Increase in net working capital		11.6	3.0	3.5	3.8	4.2
21						
22 Cash outflow		17.7	12.9	5.6	15.2	16.7
23						
24 Annual cash flow		−7.5	0.2	9.4	2.9	3.5
25 Terminal value						103.8
26						
27 Total cash flow	−50.0	−7.5	0.2	9.4	2.9	107.2
28						

Item					IRR	17.0%
29 NET PRESENT VALUE @ 13%		10.0				
30						
31 Interest @ 11%		1.7	2.0	2.3	2.2	2.5
32 Tax relief		0.8	0.9	1.0	1.0	1.2
33 Net interest		0.9	1.1	1.2	1.2	1.4
34 Increase in debt		3.5	2.1	−0.4	2.8	2.9
35						
36 Equity cash flow		−4.9	1.1	7.8	4.5	5.0
37 Terminal value						75.7
38 Total equity flow	−35.0	−4.9	1.1	7.8	4.5	80.7
39						
40 NET PRESENT VALUE @ 16%		7.6			EQUITY IRR	20.6%
41						
42 Net P&E + other	30.0	30.1	34.0	29.3	34.8	40.4
43 Net working capital	20.0	31.6	34.6	38.0	41.9	46.0
44 Capital employed	50.0	61.7	68.6	67.3	76.7	86.5
45						
46 Debt	15.0	18.5	20.6	20.2	23.0	25.9
47 Equity	35.0	43.2	48.0	47.1	53.7	60.5
48						
49 Return on capital		7.5%	10.9%	12.0%	17.1%	16.2%
50 Return on equity		8.4%	13.1%	14.6%	22.0%	20.8%
51 Capital growth		23.3%	11.2%	−1.8%	13.9%	12.7%
52 Equity growth		23.3%	11.2%	−1.8%	13.9%	12.7%
53 Interest coverage		7.7	8.5	9.5	11.9	11.5
53 Debt/capital ratio	30%	30%	30%	30%	30%	30%

EXHIBIT 13-5   Seller–Buyer Comparison

Price for Business ($millions)		Equity Basis			
		Seller		Buyer	
		NPV ($millions)	Foregone IRR (%)	NPV ($millions)	Forecast IRR (%)
0.0		− 12.9	47.9	27.6	42.6
10.0		− 4.9	23.4	20.9	35.6
17.0	S	0.1	16.0	16.3	27.6
20.0		2.2	13.6	14.3	25.8
30.0		9.3	7.7	7.6	20.6
40.0		16.3	3.6	0.9	16.5
41.5	B	17.4	3.1	− 0.1	16.0
50.0		23.4	0.5	− 5.7	13.1

If there are traded public companies that are largely in the business in question or if there have been recent acquisitions of similar public or private businesses, the seller should study the information carefully for its implications on probable selling price. One approach to setting the price is to treat the present value of the business as being equivalent to a market price and apply a typical acquisition premium without running a buyer's case. What this method will miss are those cases in which the business is worth much more to the buyer.

Leveraged buyouts have been around for a long time but have recently gained much publicity and become modish. In an LBO most of the money is borrowed, some secured by assets and some unsecured, and the primary need is to have sufficient reliable free cash flow from operations to meet the required interest and principal payments on the initial borrowings. Later rounds of financing, such as the venture capital industry provides for entrepreneurial companies, are not expected. Exhibit 13-6 shows a case for buying the example business for 20 million dollars. It is assumed that the managers can improve performance and that they can borrow 90 percent of the money required to finance the purchase, the working capital, and the first two years of capital expenditures. The debt repayments shown are the sum of the repayments demanded by the various lenders. Repayment down to a more normal debt level is usually fairly rapid, although not necessarily so rapid as in this example. The calculated IRR for the equity participants at 31 percent is handsome by corporate standards but is below the requirements of many LBO groups, shown as 35 percent in this case. However, this proposed LBO would not work because the negative equity cash flows shown for the first four years indicate that the prescribed debt service cannot be met. This example is meant to show not that LBOs cannot work, but that the criteria are different from corporate criteria. Before becoming deeply involved with an LBO proposition it is essential to explore the expected financial commitments and judge whether the business can meet them. Experienced and reputable LBO organizers are willing to cooperate, since they want neither to waste time nor make a mistake. There are situations in which an LBO can be the ideal solution. If the owner corporation intends to liquidate the business, an LBO might avoid the economic and human costs of dismissing the employees and be beneficial for all parties. Seasoned LBO groups are experts at operating mature businesses for cash flow and provide high incentives for management to succeed in implementing the necessary operating plans. The business receives intense attention, whereas otherwise it might have been neglected as a disfavored part of the company. There is an infinitude of complex legal and financial structures encompassed by the LBO label that makes it dangerous to generalize. However, because of the difference in financial criteria, it is frequently found that the price an LBO can afford to pay gives the corporation no incentive to sell.

Another means to eliminate a business is to spin it off to the public or the stockholders as a new company, possibly with the seller company retaining partial ownership. The business has to be able to stand alone and look reasonably attractive in the market. If the value of a business is hidden within the large parent, the stockholders can benefit by having it become visible as a separate company. A spinoff can also permit the business management to operate in a more entrepreneurial manner with greater opportunities for participation in equity incentive plans. However, a spinoff is still a sale, to a public market rather than to a private buyer, and should be considered only if it is the best way to benefit the stockholders of the parent company.

Bookkeeping effects should not be determinants of the decision, but management should be forewarned of their nature. Bookkept losses have to be reported in the quarter in which the decision is made, not when the deal closes.

CONCLUSION

Divestiture is not an easy process, and there will usually be several crises of doubt between the first suggestion that a business might be a candidate and the decision to proceed. This is appropriate since large sums of money are involved, many lives are affected, and the future shape of the company is changed. Divestiture is not something that should be undertaken in a casual or cavalier fashion. If the divestiture makes sense and rationality prevails, the company will benefit from the pruning.

Divestiture is a low-risk endeavor in that the seller should know enough about the business to avoid selling for less than its indifference value and during negotiation the seller has the advantage of knowing more than the buyer. Also, when a divestiture is over it is over. Unlike acquisitions or other investments that are here to proclaim their success or have their failure

EXHIBIT 13-6 LBO Case

1 Year	0	1	2	3	4	5
2 Price for business	20.0					
3 Price for inventory	20.0					
4 Sales ($millions)		105.2	114.0	121.2	128.9	133.6
5 Operating margin		12.0%	14.0%	15.0%	16.0%	16.0%
6						
7 Operating income		12.6	16.0	18.2	20.6	21.4
8 Tax depreciation		4.0	4.4	5.4	4.7	5.0
9 Interest @ 14%		5.0	5.9	5.8	4.4	3.3
10						
11 Pretax income		3.6	5.7	7.0	11.5	13.1
12 Income tax		1.6	2.6	3.2	5.3	6.0
13 ITC		0.6	0.9	0.2	0.6	0.4
14						
15 Net increase to equity		2.5	4.0	4.0	6.8	7.4
16 Tax depreciation		4.0	4.4	5.4	4.7	5.0
17 New debt	36.0	13.1	8.2	0.0	0.0	0.0
18						
19 Cash inflow		19.6	16.6	9.3	11.6	12.4
20 Debt repayment		7.2	8.4	10.4	7.8	5.9
21 Capital expenditures		6.1	9.1	2.1	6.2	3.8
22 Increase in net working capital		8.4	2.4	1.9	2.1	1.3
23						
24						
25 Cash outflow		21.7	19.8	14.5	16.1	10.9
26						
27 Annual equity flow	-4.0	-2.1	-3.3	-5.1	-4.5	1.6
28 Terminal value						42.2
29						
30 Total equity flow	-4.0	-2.1	-3.3	-5.1	-4.5	43.8
31						

13.32

32 NET PRESENT VALUE @
35%

		−1.0		EQUITY IRR		31.1%
33						
34						
35 Net P&E + Other	20.0	22.1	26.8	23.5	25.0	23.7
36 Net working capital	20.0	28.4	30.8	32.7	34.8	36.1
37 Capital employed	40.0	50.5	57.6	56.2	59.8	59.8
38						
39 Debt	36.0	41.9	41.7	31.3	23.4	17.6
40 Equity	4.0	8.7	15.9	25.0	36.3	42.2
41						
42 Return in equity		40.2%	32.4%	19.5%	22.3%	19.0%
43 Equity growth		116.3%	83.7%	57.3%	45.4%	16.2%
44 Interest coverage		2.5	2.7	3.1	4.7	6.5
45 Debt capital	90%	83%	72%	56%	39%	29%

analyzed and explained, divestitures are gone and people turn their attention to the business in hand. If the seller has got an adequate price and the business succeeds under the buyer's control, the decision was probably a good one that worked to everyone's advantage. If the business fails under circumstances that were believed to give it better prospects, the seller is unlikely to have regrets.

CHAPTER 14

Marketing Planning

LORRAINE C. SCARPA

DEBRA J. ROSENFIELD

LORRAINE C. SCARPA is currently Corporate Vice President, Customer Information Marketing, at Dun & Bradstreet Corporation. Prior to joining Dun & Bradstreet, she was President of Data Development Corporation, a nationally known marketing research company. She also served as Corporate Director, Marketing Services, at Heublein, Inc., where she was responsible for managing the provision of marketing research and media services to Heublein's worldwide operations in alcoholic beverages, fast foods, and grocery products. Dr. Scarpa received her Master's and Doctor of Philosophy degrees from the Johns Hopkins University. She was Assistant Professor of Management and Associate Dean for Academic Affairs at Vanderbilt University's Graduate School of Management. A member of the Consumer Psychology Division of the American Psychological Association, she has been a guest lecturer of various universities, chapters of the American Marketing Association, and The Conference Board.

DEBRA J. ROSENFIELD is currently a member of the Corporate Strategic Planning Division of Pfizer Inc. Prior to that she held planning and operations positions in the business development, financial, and marketing departments of Pfizer's Hospital Products and Agricultural divisions. Ms. Rosenfield is a director of the Westport Center for the Arts and a member of both the New York Academy of Sciences and the North American Society of Corporate Planners. She has done financial consulting for various private schools in her hometown of Westport, Connecticut and has been a contributing author for a textbook on new product marketing. She holds a B.S. from Cornell University and an M.B.A. from New York University.

OUTLINE

It is only in recent years that marketing and strategic planning have begun to converge in the management of consumer-oriented businesses. Since the late 1940s, marketing, while waxing and waning in importance to the corporate structure, has been philosophically and organizationally dedicated to the tactical operations necessary to efficient delivery of goods to the consumer; marketing plans have been "annual" in scope, focusing for the most part on timing of programs for existing products. In contrast, strategic planning grew to its most influential stature in the 1970s via emphasis on businesses as financial units to be moved, over a designated time frame, into and out of a portfolio that defined the corporate entity. The methodologies, languages, and concerns of each were distinct and communication was limited.

Major environmental changes occurring into the 1980s, all of which may be subsumed under the general notion of competition for consumer disposable income, are forging a potential for convergence. The implication that the era of the 1980s requires new relationships among management is clear: strategic planning and marketing must find common ground.

This chapter identifies that ground and provides a basis on which strategic planning and strategic marketing can stand as partners in the all-important process of strategic management.

PHILOSOPHIES OF GROWTH IN CHANGING ENVIRONMENTS: MARKETING SINCE WORLD WAR II

It is no secret that management owes the contemporary definition of the marketing concept to the General Electric Company. Its nucleus, as emphasized over many years, is the notion that the successful firm markets products customers want or need, rather than those it finds most convenient to produce; hence marketing must determine the existence of those needs and wants and estimate the span of time in which their repeated satisfaction will yield sustaining, profitable returns to the firm.

Adoption of this marketing concept was widespread through the years following its articulation in 1946, and the business objectives of American industry evolved, as J.B. McKitterick of GE said in 1957,

> first from a focus on profit for the owner, to a striving for market position and success against competition, and most recently to a focus on growth in which there is a continuing planned effort to enlarge the size of the market . . . . So the principal task of the marketing function in a management concept is not so much to be skillful in making the customer do what suits the interest of the business as to be skillful in conceiving and then making the business do what suits the interest of the customer.[1]

The years that followed were, in retrospect, the era of marketing's preeminence, with a marketing orientation being accepted as both essential to the corporate culture and highly influential on the course of the firm's development via marketing's guidance of choices of both products and markets.

An important, but little-emphasized, assumption of the marketing concept was that, in proper proximity to a product that satisfied a want, the consumer would respond with the desired response: sustainable repeat purchasing. Marketers came to believe deeply in such stimuli as advertising, merchandising, and promotion. Given appropriate distribution, the consumer came to be viewed as a largely predictable entity. That the assumption was tied importantly to a growing economy was not much discussed.

Since 1978, the economic game has changed. In the face of serious recession, slow economic growth, deregulation, an aging population, changing social values, and innumerable other factors, today's marketing management finds itself compelled to create models of competition based on static overall volumes. As Exhibit 14-1 highlights, one of the seemingly most volatile consumer categories — fast foods — has been altered by external realities with concurrent shifts in concepts of growth potential.

LINKING STRATEGIC PLANNING AND MARKETING: ENVIRONMENTAL FACTORS

There have been significant shifts in the corporate growth concept in response to a list of driving environmental factors. Those with most overt impact are recapped below.

1. *Industry Concentration in the Face of Declining Growth Rates.*   Dramatic increases in industry concentration occurred in the 1970s in a range of industries where growth rates had eroded significantly:*

---

*Data from Federal Reserve Board, Industrial Production Indexes.

	Growth Rates	
Industry Sector	1960s	1970s
Airlines	12.9%	6.8%
Beverages	5.5	4.9
Food	3.5	3.0
Household appliances	7.0	1.5
Textiles	4.9	2.0

2. *A Rise in International Competition.*   International competition resulted in the rise of nontraditional competitive structures, such as domesticated markets, and competition within the U.S. domestic market was intense.

3. *Shifting Domestic Demographics.*   Traditional market segments within the U.S. economy were restructured through the entry of women into the labor force, resulting in the multiwage-earning household as a new economic unit. The substantial number of divorces created a second new economic unit, single-parent households, thus generating other target audiences. Contemporaneous occurrences in demography yielded a new concentration of wealth away from the 18–34 market and an overall "geriatric" shift occurred.

4. *Changing Consumer Needs and Wants.*   A series of shifts in values and lifestyles (portrayed over 15 years in the Yankelovich *Monitor* and SRI's *VALS*) has resulted in current configurations of attitudes toward self (e.g., concern with physical fitness) and achievement that correlate with new growth in certain industries (e.g., sportswear, fitness centers) and with new attitudes toward work and financial reward.

These and other socioeconomic forces operating worldwide have moved within a framework of flat real-consumer-disposable income, creating enormous pressure on consumer businesses. Without the inflationary growth of the post-World War II era to rely on for profit, *sustainable* competitive advantages have become the key to growth into the 1990s. It is in the search for the competitive edge that marketing and strategic planning now find convergence.

THE CHALLENGE TO STRATEGIC MARKETING PLANNING

The challenge, as defined by Jack Welch, chief executive officer at General Electric, has emerged:

> The desire for sure things and the long-view vacuum left by marketing [in the 1970s] brought in strategic planning. At financial planning, at resource allocation

EXHIBIT 14-1 Change in Focus of the Growth Concept: An Overview of the Quick-Service Restaurant Industry

Era	Unique Business Aspects	External Modifying Factors	Corporate Growth Concept	"Quick Service" Marketing Concepts
1950s	Post-World War II economy Rapid growth through industrialization and standardization Entrepreneurship	Rapid population growth Growth of middle-income families Growth of television/advertising awareness Low entry barriers	"Formulas" for success and expansion Family-sized packaging and selling; "bigger is better" Entrepreneurial corporate spirit	Limited menu Drive-in service Low price Non-urban areas "Takeout" philosophy
1960s	Acquisitions Franchising growth Increased competition	Easy entry by competition, especially by capitalizing on inroads paved by the largest chains; "copycat" strategy	Expansion through franchising Expansion through acquisition of existing stores/chains Vertical integration of suppliers Segmentation based on products	Limited menu Saturation of nonurban areas High profit margins Give-away promotions common
1970s	Divestitures Company repurchase of franchises	Recession/inflation High unemployment More women entering work force	More reliance on contracts with vendors for supplies (rather than integration) International expansion Redesigning stores for upscale look	Expanded menus to ease profit squeeze Expansion into urban areas Product quality became segmentation factor Eat-in philosophy
1980s	Giving the corporation a unique identity as a response to segmentation of market by population demographics Return of the entrepreneur as the new competition	Increasing disposable income More single-parent families Greater reliance on prepared food as a routine part of a family's diet Competition from independents opening "gourmet-type" fast-food stores	Cooperative provision of products/services between restaurant chains and suppliers Growth through further penetration of international markets and institutional contracts (e.g., prime vendor contracts) Market segmentation relies on "niche" philosophy as determined by new population demographics	Expanded hours of operation Menus reflect increasing consumer health concerns Purchase with purchase promotions

EXHIBIT 14-2 *Conceptual Overlaps and Key Differences between Strategic Planning and Marketing as Linked by Strategic Marketing Planning*

Concept	Marketing	Strategic Planning	Strategic Marketing Planning
Emphasis derived from:	Brand awareness (external)	Corporate overview (internal)	Strategic business unit (SBU)
Structure:	Decentralized: P & L responsive	Centralized	Decentralized at SBU with dotted line to strategic planning
Strategic objective:	Focuses on building P & L profitability for brand and increasing market share.	Encompasses total corporation addressing how the responsibility for increased profitability for shareholders will be achieved over the long term.	Focuses on medium-term profit objectives of operating unit in view of corporate long-term goals
Response to competitive pressures:	Reevaluate tactics (advertising, promotion, pricing, sales program effectiveness, etc.)	Reevaluate long-term goals to maximize shareholders' wealth, keying in on allocation of resources for R & D, distribution, production, finance, and specific marketing issues affecting the corporation.	Reevaluate competitive frame, consumer demand, product quality, sales forecasts in view of corporate long-term goals; results are projected to corporation in terms of financial returns (working capital consumed/generated) through asset utilization

. . . the internalities . . . strategic planning did well . . . but not too well at marketing, the crucial externality. Comfortable with quantification, strategic planning *mapped* the external world beautifully . . . but strategic planning didn't, or couldn't *chart a market course*. It didn't navigate . . . it didn't lead . . . and, unfortunately, too often it was seen to replace marketing.[2]

On one hand, strategic planning was situated organizationally to encompass the macro responsibilities of achieving financial soundness and viability for the corporation; on the other hand, the marketing department was charged with reacting to external events in order to increase market share of the brand. There were few, if any, links between these two vital areas that would allow for the setting, communication, and implementation of goals necessary to "chart a market course."

Strategic marketing planning proposes a mechanism that bridges this gap both logically and organizationally. The conceptual overlaps and key differences between the planning and marketing areas and the bridge presented by the strategic planning process are shown in Exhibit 14-2.

ELEMENTS OF THE STRATEGIC MARKETING PLANNING PROCESS

Strategic marketing planning borrows both a process orientation and a horizon from strategic planning. It differs from marketing as applied to date by emphasizing the strategic concerns of the business rather than the tactical options for a given brand. In doing so, strategic marketing planning has a distinct responsibility (much akin to that of strategic planning corporately) to the corporate management function. If, as Cross defines it, strategic planning is "the process of sensitizing a business to the external environment, of determining what objectives are desirable and possible, and of deploying resources to match these objectives,"[3] then strategic marketing planning has comparable characteristics. It is a process by which management (both at Corporate and in the SBU) is sensitized to external environmental changes that can impinge on the effectiveness of marketing programs. These data are incorporated into assessment of the congruence of marketing objectives with the overall mission statement of the business. Similarly, they are employed in the construction of scenarios by which management can judge the viability of strategies designed to achieve both long- and short-term objectives. Success in the process is impacted by the degree of corporate commitment to data-driven action and by the amounts of time and staff resources allocated to the process.

In summary, strategic marketing planning includes three major elements in a process that must, by definition, be iterative: the construction of a theory of competition; the articulation of strategic alternatives and contingency plans; and the organization of implementation and feedback programs that function on an interproduct (or inter-SBU) basis. This process (shown in Exhibit 14-3), which occurs with specific reference to categories, brands,

EXHIBIT 14-3   A Simplified Model of the Process of Strategic Marketing Planning

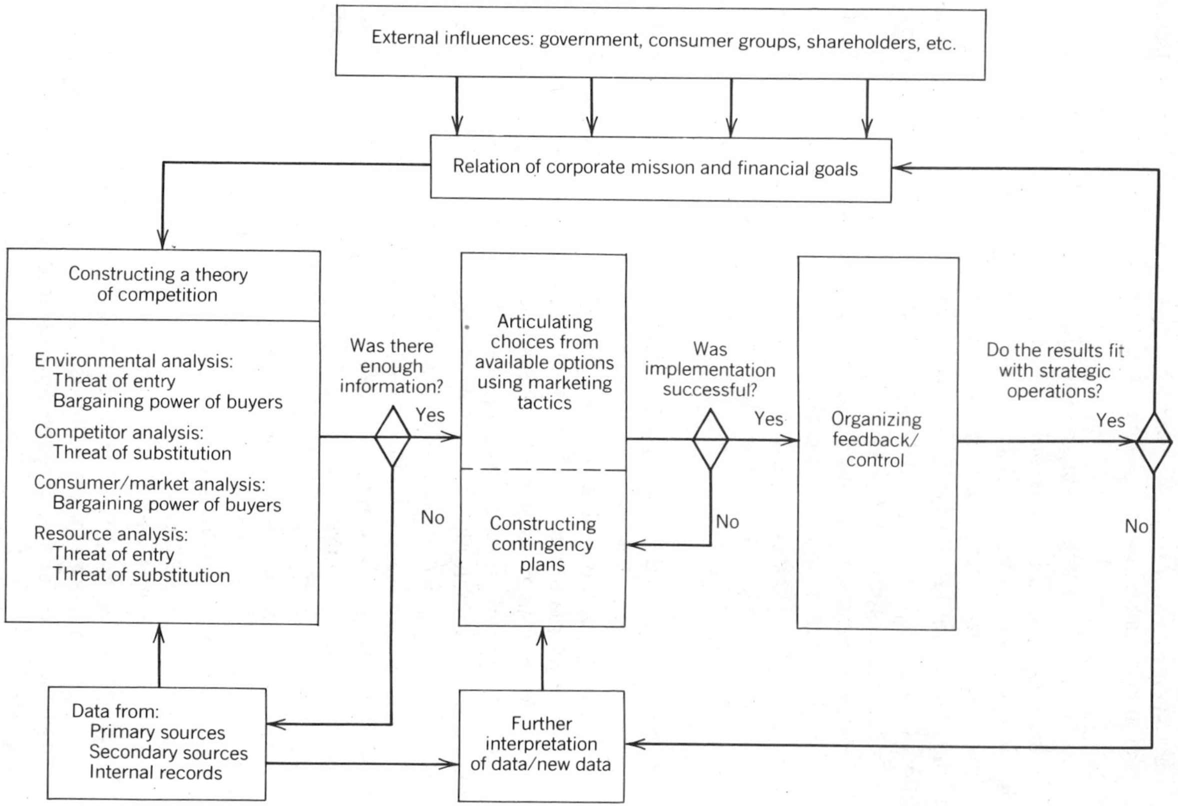

External influences: government, consumer groups, shareholders, etc.

Relation of corporate mission and financial goals

Do the results fit with strategic operations?

Yes

No

Organizing feedback/control

Was implementation successful?

Yes

No

Articulating choices from available options using marketing tactics

Constructing contingency plans

Further interpretation of data/new data

Was there enough information?

Yes

No

Constructing a theory of competition

Environmental analysis:
Threat of entry
Bargaining power of buyers

Competitor analysis:
Threat of substitution

Consumer/market analysis:
Bargaining power of buyers

Resource analysis:
Threat of entry
Threat of substitution

Data from:
Primary sources
Secondary sources
Internal records

14.8

segments, and programs, is nonetheless reflective of both the aggregate corporate financial goals and the culturally approved, qualitative goals of the mission statement, the fourth major element in the strategic marketing planning process.

Relation of the Corporate Mission and Financial Goals

The ultimate mission of any corporation is to maximize the value of the corporation to its owner(s). Favorable results are generally reflected through the analysis of the corporate portfolio comparing financial results with similar businesses within the given industry. Maximization of the indicators reflected is a function of strategic planning, which disseminates information on these target growth and profitability rates to the individual SBU and consolidates SBU results companywide to determine compliance with projected returns.

Strategic marketing planning, as the link between strategic planning and marketing, is charged with turning the targets of individual components of the portfolio into the financial results needed to optimize overall corporate profitability goals and shareholder wealth. Drawing upon information from corporate, SBU, and external sources, an individual SBU can be categorically positioned within a market growth-share matrix [4] that has heretofore been the sole domain of the corporate planner.

To achieve desired changes in rate of growth, the role of the SBU must be evaluated within the context of the corporation's current portfolio of businesses. Once this relative position is established, then appropriate marketing scenarios addressing questions of cash flow, growth of the business through merger or acquisition, redeployment of resources, and other corporate strategic considerations may be characterized for action. It is our thought that any action taken at this point should necessarily be the logical culmination of a complete iteration of the strategic marketing process as outlined here. A thorough examination of the competitive and environmental factors, plus written articulation of choices and contingencies, may provide scenarios previously considered to be nonworkable or premature when analyzed within the corporate framework. Reassessment of changing externalities can alter the growth-share positioning and result in the inclusion of strategic alternatives that had been deigned useless before. Furthermore, upon examination of the relative performance of each SBU within the corporate framework, goals previously set for the division may have to be altered to fit specific corporate growth objectives. Exhibit 14-4 graphically demonstrates the potential impact as parameters of each of the four quadrants change due to market dynamics or on behalf of senior management's willful manipulation of stated goals.

Similarly, written expression should be given to corporate values, such as largely noneconomic reasons for being in a business. Management's behavior is not that of the perfect economic man. Rather, corporations have historically continued to respond to such factors as (1) pressure from "vi-

EXHIBIT 14-4   The Growth-Share Matrix

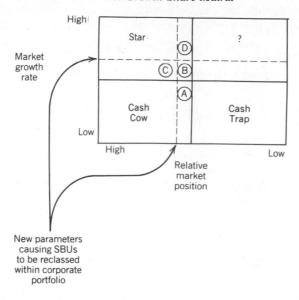

sionary" shareholders, especially board members or family-controlled blocs, to pursue growth in specific SBUs, or (2) belief in potential synergy with another division over time (such as one division's supplying raw materials to another that will allow the latter to be cost competitive). For example, Baxter Travenol has succeeded in this course by initiating a low-profit hospital management consulting operation just when the U.S. government began implementing changes in Medicare reimbursement rates. Data collected in the hospital consulting division can impact the assignment of corporate resources among those fields of medicine warranting large capital investment.

Thus the corporation is a truly dynamic entity operating under a set of qualitative and quantitative rules to maximize a chosen set of goals. From a strategic marketing planning perspective, the link between strategic planning and marketing may be facilitated: first, by integration of these financial and noneconomic objectives; and second, through recognition of the dynamics of the industries in which the corporation competes, as well as the dynamics within the corporation itself. The linchpin is an effort to articulate the corporation's actual and implicit theory of competition.

Constructing a Theory of Competition

For many years, the divorce between strategic planning and marketing precluded the construction of integrated theories of competition. Marketing emphasized regions, demography, product benefits, pricing, and channels of distribution, largely as givens in an equation that presumed that consumers responded predictably to a limited set of marketplace stimuli. We have elected to categorize these as environmental, competitor, consumer/marketing, and resource analyses in Exhibit 14-3. Strategic planning emphasized longer-range advantages of financial resources, patents, and captive markets, attributing power to the dynamism of key organizational concepts and players. It is only recently that the construction of a theory of competition has been postulated as the antecedent to the strategic audit and/or construction of functional plans, an argument Porter has made effectively:

> The essence of formulating competitive strategy is relating a company to its environment. Although the relevant environment is very broad, encompassing social as well as economic forces, the key aspect of the firm's environment is the industry or industries in which it competes. Industry structure has a strong influence in determining the competitive rules of the game as well as the strategies potentially available to the firm. Forces outside the industry . . . usually affect all firms in the industry . . . [so] the key is found in the differing abilities of firms to deal with them.[5]

Porter's model of structural determinants of competition could serve marketing planning well by providing a direct linkage with strategic planning, since Porter seeks to identify those forces that drive competition as inherent characteristics of idiosyncratic industry structure. Porter's five competitive forces — threat of entry, threat of substitution, bargaining power of buyers, bargaining power of suppliers, and rivalry among current competitors — are conceptually broad enough to subsume the spectrum of strategic planning issues while providing a previously absent scope to marketing planning. A schematic representation of these forces in its marketing planning analog is shown in Exhibit 14-5.

This structure presumes that all competitors are continually assessing their relative and absolute strengths vis-à-vis the consumer as products or services (i.e., clusters of benefits worth a particular price), while defending against revisions in industry fractionation or consolidation. Since these "revisions" derive from such factors as R & D capability, capitalization, mass, government protection, and equity structure, the linkage is in an assessment of how one's competitors *can and might* employ corporate assets in the marketplace.

Threat of Entry

Analysis within an industry of barriers to entry typically covers a range of factors such as capital requirements, economies of scale, and access to distribution. From a marketing perspective, the key considerations in either originating or defending against entry are the degree of product differentiation of different brands and the access each player has to channels of distribution.

Product differentiation creates competitive insulation (and inelasticity) by delivering to all or part(s) of the market uniqueness on one or more product dimensions. Differentiation may include advantageous access to distribution (e.g., McDonald's network of prime sites) or be facilitated by distribution

EXHIBIT 14-5   Structural Analysis in Strategic Marketing Planning

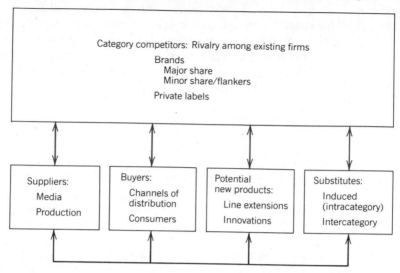

(e.g., selective distribution in upscale malls), but the assessment of the interaction of these factors is critical to judgments of price elasticity relative to competition. An example of such interdependence can be drawn from Kentucky Fried Chicken's ability to turn around its share and profitability in 1978: its absolute distribution (and the lack of a direct competitor with a comparable national base) was not sufficient to overcome consumer dissatisfaction with its declining product quality. Repositioning was effected successfully by a shift from reliance on a distribution-based positioning to a product differentiation strategy that emphasized product formulation uniqueness versus competition, both direct and indirect.

Even when coupled with parity position on distribution, capital, and leverage over suppliers, product differentiation is a formidable obstacle to competitors' moves. Differentiation creates the opportunity to brand, and branding leverages advertising, merchandising, and promotional effectiveness. Of all the elements of the marketing mix, differentiation is the most profitable and is intrinsically the area in which the best data ought to be obtained. Assessment of absolute and relative market share opportunity should be tied to clear understanding of differentiation, as should the brand-specific pricing strategy. Both can be clarified by a range of data: product testing, segmentation studies, usage and substitution tracking, price elasticity analysis (via conjoint), and perceptual mapping are but some of the ways marketing management can conceptualize and quantify the value of differentiation.

Threat of Substitution

In both the processing of raw materials and in the production of finished goods, the acceptability and availability of substitutes contribute to attainment of least-cost producer status. These tolerances of product formulations have their analogs in substitute finished goods. It is extremely important in strategic marketing planning to assign a probability (preferably known) of substitution to every product, even to truly differentiated products.

In highly advanced, consumer-oriented economies, the range of alternatives from which consumers can choose to meet needs and wants is extremely broad, both for necessities and discretionary goods and services. Strategic thinking about consumer markets must embrace the concept of substitution. Management must formally search the boundaries of category usage for other products and services that perform the same function (and are primary competitors) or perform only a similar function, despite the existence of product attributes that are not particularly relevant to the primary benefits sought. Examples are legion: intense competition among brands in consumer financial services is creating consumer confusion about selection among direct banking competitors and is drawing hitherto irrelevant competition (i.e., brokerage) into the mix. Similarly, the growth of white goods in the 1970s was interpreted by many in liquor industry as a competition between rum and vodka. Management failed to understand the real lack of substitutability that the consumer perceived between these two subcategories.

In virtually every category or industry it is possible to determine the threat of substitution if usage and substitution data (both attitudinal and behavioral) are tracked over time. Collecting such data from end users has two key results: first, the data can delineate the user definition of the served market, adding importantly to the ability to identify emerging trends in substitutes; and second, the decision to defend against or incorporate substitute products in one's SBU can impact materially on marketing's ability to manage the product's life cycle. (Such data can also be critically important to strategic planning in guiding diversification of the corporate portfolio. For example, if poor performance of the equity markets is leading investors to substitute other forms of investment, it pays brokers to have a presence in those sectors; the analogy applies to consumer businesses even more broadly, since the range of options in macrocategories, e.g., beverages, is so extensive.)

Bargaining Power of Buyers

In traditional marketing, the bargaining power of buyers is represented by brand switching and its corollary, multiple purchasing. That buyers have more power in undifferentiated or commodity categories is evident, and the marketing cost is tallied in promotional expenses at both the trade and consumer levels. Similarly, buyers confronted with added value associated with any element of the marketing mix are less powerful. (For example, decisions about food-away-from-home are constrained by physical distribution.) Least powerful are buyers for whom value-added product differentiation is based on tangible product differences (formulations) or technology (patents).

Strategic marketing planning assumes consumers are powerful and make tradeoffs based on the utilities of different options. Strategic decisions, however, can be optimized by recognizing variability in buyers' power. Benefit segmentation studies of consumer markets can enable truly targeted marketing, which takes into account not only the traditional variables of demography, lifestyle/values, and benefit orientation, but also the degree to which category usage represents loyalty and price inelasticity. As Porter emphasizes:

> A company's choice of buyer groups to sell to should be viewed as a crucial strategic decision. A company can improve its strategic posture by finding buyers who possess the least power to influence it adversely — in other words, *buyer selection*. Rarely do all the buyer groups a company sells to enjoy equal power. Even if a company sells to a single industry, segments usually exist within that industry which exercise less power [and that are therefore less price sensitive] than others.[6]

Bargaining Power of Suppliers

The leverage of suppliers across the players varies by industry and reflects the influence of each of the other four determinants within the competitive frame. Nonetheless, suppliers are generally powerful in their absolute ability to raise price and/or lower quality of a product or service's integral components. The extent to which their influence cannot be passed on to the consumer affects industry profitability.

Apart from the more obvious considerations of access and pricing of raw materials, the power of suppliers is also recognizable in such areas as communication and distribution. In consumer communication, the selection of a medium must be based on both its absolute efficacy in encouraging demand and in its cost efficiency in reaching target audiences. In network television, particularly, the ability to buy "upfront" may prove crucial to achieving programming and scheduling objectives of a marketing strategy. The power of the networks as suppliers varies by year and by day-part, but is a real influence on all players in a given industry. Similarly, promotional expense can be necessary to secure comparable distribution objectives to support a given marketing objective. Competitors must be analyzed for relative strengths in marketing clout (combination of dollars and expertise) within the industry, but the industry as a whole will suffer in its posture with suppliers to the extent that the industry itself is the underdog in degree of industry concentration, ability to employ surrogate components, and generic dependence on the supplier.

Suppliers can include such diverse constituencies as the Screen Actors Guild (a labor group over which marketers have no true influence but on whom they depend for commercials); respondents in test markets (whose compliance as "subjects" in these experiments can be the necessary element in reading a marketplace); and the Federal Trade Commission (FTC), whose very real ability to control access to consumption is a function of present and future governmental policy.

Intensity of Rivalry among Existing Competitors

As Exhibit 14-5 makes clear, the preceding four determinants affect the behavior of competitors within an industry. (That their responses provoke alteration in the environment of each determinant is also implicit, and so all possible two-way interactions are diagrammed as well.) The highly specific and culturally unique way in which each competitor has historically responded, jockeying for positions within the industry, is important input to the construction of alternative scenarios in the strategic planning of marketing programs. The reality of mutual dependence customarily leads to moves and countermoves associated with growth objectives for share or profitability.

A key to the understanding of competition lies in a firm's willingness to accept (and understand) rivalry in different forms. Not all players maximize the same goals or play within the same constraints. In the U.S. wine industry, the 1970s were heady years of growth in penetration and per capita consumption that masked the influence of major differences among key competitors: E. & J. Gallo Co. (privately held and family-controlled) answered to its owners' goals for growth in contrast to Heublein's United Vintners (publicly held and laboring under an FTC lawsuit) and Seagram's Paul Masson (a U.S. subsidiary of a Canadian family-controlled business). Analysis of the varying corporate motivations consistent with widely different legal and financial constraints is necessary to understand a significant portion of the erosion of profitability that occurred as selling costs skyrocketed, foreign imports increased, and prices remained relatively constant.

Rivalry can be summarized in terms of critical factors, such as the number and balance of competitors, industry growth, and degree of involvement with the industry exhibited by management. Such concepts as the product life cycle can be useful in constructing matrices that summarize industry rivalry, but strategic marketing planning must be based on data about each significant competitor (or groups of competitors) whose resources, attitudes, and behaviors can provide the error band around a marketing strategy.

Articulating Choices

Porter's thesis is that an SBU's competitive strategy is an adoption of one of three generic strategies. As a consequence of a strategic audit of a company's position with suppliers and buyers, vulnerability to new entries and substitutes, and ability to sustain a competitive encounter, Porter's scheme enables classification into "differentiation," "overall cost leadership," and "targeting" strategies, as shown in Exhibit 14-6.

At the categorywide level these strategies have numerous components. At the subsegment level they are keyed by product differentiation as expressed by price elasticity.

Porter's approach is but one method of strategy selection. Robertson and Wind set forth four concepts for selection of a marketing strategy.[7] When these are compared with traditional management orientations, it is clear how careful conceptual analysis can be designed to ameliorate the possible omis-

EXHIBIT 14-6   Strategic Marketing Strategies

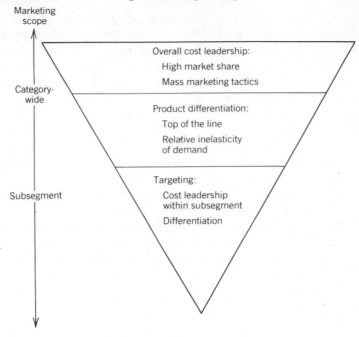

Marketing
scope

Category-
wide

Subsegment

Overall cost leadership:
High market share
Mass marketing tactics

Product differentiation:
Top of the line
Relative inelasticity
of demand

Targeting:
Cost leadership
within subsegment
Differentiation

sion of key strategic choices (see Exhibit 14-7). Consistent selection of only one of the four concepts should be a signal to the market planner that proper investigation of alternatives has not been made, or that it may be necessary to analyze the market from a different perspective, simply because markets and competitors are dynamic.

EXHIBIT 14-7   Traditional Concepts of Marketing Strategy

Concept	What It Is	Traditional Orientation
Market segmentation	Selection of key market segments	Operations-oriented
Product/ competitive positioning	Selection of products according to consumer wants and needs	Consumer-oriented
Marketing mix	Design of marketing programs geared toward sales of specific products through predetermined distribution channels	Sales-oriented
Life-cycle management	Theory that a product/brand goes through a de-velopment process consisting of introduction, growth, maturity, and decline. This pattern may be managed to forestall a stage or to aid in de-velopment of product line extensions designed to bring regrowth of the brand.	Technology-oriented

Constructing Contingency Plans and Checkpoints

Strategy selection can often be an agonizing process, especially in cases in which the product is a commodity item and the segmentation of consumers is unclear. Thus a system of checkpoints and contingency plans is necessary to provide benchmarks for comparison. These include:

1. *An Explicit Plan.*   The selected strategy should be *written,* providing rationale, key assumptions, and backup for the selection, if for no other reason than to reinforce the original decision, should positive feedback lag. Too often strategies are scrapped midstream before allowing adequate time for results to show. Secondly, contingency plans should be fully fleshed out should the need to alter strategies suddenly arise, due, perhaps, to an unexpected disturbance in the market. Contingency plans should be drafted representing those assumptions most likely to change. A third, but no less important, reason for committing the plan to paper is to provide for continuity should the person responsible for the strategy leave the corporation. Finally, written plans allow all parties involved in the strategy to participate in the implementation from a common ground.

2. *Measurable Results.*   The written plan should clearly define the desired results in measurable terms. For the marketing concepts described above there are distinct units of measurement that apply, with changes in sales volume and the bottom line being applicable to all:

Concept	Example of Measurable Results
Market segmentation	Percent penetration of selected markets through chosen distribution channels
Product/competitive positioning	Percent increase in consumer awareness/performance/intent to purchase Halt of sales erosion/brand switching
Marketing mix	Percentage increase in operating profit margin

Life-cycle management	New product:
	  Achievement of specified percent share of market or percent of awareness
	Growth product:
	  Increase in share of market
	Mature, old product:
	  Maintenance/increase in share of market for current product
	Increase in return on assets

Organizing and Implementing Feedback/Control Loops

Strategic planning and marketing implications must converge after the application of marketing tactics. Feedback and control are critical to the process because, in reality, they close two loops.

Feedback resulting from the implementation of the strategy indicates the success of the strategy and whether to continue along the same course of action, alter some of the tactics based on controllable variables, or switch to a new or contingency strategy. The adage, "If it ain't broke, don't fix it" finds a place many times when "it" is about to break, but situational analysis has not addressed the proper variables and impending change has not yet been recognized.

This is the justification for the second form of feedback — from strategic planning. An ongoing review of marketplace externalities and key corporate financial indicators should reveal subtle changes in competitive strategy that could be the harbingers of disequilibrium; such knowledge would result in a competitive edge heretofore unavailable.

Thus there is need for the routine collection of competitive intelligence organized at both the SBU and corporate strategic planning levels to be used as input to the process of modifying strategy selection. Strategic marketing planning is charged with maintaining strategies as well as with making a case for contingency implementation as needed. (There are numerous examples of companies taking an inactive stance on market signals and competitive thrusts. Warner Communications suffered significantly from its failure to manage Atari's position in the home video game market, which peaked in response to rapid growth of personal computers.)

Corporations most dependent on a high user involvement can suffer most from a lack of feedback/control simply because assimilation of market research data may consume valuable time, thus reducing the ability to react. For example, in the automotive industry, new models are in production before data on current models can be assimilated, thereby forcing a one-year lag time. Similarly, dry goods retailers are at a disadvantage when they lack accurate daily inventory/sales feedback during the pre-Christmas period, the result of which can be a huge inventory of seasonal items that must be liquidated at low margins in order to finance restocking for the spring season.

Competing successfully requires corporate commitment to information retrieval and to better methods for collecting and assimilating data about competition on a timely basis. The successful strategy, however, can also be in jeopardy should management of other SBUs within the corporate portfolio dictate change. For example, the cash cow, consistently generating working capital for the corporation and safe in its expectation in this role, suddenly may become one of two such SBUs within the corporate portfolio. In the need for constructive intervention by strategic marketing planning, becomes clear in such a situation.

INFORMATION ESSENTIAL TO THE STRATEGIC MARKETING PLANNING PROCESS

Effective, strategically minded marketing planning requires *adequate, timely,* and *relevant* information on historical behavior of each of Porter's five determinants, combined with current indicators and projections of likely trends. Across the five determinants, strategic marketing plans must be based on information that reflects changes in major components of the industry. This information may be characterized as based on data of four types: environmental trends, competitor intelligence, consumer behavior and internal resource allocation. Such data can be internal or external, shared or proprietary, projectable or qualitative — each has its utility. Management's ability to employ data to guide its judgment and reduce risk is ultimately validated in the marketplace, and data should be collected relative to this standard of usage.

Environmental Research

Marketing occurs within economic and sociocultural realities and must adapt to changes in those realities. Demographic trends, microeconomic projections, and changing social values and lifestyles are among the many indices of the marketplace that must be understood, tracked, and incorporated into marketing planning.

Competitor Intelligence

Increasing publicity and governmental scrutiny of public corporations has sensitized management to the availability of information about competitors. Public documentation of plans and marketing strategies is more widely available than most corporations believe. The collection of specific reference sources should be organized on a sustaining basis; such sources as *Advertising Age,* security analysts meetings, business weeklies, and other media through which corporations seek to influence investor interest and confidence should form the core of such a collection. The application of military intelligence-gathering concepts and systems is growing within consumer goods and service institutions and can be directed at collecting widely divergent insights into areas such as new product testing, anticipated media buys, and sales-force programs. The aggregated information can provide pieces to the larger puzzle, which can be reinterpreted over time via such information systems.

Consumer/Market Research

The focus of budgets and human resources in consumer-oriented businesses is largely on product. Segmentation, positioning, copy execution, product formulation, test marketing, and tracking are major tools in the delineation of consumer reactions to the matrix of marketing strategies used by existing competitors. Properly constructed (in terms of objectives and measurement criteria) and executed, such methods can be used to read the pulse of the current competitive frame while simultaneously providing "distant early warning" of likely reactions to major revisions of positioning or product differentiation.

Exhibit 14-8 summarizes the major tools available to obtain data about end users of goods and services. The use of these tools presumes a management focus on large numbers of consumers whose aggregated behavior "is" the category. Variations of sampling and problem definition can nonetheless accommodate qualitative usage of quantitative tools in the interest of understanding small numbers of major, key accounts/buyers. The "end user" focus is the critical element of strategic marketing planning in that it

EXHIBIT 14-8   Input to a Theory of Competition

Force Driving Competition	Strategic Marketing Issues	Relevant Market Studies
Threat of entry	Product differentiation/competitive insulation Access to channels of distribution	Product testing Usage tracking Segmentation studies Perceptual mapping Price elasticity analysis
Threat of substitutes	Lack of differentiation Price elasticity Changing consumer values/lifestyles	Product testing Substitution tracking Conjoint analysis Perceptual mapping Segmentation studies
Bargaining power of suppliers	Access to media Production/distribution constraints Promotional efficacy	Segmentation studies Advertising testing (post- vs. pre-) Scanner data Test marketing and simulation
Bargaining power of buyers	Degree of differentiation Brand switching Openness of channels of distribution Price elasticity Market segmentation	Substitution tracking Usage tracking Price elasticity tracking Perceptual mapping Segmentation studies
Rivalry among existing firms	Lack of differentiation Pricing strategy/inability to accept lower than average ROI Industry/category growth trends	Product testing Price elasticity tracking Perceptual mapping Substitution/usage tracking

seeks to understand the dynamics of current demand as input to forecasts of reaction to changes.

Resource Analysis

Realistic appraisal of one's corporate capability to meet competition in marketing is essential to strategic marketing planning and must range widely over financial and human resources issues, franchise strengths and weaknesses, the value of patents and brands, and the all-important ability to exercise flexibility in the marketplace. All too frequently, corporations set de facto limits on their ability to think and act strategically via their organizational and compensation practices. Allocating headcount and expense to tactical personnel produces tactical marketing, as does providing inadequate amounts or quality of analytic support to marketing. Data bases, which work to support the tactical needs of marketing, can also be constructed to support the longer-range needs of strategic planning if adequate time and talent are provided. At a minimum, regular review of marketing data bases should be scheduled with strategic planning to preclude expensive, reactive studies of marketplace phenomena.

ORGANIZING TO ACHIEVE STRATEGIC MARKETING PLANNING: MAKING IT WORK

Once again, philosophical differences arising in business training and fostered by political "empires" within corporations have precluded smooth communication and transition of information between strategic planning and marketing. The marketer is trained to emphasize marketing programs and to control the P & L from the sales line down to operating profit. Conversely, the corporate planner concentrates on "below-the-line" expenses and balance sheet changes, while tending to lump direct marketing/selling expenses into one category. The value of a mechanism with the ability to link these two areas is of obvious benefit to the corporation as a whole — benefits such as, but not limited to, continual review of competitive information, coordination of new product/technology reviews, assessment of new markets, and "fit" of acquisition or merger candidates. While we leave the design of such a structure to the specialist in organizational behavior, a single consideration will influence the ultimate effectiveness and implementation of the strategic marketing planning process: *senior management's commitment.* It should be clear that functional interface between marketing and corporate planning will, by definition, need the commitment of senior management. Philosophically, marketing has centered on empirical market assessment reports and studies quantifying consumer attitudes, awareness, and other "soft" data. While it has been demonstrated that there are quantitative, measurable results associated with these endeavors, only a few companies have articulated the role such data will play in managing resource allocation across the corporation. Senior management alone is capable of requiring organizational integration of the disparate data (and hence organizational linkage) of strategic planning and marketing.

POTENTIAL UTILITY OF THE STRATEGIC MARKETING PLANNING PROCESS IN THE ENTREPRENEURIAL EIGHTIES

As the eighties yield to the nineties, competition in marketing will drive marketing management harder than ever. The hallmark of the era is already evident in the much-touted pursuit of excellence, defined in strategic marketing terms as the sustainable competitive edge.

In intensely competitive environments, the need for strategically oriented marketing thinking is acute. Strategic marketing planning is essential to the achievement of the larger vision of a long-term, dynamic, and truly competitive position in an industry, because thinking strategically about the market is synonymous with entrepreneurial behavior.

Entrepreneurs "see" voids in the market and fill them, but are not content merely to stimulate the market. Their behavior is characterized by continual searches of the environment for evidence of their continued success or vulnerability to the competition. This driving need for information about the potential for change underlies strategic marketing planning. Its essential premise is that the environment is powerful: that consumers do have alternatives and do make choices, that suppliers do impact inflation pass-through, and that competitors are versatile and entrepreneurial as well.

That this focus on competition is serious is evident across domestic and international markets: the liquor industry faces worldwide trends to lower consumption; the information industry is exploding as both a hardware and a service sector; and franchising has resurfaced as a major means of propelling business growth in both the retail and service sectors. Indeed, franchising may well provide the prototype of competition, encompassing a host of players from mom-and-pops to multinationals. Franchising is a world-favorite means by which companies reduce expansion capital requirements while reducing the risk borne by the individual entrepreneur. Franchising can erode the sustainability of a competitive distribution edge in categories as diverse as hamburgers and dentistry. To fail to account for sources of competition that can arise from such leverage is ultimately to fail to think strategically about a corporation's future.

Our premise is that strategic planning's horizon must be married to marketing's perspective on value-added consumer choices if marketing is to be truly integrated into the corporate plan. Systematic searches of data that inform about actual and potential competitors, and about consumers and suppliers, are mandatory but rewarding investments, if the goal of charting the market course is to be realized.

NOTES

1. J.B. McKitterick, "What Is the Marketing Management Concept?"; in F.B. Bass, Ed., *The Frontiers of Marketing Thought and Science*, American Marketing Association, Chicago, 1957, pp. 71–82.

2. J.F. Welch, "Where Is Marketing Now That We Really Need It?," The Conference Board, New York, Oct. 18, 1981, in *Marketing Science Institute Working Paper*, Massachusetts, April 1983.

3. H. Cross, "New Directions in Corporate Planning." An address to Operations Research Society of America, Milwaukee, Wisconsin, May 10, 1973. Reprinted by Executive Reprints, Corporate Publications, General Electric Company, Schenectady, New York.

4. B.D. Henderson and A.J. Zakon, "The Growth-Share Matrix in Corporate Growth Strategy," K.J. Albert, Ed., *The Strategic Management Handbook*, McGraw-Hill, New York, 1983, Appendix.

5. M.E. Porter, *Competitive Strategy*, Free Press, New York, 1980, p. 3.

6. Ibid., pp. 26–27.

7. T.S. Robertson and Y. Wind, "Marketing Strategy," in K.J. Albert, Ed., *The Strategic Management Handbook*, McGraw-Hill, New York, 1983, pp. 11-8–11-21.

CHAPTER 15

Manufacturing Strategic Planning in Capital-Intensive Industries

DANA G. MEAD

THOBURN MILAR STAMM, JR.

DANA G. MEAD is Vice President and Group Executive, White Papers Group, International Paper Company. He has managed this group since 1981, and the group continues to be the market leader in uncoated white papers. Mr. Mead held positions within the International Paper Company as Director–Corporate Management, Director–Corporate Staffing and Personnel Planning and Vice President–Human Resources. Prior to joining IP, he was a professor and deputy head of the department of social services at West Point. He has also served as staff assistant to the President while a White House Fellow and as Associate Director and Deputy Director of the Domestic Council in the White House. Mr. Mead has received a B.S. degree in Engineering from West Point and M.S. and Ph.D. degrees from M.I.T. in Political Science and Economics.

THOBURN MILAR STAMM, Jr. is Director–Strategic Planning, Pulp and Paper Sector, International Paper Company. He has been involved in a 2-billion-dollar manufacturing facility investment program that included three large mill reconfigurations, adding over one million tons of new low-cost pulp and paper capacity. Mr. Stamm has held positions at IP as Manager of Organizational Planning, Project Manager–SURF CORR, and Manager–Strategic Planning. Prior to joining IP, he spent 11 years with Exxon Corporation in various executive positions, both in the United States and abroad. Mr. Stamm received a B.B.A. and M.B.A. in Accounting and Finance from the University of Michigan.

OUTLINE

Capital-intensive industries in the United States, such as steel, petroleum, paper, chemicals, and automotive, have experienced many of the same strategic planning fads over the past 30 years that other American industries have. These include such familiar strategic concepts as "harvest versus grow," "low-cost producer," "experience curves," "corporate culture," and so forth. However, planning in capital-intensive industries should differ from these approaches in focus.

The future profitability of a capital-intensive company is frequently at stake when major strategic investment decisions are being made. Therefore, senior management must spend considerable time and effort in evaluating and prioritizing their capital investment programs.

Many capital investments (including ongoing maintenance activities and environmental compliance projects) are nondiscretionary in nature. However, the majority of capital investments—such as new capacity, plant modernization, product enhancement, or cost reduction—are discretionary. Investment for a new plant, for example, can easily exceed one billion dollars. The magnitude of this investment requires sound strategic planning and analysis.

Capital-intensive industries are defined here as those industries with high ratios of capital to both sales revenue and employees. These industries have relatively low capital turnover; their products require high gross sales margins to provide acceptable returns. The supermarket business, in which high capital turnover and low gross margins prevail, is nearly the opposite of a capital-intensive industry.

Capital-intensive industries generally are quite mature, and technological change in them is moderate. Products are commodity-oriented, and there is limited opportunity for differentiation. Frequently, market share does not offer significant scale advantages in either manufacturing or marketing. For example, the largest newsprint paper machine that can be installed today represents less than 2 percent of the market. This inability to gain a meaningful cost advantage through scale is further compounded by limited opportunities for proprietary manufacturing or product technology. These observations suggest that it is difficult for any individual competitor in these industries to gain a competitive edge.

Capital-intensive industries have a relatively narrow dispersion of returns on investments, as shown in Exhibit 15-1. This means that any individual competitor has greater difficulty in differentiating its performance from the norm for the industry. This should be expected in industries in which com-

EXHIBIT 15-1   Dispersion of Five-Year Average ROI among Industries (1976–1980)

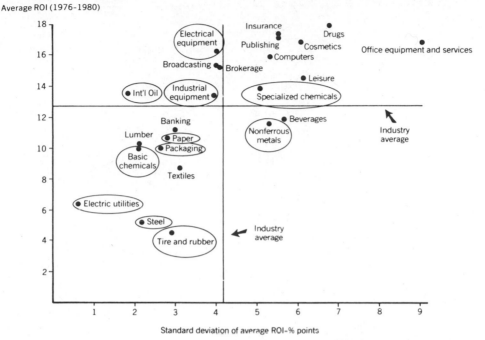

Source: "Annual Report on American Industries," *Forbes,* January 14, 1985, p. 46.
Note: Circled items designate capital-intensive industries.

petitive advantages are difficult to find. A contributing factor to this phenomenon for capital-intensive industries is the sheer size of the capital investments required, what economists often call the "lumpiness" of capital.

As demonstrated in Exhibit 15-2, industry leaders in many of the not-so-glamorous industries—including capital-intensive industries—have outperformed many of the most attractive and best-managed high-growth companies. The study from which Exhibit 15-2 is taken suggests that if a particular company is truly well-managed, it will earn an exceptional return regardless of the economic structure of its industry.

MANUFACTURING STRATEGY

Strategic planning in capital-intensive industries is characterized by a preoccupation with greater volume. Higher volume offers the dual benefits of incremental sales revenue and lower unit cost. These benefits have tremendous financial leverage when achieved with little incremental capital. This results in manufacturing objectives that are derived only indirectly from marketing or sales projections, and even less so from new market or product demand

EXHIBIT 15-2 Financial Returns and Growth Rates (1975–1979)

	Average Return on Equity	Average Return on Capital	Annual Revenue Growth Rate
Leading Companies in Eight Basic Industries			
Goodyear	9.2%	7.0%	10.0%
Inland Steel	10.9	7.9	11.4
Paccar	22.8	20.9	14.9
Caterpillar	23.5	17.3	17.2
General Motors	19.8	18.0	13.2
Maytag	27.2	26.5	9.1
G. Heileman Brewing	25.8	18.9	21.4
Philip Morris	22.7	13.5	20.1
Average	20.2%	16.3%	14.7%
Leading Companies in Other/More Rapidly Growing Industries			
Technology			
Xerox	17.8%	14.4%	15.5%
Eastman Kodak	18.8	17.7	11.8
Texas Instruments	17.2	16.3	14.6
Digital Equipment	17.0	15.5	37.4
Diversified			
General Electric	19.4	16.9	10.5
United Technologies	18.3	12.6	19.0
"Blue Chip"			
IBM	21.9	21.2	13.5
3M	20.7	17.7	13.1
Average	18.9%	16.6%	16.9%

Source: William K. Hall, "Survival Strategies in a Hostile Environment," *Harvard Business Review*, September–October 1980, p. 75.

analyses. In industries in which the plants and production lines are large, it is extremely difficult, or even impossible, to significantly shift the product mix quickly or to enter new markets, a difficulty that further reinforces management's preoccupation with volume.

In the slower-moving, less-competitive markets of the past, this approach to planning often worked—the long-term profitability of steel, paper, and chemicals, to name a few, is proof that it worked quite profitably indeed. However, as the capital structure of these industries aged and became less efficient, and their cost position deteriorated, they became vulnerable to the intrusion of substitute products and to competition from newer, more cost-efficient facilities. More comprehensive planning that integrated all the relevant aspects of a company's activity became unavoidable. For companies to remain competitive, and even to survive, manufacturing strategy and investment decisions had to take greater account of geography, raw material availability and costs, labor, technology, asset maintenance, competitive position in the industry and of each facility in its respective business, market demand, pricing, and product substitute trends. To survive, manufacturing decisions had to be the product of an integration (to use the overworked term) of every aspect impinging upon profitability and survivability.

The planning processes through which manufacturing companies achieve this integrated planning are as varied as the companies themselves. However, there are five basic objectives of manufacturing planning, each leading to an investment decision:

1. Optimize the profitability of existing facilities and technology. This seems to be a "motherhood" objective but actually involves a complex and difficult set of analyses and second-level decisions. Optimization is often done by shifting the product mix, i.e., moving products that are high- or average-cost at one facility (or on one line or machine) to other facilities where the product can be made at lower cost. They may seek noncommodity products that can be made on existing equipment or products that fall into more protected market niches.

2. Seek affordable technology that can improve the productivity of existing facilities, lower the basic costs of production at the current facilities, or help produce new or modified products with competitive/market advantages.

3. Continue maintenance capital investment programs in current facilities, enabling efficient operations without degradation of profitability or operations. In a traditional "harvest" strategy this might be the bulk of any strategic manufacturing investment.

4. Invest in cost reduction projects, usually incremental ones, to improve the competitive cost position of the line, machine, or facility.

5. Invest in *new* facilities or equipment to capitalize on expanding existing markets or to enter new ones. A recent variation of this investment strategy, necessitated by the extremely high cost of new "greenfield" facilities, is the major reconfiguration, in which valuable existing assets are preserved and "reconfigured" into essentially new facilities whose cost structures often approximate new plants, thereby offering higher returns. Recent major mill reconfigurations in the paper industry have resulted in capital costs per daily ton of paper of 50 percent less than those of comparable greenfield facilities, for example.

For manufacturing strategic planners to achieve these complex and difficult objectives, they must first understand their own company and how it is positioned in its industry. Second, they must understand how internal and external factors can be employed to improve its position. The remainder of this chapter will be devoted to describing the major considerations and issues that planners in capital-intensive manufacturing industries must address if their investment decisions are to achieve their profitability objectives.

IMPROVING PERFORMANCE

How can a competitor in a capital-intensive industry gain superior financial performance? Four concepts stand out:

Avoiding strategic errors
Operating efficiently
Gaining competitive advantages
Management agility

Avoiding Strategic Errors

There are three key elements to avoiding strategic errors. The first is to understand that each industry has its own life cycle. An important consideration is that an industry's life cycle is an evolutionary process in which the only guarantee is ongoing change. Many industries have a history of going from a high growth period to a maturing, slower growth period, and then eventually to a declining period. These industries typically have great difficulty in recognizing the transition between periods and in adjusting to them. It is common to see producers adding capacity that has been justified as being low-cost in the face of a declining market. These additions frequently prove to be disastrous investments as prices weaken from increasing supply and decreasing demand. For example, the rubber industry did not adjust very quickly to higher-mileage tires, which had a major negative impact on demand.

The second key element is recognizing market substitution, which frequently is the primary cause of a change in the life cycle. Substitution may merely involve the introduction of one product for another without any dramatic impact on the overall industry, but it can have a dramatic impact upon individual companies in that industry. Unleaded gasoline did not affect overall gasoline demand, but it had serious implications for the Ethyl Corporation, which produces lead additives. Market substitution is particularly important for higher-growth industries such as chemicals and is just as important in customer or supplier products. For example, market pulp producers were just as seriously impacted when plastic and aluminum wraps substituted for cellophane as they would have been had cellophane producers replaced wood pulp with a new base stock.

Market substitution can have strategic implications beyond demand. It plays a major role in the pricing of many products. Not long ago petroleum industry experts were predicting that crude oil prices would be up to 100 dollars per barrel today. While these experts overlooked the full potential of conservation, an equally serious error was their failure to recognize the substitution interplay between coal and oil. Approximately 37 percent of all oil consumed in 1979 in the United States was used in large industrial boilers. When the price of oil reached 34 dollars per barrel, it became economical to convert and/or replace these boilers. Since the supply of coal is relatively unlimited and very cost-driven, it was only a matter of time before oil prices would drop to discourage these conversions.

The third element in avoiding strategic errors is the most complex. It is understanding an industry's cost competitiveness and each company's cost position within that industry. Cost competitiveness for capital-intensive industries is typically international in focus, so that exchange rates and international politics, which are very difficult to predict, also become part of the cost equation.

It is just as important to understand competition's costs as it is your own, for it is your relative cost position that determines your margins. Having a reasonable approximation of competitors' costs should also help to identify opportunities to improve your own cost position.

There is a great deal of public information available for most industries. Local, state, and federal regulatory agencies offer a wealth of information. Trade publications are another major source. For example, in the paper industry such trade publications as the Lockwood's and Post's directories provide valuable information on major pieces of equipment at a competitor's facilities. Reviewing typical consumption and yield factors with your own engineering department and with equipment suppliers enables you to model industry cost. Analyzing competitor products provides a reasonable estimate of their chemical makeup. Raw material costs, freight adjusted, are readily available, and site-specific energy costs can be developed by calling the local utilities. Personnel levels and wage rates can frequently be found in trade publications. Exhibit 15-3 is a typical industry cost curve developed for un-

EXHIBIT 15-3   *Industry Cost Curve—Uncoated Free Sheet*

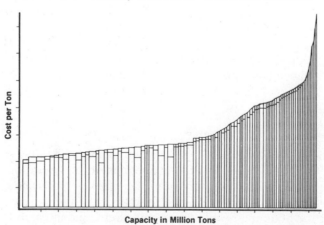

Cost per Ton

Capacity in Million Tons

coated printing and writing papers by modeling information in the manner suggested above.

However, analyzing cost competitiveness is more complex than just modeling an industry's cost curve. Technology and a company's specific experience with it can dramatically impact a product's cost. It is common to see two competitors investing at the same time using differing technology. For instance, General Motors had a very different experience with diesel engines than did Mercedes-Benz.

The significance of avoiding strategic errors for capital-intensive industries cannot be overstated. A typical return on a major capital investment may be 4 percent to 6 percent in real dolars. It is very difficult to increase the return to 7 to 8 percent. Competitive advantages are not very common and usually are quite small, particularly in comparison to the size of the investment. For example, the operating-cost profile for most new paper mills built in the last 20 years for the same products will be within a range of no more than 50 dollars per ton, or approximately 10 percent of the paper's cost. The reasons for this are the lack of major technological advances and a relative absence of proprietary technology. This 50 dollar advantage translates into an after-tax savings of perhaps 15 million dollars, which is modest when the investment is perhaps 1 billion dollars. Therefore, to make several major capital investments that will earn 7 to 8 percent returns is an extraordinary accomplishment.

What is not rare at all is to make an investment that has a negative return in real, if not absolute, terms. That one investment error can easily offset four or five extraordinary investments. Understanding your industry's life cycle and market substitution forces, and your relative competitive cost position, will minimize the risks of making that investment error. It is also important to evaluate the magnitude of risks inherent to an investment proposal. For example, a cost-reduction project at an existing efficient facility will normally entail lower risks than will a comparably sized investment in new capacity.

Avoiding strategic errors, however, should never be an excuse for not taking reasonable, calculated risks. Risk averters will ultimately be left behind by those competitors who can install well-planned innovation throughout their organization. It is a continuing challenge to management to determine the delicate balance between minimizing strategic errors and innovative risk taking.

Operating Efficiency

There are three key elements to operating efficiently. The first is to have a system that accurately measures the economics of the operation. Both the steel and automative industries were praised in the late 1950s and early 1960s for their very advanced standard cost systems. Yet their systems did not forewarn of forthcoming problems or help them against such formidable competitors as the Japanese.

   Measurement systems frequently fail because their design and operation have been left almost exclusively to accountants. They have been designed to be introspective, financially oriented, and backward-looking. The result is that these systems do not address critical questions such as how one company's cost compares to competition, or how additional cost enhances (or impedes) market position or penetration. Such comparisons for capital-intensive industries generally need to be international, as well as national, in focus. Ideally, a capital-intensive company wants to be in an area of the world offering low-cost opportunities, and then would like to be a low-cost producer in that area. Perhaps the most serious pitfall of measurement systems is their inability to provide an understanding of the underlying economics of operating efficiently. For example, some measurement systems distribute costs among common products derived from the same raw material source by allocating costs based on each product's sales revenue. These systems do not tell the operator such things as what temperature level, raw materials mix, and additive levels for a particular vessel will give optimum product yield, energy consumption, emission discharge, and so on. Consequently, line management typically has to develop its own informal measurement system. This is a most serious indictment of management—particularly American management—when one considers the enormous amounts of both time and money that are spent on formal, primary measurement systems.

   The second key element to operating efficiently is the effective application of technology. For many decades, the two leading countries in new patents have been the United States and Great Britain. Yet industry in Great Britain is well known for being antiquated. The United States is now no longer looked upon as being the technological leader in many capital-intensive industries.

   The Japanese today are highly respected for their technology leadership. This reputation is not founded on any major scientific breakthroughs, but rather on the Japanese dedication to keeping abreast of the latest technological advances and aggressively applying them. This includes not only advances in new equipment, processes, and products, but also advances in getting more out of existing equipment and products. Firsthand knowledge of the latest advances is critical to success. The Japanese are well known for traveling throughout the world to seek the latest advances, and for being quick-footed in using them when they are found.

   The importance of the role of technological advances in improving profitability in capital-intensive industries should not be overstated, either. Competition is continuing to invest in productivity through new technology and improvements to existing technology. However, most of the resulting cost savings are ultimately passed through to their customers in the form of real price erosion. Typical commodity products experience real price erosion of 1 to 2 percent annually. Exhibit 15-4 is an example of real price erosion for uncoated printing and writing papers. It shows that price has eroded by 1.1 percent annually over a 20-year period. The significance of price erosion is that every competitor must constantly reduce costs just to stay even. Standing still is a guarantee for eventual bankruptcy.

EXHIBIT 15-4   Uncoated White Papers Industry

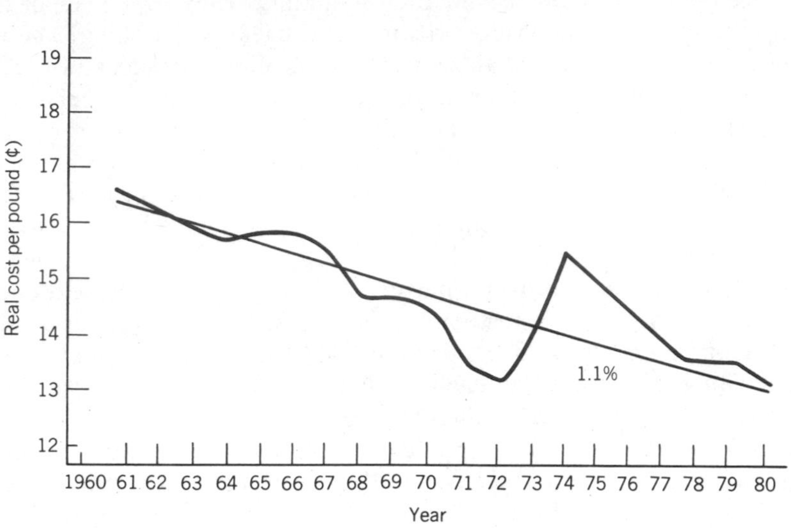

[Line chart titled with y-axis "Real cost per pound (¢)" ranging from 12 to 19, x-axis "Year" from 1960 to 80, showing a declining trend line labeled "1.1%"]

Note: During the 1961–1980 period, real prices eroded at a compound annual rate of 1.1%.

The third element of efficiency is communications. Each employee is a member of a team that is competing. A good measurement system must communicate a company's objectives and relative competitiveness to all employees, even on such delicate subjects as productivity, wage rates, staffing levels, and quality. The communication process required to do this successfully is just as important as the equitability and accuracy of the measurement system. Without it the company will be unable to make the organization, compensation, training, and facility adjustments required to keep it competitive and profitable.

Other Competitive Advantages

Gaining a competitive advantage is the most difficult challenge for any competitor. A competitor must distinguish itself in some manner if it is to earn a return higher than average and to reap the benefits that accrue to a profitability leader.

The two most important strategies used to gain competitive advantages are avoiding strategic errors and operating efficiently. Unless these two hurdles are negotiated successfully, no business can hope to achieve its profitability goals by shifting product mix, incorporating technology, reducing costs in current facilities, or investing in new ones.

Two additional strategies frequently espoused are to be the "low-cost producer" and to be the "market share leader." However, these two concepts as strategies per se are overworked. If one were to survey the top 100 companies and ask the question, is being a low-cost producer a key strategy of your company?, nearly all would say yes. Obviously, only a few can ever achieve it. This is not to say that being high-cost is desirable, but rather that being low-cost should be an outcome of other strategies that promise a stable long-term position, rather than a strategy in itself.

Market share is another strategy that in many (but not all) capital-intensive industries is not a major competitive advantage. Increasing market share is a much more appropriate strategy for specific market niches, where scale opportunities in either manufacturing or marketing are more prevalent. For example, in a large commodity market such as petroleum, market share leadership has not been an advantage. The past 20 years has been an era of the major petroleum companies' pruning back their service-station networks to enable them to compete against lower-cost independent operators. Their large market share positions did not offer any significant manufacturing scale advantages. This is not unusual in capital-intensive industries, in which a modest 2 to 3 percent share position will itself support a large, world-scale manufacturing facility.

Market share in most commodity-oriented industries also fails to provide the leverage on pricing that it may in specialty markets. Where fragmentation is the rule, market share increases are often gained only at great costs—eroding prices, market confusion, and competitive bloodletting.

If investment or business decisions regarding product shifts or mix enrichments provide only limited potential for higher profitability (unless they lead to market niches that are protected from competitive forces), and if technology, cost reduction, and greenfield investments promise only average returns in most capital-intensive industries, how or where does the manufacturing planner look for competitive advantage? We would point to a number of other strategies that can offer competitive advantages, including:

Site-specific factors
Market niches
Innovation
Quality and service

Homestake Mining is a low-cost U.S. producer of gold, due in large part to the large, high-quality gold veins that it mines. This is an example of a resource site-specific competitive advantage. Other examples of closeness to key resources include a pulp mill located in Brazil next to rapidly growing low-cost wood fiber, or a mini steel mill located in close proximity to recyclable waste centers.

There are other forms of site-specific advantages. An aluminum factory with its high electricity requirements has a major advantage when located next to its own hydrogeneration facility. Also, a new facility can frequently obtain governmental subsidies by locating in certain areas. Prevailing low wage rates or the availability of skilled labor may also be very important competitive advantages to specific sites.

There are numerous tactics for "protecting" site-specific advantages. In the increasingly rare instances when a greenfield paper mill is being built in a locality of ample wood supply, a series of satellite wood products plants can be built to insure that the mill can capture their low-cost fiber by-products for a high percentage of its needs. (This tactic has a flaw that the 1982–1983 downturn underscored: when the demand for solid wood products disappears, keeping the plants running to produce only the by-products is very expensive.)

Exploiting a market niche is an entirely different competitive advantage. In the paper industry, both James River and Pentair have performed well by concentrating in specialty markets. They both benefited from having small, slow paper machines that were best suited for specialties. In the automotive industry, Rolls-Royce and Mercedes-Benz have performed very well by concentrating on the upscale end of the market. Specialty steel producers, such as Timken, have performed much better than the steel industry in general. Market niche strategies are becoming more popular as competition intensifies. In the automotive industry, the convertible is attracting new competitors after being completely abandoned only a few years ago.

Market niches are frequently transitory in nature. The four-wheel–drive automobile market is a market niche that for many years was not fully appreciated by its two primary suppliers, American Motors and International Harvester. American Motors failed to build on its strong Jeep product line, but rather kept investing scarce capital in an attempt to regain a foothold in the passenger car market. The result is that American Motors has now lost what was practically a sales exclusive with the U.S. Government for Army Jeeps, and has also seen its share in the consumer four-wheel–drive market seriously erode with new competition from Ford, General Motors, and imports. International Harvester had to withdraw from this market for lack of capital to retool its Scout line, due primarily to problems in its other product lines. In time, this niche attracted both more competition and tougher competition. Companies often become complacent, and their relative advantages can disappear quickly with the entry of new competition.

Innovation offers another attractive opportunity for competitive advantage. Product and process innovations in the chemical industry have provided substantial rewards. For example, the DuPont Company in its earlier years made fortunes with such new products as rayon and nylon.

Paper producers, on the other hand, particularly on the commodity products side, have derived little benefit from technological innovation. The industry invests notoriously small amounts in research and development. The absence of proprietary information in an industry in which there were few secrets made it difficult to gain any advantage from innovation, so there was little incentive to spend much on it. The relatively unsophisticated and slowly developing end uses of the commodity products encouraged an emphasis on consistency and predictability rather than on innovative products. In fact, the major innovations in commodity papers—uncoated reprographic papers and high-speed forms bond for nonimpact printing—were both imposed on paper manufacturers by customers.

Quality and service can offer major competitive advantages. There have been numerous articles in recent years on the cost of quality. Avoiding mistakes in all aspects of business, ranging from producing *no* product rejects to writing errorless correspondence, adds up quickly. Highly regarded quality consultants such as Drs. Juran and Deming estimate that quality failures are equal to 10 to 20 percent of sales revenue for most companies. Many companies are incorporating quality as a major strategic objective.

Service can offer competitive advantages, too. The Caterpillar Corporation has built up a reliable customer base due to its ability to service customers over the life of its products through a strong dealer network and has done so despite charging premium prices for its products. Also, providing superior service can enable a competitor to operate its facilities at a utilization rate significantly higher than that of the industry itself. This is a major advantage in capital-intensive industries, in which a few additional percentage points in the operating rate can translate into millions of dollars of profits by keeping expensive facilities running.

Many capital-intensive manufacturing industries have been slow to grasp the benefits that superior service can bestow. Relatively small investments in warehousing and inventory, automated information systems, and customer response programs can often protect the profitability of a billion-dollar investment. But many of these advantages (often incommensurable in the financial vernacular and cost systems of today) are missed because they require actions that fly in the face of conventional wisdom. In paper, for instance, the competitive situation dictates that the producers hold more and more inventory for their customers, who will not hold expensive inventories in slow markets. Yet with only an occasional exception, new capacity has not been accompanied by the necessary amounts of finishing, staging space, and warehouse space to service these customer needs.

The ultimate test of any competitive advantage is profit. The advantage must be quantifiable by either increasing revenue or decreasing costs. Avoiding strategic errors and operating more efficiently, by definition, improve returns. Site-specific factors, market niches, innovation, and quality/service also offer opportunities to enhance returns.

It is important not to overestimate the importance of these other competitive advantages. For example, the Japanese are remote from their raw materials, energy sources, and customers, yet they have performed very well. Good management, by avoiding strategic errors and insuring efficient operations, can compensate for shortfalls in any area.

Management Agility

The fourth element in successful planning is management agility. Capital-intensive industries are evolutionary in nature, and management must be willing to adapt. This is perhaps the most difficult challenge to planning. For all the reasons we have enumerated, it is too easy to repeat what was right *yesterday*. It is most difficult to appreciate that business analyses and assessments do change, sometimes very rapidly. There are rarely absolute facts on which to base strategic judgments. Key management involvement with an open mind and keen interest can make the difference between a lethargic company and a dynamic company.

An example of management agility is found in the Duke Power Company. Most nuclear plants in the United States have had major cost overruns for a multitude of reasons, with many costing 10 or more times their original estimates. Once completed, these plants have been operating at a relatively low average utilization rate of 55 percent. Nevertheless, the Duke Power Company has been able to build three nuclear complexes without one major overrun and has been able to operate them at a very high 79 percent utilization rate. Also, Duke Power was agile enough to recognize early that another complex would not be a success and was able to cancel it at a very small cost. Duke management obviously made all the difference.

Relative amounts of management agility among companies underscore two potential pitfalls to a successful planning process that are somewhat different for capital-intensive industries. The first is that lack of time is not an acceptable excuse for incomplete analysis. These industries do not change dramatically in short periods, and this affords them the luxury of ensuring complete analysis. However, care should be exercised that this luxury does not become an excuse for not making decisions. The second is that, by the sheer financial size of these industries, they can, and generally do, employ large planning staffs. The existence of large planning staffs can erroneously encourage senior management to delegate planning, rather than to request specific supporting analysis needed for developing a strategy that they themselves are committed to. Successful planning by senior management is both very difficult and very time-consuming. It cannot be delegated and, above all else, requires a great deal of common sense. Reaching the kind of understanding that will prevent errors and assure profitability is neither technical nor very complicated. But it is time-consuming and often laborious work.

A CASE EXAMPLE

A number of examples have been used in this chapter to illustrate the importance of avoiding strategic errors, operating efficiently, and gaining competitive advantages and management agility. A test of these concepts by review of the domestic steel industry experience will help illustrate the investment results, or nonresults, of its strategic understanding.

The steel industry has one of the poorest financial performance records in recent years. Industry spokespeople have laid much blame on unfair competition from imports, due in large part to governmental subsidies and "dumping" activities. Yet, imports may be the result, rather than the cause, of the domestic steel problems.

A review of supply/demand shows that demand for steel has decreased rather steadily for over 20 years. The industry was in the declining stage of its life cycle. Substitution—first by aluminum in the 1950s and 1960s and then by plastic in the 1960s and 1970s—was rapidly making inroads into demand. Although this substitution took years, it came in an orderly fashion. Steel producers nevertheless kept anticipating an eventual rebound for their products, as evidenced by an unwillingness to close underutilized, high-cost capacity. This extra capacity had to siphon off cash that otherwise might have been invested to modernize or reconfigure the best facilities.

The domestic industry did not understand its cost competitiveness. The production of primary steel was obviously a very competitive business—a commodity product. Utilizing the latest cost-effective technology should have been a critical concern, as should have been large amounts of incremental cost reduction investments. Unfortunately, the U.S. industry virtually sat still for 20 years as the rest of the world installed new open hearth furnaces. Predictably, many U.S. facilities became obsolete. In addition, staffing and wage levels were not competitive on a worldwide basis. Mills built when capital was relatively expensive and labor cheap failed to make the painful adjustments necessary when the cost of labor in their labor-heavy facilities soared. The industry simply was not cost-competitive.

It is not unusual to read how efficient the Japanese have become. In steel, Japanese producers have been able to achieve relatively high efficiencies in the use of open hearth furnaces that U.S. producers were so slow even to install. This situation was further compounded by the good Japanese labor practices and staffing levels, which the U.S steel industry could not duplicate. It is interesting to note that steel is the same industry that was a leader in advancing the standard cost-accounting system.

Despite its overall poor record, there are two success stories in the steel industry. Mini steel mills have grown dramatically and now represent a 25 percent market share. These mills are cost-competitive, partly because of locating close to both low-cost recyclable waste supplies and their customers. The specialty steel producers who manage to find attractive market niches are also successful.

In summary, a successful strategic planning effort should encompass the above four concepts:

Avoiding strategic errors
Operating efficiently
Gaining competitive advantages
Management agility

Whether to have a formal or informal planning process is not the issue; planning is not an end in itself. Rather, planning must be a part of the management process. Senior managers are the planners and are indirectly, through delegation and proper control, the operators, too. Sound management and good strategic planning have to be synonymous for capital-intensive industries.

The more profitable companies most often build their success by repetitively achieving small successes throughout their operations, rather than by achieving one or two spectacular splashes. They also never lose sight of the fact that they are in business ultimately to serve their customer efficiently with high-quality products and service. Good management can make a big difference if it is agile enough to recognize and adapt as the competitive environment changes.

CHAPTER *16*

Strategic Research and Development Planning

MARTIN COOPER

MARTIN COOPER is Chairman of Cellular Business Systems, Inc., a company dedicated to providing comprehensive integrated software and services to the cellular radiotelephone industry. He has been a pioneer in the land-mobile industry, and was responsible for many of the technological concepts behind today's paging, mobile radio, and radiotelephone business. During his 29 years with Motorola, Mr. Cooper introduced the first practical high-capacity paging terminals and radio pagers, developed, with the FCC, the trunked mobile radio approach behind the SMRS, and participated in the regulatory activities and hearings that resulted in the cellular industry. His development teams created the IMTS mobile radio system and, in 1973, the first cellular portable radiotelephone, as well as numerous other mobile, portable, and paging products. Mr. Cooper is a fellow of the IEEE and of the Radio Club of America and a recipient of the IEEE Centennial medal. He has served on numerous industry committees and boards. He has been granted seven patents and has bachelor's and master's degrees from the Illinois Institute of Technology, in Chicago.

OUTLINE

Inspiration can't be scheduled nor inventions planned. Breakthroughs don't usually appear on demand, and we have trouble defining creativity, never mind managing it. All of these creative processes can, however, be guided, stimulated, encouraged, and channeled. Few organizations can afford the luxury of supporting unbounded creativity, no matter how inspired, if the product of that creativity does not someday benefit humanity.

Creative people work best with a minimum of structure, but even the poet sooner or later fashions words, language, into a pattern attractive to others. The sculptor has a vision bounded, at least, by the shape of his marble, and the artist to the size of her canvas and the properties of her oils. So the scientist, engineer, and inventor must have a vision. They must have goals so that they know when they have succeeded, when it's time to take a new approach, or when retrenchment and a new approach are called for.

It is the thesis of this chapter that the establishment of goals can involve a scientifically valid process, and that this process, coupled with an appropriately stimulating environment, can improve the productivity of a research and development activity, increase the relevance of its product, and reduce the risk of failures of programs that appear successful but result in curiosities having no societal merit.

This is not a process guaranteed to produce success, and there are some dangers. Overly enthusiastic application of structure will result in bureaucracy that can throttle inspiration and smother innovation. Force-feeding the process, rather than selling it, can generate resistance and resentment. The fact is, the precepts discussed here are just additional weapons in the innovators' arsenals, just tools to help them achieve their goals. The process of strategic R&D planning must evolve uniquely for each organization, and if not embraced by the innovators and researchers themselves, it will fade away or, worse, become a detriment and a hindrance. Successful management of research and development requires the soft touch and the gentle nudge, not the mailed fist; it requires intelligent persuasion, not rigid command; it requires leadership and stimulation, not obedience and submission.

PAYING ATTENTION

Organizations tend to be successful at those things to which they pay attention. Financial performance is almost universally regarded as a high-priority, top-management concern, and management treats the subject accordingly. Financial performance is discussed, measured, reported, analyzed, planned, and projected, and every level of management, to the very top, participates. It's not surprising that most companies have clear financial goals and objectives and most effectively understand and manage their financial performance. Research and development, in contrast, is generally treated as an abstract, unmeasurable art. Management goals tend to be marketing- and budget-oriented. Management leans highly on intuitive technical management or on the insight and experience of top management, where that skill exists. Experience *is* important, but experience can, in many respects, be quantified and documented. Intuition and insight are valuable, but they can be enhanced and strengthened by deductive analysis of existing and historical facts.

Three generalized tools are presented in this chapter:

1. *The Technology Roadmap.* A synthesis of predictive tools that aid in guiding research and development programs and help to establish short- and medium-range goals.
2. *The Technology Steering Program.* A participative system for stimulating and directing longer-range, research-oriented programs.
3. *The Technology Review.* A means for encouraging management participation in the research and development process.

These tools are not intended to be exclusive. Financial planning, PERT charting, and scores of other management tools may be useful and may complement the management style of a company. Nor can these tools, or any other for that matter, be forced upon the people in an organization. Where the tools have been used successfully they were sold to the R&D community and to management. They became an integral, routine part of the decision-making process. They became living, growing, self-perpetuating systems, adapted, changed, and improved by the people who relied on them. Conversely, the tools failed to have impact or survive where procedures were undertaken in response to management requirements with no relation to day-to-day activity and decisions.

STRATEGY

The emphasis here is on strategy. Strategy, as we use the term, is the combination of policy, direction, and attitude of an organization that favorably distinguishes that organization from its competitors and generally stimulates a cohesive drive toward success by the people in that organization. The substance of strategy is the competitor, which is usually real, but which may be fabricated when the real competitors are not strong enough to generate the desired stimulus. Plans, objectives, and goals are all important elements of the planning process, but the strategy is the basis of the thinking process.

The use of tools like those described here is, in itself, a basic strategy, but it is important to maintain a focus on competition, real and potential, in every step of the process.

THE TECHNOLOGY ROADMAP

The technology roadmap is a compilation of management tools that comprehensively describes the product line of a business—past, present, and future—and that states the strategy and the plan for achieving success. The intent of the roadmap is to insure that the tools are understood and available. No one can force their use, but effective tools will be embraced by the product team as soon as they are constructed and their worth is recognized.

The outline below suggests a specific format for the technology roadmap. Each organization should create its own version, but the strategic tools should always be used. These tools are briefly discussed in the following pages.

OUTLINE
TECHNOLOGY ROADMAP

1. The business
    Business mission
    Strategy
    Sales history and forecast
    Share of market
2. The strategic tools
    Product life cycle
    Experience analyses
    Competitive analyses
    Technology trends
3. Measurements
    Projects and programs
        Descriptions
        Status reports
        Summary reports
    Patent portfolio
    Quality performance
    Unfunded projects
4. The plan
    Product plan
    Manpower loading plan
    Quality improvement plan

THE PRODUCT LIFE CYCLE

The product life cycle curve appears in Exhibit 16-1 in its basic form. Most products exhibit low sales growth immediately after introduction. The length of the introductory period depends on control of the sales force, product complexity, market awareness, advertising and promotional effort, and so on. After the product's value is established, the growth phase occurs, but growth slows as competition matches or improves upon the product, the market becomes saturated, the product approaches obsolescence, or any combination of these factors takes place. Finally, the product reaches obsolescence and sales slow until termination occurs. Clearly, we cannot conduct a business on the basis of a single product cycle; we would be forced to liquidate soon after reaching the maturity stage. To achieve the steady growth that characterizes a healthy business, a next-generation introduction should occur just as growth starts to slow, perhaps even during the growth stage. It's certainly better to put yourself out of business than to have a competitor do it. Exhibit 16-2 shows an idealized series of products creating a steady growth curve. Exhibit 16-3 is a real-life example (although brand and generic names have been removed to protect the source). A cursory examination of Exhibit 16-3 reveals that:

Product life cycles have been running at 10 to 11 years in this product line.

The overall market is growing at about 22 percent.

Product B should have been introduced two years earlier to avoid the severe 1971 dip in sales.

While this may not have been predictable in the late 1960s (when product B engineering was due to start), a similar dip in sales occurred in 1975. *That* could have been predicted.

A predictable slowdown in sales occurred in 1981 because product E was late.

EXHIBIT 16-1   A Single Product Life Cycle

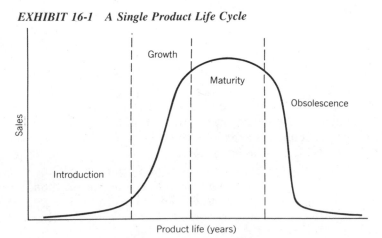

EXHIBIT 16-2   An Idealized Business Life Cycle

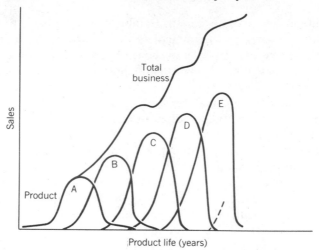

One conclusion to be drawn from Exhibit 16-3 is that the product group was starting its next generation development programs when the preceding generation had already matured and was, as a result, losing market share and inhibiting market growth. This product group could not attune itself to start working on a next generation while the previous one was still in its growth stage. The obvious solution would be use of life-cycle data to signal the need for a new development. An alternate solution (actually used) would be creation of a separate competitive group to work alternate generations and thus to keep market share loss in-house.

The product life-cycle curve has its greatest value when several generations of a specific product can be observed, but once an industry characteristic is known, much can be learned from a single cycle.

THE EXPERIENCE CURVE

Modern experience-curve theory is based on an important analysis published by the Boston Consulting Group some years ago.[1] It has evolved and has been practiced widely since. The remarkable discovery was that, in a large number of industries, product cost (in constant dollars) dropped at a uniform rate relative to cumulative experience. In simpler terms, each time the number of units manufactured doubled, the cost, with inflation removed, dropped to a fixed, but constant, percentage of the original cost. For semiconductor integrated circuits, the experience curve rate has been about 72 percent. That is, if x units of a specific device type had been manufactured up to a given time, and the cost of manufacture at that time was a, then, when an additional x units were made, the price would have dropped to $.72a$. For the television industry the rate was 69 percent, and for electric power it was 80 percent.

EXHIBIT 16-3   Business Life Cycle—Real Example

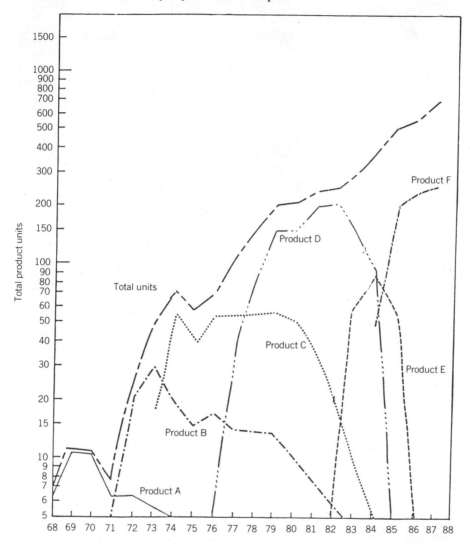

This is an amazing observation and not at all self-evident. After all, product cost drops as a result of a combination of, among other things, (1) material cost, (2) changes in product design technology, (3) manufacturing process improvement, (4) "learning" among production workers, (5) specialization, and (6) better inventory control. None of these factors alone can account for the experience-curve rate. The impact of each factor is very different in different industries.

From the above we may conclude that the producer having the highest unit volume will have the lowest cost, will be able to set industry prices, and will have the highest profitability. The experience curve concept teaches that share of market is a measure of success.

EXHIBIT 16-4   *Product Average Selling Price and Average Product Cost (constant $1972)*

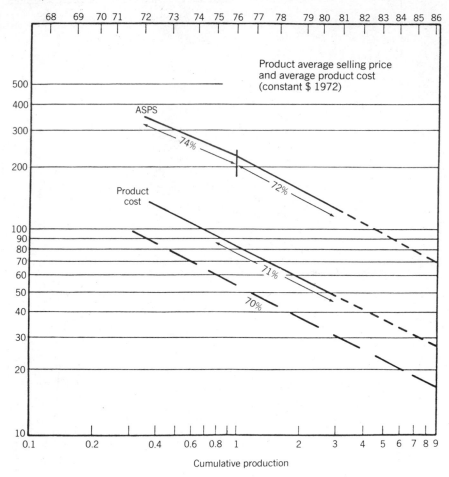

If there is sufficient cost history for a product line, the rate can be derived by plotting, on logarithmic scales, cost as a function of cumulative units produced. The slope of the resultant straight line is the experience-curve rate (see Exhibit 16-4). For most industries, the rate appears to be somewhat independent of specific product line, so that it's possible to derive the benefits of experience-curve management even for new products.

What are these benefits? Consider that, if we know our product cost and experience-curve rate, we can apply the forecast of unit sales and determine, with reasonable confidence, what our cost will have to be each year in the future. We can use these experience-curve–derived costs as goals for the manufacturing and product design teams—goals that they can really believe in. When it becomes clear that longer-range goals will be difficult, we can use the experience curve to stimulate our research people to focus on a cost breakthrough, in contrast with a performance-oriented effort. In short, the experience curve is a valuable motivational tool—if the objective is achieving high share of market.

The price-experience curve is a corollary of the cost-experience curve and was similarly derived empirically. The price-experience curve is developed in the same manner as the cost-experience curve, except that the *market* price is plotted as a function of cumulative *market* experience. This means that, unless the company for whom the curve is drawn has a dominant share, the curves should be drawn on separate graphs.

Some potentially useful conclusions can be drawn from a price-experience curve. If the slope is steeper than the cost-experience curve for a particular product line, the curves are converging and profitability will evaporate unless a more aggressive cost curve is achieved (it's also possible to raise prices—*if* competition permits). Future prices can be tested against price-elasticity criteria; targets for new markets and new applications may be envisioned; business plans can be examined for rationality.

It is my experience that something can be learned from application of the experience curve to *any* product line, even when no history exists, in which slopes of similar products are assumed. If there is an obstacle to the use of this tool, and others discussed here, it is disbelief and lack of understanding of the value of the technique. The common response to an exhortation toward derivation and analysis of the experience curve is, "Looks good—but it doesn't apply to my product line."

The fact is that it *does* apply, as long as it is recognized that the experience curve is a tool rather than a precise set of answers—a tool for motivation and communication rather than a producer of absolute conclusions.

In practice, plots of costs and prices do not lie precisely on a straight line. There is a tendency to force bends in the curve, especially where pricing is aggressive in anticipation of future sales growth. It is rare that a change in the slope of a single curve is appropriate. This happens only when a major cost or market force causes an entirely new design or marketing strategy.

Imagine knowing, with reasonable credibility, what the cost of a proposed product must be before the product is designed. Imagine knowing how the competitors will price their next-generation products. Of course the tool is approximate, but it is rational. It can be adjusted and manipulated, and when it has become part of the R&D planning culture, it is believable.

COMPETITIVE ANALYSIS

Since a prime objective of the R&D planning process is establishing or maintaining superiority over competition, knowing the competition is vital. The criteria and the means for collecting data vary with industry and product, but the results should be organized and documented so that they can be integrated into the planning process. An example of a format useful in sum

EXHIBIT 16-5　Product Technology Roadmap—Competitor/Technology Matrix

Competitor/Technology Matrix

Products or applications	This Company	Company "A"	Company "B"	Company "C"	Company "D"	Company "E"				
Aluminum etching	4 · 5/1	4 · 4/4	2 · 3/1	2 · 3/1	5 · 5/5	4 · 4/3				
Oxide etching	4 · 5/1	4 · 4/3	2 · 2/1	2 · 2/1	5 · 5/5	3 · 3/1				
Silicon etching	4 · 5/3	5 · 5/5	3 · 3/3	3 · 4/3	5 · 5/5	5 · 5/5				
Photo resist ashing	5 · 5/3	3 · 2/2	4 · 4/3	2 · 2/1	5 · 4/4	2 · 3/2				
Photo resist development	4 · 5/3	0 · 1/1	2 · 3/3	3 · 3/4	0 · 1/2	0 · 0/0				

Scale 0–5
　0 = no effort
　5 = leader

Today | Next 3–5 years / Last Year

Notes: 1. No intensive effort among Japanese companies.
2. Antipollution laws may intensify effort.

marizing a comparison of production-process capability among a number of companies is the matrix shown in Exhibit 16-5. While there is a great deal of general information in the matrix, it is essential that the matrix be supplemented with organized narrative about each competitor—narrative that relates details about the strengths and weaknesses, superior and inferior processes, and development capability of the competitor.

The product-line manager is expected to be an expert on the subject of his or her product line, and that expertise must be clearly demonstrated and used in the technology roadmap.

TECHNOLOGY TRENDS

The technology forecast provides the focus of R&D effort, and an organized approach to documenting the forecast can insure that specific technologies are not neglected or forgotten. The forecast of trends is no better than the quality and completeness of the information it contains, but documentation and the use of trend charts permit continuous adjustment and updating. An example of a trend chart appears in Exhibit 16-6. This curve of semiconductor chip density was drawn in the late 1970s, but continues to have validity 10 years later.

The matrix in Exhibit 16-7 shows how the trend in a number of technologies can be outlined to force research activities supporting a product line.

EXHIBIT 16-6   Technology Roadmap—Technology Trend Chip Density

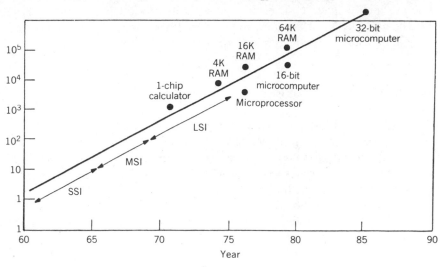

EXHIBIT 16-7   MOS Technology Roadmap

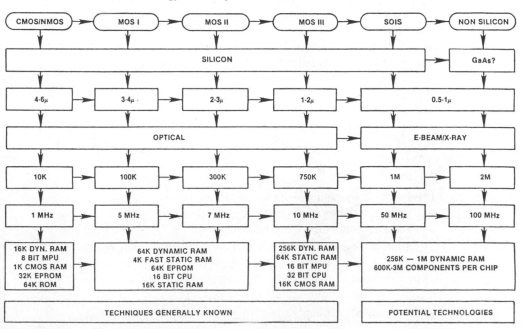

The curves, charts, and narrative forms used in each industry and product line are highly specific. Their use must be institutionalized and disciplined. The cost of guesswork and incomplete analysis are too high; the cost of the organized tools in the technology roadmap is minimal.

THE TECHNOLOGY STEERING PROGRAM

The technology roadmap, disciplined by management attention in the form of regular reviews, has proven to be a remarkable tool for managing research and development. However, as these techniques are embraced by the product organizations, it becomes evident that they focus attention on, and enhance decision making about, the next-generation product, and perhaps even the product of the generation beyond that. They also address, in the technology trends analysis, the underlying technologies that support the basic product technologies. For example, if the product is a radio, the technology roadmap should drive the cost and performance of the end product, but should also reach for new component technologies in the semiconductor, speaker, and antenna fields.

While the people who prepare and use the technology roadmap must be expert and totally knowledgeable about their product and competition, they may not be the best people to examine and drive the underlying technologies that must be available to the product engineers before they can even start a next-generation design. The following paragraphs discuss an organizational tool that focuses expert attention on key underlying technologies and provides management with a line of communications to the engineers and scientists who are most capable of evaluating the company's needs and of stimulating progress in advancing the company's position in these areas.

The mechanism for attacking this opportunity is the long-range technology steering committee. A suggested procedure is to generate a list of all of the technologies that comprise the company's product line. These will generally fall in the categories of materials, devices, process, and systems. Within these and other categories there will be a hundred or more specific areas. After this list is generated, the formation of the steering committee involves three major steps:

1. Product management, using the technology roadmap, identifies those underlying technologies that pace the progress of their products or offer opportunities for excellence.
2. Technologists are identified who represent the best expertise in the company in each underlying technology. In cases in which voids in expertise exist, outside consultants may be identified to create a balanced, complete coverage of the technology.
3. A long-range technology steering committee is formed.

The steering committee is charged with the following responsibilities:

1. Evaluate the capability, expertise, or any appropriate measure of the company in the designated area of technology.
2. Determine, as completely as possible, the same measure of capability for the best companies in the field.
3. Compare the above and establish a judgment of the strengths and weaknesses of the company in the designated area of technology.
4. Recommend to management any changes that can improve, enhance, reprioritize, or otherwise correct any competitive shortfalls, or that will present market opportunities to the product teams.

It is reasonable to expect that a company of moderate size and complexity may maintain from five to ten active steering committees and a comparable number who have met, performed their function, and now meet only occasionally to review progress in their field.

The first recommendation of almost every steering committee is to assign more R&D resources—people and money—to their technology. Committees have made, however, a number of very constructive and creative proposals that were practical, had high returns, and cost little or nothing. In one such example, a proposal was made to rationalize R&D in a specific area throughout the company. It was found that six independent groups were pursuing the same line of research, and that all of them were below critical mass. Although all of the groups could not be persuaded to yield their prerogatives, three efforts were consolidated into one effective program, and the company benefited enormously.

Other recommendations have proposed reprioritizing, purchasing technology from a foreign source, and abandonment of subcritical work where it was clear that the company could not maintain a viable technological presence in a particular product line.

Even when the recommendations have not been considered, the cross-fertilization occurring in most meetings has been beneficial enough to make the effort worthwhile. The greatest benefit has been the improved *esprit de corps* within the technical community resulting from management's interest and willingness to listen.

THE TECHNOLOGY REVIEW

Leadership can assume a wide variety of forms, from inspiration to fear; from charisma to intellectual respect. The key to all of these forms is the communication that occurs between leaders and those they wish to lead. The communication is seldom purely verbal. In fact, some of the most effective leaders lead by example and by action rather than by direction. There is a danger that the perception of leadership may be quite different from what is intended by the leader.

When management focuses strongly on fiscal performance (as it properly should) to the exclusion of strategic performance (as it does not intend), the organization can perceive this as a deliberate ranking of the financial team ahead of the technology team. When factory performance is examined frequently and engineering performance rarely, the engineers will ultimately relate to the production line, perhaps to the detriment of innovation and creativity, and certainly in contrast to the real desires of management—all of this despite the verbal protestations of the leaders. The management of a well-run company wants to maintain a proper balance between the various elements of corporate success and wants to finely tune the degree of emphasis in concert with the changing environment. The technology review is such a means of communication and of creating balance. The people in an organization know when management meets to discuss financial results, to approve capital purchases, or to plan marketing programs. In their desire to participate and to follow, it is not unusual, then, for R&D people to emphasize financial performance, equipment purchases, or marketing impact to the detriment of the most important R&D role—achieving technological dominance.

The technology review is simply a meeting involving top management and all levels of technology management in an organized review of strategic and operating technological performance. The level of management in attendance will communicate the degree of importance of the meeting to the R&D attendees. The meetings can be as short as an hour or two, or as long as a day. The meeting may embrace one product line or an entire division, but the attendance, the agenda, and the discussion in the meeting will create an image of strategic balance far more effectively than any number of orders, memoranda, or harangues.

The following list is a suggested agenda for a technology review. The details are not important and will differ between and within companies. It is vital, however, that each topic, long- or short-term, get *some* attention at each meeting. The desire to spend an entire meeting on a single product problem or on an interesting new technology must be resisted. This is a management review, not a decision-making meeting or, at the other extreme, a classroom tutorial.

Time (minutes)	Subject	Speaker
15	Introduction; marketing and business overview	Division manager
	Business A	
60–90	Schedule summary; technology roadmap summary; competitive analysis; quality review	Operations or product manager

30	Long-range topics and tutorials	Chief technologist
15	Unfunded programs and adversary positions	
30	Discussion	

Business B
(Repeat pattern of Business A)
Business C
(Repeat)

When product lines within the organizational entity under review are sufficiently different, several product lines or businesses can be covered serially, as shown in the example agenda. But the structure is relatively unimportant.

If the technology review is to become a meaningful institution, a device for focusing attention on research and development, and a means for disciplining an organization to pay appropriate attention to research and development issues, then certain fundamentals *must* be adhered to:

Reviews must be regular (even once yearly is regular), scheduled, and not postponed. Rescheduling, no matter how important the reason, will be perceived as a management shift in priority—downwards. The purpose of the technology review is to raise the priority and awareness of the research and development process.

Top management attendance is vital; it can't be delegated. This imposes a large burden on a chief executive or sector head, especially when he or she does not have a strong technical background, but there is no alternative. If the leaders attend regularly scheduled reviews, the operating managers will be there; if not, the meeting will deteriorate into a review of technologies by the technologists who live these technologies.

The balance between short- and long-range issues must be maintained. The temptation to bear down on a specific program to the exclusion of others must be resisted or the strategic value of the review will be lost in favor of operational issues. The latter will be vital—and should be pursued elsewhere.

Every program, project, or effort should be covered, if only by the briefest reference (by a schedule summary, for example). Allocation of resources is the very substance of research and development management, and that means *all* resources. It's easy to focus on one problem program and neglect a group of smaller ones that cumulatively represent a higher strategic value.

Someone in every organization has an adversary position—doesn't agree with the way things are being done, or thinks the wrong programs are being funded. As difficult as it may seem (and it is difficult), the adversaries should be heard, and they *will* be if management asks to hear them. Each review should incorporate some effort to hear someone—or some view—that contrasts with the establishment.

Beware of overdoing it. The intent is to raise an awareness of the importance of technology, not to create a bureaucracy.

NOTE

1. "Perspective on Experience," Boston Consulting Group, 1970.

CHAPTER *17*

Human Resource Planning

FOSTEN A. BOYLE

ALAN A. YELSEY

FOSTEN A. BOYLE is Vice President, Corporate Human Resources for Honeywell Inc. He is responsible for all human resource functions at the corporate level. Mr. Boyle has been with Honeywell for more than 18 years in a number of division, group, and corporate human resource assignments. A graduate of the University of Minnesota and the Harvard Business School Program for Management Development, Mr. Boyle serves on the Dunwoody Institute Board of Trustees, and is cochairman of the Minneapolis Joint Labor/Management Council. He is a member of the Twin City Personnel Association and the American Society for Personnel Administration.

ALAN A. YELSEY is Manager, Corporate Human Resource Planning for Honeywell Inc. He has been a human resource planner for Honeywell for over five years, and has worked at division, group, and business levels before joining the corporate staff. Prior to joining Honeywell, Mr. Yelsey was a regional planner. A graduate of the University of Minnesota and the University of Massachusetts, Mr. Yelsey holds a master's degree in Educational Psychology and Social Studies Education, and has completed coursework toward a Ph.D. degree focusing on dynamic systems analysis and policy analysis. He is a member of the Human Resource Planning Society and the North American Society of Corporate Planners.

The authors would like to recognize the following individuals for their important contribution to the development of this chapter: Dr. Lorenz P. Schrenk, Larry M. Smith, and Charles S. Anderson. Special thanks to Robert E. Gustafson and Pamela K. Burdick.

OUTLINE

AN OVERVIEW OF HUMAN RESOURCE PLANNING

Human resource planning provides a framework to improve organizational performance through people and the systems used to manage and involve people. It is a process that considers where an organization is and where it is going in the context of its environment. It then identifies what an organization needs to do with regard to human resources to best meet the challenges of the future. Three elements that form the basis for human resource planning and contribute to overall organizational performance follow:

1. *Human Process.*   Individual and group values, norms, culture, attitudes, and patterns of interaction.
2. *Structure.*   Formal organizational systems such as organization design, job design, management processes (rewards, appraisal, recruitment, succession, etc.), information flow.
3. *Knowledge.*   Individual and group knowledge of technical, administrative, and human process subjects.

Human resource planning is a future-oriented thought process that assures a match between the business and social objectives of an organization and the structure, knowledge, and human process of the people who make up the organization, within the context of the operating environment.

The costs of acquisitions that do not work, of business thrusts that fail, of relocations that don't perform, of products that can't compete, of organizations full of frustration, of minds that cannot relate, and of structures that immobilize surely exceed the costs of prevention. These costs are often attributable to a failure to consider and utilize human resources and management systems adequately and are not, in isolation, a failure to make the right business decision. Their ultimate origin can often be attributed to a faulty human resource decision that occurred years before a problem arose.

Human resource planning is a relatively new, evolving activity. It is not widely institutionalized, as many other planning functions are, and organizations differ markedly in terms of both the amount of attention they devote to human resource planning and their methods of implementation.

While this chapter is devoted primarily to organizationwide planning, human resource planning can and should be practiced in some form by departments, by programs and projects, and by the operating subunits of any corporation or institution.

In this chapter we identify and describe the basic components and steps of human resource planning. We begin by describing strategic human resource planning and operational planning, and then identify an organizational performance model that represents a new trend for human resource planning. Major themes in human resource planning are then addressed, followed by models and calendars that visually represent the planning process. We close with a section describing a talent and succession subplan and a summary.

A Technical Framework

There are many choices an organization has to make that determine the flavor and composition of its own brand of human resource planning. Every organization is encouraged to select from the planning framework on the following pages what seems to fit its needs. In presenting models and tools for human resource planning, we recognize that, depending on whether your organization is large or small, old or new, public or private, people-intensive or capital-intensive, needs will differ. The intent is to present what is regarded as a "leading edge" approach to human resource planning in order to spark new ways of looking at organizational planning in general, and strategic human resource planning in particular. In summary, the following is intended not as the only correct approach to human resource planning, but as a solid basis on which individuals may form their opinions.

Ethics

We would like to start with a brief comment on the ethics of human resource planning. Planning helps insure the effective functioning and future viability of an organization. It can also be regarded as a commitment to the people in an organization, their families, and society as a whole. Behind the numbers and concepts of human resource planning are real people. It is easy to forget that. Effective human resource planning can help not only an organization, but also the lives of many people within and without the organization. Decisions about hiring, relocation, layoffs, training, succession, benefits, reorganization, acquisition, and divestiture have enormous implications for the people involved. It is incumbent on all those involved in human resource planning to establish a commitment, small or large, to the human dimension of planning and to perform with the best resources and the highest commitment to comprehensive, quality thinking.

Strategic and Operational Planning

We have chosen to distinguish strategic human resource planning from operational human resource planning. It is helpful to view human resource planning in two related stages of thinking. In the first, strategic, stage, organizations are concerned with the identification of critical long-range issues and the strategies and objectives to address them. In the second, operational, stage, organizations concern themselves with what they need to do the following year to implement the strategies and objectives. The distinction lends clarity and focus to the planning process and helps avoid unnecessary confusion and complexity.

STRATEGIC PLANNING

Human resource planning guidelines and processes that are focused, brief, and to the point encourage involvement and participation. The following outline serves as both a planning guide and a review guide. It is meant to encourage clarity, brevity, and thought, rather than heavy documentation. It presumes that significant information collection and analysis will occur to provide a solid business and environmental base.

Basic Strategic Human Resource Plan and Review Outline

A. Planning Parameters

1. *Purpose.*   To develop clearly defined human resource strategies that are necessary to implement the business plan.
2. *Basic Data*
   Business strategies (formal and informal)
   Social policy directions (i.e., principle statements, mission and charter statements, etc.)
   Major organizational goals and objectives
   Human resource research and scan information
3. *Time Frame.*   Three to five years
4. *Length.*   Five to ten pages
5. *Process.*   Participative

B. Planning Process

1. Summarize your core organizational strategies and characteristics for the next three to five years.
2. Identify major shifts in internal and external environmental factors.
3. What shifts do we foresee in terms of the following business factors?

Products	Competition
Product mix	Financial goals
Markets	Information management
Engineering and technology	Other
Production	

4. What technical, political, and cultural implications do these shifts have for changes in our human resource strategies? (After a review of the list of implications, what major human resource issues are identified?)

Selection	Management style
Appraisal	Productivity initiatives
Rewards/recognition	Communication and data
Skills mix	management
Organization structure	

5. What are the social policy directions of the organization, and what implications and issues do they have for our human resource strategies?

Climate and culture change	Safety and health
Affirmative action	Other
Community involvement	

5. What are the major human resource strategies and objectives necessary to assure achievement of both business and social policy objectives?

Provide summary for business plan

7. What are the major resource investments you foresee over the next three to five years to implement strategies?

We have purposely ordered the steps in thinking about human resource planning to begin with core organizational characteristics. Words or phrases that describe the current organization form a useful starting point that serves an important reference function when you get to the point of considering strategies and actions. How do your plans compare to the current organizational environment? How much change is required? How best to approach the change? This first step helps.

Next we selected external, then internal, trends before evaluating business trends. Our rationale for this is quite simple. Business plans, whether written or transmitted informally, are not always effectively prepared. We ask the human resource planner to understand the internal and external environment and organization characteristics prior to considering business strategies and shifts. It is a check and balance on the business planning process, offering the human resource planner an opportunity to evaluate the business plan for its compatibility with people and organizational trends and characteristics. Mismatches become issues.

Human resource external environmental scans can be conducted by an organization or selected from a variety of private and institutional vendors. Some large companies have banded together to jointly fund an external human resource scan. Rather than go into depth with regard to external and internal environmental scans, we will address them by providing checklists of variables that can be considered when scans are conducted.

External and Internal Environmental Scanning Checklist

External Environmental Scan (local, state, regional, national, international)
   A brief outline of some variables to be considered in an external environmental scan are:

Workforce Demographics
   Age patterns
   Composition
   Participation levels
   Supply
   Mobility
   Population shifts, etc.
   Immigration and regional trends
   Factors influencing organizational relocation

Economic Conditions
   Unemployment
   Inflation
   Productivity
   Raw material costs
   Mergers and acquisitions
   Business trends

Legal and Regulatory
   IRS and governmental trends
   Labor laws and regulations
   Health and safety
   EEO/affirmative action
   Comparable worth

Technology
   Key trends and changes
   Partnerships

Workforce Social Trends
   Employee attitudes and values
   Special interest groups

Education and Training
   Assessment of sources and quality
   Partnerships
   Key trends and changes

Union and Collective Bargaining
   Key trends and changes

External and Internal Environment Scanning Checklist (Continued)

International Developments
    Labor markets
    Trade and foreign competition
    Multinational employment policies
    Key trends, changes, and issues

Human Resource Management
    Societal needs
    Trends regarding productivity, quality, and performance
    Trends involving cost, such as compensation, benefits, health care
    Trends in recruitment, development, training
    Trends in work structuring and worklife

Internal Environmental Scan (job groupings, locations, divisions, functions, corporation, demographic groupings)

A brief outline of some variables to be considered in an internal environmental scan follows:

Workforce Characteristics (current and projected)
    Age
    Years of service
    Race
    Sex
    Handicaps
    Salary
    Benefits
    Education and skills
    Mobility
    Grade
    Performance
    Attrition
    Retirement
    Succession depth and breadth
    Attitudes and perceptions
    Family and personal needs

Organizational Characteristics (current and projected)
    Physical environment
    Locations
    Culture
    Organizational performance and measurement
    Organizational structure and systems
    Management and information systems
    Technical and technological change
    Health and safety

The intent of an external human resource scan is to identify critical factors that may influence an organization's decision making over the next five years or more. The identification of significant external forces often requires a merging of many variables into recognizable themes that impact your organization and that demand proactive or reactive action. A similar comment can be made about the internal environmental scan.

Internal environmental scanning involves the analysis of both employee and organizational characteristics and trends. The planner is looking for issues that stand out on their own, or become issues when considered along with external or business trends.

Business plans differ widely in quality, but seem to be improving steadily. We encourage organizations preparing strategic human resource plans not simply to accept the business plan as golden or inevitable. Talk to as many knowledgeable people as you can, and look for inconsistencies and major differences of opinion. Organizations should either seek clarity on these points or build a number of scenarios into the human resource planning process.

If the future appears vague or uncertain after reviewing scan information and business information, it seems to make sense for you to develop a number of scenarios based on this information and identify for each scenario the issues, strategies, and actions necessary. This multiple scenario plan certainly will involve ambiguity, but it presents your best look at the future.

Given environmental information and business shifts, the next step is to draw human resource implications from these shifts. Implications can be such phrases as "fewer engineers," "job redesign changes," or "health cost increases." This list of implications can be grouped and prioritized, and then considered for major issues. While implications are narrow, brainstormed links to environmental and business shifts, issues are broader problem statements that often encompass a series of implications. Sometimes, along with an issue statement, the estimated impact of the issue upon the organization is identified.

Social policy directions are then identified. They are separated here from business shifts to insure that they are attended to. Social policy shifts pertain to organizational objectives not directly linked to profit, but rather to social responsibility. Once social policy shifts and their implications have been addressed, and associated issues identified, all issues are reviewed, grouped, and prioritized.

Strategies address issues, although not necessarily one-to-one. Strategies should be limited to a small number. The strategy statement is important. It preferably includes a focused statement of human resource direction that references both the driver (cause) for the strategy and basic actions linked to strategy implementation. For example, a strategy statement might read: Establish a follow-on business venture through the commitment of resources and a development team to reduce the risk of engineering layoffs.

Objectives identify measurable results linked to both the issue and the strategy. Some planning processes start with objective statements, and from there they develop strategy statements. This is not a big issue, but strategies that drive objectives are our answer to this "chicken/egg" dilemma. A direct, written tie-in between the strategic human resource plan and the published business plan is encouraged.

Assessment and Plan Development Tool

The following strategic human resource assessment and plan development tool (Exhibit 17-1) has been successfully used in large and small, public or private, organizations. Phases one and two are completed typically in a small group session, and then reviewed with others in the organization until consensus and clarity are reached. The difficult stage consists of considering all of the items in phases one and two together for human resource implications. After implications are grouped and prioritized into issues, strategies, along with a few key actions, are identified for each group of implications (issues). Care should be taken to avoid compartmentalizing or departmentalizing implications and strategies.

Business Event Strategy Chart

The business event/human resource strategy chart shown in Exhibit 17-2 provides an example of how an organization can clearly and graphically display the link between business and human resources. Using a series of human resource strategy groupings as a guide, business events are identified and highlighted in the appropriate time frame, and human resource strategies and key actions required by these events are identified according to when they need to occur.

Management Strategies Chart

For communication purposes, a chart such as Exhibit 17-3 can be used to visually identify those strategies that demand significant increases in attention over the next three years.

OPERATIONAL PLANNING

Operational human resource planning consists of a one-year action plan that defines the activities to carry out the strategies and objectives of the strategic human resource plan. We suggest that during the operational planning period an organization also produce both headcount forecasts and skills analysis. Once strategic plans have been developed and distributed, long-range information is available to guide the identification of program needs and strategic skills. Further, operational planning, while linked to the strategies of

EXHIBIT 17-1   *Strategic Human Resource Assessment and Plan Development Tool (Honeywell)*

HONEYWELL

STRATEGIC HUMAN RESOURCE ASSESSMENT AND PLAN DEVELOPMENT TOOL

PHASE I			PHASE II	PHASE III	
IDENTIFY CORE CHARACTERISTICS OF CURRENT ORGANIZATION (LABEL A1, A2, ETC.)	IDENTIFY MAJOR SHIFTS IN EXTERNAL ENVIRONMENT (LABEL B1, B2, ETC.)	IDENTIFY MAJOR SHIFTS IN INTERNAL ENVIRONMENT (LABEL C1, C2, ETC.)	IDENTIFY MAJOR BUSINESS SHIFTS (LABEL D1, D2, ETC.)	HUMAN RESOURCE IMPLICATIONS (LIST, PRIORITIZE AND GROUP) (LABEL E1, E2, ETC.)	MAJOR HUMAN RESOURCE MANAGEMENT STRATEGIES AND KEY ACTIONS
	FROM TO	FROM TO	FROM TO		STRATEGY — ACTIONS

Phase I — External environment categories:
a. Economic
b. Technical
c. Social/cultural
d. Governmental
e. Legal
f. International
g. HR Trends etc.

Phase I — Core characteristics:
a. Values
b. Identity
c. Ongoing themes & missions etc.

Phase I — Internal environment:
a. Demographics
b. HR Trends
c. Changes
d. Attitudes
e. Structure
f. Leadership
g. Location
h. Vision

Phase II notes:
a. Phase I shifts should be consistent with Phase II shifts
b. Both expert & perceived strategies
c. Include social policy shifts

Human Resource Implications notes:
a. Base on phases I and II
b. Try first for broad implications
c. Try second for component HR system implications

Strategy notes:
a. Try first for integrating strategies
b. Try second for component strategies
c. Consider structure, human process, strategic positioning, knowledge & non-human resource

HS-667

17.10

EXHIBIT 17-2 Business Event/Human Resource Strategy Chart

	BUS.	AREA.	OP.	DIV.	GROUP(S)

HR Strategy Groupings	1982	1983	1984	1985	1986	1987	1988	1989	1990	1991	1992

Technical Development

Increased professional development and competence
— Systems
— Strategies — Production transitioning
— Technologies

Increased interdepartmental mobility and intradivisional coordination
Performance improvement emphasis
Strengthened human factors focus

Future management needs forecasting — Possible increased international marketplace focus
Talent and skill development/recruitment

Strengthened human resource planning/ — Heightened risk of business instability
Business planning/ — more eggs in one system's basket
Decision support skills — smaller organization units

Organizational Change/
Mgmt. Structure Change

Performance measures reevaluation
Participative management
Talent management/development
Decentralize human resource planning
Sensitive to change management
Organization design analysis
— Trend toward new organizational and management structures
— Divisional
— Operational
— Departmental
— Business area
— Heightened organizational experimentation

Notes: Business events are business, internal or external trends, shifts, or events that require a significant change in the strategies and practices currently utilized in the management of human resources. Events may fall into more than one human resource strategy grouping. Human resource strategies identify priority action strategies that anticipate and respond to upcoming events. They also identify in coded form the individuals or groups responsible for the management of each Human Resource Strategy.

EXHIBIT 17-3   Human Resource Management Strategies

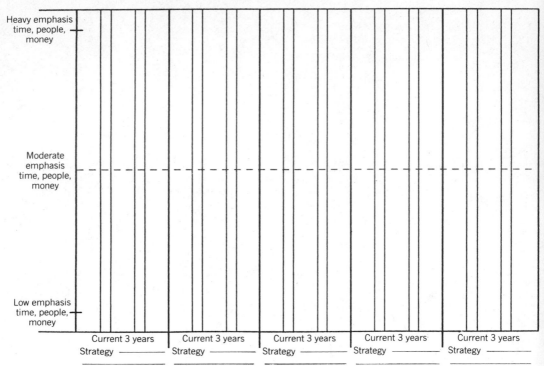

the strategic human resource plan, should include functional human resource systems planning as well. Examples include:

Organization structure
Organizational development
Management succession
Career development
Affirmative action
Compensation
Employee assistance
Community relations

Recruitment and retention
Labor relations
Management development and
   employee development
Executive education
Sales training
Technical training
Communications
Safety and health

The primary purpose of the operational human resource plan is to bring the strategic plan to fruition. Detailed functional planning should be closely attuned to strategic and operational planning, but should remain a secondary priority, the responsibility of the functional administrators or specific task teams.

Operational human resource planning begins with human resource strategies. It brings the organization up to date and assesses past performance. Skill needs and headcount forecasts are then reviewed. Information also is reviewed on performance criteria, if available. Then, actions are prepared for the next year to address human resource strategies. The action plan presents the issues and their causes, the strategies, and a statement of action related to each strategy. Skill and headcount information should be taken into account. For each action statement, the time the activity should occur, the person or persons responsible, and any appropriate measurement criteria associated with the actions should be developed. It is important to recognize special resource needs. Upon completion of operational plan development, preferably through a participative process integrated vertically and horizontally, specific appropriation requests should be developed, if needed, for presentation during the budget process, or for inclusion in individual budgets. See Exhibit 17-4 for a suggested operational plan format.

The term "human resource management" is being used more widely to describe human resource planning, the implementation of the plans, and day-to-day management. The term is meant to include the action component missing from human resource planning. While we have drawn distinctions between planning and implementation, the boundaries are artificial. As discussed later in this chapter, the people developing the operational human resource plan, by necessity, should be among the people responsible for implementing the plan. If operational planning is developed with strong involvement, top to bottom, it becomes a framework for actions tied not only to strategies, but also to day-to-day management. Exhibit 17-5 is a pre-planning tool that records stakeholders and desired participants in the development of actions for the operational plan.

Basic Operational Human Resource Plan and Review Outline

A. Planning Parameters

1. *Purpose*
   To develop specific actions that will be taken over the next year to implement the strategic HRP
   To outline key information critical to human resource management
   To link operational HRP to budget cycle
2. *Basic Data*
   Strategic and operational business plans
   Strategic HR plan
   Major actions initiated—strengths and weaknesses assessment
   New events requiring reassessment
   Skills needs

EXHIBIT 17-4 Suggested Operational Plan Format

Driver	Issue	Strategies/ actions	1983		1984				1985	1986	1987	Measurement	Responsibilities
			3rd QRT.	4th QRT.	1st QRT.	2nd QRT.	3rd QRT.	4th QRT.					
		Strategy Action 1 Action 2											

EXHIBIT 17-5   Identification of Task Team Participants for Strategy Conversion to Actions

HR Functions

	Safety and Health	Environment	Labor Relations	Security	Legal	HRP	HRDI AA	Staffing	Compensation	Communi-cations	HR Reps	Community Relations	Line Management	Executive Management	Government	Customer	Community
Human Resource Strategy A																	
Human Resource Strategy B																	
Human Resource Strategy C																	

    Basic Data (continued)
    Headcount forecasts
    Survey, research, and measurement data
3. *Time Frame.* 1 year
4. *Length.* Five to ten pages
5. *Process.* Participative

B. Planning Process

1. Summarize your strategic human resource plan.
2. Are any midcourse adjustments required? Integrate these into the plan.
3. Assess the strengths and weaknesses of your major actions taken so far to implement the strategic HR plan.
4. Present skill need shifts over the next three to five years.
5. Present forecasts for headcount and staffing/placement over the next three to five years.
6. Present objective and subjective measurement data, preferably longitudinal, relating to organizational performance and change management.
7. Identify major actions for each human resource strategy. Include specific focus, accountability, time frame, resources needed, and measurement.
   Provide a summary for the business plan.
8. Tie the plan to budget recommendations.

Both skills analysis and headcount forecasting remain key features of the human resource planning process. We suggest that, although this information should be referred to during the strategic planning cycle, the effort to prepare accurate skill need assessments and headcount forecasts logically should occur after the strategic business cycle. This usually leaves the forecasting effort for the operational planning cycle. Once the strategic planning cycles are over or once an organization has agreed on strategies, skills analysis, headcount forecasts, and other long-range projections should take place.

Skills Analysis

Skills analysis is the identification of significant mismatches between the current skills of the organization and its future needs. The mismatches can consist of a lack of either quantity or quality, and can be due to both internal and external factors. The purpose of skills analysis is not to track every skill, but rather to review skills in light of internal and external scans, business plans, and strategic human resource plans for only those skill issues that merit significant attention.

Some factors to consider when identifying critical skill needs include:

Emerging technologies
Skewed populations
Limited availability
Technical bottlenecks
Quantity and quality mismatches

The following review outline suggests some steps in skills analysis.

Identifying Critical Skills

1. Review external and internal trends.
2. Review business strategy.
   Financial/performance
   Markets
   Products
   Engineering and technology
   Production
   Product mix
   Competition
   Customer trends
   Technology trends
3. Review human resource strategy.

   Identify critical skills generally.
   Emerging technology
   Skewed population
   Technical bottlenecks
   Performance problems/technical competence
   Business change implications
   Identify critical skill jobs.

   Functions changing significantly over time
   New functions
   Functions with significant strategic implications
   Functions with significant current performance implications
   Customer concentration
   Potential bottlenecks

Once you have collected the necessary information, it may be useful to record major skills needs on a chart similar to the one shown in Exhibit 17-6. This

EXHIBIT 17-6 Skills Analysis

Division/Org. _____ Date _____

Scenario A _____ Brief Description of Scenario

Major Skill Needs	Drivers (what is causing the skill change)	Dimensions of the Problem. (Quantity & Quality gap between future need & Current Availability.)	When a Problem 1982–1988	Primary Remedial Actions	Action Responsibility

chart could become a part of the operational human resource plan and a reference for the next cycle of strategic planning.

Headcount Forecasting

Headcount forecasts are the very visible, and often referenced, output of human resource planning. Accurate projections and trends play an important role in organizational planning. Applications for headcount forecasts include:

Guidance for recruitment and training and development activities
Evaluating risks to employment stability
Planning capital, facility, and support resources
Determining growth opportunities to improve EEO/AA
Identifying employee mix changes
Ensuring adequate knowledge and capacity

On the subject of headcount forecasting, we offer the following comments and suggestions:

1. Consider forecasts not as a reactive number exercise, but a proactive opportunity to affect the level and mix of your future organization and to point out problems.
2. You may wish to prepare a forecast for each scenario of the future that your organization has recognized.
3. Combine charts with words and graphics to provide a clear, descriptive method of presenting the forecasts. The reader should understand by looking at this one chart what your basic assumptions were, what the trends look like, and what the key implications are.
4. We encourage the inclusion of historical information.
5. Unless clearly warranted, forecasting should be a people exercise rather than a computer exercise. Too often, historical trends between people and sales dollars are extrapolated into the future, and they become organizational headcount forecasts. We support an approach that stresses thought and input from many people in the organization. Computerized number crunching may be quick and scientific, but often it does not help the organization view those numbers as valid, and it fails to consider many variables that can significantly impact headcount.
6. Combine a top-down forecast with a bottom-up forecast to produce one tied to both scan information and business and human resource strategies.
7. If your sales dollars consist of labor dollars and material dollars, it is important to get an accurate appraisal of future trends in the mix

between material content and labor content of future sales. It is seldom adequate to forecast strictly on the basis of sales or orders.

8. The human resource planner should extend a great deal of effort to understand the organization's products and services, and the direction they are going in the future. This is the critical step in human resource forecasting: understand the business and the business environment.

9. Consider using a variety of forecasting types to present key points:

   Nonintervention forecasts that project using only in-hand or imminently in-hand sales and orders. This type of forecast, when compared to your projected sales forecast, presents a gap that often goes unheeded, and may require remedial action.

   Milestone forecasts that compare predetermined performance standards against your plotted numeric forecasts, enabling comparisons of forecasts to organizational headcount objectives.

10. Headcount forecasts should be educational documents that graphically portray trends, assumptions, and implications. The chart shown in Exhibit 17-7 provides an example.

A menu follows that includes some of the decisions that organizations have to make when planning for forecast development.

Headcount Forecasting

1. **Time Frame**
   Short term
   Long term
2. **Organizational**
   Program
   Business area
   Department
   Job category/skill category
   Division
   Function
   Location
   Cost center
   Direct/indirect labor
   EEO
   Level
3. **Focus**
   Headcount
   Hiring

EXHIBIT 17-7 Headcount Forecast

HEADCOUNT FORECAST

Scenario A _____

Brief Description of Scenario

Division/Organization _____

Date _____

	Actual	Estimate			Forecast		
	1982	1983	1984	1985	1986	1987	1988

Sales
Value Added Sales

2000

1500

1000

500

0

Officials and Managers – – –
Professionals
Engineering xxxxx
Administrative and other 00000
Technicians/aides ++++
Clerical ......
Hourly/crafts/operative/
Laborers/Service workers *****
Total employees _____

1982	1983	1984	1985	1986	1987	1988

KEY ASSUMPTIONS/ANTICIPATED PROACTIVE
   TRENDS:

COMMENTS AND ANALYSIS:

RECRUITMENT/HIRING SUMMARY:

IMPLICATIONS:

1982	1983	1984	1985	1986	1987	1988

17.21

    Mismatch
    Reporting
    Trend/issue identification

4. **Forecast Control/Leadership**
    Proactive
    Reactive

5. **Emphasis**
    Future-oriented
    Historically oriented

6. **Types of Forecasts**
    Multiple scenario
    Multiple variable forecasts
       high/medium/low
       probability
       what-ifs
    Multiple purpose forecasts
       actuals
       nonintervention
       dynamic
       goal- or milestone-oriented
    Numerical/nonnumerical forecasts

7. **Forecast Processes**
    Delphi/participative group/nominal group technique
    Bottom-up survey
    Top-down survey
    Statistical formulas and relationship (historical)
    Statistical formulas and relationship (future-oriented)
    Computerized/noncomputerized

8. **Update Capability**
    Immediate
    Monthly/quarterly
    Annually
    As needed

9. **Causal Variables**
    Attrition and mobility
    Replacement rates
    Sales and orders
    Value-added sales
    Projected units of production
    Productivity

Work process changes

Automation

Workforce stability policies and programs

Business strategies (such as cost goals, financial performance, new products and services, etc.)

Human resource strategies (such as organization restructuring, job design)

External labor supply

Computers

Computers, combined with careful organizational analysis and management participation, can be very useful aids in headcount and recruitment forecasting. Computers can help particularly with data rollups and "what-if" analysis. In the area of skill and talent analysis, a combination of a decision support system and a data base management system can help an organization accurately assess its skill needs. We caution against an across-the-board skill tracking system, unless it is carefully reviewed for utility and maintainability. Instead, we encourage a strategic skill data base that traces select individuals and groups.

Good, accurate skill, headcount, and recruitment forecasting often can be very complex tasks. Changes in job roles, organizational structure, markets, technology. attrition and mobility, automation, and productivity all demand consideration. Even more difficult is a recognition that proactive management decisions can play a large role in the number and type of people needed in the future. As planners, we have a responsibility to help guide the future. This is why we tie forecasting to a comprehensive human resource planning process, and not to a fixed formula computer program that considers only a few variables.

HUMAN RESOURCE PLANNING MODELS

Organizational Performance

A useful model for organizational performance contains these five levers:

1. Human process
2. Structure
3. Knowledge
4. Nonhuman resources
5. Strategic positioning

Not only must these levers mutually support each other, but they must continue to advance in order to ensure consistency with future changes and challenges. The five levers of performance must be integrated and dynamic. If structure is not consistent with human process, or if the business moves ahead while knowledge and the other categories lag behind, an organization will not perform effectively.

If we assessed the five levers and, if after evaluating each of them for mutual continuity and support for overall business strategies, we found structure and human process sadly lacking, we would, as many companies are now doing, begin to emphasize those performance components. If, like Apple Computer, an organization had good human process, structure and knowledge but lacked long-term market positioning and applied nonhuman resources, it would revise those components so that they fit. If, like GM, an organization had good strategic positioning, nonhuman resources, and knowledge but lacked structure and human process, it would move them into a matching, complementary position. All five components of performance, the action levers, need to be integrated. None can be out of step without the organization's suffering. Every business plan should contend with these or similar components, and not just with strategic positioning and nonhuman resources. Looking back over the past 20 years, we have gone through cycles where one or the other of these components was emphasized, but a systems perspective demanding that all components be managed together has been seldom, if ever, employed.

The concept of organizational performance and the use of a model such as the one above are becoming more widely accepted and implemented. The model seems simple, yet allows an organization to plan and implement relatively complex changes without neglecting key factors. We introduce this concept because we believe it will influence the direction human resource planning will need to take in the future. It also points out vividly the importance of human resources to the overall success of an organization. Exhibit 17-8 represents a model of organizational performance. Exhibit 17-9 includes human resource events that can be brought to bear on the performance levels.

Implementation of Human Resource Planning

Human resource planning, like any planning process, takes time to evolve. We encourage people initiating a new or revitalized planning process not to take on the whole process at once, but rather to pay special attention to some key themes:

Plan the planning process.
Emphasize clarity and simplicity in the process.
Involve your organization.

EXHIBIT 17-8   *Organizational Performance*

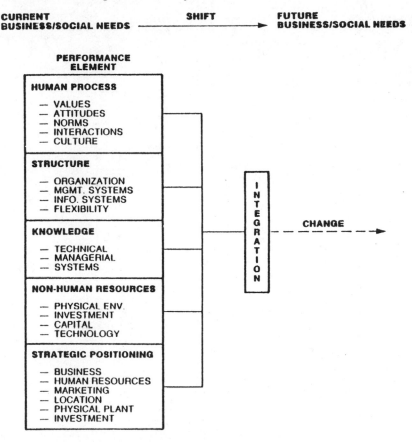

Separate strategic thinking from operational thinking.

Ensure a bias toward action, rather than bureaucracy.

Link to business, social policy, and budget.

Tie to appraisal and rewards.

Planning Human Resource Planning

Practice what you are going to preach. The basic steps in most human resource planning processes are the following:

1. Environmental analysis

    Consider current organizational characteristics

    Examine internal and external environments and future shifts

    Review business and social policy strategies and future shifts

EXHIBIT 17-9   Organizational Performance: Integration of Human Resource Systems

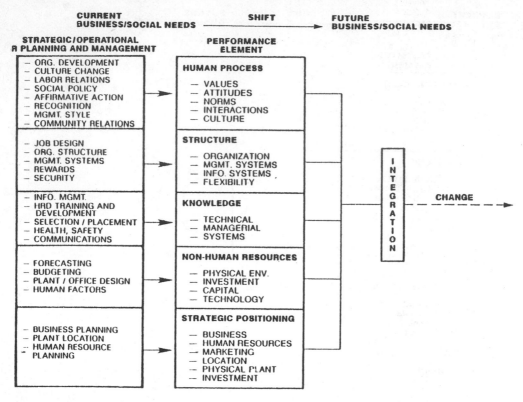

2. **Issue identification**

    Consider environment for human resource implications

    Consolidate and prioritize implications for:
    Human resource management
    Social policy
    Business decision making

3. **Plan development**

    Strategic (3–5 years)
    Develop strategies and objectives
    Process and focus

    Operational (1 year)
    Develop actions and tactics
    Resources
    Responsibilities
    Time frame
    Measurement

4. Plan implementation
    Human Resource Management
        Functional and cross-functional activities
    Monitoring and Feedback
        Measurement
        Progress reviews
        Performance feedback and reinforcement
        Dynamic planning and implementation (change them if they cannot
        be effective)

When organizations review their environment to plan human resource
planning, the following should be considered:

the internal political environment
the internal cultural environment
prime areas that can bring a return on investment in HRP
key organizational concerns
key business challenges
key supporters, players, and impediments to change

When planning the planning process, potential issues can be identified
and acted upon. Gaps such as the following are important to think about:

the degree of change desired/necessary versus the organization's capacity
for change
the level of investment required versus available resources
risks required versus the willingness to take risks
level of support and buy-in versus the level required
critical blockages versus critical supporters
the quality of business planning versus the quality required
the commitment to doing versus talking
your own skills versus those required
measures of success for the function versus desired measures for success

When strategists plan for human resource planning, they should refer to
a checklist of options such as the one below. The more options they use,
the broader the planning process will be.

1. Scope of planning
    Succession planning
    Manpower planning
    Human resource program/project planning

Human resource functional planning
Organizational human resource planning
2. Horizontal involvement
Human resource planner
Business planner
Human resource function
Line/staff multifunctional human resource planning task team
Line/staff multidivisional human resource planning task team
Societal involvement
3. Vertical involvement
Low-level staff involvement
Low-level line involvement
High-level staff involvement
High-level line involvement
High-level executive involvement
4. Integration
Talent/succession planning
Employee development planning
Rewards
Appraisal
MBO planning
Budget planning
Business planning
Societal planning
5. Timing
Strategic HRP during and after the strategic business planning cycle
Strategic and operational HRP before the budget cycle or process
Strategic HRP before functional HRP cycles such as:
    Talent/succession planning
    Employee development planning
    Compensation planning
6. Users
Human resource function
Upper-level management
Only people involved in HR planning process
All managers
All employees
7. Process
Staff developed; review with executive management
Line developed; review with executive management

Staff/line developed; review with executive management
Staff/line/executive developed
All employee involvement

Regarding plan implementation, an organization may wish to:

Match plan implementation with the planning process.
Assure that the doers are also the planners.
Avoid creating expectations beyond the organization's ability to produce.
Insure that this planning process, which really is a thought process, continues throughout the year, rather than being switched on and off by requirements.
Insure communications and feedback to participants about what is happening and about how effective it is.

Human resource planning serves as both an information-gathering activity and a decision support system. The best human resource planning is not necessarily determined by the largest document, the most perfect strategies, or the flawless completion of planning steps. As Noel Tichy, Associate Professor of Organizational Behavior at the University of Michigan, suggests, it is a matter of jointly pursuing common objectives through consideration of technical, political, and cultural means. The most common error in planning is the organization's emphasis on the technical planning function, and neglect of political and cultural factors. Human resource plans must not only look good, but also ultimately become an integral part of the organization's functioning. They have to match the needs of the organization, have a buy-in by the organization, and produce measurable subjective and objective results. Doing a good job of planning the human resource planning process will help assure that the gap between planning and implementation, between paper and practice, is closed. Clarity in plan development will help insure that an organization's human resource and business decisions are documentable and more effective.

Business/Environment Trends	Human Resource Planning Issues/ Implications	Human Resource Planning Strategy
From: Financial Planning To: Organizational Planning From: Number Management To: Change Management	Human resource planning must address the shift from forecasting and succession data preparation to organizatonal change.	Manage human resource planning as a change process

Emphasize Clarity and Simplicity

From the viewpoint of the participants in planning, and of plan recipients and implementors, the process and outputs need to be attuned to what can be understood and utilized. In a very real sense, strategic human resource planning functions the same way that information management functions. Large amounts of complex information are gathered, analyzed, reprocessed, and converted into decisions. The planning process is a large decision support system that focuses on one arena of decisions–human resources. The task is to help people work through the information, make sense of it, put it into a workable context, reach conclusions about it, and implement whatever decisions are reached.

Multiple participation in the planning process makes this a particularly challenging task. It is much easier when only one person is involved. When the process includes business planners, department managers, executives, etc., the questions asked have to be clear and brief, the responses have to be honed into crisp statements, and the entire organization has to be understood, not only in today's terms, but in future terms as well. Several suggestions come to mind that are critical in communicating and educating during the planning process, as information is collected, analyzed, and formed into strategies.

1. Guidelines for planning, and the plans themselves, should be brief. Rely on outlines and examples to present guidelines. Use no more that five to ten pages for the strategic portion of your plan, and seven to ten pages for the operational portion of your plan. Provide simple tools for planning. Let people wrestle with content, not formats.
2. Issues and strategies should be limited in number.
3. Graphics should be utilized as much as possible. Commentary should accompany the graphics.
4. Include the flow of logic (from trends to issues to strategies to actions) as much as possible on one page.

Strategic human resource planning is not an academic exercise, yet it is often conducted as such. It must reflect the reality of your organization, yet encourage the organization to move beyond its current boundaries. The simplicity of the process should not deter an organization from looking wholly and comprehensively at itself and its environment. It should help bring complex issues into focus. The term "nuggetizing" is becoming popular in describing the rather sophisticated skill of coining a few words to communicate a complex concept. Planning guidelines, the actual process of planning, the written outputs, the reviews, implementation procedures, and measurement all can be designed for simplicity and clarity. Communications skills become increasingly critical, and the role of planner becomes meshed with those of facilitator, measurement specialist, and change manager.

Business/Environment Trends	Human Resource Planning Issues/ Implications	Human Resource Planning Strategy
From: Moderate complexity and narrow managerial job responsibilities	Efficient yet effective line involvement in human resource planning	Develop human resource planning as a streamlined yet comprehensive thought process
To: Increasing complexity and broadened managerial job responsibilities		

Involve Your Organization

The responsibility for human resource planning can rest with quite a variety of individuals. Determining who has management responsibility should be done through careful organization analysis during the planning process. Ultimately, the most important criterion for success in human resource planning, and the greatest challenge, is to insure that the line owns human resource planning.

The greatest criticism of business planning has been the perception that it is a bureaucratic, isolated paper process that seldom is effectively prepared or implemented. There has been, and continues to be, some truth to these criticisms. The criticism stems from a chronic failure to consider people and the process of planning and organizational change adequately. Using the organizational performance levers, for example, if we were to critique planning in organizations over the past decade we could conclude that:

Little attention was placed on culture and participation. (human process)

The structure was rigid, formal, and top-down. Rewards continue to support short-term performance. Planning was staff-driven. (structure)

People carry relatively narrow knowledge bases. There was little interfunctional communication at the necessary depth and breadth. (knowledge)

These characteristics did not fit with an environment of change, and with a recognition from a strategic perspective that the best strategies in the world will not be effectively accomplished without equal or greater attention to human resources.

If an organization wants a process that educates, that is supported, and that is implemented, it is crucial that it plan for considerable employee involvement. The model whereby the staff prepares the plan and then runs it by management for their review seems to be ineffective when the objective is not just a plan, but successful implementation. We encourage the broadest possible involvement, from top to bottom and across the organization. We encourage consulting with community members and government personnel. This is more easily said than done; it takes more work, requires that the groups see a benefit for their involvement, and demands the kind of clarity and structure identified in the previous section. Yet the return on participative human resource planning far exceeds that of narrow efforts. Making the plan an organizational plan rather than a human resource department plan brings the following benefits:

1. It provides more accurate information and leads to more effective human resource management.
2. It leads to improved buy-in and implementation.
3. It ties to business issues better.
4. It links to budget and resources to get things done.
5. It provides clear guidance for managers concerning their priorities and helps them organize their efforts.
6. It sensitizes an organization to the need for cooperation and integration of efforts.

At Honeywell, the Military Avionics Division and Underseas Systems Division employ participative planning processes. The Military Avionics Division involves line managers through the use of human resource department facilitators. The Underseas Systems Division planning is led by a task team of line and staff managers. Their outputs and success with implementation are exceptional. Once the organizations agreed that a certain strategy was needed, the resources and individual actions key to implementation followed immediately. No gap existed between plan and implementation. The doers were the participants. Their strategies were top-quality, and management looked good across the board because they knew what they were going to do, and why. More than anything else, that feeling of clarity, in what can be an overwhelmingly complex environment, reinforces involvement. Streamlining the process is vital.

The business planning department can lead the human resource planning effort, but most often it is the human resource department that drives the process. Honeywell Europe has successfully pursued planning as an explicit task of each general manager. The goal is line leadership.

A crucial point is that often the plan, when driven by the human resource department, becomes the human resource department strategic plan, and not the organizational strategic plan. The difference is great. The departmental plan focuses strictly on departmental strategies and actions. More often than not, issues identified by an organization require strategies and actions that are not restricted to the human resource function. Even if all responsibility did happen to fall in the human resource department for implementation, without buy-in from the rest of the organization the effort would be ineffective.

An issue that can arise from participative human resource planning is an inconsistency between what was arrived at bottom-up versus what was arrived at top-down. Imagine a task team, one that does not include top management, that upon presentation of its plan to top management finds itself without support for its strategies. Clearly, one way to avoid this problem is to insure top-management involvement during the plan development process. Another is to establish a bridging team that takes bottom-up tentative plans and top-down tentative plans and attempts to merge the two. Isolated top-down human resource planning is often as ineffective as isolated bottom-up human resource planning. A healthy merging of the power base of an organization with middle- and lower-level organization personnel can open lines of communication and mutual respect, and can lead not only to education, but also to innovation.

In larger organizations, when there are many divisions producing plans that are presented to top corporate levels, a similar bridging should take place. Divisional issues and strategies can be analyzed, summarized, prioritized, and compared to corporate perceptions of issues and strategies. The dialogue between representatives of the two groups can take the best thinking from both sources, and insure buy-in not only at the corporate level, but also at the divisional level.

Participation is a commitment to cooperation, coordination, and compromise. Properly managed, it can lead to better results and an organizational willingness to act.

Business/Environment Trends	Human Resource Planning Issues/ Implications	Human Resource Planning Strategy
From: Human resource planning by human resource planning departments	Cross-departmental planning integration Planners link with doers	Integrate human resource planning with other planning processes.
To: Strategic human resource planning and management by organizations		

Separate Strategic Thinking from Operational Thinking

Human resource planning is a partner in business planning. If the business planning cycle is split into strategic and operational cycles, human resource planning should also follow those cycles. In smaller organizations, there may be one formal planning period. Human resource planning should occur during that one formal period. Human resource planning should overlap with the actual formal business planning cycle and should trail it a bit in order to benefit from full access to information. Planning is dynamic and should not be restricted solely to schedules and cycles. Do it when new information seems to require an immediate modification of a strategy or action. Planning flexibility, particularly during a period characterized by high change, is an important link to action. The concept of logical incrementalism, the gradual development of clarity and strategy, suggests that organizations should recognize our inability to accurately consider the future with a single snapshot of information.

It is useful to differentiate between strategic human resource planning and operational human resource planning. The former consists of an evaluation of the long-term directions of the business, key environmental shifts, social policy shifts, implication/issue identification, and strategy and objectives identification. Operational human resource planning consists of a review of previously identified issues, strategies, and objectives, and the identification of an action plan. Typically, skills analysis, manpower forecasting, human resource development, and succession planning occur after the strategic cycle, when information is in place about what the future holds from both a human resource and business perspective. The operational plan links to the budget cycle, providing input for resource requirements. In larger organizations it is helpful to split the planning process into two separate time periods—one for strategic (typically early in the year) and one for operational (typically later in the year). This helps an organization to focus, first on a broad scale, and then on a more detailed action plan. Even if an organization does not split the process into separate planning cycles, it may want to distinguish them from each other for both impact and communication.

Separating strategic human resource planning from operational planning also seems to help with plan implementation. By focusing energy first on

Business/Environment Trends	Human Resource Planning Issues/ Implications	Human Resource Planning Strategy
From: Moderate change and low complexity planning	Emphasize clear process	Conduct human resource planning in two thought stages:
To: High change and high complexity planning	Utilize planning resources effectively	1. Strategic
	Tie HRP to business cycle	2. Operational
From: Financial planning		
To: Business/human resource linked planning		

long-term issue analysis and strategy development, and then on operational planning—which consists of action plan development and includes forecasting and skills analysis—the entire organization understands with some clarity what it is trying to accomplish. The operational planning process is dedicated to action. All the involved people pursue the best route to accomplish their respective strategies and objectives. Meshing the two without any distinguishing time frame or boundaries can bog down an organization, lengthen the time required for individual participation, and reduce clarity and crispness, which seem to be huge reinforcers for planning.

Ensure a Bias toward Action, Rather than Bureaucracy

The six other themes in this section all have an action bias. In addition to these themes, there is the need to provide people in an organization with feedback on implementation successes and failures. Too often, positive efforts with measurable returns go uncommunicated. Feedback to the organization is crucial to an action orientation.

Link to Business, Social Policy, and Budget

This theme has been addressed through some of the previous discussion. In recent years, the key message has been to tie business planning to human resource planning, and vice versa. Human resource planning should also be linked to organizational social policy. Roughly, social policy refers to the "nonbusiness"-driven commitments of an organization, such as community support, affirmative action, and societal objectives. With the bias for action we just spoke of comes an additional, critical linkage. Human resource plans should be tied to the budget process, with resource needs introduced carefully into the budget process and priorities clearly communicated.

The people who plan for business, and plan for budget, should be involved in the planning for human resources. Institutionalizing these linkages should be a goal of every organization. Linking means the cross-involvement of people, the sharing and inclusion of content in the plans, and the disappearance, ultimately, of the boundaries that distinguish business plans from human resource plans, and functional plans from each other.

Business plans should consider human resource factors and include key human resource variables among their strategy and action outputs. Human resource plans should consider the overall business plan, and the functional plans of an organization, in their considerations and outputs.

Organizational performance is the ultimate integrator. The gradual merging of human resource planning with business planning, while retaining the distinctiveness of the thought process, seems to be the direction for the future. Executives throughout the United States are learning about change management and culture change. Management throughout the world is becoming sensitized to the human resource dimension of business success. A holistic view of organizational planning seems desirable.

Business/Environment Trends	Human Resource Planning Issues/ Implications	Human Resource Planning Strategy
From: Business management To: Business/people/ environment management	Employ a broad system approach to human resource planning Integrate human resource planning with business planning	Retain a discrete human resource planning identity while up-grading the responsibility and ability of line management to perform strategic human resource planning as an integral part of business planning

Tie to Appraisal and Rewards

We spoke earlier of the need to integrate structure with rewards and human process. There is no better opportunity to apply that thinking than when dealing with human resource planning. If MBOs, formal appraisals, compensation, and recognition do not link to human resource planning, and are not supportive of it, little headway can be made in institutionalizing human resource planning, or even in supporting its existence and improvement. Changes in these systems cannot be made overnight, but gradual integration of these systems with the process and outputs of human resource planning separate serious planning efforts from superficial ones. Measuring the progress of human resource planning against objectives, and quantifying the impact of human resource plan implementation on an organization, while difficult, help to document and legitimize human resource planning. Longitudinal measurement, both objective and subjective, is a prerequisite to organizational appraisal and group rewards.

MODELS

How It Fits

Exhibit 17-10 portrays the relationship strategic and human resource planning have to each other and to business planning and human resource management. While the model presents these four components in a discrete order for clarity, they can, and should, be more integrated than this portrayal indicates.

Systems Integration

Human resource functions and line functions should not be looked at separately when one considers strategies and actions. It is more effective to

EXHIBIT 17-10   Human Resource Planning: How It Fits

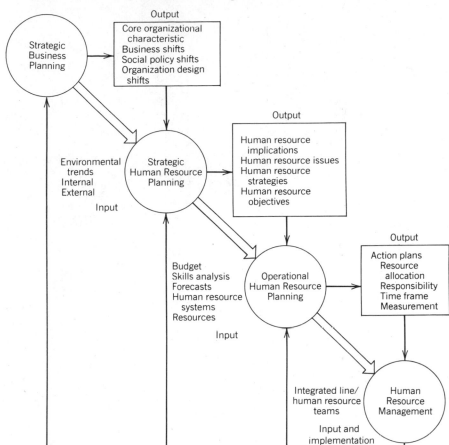

identify, whenever possible, integrated approaches that tie together resources and thrusts from many functions. This integration is depicted in Exhibit 17-11.

Planning and Management Cycles

There seems to be a rational order for human resource thinking. It also seems that human resource systems should clearly link to business planning and budgeting. The best human resource organizations provide these linkages through a combination of scheduling and involvement.

Exhibit 17-12 portrays the scheduling of human resource planning in a large organization. It includes a representative example of a human resource subplan schedule—in this case, that of management talent/employee development.

EXHIBIT 17-11 ***Human Resource Systems Integration***

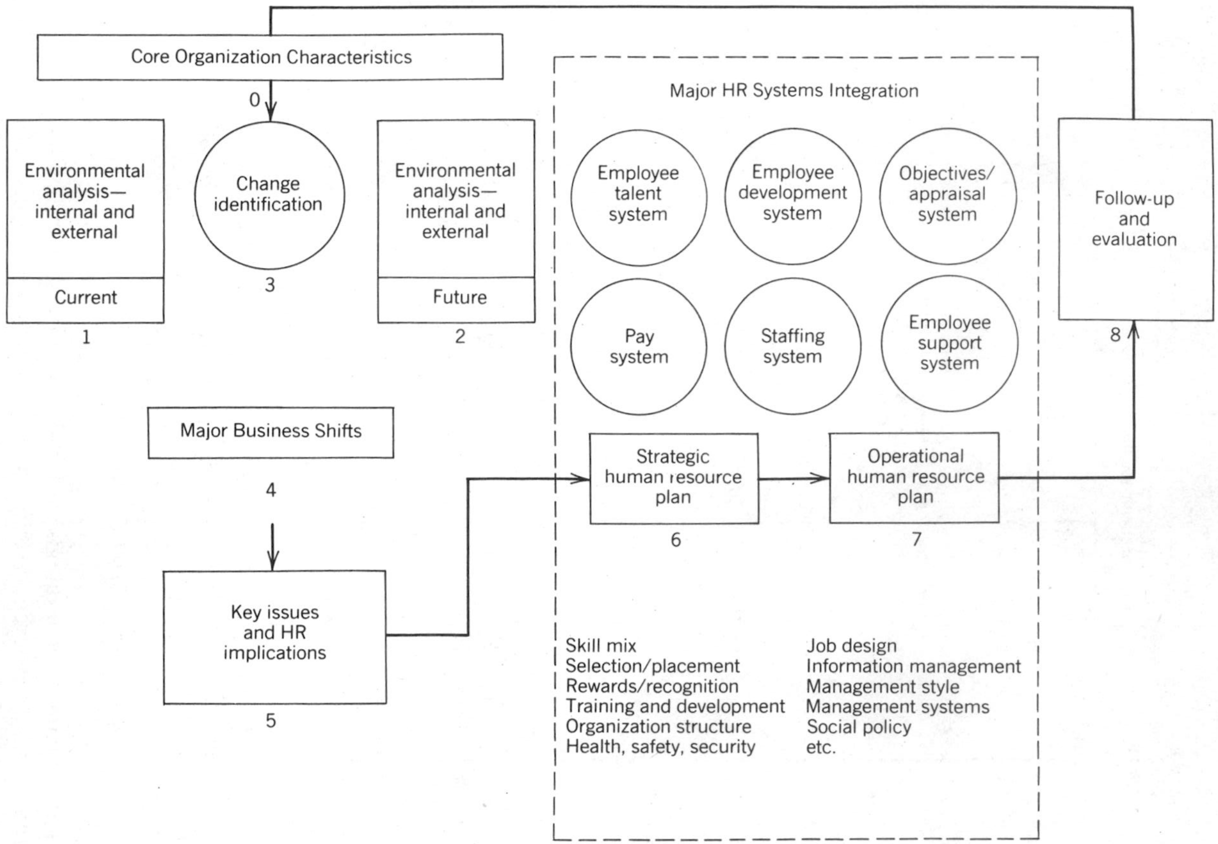

EXHIBIT 17-12 Major Human Resource Planning Systems Schedule

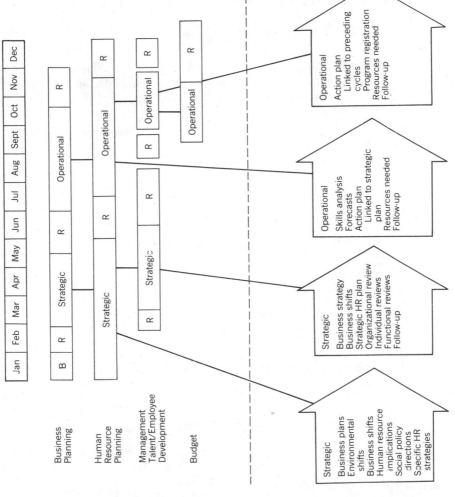

	Jan	Feb	Mar	Apr	May	Jun	Jul	Aug	Sept	Oct	Nov	Dec
Business Planning	B	R	Strategic		R	R	Operational			R		
Human Resource Planning		Strategic				R	Operational			R		
Management Talent/Employee Development		R	Strategic			R			R	Operational	R	
Budget									Operational		R	

Strategic
Business plans
Environmental shifts
Business shifts
Human resource implications
Social policy directions
Specific HR strategies

Strategic
Business strategy
Business shifts
Strategic HR plan
Organizational review
Individual reviews
Functional reviews
Follow-up

Operational
Skills analysis
Forecasts
Action plan
Linked to strategic plan
Resources needed
Follow-up

Operational
Action plan
Linked to preceding cycles
Program registration
Resources needed
Follow-up

Integrated Systems Calendar

Without promoting specific times for planning, Exhibit 17-13 provides an example of planning that is timed to encourage logical information flow, integrated planning processes, and systems thinking. Overlapping planning cycles, staggered review scheduling, and the planned availability of pertinent information are key features of this large organization calender.

Subplan Example: Management Talent System

The following outline walks through a basic process of talent identification, with emphasis on succession and development. It is included here for several reasons. First, management succession and development often are tasks of organizational human resource planners. Second, it provides an opportunity to display how subplans can link to business and human resource plans.

Management Talent Plan and Review Outline

A. PLANNING PARAMETERS

1. *Purpose.*   To review and assure the appropriate assignment/development of people and the most effective structure to meet long- and short-range organizational needs.
2. *Basic Data*
   Business strategies
   Strategic human resource plan
   Organization charts (current and future)
   Previous talent review data
   Relevant assessment and development data for individuals
   Functional human resource data
3. *Time Frame.*   Strategic: three to five years; operational: one year
4. *Process.*   Linked to business and HR planning

B. PLANNING PROCESS

Section 1 (three-page summary)
   Background
      Business Strategy.   Briefly overview the current business and your strategy for the business over the next three to five years.
      Strategic Human Resource Plan.   Briefly review the key human resource issues and strategies (including social policy directions) identified in your human resource plan.

EXHIBIT 17-13 *Suggested Human Resource Systems Integration Schedule*

	Jan	Feb	Mar	Apr	May	Jun	Jul	Aug	Sept	Oct	Nov	Dec
Integrated System												
Primary Cycles												
I. Business planning		Strategic		Strategic reviews				Operational			Operational reviews	
II. Human resource planning												
Smaller organizations				Strategic		Strategic reviews			Operational			Operational reviews
Larger organizations				Strategic		Strategic reviews		Operational			Operational reviews	
III. Budget								Strategic and operational				Strategic and operational reviews
Integrated System												
Secondary Cycles												
A. MBO/goaling	Operational goaling						Strategic goaling					
B. Employee/AA development	Talent review follow-up				Strategic		Service provider reviews		Operational course registration system		Talent review follow-up	
C. Management talent			Strategic	Division talent reviews		Group/business talent reviews		Corporate talent reviews		Operational		
D. AA Planning		Strategic					Operational					
E. Appraisal		Strategic			Pay delivery							
F. Pay					Pay delivery						Pay delivery	
Planning Information												
Dissemination Cycle												
1 Plan specifications												
2 Internal and external data												
3 Survey research data			Strategic					Operational				
4 Summary of previous planning activity												
5 Measurement feedback data												
6 Consultants												

17.41

Organization.

What is your current organization (organization chart), and how does it fit your current business?

How will your business environment change within the next five years, and what impact will such change have on your future organization with regard to:

> Structure
> Human process
> Knowledge
> Nonhuman resources
> Strategic positioning

Present a future (three to five year) organization chart and describe how it will fit future business. Consider relationships among organizational units.

What managerial skills have been identified in your present and future organization as critical to support the business strategies (general management, technical management, administrative management)? Where are the gaps between what you have and what you need?

Relevant Statistical Summaries (5-year).   Affirmative action, headcount forecasts, demographics, skill need projections, etc.

Section 2

Key people/position review

Section 3 (Summarize in two to three pages)

Assess your functional departments in the context of section 1. Include:

Marketing	Quality
Engineering	Procurement
Production	Information systems
Human resources	Program management
Finance	

Discuss the breadth, depth, and quality of talent.

> Do you see any structure, staffing, and development problems because of:
>> Organizational changes
>> Changing business strategies
>> Age distribution of incumbents
>> Business expansion or contraction
>> Departure because of health or other personal reasons

> Identify key high-potential managerial and technical talent by function for people below the director level.
>> Consider potential for growth.
>> Consider development and placement needs

EXHIBIT 17-14 Human Resource Action Register

Name	Title	Function	Initial Review Date	Issue	Type of Action Required	Key Responsibility	Time Frame and Comments	Completion (Yes/No) Date
1								
2								
3								
4								
5								
6								
7								
8								
9								
10								
11								
12								
13								
14								
15								
16								
17								
18								
19								
20								

Objective: Follow-up tool to be used during management talent/technical talent planning and review meetings.

EXHIBIT 17-15 Management Development System

PRIVATE

NAME		SEX	RACE/HANDI.	REVIEW DATES		
				YEAR	MONTH	SUPVR. INITIALS
DIVISION/DEPT.		HIRE DATE		19 TO PRESENT		
EDUCATION		OPTIONAL		19 TO		
ASSIGNMENTS				19 TO		

ASSESSMENT PROFILE
(Adjust as needed after each review)

ELEMENT	NEEDS SIGNIFICANT DEVELOPMENT	—GOOD— SOME DEV. NEEDED	—EXCELLENT— MAINTENANCE NEEDED
HUMAN PROCESS MANAGEMENT	CURRENT LEVEL FUTURE/DESIRED LEVEL COMMENTS:		
STRUCTURE MGMT. – ORG – MGMT. SYSTEMS – INFO. SYSTEMS – FLEXIBILITY	CURRENT LEVEL FUTURE/DESIRED LEVEL COMMENTS:		
SPECIALTY/TECHNICAL KNOWLEDGE	CURRENT LEVEL FUTURE/DESIRED LEVEL COMMENTS:		
MANAGEMENT/ BUSINESS KNOWLEDGE	CURRENT LEVEL FUTURE/DESIRED LEVEL		

DEVELOPMENT PLAN

Identify key employee or supervisor initiated plans & activities in three areas of development:

1. Education & training
2. Job assignments & job redesign
3. Coaching & relationships

	ACTION	PLAN IMPLEMENTATION DATE	ACTUAL COMPLETION DATE
A			
B			
C			
D			
E			
F			

COMMENTS:

NON-HUMAN RESOURCE MANAGEMENT
- PHYSICAL ENV.
- INVESTMENT
- CAPITAL
- TECHNOLOGY

CURRENT LEVEL   G

FUTURE/DESIRED LEVEL   H

COMMENTS: I

STRATEGIC POSITIONING

CURRENT LEVEL

FUTURE/DESIRED LEVEL

COMMENTS: J

(Contact HRD clearing house _____ for resource information and support)

FUTURE PROFILE

READINESS FOR POSSIBLE ASSIGNMENTS
POSSIBLE ASSIGNMENTS:

WHEN READY:

INDIVIDUAL'S OBJECTIVES AND COMMENTS:

SUCCESSION PLAN

BACKUPS AND THEIR READINESS
BACKUP:

WHEN READY:

REMARKS:

NAME

NAME

SUPERVISOR   DATE

HE-408   OBJECTIVE: Longitudinal development tool for supervisors/managers   Form HC-775 (Rev 3/84) serves as a supplementary tool

17.45

Section 4

Prepare an action register that contains action plans resulting from this review. The human resource action register is a simple, yet effective, recording and programming tool that helps assure follow-up after discussions about people take place.

Section 5

Review priority topics and action register on a quarterly basis.

SUMMARY

As described in the five-lever organizational model presented early in this chapter, human process, knowledge, and structure all have to support human resource planning and the strategies and actions that are its end products. If people are not appraised for these efforts, not rewarded for them, not taught how to plan, and not organized correctly for involvement in the process, our efforts will have a difficult time succeeding. Human resource planning must pay off in order for it to be a viable function. The return on the investment in human resource planning can be both quantitative and qualitative. Organizations are encouraged to measure both. Mistakes not made are hard to measure. The merging of business decisions with people decisions can help to avoid mistakes and address corrective actions for those already made. Unified planning, conducted with clarity, crispness, and organization involvement and linked directly to action, serves the integration role of human resource planning and serves all the stakeholders, from individuals to society.

CHAPTER *18*

Public Affairs Planning

JAMES C. BOWLING

JAMES C. BOWLING is currently a consultant to Philip Morris, Incorporated and to Burson-Marsteller. He is chairman of the Public Affairs Council. He was previously a senior vice president, member of the board of directors, and assistant to the chairman of the board, and director of corporate affairs. He also served on the boards of Miller Brewing and the Seven-Up Company. He has held many managerial positions in the area of public relations and sales during his long career at Philip Morris. James C. Bowling received his degrees at both the University of Kentucky and the University of Louisville. He was given an honorary Doctor of laws degree from Murray State University; he received from the University of Kentucky the Distinguished Service to Agriculture Award of Merit and a Doctor of Laws degree.

OUTLINE

BACKGROUND

Public affairs—or "Corporate external relations," as it is termed in a recent study by the Boston University School of Management—is a relatively new function for the majority of companies, but public affairs problems for private enterprise have been with us almost since the beginnings of the industrial revolution.

In the heyday of massive industrial growth in America, the problems of doing business were too often viewed as gnats getting in the way of all-important progress, subject to empirical solutions designed by industry entrepreneurs.

But the great new American democracy, which had made it possible for anybody to become a satrap, or even a king, of industry, began to prove that its protective powers *really* applied to everybody; that it was *all* the people who had the power—not a few favored princes. For the self-appointed American "royalty," it was a hard lesson to be learned the hard way, starting in the late nineteenth century when public feeling began to run high against the enormous trusts, which then dominated the business landscape.

John D. Rockefeller and the Standard Oil trust became particular targets. He and his company were criticized and vilified with a venom that makes Ralph Nader sound like a little Lord Fauntleroy. So upset and anxious did Rockefeller become from the constant attacks that, at the age of 56, all the hair on his head fell out, including his eyebrows. Even after Standard Oil was broken up under the Sherman Act, and Rockefeller became a full-time philantrophist, it never grew back. Until he died at 97 he wore a wig.

A few years later the tobacco trust came under the gun, with James Buchanan Duke in the Rockefeller role. But he played differently. Instead of stewing, Buck Duke went to see the number-one trust buster, President Theodore Roosevelt, and stated his case along the following lines: "I have read the law, Mister President, and I realize that in the long run we are bound to lose. But we can fight you through the courts and delay things for years if we choose to. So here is my proposition. I will break up the trust myself—right now—if you'll let me do it in a way that takes care of the men who helped me build it."

And that is what happened. In place of the trust, four independent, competing, domestic companies were set up: American Tobacco, Liggett & Myers, P. Lorillard, and R. J. Reynolds. All foreign business was assigned to a fifth company, British American Tobacco, based in England. Seventy years later that structure designed by Buck Duke is still in place—the chief improvement to it being the addition of Philip Morris, which began to be a factor in the industry in the early 1930s and has now grown to number one.

Clearly, then, public affairs problems are not a new thing in the lives of great corporations.

As for *strategic* public affairs planning, the professional will quickly recognize two standard management responses—even today—to "gnatty" public relations problems that become so important as to threaten the very existence of the corporation itself. To the frustrated entrepreneur the choice seems to be the classic one pondered by Hamlet: "whether to suffer the slings and arrows of outrageous fortune," as did Rockefeller, or "to take arms against a sea of troubles," as Duke did.

But I won't press the parallel too far. Certainly no modern chief executive officer would allow a public affairs matter to bring about sudden baldness. That's what he or she has public affairs people for.

And it is equally hard these days to imagine any president of the United States cutting a deal with a captain of industry like the one cut by Teddy Roosevelt and Buck Duke. Not that some of our recent presidents would have hesitated—I'm thinking of the corporate CEOs. Their lawyers would never have let them.

In any event, the choices have long since ceased to be either/or propositions. The experiences of twentieth-century corporate history—prompted by vigilant government and a highly enlightened public—have generally removed the temptation of business brinkmanship for most modern managers.

Yet today, roughly 100 years after the classic show of public strength in dissolving the seemingly invincible trusts, the lesson of the power of the people is still being learned—and again, apparently, the hard way.

To those who consider themselves to be old-timers in the public relations business, the Boston University School of Management study, mentioned above, might prove to be an eye-opener. It found that of 400 companies with public affairs departments—no matter how that function is defined by the individual companies—60 percent had established them since 1972. As for the rest, public relations is still largely a do-it-yourself proposition, but the rapid, continuing growth of this corporate function is based on modern reality.

In the early 1970s, the average chief executive officer could expect to spend about 90 percent of his or her working day running the business and making a profit for the company's investors. Today, it is generally estimated that the CEO of a major corporation spends more than half of his or her working time dealing with external matters that will allow the company to function in the first place.

The traditional American corporate response to any major problem facing a company—no matter the origin or area—has been to put somebody in charge. The spectacular growth of the public affairs field just in the past 10 years gives evidence that corporate management has become increasingly aware of, and involved in, the very serious problems of corporate external relations.

Whether recently established or long-existing, public affairs departments are now part of the table of organization of nearly all large companies, and of many smaller ones as well. The work itself is beginning to assume a broadening dimension within America's business and industrial complex. Yet, in most corporations, I suspect that the function has a long way to go—particularly for those departments that came into being only within the last few years.

In some instances the establishment of these may have been prompted by a genuine desire on the part of senior management to give public affairs proper importance as a corporate function. But new trends and fads in corporate organization can generate a lot of routine imitation, too. And there is a big difference between starting a public affairs department and making a thorough corporate commitment to the perceptive, resourceful, and constructive handling of public affairs.

What prompts my skepticism is the discrepancy between the large proportion of companies with public affairs departments and the very small proportion that have given recognition to public affairs at the board-of-directors level by appointing a standing committee of the board to provide policy direction and oversight in this area of such great significance. The facts are that in two recent surveys of the standing committees of the boards of America's largest corporations—Fortune 500 and Fortune 50–caliber companies— only one in eight reported that its directors had established a committee on public affairs. An even more recent survey by the Conference Board confirms these findings, with only 103 of more than 1000 responding companies reporting board committees on "public policy" (under 24 different titles, incidentally). Of these, 42 had been established in 1975 or earlier, and 61 were established since; the pace of formation, while it is stepping up, is far from headlong.

In most corporations the things that count do get to the board, which is to say that *until* something gets to the board, it doesn't really count. In the large majority of companies, public affairs has not yet crossed this Rubicon. Doing so, it seems to me, is the single most important challenge to the profession.

I write with such conviction because, at Philip Morris, public affairs has crossed that Rubicon. Our board of directors does have a standing committee on public affairs and social responsibility—and what a difference it has made! I would like to claim that our exceptional wisdom and foresight caused us to take this step. The fact is that we were forced into it. The Surgeon General's report of 1964 was a serious blow to us and every other cigarette company: the need to do research on the health effects of our principal product, being forced to put a health warning on every package, the possibility that our company and industry (which had come to depend heavily on broadcast advertising to generate sales) might have to offer to take our commercials off the airwaves. This, of course, happened. These and many similar questions involving government actions and the public attitudes of both users and nonusers of cigarettes became the company's dominant concerns. Every important decision was affected by them: whether to introduce a new brand, enlarge a plant, or buy new equipment, diversify at home, expand abroad, and so on.

This necessary preoccupation with external relations and opinions, by increasing our general sensitivity to the world around us, in turn caused us to develop a major corporate social responsibility program long before most other companies did. We began trying to make friends actively instead of simply reacting to outside pressures. This was a great step forward, to be sure, but one that soon called for substantial dollar commitments with no direct cost-benefit relationship to our business—commitments that had to be made almost wholly on the basis of public affairs judgment.

Finally, with our acquisition in 1970 of Miller Brewing Company, we entered a highly regulated industry with extensive public affairs problems peculiar to *it*—including plenty of critics and enemies.

For a good part of this period, the Philip Morris board was composed largely of inside directors—among them George Weissman, chairman and chief executive offier, who had acquired a broad background in public relations prior to joining Philip Morris. So, though many board discussions ended up gravitating to the critical area of public affairs, for most of us this represented only an extension of what we were dealing with and talking about to each other every working day.

As the board became larger, however, mostly through the addition of outside directors, a less clubby, more formalized approach became necessary. In 1973 a standing committee of the board was formed with special responsibility for public affairs. I became, and continue to be, its chairman. Eight of our 23 directors are members.

As we and other companies brought more public policy people to our boards, including government officials and academicians, the public affairs committee gave them a mechanism for being effective. What this means is that a significant proportion of those individuals who are ultimately responsible for the current well-being and future progress of Philip Morris also carry specific personal responsibility for our progress, or lack of it, in the area of public affairs. This has caused them to develop both knowledge and interest, including a rooting interest, in that rather specialized subject— something that otherwise simply could not be expected of a group of business generalists with heavy demands on their time. As a result, those of us who discharge the public affairs function inside the company have had not only support, but active assistance, at the company's highest level, toward doing what we think needs to be done—meaning both programs and the money to pay for them.

At Philip Morris we have three departments dealing with public matters; all of them report to me. The corporate communications department is responsible for the annual report; quarterly reports; the annual stockholders meeting; all dealings with the media, including the financial press; all internal publications, bulletin boards, and so on; communications research, all presentations, speeches, films and audiovisual materials; our large program of sponsorship of major art exhibitions; and our corporate advertising programs.

The public affairs department also has first-line responsibility for government affairs, for issue tracking, for working and establishing relationships with a vast array of consumer groups, caucus groups, and governmental and quasi-governmental organizations. It also oversees corporate contributions and is the link with the public activities of our six operating companies.

Each of those companies (Philip Morris U.S.A., Philip Morris International, Miller, the Seven-Up Company, and so on) has its own public affairs department as well, responsible for internal communication, for dealings with local, regional, or foreign media, and for relations with state governments—the latter being especially important to Miller.

I should add that, in terms of promotions and transfers, there is extensive two-way traffic between the corporate staff and the operating companies. Public affairs people also move rather frequently into important non–public-affairs jobs; two of Miller's senior officers and the financial vice president of Philip Morris Industrial are recent examples of those who have been promoted.

Finally, reporting to me is the corporation's Washington office, which functions as a listening post and early warning system on legislative and regulatory developments of potential interest to us—everything from safety codes in the workplace to tax rulings on the repatriation of foreign balances. While this tends to be a defensive operation (against the passage of such-and-such a bill, for instance, or to modify this-or-that regulation), we try for positive results when we can. To cite one example, in the recent efforts to attain a lowering of trade barriers by Japan, our Washington office played an active, and we think helpful, role in the successful outcome.

It all adds up to a very comprehensive public affairs program. Needless to say, it doesn't come cheap. Furthermore, we keep adding to it. Within the last several years, we have created an information transmission program to help us manage our government affairs better—a computer system that tracks all federal and state legislation for the corporation and each of our operating companies. The feed-in of data is constant, and the system is also tied into the formation banks of Martin Ryan Haley, the *New York Times,* the *Congressional Record,* the Tobacco Institute, and others. That, too, costs money. It represented the sort of outlay that, in a sluggish economy, many boards of directors might well have questioned. Ours did not, because the board's own public affairs committee was well-informed about it and solidly behind it. A lengthy report on our entire program is the main event of one Philip Morris board meeting each year.

I have gone into some detail on Philip Morris' organization, function, responsibility and follow-through in public affairs only to establish the point that *nothing* really works, or happens in a corporation, sans the full support—*and* commitment—of management and the board of directors. Without that, it is virtually useless to try.

RELATIONSHIP TO MANAGEMENT

Strategic public affairs planning becomes a wasted exercise if its object does not relate directly to the objectives of management; if the entire program is not a program of *management* and the *board.* It follows, and is taken for granted, that the public affairs department must also have their trust and respect.

The evolution of public affairs came about as a business function in a fairly typical form, starting with the traditional penchant of management for putting somebody in charge of problems. As government has become increasingly involved in business, business has increasingly tended to put somebody in charge of the areas being affected by government involvement. In recent years, it has become much more than having a Washington office to monitor and report on what's happening there, than working with Congress and the various government agencies, or than adhering to any of the stereotyped job descriptions of any company's Washington presence. The sophisticated government relations operation of public affairs today is a major management function that extends from the boardroom to the office of every manager, from the CEO to the one in charge of a purely local operation.

The same evolution may be found in the development of public affairs people and skills to handle any of the major external problems that may affect a company's ability to do business. But with the burgeoning of external problems and the increase of public affairs experts to handle them, it is apparent that a major deterrent to effective, strategic public affairs planning can easily arise from the very problem of all disorderly management: of properly assembling, organizing and digesting the information required to make the right decisions beforehand.

Fortunately, the era that has given industry its greatest and most complex problems to date has also ushered in its best ally: the computer. Information and knowledge that once may have taken centuries or decades to communicate can be transmitted instantly. Whatever later historians may call the present era, many modern thinkers see it as the end of the industrial age and the beginning of the communications age. Harvard's Assistant Vice President for Information Services and Technology has called the computer "the machine that magnifies mental power as earlier machines magnified muscle power."

Withal, the computer and its latter-day offspring are simply tools or devices that enable us to acquire and dispense information more quickly and more accurately. The job of the human mind is still to discern the worth of that information and make proper decisions as to its use. In that connection, we have created a number of our own systems at Philip Morris, designed specifically to provide accurate information on areas and situations vital to *our* company. In planning strategic public affairs programs and actions, the key phrase is *absolute pinpointing* of accurate information. One of our homegrown systems, called GAMBIT (Government Affairs Management By Information Tracking), provides us with a daily updating on all bills and situations vital to us: the legislative history, the congressional/government people and committees/agencies involved, our relationship with and access to them, and so forth.

It is, of course, of no use to us if we settle on what turns out to be the *wrong* strategy, but it is an invaluable guide in helping us make the right decisions—even in those situations that are heavily weighted against us, and where there is little chance of any success.

We also have GAMBIT programmed to provide us with similar information on state and local municipal legislation and/or ordinances. The players and the approach may be slightly different, but the outcome there can be just as vital—sometimes even more important, because by extinguishing a localized blaze you sometimes can avert a national conflagration.

Thus, the strategic plan of public affairs programs/actions must start with vital information, culled and ready for use. With such knowledge, you know what it is that you have to accomplish, and you know the extent, the severity, and the imminence of the problem. The plan design, itself, is limited only by the expertise of the planner and management's commitment to solving the problem. In the end, no theory on paper will work in practice without the full support of management.

In the best of worlds, the most successfully executed plans are those that are handled through a coalition composed of people and organizations whose goals are similar to your own. Sometimes such groups are created for the express purpose of taking on a specific problem, and in some instances there are existing trade associations and/or other industry entities that you can work with or through. In those cases, it may not be necessary to send in your own corporate public affairs team; you may simply decide to have a means of being supportive of whatever that group may be.

In our strategic planning at Philip Morris, we prefer to work through established associations for three basic reasons. First, it is much more efficient. You help keep the industry or group together, and you reduce expenses proportionately by having the individual companies pay only a portion of the commonality of interests. Second, you save your management's time, the company's money, and the time of its people in answering the calls and doing all the field work. Third; by keeping within a group, your communications are better and you sometimes can prevent one or more members of that group from going off on a tangent and making snap decisions that might be destructive to the interests of all. In addition, a combined voice—no matter the makeup of the coalition—is always a stronger voice. For us, then, it is logical to look first for support and help from the companies in our own industry as often as we can, although we certainly know that there are certain issues that may not be suitable for an industrywide effort. Because ours is a highly competitive, consumer goods business, we hardly expect that our competitors in tobacco, beer, and soft drinks will share our own interest in every public issue. Not only do companies in the same business have a wide variety of interests not necessarily shared by the others, they also might not even agree with any other company's position on a given issue. Effective strategic planning in any public affairs program for any company starts with a frank recognition of that timeless business reality, and that is the point at which the wise planner begins to earn his or her keep.

OBJECTIVE

The *real* objective of public affairs in any company is to help create the kind of atmosphere that will allow *that company* to do its own job (at which it is presumed to be expert, or it wouldn't be in business in the first place). It deals knowledgeably on matters related to governments and other publics to build support for *that* one company, its products, goods, and services. The public affairs department does this in a great variety of ways, but, in the end, it is judged on its ability to rally public sentiment in favor of the company and its positions on public matters. One of Abraham Lincoln's notable observations about the American way of life was that, in this country, public sentiment is everything—without it nothing can succeed; with it nothing can fail. That Lincoln truism certainly applies to strategic public affairs planning. Whether or not a company has the backing of its own industry in a given situation, it is obliged—if it wishes to succeed—to build and maintain a constituency of its own. It cannot assume, no matter the situation, that it will be supported automatically by any given group of people simply because their interests seem to be similar or because it had enjoyed that group's support on other issues in the past. The safest assumption is that you might not have any public support at all. And, in order to get it, you will have to reapply all of the standard communications tools of public relations—press releases, media interviews, speeches, films, news clips, publicity programs, special news-making events. It is a poor plan that takes anything for granted or neglects to include any communications opportunity, no matter how obvious.

Beyond the laundry list of standards, the plan must account for a great many other factors, not the least of which is the specific use of, and purpose of, those communications devices in presenting the message and the need, and in identifying those entities and people for whom the action is important. It is in this phase of planning that the program begins to take on flesh. Whether it is a defensive action or an offensive action (i.e., to create a better circumstance of a better working climate, to alter negative public opinion or sentiment, or to remove a stultifying obstacle) you are still up against the same odds. Whatever the situation, you are out to change *something*—and change does not come easily.

Where should you start in building a supportive constituency? "Natural" allies abound—depending, of course, on the action. The logical place to look is right at home, and fan out from there. Whose jobs depend on the success of the company? What suppliers are affected by its ability to keep its production or service lines moving? Which are the transportation companies, the wholesalers, retailers, warehouse, and others, whose own profits are directly tied to the company's ability to make and market its goods or services? What consumer groups will benefit, and how, from a successful result of this action? Where and how do all, or any, of these *inside* groups relate to other sectors of the general public—as citizens, taxpayers, home owners, parents, volunteers, supporters of local institutions, and, of course, as voters? Can their influence be extended to those sectors?

This is not to imply that any company can expect to start from ground zero and build an immediate constituency for an isolated public affairs program. Rather, it is to suggest logical areas in which the company may reasonably seek to enhance continuing public support for its business and/or social endeavors. It is obvious that short-term success in getting out the troops for a single battle largely depends on building and maintaining a standing constituency for the long term.

GOVERNMENT RELATIONS MANAGEMENT

For example, in the manner of government relations, it is very important that your position has the votes in Congress, the state legislature, or the municipal council to support it at the official level when the chips are down. Despite all the charges and countercharges having to do with PACs and/or special interest legislators, in the real world of politics, the only thing that really counts to an elected official in the long run is the voter who elects him or her.

The well-designed plan for public affairs recognizes the power of the voter and seeks to influence legislators through the entity that puts, and keeps, them in office. The best strategy of all is a good, positive community program in a congressperson's district. That applies, equally, to mayors, governors, and other elected officials. Even as the elective official continually sounds out the electorate on its opinions, wants, and interests, a company that seeks to establish a strategic plan in public affairs must keep its ear to the ground on all these matters, trends, and signs of change that may guide public sentiment.

Access to such information is vital; here the computer is an invaluable tool. Not only can it help in building a company's support constituency program, but it also can provide telling data, in detail, on the issues and the public sentiment that supported an elected official in his or her bid for office and in any part of the process along the way in getting there. It can supply the kind of information needed to identify the people, the groups, and the organizations who can help or hinder the progress of the company's public affairs action. Certainly it can pinpoint the strengths and weaknesses in the elected official's own support and provide important insights into the company's opportunities for winning his or her backing on any given measure that will come before a vote in his or her chamber.

In this era of multiplying pressure groups, burgeoning citizens' lobbies, and instant communications, modern planning for public affairs programs must allow for a wide variety of options in approach and execution. In the political arena, particularly, what may be seen as today's iron-clad opportunity could be tomorrow's iron-clad trap. In recent memory, corporations that have locked themselves into an untenable, perhaps old-fashioned, position on any given issue often have suffered the same fate as the political aspirant who seeks election by championing the wrong issues before the wrong constituency.

With the affairs of business so inextricably woven with the affairs of government and, in turn, with the will of the people, the successful company really has little choice in its public affairs programs, except to be prepared for all possible contingencies.

The task is formidable, and may even sound impossible, but a crystal-clear understanding of the objective makes it less so. Unforeseen contingencies are natural phenomena of life itself, and no plan will work that doesn't allow for them. That is to say, in short, that strategic planning for public affairs is akin to planning one's own life. You know the pitfalls and traps are out there. The best you can do is to be aware of them, study the possibilities, and forge ahead. At the least you know what it is that you want to accomplish, and you have the benefit of previous experiences—both good and bad—to help you make the best possible choices as you progress. Even so, as the poet Robert Burns noted, "The best laid schemes o' mice an' men/gang aft agley," and just having a good plan is no guarantee that you will achieve your objective.

While strategic public affairs planning must necessarily deal with all of the known negatives and foreseen problems in trying to achieve the planned objective, it must also be alert and ready to take advantage of new opportunities by changes that regularly occur on the public scene.

Current law makes it possible for corporations to form political action committees (PACs) to which the people of the company or the entity (e.g., stockholders) can contribute. That allows the company, through its own people, to do the most important thing of all in building its public political base—directly support candidates for election or reelection to Congress. It is not just a matter of pulling friendly names out of a hat, but a scientific selection of candidates whose election will add strength to the company's public affairs mission.

Obviously, the work of the company's political action committee, besides organizing the action group and raising funds for the effort, is to identify very carefully those candidates who are of key interest to the company on the basis of (1) their standing on the committees that deal with issues and legislation of particular importance to the company, (2) their past record of support (or nonsupport) of key legislation, or (3) the makeup of their constituency as it relates to the company's own area of special interest (e.g., does the district include a number of the company's employees, i.e., is it in a plant city or is it located in a major supplier or customer area?).

Since the actual funds any PAC can contribute to a candidate are minimal at best, its support means far more than money to the office seeker. The real power of the PAC is the voluntary action of like-minded people in supporting the candidate's election drive. In turn, the concerted effort of the employee political team in the real world of politics sharpens employee awareness of the issues that bear on the company's ability to do its work. And it opens new vistas and possibilities for further building the company's constituency.

Knowing who your friends are—and rallying them to your support—long predates the age of civilization, but over time the process has become both an art and a science. Today, building constituencies of support is the backbone of what is now generally called "public affairs"—a catch-all phrase encompassing everything an individual or an entity may do, say, or think beyond the confines of an inner chamber.

If the process is ancient, the methods and the tactics have become increasingly sophisticated and, no doubt, will improve a great deal in times to come. In the effort to alter public opinion so that it may favor a company and/or its position on a given issue, public affairs is an educational process. It reaches and teaches people who otherwise might not even realize that they could be affected by a given issue. It provides information on, and insights into, the legal processes through which they can make their influence felt. It develops systems and methods for study and follow-up action. On company-involved bills before Congress, state legislatures, and municipal bodies, the public affairs operation becomes a research and communication center, providing its constituency with the knowledge needed (including the names and addresses of key legislators and elected officials) to become actively influential in the passage or defeat of the proposed measure.

The jobs of building constituencies and participating in the political processes have become such an important part of public affairs that a number of specialists in the field are developing new systems designed expressly to create groundswells of public sentiment and supportive public action on matters vital to protagonist entities. The sophistication of modern constituency building may be judged by the relatively recent successes of various citizens' lobbies in influencing the passage (or defeat) of milestone social legislation in the United States Congress.

The careful student of what is happening in society today that may sooner or later affect a company or any entity will surely touch all the bases, not only monitoring what is in the press but culling the facts from key research studies, opinion polls, etc. The process results in the identification of issues and knowledge of where the public stands and how it feels about them. The study extends to the local, state, and federal legislative action to date on those issues. In this management of issues, the company's public affairs people can fairly well anticipate resultant legislation, if any. But public affairs is far from an exact science, and new challenges frequently come as a total surprise.

For example, a member of some state legislature may well enter a bill, not in the company's interest, that has to be dealt with immediately. That takes us back to my earlier observation that in public affairs, nothing can be taken for granted. And it makes the argument for strategic planning even stronger. Valid strategic planning must at least have anticipated the need to work with that legislature at some future point on some issue. The logical public affairs purview of any company encompasses every state, municipality, and territory where it does business and/or markets its products. Anticipation of someday working with a given state legislature, city body, or any key public group would, in turn, call for at least a standby constituency support program that could be activated at once.

As for the "surprise" of a suddenly proposed bill, the only surprise should be in its unexpected introduction—not in its general content or in the company's unpreparedness to respond. Effective public affairs planning first calls for a thorough knowledge of all issues that *could* affect the company and a thorough understanding of how to direct the forces in the field—be they paid lobbyists, company employees, or local constituents—in taking the company's message to the legislative committees and the key officials who will be dealing with the bill.

PUBLIC AFFAIRS MANAGEMENT

The ability to move quickly and effectively in any public affairs effort—the *art* of public affairs—arises from the company's astuteness in *issues management,* the *science* of strategy planning. Issues management involves the anticipating of possible problems, planning on how to deal with them, recognizing societal trends, thoroughly researching and studying all possible issues that may relate to the company, interviewing people who are involved or affected, and closely watching and studying new things as they emerge.

All too frequently, the public affairs arm of a company is regarded by management as a defense force to be called on in time of trouble. Its genius in creating special events and communicating positive company news is often regarded as some sort of extension of the company's marketing arm. In fact, the public relations operation of many companies is still confined to promoting and publicizing products.

Over a period of some 30 years as an active participant in my company's public affairs development, and as an interested witness of what other companies have done, I have come to a few conclusions about the field that may be of interest to those who would like to strengthen their companies' commitment to it.

Until very recently, schools of business and management have not generally concentrated on public affairs as a required management skill. Many top managers—who often come from backgrounds of engineering, finance, sales, or law—are not well-versed in the nuances of public affairs. In an era that has increasingly called for management's attention to external matters that are too often beyond the manager's control, the tendency is to be uncertain and uneasy about the societal problems companies are forced to face today.

This causes many top managers to look on public affairs differently. It leads them to view the public affairs professional as the expert in charge of repelling any external attacks that may threaten to penetrate that shield—preferably with minimum risk and at minimum cost. Or, if I may mix metaphors, the "pro" is supposed to put out the fire without giving away the store.

To be viewed as an expert in this way—to be relied on by great corporate chieftains to do something that they don't know how to do—can be very heady stuff. It feeds the ego. It gratifies one's sense of professionalism. It can make the professional feel special, a breed apart from those in the company with less "glamorous" jobs.

But if a company adopts a fire-brigade view of public affairs, what happens after the fire is put out? It doesn't take very long for the highly-priced expert to be viewed as an unneeded alien, outside the company's mainstream. The very professionalism in which the expert takes such pride may even contribute to this. Robert Stuart, the chairman and chief executive officer of Quaker Oats, has asserted that public affairs people "are more apt to be simply interested in the technical handling of the issues and the communications involved. But they are too often unaware of its impact on the strategy of the company."

This "hired gun" syndrome militates against strategic public affairs planning right from the beginning. The crucial public affairs problems that keep cropping up in the business/industrial world of the late twentieth century are the *company's* problems, not show-and-tell exercises for the skilled specialists.

The recurring frequency of public affairs *emergencies* tells us that societal problems cannot be regarded as isolated headaches, but rather as a permanent condition of being in business as the twenty-first century approaches. No single expert, or department of specialists, can be expected to be the lone keeper of the company's social conscience. Effective public affairs planning can be accomplished only in a company whose *management* accepts full responsibility for the entity's public posture.

To put it another way, in my view the single most important ingredient of a successful public affairs program is not professional competence or adequate budget, but management involvement. And the most valuable contribution a strategic plan can make is to bring about that involvement. It may not come easily. Many company chairpersons and presidents will resist. Thoroughness in reporting to them is a vital first step. Both spending time with them to make them understand the company's public affairs problems and soliciting their views on them are fundamental. Being on the lookout for ways to persuade or push them out front—to speak, to testify, or simply to appear for the company—should be a constant concern. The best public affairs people are also good businesspeople with a thorough knowledge of the company and its strategies.

A company's political action committee provides an excellent vehicle for involving management. Managers contribute their own money to PACs, and there are strong public affairs implications in how that money is distributed. More important, managers at all levels who contribute to PACs usually become more informed and concerned about politics.

Once management does become involved, good things begin to happen. In the long run, perhaps, there may be a board committee on public affairs, the formation of which certainly won't happen unless management presses for it.

A PRACTICAL APPLICATION

A few years ago, it became important for Philip Morris to make a formal appearance before the Legislature of Virginia, where our largest cigarette plant is located. The reason was not new: a difference of opinion about taxes. Any number of executives could have represented the company appropriately, but we went to the top and asked our vice chairman, Ross Millhiser, to take on the duty. Ordinarily he might not have paid much attention to the matter, but since he was going to appear personally, he wanted to do the thing well. He thought it would be good to point out to the city fathers just how much Philip Morris meant to Richmond and to Virginia in terms of jobs, payroll, purchases, taxes paid, and so on—facts and figures, dollars and cents. Some data we could get easily and some not so easily, but it made quite a show when it was all done, and Millhiser impressed them.

So he said, and we agreed, "Wouldn't it be good if we had figures like that not just for Philip Morris and Virginia but for the entire tobacco industry and the whole country?" If people could see what an enormous economic contribution we make, maybe we'd gain a different dimension of understanding and support. That was the genesis of a study conducted by the Wharton School of Business and financed by the Tobacco Institute—a study that makes our industry more completely and reliably documented than any other in terms of its economic contribution to each individual state and the many individual communities. We can now say, Increase the taxes on our product or discourage its use, and here's what will be affected: so many jobs, so much in sales, so much in taxes. It's all there—and the involvement of cooperative top executive, in one relatively minor public affairs chore, is what caused it to be there.

If the result in this instance of strategic planning went well beyond the initial objective, and certainly beyond our expectations, it was a consequence of top management's involvement from the very beginning. The example also illustrates how proper planning can turn an essentially defensive action into an important offensive program. That is the most rewarding aspect of public affairs activity, and should be the end objective of all public affairs planning.

When a company has identified something that can be made better or, through change, might benefit its constituency, it has an opportunity to move its entire public affairs thrust from the negative to the positive. For example, a company's or entity's initiative and/or action may concentrate on getting a burdensome tax or trade barrier removed. The results of such a mission, if successful, could benefit many other entities, in addition to allowing the company to work more effectively or more efficiently.

When the company attempts to make such a constructive change, its role becomes one of *leadership,* rather than one of necessary involvement. Marshalling the support constituency requires a program of education—of preparing (in writing) the program or proposed legislation and getting the logic of it understood. The company then must use its own access to key leaders, particularly those in state legislatures and in Congress. Who is the right lawmaker to introduce such a bill? What help can the company or entity provide in formulating the bill or whatever measure will be required?

If the initiative involves the removal of a trade barrier, the company will know that it is not alone in this goal, and it logically will want to involve all companies and individuals who are affected. It will seek access to influential officials of the foreign government that imposes the barrier, while working through our own government to help negotiate a more beneficial agreement. Astute planners recognize and understand the importance and implications of involving the American people and their areas of influence—the State Department, the Departments of Commerce and Labor, special trade representatives, the states that supply raw materials, purchasers of the foreign country's export goods, unions and union leaders, etc.

Whereas a purely defensive action may be restricted by preordained conditions, the latitude and bargaining power afforded by positive public affairs initiatives more often than not make for a successful mission. This statement is based on the assumption that the company is truly acting in the public interest, and if there is something wrong, the entire plan will quickly go back through the system, including top management and the board, for correction. More often than not it will be rejected.

If a company *is* doing something wrong, the best program on earth won't save it. Strategic planning for public affairs is a wasted exercise for any company, today, whose object is to fool the public. Enlightened management may, occasionally, "back into" a public affairs opportunity that turns into a major commitment. The company may experience ensuing years of dedication to, and work in behalf of, a cause that will become an integral of its public affairs plan.

More than 30 years ago, Philip Morris became involved with, and took leadership in, a fledgling effort of the private sector to help clean up the environment. It was, and still is, called "Keep America Beautiful;" it has since evolved into a worldwide organization, "Clean World International." I have been involved officially with the movement from its inception, and served as cofounder of the national KAB organization with several other like-minded corporate executives. Although the early years of the effort were gratifying—aided primarily by the voluntary support of the Advertising Council—the movement enjoyed its greatest national boost in the mid-1960s with the personal involvement and vigorous support of then-First Lady Mrs. Lyndon B. Johnson. I continued to serve the cause, successively, as an officer, committee chairman, vice president, president, and chairman of KAB. I was involved in founding the worldwide organization and, today, serve as Vice Chairman of Clean World International, and continue as a board member of KAB.

Reflecting on an era in which the environment, per se, became an international *cause célèbre* and the key subject of a number of international conferences, I would *like* to say, as a professional, that Philip Morris' involvement was the result of some carefully thought-out public affairs considerations—even a *strategic* plan. However, it was not.

The truth is that, in addition to our natural desire for a cleaner national environment, we were interested in the KAB concept of litter control because we manufacture "disposable" consumer products. At that time, it was only cigarettes; later we added beer and soft drinks as well. We saw that our products were a part of the litter, the litter was becoming a major societal problem, and that we were obviously involved in it.

It was a very pragmatic decision. Even if one were to try to rationalize on the basis of any one company's culpability for careless or thoughtless acts of the public, the decision was a valid one for a company that highly valued its reputation as a good corporate citizen. Looking to the future, as judged by past, unchecked carelessness, we knew that our products would be increasingly involved in litter and, frankly, we did not wish to advertise our quality brands in clutters of roadside rubbish.

Initially, the organization tried to eliminate the problem, primarily through long-term educational programs. In fact, the day-to-day work of KAB today is largely involved with educational programs, and is particularly directed to and through the younger generations.

When it became clear that litter itself was only one part of an increasingly larger environmental problem, KAB set out to help change the *system* in order to create a better circumstance. It initiated and took on an exhaustive and intensive study that spanned several years, and that resulted in the creation of the "Clean Community System," which then had to be tested and improved through practical application within volunteer test communities. The design and the practical testing of the system were closely coordinated with the Public Works Association of the United States, which endorsed all of our programs and concepts.

As for my company's planning for this public affairs program in the ensuing years, our strategy has been to continue and increase our presence. The KAB has been an important and successful venture for America. Its programs such as the "Clean Community System" truly have improved the conditions and the workings of American communities. That its example is being followed across the world speaks for its societal value and timeliness.

For Philip Morris, KAB has provided not only an opportunity to enhance its public stature—or even stave off an impending public problem—but also a source of first-hand information and invaluable experience for taking on the role of improving the quality of life in all of its "hometown" communities around the world. Our company's involvement in the work of the KAB has led to our gratifying environmental participation everywhere that Philip Morris has a presence.

Strategic planning for public affairs certainly includes the retention of good programs that are already working for the company—including those that the company happens to "back into." Astute planning also includes the constant search for new ideas and possible new programs that might improve the public *style* or character of the company.

Philip Morris' considerable reputation as a corporate sponsor of cultural events, particularly in visual arts, began 26 years ago in an era when the federal government was taking over the funding of philanthropies that had been routinely supported by the private sector for decades, principally in health, education, and welfare. Our company, too, had important commitments in these areas—and still does—but the public reaction to any such contributions had become tepid. How could any company, in an area dominated by the dollars and the public-affairs clout of the federal government, expect to realize any exceptional return in public goodwill on its investment in philanthropies that had become routine and expected by the public?

At that time, the field of visual arts was seriously underfunded and underpromoted. Philip Morris management, with the enthusiastic prompting of Chairman George Weissman, decided to become an active sponsor of cultural events. It was, in some measure, an intuitive decision, guided by little, if any, public affairs research and few, if any, existing studies on corporate support of the arts. But, by looking at trends, we saw that in the 1920s, 1930s, and 1940s, virtually all business contributions were made to health and social welfare programs. This was due to the growing awareness of company managers of some obligation, even if unspoken, to do something to improve life in the communities in which they lived and worked, and on whose prosperity their own welfare was dependent. The whole area of health and welfare was increasingly, and properly, preempted by governments— local, state, and national—a change that the companies themselves helped bring about.

Private business then turned to education, and in the post-World War II era, education became the principal philanthropic thrust of business giving and corporate support. As that area, too, started to become a principal province of governments, we began to wonder what would be next. Our own belief, from watching trends, was that it probably would be cultural affairs. We saw a need there, and our own cursory research told us that the public was, indeed, interested in the arts.

Our initial program was small and tentative, but it was apparently doing its job with the people and groups who were exposed to our sponsored events.

Philip Morris was about three years into the program—which kept expanding—before it commissioned the Louis Harris research organization to conduct a major study on art show attendance and on the involvement of the corporation in public cultural affairs. The findings startled even us, although the evidence had certainly seemed to be there. Among other positive findings—including the enhancement of our corporate image as a sponsor and partner in this phase of public life—the study (the first of its kind, incidentally) showed that, in a given year, more people attend art events and frequent museums of art than those who, combined, attend all sports events, both national and local.

Obviously, Philip Morris has retained this program in its strategic planning, and its involvement has increased over the course of time, culminating in the sponsorship of *The Vatican Collections: The Papacy and Art,* which enjoyed record attendances and massive public interest. Aside from emphasizing our corporate character, the program gives us unique access to thought leaders; it is very popular with the public, and we're doing something that greatly appeals to our employees.

THE ROLE OF STRATEGIC PLANNING

Strategic planning, then, also calls for *creative* planning in finding and selecting those programs that may be new and may differ from the company norm. "Intuitive" ideas, most usually, come from a company's desire and determination to set a distinctive corporate style. In the design of its plants and office buildings, and in its interior decor and its art acquisition program to beautify the exteriors and interiors of its structures, Philip Morris has reflected its own corporate style as a creative maker and marketer of quality products. It is not by chance that its employees also reflect that style and share the company's enthusiasm for the visual arts. As stated in one of our recent corporate advertising series, *It takes Art to make a company great.* After a quarter of a century of vigorous arts support, it is difficult to say whether our style is a consequence of our involvement with the world of art, or whether our involvement is a consequence of our corporate style.

Proper strategy in public affairs for any company calls for programs that are in harmony with the company's corporate character—or, at least, are pointed toward the style or character the company wishes to achieve. Without it, even a good program, no matter how well-intended, has a slim chance of working.

Effective public affairs planning is based on constant, up-to-date study of all public factors and issues that can affect a company. Some *new* ideas, however, may be so old and so taken for granted that they can be overlooked entirely. One example of such an idea is the spirit of American voluntarism, which dates back to this country's discovery and early settlement. It is this ingrained trait of help and interdependence of a people, free of the dictates and fiats of sovereign rule, that conquered and civilized the vast reaches of our land.

Voluntarism is not only good for America and its society, but is also very good for the individual who volunteers to help a neighbor, a group, or a cause. Societal volunteers probably end up as better citizens and as more active participants in the country's democratic processes. Their exposure to important public needs also tends to make them more aware of the community's political system, they are very apt to be more active in the community's political affairs. Philip Morris, which has encouraged—even urged—voluntarism and citizen involvement also has found that the employee who is active in outside volunteer work is also more likely to be supportive of company programs. So, the combination of all such volunteer activities creates a coterie of good citizens, which then serves not only the community in which these people live and work, but the company they represent as well.

Several years ago, at a planning session on public affairs, Chairman Weissman suggested that the corporation do something to recognize Philip Morris employees for the fine community services they were performing voluntarily above and beyond their regular work days at the company. The result was a special issue of the company newspaper, swollen to more than ten times its normal publication size. The examples of voluntarism and services performed by our people were so many and so important that the story simply could not be contained in one issue, no matter how swollen. As a result, the subject of employee voluntarism has become a regular feature, and one of the best-read parts, of our company paper.

Thanking one's own employees for unusual performance is a logical exercise in public affairs. Employees, after all, are the closest and most important constituency a company has. A company regarded by its own people as a good place to work finds a bonanza of goodwill in its external public affairs, and a reliable source of internal support for its stand on external issues.

But this example of a "logical" exercise in public affairs had unexpected, and far-reaching, results. When the Reagan Administration selected American voluntarism as a vital means of accomplishing its newly proposed programs, our company found itself in the very pleasant position of corporate leadership. The special voluntarism issue of our company newspaper was reprinted several times and sent to other companies as an example of the theory in action. Our employees were recognized, individually and collectively, by numerous local and national volunteer organizations. The corporation, itself, was cited for its encouragement and support by a number of important public institutions and leaders, including the President of the United States.

I have given a few examples of specific experiences at Philip Morris—not to set the company up as a paragon, which it is not, or to offer suggestions of programs that others might wish to duplicate—but to illustrate the workings of strategic planning. If a given program is truly in the public interest (that is, to *any sector* of the company's, or entity's, public), if its activities are properly motivated, and if it is totally honest, the resulting good can often go beyond the planned objective. In fact, good strategic planning, based on these caveats, can be *expected* to produce public affairs bonuses.

One of the main things to remember in strategic planning is to build everything on a carefully identified, sturdy base. The best starting base is the community or communities in which the company operates. A company's core constituency consists of the people of that community. They and their elected representatives, starting with the mayor or manager and officials of the local governing structure, must be given good reason to know that the company is operating in *their* best interests: providing employment, paying taxes, and being a good citizen in, and supporter of, the community.

I have emphasized the political implications and political involvement that attend strategic public affairs planning. Any public affairs activity that translates into good for society translates, in turn, into public support. When the chips are down, public support means legislative and governmental support. The process is very pragmatic.

CHAPTER *19*

Venture Capital Planning

KENNETH W. RIND

KENNETH W. RIND is the cofounder of Oxford Partners, a venture capital firm. Dr. Rind's past experience includes five years with Xerox Development Corporation, where he was responsible for introducing such venture capital opportunities as Paradyne, Apple Computer, and Tran. Prior to his work at Xerox, he was a vice president of corporate finance at Oppenheimer & Co., Inc., and served as general partner of its venture capital fund. Dr. Rind helped finance many companies that were sold to such companies as Monsanto, Data General, Johnson & Johnson, and Motorola. He also has been associated with the Rockefeller family and with Quantum Science, where he managed investments and worked in venture capital. Dr. Rind was a founder and initial director of the National Venture Capital Association, and he is currently president emeritus of the Connecticut Venture Group. He is a director of the Baillie Gifford Technology Fund and a member of the Connecticut Governor's High Technology Council. His education includes a Ph.D. in nuclear chemistry from Columbia University and a B.A. in chemistry from Cornell University.

OUTLINE

Venturing can be an effective tool for strategic management. Among the venture techniques available for the corporate planning and development function are new venture divisions, wholly owned ventures, R&D partnerships, spinouts and divestitures, new-style joint ventures, direct venture investments, outside partnership investments, and venture monitoring.

The benefits that may be gained from venturing include enhanced innovation, earlier discovery of relevant technologies, better acquisition knowledge, lower-cost/higher-quality products, more direct information on market/government/business developments, greater assurance of supplies, assistance to customers, lower-cost financing of developments, and financial returns exceeding normal corporate hurdle rates.

This chapter will focus primarily on the techniques that have gained recent popularity: direct venture investments, investments in outside partnerships, R&D partnerships, and divesting operations with the help of venture capital.

The strategic utilization of venture capital investments by industrial corporations is a rapidly growing phenomenon. Among the recent participants are some of the largest U.S. corporations, including AT&T, DuPont, IBM, General Motors, and Kodak. They have joined such other Fortune 100 industrials as General Electric, Xerox, and Standard Oil of Indiana, all of which continue active direct venture investment programs, despite the well-publicized problems of Exxon's venture capital subsidiary, Exxon Enterprises.

VENTURING AS AN INNOVATION SOURCE

Venture capital provides a low-risk path to innovation for large corporations which typically find it difficult, if not impossible, to implement new ideas.

While the importance of innovation is accepted by all corporations, countless dollars and hours spent in attempting to foster this quality internally have often yielded frustratingly poor results. As a result, venture capital investments have come to be regarded by a growing number of large businesses as another "arrow in the corporate quiver"—an arrow that can be directed on target with minimum risk and maximum efficiency.

Venture capital investing can provide the large corporation with what is essentially a cost-free insurance policy, since returns are usually positive. Further, strategic venture capital investments provide large companies with a window into new technologies and an arena for testing new ideas.

The value of venture investing extends through all stages of innovation. It is in small companies that new technological breakthroughs are frequently made, and these small businesses provide the ideal environment in which the practicality of such new concepts can be assessed. Finally, commercialization of products or services is an area in which the large and small corporations can work together successfully.

The risk/reward for corporations invested in ventures is optimal. Properly structured venture investments have no negative earnings impact on the corporation during the early development stages. The capital outlay required by these investees is relatively small, while results in small companies occur much more rapidly. The large corporation can obtain innovative results with no drain on its personnel and minimal senior staff involvement.

Venture capital is not a substitute for other corporate development techniques such as internal research and development, university sponsorship, outside contracting, venture management, joint ventures and, of course, acquisitions. Nor should it ever be considered a method to be employed for major diversification.

Venture capital is just one of a number of means that should be utilized by the large corporation in its quest for constructive growth and change. Because of venture capital's low risks and high rewards, it is a strategy increasingly being utilized by many large corporations.

The frequent failure of internal corporate venture programs has in no way diminished recognition by large companies of the need to utilize venture capital as a primary innovative technique. Today, more and more of them are finding ways to use external venture capital investment as a means to this necessary goal.

Small Versus Large

Innovation is not synonymous with invention. Inventions may proliferate within the R&D sector of a corporation without successful commercialization. Innovation implies the implementation of change—in planning, in philosophy, in product development, and in marketing strategy—which permits the growth necessary to survival in a competitive environment. Innovation means the transformation of creativity or invention into a successfully implemented policy or action that provides a corporation with new growth and financial return. The implementation of innovation requires flexibility and the ability to respond easily and quickly. All too frequently large corporations lack these characteristics.

Studies have shown that large established corporations spend their R&D

dollars four times less efficiently than do small ones, and that since 1953 the majority of innovations in the United States have come from small companies.[1] Two other studies have shown that, while seven to ten years are required for large companies to bring innovation to the marketplace,[2] small companies accomplish this in three to five years.[3] In fact, during the commercialization of a product, small entrepreneurial groups are given an A or B rating at producing innovative products and introducing prototypes, thus complementing the skills of large companies, which are best at volume manufacturing and marketing (see Exhibit 19-1).

Why Small Companies Are More Innovative

A variety of hypotheses exist as to why small companies are better able to utilize innovative ideas effectively. Most of these appear obvious upon consideration and result from factors inherent in size.

1. The necessary bureaucracy frequently deprives large corporations of flexibility and the ability to make rapid decisions.
2. Employees and top management of small corporations are more strongly motivated and work harder because they have a sense of personal accomplishment as well as a sense of personal accountability.
3. The financial rewards of success and the harsh consequences of failure in small companies contribute to this motivation.
4. Small companies provide a freedom from constraints, an informality, a sense of immediacy and closeness to the inner workings of the business, a chance for flexibility, and enhanced communications, all of which lead to rapid decision making and superior efficiency.

EXHIBIT 19-1.   *From Invention to Commodity*

Stage	Large Company Capability Rating	Small Company Capability Rating	Best Approach
Basic discovery	D	F	Individual/laboratory
Innovative production	C	B	Engineering team/R&D partnership
Prototype introduction	B	A	Entrepreneural group/VC start-up
Volume manufacturing and marketing	A	D	Large company/merger
Market maturity	F	C	Focused management/ divest (leveraged buyout)

VENTURE CAPITAL TECHNIQUES

In selecting a venturing approach, companies may choose to use one strategy or a combination of several strategies. These can be classified as new ventures divisions, wholly owned ventures, R&D partnerships, spinouts and divestitures, new-style joint ventures, direct venture capital, outside partnership investments, and venture monitoring.

New ventures divisions are responsible, as a rule, for investigating new business opportunities, developing business plans for new ventures, and managing the early commercialization of these ventures. They usually start by developing internally generated new product or service concepts. Management is drawn from inside the company, is not given entrepreneurial rewards, and returns to positions inside the parent corporation if the new venture fails. While 30 percent of the Fortune 100 companies have tried this approach,[4] it has rarely met with success.

Wholly owned ventures represent a modification of the new-ventures-division technique. The entrepreneur is kept or thrust outside the company (giving up any rights to return), talent is added from outside, and provision is made for appropriate rewards, with project closure if the new venture fails. Companies such as Xerox, Burroughs, and Teradyne have reported success with this method.

R&D partnerships involve the corporation as the general partner, and usually individual investors as limited partners, in an independent entity designed to develop a specific product that is to be produced and marketed by the parent corporation.

Spinouts and divestitures are methods by which corporations may get their greatest value from operations that are no longer strategically relevant. A divestiture to a leveraged buyout group can frequently be concluded at a high price because of tax considerations. In some cases, the corporation may also retain a part of the equity on which it can cash in after a public offering, which may be made at a higher price/earnings ratio than that carried by the parent.

New-style joint ventures are arrangements whereby a large company engages with small companies through marketing agreements, technology licenses, exclusive manufacturing rights, or even earn-out acquisitions. These arrangements may take the place of direct venture investments or supplement the direct approach. However, it should be noted that results have been mixed.[5]

Direct venture capital has become more and more popular in the last five years,[6] and outside partnership investment is the most rapidly growing venture technique. It is estimated that some 100 industrial companies have invested one billion dollars in over 100 partnerships for strategic purposes.

Venture monitoring is the systematic tracking of firms backed by venture capitalists, and while conventionally it is carried out in conjunction with outside partnership investments, it may also be divorced from that approach.

THE VENTURE CAPITAL INDUSTRY

The techniques listed above can best be understood through an examination of the venture capital industry and by a review of its history.

Definition of Venture Capital

Venture capital can be optimally defined by considering what venture capitalists do. They create new businesses, as well as expand or revitalize existing ones, by making high-risk, high-reward investments in entrepreneurs. They carry out intensive analyses and investigations prior to investment, much like the work done by a corporation for a potential acquisition.

Venture capitalists negotiate financial structures using individualized investment instruments, and they maintain a long-term orientation toward their portfolio companies, as would be expected with such generally illiquid investments.

Venture capital is unique in relation to all other types of investing because of the value added to portfolio companies by the direct and continuing involvement of the investors.

Venture capitalists try to maximize the growth of their investees, since they usually receive, as incentive compensation, a percentage of the capital gains after return of capital.

History of Venture Capital

It is difficult to date the precise inception of the organized venture capital industry in the United States. In fact, groups of domestic and European investors in the late nineteenth and early twentieth centuries were responsible for financing the development of several new industries, including railroads, steel, petroleum, and glass. However, a landmark date for the computer industry was 1911, when a group of wealthy individuals financed and merged three weak companies—International Time Recording Company, Tabulating Machine Company, and Computing Scale Company—into a single manufacturer and marketer of office equipment. They were wise enough to recruit Thomas Watson as its president in 1914. In 1924, the firm's name was changed to International Business Machines.

The modern venture capital era is generally considered to have begun after World War II; it was given much of its impetus by Laurance Rockefeller, who even prior to that time had helped finance Eastern Airlines in 1938 and McDonnell Douglas in 1939. Other wealthy family groups, many of whom had made their fortunes in earlier ventures, also became active venture capitalists. These included the Phippses (Carnegie Steel) and the Whitneys (John Hay Whitney and his sister Joan Payson, heirs to the Vanderbilt fortune).

The formation of American Research and Development (now part of Textron) in 1946 was another landmark event because AR&D was the first venture organization open to public investment, and by being the sole backer of Digital Equipment Corporation, turned a 70,000-dollar investment into 490 million dollars market value.[7]

The 1950s saw several new companies founded, with government R&D contracting as their major business. Several not-for-profit research groups associated with universities spun out and prospered in defense-oriented areas. These included Itek, now a part of Litton, in reconnaissance; GCA in geophysics; Tracor in undersea warfare; and Conductron, now a part of McDonnell Douglas, in radar signal processing.

In the late 1950s and early 1960s, a number of successful organizations were formed by large groups that left the major data processing companies. Examples are Control Data, founded in 1958 by a group from Univac; Memorex, now a part of Burroughs, founded in 1961 by people from Ampex; Scientific Data Systems (later acquired by Xerox), founded in 1964 by Packard-Bell personnel; and Mohawk Data Sciences, founded in 1965 by a Univac spinout. Two successes of this period can be traced to the concept of gathering a number of smaller technological firms under a single corporate wing. Litton Industries, founded in 1952, and Teledyne, founded in 1961, were created in this manner. Other venture-capital-backed success stories, such as Digital Equipment and Raychem, spun out of nonprofit organizations to commercialize new products.

Drawn by the large gains, many new groups entered the venture capital field in the 1960s and 1970s. Unfortunately, the decline of the public market for new issues in 1970, followed by its collapse in 1974 and 1975, drove most of the new entities from the arena (see Exhibit 19-2).

Resurgence of Conventional Venture Capital

The conventional venture capital industry blossomed again after 1978 for several reasons, including the capital gains tax reduction, improved liquidity that resulted from changes in SEC regulations, attractive acquisition prices for small technological companies, and a revitalized public market for high-growth companies. These factors led to substantial portfolio returns for most venture capital partnerships over the past five years (generally ranging from 20–40 percent compounded annually), as against a flat stock market.[8] In turn, these high returns led to a resurgence of the industry and the formation of many new independent private firms. In 1984, these firms raised 3.2 billion dollars (up from 170 million dollars in 1979) and about 80 corporations contributed 419 million dollars of this total (see Exhibit 19-3).

Current State of the Industry

In the last several years, high interest rates and the tight money environment for small companies have made funding growth through venture capital a very attractive alternative. In addition, the volatile new issues market has

EXHIBIT 19-2.   Small Company New Issues

Year	Number of Companies	Total Raised ($ millions)
1968	358	$ 745
1969	698	1367
1970	198	375
1971	248	551
1972	409	896
1973	69	160
1974	9	16
1975	4	16
1976	29	145
1977	30	118
1978	37	206
1979	73	368
1980	185	1306
1981	390	2646
1982	153	1131
1983	611	5740
1984	265	1682

Note: All statistics on the venture capital and new issues market have been compiled by *The Venture Capital Journal,* Capital Publishing, Wellesley Hills, Mass.

been an uncertain funding source. Thus, companies have found it preferable to accept money at lower valuations from venture capitalists, rather than to rely on the uncertain public market. While 1983 was a record year for IPOs, with 611 small companies (companies with net worth less that 10 million dollars when they went public) raising about 5.7 billion dollars, the new issues market was very depressed in 1984.

The number of new issues, historically, has varied considerably. In fact, in 1969, more companies went public than in 1983 (698 small companies), while in 1975, only four small companies went public, raising 16 million dollars.

EXHIBIT 19-3.   Capital Commitments to Independent Private Firms

	1979	1980	1981	1982	1983	1984
Pension funds	$ 53	$197	$200	$ 474	$1070	$1085
Individuals and families	39	102	201	290	707	573
Insurance companies	7	88	132	200	410	467
Foreign	26	55	90	188	531	463
Corporations	28	127	142	175	415	419
Endowments and foundations	17	92	102	96	267	178
Total	$170	$661	$867	$1423	$3400	$3185

In contrast to the fluctuations of the public market, the venture capital community consistently increased the amount of money put into small companies (see Exhibit 19-4). In 1975 there were new capital commitments of 10 million dollars made to venture capital groups, and 4.2 billion dollars in 1984. This dramatic influx of venture capital brought about the question, Has too much money come into the venture capital business?, but in 1984 commitments leveled off. However, even in 1983, consideration of the other columns in Exhibit 19-4 shows that there was at no time an excess of venture capital. The second column shows disbursements to portfolio, which had been higher than new capital commitments every year until 1983. In 1983, for the first time since 1978, new capital commitments into venture capital groups (4.1 billion dollars), exceeded disbursements to portfolios of 2.8 billion dollars. Industry size, which includes committed capital, has grown quite substantially, from 2.5 billion dollars in 1975 to 16.2 billion dollars in 1984. However, the venture capital community does not take all its money down at the time it is committed. Typically, the large funds will take down money over a period of three to five years, and even the funds that take all their money up front will invest over a period of two or three years. Thus, even in 1983 the situation that actually existed was that of a money shortage.

The most important comparison is that between industry liquidity and disbursements to portfolio. It can be seen that there has been about one year's worth of liquidity in the system. What this means is that if the venture capital community were to cease raising money, it would run out of money within a year. The venture capital community is, therefore, always in the process of raising money to keep itself in business for another year.

Industry liquidity is defined as the amount in money equivalents available to venture capitalists, as opposed to capital that is locked up into investments or still in the hands of investors who have not yet provided all the funds committed to partnerships.

EXHIBIT 19-4.   *Venture Capital Industry Fundings and Disbursements ($ millions)*

Year	New Capital Committed to V.C. Groups	Disbursements to Portfolio	Industry Size	Industry Liquidity
1975	$ 10	$ 250	$ 2,500	$ 200
1976	50	300	2,700	300
1977	39	400	3,000	400
1978	570	550	3,500	500
1979	319	1,000	4,000	500
1980	900	1,100	4,500	1,000
1981	1,300	1,400	5,800	1,200
1982	1,750	1,800	7,600	1,600
1983	4,100	2,800	11,500	3,000
1984	4,200	3,000	16,200	2,400

Of the 4.2 billion dollars that came into the venture business in 1984, about 3.2 billion dollars was raised by partnerships. Two hundred million dollars was raised by the SBICs, and 800 million dollars came into the banks, insurance companies, and industrial corporations, adding to their previous investments. (That 4.2 billion dollars exceeds the 3 billion dollars invested, and it increased the capital base 41 percent, but industry liquidity actually declined 20 percent).

One concern is whether this money is attracting inexperienced individuals into venture capital who lack the ability to assist their investees. However, only 43 new firms entered the field in 1984, increasing those active to about 340, up only 11 percent. Furthermore, most of the new firms were started with at least one experienced venture capitalist as a partner.

A breakdown of where the 16 billion dollars resides is given in Exhibit 19-5. Private venture capital partnerships (about 274) have about 11.4 billion dollars available for ventures. Wealthy individuals and families constituted the earliest venture capital sources and some—such as the Rockefellers (Venrock), Phippses (Bessemer Securities), Rothschilds (New Court), Watsons and Cornings (Greylock), and Whitneys—continue to be very active. "Wall Street = organized" partnerships—such as those sponsored by Hambrecht and Quist; Smith Barney; Paine Webber; Donaldson Lufkin; L.F. Rothschild, Unterberg, Towbin; Robertson, Colman; and Alex Brown—have been more recent venture capitalists. Independent organizations funded by financial institutions, pension funds, and corporations are the newest, but fastest-growing, group. Old-timers in this category include T.A. Associates, EMW Ventures, and Institutional Venture Associates.

Small business investment companies (SBICs) are licensed by the government to invest in "small" companies. Businesses with net worths under 6 million dollars and average after-tax profits of under 2 million dollars, for the previous two years, or who meet industry-based employment tests, are

EXHIBIT 19-5.   The Venture Capital Industry

Source of Venture Funds	Amount Available ($ billions)	Number of Contributors
Private pools	$11.4	274
Wealthy families		
Investment banker affiliates		
Independent entities		
SBICs	1.6	360
Financial institutions	1.6	25
Bank SBICs		
Insurance companies		
Industrial corporations	1.4	40
Total	$16.0	340+

eligible. There are currently about 360 active SBICs commanding about 1.6 billion dollars.

Financially related corporations seeking high returns on investment have been important participants in the industry for some time. There are currently about 25 active groups, including insurance companies such as Allstate, Prudential, John Hancock, and Aetna, and banks such as Citibank, Manufacturers Hanover Trust, BankAmerica, First Chicago, Continental Illinois, Security Pacific, Wells Fargo, and Bank of Boston. They are estimated to have approximately 1.6 billion dollars set aside for venture capital.

Industrial corporations comprise the smallest pool of venture capitalists. About 40 U.S. firms are believed to have set aside about 1.4 billion dollars for this purpose.

Where Do Venture Dollars Go?

In 1984, about 1337 companies were financed out of 10,000 proposals presented to the venture capital community. Venture capitalists are still quite selective, and are not running out of entrepreneurs in need of financing.

Most of the money goes into the technology areas (see Exhibit 19-6)—72 percent to the information industry, 10 percent to the medical industry, 2 percent to energy, 5 percent to other technologies such as lasers, and 11 percent to nontechnological industries. That nontechnology sector on the table includes leveraged buy-outs. The leveraged buy-out industry is included here as part of the venture capital industry, even though it is in many ways quite different.

Early-stage deals take about 34 percent of the money (see Exhibit 19-7). Three percent of these are seed financings. Seed financing occurs when a group, having just left an organization, is provided with a small amount of capital to prove a concept or to write a plan. Start-up financing, with 13 percent of venture dollars, is for product development, not for research and development. Except for a few specialized funds, venture capitalists do not

EXHIBIT 19-6.   Where Venture Dollars Go

1337 Companies out of 10,000 proposals		
72% Information industry		
10% Medical		
2% Energy		
5% Other technology (lasers/instruments/robotics)		
11% Nontechnology		
Seed/start-ups:	300 Companies:	$2.0 million average
First stage:	280 Companies:	2.7 million average
Later-stage:	640 Companies:	3.6 million average
LBOs/other:	120 Companies:	3.6 million average

EXHIBIT 19-7.   *Disbursements by Financing Stage (Percent of dollar amount invested)*

	1981	1982	1983	1984
Seed	2%	2%	2%	3%
Start-up	22	17	12	13
Other early stage	18	17	21	18
Total early stage	42	36	35	34
Second stage	28	30	36	36
Later stage	16	22	18	18
Total expansion	44	52	54	54
LBO/acquisition		8	9	9
Other		4	3	3
Total Other	14	12	12	12
TOTAL	100%	100%	100%	100%

typically provide money for research and development. Venture capitalists try to invest in companies that are trying to commercialize development within a year. First-stage financing, at 18 percent, is used to initiate manufacturing and begins after the prototype has been developed.

Expansion dollars (with 55 percent of venture dollars invested) is the next broad category.

Second-stage financing takes place when a company is shipping its product, but is still unprofitable and needs the money to finance its growth. Third-stage financing takes place when a company is profitable, but needs expansion capital. Fourth-stage is a bridge financing to a public offering/merger. Sometimes the later stages disappear when the public market is very aggressive and investment bankers are willing to underwrite even companies that are losing money.

EXHIBIT 19-8.   *Venture Capital Investments by Industry (percent of dollars)*

	1980	1981	1982	1983	1984
Computers	26%	30%	42%	46%	43%
Electronics	10	12	14	10	13
Communications	11	11	10	13	16
Genetic engineering	8	7	3	3	2
Medical/health	9	6	6	9	8
Energy	20	10	6	3	2
Industrial automation	3	4	3	2	5
Consumer-related	2	5	5	7	6
Other	8	10	7	5	5
	100%	100%	100%	100%	100%

EXHIBIT 19-9.   *Disbursements by Geographic Area*

	1970–79	1981	1982	1983	1984
West Coast	30%	42%	48%	52%	48%
Northeast	33	25	26	24	26
Southwest	12	16	13	10	12
Midwest	12	8	8	7	8
Southeast	10	5	5	7	8
Other	—	4	—	—	—

The final category includes turn-around investments made to sick companies, leveraged buyouts, and public market investments. The purchase of stock over-the-counter would not be considered a venture capital investment unless the venture group was also involved in providing assistance to the investee.

To illustrate the course of disbursements by the industry over the years, Exhibit 19-8 shows that investments in computers have grown relative to other types. Genetic engineering, which was quite popular back in 1980, and energy have declined, while most of the other areas have remained in relatively the same position.

It is also interesting to note disbursements by geographic area (see Exhibit 19-9). As might be expected, Silicon Valley and the West Coast have grown in importance. California alone now commands about 44 percent of all venture dollars invested. The Northeast remains at 26 percent. Massachusetts, with Route 128, another famous technological center, has received about 14 percent of venture dollars.

Recently, there has been a move toward formation of groups in other parts of the country, in the hope that when money becomes available entrepreneurs will materialize.

There is also a small amount of venture capital being invested outside the United States by venture capitalists. Of the disbursements to portfolio of 3 billion dollars in 1984, less than 100 million dollars went outside the United States.

THE VENTURE PROCESS

It is important to understand the venture process in order to understand what the next decade is likely to hold in store.

Venture capital funds show good results because small companies afford excellent investment prospects or risk/reward ratios. They typically outperform large companies in terms of their ability to grow rapidly. These small, rapid-growth companies are valued highly in the marketplace—in the public market as well as by large companies. They make excellent acquisitions for large companies that are anxious to acquire their technologies and move them into their manufacturing and marketing channels.

Venture capitalists are also able to structure favorable instruments. The venture capitalist is able to invest at lower price/earnings ratios than are available in the public market. If the public market is going to pay ten times earnings for a company growing 25–30 percent a year, the venture capitalist might pay five times earnings. The venture capitalist almost never buys common stock. But, if he or she should, he or she always sets some priorities over the common held by the entrepreneurs. However, most frequently the venture capitalist purchases some sort of senior security—a convertible preferred, a convertible debt, or debt with warrants. The venture capitalist always obtains a senior position, so that if the company should not prosper and should have to be sold at a low price, he or she can get out first, leaving the entrepreneur with virtually nothing. While that may seem unfair, it is the venture capitalist's protection against the entrepreneur's walking away or trying to sell the company, leaving the investors with a loss. Frequently, there is an adjustable share price, so if the company does not make its projections or does not perform as expected, or if additional money comes in at a lower price, the share price goes down. Venture capitalists have a variety of protections on their investments that are impossible to get in the public market.

A great deal of value-added exists in the venture investment process in the way it is performed by experienced venture capitalists. That comes about through selection from the deal stream, monitoring/control, and the augmentation of the entrepreneur as appropriate.

The first step in the venture capital process involves selection from the deal stream, the proposals that are received by a venture capitalist. Typically, the first three years of a venture partnership are spent looking at these proposals, analyzing them, and making investments. The next eight years comprise the monitoring and control stage, and are spent in assisting the investees. From the fourth year to the eighth year, exiting from some of these investments takes place.

In selecting from the deal stream, the typical venture firm sees 50–100 business plans a month, generally makes quick checks on 40 percent of them, meets to discuss 20 percent of them for more than an hour, makes counterproposals to 4 percent, and investments in 1–2 percent. It is a very selective process (see Exhibit 19-10).

Proposals may come in directly from the companies, from finders, or from other venture capitalists. Greatest attention is paid to opportunities that come from other venture capitalists, because venture capitalists like to coinvest in order to expand the expertise that can be provided to their portfolio companies.

After the proposal arrives, it is logged in, a rapid assessment is made, quick checks are done, priorities are determined, brief meetings are held, and, generally, a counterprorosal on price and terms is made to the few

EXHIBIT 19-10.   *Investigating a Venture Deal*

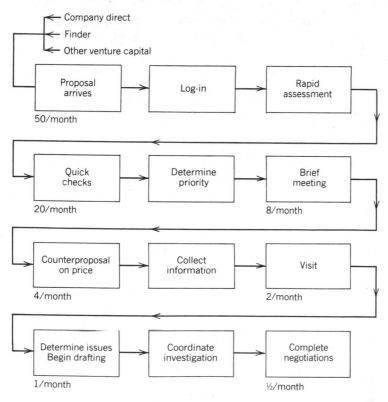

Process takes 1-6 months

deals that remain active prospects. It is rare for the valuation proposed by the entrepreneur to be accepted by the venture capitalist. Then, information is collected, visits are made, and negotiating issues are determined. That process can take as long as six months.

Venture capitalists use certain criteria to select those deals from the deal stream that are worth spending some time with. First among these is compatibility of goals. Venture capitalists are not interested in an entrepreneur whose ambition is to build a 5 million-dollar company that will provide him or her with a high salary. They seek, rather, the person whose goal is to develop a major corporation—one that is unique and preeminent in its field—from which he or she will get rich, either by having the company go public or by selling it to another large corporation. There are entrepreneurs who say, "I have just left a large company and have no intention of losing my independence again." Those would not be suitable venture capital investments, because many venture capital investments are liquidated through sale to a larger company, and such a sale usually requires that key management agree to stay on.

The size of the financing is another important factor. If the entrepreneur wants only $50,000, his or her business will probably be too small to attract venture capitalists.

Venture capitalists examine the pricing and the risk/reward. The kind of return venture capitalists are looking for is the ability to make ten times their money over a five-year period if the company sells at a ten-times price/earnings ratio.

A committed, strong lead investor, such as another venture capitalist, will influence the way a venture capitalist views an opportunity. If there is not a strong lead in the present round, it is desirable that there should have been previous strong investors working with the company over some period of time.

Venture capitalists look for a complete management team. They want a company to have reasonable long-term capital needs, so that it will not be necessary to rely on the public market for financing. They usually want positions on the board of directors. Familiarity with the industry—on the company's part and on theirs—plays a decisive role in venture capitalists' investment decisions. They are looking for people who are sophisticated, so that excessive effort is not required in order to negotiate with them and introduce them to the ways of the venture capital community. Venture capitalists also look for geographic accessibility, but most technological companies do locate themselves conveniently.

After a company has qualified as having met the initial criteria, venture capitalists then look for three particular factors before making an investment:

1. Innovative, superior products and/or services based on proprietary capability and broad technology that offer clear customer benefits. Venture capitalists do not want to be involved in the third company to make an IBM-compatible computer. They are looking for something innovative and unique that can be defensible in the marketplace. That provides better lead time over competition and provides better margins for the company; that, in turn, makes it a valuable acquisition candidate and gives it a high price/earnings ratio in the public market.

2. Companies that are addressing very large rapid-growth markets that will permit the company to grow to 50 million dollars' worth of revenues within five years. What is generally required is a market of at least 100 million dollars that is growing at least 25 percent a year and that has no dominant leader.

3. Superior management, which, to venture capitalists, means a complete management team with integrity, initiative, confidence, commitment, comprehensive business skills, prior profit and loss responsibility, and direct experience in the industry.

Unfortunately, it is not always possible to fulfill all of these desires. But, a perfect deal would be one where the company's goals are to build a profitable, preeminent company with experienced, dedicated people willing to go public or to merge (whichever is better for the shareholders).

Once it has been decided that a company meets the criteria for an investment, further checks are made. These include personal checks on each of the people involved (with their superiors, their peers, and their subordinates), checks with their competition (who are usually quite willing to present arguments against investing in a new competitor), checks with their customers (both current and potential), checks with their suppliers, bankers, CPAs, attorneys, consultants, experts, and trade associations, and, of course, with their prior investors and investment bankers.

That is just the front end of investment, which comprises soliciting proposals, selecting opportunities, analyzing business plans, and negotiating investments. That requires about 30 percent of a venture capitalist's time. About 70 percent of his or her time is spent actually helping the companies: serving as a director, monitoring the company's progress, acting as a consultant and strategic planner, recruiting management, assisting in outside relationships, and exiting.

Among the specific kinds of assistance given by a venture capitalist to portfolio companies are help with budgeting and control techniques, policy matters, personnel recruiting, technology interchange, legal assistance, providing credibility with suppliers, and customer introductions. He or she also may recommend supporting professional services such as attorneys, various kinds of consultants, and recruiters. He or she provides them with advice on their future financing needs and will frequently get involved with important business negotiations. But most of all, the venture capitalist acts as a sounding board for the entrepreneur, so that there is somebody to lean on when assistance and support are needed.

A number of studies have shown that companies backed by venture capitalists have a much higher success ratio than companies that are not. That positive correlation is due to the kind of help given by venture capitalists to growing companies.

DIRECT CORPORATE VENTURE CAPITAL

Despite the relatively small size of their venture capital commitment until very recently, corporations have directly participated in some extremely important ventures throughout this century.

History of Corporate Venture Capital

The first corporate venturer was probably DuPont. In 1919, when one of its important new customers ran out of funds, it purchased a 38 percent equity interest and brought in a new president, Alfred Sloan. General Motors has grown substantially since the time of that investment.

After World War I, American Telephone, General Electric, and Westinghouse bought out the British interests in American Marconi. They subsequently changed the name of their venture to Radio Corporation of America, now RCA.

Right after World War II, a small company named Haloid Corporation funded the commercialization of a new technology developed by Chester Carlson and the Battelle Memorial Institute. Haloid later changed its name to Xerox Corporation.

Another corporate venturer probably became interested in the concept because its largest stockholder was a man whose father had previously been the venture capitalist behind the formation of IBM. Fairchild Camera and Instrument financed a group of eight technologists leaving Shockley Transistor in 1957, and later acquired this venture, Fairchild Semiconductor, the grandfather of many of the companies now populating Silicon Valley.

In the 1960s, many corporations became active venture capitalists seeking a "window on technology." However, the lack of profit orientation and the decline of the market in 1970 brought about the exit of most of those established corporate venture capitalists, including such major names as DuPont, Ford, Alcoa, Union Carbide, Northrop, Scott Paper, and Singer, as well as some newer venturers such as Memorex, California Computer, Dataproducts, Electronic Memories, Mohawk Data, and Applied Magnetics.

Public interest in the stock market recovered in 1971 and 1972, before almost entirely collapsing in 1974 and 1975, driving many other corporate ventures from the business.

Corporations Become More Active

Corporate venture capital activity began its resurgence about the same time as conventional venture capital,[9] fueled mainly by a desire to keep pace with technology developments coupled with an awareness of the success of a few corporate venture groups.

One particular trend has been for domestic and foreign corporations to invest in semiconductor manufacturers in order to assure a viable supplier. The success of such attempts remains to be proven, but the trend has not yet abated. Recent examples include Intel, International Microelectronic Products, LSI Logic, Siliconix, VLSI Technology, Xicor, and Zymos.

Also, at least 35 U.S. Biotech companies have been financed by 38 strategically oriented industrial companies. These include Advanced Genetic Sciences, Biogen, Cetus, Collaborative Research, Genentech, and Genex. Substantial strategic investors in biotechnology start-ups include Allied, American Cyanamid, Dow Chemical, FMC, Inco, Johnson & Johnson, Koppers, Monsanto, National Distillers, Rohm & Haas, Schering-Plough, Standard Oil of Indiana, and Standard Oil of California.

Some noteworthy companies that presently have, or have had, participation by corporate venture capitalists include:

Computers—Amdahl, Apple, Convergent, Cray, Stratus, Tandem, Wang

Medical Electronics—ADAC, Coherent, Cordis, Kolff Medical, Orion Research

Telecommunications—Intecom, Lynch Communications, MCI, Network Systems, Paradyne, Quotron, Rolm, Ungermann-Bass

Terminals—Datapoint, Four-Phase, Lee Data, Ramtek, Syntrex, Telxon

Peripherals—Centronics, Computer Memories, Decision Data, Evans & Sutherland, Seagate

Instruments—Analog Devices, Nicolet, Waters Associates

Miscellaneous—Data Card, Data I/O, Dysan, Federal Express, Key Pharmaceutical, Siltec, Scope, Xidex

A Most Active List

Many corporations have made a single venture capital investment, have entered into a "new-style joint venture" to obtain access to a unique technology, have spun off a single new entity, or have found themselves unwittingly with a share of a customer unable to pay his or her bills. The following discussion, however, lists those industrial companies that seem to be most active in directly providing venture capital.

General Electric has been the most active corporate venture capitalist. However, it has recently shifted its emphasis back to financial returns from strategic considerations.

Xerox has reported the most successful direct venture program, both in terms of corporate impact and financial performance,[10] and continues to be active.

Inco has probably been the most active metals company, and *Johnson & Johnson* is the most active medically oriented venturer, though *Warner-Lambert* has recently become active.

Monsanto and *Emerson* have been investing in technology across the board through an outside partnership, Innoven. Monsanto, in particular, through its investment in Innoven, was able to follow such areas as biotechnology, biomedical, chemistry, radiation equipment and materials, process control, and semiconductors, and subsequently launched a similar fund in London.[11]

Textron (American Research and Development) continues to be an important participant in the financing of technology ventures.

Control Data is investing through a recently formed SBIC and is promoting additional loans and consulting to small businesses through other entities.

Lubrizol has been very successful in biotechnology investments.

Greyhound has been financing primarily computer-related companies, where its leasing activities provide additional benefits.

Perhaps inspired first by *Xerox's* active program, and then by *IBM's* investments in Intel and Rolm, several computer-related companies have recently made several venture investments, among them *Burroughs, NCR, Honeywell,* and *Wang.*

General Instrument and *M/A-COM* have active programs aimed at telecommunications ventures that will utilize their equipment.

Despite the termination of *Exxon's* direct venturing program, several other petroleum companies have become active venture capitalists, including *Texaco* and *Standard Oil of Indiana,* which is also funding *Analog Devices'* active program.

Others who have recently set up organized programs include *Ameritech, Bechtel, Safeguard Scientific, Emerson Radio,* and *Dysan.* The latter is interesting because *Dysan* is itself a venture capital investment of *Rhone-Poulenc* and has financed *Seagate,* which recently invested in *Applied Circuit Technology,* making that the first known great-grandchild corporate investment.

Active foreign companies investing for strategic reasons include *Olivetti* (now working in conjunction with its partial owner, AT&T), *Siemens, BMW, CGE, Kyocera, Mitsubishi,* and *C. Itoh.*

Among the different approaches to corporate venture capital are the following:

Setting up an in-house fund that invests solely and directly into venture situations, like *TRW* and *Kollmorgen.*

Organizing a fund that first invests in partnerships, then begins to invest alongside the partnerships, and finally invests directly into venture companies, such as *Texaco.*

Creating an entity through which the corporation shares the venture capital responsibility with an outside group, *Westinghouse, Ferranti, Elf, BMW,* for instance.

Leveraging an inside group by managing outside limited partnership funds, for example, *Analog Devices, Olivetti, Inco.*

Following the investments made by outside venture capital firms in which the pension fund is investing, such as *Eli Lilly, Sperry, American Hospital Supply.*

Obviously, most companies mix these approaches in various ways. The following pages list many of the most active corporate venturers and the approaches that they have chosen.

Strategic venture investing has spread beyond corporations to political entities. In the United States, several states, including Massachusetts, Connecticut, New York, Minnesota, and Michigan, have organized small venture capital-type entities. Other states have encouraged their pension funds to invest in locally organized venture partnerships, as has been done in Ohio. Various cities, such as New Haven and, prospectively, Cleveland and Cincinnati, have organized funds.

Canada Development Corporation was set up by the federal government to make direct venture investments to create jobs. More recently, Ontario organized IDEA Corporation to fund other venture partnerships, while Alberta has sponsored Vencap Equities Alberta Ltd. to sponsor economic diversity.

European political entities that provide funds to U.S. venture situations and/or partnerships for the purpose of attracting business include England (as well as several municipalities therein), Scotland, Belgium (Flanders and Wallonia, separately), the Netherlands, and Finland.

Corporate Investors Have Advantages

A corporation that invests directly in venture situations can offer many benefits beyond, or different from, the valuable assistance provided by conventional venture capitalists. Corporations may provide:

Assistance in almost all facets of corporate endeavor, for example, setting up financial systems, qualifying suppliers, and meeting government regulations.

Credibility with customers, banks, and other investors, both from a technical and financial standpoint.

Relief, if desired, from the full range of corporate activities; for instance, the corporate investor may take on marketing responsibilities or may license the product.

Immediate income from an R&D or consulting contract, if appropriate.

Customer interface with an interested party.

An investor with an infinite lifetime, though his or her time horizon for profitability will be shorter.

Additional forms of capital, such as lease guarantees, where warranted.

A merger partner, if and when appropriate.

A more flexible financing package, since return on investment may not be the only criterion.

Many Corporations Have Failed as Direct Ventures

Many companies that once were active in the venture capital business are no longer direct participants. A partial listing of former corporate investors includes the following:

Alcoa	Hercules
American Hospital Supply	Hughes
Applied Magnetics	Itel
Boise Cascade	Memorex
Boothe	Mobil
California Computer	Mohawk Data
Chemetron	Monsanto
Diamond Shamrock	Northrop
Dow	Reliance
DuPont	Schlumberger
Eaton	Scott Paper
Electronic Memories	Singer
Exxon	Studebaker
Firestone	Sun
Ford	Tracor
General Dynamics	Union Carbide
General Telephone & Electric	Weyerhaeuser

A recent survey of corporate venture capital organizations made by Tektronix states that only seven percent of corporate venture capital organizations regard themselves as being very successful, with over half not even rating themselves as marginal successes.[12] The difficulties experienced by a corporation seeking to become a venture capitalist usually arise from one of the sources dicussed below.

Lack of Appropriately Skilled People

A venture capitalist must be entrepreneurially motivated, patient, realistically optimistic, proficient at negotiations, persuasive, and able to evaluate people, as well as businesses, skillfully. He or she must also be more than merely familiar with accounting principles, tax regulations, corporate finance structures, securities analysis, and securities law. Good internal people frequently are unwilling to leave a company's mainstream activities even if they possess the appropriate skills. Experienced people from the outside are difficult to attract and retain without special compensation packages, which are almost impossible to structure, since corporations find it difficult to provide an incentive bonus arrangement.[13]

With the improved environment for conventional venture capital, corporations have lost qualified people at an accelerating rate as independent partnerships have become more and more financially rewarding.

Contradictory Rationales

A corporate venture capital program may find it difficult to act in the best interests of both the investee company and the parent. For example, if the goal of the venture group is to acquire, then equity financing by others is undesirable; if the rationale is an exclusive marketing arrangement or a preferred supplier role, then the investee's operations may be unduly limited. A parent company's desire for continuous profit increases is also incompatible with the normal results of a venture operation.

The entire problem can be exacerbated by a skewed or shifting reporting structure. For example, having the venture group report to the vice president of finance is likely to shift the focus to profitability. Similarly, the group's reporting to the vice president of R&D might shift the focus to technology, and reporting to the vice president of corporate planning might shift the focus to market information, and so on.

Through the utilization of an outside partnership, the interface can remain consistent, even if the rationale for venture investing changes. In addition, the partnership can insure that the benefits are exposed to all the appropriate corporate groups.

Legal Problems

A corporate venturer must be extremely careful to organize the activities so that they will not run afoul of conflict of interest problems, including fiduciary responsibility and corporate opportunity doctrines, which, respectively, require the substantial investor to scrupulously maintain the rights of the other investors and require the corporate director to give first refusal of new business opportunities to the investee, rather than to his employer. Several corporations have left the field incorrectly believing that such legal strictures precluded their deriving strategic benefits from a venture activity. Nevertheless, problems can arise unless the investments are made by a group sensitive to the necessary legal procedures. Separating the responsibilities for assisting the investee and for obtaining strategic benefits can be helpful in this regard.

Inadequate Time Horizon

A venture portfolio usually experiences its losses and problems early, while the successes take more time to develop than anticipated. Unless a firm commitment is made for at least seven to ten years, a corporate venture fund is often terminated during those early problem years. This is one rationale for investing through an outside fund, where the individual investments are insulated and the internal corporate group does not have to divert its efforts toward explaining why a particular investment is not meeting its forecasts.

In addition, venture investing frequently has been the "baby" of a single member of management and has been cancelled at his or her departure. Finally, internal people often regard venturing as a temporary assignment, and hence do not have the appropriate long-term orientation necessary for success in venture capital.

The longevity of even successful corporate funds seems not to extend beyond six years. Though the reasons are varied, they frequently seem to involve staff departures during a healthy economic environment, funding cancellation in a recession, and change of emphasis by a new CEO.

Outside Partnership Investments

For these reasons many corporations have begun to invest in venture capital partnerships either as an alternative, as a first step, and/or as a supplement to a direct venture capital program. The following list names a few of these companies.

As an Alternative	As a First Step	As a Supplement
3M	Texaco	Xerox
American Hospital Supply	WR Grace	Koppers
GTE	Inco	General Electric
Monsanto	Westinghouse	Olivetti

Several corporations that have arranged to share the general partner role in outside partnerships include Westinghouse, Siemens, Olivetti, and Standard Oil of Ohio.

Others that have provided funds to groups with whom they then work closely to supplement their own programs include Xerox, GE, Koppers, Olin, Merck, Eli Lilly, Raytheon, Northern Telecom, Honeywell, United Telecom, Schering-Plough, EG&G, Tandy, Corning, Texaco, and Allied.

Many corporations monitor venture activities through the partnerships in which their pension funds have invested. These include AT&T, GTE, US West, Warner-Lambert, Owens-Illinois, Pitney-Bowes, and Eaton.

Making Direct Venture Investments

As we have seen, the advantages of direct corporate venture capital may be outweighed by the disadvantages unless the activity is organized with great care.

Direct venture investment offers the advantage of permitting the structuring of unique relationships and provides an avenue for the development of rapport with the investee companies. However, the disadvantages are many: difficulty in obtaining appropriate staff, potential legal liabilities, expectation of being the funding source of last resort, and vulnerability to internal shifts that confuse the program. Furthermore, corporate venture capitalists are not well-received by the venture capital community, because of suspicion regarding their motives and doubts of their longevity and thus the flow of projects is restrained.

In addition, corporate venture capitalists must spend the great majority of their time working with the venture situation in ways that do not benefit their corporations' strategic needs, but are required of credible venture capitalists. They must spend their time soliciting proposals, analyzing business plans, investigating opportunities that pass the initial screen, negotiating investments, serving on boards (monitoring the companies' results), acting as consultants (particularly in strategy and financial planning), recruiting management, and assisting in outside relationships by making introductions, lending credibility, and helping in negotiations. Thus venture capitalists can rarely work effectively with more than five corporations. If they do not share in the work of assisting the investees, they will not be invited to participate in other venture capitalists' investment opportunities.

Nevertheless, a direct venture operation can be carried out inside a corporation by appropriate planning and organization of the activity, within the following parameters:

1. *Motivation/Goals.* Set the objectives clearly. Make sure that everyone understands and agrees with them. For example, if the group is expected to undertake high-risk technology start-ups, early losses and some liquidations should be anticipated.

2. *Staffing/Compensation.* Combine experienced venture capitalists with corporate staff. While there is no substitute for venture investment experience, executives from inside the company should also be encouraged to join the program. In this way, optimum and mutually beneficial coupling can be made between the strategic planning function and the group. An imaginative compensation scheme that facilitates the attraction of outside and inside personnel is a must.

3. *Investment Rate/Size of Group.* Provide realistic resources. Do not set up a group that is too small for the desired investment program. In addition to monitoring and assisting five venture investments, an individual can add about two new ones a year.

4. *Reporting/Decision Making.* Permit appropriate autonomy. Venture groups need flexibility in order to work effectively with rapid-growth businesses. If the group reports at a low level and requires concurrence from other parts of the corporation for its actions, then timely decisions will never be made.

5. *Longevity/Time Horizon.* Make a long-term commitment. Problems will arise, and the venture activity will experience criticism. Unless

it is the firm intention to continue the program for at least seven years, a venture activity should not be organized.

6. *Coinvesting/External Visibility.* Become well-known. Join industry associations and discuss your motivations. Successful venture capitalists syndicate projects among themselves. It will take time to be accepted, but bringing in experienced people from the outside will help in this area.

XEROX DEVELOPMENT CORPORATION: A DIRECT VENTURE CAPITAL SUCCESS STORY

Xerox Development Corporation (XDC) is the best example of a direct, strategic venture capital program that was totally incorporated into the corporate development and corporate planning process, and was the most successful program of its kind.

XDC was started as a wholly-owned subsidiary of Xerox in 1975. People with venture capital experience were brought in from outside Xerox to meld with corporate planners from inside Xerox. It was the first corporate development venture capital program to provide incentives in order to bring in people from the outside. It was structured as a partnership, with each of the individuals having the title of Principal and with a shared bonus incentive. XDC was organized in a rather free-form manner, really on a project task basis.

The charter of XDC was very broad. XDC was in charge of acquisitions, divestitures, joint ventures, licensing, strategic planning, wholly owned "new ventures," and venture capital for Xerox. Venture capital was just one of the arrows in Xerox's corporate development quiver. XDC's staff included three very experienced venture capitalists, two experienced investment bankers, several entrepreneurs, two full-time attorneys, a financial vice president who had been financial vice president of one of the Fortune 500 companies, security analysts, corporate strategists, a technical wizard, and a management audit person, who did an audit of people and their goals and aspirations alongside the legal and financial audit. Altogether about 16 people worked on the program at its peak.

Among the investment criteria for XDC was the guideline that each investment had to be in a business area appropriate for Xerox and its interests. For example, XDC did not go into biotechnology, despite the awareness that it was probably a good growth area. The other criteria followed by XDC were clearly stated. XDC invested only in management teams led by entrepreneurs and insisted that the investments provide an attractive, although not a maximum, financial return. Most importantly, XDC invested only in companies that were willing to work with Xerox in whichever way Xerox wanted to work with them. That could involve a technology transfer, a marketing information transfer, etc. Because of potential legal problems, XDC was organized so that before an investment was made, a contractual arrangement was finalized whereby all information transferred was nonconfidential. To avoid some of the corporate opportunity problems, XDC did not take any board positions. The responsibility for each investment was split between someone who monitored the progress of the company and another person who insured that the company's technology, market information, and other assets were flowing back into Xerox.

The information received through its venture program led XDC, in turn, to bring Xerox into a number of excellent acquisitions. The ventures were in areas such as telecommunications, data communication, voice recognition, home computers, computer stores, power supplies, CAD/CAM, PROM programmers—all areas that held interest and potential for Xerox. The areas that Xerox entered through acquisition include peripherals, now worth over a billion dollars for Xerox; telecommunications, eventually divested at a profit, and software. These acquisitions came about because of information received through the venture capital program. The business areas explored by Xerox through venturing form a long list. The areas that Xerox entered because of information it obtained from its venture capital program include peripheral equipment to OEMs, local area networks, software packages, disc media, slide making, computer systems, data base services, retail stores, leasing, telecommunications services, optical character recognition, personal computers, and electronic typewriters. Although Xerox has subsequently divested itself of several of these areas, it has, overall, done so at a substantial profit.

Of equal benefit was the fact that information gleaned from the venture program prevented Xerox from entering unsuitable areas, such as merchant semiconductors and PABXs, that resulted in high losses to other large corporations.

Xerox Development Corporation, during its five-year tenure, led Xerox into new, profitable areas, developed new products for them, commercialized outside technology, and provided for a strategic plan in microelectronics, the introduction of new marketing concepts, the acquisition of two venture companies, and a return on investment of over 100 percent per year compounded.

PARTNERSHIP BENEFITS

Many corporations have invested in outside partnerships for strategic purposes, as either a replacement for or a supplement to direct venture investing.

An investment in a partnership has several advantages. It provides the opportunity to attract good people; problem investments become less visible; management time is conserved; a long-term commitment is assured; many legal liabilities are eliminated; and, if desired, additional opportunities can be provided for direct investment, acquisition, or obtaining information.

Partnership investment can also serve as a supplement to direct corporate venture capital, in that the internal group can utilize the partnership to handle much of the monitoring and assistance load. The main disadvantages of relying solely on indirect venturing are that there will be lesser concentration on areas of interest and there could be potential embarrassment from an investment in a competitor, unless there is an agreement in advance on areas in which to invest. The corporation will, in addition, have to utilize some of its newfound time to establish direct rapport with important investments.

Selecting a Venture Capital Partnership

In picking a venture capital partnership in which to invest, it is important to consider the track records and backgrounds of the proposed general partners. Have they been involved in all the phases of venture capital—in finding and analyzing the investment, in negotiating the transaction, in assisting the entrepreneur, and in exiting? One should obtain references from companies in which they have had investments and from individuals who have coinvested with them. However, to a corporation, the most important considerations will be the managers' sensitivity to normal corporate procedures, which can be best assured if they have worked inside a corporate venture capital situation previously, and if they are willing to work closely on strategic needs.

The corporation, having decided to invest in an independent venture capital partnership, has two alternatives. The investment may be made in a traditional firm that tries to maximize return. Such firms will not accept much, if any, direction from their investors, but they also relieve the corporation of involvement in the investments while providing a window on the industry.

A comparatively recent alternative is the semidedicated group, which attempts to maximize the strategic benefits of venture capital for its investors. Such firms will expect and accept corporate involvement and direction.

A semidedicated venture partnership can provide the corporate investor with memos on all investments, giving a description of the technology and the market size and growth; make introductions to investee companies; provide a summary of all rejected investments; hold quarterly meetings to review the activity and forecast trends, and offer consulting sessions in which important developments and suggested projects can be reviewed in depth. The partners may also provide consulting assistance in strategic planning, acquisition evaluations, internal venture analysis, and commercialization of unwanted corporate technology.

In a typical relationship with a semidedicated venture partnership, the corporate investor will assist in evaluation of projects that are within his or her area of interest, provide a test bed for new products, pass along investors whom the corporation does not wish to assist directly, suggest areas for investment, act on an advisory panel, and occasionally provide consulting to investee companies in specialized areas such as patents or foreign relationships.

SPINOUTS AND DIVESTITURES

A spinout or divestiture can be facilitated by the use of leveraged buyout techniques. The leveraged buyout (or LBO) is the purchase of an entity with largely borrowed capital. There are at least 50 venture groups specializing in this type of transaction, and many others participate occasionally. It has been estimated that as many as half of all divestitures may now be financed using such techniques.

The advantages of an LBO to a divesting company are several:

1. The highest price may be available because the buying group will be able to deduct interest on the borrowed funds and will generally be able to deduct high depreciation charges from taxable income. (In one variation, where assets are sold for less than book, a tax refund may be obtainable.)
2. Employees will be able to participate, thereby building good feelings, while a divestiture to another operating company will usually result in redundant management.
3. Retention of some of the equity may be possible, resulting in a capital gain opportunity if the divested entity is successful.
4. Most importantly, new entrepreneurial management which can have a dramatic impact on profitability, can be attracted through stock ownership.

An excellent example of this approach was the divestiture by Campbell Soup of its biotechnology research into DNA Plant Technology.

R&D PARTNERSHIPS

The use of R&D limited partnerships by start-up companies as a less expensive method of financing has been popular since 1974, when it became clear that expenses could be deducted from an individual's income. Notable failures include Lear Fan, DeLorean, and Trilogy. In recent years the technique has begun to be used by major public corporations, such as Emerson, Control Data, Becton-Dickinson, Cummins Engine and Storage Technology, as well as many biotechnology firms that are not yet profitable.

In both cases, this venture capital–related technique permits a corporation to develop new products with no immediate impact on earnings, with limited impact if the project is unsuccessful, and generally with less impact on earnings per share even if the project is successful (although highly successful programs may eventually be more expensive).

Equity R&D partnerships broadly involve the corporation's acquiring the position of the limited partners in return for shares upon successful termination of the development phase.

Royalty R&D partnerships provide for the licensing of the technology back to the corporate sponsor (who manufactures and markets products using the technology) in return for royalties, which enjoy favorable tax treatment.

In either case, individual investors are willing to provide funding on improved terms because of the favorable tax considerations. Thus, several major brokerage firms have assembled "blind pools" to finance such partnerships, while others package groups of such partnerships or sell individual ones separately. Nonetheless, at this writing, returns to investors in R&D partnerships have predominantly been negative, and thus the phenomenon may be short-lived.

CONCLUSION

Venturing can provide strategic benefits. A recommended approach is to assign the corporate development/planning group to make three or four investments in geographically dispersed partnerships interested in the benefits of a mutually rewarding interchange of information. Subsequently, direct investments can be made alongside venture capitalists, and later, if properly organized, exclusive investments may prove rewarding.

APPENDIX

Venture Activity by the Leaders in the Electronics* Industry 1984

Company	Dedicated Groups	Direct Venturers	Investors into Partnerships
IBM		X	
AT&T Technologies			X
ITT		X	
General Electric	X	X	X
RCA			
Hewlett-Packard		X	
Motorola		X	
Hughes Aircraft			
United Technologies		?	
Honeywell		X	X
Xerox	X	X	X
Sperry	X	X	X

*Order of list from *Electronic News,* August 6, 1984.

Company	Dedicated Groups	Direct Venturers	Investors into Partnerships
Texas Instruments		X	
N.A. Philips			?
Control Data	X	X	
NCR		X	X
Digital Equipment		X	X
Raytheon			X
Westinghouse Electric	X	X	X
Litton Industries			
Burroughs		X	X
Tandy		X	X
TRW	X	X	X
Northern Telecom	X	X	X
General Motors	X	X	
Rockwell International		X	X
Allied	X	X	X
Schlumberger		X	X
Wang Laboratories	X	X	X
GTE		?	X
Harris		X	
National Semiconductor		X	
Eaton		X	
Zenith Electronics			
Intel		X	
Gould			?
Tektronix	X	X	
Penn Central	X	X	
Avnet			
DuPont		X	
AMP		X	X
Ford			
Singer		X	
Teledyne			
Data General			
Storage Technology		X	
Varian Associates		X	
Perkin-Elmer			
Amdahl			

Corporate Venturers in the Telecommunications Industry

Company	Dedicated Groups	Direct Venturers	Investors into Partnerships
AT&T		?	X
GT&E		X	X
Ameritech	X	X	
Bell Atlantic			X
Bell South	X		X
NYNEX		?	X
Southwestern Bell		?	X
SNETCO	X		X
Northern Telecom	X	X	?

Venture Activity by Chemical Corporations

Company	Dedicated Groups	Direct Venturers	Investors into Partnerships
Olin	X	X	X
Koppers	X	X	X
W.R. Grace	X	X	X
Owens-Illinois		X	X
Gulf & Western			X

Venture Activity by Pharmaceutical Corporations

Company	Dedicated Groups	Direct Venturers	Investors into Partnerships
Warner-Lambert	X	X	X
Merck		X	
Becton Dickinson		X	X
Eli Lilly			X
3M			X

Venture Activity by Energy Corporations

Company	Dedicated Groups	Direct Venturers	Investors into Partnerships
Texaco	X	X	X
Standard Oil of Indiana	X	X	X
Standard Oil of Ohio		X	X
Tenneco	X	X	X
Fluor	X	X	
Bechtel	X	X	X

Venture Activity by European Electronics Corporations

Company	Dedicated Groups	Direct Venturers	Investors into Partnerships
Siemens	X	X	X
Olivetti	X	X	X
CGE		X	X
MATRA		X	X
Bull		X	X
N.V. Philips			X
GEC			X
Plessey	X	X	X
Thorn/EMI	X	X	X
Ferranti	X		X
STC/ICL		X	
Nixdorf		X	

Venture Activity by Asian Corporations

Company	Dedicated Groups	Direct Venturers	Investors into Partnerships
Kyocera	X	X	X
Sony			X
Mitsubishi	X	X	X
C. Itoh	X	X	X
Nichimen		X	X
Singapore		X	X
Hyundai		X	

NOTES

1. National Science Board, "Science Indicators—1976," in *Report of the National Science Board 1977*, National Science Foundation, Washington, D.C., 1977.

2. R. Biggadike, *Corporate Diversification*, Harvard University Press, Cambridge, Mass., 1979.

3. L. Weiss, *New Business Startups*, American Scientific Enterprise, Inc., Great Neck, N.Y., 1979.

4. N. D. Fast, *The Rise and Fall of Corporate New Venture Divisions*, UMI Research Press, Ann Arbor, Mich., 1978.

5. E. B. Roberts, "Corporate Growth and Diversification through New Technical Ventures," Massachusetts Institute of Technology, Cambridge, Mass., December 1979.

6. K.W. Rind, "Dealing with the Corporate Venture Capitalist," *Guide to Venture Capital Sources*, Venture Economic Inc., Wellesley Hills, Mass., 1985, p. 97.

7. P. R. Liles, "Sustaining the Venture Capital Firm," Management Analysis Center, Inc., Cambridge, Mass., 1977.

8. S. Wittebort, "Tips for Playing the Venture Capital Game," *Institutional Investor*, New York, July 1980.

9. See S. E. Pratt, "Major Corporations and Venture Capital," *The Venture Capital Journal*, Capital Publishing Corporation, Wellesley Hills, Mass., June 1980, pp. 12–17. *See also* M. Rosene, "The Corporate Venture Players," *Venture*, New York, August 1980, pp. 53–56.

10. K. W. Rind and G. I. Miller, "Corporate Venture Capital in the Computer Industry," in *Proceedings of the National Computer Conference*, AFIPS, Washington, D.C., 1980.

11. L. Klein, *New Ventures that Succeed*, The Strategic Planning Institute, Cambridge, Mass., November 7, 1983.

12. E. Tempelmeier, "Venture Capital: A New Ventures Technique for Industrial Firms," Tektronix, Beaverton, Ore., January 1978.

13. K. S. Colmen, M. Perel, and L. Buffington, "Developing Internally Generated New Ventures," SRI International, Menlo Park, Calif., May 1979.

5

SPECIAL CASES

CHAPTER *20*

Strategic Entrepreneurship in High-Technology Companies

WILLIAM E. JOHNSON

RAYMOND D. LUCAS

WILLIAM E. JOHNSON is President of William E. Johnson Associates, a New York-based management consulting firm that carries out strategic studies involving in-depth evaluation of strategic options and preparation of a thorough foundation for managing strategy execution. The firm's experience covers a broad range of industrial and consumer products and service businesses, both domestic and international. Prior to starting his firm in 1978, Mr. Johnson was the Senior Vice President, Finance and Planning, and Chief Financial Officer for Standard Brands. Besides financial functions, he had responsibility for strategic planning, market research, management information systems, investor relations, and commodities planning. Before joining SBI, Mr. Johnson was a partner at McKinsey & Company, where he focused on building the firm's strategic planning practice. Mr. Johnson received his undergraduate degree from Yale University and an M.B.A. from the Harvard Business School, where he was a Baker Scholar.

RAYMOND D. LUCAS is Vice President for Planning and Business Development of the GTE Diversified Products Group (DP). He is responsible for coordinating and directing the business planning and new business development activities and resolution of marketing, technical, and operations issues that require DP action. Mr. Lucas has held several managerial positions while with GTE. In 1960 he joined the company as an engineer with The Sylvania Systems Group, Western Division and subsequently held a broad range of engineering and managerial positions with that group. Mr.

Lucas received bachelor's degrees in arts and science from Rice University and a master's degree in Electrical Engineering from Stanford University. He also is, a Sloan Fellow graduate of the Stanford Graduate School of Business.

OUTLINE

HIGH-TECH DYNAMICS

The only thing we know for sure is that some of our plans will be wrong.

High-technology companies pose a special planning challenge. They have a number of characteristics in common that differentiate them from traditional firms:

Reduction or collapse of product life cycles

Impossibility of accurate forecasting

Rapid change and unpredictability in technology and product performance

Uncertainty as to who are, or will be, the key competitors

Abnormally wide latitudes in basic economics

Great uncertainty about customers and their needs

With such uncertainty and rapid change, some managers will argue that strategic planning and high technology don't mix—the pace is too fast; there are too many competitors; invention is unpredictable; the market is too tough to read; and success is too dependent on individuals. In this environment, the argument continues, strategic planning ends up as an academic exercise that is not tied to actual operations and is independent of the course of events.

Nevertheless, we believe effective strategic planning and decision making can be accomplished in the high-technology company, and we will present a workable model for that purpose in the following pages.

This model has two components. The first is a generic approach to strategic decision making in any business going through significant change. We call it strategic entrepreneurship. The second component represents the specific structure for applying strategic entrepreneurship to the high-technology business. We'll start by describing how and why it was developed.

FORMATS AND BIG PICTURES

Many of the approaches to strategic planning that were popular in the 1970s do not lend themselves to today's sophisticated managements and dynamic environment. They are too rigid, methodological, and format-oriented to be effective, especially in the volatile and uncertain situations that high-tech companies face.

These approaches were originally developed for situations in which there was strictly a budgeting and operating view of planning. In this context, they provided a useful start for strategic planning. They developed information on the external environment and the underlying technology and economics in order to make opportunities and threats more understandable. They forced explicit consideration of broader and longer-range strategic directions, and they installed planning as a regular discipline, providing management the opportunity, at least once a year, to withdraw their attention from day-to-day operations to look at where they were taking the business longer term.

While they were useful in developing the initial fact base, these approaches were less useful in fulfilling strategic planning's promise of sound strategic decision making and operating execution. Several implicit or explicit characteristics limited their value.

Too often, they were based on unspoken precepts that (1) if you provide the vision, someone else will figure out how to make it work and (2) strategy is where you want to go; tactics are how you get there. As a result, the "big picture" was not grounded in the realities of execution in the first place. Even if the vision was solid, the means of execution were frequently inconsistent, ineffective, or misdirected. This weakness stemmed, at least in part, from the idea that strategy was separate from operations. While this distinction may have been necessary to get managers away from a strict short-term view of the business, it ultimately sowed the seeds of its own ineffectiveness. Excessive differentiation between "strategy" and "tactics" undermined building of an effective link between basic strategic priorities and their effective execution in daily operations. And, while much emphasis was placed on avoiding risks and developing contingency plans, too little emphasis was placed on preparing for and creating success.

Furthermore, the heavy data orientation, annual reviews, and preparation of "the books" often became an end in themselves. This weighty administrative process frequently became divorced from the real strategic decision making.

Once embroiled in the mechanics of the planning system, it became more and more difficult to break out. It was easier to circumvent than to replace. Indeed, many companies used task forces to evaluate a specific business or issue for the real decision making, and then used the planning process for later documentation. By getting stuck in the early data and structure-creating phase of its development, the planning process had become more administrative red tape than a real strategic decision-making tool.

However, while highly methodological approaches don't work for companies facing fast-paced change, neither does reliance on ad hoc and spur-of-the-moment decision making. Lead times may be long. Often large commitments need to be made. Once made, they may be tough to change suddenly. The challenge is to find a happy medium—the strategy itself needs to be well-defined yet flexible enough to be adjusted as conditions change.

STRATEGIC ENTREPRENEURSHIP

It is important to remember that while strategic planning is difficult, it is also fundamentally very simple. It is simple because it is nothing more than a series of decisions and actions to be taken over time. It is difficult because making sound and executable decisions requires vision and focusing analytical depth selectively when it counts and where it counts. What is needed is not a strategic planning process or technique per se, but rather a strategic thinking framework. This framework must foster development of a game plan for operating the business today while preparing it for tomorrow. It must encourage aggressive execution of past decisions while preparing to choose among the range of options still open that will determine the business's future. It must provide the means not just for containing risks but for preparing for success. Its inherent focus must be on decisions, not plans.

We call this strategic-thinking framework *strategic entrepreneurship*. It is a context within which to create and manage strategy, rather than a technique for doing so. It includes a number of important dimensions, which, taken together, reinforce each other. They are depicted in Exhibit 20-1 and briefly characterized as follows:

> The strategy and its execution must be tightly *linked*. Day to day operating actions and programs are simply the front line of the strategy. The linkage must be consistent, clear, and regularly reassessed.
>
> Effectively making this linkage requires concentrating on *critical success factors*—those things the business must do extremely well to succeed.

EXHIBIT 20-1. *Strategic Entrepreneurship*

STRATEGIC ENTREPRENEURSHIP

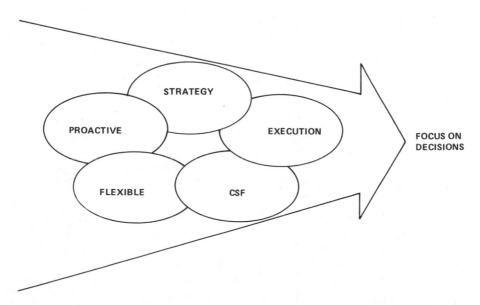

The emphasis on critical success factors is not only essential for a viable business game plan but also crucial to allow meaningful tracking of results.

While the framework must be specific enough to provide a basis for operating the business, it must also be *flexible* enough to allow for change—because that is one thing that will surely be needed.

Dealing effectively with the inevitability of change requires seeking change *proactively* rather than resisting or reacting to it. Changes will be needed in both the strategy and its execution. Just as there will be phases of a businesses development, so too must there be phases of its strategy. A range of strategy alternatives always exists—the issue is when and how to shift from one to another as conditions change.

Most importantly, the strategic framework must focus on *decisions* that are the basis for major actions. The planning process and schedule must be tailored to these decisions, not vice versa. The structure and formats used are not important; the relevance and quality of the assessments of these decisions are crucial.

Created in a context of strategic entrepreneurship, the strategy becomes as dynamic as the business itself, emphasizing proactive management of both the strategy and its execution. While the resulting strategic framework is unique to each business, we've found that several concepts are often useful in applying the principles of strategic entrepreneurship to a high-technology business:

The first involves defining the market in terms of the potential that is opened up by the technology itself—both at its known limits and at its current state of development. These two added perspectives supplement the view of the actual current market. Taken together, they indicate how much potential has been realized at any point in time. Comparing these three views of market potential helps define key issues and set priorities for both technical and marketing efforts.

The second concept involves breaking down the traditional growth phase of the business life cycle into a series of manageable subphases. In each subphase, there are important shifts in success factors and emerging strategic issues and decisions that must be dealt with in order to move through that phase successfully. It is essential to anticipate these issues for effective preparation and timely action.

Managing varying dimensions of strategy often separates success from failure in the high-technology environment. In this environment, there is little room for error, and frequently there is no second chance. The most important contribution of strategic thinking is to address the issues that will be crucial to the company's future before it becomes obvious, in hindsight, that they were.

MANAGING THE MARKET OPPORTUNITY

A proactive strategy manages the market's potential, as well as its exploitation, to create and sustain growth.

Price/performance is an important determinant of the potential market. By price/performance, we mean the amount of performance received per unit of price or, alternatively, the price per unit of performance. For purposes of this discourse, we assume that price reflects cost, to separate the effect of pricing strategy. Improved price/performance does not necessarily imply enhanced performance, or a more sophisticated, "high-end" product. In this context price/performance can be improved by either lower cost or higher performance, or a combination of both. Gauging how much of each is needed and is possible at different times often determines competitive success in the high-technology business. The right balance improves the ability to exploit current markets and also opens new uses, users, and usage, thereby expanding the potential market.

Market growth simply indicates how fast the gap is being closed between the existing market and the potential market. Sustaining that growth depends on continuing to expand the potential market ahead of the current market. Management does this by improving price/performance to create new uses, users, and usage.

In this context, we've found it useful to distinguish between three views of the market: the maximum potential, based on the perceived limits of the technology; the current potential, based on existing products; and the realized potential, which is the actual market. Different choices and actions are implied to manage each of these "markets," and relative priorities need to be chosen and regularly reassessed between them.

1. *Maximum market potential* (MMP) represents the long-term ceiling on market size; thus it indicates how much room there is for long-term growth. It is based on perceived performance limits of the technology and the maximum population of potential users addressable at those limits. Thus the issue is how far and at what cost can technology limits be pushed to raise this ceiling, and the decision required is how much short-term commitment to place on this goal.

   The appropriate definition for "limits" will depend on the business situation. In some cases limits may appropriately be defined as the theoretical technical limits; in other cases they can be defined as specific improvements that we know to be achievable; in others they represent improvements achievable within a specific time horizon.

2. The *technical capability market potential* (TCMP) is the proportion of the maximum market potential that can be served with the price/performance capabilities of today's products. The choice issue is how much emphasis to place on improving current price/performance ca-

pabilities through enhancements or new products to increase near-term market potential and provide room for short-term growth.

TCMP varies by competitor. An industry curve over time will really be a band of different competitive capabilities. It is important to understand how your TCMP differs from that of your competitors—both overall and for specific market segments—and the reasons for the differences. This comparison will define zones of competitive advantage and disadvantage, and is the basis on which competitive actions and share objectives can be established.

3. The third action area is the exploiting of existing products in the marketplace to realize some of the market potential today, and to drive actual market growth in doing so. The significance of this *realized market* (RM) is not just sizing today's market. Rather, the issue is where to apply resources to close the gap between the realized market and the technical capability market in individual market segments. Where is potential being realized, and why? What options exist to concentrate resources in areas where there is still significant upside opportunity? How can we exploit zones of competitive advantage in our potential market versus our competitors' potential markets?

We've found these three market definitions useful as a framework for identifying options and for trading off priorities between developing the immediate, near-term, and long-term market potentials.

SHIFTING COMPETITIVE SUCCESS FACTORS

Developing any competitive strategy requires identifying and managing critical success factors—things a company must do especially well in order to succeed in its environment against its competitors'. Critical success factors are not constant. In most industries they change as the business matures throughout its life cycle or as new conditions emerge. Competitors change. Their strategies change. Technology changes. Markets mature or are saturated. All have an impact on success factors.

The idea of success factors shifting with an evolving business has been usefully applied for some time. In the early 1970s, one of the authors was part of a small McKinsey & Company and General Electric team that developed a portfolio approach to strategic planning. Properly done, this approach assesses the likely long-term profit potential of the market (market attractiveness) and evaluates ability to build a long-term profitable competitive position by comparing company strengths to critical success factors (competitive strengths). Business segments are then classified into nine categories with different strategic challenges, which can be summarized into three broad strategic thrusts: invest for growth, manage selectively for earnings, and harvest for cash. These three thrusts also represent the shifts in strategy appropriate during the extended life-cycle phases of a business—

growth, maturity, and decline. This portfolio "positioning" was not intended as an *end* in itself (although it has sometimes been used as that), but rather as a *beginning*. Different issues and success factors tended to be important for each strategic category. Appraising existing plans and actions to see how they addressed these issues and success factors helped management determine where additional attention was needed and the specific issues that warranted in-depth review.

In the high-technology situation, however, focusing on critical issues and success factors is more difficult. Conditions change more rapidly, often overnight, as the company moves quickly through the growth phase of its life cycle. Constant adjustment is required to compete and to sustain growth. There is no promise of a stable and extended period of maturity and a gradual decline. Competition may make the product obsolete; the market may shift away. The business needs to be reenergized continually during the growth phase, since that phase of the life cycle may be all there is.

Therefore, the core issues in a high-technology firm become how to manage through the growth phase and how to create the next growth phase before obsolescence sets in. This isn't just a matter of "trying harder." What is required is a proactive bias to challenge basic assumptions continually, to reevaluate success factors, and to take immediate action. We've found it useful to segment the growth phase into four subphases, in order to better focus on changing critical issues and choices.

THE FOUR GROWTH PHASES

During the growth phase of a high-technology business, it typically passes through four subphases. Each of these phases requires dealing with new strategic issues in order to manage success in that phase and to prepare for the next. The four phases are described below and depicted in Exhibit 20-2.

Threshold Phase

The threshold phase might be called the "incubator" stage, before the market takes off. During this phase, market development is constrained. User needs may not have developed adequately. Technology does not provide the necessary price/performance. Other constraints to significant market development exist—perhaps legal, regulatory, or technical. Most high-technology markets may stay in this stage for an extended period while customer needs and technology capabilities converge, or while constraints are eliminated. This convergence is followed by a rapid opening up of opportunity. Experience shows that it is almost impossible to predict precisely when this "threshold" will be reached and when the market takeoff will be triggered, much less how fast the market will develop afterward.

The key strategic issues during this stage involve anticipating and managing the threshold, and deciding how to keep risk and exposure acceptable.

EXHIBIT 20-2.   Managing the High-Technology Growth Phases

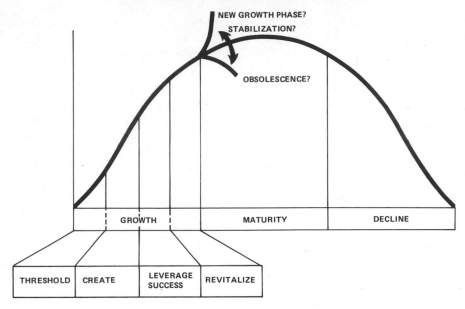

Exhibit 20-3 depicts the relationship between the three measures of market opportunity during this threshold stage. The technical capability market potential (TCMP) and realized market (RM) both lag the maximum market potential (MMP) significantly until the technology or market receptiveness reaches some threshold where potential growth constraints are eliminated. At this threshold, the TCMP and the MMP may rise very quickly because of a breakthrough, or more slowly if they are affected by such factors as greater market acceptance or the gradual deterioration in the relative economics of a competing substitute.

Create Phase

This is the "takeoff" phase—the stage at which industry participants literally *create* the market by driving price/performance and new applications ahead to expand the technical capability market, and by developing the realized market with aggressive marketing. It is turbulent, volatile, and uncertain. Commitment and focus need to be balanced with the need for flexibility, speed, and coverage.

Leveraging-Success Phase

During this phase, the focus shifts. Competition has become intense. Customers are more sophisticated. A reevaluation of technical, marketing, and manufacturing approaches becomes necessary. While technology continues

EXHIBIT 20-3.   Three Measures of Market Potential

ILLUSTRATION

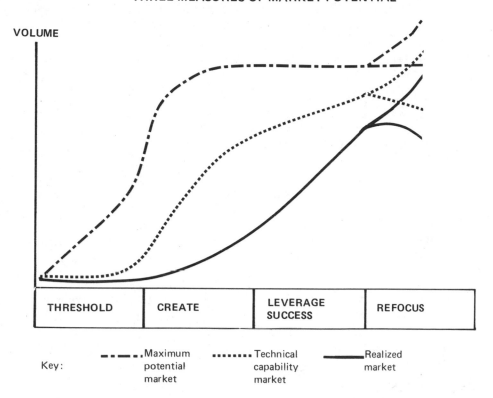

THREE MEASURES OF MARKET POTENTIAL

VOLUME

| THRESHOLD | CREATE | LEVERAGE SUCCESS | REFOCUS |

Key: —··—··Maximum potential market   ·······Technical capability market   ——Realized market

as an important driver in the market, the market now has developed considerable momentum of its own, and marketing and manufacturing have become increasingly important success factors. Two basic issues must be addressed: how broadly to compete, and how far to integrate vertically. During this leveraging-success phase, the "gaps" between the immediate, near-term, and long-term market potential begin to narrow.

Revitalize Phase

In this phase, the current products and business are approaching the end of their growth phase, the three market potentials are approaching convergence, and room left for growth is diminishing. The chances of a nice, comfortable plateau in maturity are often slim. If revitalization is possible, will the business be one of the instigators of the new phase of growth or one of the victims? This is more than just the next new product enhancement—that's been going on throughout the growth phase. It typically involves new technology and market opportunities that require recreating the business on a wide range of dimensions beyond simply the product. The objective is to revitalize and redefine the maximum market potential and technical capability market potential through expanding the limits of technology, applying a new technology, opening major new uses, developing new users, or broadening the business scope (e.g., service as well as manufacturing). Failing that, management must face the issue of whether, and how, they can stabilize the business or manage its decline.

In the following sections, we will discuss some of the specific strategic issues that typically need to be anticipated well in advance as a high-tech business advances—or perhaps rushes—through these four phases.

THE THRESHOLD PHASE

The threshold phase is the early incubation period before the events that trigger market takeoff. It is characterized by undeveloped technology and undefined user needs.

During the threshold phase, the fundamental choices to be made by the high-technology company relate to its degree of aggressiveness in driving the market to the takeoff point. The company has three basic options:

1. Seek *leadership* through aggressive innovation and development
2. *Position* itself with adequate technology and market access to be able to pursue the market quickly as the potential becomes clear
3. *Monitor* developments with minimal current investment, with an intent to apply resources once others have demonstrated the feasibility of the opportunity

Timing is critical during this phase. If a company misses the takeoff window, it can have a tough, perhaps impossible, task of catching up. It may then be dependent on a technical leapfrog. It will need to offset competitors' head starts in obtaining customer bases or installed equipment bases, and in gaining scale economies on marketing and support activities.

On the other hand, if the company acts too early, with too heavy a commitment, the profit and cash drain may be unacceptable. Then, on the rebound, the firm may cut back excessively and miss the opportunity later as others seize it. The old adage "Timing is everything" applies here. The trick is to match commitments with the right technical and market conditions.

Thus, during an extended threshold phase, the effective competitor will operate on all three of these strategies at various times—ideally, moving from the monitor to the position to the leadership strategy just in time to capture an early advantage, but without excessive waste in premature spending. Exhibit 20-4 characterizes this progressive commitment, as well

EXHIBIT 20-4. *Threshold Phase*

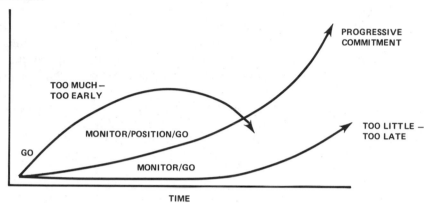

as the "too little, too late" (monitor/go) and "too much, too early" (go) scenarios.

In evaluating these choices, it is essential to maintain a dispassionate view—neither the excitement about potential nor the fear of financial exposure should get out of perspective in making the tradeoff between the added risks versus the added advantage of a more aggressive strategy.

In weighing the risks, three issue areas need be dispassionately assessed:

1. What gaps in market and technical development need to be closed to stimulate the takeoff? What specific barriers need to be overcome to close those gaps? What is the feasibility and difficulty of overcoming those barriers?

2. What are the capabilities of the company to overcome these barriers? How do these capabilities compare to its competitors? How can the company and its competitors add to these capabilities?

3. To what extent can risks be contained? What front-end resources need to be applied before significant feedback can be gathered? How easy is it to change course or back off in midstream? Are parallel efforts needed? The issues to be faced here are the exposure and risk inherent in the task and the options, flexibility, and feedback available to manage it.

The other side of the issue is the payoff. What total business results and preservable competitive advantage will be achieved if the company succeeds in triggering the threshold first? This requires assessment of:

1. The market potential—the three views previously discussed.
2. How fast the markets are likely to develop once they are triggered, and what the time window for catching up is likely to be.
3. What barriers will exist, or can be created by the leader, to forestall followers, how important early technical and application experience will be, and how important an installed base, or early control of distribution will be?
4. How well the company is geared to play the fast-follow role, from either a *position* or *monitor* strategy, whether it has strong and fast response technology and applications development capabilities, and whether it has distribution already in place to serve the likely market.

Resolving these issues will lead the company to select an appropriate initial strategy. Managing and shifting this strategy as the threshold phase progresses requires carefully and continuously assessing the readiness of both the technology and the market, then resetting priorities for development of both to stimulate the market itself.

WHEN IS THE TECHNOLOGY READY?

It is especially difficult to decide when the technology should move out of the labs and into the marketplace. The critical question is, when is price/performance good enough to stimulate real buying? A follow-up question to this is, can that price/performance be produced economically at modest volume levels, so that the business will be viable while the market experiments before strong purchasing occurs? Unfortunately, it is rarely obvious what the "right" price/performance is, when it will be right, or what it will cost to produce when it is.

The "Baseload" Application

Finding the answers to these questions is an iterative process of analyzing and testing the technology and economics against possible applications. The goal is to find a "baseload" application that will start the market takeoff, fund further development, build cost leverage, and provide a foundation for other applications.

Video conferencing is a case in point. For decades people speculated about when the market would be ready for two-way video conferencing. The problem wasn't the market—people liked the idea. The problem was cost and performance. Recently, new video compression technology and lower transmission costs promised improved price/peformance. But while two-way video still limped along, companies moved aggressively to one-way video broadcast. Here the threshold was more favorable. There were many more useful applications for a system that could broadcast key product, marketing, and management information to multiple locations. Further, since it was one-way in nature and covered many locations, the cost per person reached per session were much lower.

Video conferencing is also an example of how the baseload application can pave the way for others by lowering the threshold for those applications to "prove in." The first application will often get equipment or costs in place, which will provide some of the resources needed for the later applications. Thus on an incremental basis they become more attractive than they were on a stand-alone basis. In the case of video-conferencing, small earth stations may be installed for one-way broadcast via satellite. However, these also could later provide the medium for two-way video or data transmission. With some of the fixed costs already in place, the threshold for two-way video is lowered.

Outside Influences

In assessing the readiness of technology, look beyond your own borders to other technical areas that could affect your price/performance capabilities. For example, lower cost and response time of memory and processors made possible the complex instruction sets needed for more user-friendly software.

Technology from suppliers or companion products can also have a significant impact on price/performance capabilities. The battery industry, not usually regarded as high-tech in itself, has developed smaller, lighter, and more-powerful batteries that make a variety of new applications possible for other electronics technology.

Finally, market potential is often driven by price/performance *relative to* competing substitute technologies. For example, improved economics for small earth stations, as well as significant forecasted overcapacity in satellite transmission, will impact the price/performance that fiber optics will need in applications where it competes with satellites.

Compatibility

A constraint on technology's readiness may be the need for standards to permit adequate interconnection and communication. Telecommunications companies have found standards critical to the takeoff of many markets. The key issue is whether to wait for an industry standard to be agreed on—sometimes a long, laborious, and uncertain process—or to go it alone to introduce a product or feature into the marketplace sooner.

Going it alone may develop the market faster in the near term, but it can lead to significant problems later. Over the years, many companies added messaging software to internal computer systems in order to transmit messages between a system's users. This resulted in many different, and incompatible, internal messaging systems within large companies with multiple computer networks. One major bank complained of having seven different messaging systems that would not communicate with one another. Thus, while rushing into initial messaging systems without standardization allowed individual pockets of usage, the next phase of system development was bottlenecked. The recent establishment of international standards for computer-based messaging systems should stimulate the market; large companies can interconnect multiple networks, and separate companies will be able to communicate with each other.

Gaining Credibility

In most new high-technology products, pilot tests with customers are needed to work out bugs and to gain marketplace credibility. However, it's easy to underestimate the time it takes to sell pilots, complete the tests, and make necessary adjustments. If a venture firm is involved, investors are often pressing for a robust forecast of exploding sales. The risk is getting locked into a set of unrealistic expectations that not only endanger financing commitments if delays occur, but that could kill the venture's chance at success. With fast-moving technologies, failure to anticipate lead time may not simply result in sales shortfalls. The real risk is that the product may be preempted. During the delay, other firms may come in with an enhanced version and steal the market.

Therefore, begin planning for pilots and lining up participants as early as possible. A larger company sometimes can do its own internal pilot. This is an attractive way both to test the product and to get information that later can be used to sell potential customers. However, it is important to set up the pilot to minimize the risk of a biased reaction. The financial organization may be a better place to test the new office automation product than the engineering organization that developed it.

WHEN IS THE MARKET READY?

There is no sure way to answer this question. Furthermore, it's frequently the wrong question. Often, what is characterized as the market's reluctance is just inferior price/performance of the technology.

The natural tendency is to work on demand forecasts in response to this question. However, these tend to estimate what might happen once the take-off *has been* triggered. The real issue at this point is what market factors must change to *unleash* demand.

Barriers and Drivers

We've found it productive to address the issue of market readiness directly by concentrating on what is holding demand back, and what would need to change to drive it forward. This understanding provides a ''model'' of what would have to change to trigger a takeoff, and isolates specific variables to be monitored or influenced toward that end. Market barriers and drivers will be specific to the opportunity and may encompass areas ranging from potential buyers' attitudes about the product or application to regulatory or legal constraints. In some cases barriers and drivers are like the front and back of the same hand. A change in buyer motivation can convert a barrier into a driver. In other cases a driver could be some positive influence that has nothing to do with an existing constraint.

Evaluating "demand barriers" is made more difficult because potential customers often are unable to meaningfully articulate their needs or potential purchase behavior at this point. Most potential customers have difficulty visualizing applications and benefits for the new technology products in the abstract. Reactions will be general, often encouraging but noncommital, and provide little protein for the specific product design choices to be made. Overcoming this barrier may require much missionary selling over an extended period; this is why pilots are generally critical to success. Often customers have to find out for themselves by testing the product in "small bites." Getting commitment to a pilot isn't easy, but the chances are increased by using examples of other applications effectively to demonstrate benefits and to help the potential user visualize the possibilities.

The success factor here is developing a thorough understanding of the customer's business, needs, and perceptions, and how they are changing. Track surrogates as indicators where possible. Experience with a related product may reduce resistance. Become knowledgeable about the customer's business, since this could relate to the new product. To be a leader, you must stay as close to the customer before the takeoff as after.

Critical Mass

Critical mass of usage or product may be necessary to trigger significant demand. For example, it is important to evaluate whether a product gives value based on individual "one-shot" use or whether a critical mass of users is necessary. In some applications, like electronic messaging, it is necessary to have both adequate *users* and also adequate *usage* before the system becomes valuable—even with many users, a regular check for messages must be made for the tool to be effective.

Critical mass may also be necessary to get effective distribution or retail support. A product line, rather than an individual product, may be needed so that distributors can substitute for other product lines or serve the full range of their customers.

THE CREATE-THE-MARKET PHASE

The create-the-market phase is the growth period that begins once product price/performance and market factors have converged to trigger major demand. In this phase, industry participants literally "create" the market.

Technical efforts not only drive for price/performance improvements but also concentrate on developing applications. Marketing becomes more aggressive. The phase is characterized by turbulence and great uncertainty.

Critical success factors for the high-tech company change rapidly when its business moves from the threshold phase to the create-the-market phase. In the threshold phase, attention is focused on anticipating and influencing the technical and market takeoff triggers. In the create phase, critical success factors both deepen and broaden to include:

Developing a realistic view of the market opportunity based on understanding fundamental drivers.

Pursuing a proactive approach to creating the market.

Balancing aggressiveness with care in seizing opportunities.

Balancing technical stretch with speed to market in introducing new products.

Using the competitive turmoil of this phase to the company's advantage— or at least in order not to become the victim of the turmoil.

Targeting opportunities to achieve competitive advantage.

MARKET FORECAST OR FOLLY?

The first step in most strategic planning exercises is to define the market for the particular product under assessment, and then to quantify the market's future potential. This assessment looks at current market size and past growth experience, then concentrates on how future growth will be determined compared to growth in the past. This assessment of future market size is based on a thorough understanding of three critical dimensions:

The current market characteristics

The specific drivers of future size and growth

How to translate these interrelationships into a quantitative market forecast

This approach works with well-established businesses but is difficult to apply to embryonic and emerging high-technology markets. In the embryonic market situation, understanding on all of these dimensions is weak. The market is just taking shape; in some cases it may barely be there at all. It is difficult to measure and forecast, even when statistics seem to be available on early usage. The early phases of the personal computer market are illustrative of this difficulty. Many studies were done on market size and future growth potential. Not only did the forecasts vary by a factor of ten, but estimates of the *current* market size were almost equally diverse. This was due to more than differences in estimates. There was no well-understood or commonly accepted definition of what specific workstation types and applications constituted the relevant market. In some cases, the definitions were different, but in many cases, the researchers did not even attempt to be explicit about what was and wasn't included. Explicitness on what is included in the relevant market must be stressed. Then, at least there's a backdrop to work against as understanding improves. Without meaningful and specific definitions, the forecasts that follow will be garbage.

In developing a forecast, the issue is whether to estimate "top down" or "bottom up." Top-down forecasting often has little substance to go on at this point, and risks too superficial a view to spend against. Bottom-up forecasting is based on specifics, but specifics are soft at this stage. The best approach is generally to do both types of forecasting and then compare and reconcile the results. At this stage, however, any estimates, even with such cross-checking, will be soft. The real value in forecasting is not in the estimates themselves, but, if it is done rigorously, is in the understanding developed about the potential customers, applications, and competitive success factors. To be useful the emphasis needs to be on market assessment, rather than on forecasting.

In doing this top-down market assessment, beware of two common traps: the "headline syndrome" and the "10 percent solution."

Headline Syndrome

It's faster and easier to justify a decision on published material rather than to do a painstaking and thorough analysis yourself. The temptation is strong to use magazine or newspaper articles as "gospel," forgetting that the authors were under as much, or more, deadline pressure as you and certainly didn't have as much at stake in being right. Unfortunately, the same applies to many "industry overview" independent research studies. Often long on weight, but short on substance, their superficial but rosy forecasts sell well because they're what many advocates want to hear.

The appropriation request that got a major U.S. corporation into the transit car business prominently displayed as backup to its glowing market forecast a newspaper article headlined "$20 billion transit car market." It referred to federal funding support, which was a key market driver. Unfortunately, the process by which spending would be approved and applied and the "make-it-up-on-the-follow-on" psychology of the competition were not understood. The result was a smaller market, and bidding practices that made profitability unlikely. Millions of dollars later, analysis showed that it would take a 40 percent market share to break even, and there were six hungry competitors pursuing the business. This manufacturer, along with a number of others, eventually exited.

The 10 Percent Solution

In assessing an opportunity for substitution, we often hear "we can certainly get at least 10 percent." This sounds easy enough, but 10 percent of the long-distance telephone market is over 4 billion dollars—no mean feat to try to capture from scratch. Similarly, one independent study projected the video-conferencing market based on its substitution for travel, asserting that 10 percent seemed to be a reasonable amount to displace. The study assumed that the video-conferencing market potential would be equal to 10 percent of the total travel expenditures, a huge number. No consideration of relative economics, user preferences, or purposes of travel versus conferences was involved. Current forecasts for the same time frame are much more conservative, and later experience has shown that productivity improvements, rather than travel savings, are the primary driver in most applications anyway. The point is that if it's a guess, say so; if it's really an estimate, then there is no substitute for thoughtful assessment.

Demand Model

The bottom-up market assessment should be based on a fundamental "modeling" of the variables that drive demand. The important thing is to have a thoughtful logic structure of the variables and their relationships. Such a model can then provide the basis for developing meaningful scenarios of alternative "futures."

In developing perspective on the market, it is valuable to define an explicit logic model of how demand is generated and then probe critical assumptions in depth. In estimating the market potential of a new PABX technology, some industry forecasts made no explicit assumptions about the rate of replacement of the old-technology installed base versus new demand. (Private Automatic Branch Exchange (PABX) is the switch in a large office that routes telephone calls inside and outside the premises.) Furthermore, deeper probing showed that many users were tied into high-penalty contracts that would delay the time when it would be economical to convert to new technology, regardless of their natural preferences. Building these factors into a demand model actually showed a depression of the available market for several years, until contracts ran out, as compared with other projections of continued growth. The demand model's output proved to be a more accurate indicator of subsequent market results.

Emphasizing market assessment, rather than simply forecasting, helps insure that it's kept an integral, not a separate, activity in the development of a competitive strategy. Market assessments should be based on the competitive concepts of how and where the business will compete. Therefore, to be meaningful, forecasts need to be developed after, not before, that concept is clearly defined. And they should be developed with the participation of the same people who developed, and who thoroughly understand, the competitive strategy. No forecast will be "right," and the real value in forecasting is in dimensioning and understanding the opportunity.

CREATE THE MARKET

Faced with this forecasting problem, one senior manager in a volatile high-technology industry commented, "The best way to predict the future is to create it."

When the focus is on predicting, the tendency is to look for some market characteristic that will tell you what will happen. Once the focus shifts to creating, the emphasis is on the capability that can be delivered, and on the potential value to specific users. This means emphasizing what you can do as well as what buyers say they want. Akio Morita, CEO of Sony Corporation, is quoted in a recent *Harvard Business Review* article as follows:

> The newer and more innovative a product is, the more likely it is that the public might not appreciate it at the beginning. In 1950, our company marketed a tape recorder. Despite the fact that it was a great achievement and a technological innovation for us, at the time it looked like a toy to the general public. Nobody thought about recording speeches or using a tape recorder to learn languages. *In the case of an entirely new product, a market must be created.*[1]

With the traditional marketing approach, we go out and ask the customers what they want, then go back and see if we can do it. The difficulty in developing new technology products and services is that customers can't define what they want independently at this stage. They don't know enough about the technology and economics to know what's possible and practical. So we need to generate possibilities, and then test them against the customers' sense of what would be useful to them. However, as Morita points out, even when faced with an idea, it is difficult for the customer to visualize uses and benefits. And even then, it's tough to give a meaningful reaction without specifics on price and performance. In high-technology products, the execution of the idea makes all the difference. A lot of computer software programs sound great as concepts, but the real issue is how easy they actually are to use.

To find out what is valuable, and how to provide it, you must understand your customers better and work more closely with them than ever before. You can't simply ask them what their needs are. You have to understand their business so well that you can begin matching the capabilities of the technology with what might be a benefit to them—working in partnership with them to let their potential uses and values drive the product.

This process demands tightly knit cooperation between marketing and engineering. With uncertain markets and rapid technical change, it's a tougher challenge for each to be current on the other's area of expertise. The only solution to this problem is a team approach, to give the engineers exposure to the market and the marketeers better understanding of the technology. This integrated approach is fundamental to developing a successful product and market strategy.

Data General is a textbook example of getting close to customers and allowing them to drive product development. Data General's first entry in the desktop computer market, the Enterprise, was a major failure because the company misread the market. The failure led Data General to change its internal product development process radically. When the company developed its next desktop computer, a new business unit was established that was physically separate from headquarters. Engineering, marketing, and manufacturing worked as a team. A key change in approach was in-depth analysis of competitor products, combined with hundreds of interviews with potential customers. Most significant was the fact that these customer perceptions became the driving force in feature and design elements, sometimes overriding the objections of engineers.

Therefore, focus on how to create the market rather than how to predict it. This leads to something more useful than a forecast—it defines actions and decisions to be taken in order to exploit the opportunity. Understanding how to provide real value to users leads to clear product development and marketing priorities. Coupled with an understanding of different purchasing motivations, it also pinpoints the most likely candidates for early adoption.

With these customer and product priorities in hand, it's possible to develop meaningful scenarios for the market's development, based on the outcomes of specific technical and marketing actions and assumptions. This provides an initial framework for forecasting and, more important, for helping manage and monitor ongoing technical and marketing efforts to develop the opportunity. It also furnishes the initial layer of a competitive and financial model of the business.

SEIZE OPPORTUNITIES—BUT CAREFULLY

Products in the high-technology environment have relatively short life cycles; a late product launch not only cuts valuable life and payback potential but also risks competitive preemption in the marketplace. On the other hand, a shoddy job can be disastrous, and even fatal. It is necessary to move fast, but also to move carefully.

Managing this paradoxical situation is a key success factor in building a strong position in an emerging market. There are some common areas where it is easy to get careless in the rush to market:

1. *Product Design.*   The most common problem is sloppy and incomplete design and inadequate attention to details. Things get left out; loose ends don't get tied up, and introduction gets delayed. One microcomputer manufacturer had major problems in the manufacture of its portable computer because of inadequate design time and attention. Potential buyers cut orders, and the company used up over 30 million dollars in venture funding before the product was fixed. By then its technical edge was blunted and its chances for long-term viability were greatly diminished.

2. *Moving from Engineering Directly to Production.*   Time pressure becomes the excuse for not thoroughly testing the product or doing pilots. As a result, an unreliable or poorly performing product gets to market. Convergent Technologies took its new portable "Workslate" PC directly to production. Manufacturing problems led to in-

adequate availability of the product after it had been introduced. Missed opportunity, loss of credibility, and other problems led to a flop.

3. *Premature Product Announcement.*   Often a tactic to preempt competitors, this can backfire if delays occur. Credibility is lost with potential buyers and distributors. Advance orders may be cancelled or reduced. If it is an enhanced, or a next-generation, product, customers may stop buying the existing product, since it will become obsolete when the new one appears. Osborne Computer announced its second-generation portable computer months in advance of actual shipping time, and was driven out of business as sales of its current product dried up.

4. *Failure to Identify and Test Key Assumptions.*   There is no substitute for painstaking homework. Define critical assumptions—those that would cause you to reconsider some important action or commitment. In the rush to expand its network, one telecommunications carrier had capacity delays on some routes because it failed to test the assumed feasibility of adding capacity on existing microwave towers, rather than building new towers, which is a slower process. The challenge is that key assumptions arc often submerged, so it is necessary to work backward from important actions to answer the question: What would cause us to miss our targets, or to do that differently or not at all?

5. *Poorly Defined Programs.*   Programs must identify not only activities and milestones but also the key choices to be resolved cn route and pivotal assumptions affecting those choices.

6. *Neglect of Marketing.*   Lack of time is not an excuse to bypass a solid analysis. By its own admission, Convergent Technologies introduced the doomed ''Workslate'' without market research and with disastrously inadequate marketing and sales expenditures. The market assessment is often left until it's too late, after the product specs are flushed out internally, positions are hardened, and advocates are beating the drums for introduction.

The question is *how* to work both fast and carefully. Ten success factors seem to distinguish companies that do well from those that don't:

1. *Develop well-defined product features* that are driven by users and an integrated marketing-engineering team. Start the external, objective marketing assessment early. Do it with potential customers, not just ''in-house'' or using secondary research. Don't get locked into an engineering version and hardened positions. Even if this process starts late, it is rarely necessary to stop everything while the marketing homework is done.

2. *Develop a detailed program roadmap,* including actions, critical as-
    sumptions and success factors, milestones, and key choices still to
    be made. It must clearly delineate how success will be measured,
    including the basis on which future key decisions will be made. This
    must cover all elements of the plan—not just product development,
    but also marketing plan completion, sales resources and rollout,
    product support and service, legal/patent activities, and any other
    area critical to success.

3. *Maintain management control* of the schedule and tasks. Appoint
    and support a leader who is responsible for the project and its timing,
    and who has the authority and top-management support to get the
    job done.

4. *Involve manufacturing early* both to build up quality control and
    influence the design for produceability.

5. *Test the product thoroughly,* and induce actual potential users. This
    isn't lost marketing time. Successful tests are important showcases
    to close other sales; unsuccessful tests mean there's more work to
    do before full introduction anyway.

6. *Announce it* only when a definite introduction date can be met, and
    carefully balance the advantages of alerting customers and potentially
    preempting competitors against risks of prematurely killing current
    products.

7. *Provide top-management visibility* to ensure commitment and to
    motivate the project team.

8. *Link rewards* to performance as part of the team, even though some
    members may be on temporary assignment from other organizational
    groups.

9. *Set up and train a competent sales/service group* ahead of intro-
    duction to sell and support the targeted user and distribution channel
    effectively from the outset.

10. *Insure communication and responsiveness* to reduce the risks and
    inefficiencies of doing many interdependent activities in parallel to
    save time. Close communication is essential. As incoming market
    feedback shifts product specifications, engineering needs to know
    immediately how to shift direction with a minimum of lost time and
    effort. As engineering uncovers feasibility problems in meeting specs,
    marketing needs to know quickly what they can and can't assume
    in order to avoid developing unrealistic objectives and strategies.

Two professors at Northeastern University's College of Business Administration studied the results of seven new product development projects that
required a quick response to a competitor's introduction of a superior product.
Of the seven efforts, three succeeded and four failed. In the four unsuccessful
cases, top management "orphaned" the projects, feedback was nonexistent,

there were no rewards for project member, and slippages were accepted. In successful cases, the project was highly visible, generating lots of enthusiasm. The failures tended to be engineering-driven, while successes followed carefully delineated product specifications and targets based on market considerations. Schedules were closely followed and project leaders were engineers with a strong business orientation.

Faced with time pressures and ambiguity, it's easy to fall into the time-trap mentality: "I'd take a time management course, but I don't have time." Scrambling is unlikely to deal with the "fast but carefully" paradox; it takes disciplined management. Time pressures are no excuse for inadequate research, control, and care. They just make them all the more essential.

BALANCE TECHNICAL STRETCH WITH SPEED TO MARKET

In discussing the threshold phase, we outlined tradeoffs in deciding how much to commit to being a leader at the start of the game. In the create phase, the game is on and the company is a competitor. The issue is how to play to win over a period of time.

There are two levels at which choices need to be made about pursuing technical leadership—one at the fundamental level of the strategy, the other at the execution level.

Fundamental Emphasis

The fundamental issue is the extent to which one emphasizes being a leader versus being a follower. Most of the considerations highlighted in the threshold phase discussion also apply during the create-the-market phase, so we'll be selective in our comments here.

The technical leadership issue is complicated because it involves tradeoffs in *both* timing and price/performance. A fast follower may be aiming at price/performance leadership. A company that is first into the market with a new product idea may enter with less price/performance than it needs to sustain an advantage because timing is critical and the company hopes to enhance it later.

It is not always necessary to be first with an innovation to be a technical leader. Sometimes the fast follower's advantage of being able to learn from the success and failure of others offsets the time lag, and the follower is able to implement an improved version and capture the market the competitor has stimulated. Matsushita Electric (Panasonic brand) has developed the fast-follow approach to an art. In fact, its key rival, Sony Corporation, which is one of the most innovative in new-technology–based products, often has no chance to reap the market rewards of its products because followers jump into the market so quickly.

In any event, there are offsets to pure price/performance leadership. The relative importance of seeking technical leadership also depends on whether a company has offsetting strengths in marketing and distribution or in brand image. A strong direct sales force already selling related products to the same decision makers can be worth significant price/performance in relation to a smaller competitor without marketing clout.

The fundamental issue is what is the appropriate basis of competition for a specific company. How essential is a price/performance edge to success? How important is it to be first? There is no generic answer for an industry. The right answer will differ from one competitor to the next, depending on the full range of capabilities. Often, smaller, newer firms will need to compete on the basis of technology innovation and timing, or a price/performance premium, taking greater technical and market risk; meanwhile, larger, more established firms may be able to rely on their marketing and operating strengths to let others test the market first. IBM is currently honing this strategic approach as it moves into new segments of the computer business once the market has been proven and has reached significant proportions.

Execution Strategy

Regardless of the fundamental emphasis selected, the challenge of technical competitiveness boils down to a year-to-year and month-to-month issue. With the race underway in the create phase, you often need to run as fast as you can just to keep up. As successive product improvements are introduced, today's leader may be tomorrow's follower, and the next day's leader.

Thus the real challenge becomes execution rather than philosophy. Whatever the fundamental emphasis, the recurring decision that must be made is how far to push price/performance before freezing it to introduce the next product or enhancement. The challenge is to balance schedule with sophistication. Added sophistication tends to have an exponential impact on complexity and manageability of the program. Trying for too much too fast risks schedule slippage, product problems, and potential competitive preemption. The question is, *Specifically* how much is enough for now, and how fast do we push? This is not simply a choice to be *made;* it is a choice to be *managed.*

One of the important issues in managing this tradeoff is establishing thorough price/performance goals. In setting price/performance targets in performance-oriented development groups, it's often difficult to keep adequate emphasis on the cost side of the tradeoff. Whether the company is positioned at the higher- or lower-performance end of the range, the issue is *relative* competitive price/performance, not just performance. Too much performance may be as bad as too little, if it's not accompanied with a significant reduction in price per unit of performance.

Furthermore, in deciding how far to stretch, it is essential to remember that the price/performance standards are moving targets. Generally they need be updated during the extended development cycle of a new product. What would be a leadership product today won't be tomorrow. Don't focus on beating today's leader if you're seeking a competitive advantage. Focus on beating the competitor who's going to beat the leader.

Success Window

Beat him by establishing a target price/performance "success window." This success window should encompass the minimum and maximum specs that are believed to be necessary to attain a competitive edge at the time of introduction. The actual program underway is aimed at a point within the window. It reflects some cushion above the minimum specs in case competition moves faster, and also reflects a gap from the maximum specs based on balancing time to market entry against extra capabilities.

Adopt your competitor's viewpoint to help assess your own options and actions. Look at your products and your competitor's from his perspective to understand what he *should do*—for example, how he should respond to your plans or how he should deal with his particular problem. Then determine what you need to do to beat the response. In the case of a major next-generation digital telephone switch under development, a thorough cost/performance analysis of a key competitor's product showed he could make several changes to approach the planned product's capabilities. A program for enhancements was undertaken even before introduction of the product in order for the company to stay competitive if the competitor responded quickly. As the ongoing market and competitive assessment better defines the success window, it will lead to a well-focused series of parallel programs aimed at future enhancements.

When aiming for the maximum end of the window, it may be appropriate to define a backup program to cover the risks on the "high-stretch" product with a "lower-stretch" version. This could be an entirely separate and parallel program with checkpoints to cut it off as key technical risks are eliminated on the high-stretch program. It's likely to be more cost-effective, however, if a way can be found to define milestones in the high-stretch program, where efforts could shift a less ambitious version if technical hurdles are not met.

A major company was launching a program to develop a leading next-generation office automation product that performed a wide range of functions. Success depended on an outside supplier's meeting its goals for a powerful next-generation processor. The new processor required redoing much of the current-generation–base software, as well as adding that required for new functions—a major software development and integration task. Weighing the risks, the company undertook a parallel program to overhaul its current-generation product with more powerful, lower-cost hardware based on proven components, which also permitted it to avoid redoing much of its software. While it did not offer the same leapfrog price/performance improvement as the high-stretch program, the backup program made the difference to survival. It provided a second chance when the processor vendor was unable to meet his performance specs on the new processor and the high-stretch program had to be aborted.

Differentiate or Duplicate?

All competitors look for ways to differentiate their products. The key choice is how to do it in ways that provide added value without creating a dead end. Focus early on whether technical or de facto industry standards are likely to emerge. Even though standards may not be necessary to stimulate market takeoff, they may become important for extending product capabilities or markets served.

In particular, as competition evolves, de facto standards often emerge. IBM's PC market entry provides an instructive case. Its PC rapidly became the de facto industry standard, and other PC makers have been forced to be IBM-compatible. Software companies have flocked to develop applications to be run on IBM equipment. This was predictable by those who appreciated the importance of the IBM monogram in developing an installed base, and the importance of an installed base in attracting needed outside software development efforts.

The lesson? Being unique is not necessarily a plus. Success requires developing the insights to know where you should be different and where you should be a clone.

Pricing Tradeoffs

Exploiting the success window requires balancing both price and performance for the maximum competitive impact. The short life cycles of high-technology products also mean that some classical pricing methods don't work well. Early "cream skimming" can be especially dangerous. It risks failing to expand usage quickly to establish a strong user base ahead of competition. Too high an "umbrella" encourages dangerous additional competition in an environment where the technology is changing quickly. A company becomes too easy a target if competitors can just add features or moderate performance improvements without being under pressure for significant cost reduction as well. The key point is to beware of the temptation to let short-term financial pressures sacrifice the future. Pricing aggressively enough early on helps extend the product's life by keeping competitors off balance, perhaps halting products already in development before they can be introduced, and forcing them to push their technology further to beat both price and performance.

While aggressiveness often is called for, pricing *too* low just "leaves money on the table." There is no substitute for a thoughtful assessment of how customer and competitive behavior are likely to be affected by successively lower price levels. Include research on alternative prices with potential customers where practical. Avoid simplistic assumptions that a lower price will always develop more usage and discourage competition—there is always a point of diminishing returns.

Thus it is a question of balance. We are in business to make money. Yet greed is rarely rewarded in high-technology businesses. Jeopardizing the future for incremental immediate earnings rarely pays off. The future comes fast in this environment—it will become the short term before you know it.

CAPITALIZE ON COMPETITIVE DISEQUILIBRIUM

Who are the Competitors?

In industries with relatively slow-moving technology, who's who in the competitive lineup generally is clear. But in the fast-changing high-technology environment, key competitors can change overnight. New or unknown competitors can come from nowhere and achieve market dominance rapidly. Management Sciences America grew to be the largest independent software supplier in only three years, with 1983 sales of 145 million dollars, based heavily on the development of the microcomputer side of their business. Yet they lost their edge just as quickly, and exited the microcomputer software area roughly a year later, due to expanding losses.

Diseconomies of Scale

In recent years, the huge R&D labs in large companies have not generally produced the "eureka" innovations. While sometimes the basic research underlying new technology has come from work in large R&D organizations, the early applications frequently have come from small, entrepreneurial organizations. These organizations are able to move a technology quickly ahead into the application phase because of diseconomies of scale. Development organizations in large companies are often "muscle-bound" by structure, long lead times, internal politics, and lack of intense drive and focus. But the start-up or entrepreneurial company can muster a highly committed and energetic group of individuals who deliver many times the productivity found in the large organizations. That productivity is a function of sheer drive, capabilities of the core group, and close, informal communication that allows problems to be quickly worked out in many cases. It is also spurred by financial participation in the company's success.

We did a comparison of software development productivity in a start-up company and a large corporate R&D lab for products that required systems integration. It showed a difference of from 10 to 20 to 1 in the amount of code per hour produced by the start-up's engineers versus that produced by the corporate lab group. Such differences can get a product to market much sooner or allow pursuit of more sophisticated capabilities within a given time horizon.

Accordingly, in many industries a shift to the philosophy "smaller is better" has taken place. The problem with the classic economy-of-scale argument for many high-technology businesses is that, in practice, the human factor can become overriding. There are limits on the ability to manage bigness and complexity with nimbleness and efficiency. Economies of scale no longer guarantee a competitive advantage in every area.

In large part, the collapsing product life cycle—which puts a premium on time to market—along with manufacturing technology changes that permit low costs with less scale, are the key causes of the emergence of the "smaller is better" argument. Rapid technological change in the manufacturing process (automation, robotics, CAD/CAM) can make big, expensive plants obsolete and economically inefficient. For example, AT&T Technologies Inc.—formerly Western Electric—has been closing large assembly operations for several years and replacing them with smaller automated plants that make a limited range of specialized products.[3] Smaller plants can be just as efficient, but they involve lower capital investment and risk.

"Small" is often more productive because scaling down the size of units and flattening organizational structure improves manageability and communication, which is essential for quality decision making and execution when time frames are short and conditions are uncertain and volatile. It builds teamwork. Individuals have a sense of ownership, and have more responsibility for decisions.

Later in the chapter we will enlarge on other issues relating to the small and large firm. Our purpose here is to warn the strategist coping with the create phase to beware of thinking he knows the competition—who they are, what they offer, what they're capable of. That's a sure way to be unpleasantly surprised. Approach competitive assessment as a continuing quest for new discoveries. Expect the unexpected.

Enter the Heavies

Frequently the early development and marketing of a new technology is done by small entrepreneurial firms. However, when the technology is well-enough established, it often attracts larger firms that have the major resource commitments necessary to take the next steps. The next stage of development of the technology may be to translate it into a broader range of applications. Or the larger company may acquire the technology, or the smaller company itself, to allow it to take the final steps into the mass market by leveraging sales and distribution capabilities.

The biotechnology industry is a good example of this. It can cost up to 20 million dollars to test a new drug. Big companies are moving in on the field, based on their greater financial resources, their marketing and sales staffs that are needed to get the product to market, and their ability to get production up to scale quickly. Start-ups have had increasing difficulty in getting additional funds, even though much of the initial development and progress in gene splicing has come from them.

In the emerging artificial intelligence industry, where computerized "expert systems" draw conclusions from masses of data, small companies like SRI International have pushed the technology to specific applications. Now, major firms like General Electric, ITT, GTE, and Hughes Aircraft have established resarch labs for AI.

For the small company that is intent on growing to be a large one from an early technology lead, key success factors are its ability to target the right customer segments and find or develop sales and marketing capabilities to exploit the technology quickly in the marketplace and develop a defensible position. If it can accomplish this, it then has the opportunity to grow with continued enhancements and follow-up products. That's a tall order, and is the reason why many start but few finish.

TARGETING FOR COMPETITIVE ADVANTAGE

Targeting

Even though you know you are going to have a better mousetrap, you can't count on customers beating a path to your door. While the product may be great, it is not always clear who will think so and who will feel strongly enough about it to purchase it, especially during the create phase, when customers are just beginning to develop familiarity and comfort with the product.

In the early stages, some marketing efforts therefore seek to expose the product to as broad a cross section of potential users a possible and let the market emerge. However, the shotgun approach is undesirable for many new high-tech products. It is simply too expensive. The education and missionary selling time required to establish the product can be enormous, and the effort can take forever if the product is poorly targeted. It is important to focus efforts on the paths of least resistance for selling results to be productive and timely.

Accordingly, many companies emphasize market segmentation to help set priorities. Unfortunately, most segmentation schemes fall short of stimulating real marketing effectiveness because they are descriptive, rather than actionable. Market segments are often defined from a market-research perspective, rather than from a general management perspective. They tend to be based on the way the data are most conveniently or traditionally organized and available. They often split the market based on what's being sold rather than on who's buying it; when based on who's buying, buyers are split by general characteristics, rather than by factors influencing why they buy; and when market segments are based on buying motivations, they often don't emphasize the criteria where an advantage exists versus competition. Accordingly, traditional market segmentation approaches may be helpful for forecasting or measuring the total market, but they provide an inadequate basis for action.

Actionable segmentation, or *targeting,* as we call it, defines the market selfishly. It specifies the customer groups with whom winning is both attractive and likely for us, and it signals what we must do to win. It involves applying multiple criteria to determine the characteristics of these target customers and, specifically, who they are. It is based on in-depth product, market, economic, and competitive assessment. Deciding on the appropriate segmentation is, in this sense, selecting the basis for the strategy, not just a convenient view of the market. Targeting defines the competitive concept for winning.

Developing the targeting approach is based on a thorough application of three screens of potential, encompassing six criteria. The screens and their criteria stress the ability to act, rather than to describe. The evaluation focuses on why potential customers differ with respect to each criterion, and thereby identifies the characteristics and specific customer types that optimize results for that criterion. The screens and their criteria are shown in Exhibit 20-5. They are:

1. *Customer potential,* based on:
    Ability to create the most value for the customer.
    Ability to serve most profitably.
2. *Competitive potential,* based on:
    Ability to beat competition on value.
    Ability to beat competition on cost and margin.
3. *Execution potential,* based on:
    Ability to get early adoption.
    Ability to keep the customer.

EXHIBIT 20-5.   Create Phase—Targeting

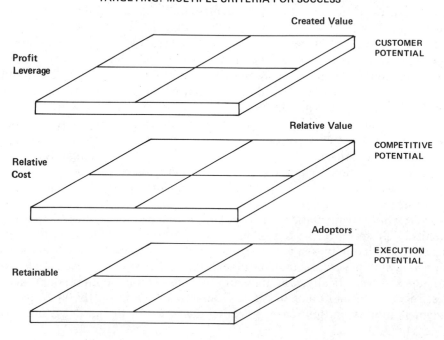

TARGETING: MULTIPLE CRITERIA FOR SUCCESS

Once they are identified, the characteristics of customers that fulfill each criterion are compared in order to arrive at a final set of descriptions. These descriptions best characterize those customers who have the highest development attractiveness and with whom the best competitive advantage can be obtained. The descriptors are used to identify actual customer sets with these characteristics, and these sets are developed into a quantitative sizing of the total potential of each customer type, as well as the foundation for the sales and service resources and operating plans. Most important, since the descriptors have been chosen based on customer attractiveness and how competitive advantage can be achieved, they define the foundation for the "winning" marketing and competitive strategies for the business.

Customer Potential—Created Value

The created value criterion is the starting point; its purpose is to identify applications or users for which the highest value is created by the product or service. This is an iterative process that involves the four steps depicted in Exhibit 20-6.

1. Identify as many potential applications as possible. Make them as specific as possible—describe them from the customer's viewpoint.
2. Determine what provides the most value in these applications. Define the specific sources of value, such as productivity improvement, substitution, or cost savings, and show specifically how they are realized. Estimate how the customers can, and will, measure the value. Assess

EXHIBIT 20-6.   Create Phase—Targeting: Customer Potential/Created Value

CUSTOMER POTENTIAL: CREATED VALUE

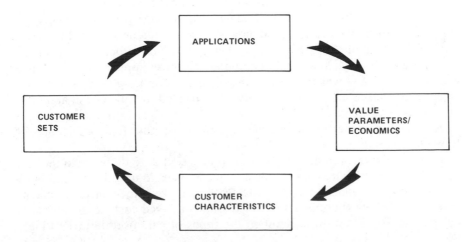

the value created, how it varies with different performance levels, and, therefore, which are the most important parameters to influence in order to maximize value.

3. Define the characteristics of customers that will distinguish whether they get high or low value. Examples of these characteristics include specific uses, geographic locations, demographics, attitudes, personal or business objectives, economics, etc.

4. Translate these characteristics into identifiable customers or sets of customers.

In assessing the value created by many high-technology commercial products, cost saving is typically important to early sales, whether through substitution, time savings, or elimination of some requirement. For example, word processors and teleconferencing were frequently justified on this basis in initial applications. In fact, since return on investment calculations are required in many companies, cost saving is usually a critical parameter for getting established in an industrial or commercial market.

However, the greatest benefits of many high-technology products are frequently not in the cost savings, but are in the less tangible, less-measurable, productivity improvements. Copiers and personal computers are examples.

In fact, the best new application is one where both productivity and cost-saving value can be created. The greatest benefit is often enhanced productivity or new opportunities, but cost savings get the new product "in the door" so that it can prove its broader value.

The real challenge is to define value added in a meaningful way. This requires clearly identifying those factors that will "drive" the value to the user. It is useful to "model" the characteristics of the user's application that drive value to him. For example, the value of a voice mail system to a sales force would be greater in those situations where the sales force was widely dispersed, where sales persons spend little time in the office, but need to place orders or communicate with other personnel frequently.

Furthermore, it is important to remember that value is usually relative to some alternative. Packet-switched data are more valuable relative to circuit-switched data in applications that are highly interactive between terminals or between terminals and a host computer. In these applications there is a good deal of time in which the transmission link is not being used. The packet approach permits a link to be used only when needed, but the circuit approach keeps the link open as long as the "session" is active. In interactive applications such as order entry or remote computing, the better utilization of transmission reduces cost.

In assessing value added to the user, it is essential to define who the real decision maker is. It may not be the actual end user. Managers at a company developing a new railcar equipment technology thoroughly evaluated benefits and defined where these benefits added value or saved costs to the railroads or car builders. Then they identified the types of cars used in these "high-benefit" situations. They found that in some cases the real purchase decision was made by the third-party fleet owners, not by the railroads or car builders who got the benefits. The resulting analysis is summarized in Exhibit 20-7. Short of the railroads' jointly mandating the technology, there was only modest economic incentive for the lessor to pay a premium for the new technology. To be viable, it would be necessary to get railroads to change their rate structure to pass some of the benefits on to actual car owners. All railroads would have to agree on it for cars to be in exchange service across the country. The uncertainty and time involved to accomplish that became a critical factor in deciding whether to proceed.

Created value assessment should be done for each major benefit. It should be carried out with a large enough sample of potential customers to clearly confirm those buyer characteristics for whom the benefits apply, and thus permit meaningful definition of target segments. It is then possible to assess both the benefits and the individual segments in terms of degree of value created, how broadly benefits apply, and "fit" between benefactors and de-

EXHIBIT 20-7.   *Created Value Summary by Feature*

CREATED VALUE SUMMARY BY FEATURE

PASS THROUGH OF FEATURE'S
VALUE TO OWNER/DECISION MAKER

Key: ◯ Good   ● Weak

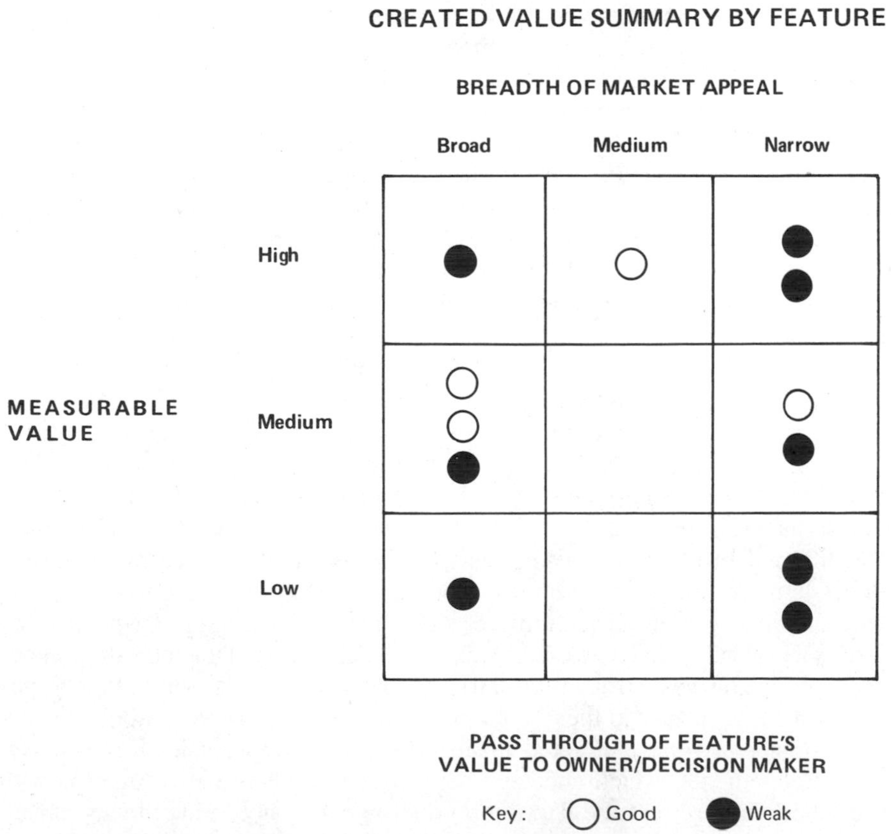

cision makers. This will help establish priorities for segments, as well as help determine which benefits should be concentrated on for the most leverage in developing the market rapidly. It will also indicate where opportunities exist for value-based premium pricing, an important input to the profit potential assessment that follows.

Customer Potential—Profit Leverage

It always feels good to create value for the customer. It feels even better when you add value and make money doing it. Frequently, too little attention is placed on quantifying the full cost profit potential of serving different customer types, and then using this as a key criterion for segmenting the market and setting customer priorities.

Most companies spend much time and effort on developing manufacturing cost projections for a new high-technology product. They do elaborate analyses to estimate how costs will decline as volume is built up. Although this is a necessary ingredient in the profit picture, the costs of selling and servicing the product are of at least equal importance but are generally given significantly less emphasis. Often costs are not meaningfully allocated to products and customer segments to define a "full-cost" profit picture. When they are allocated, they frequently are estimated in gross terms as a percentage of sales or on some other relatively macro basis, perhaps building in some allowance for early start-up efforts.

This approach is neither accurate nor helpful in making key marketing decisions. For example, someone has to decide how many salespersons to employ to reach the revenue goal and who should be called on to best achieve it. This requires specific (even if implicit) assumptions about specific factors that drive the productivity of the selling effort—hence what sales level per salesperson is obtainable and, accordingly, the sales cost to generate revenues.

Working out the productivity potential and cost of serving specific customer groups requires a thorough economic analysis of the sales process for each customer type. The decision process for high-technology products is often complex and involves multiple decision makers. Consider the selling effort for a high-technology medical product. One manufacturer did an in-depth analysis and modeling of the sales process for each type of hospital for different products in varying geographic areas. It showed major differences in travel times, the number of people to be contacted, duration of the calls, number of demonstrations required, order sizes, likely "win" ratios, after-sale revisit frequencies, and support requirements. Dramatic differences emerged in the cost of gaining market share in different product/customer sets and consequently in their profitability. In addition, the geographic density of customers strongly affected profits through different sales-force travel-time requirements, which impacted their effective selling time. Analysis with the model showed that the flagship product was actually losing money except where it was sold in multiple units, and that certain combinations of geographic areas, products, and types of hospitals were unprofitable on a full-cost basis. The result was a significant restructuring of both marketing and product development efforts to focus on specific types of hospitals in certain metropolitan areas with a "basket" of products designed to permit multiple productive contacts with these hospitals on a given visit to get maximum leverage out of the salesperson's time.

Carrying out this evaluation not only helps identify high- and low-profit leverage segments, but also shows how the actual marketing process should be managed to be productive. A company introducing a high-technology product into the otherwise low-technology automotive repair business was growing rapidly, yet its growth was unprofitable because of high marketing expenses due to low salesperson productivity. Analysis showed that less than half of the available market was composed of possible buyers, and of those only 20 percent were near-term prospects. Yet at the time 70 percent of the effort was being spent on "non-near-term prospects," and only half of the actual buyers were ever contacted. Sales processes were modeled in terms of which customers should be "forgotten" and which were worth monitoring, developing over time, or pursuing immediately. This model provided the foundation to define approaches and allocate selling time for each category—focusing on customers with payoff potential and covering longer-term prospects through more cost-efficient means. Sales productivity was improved over two-thirds in the first six months, and selling costs were reduced by 20 percentage points.

It is important to look at both the profit potential of individual segments and also how much of the total market can be served economically. For example, in most service businesses assets and people resources must be geographically located in the local markets they serve. Given a minimum local cost structure, it is essential to carefully analyze which markets have adequate potential to be served profitably. Exhibit 20-8 shows the analysis for one high technology–based service business which has both heavy centralized costs and significant local costs. High-density, high-potential markets are added first to spread fixed local marketing and service costs across their larger volume potential, thereby giving lower unit costs. As markets are initially added, fixed system overhead is spread more broadly, bringing down overall unit overhead costs further. However, as more and more markets are added, low-density, low-potential markets begin to boost system-wide costs again because of inefficiencies and high local fixed costs. As for margins, they improve as markets are added initially because of growing critical mass and leverage on direct product costs. However, eventually margins also deteriorate because of inefficiencies and poor product mix in smaller markets. Taken together, the analysis showed a discrete band of coverage in which operating profitability would be highest. The decision was made to significantly restructure the markets served, trimming back to a concentrated geographic strategy.

EXHIBIT 20-8.   Profit Leverage Varies with Geographic Coverage

PROFIT LEVERAGE VARIES WITH GEOGRAPHIC COVERAGE

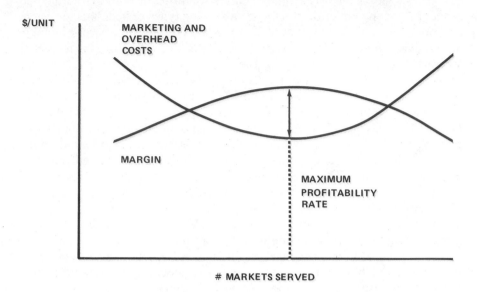

While the profitability of serving specific segments and the economics of broader coverage may be the most frequently underevaluated areas in assessing the market profit potential, there are several other areas where payoffs usually follow careful probing:

1. The newer and more unique the product, the greater the challenge in setting an initial price, since it is tougher to find some baseline against which to assess price/performance. The value analysis discussed earlier is the key, if it has been done thoroughly it will provide a good starting point.

2. Higher price may be supportable in some segments based on greater benefits, with only minor differences in the product or support costs required to provide them.

3. Some customers will tend to use larger or more enhanced versions of the product, meaning higher value per order, often with little or no increase in selling effort, hence sales costs.

4. Some customers tend to buy in quantity. While this generally reduces the cost of sales, it is necessary to establish whether pricing that results from a bidding process or competition reduces margins more than the efficiencies improve them.

5. For many products, the initial sale is only the beginning. Assess the "razor blade" potential, whether due to maintenance, parts, future enhancements to the products, or continuing usage revenues. For

technology-based service businesses, this is generally the predominant factor on which the economics depend. For example, in the long-distance telephone business, customer profit potential is driven by acquisition costs versus monthly revenue potential and the probable rate of loss of customers over time to competition. Different segments vary in these characteristics, and these are the critical success factors to be managed.

We've emphasized actionability. The purpose of this segmentation by profitability, then, is not to measure it, but to figure out how and where we can best achieve it. Profit-leverage assessment will identify those customers with whom we can obtain the highest profit potential. However, our success at capitalizing on both profit leverage and created value opportunities will ultimately depend on our relative competitive position in serving these customer segments.

Competitive Potential—Relative Value

With customer potential defined, emphasis shifts to determining competitive potential—with what customers in what circumstances the company has the best chance to beat competition. This requires segmenting the market in "selfish" terms.

An important dimension of competitive potential is the relative value provided to various customers by our product offerings versus those of the competition. The created value assessment described earlier provides the foundation for this evaluation. It will have defined which users get the most value and how they get it, as well as the parameters that are likely to drive the purchase decision for different users. We can then compare ourselves to key competitors on those parameters. This will reveal those parameters where we have competitive advantages and those where we have disadvantages. Since the earlier created value assessment showed which customers should care the most about which parameters in making their purchase decisions, we can define the characteristics of "winning" customer groups—those customers or applications where our particular advantages are most important—our best targets. By identifying and quantifying these customer sets, we will also have a picture of the size of the market where we have a competitive advantage. Similarly, those customer sets where we have disadvantages will also be evident, so we can quantify how much market can be "opened" by improving performance on parameters where we are weak. The resulting profile of the market in terms of relative competitive capabilities provides a tangible basis for decisions on how to improve existing products and which new ones to develop. The market affected by resource commitments to improve specific features or performance parameters can be clearly defined and quantified, and the potential returns can be evaluated.

This kind of segmentation is actionable. In one sophisticated power

EXHIBIT 20-9.   Define Relative Competitive Value

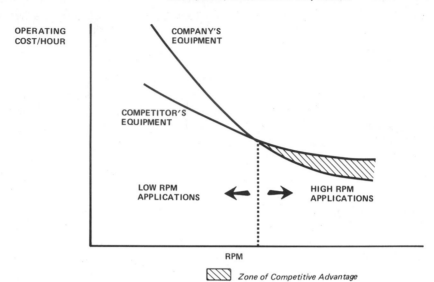

equipment business, a smaller competitor sought to build share profitability against the dominant market leader. Fuel costs were a critical element of user life-cycle costs. As shown in Exhibit 20-9, assessment showed that while the market leader's technology gave better fuel economy at lower RPMs, the smaller competitor had an advantage at higher RPMs. The smaller manufacturer therefore defined and concentrated on applications that had high-RPM modes. The cost for the larger competitor to change its technology to improve its performance was high and time consuming and would require sacrificing much of its advantage at the lower end. The smaller competitor was able to carve out a significant piece of the market while commanding a price premium. It gained volume economies and built a support structure to protect its share while the larger competitor struggled to find a means to improve its performance in those ranges without sacrificing its own advantages in the rest of the market. Once the smaller competitor, that business now has equal share with the formerly dominant competitor and competes toe to toe.

The competitive value assessment, building on the customer value assessment, leads to a clear picture of which customer groups not only receive high value from the product but also will receive higher value from us than from our competition. This permits targeting on customers who should care most about the capabilities where we have a competitive advantage and care least about those where we are at a disadvantage.

Competitive Potential—Relative Costs/Profits

The next crucial question is which customers can be served more or less profitably by us than by our competitors—through either cost or price differences. This requires appraising our competitors' relative costs and price potential in serving important segments. Do not limit cost comparisons to different products, customers, and applications. Frequently geographic differences are especially important, since much selling, marketing, and after-sales service cost tend to be geographically based. Hence significant differences will exist in serving lower- versus higher-density geographic areas, or areas with a small versus large existing installed base.

Our topic is not of how to do a basic competitive cost and price comparison. But with this assessment complete, it should be used to define and measure segments of the market in which a competitive advantage can be obtained based on price-value differentials, cost differentials, or both. Similarly, it shows where economic disadvantages exist. This comparison can be used either to determine where higher profitability can be achieved—through lower costs and/or pricing to recover higher value—or where an advantage can be used to leverage share and volume. Exhibit 20-10 illustrates examples of issues and options that are typically raised in following through

EXHIBIT 20-10. *Create Phase—Targeting: Define Segments/Set Priorities Based on Competitive Value and Cost/Profit Differentials*

TARGETING: DEFINING SEGMENTS AND SETTING PRIORITIES

COMPETITIVE VALUE DIFFERENTIAL

	Favorable	Unfavorable
Favorable	**CONCENTRATE** • Segment size adequate to merit concentration? • What optimal tradeoff on premium price vs. share emphasis? • Can competitor correct deficiencies; can we stay ahead?	**COST FOCUS** • What performance/segment emphasis best exploits cost advantage? • Is low price/performance segment viable? • What enhancements possible?
Unfavorable	**VALUE FOCUS** • Value pricing potential? • Cost reduce/outsourcing without sacrificing value advantage?	**REPOSITION** • Avoid? • Restructure? • Incremental?

COMPETITIVE COST/PROFIT DIFFERENTIAL

this process. This segmentation thus provides a framework with which to identify and evaluate specific actions in order to achieve a competitive advantage with different customer groups.

Execution Potential—Early Adopters

Ability to execute quickly is a crucial consideration in trying to create the market for a high-technology product. Once target groups have been prioritized on customer and competitive criteria, it is important to identify the specific companies or groups within them that are likely to be the initial tryers.

While the characteristics of early tryers will vary from the industry and market to the next, there are some characteristics worth looking for in screening the market.

1. A simple decision-making structure is a real plus in a situation where missionary selling is required. For example, most banks have very complex telecommunications and data processing organizations. A data communications offering may require agreement of a half dozen groups spread among different staff areas, with reporting relationships that do not converge until near the top of the corporate structure. Consummating a sale in that situation is difficult and time-consuming.

2. The interest of top management is almost invariably a critical parameter in the introduction of new technology, since a significant investment is required and returns are uncertain. An analysis of teleconferencing usage growth across a large sample of companies clearly indicated an enormous difference in utilization in those companies where senior management took not only an interest in the application, but where they literally mandated its use. It became the norm, and was politically desirable. This is especially important for products that require a critical mass of usage before productivity benefits are realized. Additionally, top-management involvement influences the appropriate sales approach. Look for signs that top management has been willing to make commitments to try new products in their company. Evidence of previous pilot systems is a good indicator.

3. In some companies, the structure or the nature of business more easily permits a pilot approach to the project with contained risk before a full adoption. Larger and geographically diverse companies are often the early tryers of new technology, because it is possible for them to test it in a particular region or part of the business without being totally committed. This requires a real understanding of the customer's business. For example, in open-pit mining, certain mines were good candidates for new products because their physical dispersion of operations around the mine resulted in many relatively independent "pockets" of operating activity where technology could be tested.

The fact is that some users are just more disposed to be "tryers"; the culture of some companies is to "try it." They are generally known within industry circles. Identify these companies—they offer the best chance of getting an early trial.

Execution Potential—Keeping the Customer

Which customer segments can be made long-term as well as short-term profit generators? The customer goes through his own usage experience cycle with the product. It is essential to understand and anticipate how that experience may change his usage, his needs, and his purchasing behavior. The high-tech customer may go through this cycle very rapidly.

The customer's usage experience cycle occurs as he becomes more comfortable and familiar with the product. As this happens his usage increases and his requirements become more sophisticated. As users of personal computer software became more sophisticated with the individual packages for word processing, spreadsheets, and graphics, they wanted to use them together, leading to development of integrated packages and window displays.

In a service offering, this may mean that although the customer will initially use an outside capability, he may eventually buy his own system. Companies using outside broadcast video services for periodic broadcasting of shareholder meetings or other major events may eventually install their own internal systems as usage increases.

This user experience cycle means that segments must be conceptualized as moving, rather than static targets. The issue is how to move with them to fulfill their future as well as current needs. For example, the management of an electronic messaging service anticipated that some of its customers would ultimately buy their own internal systems. Rather than simply fighting the facts, it effectively put the customer in the business at the appropriate time by offering to integrate, install, and manage the system. This saved the customer installation headaches and eliminated the need to build a competent staff to operate and enhance the system. The service company retained the revenues from transmission and management of the system and expected to offset lost revenues with the additional growth in customer usage.

For service businesses and equipment businesses where there is a "razor blade" follow-on profit stream, understanding changing user priorities is critical to minimize the customer "churn." The cost of acquiring new customers simply to replace the churn and stay even can become overwhelming as the size of the customers' base increases, especially when the primary growth of the business slows.

A critical success factor is renewing competitiveness with the important customer segments as they develop. An early sense of this preservability is an important consideration in prioritizing target segments. Effectively, we are anticipating how customer needs are likely to change as the business makes the transition to the leverage success phase. Again, the task is not just finding preservable segments but determining how to make them preservable and laying the groundwork early to do so.

Actionable Segments

The end product of the six screening criteria described above is often not one but several different layers of market segmentation. The result is a framework of opportunities defined in terms of what we can do about them.

THE LEVERAGE-SUCCESS PHASE

Once the basic market has been successfully developed in the create phase, it begins to build momentum on its own. Then, the opportunity exists to get maximum leverage. However, at this point, shifts start to occur in some of the factors driving the market and competition. There are more competitors, and competition is stiffer. The balance between added performance and improved price begins to change in favor of price. Customers and distributors become increasingly selective and demanding with regard to quality, service, and price. They look for vendors to simplify an intelligent purchase decision. The customer base may fragment into even more discrete groups that represent different purchase motivations.

In this context, critical success factors change, too. Timely strategy shifts are necessary to maintain success. Typically, several changing requirements emerge:

The need to maintain product-line integrity

The need for greater marketing leverage

The need to redefine the boundaries of competitiveness

The need for manufacturing integration

PRODUCT-LINE INTEGRITY

"Leveraging success" means consolidating what you've got and building on it before the dust settles. The pressure is on to exploit technology quickly once the basic market has been created and has achieved its own momentum. Companies move quickly to deepen and broaden both the products categories and markets they serve.

Years ago the artificial-fiber producers were excellent at doing this; as a synthetic fiber came out, it was quickly moved downstream into the different yarn and fabric manufacturing applications, and thence into a wide variety of end uses for which its particular attributes were best suited. Today we see this happening in computer software. Building on its initial MS/DOS success, Microsoft produced a broad variety of products: seven languages, three operating systems, four applications products, games, computer books, and even some hardware.

Proliferating Complexity

There is a lot of leverage from success; however, if rapid exploitation is done carelessly it can often lead to major problems of incompatibility and inconsistency, which prove hard to correct later. Product-line integrity can be lost; once lost, it is extremely difficult to restore without major reworking and loss of credibility.

Thus it is not only necessary to move quickly to exploit the initial successes, but also to do so with careful discipline, coordination, and sensitivity to changing conditions. For example, to spur entrepreneurship, it may make sense for different groups within a large company to move in parallel to develop products and markets faster, but there needs to be overall coordination. IBM produced a jumble of incompatible office systems over the years—over half a dozen overlapping systems in word processing, office automation, and small computers. This incompatibility left it vulnerable to competitors like Wang, DEC, and Data General. The company later committed itself to making its systems work together—a major and lengthy undertaking to eliminate inconvenience and frustration for both IBM and its customers.

Integration

Preserving the integrity of the product line requires alertness to needs for integration. For instance, it may be critical to insure that new products are compatible with an installed base. In 1983 DEC introduced desktop computers. However, they were not compatible with DEC's family of Vax super minis, because DEC did not fully realize the importance and marketing implications of the workstation.

Integration can sometimes be required between areas that are, on the surface, even more dissimilar. For instance, technology's leading markets sometimes converge. Hewlett-Packard found that two of its markets were converging as customers wanted to link test instruments with personal computers, both of which it made but sold separately through different sales forces. HP combined the sales forces and sold both products as an integrated system.

The main driver for integration and simplification is the customer. If product lines become too fragmented and complex too quickly, even sophisticated users may find themselves overwhelmed. There is a limit to how much confusion and fragmentation customers are willing to put up with. Furthermore, as technology moves into new areas it must be introduced to less-sophisticated users who are unfamiliar with it. A clear, well-integrated approach to the product line is important to give customers confidence in their ability to make intelligent purchase decisions. They will look to the major suppliers to play more of a role in simplifying, integrating, and packaging as product offerings proliferate. The suppliers who do offer such improvements have a competitive advantage.

Microcomputer software represents a classic example. Individual application areas such as spreadsheet, word processing, data base management, and graphics programs have burgeoned from simple initial offerings to a snowballing of more sophisticated programs. As applications fragmented, increasing attention focused on the inability to run these programs together. The first integrated programs followed, led by Lotus 1-2-3. Before long, integrated programs also began to proliferate. That, of course, led to the desire to work with programs simultaneously, fostering multiple window approaches for more effective integration. Then, as these broader capabilities evolved, they stimulated more power needs and more sharing of resources, thereby fostering multiuser capabilities that share data bases and central storage. As this developed, it led to more and more emphasis on communications, including eventually, person-to-person conferencing using PCs as the medium for simultaneous reviewing and editing of information. The next issue would seem to be whether the more integrated programs will provide adequate capabilities in their individual program elements to meet the increasing sophistication of users. Failure to do so would cause many users to move back to more specialized programs, creating a shakeout of the weaker integrated programs.

The pattern becomes clear. As depicted in Exhibit 20-11, each product

EXHIBIT 20-11. *Leverage Success Phase—Product Line Integrity*

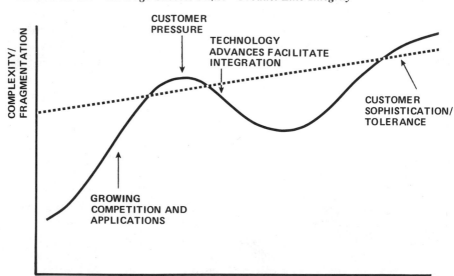

or system advance leads to a proliferation of capabilities and hence to complexity. This is followed by some type of integration approach to handle the increased complexity and reduce its effect on customers. Then this integration advance itself proliferates and is followed by another integration advance, and so on. Meanwhile, the customer's sophistication increases in parallel. A critical success factor is alertness to the opportunity for integration that will provide a basis for the next advance—and all the while remembering that the customers' capabilities and experience with the technology are changing too. Customers expect not only depth and breadth of capabilities offered, but also ease of use and reduced complexity of their purchase decisions. Their needs become increasingly hard–soft. Sophistication makes them more demanding on some dimensions and more tolerant of complexity on others. The challenge is to stay on top of and adjust to this changing texture of customer requirements as they evolve. Doing so effectively will help maintain the product-line integrity needed to support continued success in the leverage success phase.

THE NEED FOR MARKETING LEVERAGE

During the leverage-success phase, marketing and distribution become increasingly important success factors. This does not imply that technological innovation and product enhancement decline in importance. However, as the market broadens, users become more sophisticated, and competition intensifies, the need for marketing skills and capabilities grows.

Higher Barriers

It becomes more difficult and expensive to overcome the "noise level." This translates into more marketing, advertising, promotion and distribution costs, and sophistication in order to achieve the same effect. VisiCorp introduced the original VisiCalc spreadsheet with virtually no advertising. Four years later, Lotus Development Corporation introduced its 1-2-3 package by spending a million dollars on advertising over a three-month period, setting a new standard for the industry. In late 1984, it took 8 million to 10 million dollars to introduce a significant new software product, and advertising costs effectively became a barrier to new competition. In this context, computer companies such as Apple are bringing in senior executives from consumer packaged-goods businesses, where retail and advertising savvy are the key success factors.

It is essential to identify what the barriers will be for the "incremental product," and to get control of them early on. These barriers include shelf space, inventory stocking, customer willingness to undertake demonstrations or pilots, approval of limited brands for purchase, and many other factors. These barriers will determine the critical success factors for either capturing the "high ground" early or developing a plan to control or circumvent them as they emerge.

The character of this marketing shift varies from one industry to another, but the common denominator is that marketing strength becomes a key differentiator between winners and losers.

Reshaping Distribution

Distribution leverage almost certainly becomes a major differentiator: important issues concern how broadly to diversify channels, and how and where to rebalance control with expediency during this phase.

Powerful marketing and distribution leverage may be critical from "day one" for the substitute product entering an already structured and highly competitive marketplace. Texas Instruments learned this lesson the hard way with its failure in digital watches. Later it entered the home computer business in the create phase, where technological capability was in fact the main success factor. It did well initially, but as the need for marketing leverage increased, TI's position deteriorated, and it (along with a number of other well-known companies) was forced to withdraw with major losses.

There is a fundamental tradeoff between the importance of the control associated with direct distribution versus the expediency and variable cost of indirect channels. Many high-tech products require a sophisticated "technical sell" and much missionary work to develop an order. Typically, if the product is complex and difficult to sell, a direct, dedicated sales and service organization is more effective. But the missionary sell means a heavy time commitment with the customer to pursue each order opportunity. This requires high productive time (e.g., by minimizing travel), high value orders, and high win ratios for good marketing productivity and reasonable marketing cost of sales. But the early market situation works against these economics. Opportunities are scattered. The installed base is too small and dispersed for significant parts revenues and service efficiencies. Buyers want to commit themselves in small bites, and many are looking, but few are buying. Building a broad, dedicated, direct approach is very expensive under these conditions and frequently is not affordable in early stages while creating the market.

Often economics and the priority to get the base established quickly outweigh early control and dedication, even when complexity and uniqueness may suggest a direct and dedicated approach as soon as it is affordable. This suggests shared or variable cost approaches with established channels: another internal sales or service force, or agents or distributors calling on the same type of customers. The challenge is to identify candidates with the necessary skills, coverage, and incentives.

The economics change as the business moves into the leverage-success phase of growth. The installed base is larger and denser, the market has momentum, order sizes are larger, chances of closure are higher, and scale economies on indirect service and support costs improve. These shifts make higher control through dedicated sales and service approaches more cost-effective and affordable.

Mixed Approaches

Many companies have been successful with a mixed portfolio approach to handling the early situation while preparing for the later transition. Exhibit 20-12 depicts one such approach. With this approach, some companies use their own direct sales force to go after a limited set of large "house accounts" or to market directly in a few major metropolitan areas. They use distributors to sell to smaller and less sophisticated users, to larger accounts that are not on the "house" list, and to all other geographic areas. Sometimes the "carrot" to encourage the distributors to accept this hybrid arrangement is giving them the service, consumables, and after-market parts business for house accounts in their area as well.

This portfolio of approaches can be modified selectively to either get greater control by expanding direct leverage or continue to broaden channels as the business moves into the leverage success phase. In the example shown, direct distribution is expanded to many markets, and new channels are opened up, while indirect distribution is concentrated on lower density markets.

In the PABX business, Rolm managed its transition in distribution in an outstanding way. Rolm was a military computer company that developed

EXHIBIT 20-12.   Shifting Distribution Strategy

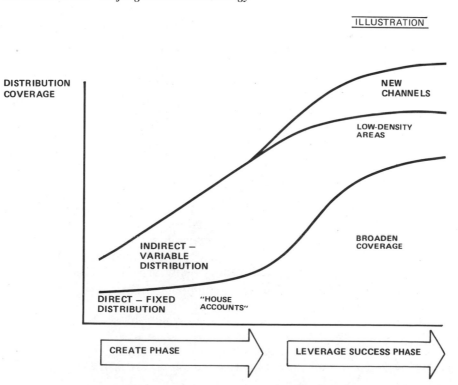

one of the first sophisticated computer-controlled PABXs, in medium size ranges. However, it had no distribution capabilities for the PABX market. Recognizing the importance of rapid exploitation of the product and "variable-izing" its sales costs to do so, it developed good relationships with a wide range of non-Bell telephone companies. The majority of its early sales were through these telephone companies, which served about 20 percent of the national market. It then carefully chose distributors to serve the balance of the country and began competing head to head with AT&T in those areas. Eventually, Rolm's reputation and installed base reached the point where its distributors were more dependent on Rolm than it was on them. Rolm began to weed out and take over its distribution system, acquiring the excellent distributors where possible, and replacing the poor ones by going direct. This further spurred its sales dollar growth. By integrating forward, Rolm captured a larger piece of the customer's dollar, since its offering then included the final sales price, installation, and service.

It is important to anticipate and plan the evolution of distribution right from the start. Selection of some early options may foreclose others or make later transition without lost sales or service gaps difficult.

BOUNDARIES OF COMPETITIVENESS

The likelihood of profitability in a market segment is suggested by the relationships among three variables: the size and growth of the market, the share required to be profitable, and the number of competitors attacking the segment. Since the incremental costs of serving a segment vary by competitor, their potentials for profitability in that segment also vary. All these variables change dramatically from the early create phase to the leverage-success phase. The market during the latter period is significantly larger and is still growing fast, but there are many more competitors. Sales productivity variables may be stable, or even in decline, after having risen as the market developed during the create phase. Breakeven share levels rise; in many segments there are too many competitors for all to reach breakeven shares. Some customer segments, some applications, and some geographic areas become uneconomical for some competitors to serve. They become marginal unless a company already has an especially strong position for cost leverage, or some other unique cost or value advantage in serving them.

The competitive economics have changed. Each competitor should redefine his boundaries of competitiveness—how broadly he can serve the market profitably today and where he should concentrate now for the best overall profit and growth.

The answers will rarely be clear-cut on a segment-by-segment basis. It is necessary to review the segments defined in the create phase and to assess what subsets are becoming less profitable to serve. For example, in spite of greater market size, some lower-density geographic areas may have become uneconomic to serve except by competitors who have already built strong bases and share positions. As applications have grown more sophisticated, they have fragmented into subsets with varying attractiveness. As a result, it is important to reevaluate which segments are most profitable to serve. The results of this assessment usually differ markedly by competitor, since share, product, and cost differences have opened up between them. Competitive advantages and vulnerabilities have changed notably, and with them the appropriate basis for a successful competitive concept for the next phase of growth.

While it is necessary to slice the market and competitive economics more finely at this point, there are considerably better data and experience to use than there were during the early create phase. There should be good understanding and evidence on how costs vary in serving various types of customers or segments, and how competitors and customers are behaving. It should be possible to build a sound, fact-based foundation for determining shifts in competitive and market focus—where to concentrate narrowly and where to compete broadly to leverage success in this next phase of growth.

MANUFACTURING INTEGRATION

How much manufacturing should the high-tech company do itself? It faces a wide range of options, from sourcing all manufacturing and a significant portion of design work, through various combinations of inside and outside sourcing for components, subsystems, assembly, and specific design elements, to a highly vertically integrated approach. The essential tradeoff is in the degree of flexibility and speed versus control and value added. The relative importance of these factors also tends to shift as the business moves from the create to the leverage-success phase.

In the create stage, flexibility and speed are usually paramount. Some outside sourcing is often desirable for components, where technology and quality control needs permit. This syndicates risk and reduces investment needs while uncertainty is highest. It offers higher volume potential faster than does putting in new manufacturing facilities from scratch, and it may facilitate obtaining needed manufacturing technology from others rather than taking the time and resources to develop it in-house.

During the leverage-success phase, cost leadership, quality control, and delivery times become increasingly important success factors in an environment of intensifying competition. Manufacturing focus typically moves toward more automation, and technological efforts emphasize manufacturing improvements as well as product development. Further, product innovations are more frequently cost oriented. This requires close integration between product and manufacturing process design to obtain enhanced product capabilities at emphatically lower costs. The result is greater complexity and tighter integration needs.

Manufacturing becomes a critical success factor, and the business needs greater control over some elements of it. While this doesn't always mean doing everything in-house, a rigorous review of the manufacturing structure is essential, even if it suggests simply being more selective on what is sourced outside. Such a review could even result in sourcing *more* from outside in some areas; for example, if manufacturing technology has stabilized enough that less expensive overseas sourcing may be possible with the greater control needed. In general, however, we've found the tendency is to go more internal at this stage for greater product-manufacturing integration and control. The key success factor is to identify the core elements of the product which dominate technical and cost competitiveness and ensure control over them.

In the microcomputer business, IBM represents an example of this movement toward internal sourcing. Long known for its "do it inside" approach and expertise in manufacturing, it opted for flexibility and speed when it entered the business. Controlling the basic system architecture, it sourced design elements and readily available components and subsystems, and even subcontracted assembly, to cut lead times and increase its flexibility in order to respond to the market. Then, as the industry became more price- and distribution-sensitive, it steadily brought manufacturing in-house, even while preparing to introduce a more powerful second-generation product, the AT.

Shifts in manufacturing strategy—as do shifts in distribution strategy—need to be addressed early to permit a smooth rebalancing of flexibility versus control. It takes time to develop the capabilities to bring more manufacturing in-house or to set up systems to ensure the efficiency of outside sources. This requires concurrent management—continuing to pursue flexible approach in the create phase while simultaneously preparing for selected integration during the leverage-success phase.

THE REVITALIZE PHASE

It is in this phase that a company must revitalize the business if growth is to be sustained. The market is still growing as the business enters this phase, but the maximum potential, technical capability, and realized markets are beginning to converge. Saturation is within sight. The issue then is whether the business can be revitalized before it plateaus or declines. The one thing for sure is that it won't stay "business as usual."

Warning Signs

When an industry is growing, most participants assume it will grow for the foreseeable future. In fact, the saturation point is difficult to diagnose well in advance. Spotting it early takes objectivity and real insight about how the market and economics of the business are changing, coupled with a well-thought-through system to monitor key indicators. There will be visible signs; however, the effectiveness at detecting them is directly related to how good a job has been done in rigorously developing the market, competitive, and economic variables discussed in conjunction with earlier phases.

If the three measures of market potential have been thought through and quantified, they will reveal the technical capability market approaching the maximum market potential, and the realized market narrowing the spread with the technical capability market. Likewise, tracking product enhancements and price/performance improvements will show them to be stretching out and slowing. If profit economics of serving important segments and introducing new products have been reevaluated and tracked during the leverage-success phase, they will show that the costs of gaining share or introducing new products have become so high that a new move must nearly be a sure thing to be warranted, and even then requires accepting an extended payback. Similarly, the viable "boundaries of competitiveness" in some segments will contract markedly as it becomes unattractive to compete so broadly. Meanwhile, breakeven share levels will be rising faster than the market is growing.

These are some of the indicators that will give early warning. However, to be valid, some of them need to have been measured and tracked well in advance of the business's entering this phase. While information generally exists to measure past product improvements on a consistent basis, it is especially difficult to reconstruct, in retrospect, historical values of the maximum and technical capability markets, specific user segments, or the economics of serving these segments. Thus laying the basis for dealing effectively with the revitalization phase really needs to be started much earlier, as part of the planning efforts for creating and leveraging growth.

Two-Edged Sword

The new opportunities or threats that can emerge in this phase are even more difficult to anticipate. If the opportunity to revitalize the business exists, it will be a two-edged sword. A new competitor might emerge with an innovation or new technology that will spur the market and render the present competitors obsolete in the process. Alternatively, the market may outgrow and move away from present products. As user sophistication increases and needs change, different products or technologies may suit them better. As we saw earlier, floppy disks alone were fine for early PC users, but as usage grew and applications became more sophisticated, the capabilities of hard disks became more appropriate and the market shifted toward them. Once started, a shift tends to accelerate as greater volume drives down costs and prices for the substitute.

Obsolete Yourself First

The trick, then, is to obsolete yourself before the competition or market does. This runs counter to the conventional wisdom about return on investment. After putting in major efforts, and perhaps after incurring significant losses over an extended period, management finds that the product is finally taking hold and beginning to pay the returns it has been waiting for. Can it really be time to think about replacement?

The problem in putting off replacement is the speed with which the market can move away from a product once a better one is introduced, or once customers' needs change. Once momentum is lost to a competitor's product, the chances of recovering it are slim. Even with a good product response, credibility must be regained with distributors and users. This can be a slow and laborious task, and the developing market for the new technology doesn't wait. VisiCorp introduced VisiCalc in 1979 and triggered the growth of the PC market with the first powerful and easy-to-use financial modeling tool. But it lost sight of its core product, milking it while it sought to move into other applications areas. As competition increased, it finally began to revise the program, but then did so in the form of minor product enhancements, rather than recognizing the need to replace it to meet competitive offerings such as Lotus 1-2-3. The response was "too little, too late." VisiCorp's business dropped dramatically, and it was later acquired by Lotus.

On the other hand, 3M is an example of a company that aggressively pursues self-obsolescence. A major participant in magnetic hard disk technology, 3M has pushed laser technology to provide a much higher-density and cheaper alternative. Early efforts had serious limitations; for instance, information on the disk could not be altered once it was implanted, limiting it to applications such as the storing of archives. But commitment paid off—3M has now found a way to revise information. Able to store 25 times the information that a comparably sized and priced hard disk can store, the new technology offers promise for major advances in the capabilities of microcomputers, and hence for a whole new range of applications. 3M didn't wait for saturation; its determination to obsolete itself, if successful, promises to revitalize not only its own still-growing business, but also could provide the foundation to spur a new phase of growth in the broader microcomputer industry.

The 3M example reveals something else about a major revitalization. The new technology may appear to be a direct substitute for the old, with vastly improved performance. But that vast improvement virtually guarantees it will not be a direct substitute. It will open up major new market opportunities. Furthermore, the new technology may only obsolete a portion of the existing product's applications—some may still be more cost/performance-effective with the older technology. The implication? A new business is generated, not just a new product. Markets, customer applications and buying motives, distribution, manufacturing, and, ultimately, virtually every element of the business will be affected.

The obsoleting triggers a new create phase. It is essential to go through the same rigorous competitive targeting and other approaches described for the create phase to define and exploit the potential. Opportunities may be relatively quick to exploit if the new product is a substitute for the existing product or if an installed base is replaceable. In other cases they may take significant time to develop.

What's Different the Next Time?

In a high-technology business success can sow the seeds of failure. Flushed with confidence from the success of their first-generation product, many high-technology companies have either met or narrowly avoided disaster in their efforts to revitalize the business with a second-generation product. It is natural to see the challenge as one of introducing a second-generation product, when the real challenge is to redefine the whole business.

This distinction is critical for several reasons. Each new generation is typically more expensive to develop and introduce, vastly changing the scale economics of the industry. Also, improved price/performance opens new markets, which change success factors in distribution, manufacturing, and support.

The tendency to see a new project as a line extension, rather than as a new business, was a factor when, in 1981, Data General brought out the Enterprise computer two years late, overpriced, and with limited software. They sold only 1200 units. DG didn't adapt to the different semiconductor technology for smaller machines, didn't focus on lower-cost manufacturing, and didn't have the right distribution channels for the product. Because they viewed it more as a line extension than as a separate business, they failed to commit the adequate resources to succeed or identify "what's different" about the opportunity. But, to their great credit, they really learned from the failure—they set up a separate team and facility for the new workstation line and ultimately developed a strong entry not only in the PC area but also in the office automation capabilities of their minis.

Dream or Reality?

When the next new technology is fresh from the labs, the excitement is high and opportunities look juicy. Before abandoning or undermining the credibility of the core product, and before investing millions for commercialization, it is worth an in-depth "sanity check" to validate that the new offering is in fact a "revitalizer," and not just a specialty product. Carrying out the targeting assessment discussed in the create phase will separate the wheat from the chaff.

A company with new triglyceride technology was preparing to spend tens of millions of dollars on a plant to produce a new food ingredient which comparison tests demonstrated would offer either much better taste or lower cost than most products on the market. However, a last-minute but thorough targeting study showed that while it beat low-cost products on taste and high-performance products on cost, it beat neither on both. Research showed the market was split between taste buyers at the high end and price buyers at the low end. The competitive value and cost segmentation revealed that there was only a narrow slice in the middle of the market where it had the necessary combination of taste and cost to take business from competitive products. Comparing that market to the scale economics of production showed dismal returns. The "future flagship product" was dropped.

Managing the Transition

When it has been established that a revitalization opportunity exists, one of the major issues faced is how to manage the dual-product business during the transition.

Scale declines for the old product while it increases for the new. Manufacturing technology is likely to be distinctly different. It takes a different mind-set to go for volumes leverage on costs in the new area while trying to keep unit costs down with stable or declining volume on the old product. Yet, while the tasks are different, it is often desirable to share overheads. Careful tradeoffs are needed to determine where operations should be shared and where they should be separate.

Some markets will overlap, and others will be clearly better served by either the new or the old product. The new product may require new selling capabilities due to technical and application differences. Thus it may be necessary to restructure the sales organization or to reinforce some channels with technical/applications specialists for the new product.

With the many adjustments, this period is often marked by a loss of overall scale and efficiency. At the time, the opportunity may seem like a mixed blessing. The business has a new bright future, but in some respects it's a step backward to the greater ambiguity, uncertainty, and confusion that characterize emerging growth business.

Starting Over

The revitalize phase is a transition phase. It has characteristics of both the threshold and the early create phases. It will either lead to another create phase or to maturity and, perhaps, rapid decline. Some of the issues in this phase are similar to those faced in the threshold phase and in the early create phase. There are two important distinctions:

1. You are assessing the upside market and technology opportunities from the baseline of an established growth business. Better experience and information exist with which to judge opportunities and risks.
2. You must view yourself, not just others, as your chief competitive target.

After working so hard to achieve success it's tough to adopt a "starting over" mind-set, yet that's exactly what's needed for a chance at revitalizing growth. It takes a renewed commitment and strong leadership to reenter the mode of aggressive ambiguity that characterizes the start of a new phase of growth.

STRATEGY ROADMAPPING

We've touched on some of the issues, changing success factors, and strategic choices encountered in managing a high-technology business through its successive phases of growth. The strategic thinking framework we've used emphasizes critical strategic choices. These choices determine the competitive approach for each phase of growth and then redefine it as success requirements change with each subsequent phase. Since it is rarely obvious when the shifts must occur, it is necessary to anticipate changes, prepare early, manage programs for the current phase and next phase concurrently, and then commit progressively to make the shift in each area as conditions warrant. This represents a dynamic, decision-oriented, and proactive approach to managing the strategy in a volatile and uncertain environment.

However, any strategy is only as good as its execution. In this case, execution means not only doing it but also continuing to make important ongoing strategic as well as operational decisions. In theory, execution is handled by the operating plan. In fact, most operating plans focus only on the action steps and not the choices still to be made. Even then, they often fail to underscore critical strategic priorities and milestones. The forest becomes lost in the trees. We've found that a supplemental tool is needed to define and manage the links between the strategy and the operating plan—both to execute strategic decisions already made and also to map out future decisions to be made on open issues. It must provide a "control board" to monitor and adjust both strategy and execution. We call this tool strategy roadmapping. We deal with it only lightly here because of space constraints and because, while it is essential to a high-technology strategy, it is a more generally applicable tool. There are several basic elements of the approach.

Clear Strategic Choices

The first element is to sharply define the choices underlying the chosen strategy. A strategy is simply a framework of decisions as to how to address critical execution areas of the business and the actions and objectives to carry them out: for example, what product cost and performance to accomplish by when, which segments to target on, what type of distribution to use, what manufacturing approach, what pricing structure, and so on. However, the character of decisions made often is submerged as they are watered down into general descriptions of directions to be taken. This dilution makes the real decisions underlying the strategy fuzzy. It opens them to broader interpretation, and is a major reason why execution often gets off track, especially when new conditions lead to reconsidering some element of the plan.

Therefore, this framework of current strategy choices needs to be clearly and precisely articulated. It must represent a working tool rather than a static description. It is important to delineate the decision in terms of options considered and document the rationale for the choice made as part of the strategy definition. Simply stating objectives or actions is not enough. In managing execution, it is important to keep what you chose *not* to do as well as what you chose *to* do in constant sight. This helps keep execution on track as well as communicate and get understanding and commitment to the strategy at the levels in the organization where execution will succeed or fail. When conditions change, it is especially valuable to be able to revisit the options with the perspective of "what's different now" rather than starting from scratch. This limits consideration to those variables which should really make a difference to the decision, keeping the forest as well as the trees in sight.

Thorough and Consistent Programs

For each of these strategic choice areas, develop programs detailing actions, timetables, performance criteria, and responsibilities. We described earlier how carefully developed programs separate success from failure. While most companies have detailed product programs, it is equally important to define specific programs in the "softer" areas of marketing, sales, legal, and so on, to support each strategy choice. Great care must be taken to ensure the details *in fact* reflect the substance of the strategy.

Decision Roadmaps

Not all decisions are finalized at the outset. Indeed, often some future options can and should be left open to be decided on later based on conditions or performance on current programs by the time a choice is needed. The important thing is to identify as many of those key future decisions as possible at the outset. This should include both future strategic choices as well as important decisions to be made during the implementation of major programs. Prepare a decision roadmap of these choices. For major future decisions, this roadmap lays out:

1. The options that are known to exist.
2. The times when choices will be made.
3. The criteria by which they will be made.
4. The actions that are required to be prepared to make effective choices at that time.
5. How decisions depend on each other in time and substance.

This provides the decision framework for managing the strategy and linking it to its execution. Exhibits 20-13 and 20-14 depict the framework of alternates

EXHIBIT 20-13. *Strategy Alternates*

STRATEGY ALTERNATES

PHASE I	• Clear decks (cost improvements, complete current orders successfully)
PHASE II	• Pursue follow-ons • Exit assembly • Exit assembly and components
PHASE III	• Enter "new" market • Exit assembly • Exit assembly and components
PHASE IV	• Go broad in "new" • Stay narrow in "new"

and the decision roadmap for a company that is seeking to reposition itself from a narrowly based and highly competitive market by pushing new technology into a series of major new markets where it hopes to create new demand or substitute for existing offerings. It has thought through a series of target "windows"—shown as junctions on the roadmap—where it could gain leverage from the success of earlier efforts by entering the new markets. At each juncture, it defined the best alternative approach available if it were unsuccessful in developing the new opportunity area, which in this case involved pruning back or exiting the current business. The preferred route was clear, but progressive commitment would be made based on proven results and conditions as each "window" was reached.

The company progressed successfully along this roadmap for a number of years. From facing huge losses associated with an exit from the assembly business at the outset, it exited this unattractive portion of the business several years later with a major cumulative net profit. Meanwhile, it established a solid position in the remaining core components business serving a broad range of markets.

Key Assumptions/Triggerpoints

Define the key assumptions that underlie the current strategy and also those that will drive future decisions. Ask what would change (or make up) our minds? Many of these assumptions will be external, but some will be based on internal performance. Work backward from key actions already committed, or from choices to be made in the future, to identify the assumptions that dominate the appropriate answer. This allows selective monitoring of internal and external factors that will "make a difference" to the strategy or to its execution. In the roadmap case shown, key assumptions were the timing of the "window" to enter new markets versus the plant's manufacturing load. Too early a window would find the plant without capacity to respond; too late would mean losses and low capacity utilization in the in-

EXHIBIT 20-14. *Strategy Roadmapping*

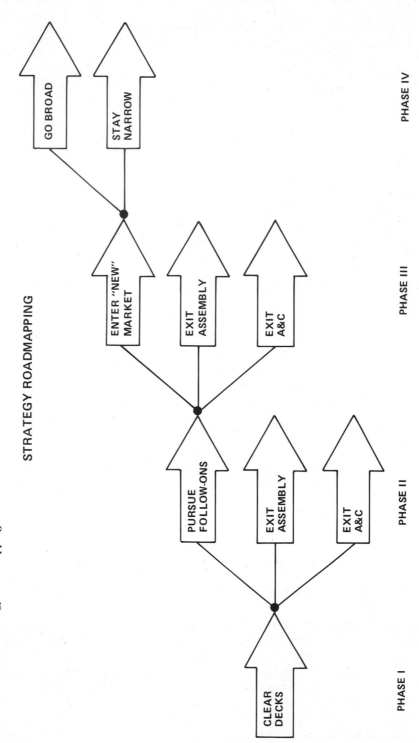

STRATEGY ROADMAPPING

GO BROAD

STAY NARROW

ENTER "NEW" MARKET

EXIT ASSEMBLY

EXIT A&C

PURSUE FOLLOW-ONS

EXIT ASSEMBLY

EXIT A&C

CLEAR DECKS

PHASE I

PHASE II

PHASE III

PHASE IV

terim. It is important to quantify the impact of such uncertainties on key assumptions in order to identify triggerpoints at which action is required. For example, slippage of more than a year in the market window for phase III would have more than offset the advantage of a successful entry over exiting the assembly business. Without some offsetting factor, an exit would have been triggered if it became clear that slippage would occur.

Critical Success Factors

Finally, yardsticks to measure progress on critical success factors must be clearly identified, continually tested, and monitored for performance. Frequently, operational reviews emphasize only after-the-fact measures of market and financial results. It is important to broaden the basis of these measures to include those that give "early warning" of performance on the fundamentals that affect competitive success *before* the ultimate results are visible. Thus in a high-growth communication service business, keeping customers is an essential success factor in recovering initial acquisition costs and reducing the overall costs of continued growth. Thus, a key success yardstick to give advanced warning is the trend in the rate of churn in important segments. Well-defined critical assumptions and success yardsticks permit the anticipation of problems before they undermine the strategy and identify opportunities while they are still exploitable.

Control Board

Taken together, the elements described above—clearly defined strategic choices, consistent operating programs, decision roadmaps, key assumptions and triggerpoints, and critical success factor monitoring—allow proactive management of the strategy and its execution in a rapidly changing environment. They provide a "control board" for managing the business within the framework of the strategy. This means more than tracking and adjusting execution. It means adjusting the strategy itself by making timely strategic choices based on shifting conditions and actual performance.

THE APPLICATION OF STRATEGIC ENTREPRENEURSHIP IN THE FIRM

To this point the discussion has centered on a framework for identifying and managing strategy in a high-technology environment. We emphasized the dynamic interrelationship of strategy and execution. Developing an entrepreneurial spirit among the business development team and maintaining it as the business grows are key to making the approaches we've discussed work. This section deals with issues of application of strategic entrepreneurship in a high-technology organization. These issues include:

Getting started
Fostering entrepreneurship
Coping with the special problems of a large or small firm
Managing
Risk containment

These issues may stand between a good business concept and business success.

Getting Started

The issues of receiving financing, selecting or avoiding a partnership with another firm, and participating in international markets are essential to consider when starting a high-technology business venture.

Financing

Besides development of a sound business plan, the biggest challenge facing either a start-up business or a new business within a large corporation is financing. The financier is looking for a sustainable high rate of return with bounded risk. High-technology businesses have problems demonstrating sustainability and bounded risk. The potential for high rate of return must be the basis of any business plan worth considering.

Most entrepreneurs learn that whatever funds they thought would be sufficient miss by a large margin—a factor of two or more is not unusual—stemming from the various perils described above, plus a number of others.

A sound plan for a high-technology business with competent management should find funding. Now that pension fund managers have decided that high-technology investments can pay, and venture capital fund management has had a decade or two to mature, the ingredients are there for continuing availability of capital for start-up, high-tech businesses. Entrepreneurship within large firms has come into vogue; 3M, and even IBM, are able practitioners. Indeed, many large firms are developing processes to encourage new business formation within the firm; some budget funds are set aside in expectation of new venture proposals.

Thus, though the challenge of securing financing is formidable, at least the financiers are listening attentively, and in expectation of investing in sound plans.

The entrepreneur's job is to demonstrate not only how to translate a better idea into a business, but also how to identify and predict the issues and assumptions on which business fortune will turn, leaving margin for the unknowns.

When Do We Need a Partner?

Every business has dependencies of many kinds that temper independence of action. Suppliers, distributors, investors, banks, employees, and others, all have significant influence on management decisions and in some way are partners in the enterprise. These relationships normally define the boundaries within which management is free to move.

The price of legal partnership is formal dependence on another party, or on other parties. If the parties can move as one, then energy can be focused on garnering the benefits. When objectives differ, operating methods or styles clash, or when the partners' relative contribution to the deal change over time, dissolution is inevitable.

Despite the price and likelihood of dissolution, there are compelling reasons for a partnership:

> When we have the technology but not the financial, manufacturing, or marketing resources to commercialize
>
> When we have the economies of scale but not the technology (e.g., equity position or buyouts of biotechnology entrepreneurs by established pharmaceutical firms
>
> When we need entrepreneurial skills or outlook
>
> When the two of us together, but not alone, have sufficient market clout or low enough operating costs to compete
>
> When we need protection from takeover
>
> When changes in the industry or market environment create major threats or opportunities (e.g., the convergence of telecommunications and information processing and the breakup of AT&T brought IBM and Rolm together, with the eventual absorption of Rolm)

A typical partnership situation arises when neither party feels he or she can capture a particular market opportunity alone. The U.S. defense industry has developed a myriad of "teaming" relationships formed for particular government contract opportunities that dissolve when the contract is done. All parties appear to benefit from such pacts. The buyer (the U.S. government) gets more bidders, firms can go after a piece of a large opportunity they could not otherwise address, and small and large firms can coexist in the market in a balance (albeit unsteady) of economies and diseconomies of scale. In effect, the teaming agreement is a catalyst that brings innovations and ability to execute together.

When the partnership starts out to be a joint venture, with each partner holding a share in a new enterprise, the enterprise, if successful, will develop its own objectives over time and most likely will reduce its parental influence to that of a financial investor.

The importance of a formal legal agreement grows as the interests of the partners diverge. If the agreement is properly drafted, the partners can extricate themselves without protracted management involvement and the consequent impact on other business interests. Buyout provisions, continuing rights in the developments of the partnership, and other details of the provisions for dissolution are of particular importance if the partners want to avoid costly litigation. The joint venture literature is full of advice and counsel and includes more information on the problems than on the benefits.

What Are the International Business Opportunities?

High-technology business crosses borders more easily than most other businesses, primarily because local defenses normally have not yet been erected. For a multinational corporation, bringing a technological innovation to international markets is an intrinsic part of business. For non-MNCs it is a difficult decision. Ignorance of foreign markets, lack of experience with customs, letters of credit, export financing, government clearance of high-technology exports, patent, copyright, and license procedures, local business practices, and so on, contribute to decisions against moving beyond domestic boundaries.

Once the state of ignorance is dispelled and the opportunity looks promising, the question gets down to export, license, foreign investment (normally, sales first, then manufacturing, and last R&D), or joint venture. Since international business ventures are dealt with in so many references, we deal only with the particular concerns of high-technology business—protection of proprietary rights and cross-license opportunities.

While a U.S. patent will protect an invention from infringement by other U.S. firms or by a foreign firm that attempts to do business in the United States, it will not protect the firm beyond U.S. borders. If there is likely to be a significant market opportunity abroad, the firm must consider filing for a patent in each country. Patent requirements differ from one country to another; in particular, in many countries patent applications must precede public disclosure of the embodiment of the concept, unlike in the United States, where up to one year is allowed before application. Thus care must be taken to keep proprietary information from becoming public prior to application to avoid loss of foreign patent rights.

Licensing foreign firms for local and/or export markets under a firm's patents or know-how has been a source of income for many who are unable to exploit those markets on their own. Some firms have also been surprised by the ability of the licensee to improve upon the know-how—to the point of entering the U.S. market with superior products that have their own patent protection. Similarly, a U.S. firm and a foreign firm with complementary technology may seek cross-license agreements that permit both firms to expand their product lines for their respective served markets.

There has been a lot of press over the past decade about the imbalance of technology flow, the implication being that U.S. firms are willing to sacrifice the long term for short-term license fees. While the trend is still evident, there is also a strong trend toward more foreign filing of patents in the United States, which suggests that the technology imbalance is being corrected.

Patent, licensing, and copyright activities are vital parts of a high-technology plan. The short- and long-term implications of various alternative arrangements with foreign (or other U.S.) firms should be factored into the strategy roadmap.

Mastering Entrepreneurship

While continued highly profitable growth, a steady stream of new innovative products and services, and low employee turnover are the objectives of most firms, they are the hallmarks of few.

Failure to achieve these objectives in a large firm is sometimes ascribed to a lack of entrepreneurship. In a small firm the problem may be addressed as lack of professional management. For both, the issue can be summed up as a question: How can we manage entrepreneurship? In order to address this issue, we will first examine another issue: how we foster entrepreneurship. Then we will turn to a discussion of how we can manage it.

Entrepreneurship involves one or a few individuals with a dream, who have the zeal to make it come true, and the ability to excite others into wanting to participate. Investment capital, bonuses, stock options, well-stocked facilities, and a hands-off approach will probably produce a long list of applicants and ideas. While both the individual(s) and the ideas are important, most successful venture capitalists will put their money on the individuals. There are always many unknowns about what problems a venture will encounter. What is key is whether the individual has the wherewithal to surmount them.

Selection of the team can fall to the entrepreneur, or the investor can share the responsibility; in either case, it is a crucial test, and is more an art than a science. With compatible and complementary people, the right tools, financing, and schedules in place, the next question is: How do we motivate them to perform?

This is treacherous ground; it is easier to demotivate than it is to motivate. Recognition, deadlines, peer pressure, and rewards all play a role here, as do fair company policies, well-oiled procedures, and investors or top management that listen well.

Recognition

Recognition helps to motivate people, whether it is accomplished through trophies, features in company publications, award dinners, vacation trips, visits by top management, having workers sign their work for the customer to see, or through some other means.

Deadlines

Few knowledgeable workers produce at an even pace; work comes in fits and starts, and there is nothing like a deadline to promote starts. More deadlines tend to be better than fewer deadlines, but there should not be so many deadlines as to create shell shock.

Peer Pressure

Peer pressure is a strong motivator. Peers are reference points. A few high producers do more than pull up the average—they inspire others. If the people selection process is properly done, even the top performers feel pushed by their peers.

Some firms go further, and pit two or more teams against each other. This has obvious penalties—it is expensive, and the losing team must deal with its failure—but when the stakes are high, it can produce results. Others have used the contention process, i.e., the challenging of ideas, approaches, design reviews by peers for refinement or eliminating of bad ideas.

Rewards

The use of large stock options or extraordinary bonuses to attract and motivate key members of the business is widespread among high-tech firms. This is an interesting contrast to the idea of achievement as its own reward, which would seem to be a part of a technologist's character. Many successful high-tech firms have used few rewards besides competitive salary and a challenging working environment, although almost all offer some opportunity to participate in the firm's success through stock purchase plans or profit sharing.

The choice of compensation packages (including employee benefits, such as fitness centers) and of perks certainly has an impact on business costs, but its impact on employee performance is less certain. The choice of elements for the compensation package is believed by most to be very important, but what are the relevant bases for decision? The conditions that argue for heavy use of stock options, and so on, in lieu of pay, are:

Opportunity for short-term payoff (e.g., go public)
Time is of the essence
Financing is very tight
Key players won't play otherwise
Competitors will be after the key players

Conversely, the conditions that suggest a more conventional pay and benefit package are:

The key players will still be key long after initial success
There are very attractive advancement opportunities within the growing business, or elsewhere in the company
The firm is not prepared to offer a variety of compensation packages

Whatever the choice, it is vital that the key players feel that the rewards are fair, given their contribution.

Company Policies and Procedures

Companies need policies and procedures to function. The challenge is to keep them fresh and effective. In general, most will agree that fewer policies and procedures is better.

Policies and procedures may be written and followed, or not followed, or "understood." In any event, they should be perceived as fair if the goal is to not demotivate. The handling of routine items, such as payroll deductions, expense reports, purchase requisitions, capital expenditure requests, vacation scheduling, and similar person–system interfaces is fraught with peril—so is office assignment, travel policy, or any other real or imagined perk.

Listening

This is the subject of whole books—it's importance can't be overestimated, but it takes time, availability (both real and perceived), and skill—all in short supply. It also takes an atmosphere of mutual respect and trust for people to open up. "Walking around" is the approach some follow; others use selected one-on-one meetings, group meetings with the boss, an open-door policy, surveys, questionnaires, or Friday night beer blasts to "listen." Personal access to the boss' ear (and the boss' boss) works best.

High Technology in the Large Firm

Large high-technology firms became large because they were successful in executing high-technology strategies. They have evolved effective organizations that can market and develop products and services, and grow. Nevertheless, a frequent topic in business journals is the absence in large firms of the innovation that made them large in the first place.

There are some special problems in fostering innovation in a large firm. As firms grow, R&D becomes structured, sometimes isolating those engaged in advancing the frontiers of science and engineering from those responsible for product development. The internal technology transfer process breaks down. This is particularly true for central research laboratories which have been likened to crown jewels—pretty to look at but without much practical value.

It's not easy to translate a laboratory's results into realizable concepts of new products and services. Even with a concept in mind, the timing of technology transfer to a "nuts and bolts" engineering department is an issue. Should a few more wrinkles get ironed out in the lab? Is this the stage of the technology's evolution that is ripe for competitive exploitation? Finally, is engineering ready to take this technology on? Formal technology development tracking and technology hand-off procedures are used by some firms to keep the heat on the technical staff and to keep management plugged in. Having responsible persons at both the generating and the receiving end of the technology transfer process is a vital part of such procedures.

It is difficult for the large firm to adapt quickly to significant outside technology developments that affect its industry. Small departures or even major breakthroughs in technology that are close to the traditional core technology of the business can be dealt with, but when the industry is faced with intrusive new technology, incumbents often falter. The arrival of solid-state electronics was the undoing of many office product firms. New digital technology and fiber optics, which paving the way for many newcomers to the telecommunications industry, threatened traditional firms. New developments in molecular biology may reshuffle the pharmaceutical industry.

Why can't well staffed and funded R&D departments quickly take on the new? Whatever the cause—NIH ("Not Invented Here"), planner's blind spots, technical ineptness, lab management smugness, or lack of anyone assigned or accountable to protect the flanks—prevention (or if late in the game, cure) is a major issue for planner and management. In short, technology is too important to the firm's future to leave its direction and focus in the hands of technologists.

Complicating the problem is the realization that mass is a multiplier in both inertia and momentum, and a large corporation has a lot of mass. Furthermore, technology is evolved by people who dedicate their training and working lives to knowing more and more about less and less. Thus the combination of a large number of people working in very narrow areas of technology may evolve very profitably for years and then be unable to revolve to an innovative new direction.

Continual renewal of the technology staff and steady investment in non-traditional technologies that may well affect the future of the industry is an expensive (at least in the short term) approach, but when well managed it has kept some industry leaders—leaders.

When the hour is late and the structural inertia is high, a fresh start may be the answer. The litmus test of a steady flow of "market-leading" new products is a signal to planner and management that their technology is well tuned and timed to the market. When market attention is drawn to someone else's products or services, the R&D process is not working. Is it too late for an evolutionary fix? That's the crucial question.

High Technology in Small Firms

The planner for the small firm is normally the chief executive, although the responsibility is often shared by a core team. The chief either needs to really know the technology central to the business, or to have someone on the staff he can thoroughly trust. Staying plugged into the latest technological developments is essential, whether it is effected through direct participation in the lab or through consultants and friends. The technical staff will have their own network within the technical community—the key is to bring more information in than flows out. A well-managed effort of participation in technical associations, with an occasional well-timed publication or paper, will maintain club membership.

As most firms have learned, patents are important, but they rarely protect a firm from competitors. Nevertheless, a proactive patent policy (i.e., anticipation of and planning for a steady stream of applications) can stimulate technical advancement and provide competitive distance. For the small firm, this means keeping a patent counsel at hand. As many participants in high-technology business have learned, the number of patents correlates more with the number of attorneys involved than with the level of technical activity. Each corporate patent attorney can do about 15 to 20 patent applications per year and, if motivated, will extract about that many out of the technical staff. Corporate patent attorneys have duties besides applying for patents. A private patent attorney who subsists on applications may do 50 to 75 applications per year. What really counts is establishing an atmosphere where innovation and creative thought are the norm, particularly innovation and creativity that are channeled to the technology that is related to the core of the business. To maintain that focus, many small businesses, whether out of studied decision or out of financial necessity, have off-loaded all but the essential core of the business to suppliers.

A crucial decision for any high-technology business to make is how fast to grow. Assuming the market is there, and that the technology is sound and provides a competitive edge, management will often pull out the stops and go for 50 percent, 100 percent, or even greater, growth per year. Once the business is established and is beyond the 50-million-dollar mark, sales or revenue growth greater than 20 percent per year is probably not stable. It's a real challenge to build quality staff, develop systems, and identify and shunt those that have peaked in a business that is growing so fast. In our experience, cracking 10-million, 100-million, or 1,000-million-dollar sales barriers are important benchmarks for the management team. One-man management may run out of steam at 100 million dollars or less. Somewhere well before the 1,000-million-dollar mark sophisticated management systems are needed. Thus the normal business planning that selects customers to be served, chooses channels of distribution, determines products or services to be offered, fosters core technology, lays out facility requirements, and allocates resources must also deal with the development of a business culture, supporting management systems, and the growth and pruning of business staff. As with patents, proactive policy pays, because catch-up may not be possible.

Managing Entrepreneurship

Now that we have fostered a climate for entrepreneurship, we need to manage it. Management is the art of getting results through the efforts of others. While the principles of good management apply to high-technology entre-preneurial businesses, the practices are tempered by the need for an environment that encourages innovation and the rapid exploitation of that innovation. This last statement assumes that the innovation that is encouraged will fill others' needs and that customers will be willing to pay handsomely for it.

While high-technology companies often find themselves with solutions that are looking for problems, they need to define, and then establish, firm roots in the market. Management's biggest challenge in a technology-dominated company is to focus (i.e., constrain) the firm's energies in that market. Artful yet sound, segmentation and a thorough understanding of each competitor's position and momentum, and of the dynamic price/value relationships in the market, provide a sound basis for high-yield innovation. This is true even (especially?) for revolutionary concepts, where the market, and the established suppliers to that market, are unaware of what is coming. Given a solid foundation in the market, management's next task is organizing and controlling the firm's resources in order to encourage and exploit innovation. One aid in resolving the issues is to determine where to manage loosely, and where to manage tightly.

Loose versus Tight Management

In short, management should keep the reins loose around the innovative core and tight everywhere else: manage what can be managed, and encourage what can't. If this approach is followed, the rules will differ for different parts of the company (e.g., with regard to working hours, dress, financial controls, and authorization). However, tight controls will be appropriate within that innovative core for many things, such as handling of proprietary information, weekly project reviews, safety, documentation and configuration controls, manufacturing cost targets, reliability, maintainability.

A related issue is deciding whether to organize around people or around functions. There is no good answer to this, except perhaps to do both. The strong individualism of both the entrepreneur and key innovators forces many firms to adapt their organizations to the strengths of those individuals and, at times, to their whims. Management's test is to recognize an individual's blind spot and weaknesses and then structure the freedom of action accordingly, and cover the weak areas with other people. This presents a real challenge.

Recent studies of innovative companies suggest two organizational keys for success:

1. Compress lines of communication between the CEO and the performing unit; i.e., maintain a flat organization. Work to avoid the belief that people in the middle don't understand the business and screw up communications, that to them it's just a job.

2. Keep business units small to throw engineers/scientists, marketing people, and financial people together. This suggests continual subdivision as the business grows, with consequent span of control problems if the organization is kept flat.

Both of these guides to entrepreneurial organization put priority on responsiveness, but require open communications and sound timely data on the factors critical to the success of the venture. Open communication alone will not do. Without a continual stream of useful, insightful information, management interaction with the business can impede, rather than aid, responsive action.

Given a well-designed organizational structure and sound management information systems, the next issue is how to cultivate R&D in fertile marketing soil.

Mixing R&D and Marketing

Engineers want to be given a firm set of specifications and guidelines on performance/cost tradeoffs, and then want to be left alone. Marketers would generally prefer not to set foot in the lab. While there are undoubtedly many exceptions to these statements, they are, on the whole, valid. Indeed, many businesses keep firm boundaries around these functions with well-controlled interchanges of information.

The project-team approach has found success in many firms. In addition to the motivation from team identification, there is presumably real payoff from the daily interchange of product/service development progress and issues and feedback from the market. The spur of a competitor's progress, the visibility of a customer's response to proposed features, and hard realities of engineering feasibility and performance/cost tradeoffs apparently have more positive impact than the advantage of sizeable, well-run functional departments.

The trick is to keep the teams focused on the critical marketing and R&D issues, to push for a hard factual basis for issue resolution, and to test all significant assumptions. This calls for real team discipline and solid analytical skills. Furthermore, interpersonal skills are tested on a daily basis to a much greater degree than they are in a functional structure, where individuals can retreat to their islands of expertise.

Teams normally include financial members, and some add manufacturing or operations—particularly when a manufacturing process or service operation is key to competitive advantage.

Maintaining the Pace

Sustained growth is a challenge few firms can meet. In high-technology businesses, it is often the people, rather than the market, that limit the business. Care and feeding of the technical staff for continued creative marketable output is a key management challenge, and thus is vital to executing the plan.

An engineer or scientist may reach his or her creative peak after being out of school about seven to ten years. There are many exceptions to this statement, but the plan should recognize that, while only 20 percent to 25 percent of their way into a career, much of the staff will not continue to grow at the same high rate and, indeed, may well slow down or burn out.

Furthermore, the continued growth of the firm depends on the sound performance of increasing layers of management. Each layer is typically five to ten years senior to those below, and is thus approximately one technical generation away. In an average-sized firm, the usual three to four layers of technical management can become increasingly insulated from the latest technical drivers in the industry. Sadly, ossification of the R&D staff is not an unusual situation in a high-technology firm that is only 15–20 years old.

Plans for periodic retreading, reorganization, and reassignment of key technical management and staff, strong links to leading universities, hiring from college every year at a forcing level (i.e., beyond real need), and close attention to the business's technical competitiveness by top management are all positive steps toward maintaining the pace. As always, it is execution that counts.

Tinkering

Technical problems are an intrinsic part of a high-technology business. Planning for those problems is part of management's responsibility. Furthermore, as the plan is executed, management must separate problems that will significantly affect an offering's market acceptance from those problems that only offend the sensibilities of the technical team. The latter problem gives rise to tinkering. Some tinkering is inevitable; it is the price to pay for keeping highly motivated technical staff whose objectives differ in marked ways from those of management. Indeed, some firms foster individual initiative by encouraging the staff to use company time and resources to develop their own ideas. Keeping tinkering under control is the challenge. A strong technical management staff with team-building interpersonal skills should be up to that challenge.

The job of the planner is to insure that the argument for freezing the product (without the latest feature) is developed beforehand, and that it is understood before emotional attachment is established and the resulting counterargument, to stay out in front, is developed.

Encouraging "G" jobs, having design and development staffs take the product into manufacturing or operations, or having new, more challenging projects always at the ready are some methods that successful high-tech companies have used to accelerate the product development process and to contain tinkering.

Location

Most high-tech firms locate wherever the founders wish them to locate. As the firm grows, the next location must be decided on. The principal criteria for choosing a new location, beyond the chief executive's personal preference, are:

Is the new location near key suppliers?

Is there a supportive university nearby with strengths in the relevant technology?

Is the location near the market?

Is it near major competitors?

Is it near a center of financial support?

Are the business economics of the area attractive, or at least not prohibitively expensive?

Is the area politically stable?

Each of these factors encompasses a long list of relevant questions that need to be asked, weighed, and answered. These questions, and the right answers, depend on the character of the business. For example, a good case can be made for locating far away from potential competitors if the firm is bent on a market leadership position. On the other hand, if the firm is following in the wake of industry leaders, locating near them has significant advantages, especially if the firm plans to hire the competitor's staff in order to rapidly move down the experience curve.

Managing Risks

High-technology business and risk aversion are not terms that are comfortable in the same sentence. Risks are a part of any business, but when the future is entirely dependent on planned inventions and market creation there are extra perils. There are many reasons for failure:

The market wasn't ready

While we were carefully testing, the competition stole the market

We missed the product development schedule

A key supplier couldn't deliver

Some key employees left to start their own company

A competitor's product was a little better in all the key features

We missed the manufacturing cost target by 10 percent, 25 percent, 100 percent

Product reliability problems caused high returns and warranty costs

We couldn't meet market demand; by the time we built up capacity, the competitors owned the market

The market didn't support our price expectations

Our major distributor went bankrupt

We couldn't get market coverage

We totally misjudged cash requirements

We had a fire

The following sections address some key high-tech business risk areas and approaches to containment.

How Can We Operate in the Range of Forecast?

The issue is *how to operate within the range of the forecast with acceptable risk.* Certainly, sound market research, including focus groups and pilots, are important to a quality forecast. A diligent effort to examine all the key assumptions, and then to test them thoroughly and be prepared to alter course if an assumption proves invalid, is an important part of a risk containment program, as is a well-planned program to capture the response from the start of the market to a new product or service. There is some danger of getting lost in the data, but this can be lessened with the involvement of quality market analysts. When the data are compared to predetermined thresholds and decision criteria, the business should be prepared to respond whichever way the market turns.

The ability to recognize and seize success, as well as to contain the cost of failure, is dependent on solid analyses of market data.

How Can We Contain the Risk of Technical Failure?

Technical competence should be at the core of every high-technology business. Nevertheless, in a world of scheduled inventions, there are risks. The key performance-feature requirements of a product should stem from the marketing and technical team effort. A good price and value analysis will determine the impact of failing to meet those requirements. A key issue is whether there are optional approaches to meeting the riskier requirements, and whether or not to pursue them in parallel. As for marketing, the approach is to test all assumptions, and clearly identify and surround all design issues.

Access to those people, in the firm or from outside, who are experts in the areas of risk can provide independent evaluation of a risk situation. The use of formal design review teams at several stages in the development, and of independent test and evaluation teams at the end of development, can also limit risks.

Killing the Project

A special problem facing management is deciding when to kill a project. High-technology businesses operate in a high-risk environment where failure is commonplace. Most, if not all, high-technology firms will have projects that fail. Is there anything that can be done through planning that can contain the damage when a project is killed?

A sound high-technology planning process will produce a decision roadmap with predetermined decision criteria. Projects will still get killed, but those involved should have a clear understanding of the rationale well ahead of time. Furthermore, if the roadmap is well designed, few projects will lead to a cliff. They should steer clear to new objectives before disaster strikes. Simply put, when the objectives are clearly stated, alternatives are developed, and the timing and bases for decision are laid out in advance, the likelihood of a total project failure is greatly diminished. The damage, if failure does occur, should be minimal.

Usually, even the most dismal failures have something worth salvaging. However, in the heat of shutdown, everything may be lost. A salvage analysis to accompany the plan alternatives provides management with a script to follow at a time when it's difficult to keep cool.

How Do We Manage Financial Exposure?

All risks have some financial aspect to them, and there are risks in every facet of the business. To minimize these risks, there is no substitute for strong financial controls coupled with some form of forward-looking business model—one that translates the impact of the latest significant news onto the bottom line.

When the business is operating on a well-constructed strategy roadmap with clear decision points and criteria for steering the business to a revised objective, management is in control. The construction of such a roadmap is no easy task.

However, consider the alternative: many firms have been caught with an idle marketing force waiting for the dramatic new product to arrive. Such delays not only drain cash, but also sap the marketing force of its vitality. While management wrestles with whether to keep the force on the payroll, the business is digging itself into a hole. A strategy roadmap for a business should have well-defined decision points to go with such delays, so that the decision to taper hiring or to lay off well before the peak is not subject to second thoughts while management's attention is focused on the crises in R&D.

How Do We Keep Secrets?

Keeping the secret sauce under wraps is a big challenge for a high-technology firm. Without conscious policy and diligent follow-through, the more important the breakthrough, the faster it will get out. The leaks are built in; technical societies, meetings, friends at other firms, publications, papers, seminars, night school, the local watering hole, headhunters, the working spouse, and rapid turnover provide a multitude of channels for ready ears. Furthermore, an ethic has arisen among some technologists that their ideas are their own property—along with any other ideas they pick up along the way. While some firms are busy controlling the copy machine, the latest development is being down-loaded into a remote personal computer.

Some firms (e.g., IBM) have been consistently successful in keeping their secrets. Those firms make it very clear that leaks damage everyone—both the firm and individual careers. They also go to great lengths to pursue leaks to the source, and take steps not only to stop the leak, but also to set an example to others that they will punish such actions.

Establishing a working atmosphere where proprietary information is controlled requires a lot of forethought. Much of it is attention to detail as in the use of the following guidelines, which will make the company's position very clear from the start, and on a daily basis:

"Need to know" as the basis for access to project information

Controlled technical notebooks for all technical records

"Company Confidential" stamps on all company data

Requiring employees to submit all papers and presentations for formal review and release by a management committee

Requiring written reports for all technical society meetings and formal briefing/debriefings at hire, upon departure, and upon start and finish of a project

Diligent follow-up at the first hint of a leak can limit the damage.

Whether or not a company takes elaborate precaution, the employees' attitudes toward the firm and their jobs are critical to company security.

People who are happy in their jobs and who understand the importance of keeping the company's secrets will do so.

STRATEGIC ENTREPRENEURSHIP IN ACTION

A good strategy is simply a series of decisions on how to address critical issues, specific programs to execute these decisions, and a roadmap for making future decisions and for monitoring and adjusting both strategy and execution as appropriate en route. But the complex and dynamic high-technology business is not only a tough place to put a good strategy together, it is also a tough place to keep it together.

The approaches we've described are built around six basic principles of strategic entrepreneurship that we believe distinguish the successful high-technology firm. These are:

1. Proactive development of opportunities. Manage and create, rather than define and pursue, the market potential. Anticipate the issues that will emerge with each successive phase of growth and prepare for success early. Define the market in actionable terms—not only in terms of where to win, but how to win—providing the competitive

concept for the business. The high-technology opportunity isn't just there—it's there to be created.

2. Constant renewal is necessary to develop and sustain competitive advantage. Market, technology, and competitors are moving; aim at future, not present, targets. Recognize that you'll never "finally get it right." There is no such thing as standing still—you're either moving forward or backward. Competitive approaches, target segments, and technical, marketing, and manufacturing strategies must shift with each phase of growth as new issues and challenges emerge. Competitive advantage determines total profit potential. Never be satisfied with it, and always be seeking the next vision for improving it.

3. Keep looking "outside the box." We're reminded of the puzzle with nine dots defining the junctions of a nine-block square. The challenge is to connect all nine dots with four continuous lines without lifting the pencil. It can only be done by taking the lines outside the limits of the square. So it is with the high-technology business—look outside the perimeters of the current business. They won't be there for long anyway. Opportunities and threats frequently emerge from outside; these may be new competition, substitutes, new technology to revitalize the business, or new uses and customers.

4. Managing complexity with rapid change takes emphasis on integration and partnership at many levels. This starts with a close partnership with the customer, and between engineering and marketing, to mesh technology's capabilities with areas of potential value. Formal partnership with outside firms may be appropriate to some objectives. Integration of the product line to handle proliferating complexity, integration between manufacturing and product design, close communications between interdependent functions and programs—all are essential to allow the business to handle its own dynamics.

5. A strategy is only as good as its execution. Make it executable by focusing on key decisions, rather than on directions, by pushing analysis deep enough to understand fundamentals and the operating realities of implementation, and by insisting on disciplined planning in spite of time pressures. Effective execution can't start without sound strategic decisions; it can't finish without maintaining a tight linkage between those decisions and day-to-day operations.

6. All this takes entrepreneurship, and the ability to foster and maintain entrepreneurial drive as the firm grows is perhaps the major challenge in fulfilling the promise of the high-technology firm. This means nontraditional approaches to managing, to motivating and rewarding, to organizing and staffing, to communicating, and to dealing with risks. It means having the courage to innovate internally, as well as in the marketplace. And when it is effective, all this becomes invisible— what emerges is the dynamism and competitive success of the firm.

NOTES

1. W. Shanklin and J. Ryans, Jr., "Organizing for High-Tech Marketing," *Harvard Business Review,* November–December 1984, p. 165.

2. "How a Flop Gave Birth to a New Machine," *Business Week,* August 1, 1983, pp. 77–78.

3. "Small Is Beautiful Now in Manufacturing," *Business Week,* October 22, 1984, pp. 152–156.

CHAPTER *21*

Strategic Planning for International Operations

ERIKA IZAKSON

ERIKA IZAKSON is Vice President and Director, International Business Strategies Group for Business International Corporation. She is responsible for managing global research and consulting activities, as well as for published reports, multiclient studies, and roundtables in such international functional fields as corporate organization, planning, marketing, technology management, and other related areas. Ms. Izakson also specializes in international strategic planning methodology. Prior to her present position, she specialized in business conditions in Western Europe. She has been a speaker at meetings of major organizations, including the Conference Board Conference on Strategic Planning and the North American Society for Corporate Planning. Ms. Izakson earned her B.S. and M.A. degrees in Political Science from Columbia University.

OUTLINE

This chapter is based on Business International research into the international planning practices of some 150 companies, as well as other related areas of corporate practice, over many years. However, the opinions expressed are those of the author.

International strategic planning is a way of thinking to help a company become as important globally as its potential allows. The three major reasons for incorporating the international dimension into corporate planning are:

1. To maximize growth and profit by focusing effort on priority businesses in priority countries.
2. To deal with the competition on a global scale.
3. To reduce the impact of shocks in the external environment.

International strategic planning—and geographic portfolio planning, which is an essential part of it—has enormous potential to help companies be successful internationally on all three of these fronts because it forces examination and resolution of such questions as:

1. Are we, as a U.S. firm, successful and secure in having 75 percent of our sales in the U.S. and 25 percent internationally, when the United States' share of the world market is now down to 21 percent, and that of the rest of the world is up to 79 percent? Admitting that most firms are strongest in their home markets because of historical roots and management affinity, is such a gaping imbalance sensible or preordained? If not, what changes are required to redress it?
2. Why are our sales in Japan only 5 percent of our sales in the United States, when the Japanese market is 36 percent of the size of the U.S. market? Granted that Japan is geographically and culturally remote for U.S. and European firms, boasts strongly entrenched local companies, and has a history of restrictions against foreign firms, are these conditions still sufficient to justify the 31-point gap in market penetration? Or can the gap be narrowed by even a few points (generally worth many millions of dollars), and, if so, at what cost and effort?
3. In the heyday of Brazil and Mexico some years ago, multiple divisions of our company hurried to take advantage of these markets. From an overall corporate point of view, was the proportion of total company assets invested there appropriate, insufficient, or excessive then? Is it now? Is hurrying to divest some of these assets a short-term response

to negative conditions, or does it fit into a longer-term corporate scenario for these countries?

4. Only two of our seven product groups have any meaningful penetration in Asia, our most profitable and fastest-growing area. How can we expand our presence there?

5. We are a young, fast-growing, high-tech company in an industry undergoing rapid technological change. At present, we are literally shifting product from point A to point B in response to export orders. We believe there is more of a market out there, but how do we go about identifying and developing it?

6. Our huge operation in Germany can no longer grow in its existing product line; in fact, we can no longer stop its downturn. The labor representatives on the board keep asking what we are doing to ensure the security of jobs. However, unless Germany is allocated a greater share of our world production (which may be uneconomical), or unless it can move to diversify unilaterally (which management resists), it has no place to go but down. How should this dilemma be resolved from a global perspective?

Conceptually, international planning is inseparable from a company's total planning activity. Its objectives and processes are essentially the same. The main difference is diversity in that which is to be planned—diversity of market characteristics and diversity of environments. Ideally, the goal is to generate a globally integrated corporate plan covering all of a company's existing and potential businesses (product areas) in all its existing and potential markets (geographic areas).

In practice, however, relatively few firms have attained such an advanced state of development in both their international operations and their planning activity. Firms whose home markets are large countries (e.g., the United States, Japan, and even Germany or France) are typically more advanced in their planning activity for domestic operations than for those outside the home country, if only because the domestic business is generally so much larger and well established.

Management's thinking then often is domestically oriented, which militates against the emergence of a global planning approach. Observation suggests that senior corporate executives tend not to apply a global perspective to planning until international sales reach at least 30–40 percent of a company's total consolidated sales (a point at which top management may also have international experience).

But they may never reach this level unless the global perspective permeates management thinking. To break this vicious circle, it may be useful to segregate the international dimension of planning, to give it recognition and emphasis, and to create some structure for it, at least until it is imbedded in the consciousness of corporate and divisional management and can be maintained on its own momentum.

THE KEY CONCEPTS OF INTERNATIONAL PLANNING

Six concepts are central to the successful evolution of international planning:

1. A top-management commitment to the idea that the company must think globally, both offensively and defensively, and must seek to achieve its rightful place in the world, and communication of this commitment throughout the company by means of some form of top-down direction.
2. An organizational structure that (a) recognizes that managing international operations and doing business in specific countries and regions of the world represent complex areas of executive expertise requiring years to master, and (b) integrates this expertise into the company's planning and decision-making process.
3. Awareness of the diversity and changeability of the external environment—the political, economic, social, and regulatory climates—within which international business is conducted, thus necessitating for planning purposes (a) close monitoring of current and future developments and (b) sufficient insight to judge the likely impact of such developments on a company's business in a given country or region, or globally.
4. Awareness of the diversity of markets in different countries.
5. Anticipation of the international competitive environment on at least two levels: individual major markets and the global strategy of each major competitor worldwide.
6. Realization that there are multiple approaches to planning for different countries, depending on the particular situation, and that some countries possess an intrinsic strategic value for a company that requires in-depth examination. The four most common such planning situations are:

    A single business in a country

    Multiple businesses in a country

    In-depth strategic country planning

    New country planning

Each of these six concepts is discussed below in greater detail.

TOP-DOWN INTERNATIONAL PLANNING

The concept of top-down global planning, whereby the managements of multinational and other corporations set broad goals for the size and direction of international operations, appears to be a basic requirement of good planning. Like all top-down guidance, top-down international direction:

Raises interest, attention, and responsiveness in operating groups

Gives a company-wide perspective to the international dimension that is otherwise lacking in large, decentralized organizations

Allows the operating groups to focus on defined goals, rather than to waste efforts on developing marginal or disallowed activities.

In evaluating the extent to which companies have established top-down international goals, one can contrast the prevalence of the three major elements of top-down planning:

1. Financial (return on investment and other measures)
2. Business portfolio or product mix (acquisitions, divestitures, resource allocation)
3. Geographic (degree, form, location of international activities)

The third is by far the most amorphous, for a variety of possible reasons. First, financial objectives and product-mix goals are conventional top-management concerns for which there is a long history of executive training and corporate practice. Geographic goal setting, on the other hand, is a barely nascent managerial responsibility for many firms, and its practice is largely undeveloped.

Second, corporate geographic goals generally are subordinated to product-related goals and decisions. Therefore, a product-related goal may supplant a geographic goal; for example, one European company that had decided to build up to 25 percent of its sales in the United States suddenly acquired another major European firm, making the original geographic goal unfeasible.

Third, some companies may wonder whether the effort of broadening and complicating the already large task of corporate planning is worth the difficulty. This is a legitimate question, answerable by the empirical evidence of a few concrete successes in solving strategic issues of the kind listed at the beginning of this chapter, or in identifying a few promising opportunities. It is also answerable by an act of faith: that it is imperative to think and act globally in order to survive.

The international corporate goals that have been enunciated by top management generally fall into the following categories:

The ratio of foreign versus domestic involvement in sales, assets, and profits. For example, one large U.S. industrial firm set a goal that international sales should rise from 22 percent to 35 percent of total sales within the time frame of its plan. A diversified medium-sized U.S. company stated the goal that 50 percent of its profits should originate outside the United States.

The distribution of the international portfolio among different parts of the world with different characteristics of market size, growth, technological sophistication, risk, and other relevant factors. One example is the decision of a large European consumer goods firm that no more than one-third of its sales should arise in developing (vs. developed) countries.

The relative priority of certain countries or regions into or from which top management wants to draw or reduce resources. For example: Asia might be a thrust area for Company A, or "We don't want to do any business with the Soviet Union" (not a common point of view).

The preferred mode of international operations. Examples include a company policy to have a presence in every country, under which the exception has to be justified; or a determination only to go into countries where 100 percent foreign ownership is possible, or, conversely, a decision to enter a country only with local partners.

These top-down enunciations may be the result of top management's innate judgment, or they may be the outcome of studies and analysis. Thus for top management to express reasoned goals, international planning capability must be available.

It should be noted that the discussion above refers to CEO-level, top-down international direction, which, where it exists, tends to be very broad. At lower organization levels—international division, worldwide product group, or regional management—top-down geographic direction may be much more specific and may include rationalization of production, changed patterns of sourcing and supply, and regional marketing strategies.

ORGANIZATIONAL STRUCTURE

Planning and organization in international operations are intimately intertwined. Inappropriate organizational structure clearly has the potential of seriously impeding good planning internationally. While appropriate organization structure does not, of course, guarantee good planning, it is a substantial facilitator to good planning.

Five elements of organizational design must somehow be intermingled in order for a complex, modern corporation to be managed: product, geography (country/region), function, market/customer, and technology. "In the past, many companies have tended to focus on one element, such as product or geography, and suffered the consequences from reduced attention on the others. Today, more and more companies are seeking to account for as many as possible of these elements (at least for product and geography) *simultaneously.*"[1]

International strategic *planning* requires more intense interelement connections within the organization than does day-to-day international *management.* Apparently, not all firms fully perceive the difference.

The main forms of organization for international operations, and their implications for international planning, are:

1. *Line International Division.*   This is a traditional concept, used today primarily in consumer goods and pharmaceutical companies, whereby domestic and international operations are split and the international division has responsibility for foreign manufacturing and marketing (sometimes only for marketing, as in the case of some computer firms). This form of organization provides intensity of international expertise but sometimes produces weaknesses in product know-how (R&D is often in the domestic operations and geared mainly to domestic markets), as well as a lack of close linkages between a firm's domestic and international operations.

2. *Worldwide Product Groups.*   Diversified industrial companies (and sometimes new divisions of consumer and health-care firms that otherwise have line international divisions for their traditional products) tend to operate in a decentralized fashion, where each product group has worldwide responsibility within its field. In this model there is no coordinating international unit at the corporate level. This form of organization is strong on product know-how—R&D, manufacturing, and applications—but often weak on international functional and country/regional expertise. Sometimes large product divisions have their own internal international division, but there is still no central, corporate international perspective. (On occasion, such a divisional international division may serve the international needs of one or more of the parent company's other divisions that lack such know-how.)

3. *Matrix.*   Some companies (notably some large chemical firms) operate in a combination of the two forms described above, thus emphasizing equally the product and geographic dimensions. Decisions and plans are made jointly. From an operating standpoint, the matrix form of organization has been found cumbersome, slow, and costly, but from a strategic planning perspective it is the most balanced form because it forces the major resources of expertise to interact from plan inception through plan implementation. However, not many firms have chosen this organizational structure.

4. *Worldwide Product Groups with a Corporate International Coordinating Unit.*   Firms that believe product know-how is supreme in the management of their businesses, but that are simultaneously committed to maximize their international operations (mainly diversified industrial firms), have opted to create a corporate-level international staff department that lends expertise to the worldwide product groups. Such an international unit may, on occasion, be just as effective as a line international division, or as a quasi-line international division in a matrix structure, in stimulating the product groups to explore their international opportunities, in participating actively in their international plans from inception, and in reviewing their plans on behalf of top management, *provided* they have CEO-given clout and a high level of credibility based on competence, and have persuaded the

product groups that they do not seek "to interfere." Lacking these conditions, a staff international unit may be very limited in its effectiveness, with power to approve exercised only at the very end of the planning or investment decision process, when changes are very difficult to make, as well as unpopular.

This organization form is a manifestation of what is sometimes described as "matrix overlay," that is, short of matrix but with some similarities. The various "matrix overlay" mechanisms to integrate the product and geographic dimensions in planning include:

Required communications and agreement between worldwide product divisions and geographic structures (international, regional, or country management, where they exist) at the onset of the planning cycle;

Preparation, preferably done jointly by international and/or planning staff and the affected operating units, *of company-wide planning assumptions,* including those regarding the external environment and its impact on the various businesses;

Required review of product groups' international plans by a corporate staff executive with a specific mandate to this effect;

Appointment of a corporate representative as country "manager" or "executive," in countries where a company may have multiple businesses, to perform certain joint staff functions and provide country expertise and strategy to all the firm's units;

Teams or task forces made up of individuals from one or more product groups, corporate functions, and corporate international staffs to work on some coordinated company-wide international issues such as countertrade, developing business with the People's Republic of China, or in-depth country planning. Teams may also be formed to help develop a single product division's plan for one or more countries (such a team may consist of as few as two people—one from the division, one from international—or may be a large multidisciplinary group);

Ongoing committees with some of the same responsibilities as those of teams and task forces, as well as responsibility for overall international planning coordination among divisions and staff officers (up to and including a corporation's executive committee).

It should be noted that these "matrix overlay" mechanisms are easily adaptable to other situations that require building organizational bridges between separate organizations; for example, between domestic and international operations, in companies that have this split, or in firms organized along functional lines, such as exploration/marketing or production/marketing (often in the fields of natural resources, computers, automotive, etc.).

The Place of an International Planning Function in the Organization

Whatever the organization structure a company chooses, it is extremely important to provide "a guiding intelligence"—a planning function in a line international division, a corporate international staff department, or an international planner or unit within a corporate planning department—to:

Spur, coordinate, optimize, and add value to the international plans of the operating groups.

Help top management allocate resources by doing the preparatory work for business and geographic portfolio analysis.

Help create a unified long-term corporate posture toward individual countries and regions.

Step in to do new opportunity planning internationally, both product- and new country-related, that falls outside the mandate, capability, or vision of the operating groups (or to participate with them in joint development teams).

Prepare top management to deal with potential contingencies.

THE EXTERNAL ENVIRONMENT

As noted earlier, two major aspects of this issue should be borne in mind:

1. Monitoring and forecasting the external environment—political, economic, and regulatory—in key countries and regions, as well as global trends.
2. Integrating these expected developments into actual plans, that is, making a judgment of the impact they are likely to have on sales, profits, and operating conditions during the plan period.

Three caveats should be kept in mind. First, it is unrealistic to expect precision. No one can predict the future. There will always be surprises, but it is possible to reduce the range of uncertainty through systematic observation and analysis of the past and the present. Since business is generally uncomfortable with uncertainty, and since it is impossible to plan sensibly in a vacuum, a narrowing of uncertainty and a greater awareness of possible scenarios are highly beneficial.

Second, it is totally useless to include general environmental forecasts in plans without making the effort to understand and integrate their implications for the business.

Third, while it is not easy to make reasonably reliable forecasts of the environment, there are competent professional firms that supply such services. However, making the linkage between these general judgments on the one hand, and their impact on a particular firm's own business on the other, is a task that has to be performed internally. Many firms do not possess the awareness and/or the skill to do it well.

There are five key concepts in terms of the external environmental dimension in international planning:

1. A global corporate approach
2. Content of environmental guidelines
3. Key points in the process of creating guidelines
4. Strategic versus operational environmental content
5. Methods of integrating environmental forecasts

A Global Corporate Approach

Many companies include external environmental assumptions in their planning guidelines, from the corporate planning or international departments to operating groups, so as to start from a common base. These political, economic, social, and regulatory assumptions generally cover a limited number of countries representing the company's key markets. A consistent world view prepared by an in-house economist or outside supplier underlies the country-by-country assumptions.

Content of Environmental Guidelines

There are two types of environmental guidelines:

1. *Country-by-country guidelines* would include for the plan period (possibly with alternative scenarios):
   The political environment and other elements affecting stability
   Economic growth, sectoral/industry growth
   Conditions affecting profitability (inflation, price controls, currency movements, profit controls, remittance controls, etc.)
   Prices of energy or key raw materials, if applicable
2. *World or regional guidelines* include:
   Top-down direction on favored or unfavored geographic areas for distribution of assets and/or profits
   Changing sourcing/supply patterns based on formation of trade blocs, local content requirements, etc.
   Regulatory developments on a sufficient scale of repetition in multiple countries to affect product or portfolio decisions (e.g., certain drugs

will no longer be reimbursed by health insurance; certain types of telecommunications equipment will no longer be acceptable to national PTTs; price controls on some goods and services make those businesses unprofitable)

Key Points in the Process of Creating Guidelines

It is useful to invite participation from as many of those affected as practical (corporate, international, operating group levels) to have different views represented, to foster a sense of partnership, and to ensure usage of the guidelines. One way alluded to earlier is to consider creating a task force, giving the lead role to the person or persons in whom most of the expertise resides, but making partners of other players from other parts of the company.

It is also important to gear guidelines as closely as possible to the various businesses using them. The environment has a different impact on different businesses; guidelines that come from above without an apparent effort to relate them to a particular business are often rejected as representing "ivory tower" thinking.

Strategic Versus Operational Environmental Content

Selectivity is called for in terms of what type of environmental content is appropriate for inclusion in planning. Not all developments in the environment, however important, affect company strategy, or affect different companies—or even different businesses within the same company—in the same way. All businesses are vulnerable to the external environment, but some are more vulnerable than others (e.g., natural resource-based, defense-related, pharmaceuticals, tobacco products, among many others).

Therefore, it is important to distinguish whether expected change in the external environment will have operational versus strategic impact on a company's plans. It is impossible to generalize which developments fall into which category because impacts vary. For example, a requirement that foreign firms may not own more than, say, 49 percent in the equity of local firms in a given country may be a nuisance to Company A, which likes to have a majority but is willing to bend; a blessing to Company B, which only wants to operate with local partners everywhere; and death in that particular market for Company C, which never shares its technological know-how. Only in the last of these cases does the regulation have strategic impact.

If developments affect more than one country, or multiple businesses in a major country, on an ongoing basis, if they affect strongly entrenched corporate policy or behavior, or if they confront a company with the possibility of having to abandon a significant market, then they generally fall into the realm of strategic impact.

Methods of Integrating Environmental Forecasts

Country-by-Country Trends

Some companies build models in which they attempt to quantify the effect of different variables in the external environment (and often other factors) on future growth and profitability. These models range from highly sophisticated formulas based on long time series relating these factors to company patterns and results, to highly informal judgments made in the process of group discussions. As a general rule, it should not be excessively difficult to generate these judgments for the major countries, given enough attention by knowledgeable individuals.

World/Regional Trends

When one moves away from the country-by-country approach, regional or world trends become more difficult to integrate into the planning process because they are not usually amenable to identification and certainly not to resolution by individual business units. In fact, the response to these trends may have to be imposed on business units, which may perceive a loss of income or status for themselves. For example, a company with manufacturing facilities in three European countries might decide to concentrate production in a single large plant in order to produce more economically in a tough competitive market.

In general, structured planning processes often fail to capture world and regional trends unless management—corporate, divisional, international, or regional, as the case may be—initiates focus on them and draws strategies from them.

One way that some companies deal with these regional or world trends is by splitting them from the normal planning process through (a) preparatory staff work addressing each "issue," possibly via an ad hoc task force, or (b) top-down resolution through an informal alternate planning system that takes the form of periodic meetings as needed.

DIVERSITY OF MARKETS

Even assuming a company can successfully market internationally the same products it sells in its home market—which is certainly not always the case—the characteristics of individual marketplaces tend to vary, the degree of variance depending on the nature of the product. In the most simplistic terms, the variance is smallest in technologically driven businesses and greatest in marketing-driven firms (e.g., soft consumer goods). But even this generalization does not necessarily hold, since technical standards and public procurement requirements often shape the marketplace, even for technology-intensive products.

Therefore, international planning in respect to the requirements of diverse markets has to be linked with various functional plans in the areas of research and development, product development, engineering, and manufacturing in order to insure that these functions are responsive to the needs of diverse marketplaces.

As to understanding and forecasting international markets, all countries (except some Communist countries) are amenable to conventional methods of market research yielding reasonably reliable results, but the methodologies to be employed and the degree of effort required may vary from a company's standards in its home country. As a general rule, companies have to set priorities for which markets they will study, since virtually no one can afford to study all markets for all businesses within a short time span. However, it is often necessary to study a *group* of countries in order to select the priority markets.

THE INTERNATIONAL COMPETITIVE ENVIRONMENT

Very few executives need convincing by now that they operate in a highly competitive world; that competition is becoming more global every day; and that global competition affects not only their international operations but also their domestic activities, thus leaving no part of the corporation immune to foreign competitive thrusts.

In this climate, maximal knowledge of competitors' strategies—and their strengths and weaknesses—has become an imperative of planning and operating business enterprises on a global scale. It is well within companies' control to develop in-depth knowledge about their competitors globally and to integrate that knowledge into their planning stategies. Yet many sophisticated companies have responded weakly to this challenge, either because they are unaware of its potential benefits or because they have found it difficult, or both.

To abbreviate sharply a large subject, there are two key issues in the international dimension of the competitive environment:

1. Generating and assessing information on the competition
2. Integrating competitive assessment into planning

Generating Competitor Information

According to a recent study, most companies follow the activities of competitors on the most decentralized basis—in the marketplace of the various countries where they operate.[2] Often this information never moves to other levels within the organization.

Some firms also select key domestic and foreign competitors, monitor their activities internationally, and attempt to develop an understanding of their global strategies, both portfolio and geographic. The firms that do this systematically on a global scale are not numerous, yet the presence of such an activity could reduce the surprise element of competitive actions significantly.

Such key competitor assessment tends to take place on the corporate level when the competitor competes with more than one of a company's businesses, or when the competitor's position in the marketplace is very powerful. Otherwise the function may take place on the divisional level.

A few companies have set up competitor assessment systems that permeate the entire organization as a subset of the planning activity, generating the information through in-country reporting upward to the corporate center, where the global assessment actually takes place.

Integrating Competitive Assessment into Planning

Once competitor information is generated and assessed, its key purpose is to gauge the impact it may have on a company's plans. That linkage requires deep knowledge of the company, the industry, and the international marketplace. To mobilize these resources probably requires group meetings or a task force.

On the whole, the aforementioned study found that international competitive assessment appears to be the weak link in the international planning process.

GEOGRAPHIC/COUNTRY PLANNING

The concept of geographic planning is simply that companies will generally be more successful if they engage in international operations by design rather than by accident. This is not to say that opportunistic decisions are bad, but that such decisions are better made within a predetermined (if frequently updated) framework of what fits, rather than in a vacuum.

An important element in the concept of geographic planning is that selected countries have a strategic value for a corporation, and that it takes a strategic corporate approach to these countries to realize this value.

Geographic or country planning can be viewed in terms of four variations that often overlap and are represented in Exhibit 21-1. (The term "SBU"—strategic business unit—is employed to denote a country operation in a given business. In fact, not every country subsidiary is viewed as a discrete SBU by many companies. Some cluster several country operations into an SBU, or even a region or subregion within a specific business. But large country

EXHIBIT 21-1 The Four Faces of Country Planning

The Four Faces of Country Planning

Country SBU Planning	SBU	SBU	SBU	SBU

Country-Wide Planning	SBU SBU ✕ SBU SBU

In-Depth Country Planning	SBU SBU ✕ SBU SBU	SBU ?

New Country Planning	?

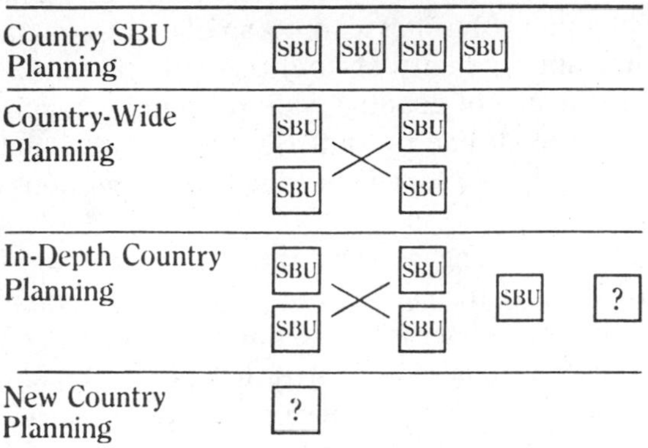

operations are generally independent SBUs. Of course, not all companies are as diversified into multiple businesses, as is shown in Exhibit 21-1.)

Country SBU Planning

Country SBU planning generally involves the planning for each separate operation or business within a country. The SBU has many linkages to other elements in the corporation that relate to its planning efforts. Two factors are major determinants of the content of country SBU plans: (a) the rigor of the requirements placed on it by the corporate planning system and by the next level up in the planning process; and (b) the inclination of the local management to plan, and the availability of resources for that purpose. Thus there are major differences, both among and within companies, in the coverage and innovativeness of country SBU plans.

A major philosophical issue with the concept of country SBU planning is that, because SBUs are generally limited to their existing (or related) product mandate, they may be structurally constrained in their potential growth. The alternative—to allow at least large country SBUs to diversify in individual ways suited to the particular environment—seems unacceptably radical for most firms.

Country-wide Planning

Country-wide planning occurs when companies with multiple businesses in a country take an overall country view of these activities, integrate the plans of the individual SBUs into a country plan, and/or generate joint strategies concerning the country.

Of course, a company's diverse businesses in a country often report to individual worldwide product groups, and the country SBU plan is integrated into that group's global plan. The multi-SBU country plan then becomes another form of plan integration—all of a company's business in country X. It can also add value, however, by juxtaposing and complementing the needs of the individual country businesses into a coherent country strategy.

The substance and intensity of country-wide planning vary widely by company. The incidence of country-wide planning is much greater in companies with international line or staff divisions or regional offices than in companies organized by worldwide product groups without such geographic structures.

Many companies that engage in country-wide planning have designated an executive as "country manager." For purposes of planning, the key issue regarding the country manager is not so much his internal managerial versus his external representational role, but rather his strategic versus his operational role. His can be either a housekeeping function (valuable though it may be) or a strategic function, depending on the intent of management and the qualifications of the individual.

The vast majority of the companies that produce country-wide plans explicitly incorporate external environmental factors. This information is produced at different levels of the company—from the country to the corporate level, or jointly.

In-Depth Country Planning

The basic concept of in-depth country planning is that, for certain important and often volatile countries, the normal ongoing business planning process is not deemed sufficient. Some companies thus designate selected countries as subjects for intensive, long-term strategic analysis to determine:

The possibilities available to the company for all or most of its products, both existing and potential

The appropriate priorities among them

The resources needed and the sequence of events in a long-term country plan

The exposure that it is prudent to have in the country given its political, legal, economic, and social climate

How this amount of resources fits into the total geographic portfolio of the company

A successful methodology of in-depth country planning employed by a number of companies is the multidisciplinary team or task force, which brings together various areas of expertise and skill and ensures a wide-ranging company view of the country. The effort involved for each country may range from moderate to large.

New Country Planning

The identification of a systematic approach of entry into new countries from a *corporate* perspective appears to be the least developed of all types of country planning examined. The majority of firms do not have a systematic approach; either they expand as the opportunities arise or they leave new country planning to operating groups. The firms that do use a more strategic approach to new country planning do so by means of specific organization units assigned the responsibility or by task forces and in-depth studies.

The identification of a systematic approach of entry into new countries is typically most developed in companies that have an international division, either line or staff. Such groups automatically view enlargement of the geographic portfolio as their mandate.

In the absence of an international division, new country planning can occur either at the corporate level or on the operating group level (a worldwide product group, for instance).

Product divisions may use a systematic approach if they have the motivation and staff resources (as stated earlier, large worldwide product groups often have their own international and/or regional divisions). If they do not, they tend to act opportunistically.

Some firms initiate such an effort from the corporate level (top management or corporate planning department), putting in place staff work (either corporate or joint corporate-divisional) to support top-down and bottom-up international planning. The most common method is identification of priority markets through systematic global analysis. Factors to consider for selected countries might include:

Share of world GNP
Overall economic growth rate
Potential share of world industry market
Growth of industry in market
Competitive situation in market
Operating environment for multinational corporations
A variety of other factors that are proven determinants of growth for the company elsewhere

These factors can be weighed according to their importance to the company, and thus countries can be ranked into classes of priority for entry. Those in the highest priority group may merit deeper market and environmental studies before they are definitively incorporated into plans.

NOTES

1. *New Directions in Multinational Corporate Organization,* prepared and published by Business International Corporation, New York, 1981, p. i.
2. *Assessing Your Worldwide Competitors: A Key to Planning and Decision-Making in the 1980s,* prepared and published by Business International Corporation, New York, April 1983.

CHAPTER 22

Strategic Planning for Financial Services Companies

CARL H. MALMSTROM

CARL H. MALMSTROM is Vice President, Corporate Strategy, Office of Corporate Planning and Development of American Express Company. He has held various planning positions, including Manager, Planning–Card Division; Director, Annual Business Planning–Corporate Comptroller's Office, and Vice President, Long-Range Planning–Corporate Development Office. Mr. Malmstrom has an undergraduate degree in Mathematics from Reed College, and a master's in Industrial Administration from Carnegie-Mellon. In 1981 he was awarded a Certificate in Management Accounting.

OUTLINE

OVERVIEW

The purpose of strategic planning in a financial services company is the same as in many other businesses: to position the company for competitive success in the future. In general, the approaches to accomplish this objective are similar. An understanding of the environment in which the company operates must be developed, its strengths and weaknesses must be assessed, and the strategies of its competitors must be understood. The successful application of these approaches in a financial services institution (FSI), however, require an appreciation of overall changes in the business climate, a recognition of the distinctive characteristics of the financial services sector, and an appropriate tailoring of management systems to the FSI's particular capabilities and culture.

A Decade of Change

As the business environment has evolved since the 1970s, management's strategic thinking and planning has become more focused—particularly in the financial services industry. In the mid-to-late 1970s the economy was in a state of rapid change, characterized by high volatility and uncertainty. This crisis economy forced companies to undertake a thorough reexamination of their expectations about the macroenvironment in which they were operating, as well as the basis of their own business economies. Much of the analysis centered on portfolio analysis, using such techniques as the BCG or GE/McKinsey grid, to help in redeploying resources and redirecting diversification efforts. Strategic thinking focused on corporate restructuring of assets and earnings bases and emphasized financial analysis of alternatives. Business strategy development was required to follow through on broad investment strategies, the keys being analysis of resource allocation and the validity of programs to ensure implementation.

These strategic planning efforts continue to be important, but as we approach the late 1980s, the changing environment continues to require new approaches. As the long-term economic outlook shows a lower level of sustained growth, companies increasingly are being faced with a shifting market-share environment. This mandates a more careful review of specific competitive strategies—closer attention to microanalysis rather than macroanalysis. The needs of the target markets are rapidly becoming the key strategic driving force. Careful customer segmentation analysis is becoming crucial, redefining the products and services to meet customer needs and rejuvenating marketing approaches to deliver the products and services. Business strategy needs to focus more heavily on product/market initiatives, emphasize innovative approaches to satisfy customer needs, and rely on market testing and research to insure the success of proposed strategies. Functional strategy development—marketing, manufacturing, distribution, and human resources—will have to be tailored to the needs of the particular product/market segments.

The Financial Services Sector

Not only is the business environment changing, but it is affecting the financial services sector differently from other sectors. Generally, manufacturing concerns face an environment of maturing product lines and the problems of product displacement, either through technical or competitive substitutions.

Customers of manufactured products tend to be experienced in product usage and are aggressive in their comparative shopping habits. Products are designed to meet particular application needs. Competition tends to be concentrated, with a few large firms representing a major share of sales in a particular market segment. Technology is hardware-oriented, aimed at reducing the production cost equation. The economics of the business are likely to be driven by production scale and production quality. The strategic leverage points in such businesses tend to be focused innovations to provide competitive advantage for share shift.

The financial services sector, on the other hand, is in a much earlier stage of development. The environment can at best be characterized as uncertain and restructuring, if not turbulent. Customers are rapidly climbing the learning curve and, as they become more experienced in making their own financial planning decisions, are becoming much more sophisticated. Products, which have historically been supplier-driven, will undoubtedly become more customer-needs–driven as this sophistication increases. Competition is highly fragmented, with over 70,000 financial services institutions in the United States alone. Technology tends to be software- and systems-oriented. The economics of the business are likely to be driven by service value and delivery productivity. The strategic leverage points, then, tend to be targeted marketing and creative service integration in the most profitable, risk-acceptable market segments.

STRATEGY DEVELOPMENT

Within this general framework of differences between the financial services and other sectors, however, three specific factors take precedence in terms of strategic development priorities: the needs of the customer, deregulation, and technology. Clearly, there are strong interactions among these factors, but each is a powerful force in its own right.

Customer Needs

We have often heard the expression "the customer is king." Certainly in the manufactured goods sector this has been a watchword for years, where over a period of time consumers have built up an extensive base of knowledge of the products available. People have become experienced and confident in their purchasing behaviors, and the manufacturing sector has had to be sensitive to those customers' needs and preferences. Unfortunately, the financial services industry has not always acted that way. It was not so long ago that banks and thrift institutions did not offer discount brokerage services or provide investment alternatives to savings accounts, which were limited to a 5½ percent interest rate by law.

Those days are gone forever, and consumers know it. The question is no longer as simple as deciding whether to invest money in stocks, bonds, mutual funds, or a savings account. Consumers regularly decide between an 8.75 percent money market mutual fund, a 9.375 percent six-month saving certificate, or a 401(K) long-term employee savings program in order to defer current income taxes. The United States has indeed become a "basis point" society.

The economic turbulence we encountered in the late 1970s and early 1980s, in part, helped to shape the new consumer. The prime rate fluctuated between 11 and 21 percent, often moving several hundred basis points within the period of a few months. Consumers of financial services were shaken to the very foundations of their financial security and began to ask hard questions of their bankers and other financial advisors. They started to become much more sophisticated about the handling of their financial management matters. Whether they were buying insurance, taking out loans, transacting business with their credit or charge cards, or paying for other financial services, individuals began to shop for the best price.

This growing consumer sophistication has had a profound effect on the financial services industry. As the Hudson Institute pointed out, "Demands of more financially sophisticated consumers have been especially powerful in pulling the financial services industry into the future."[1] Firms have had to become much more sensitive to the needs of the public. The product life cycle of a company's offerings has in many instances become very short, sometimes in the category of fads, such as the Rubik's Cube or the Cabbage Patch doll.

Financial services managers who recognized this rapidly changing consumer environment and responded by building flexibility and speed into their management decision-making processes have been in a better position to react to, and anticipate, the changing needs of their consuming public. In many cases this has allowed previously successful companies to differentiate themselves and new entrants to flourish by providing "one-stop financial shopping."

To react to this changing consumer environment, of course, the financial services industry has had to develop an understanding of customer needs and priorities. This is where market segmentation becomes extremely important. The process of dividing a market into groups of customers who have similar needs and desires may be one of the most important efforts a company can undertake. If an FSI does this better than the competition, it can achieve a differential advantage by designing a value-added service specifically targeted to the needs of that particular segment. The narrower the target group that can be defined and the needs of that group determined, using such techniques as focus-group marketing research, the better the chance of gaining a differential product/service advantage.

A starting point in this segmentation analysis is to look at the consumer's financial life cycle. Exhibit 22-1 shows the types of services needed by in-

EXHIBIT 22-1   Consumer Financial Services Life Cycle

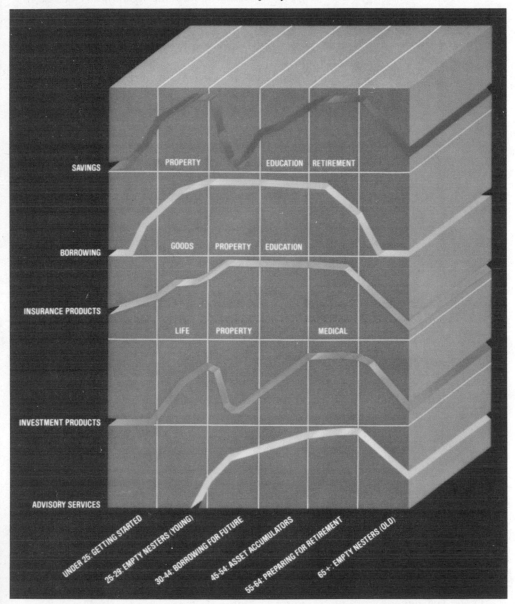

dividuals as they age. In the under-30 age group, savings are being accumulated, along with a certain level of debt, to establish initial homes, careers, and families. Between the ages of 30 and 44, income, savings, and investment funds are being used to purchase property and to further increase an equity base. Between the ages of 45 and 64, income production peaks, and growing assets are directed toward educating children and preparing for retirement. Finally, in the over-65 age group, increasing the income from the assets accumulated during the previous decades becomes a key goal, as well as conserving those assets for later generations. Certainly, these typologies overlap, but they do serve as a starting point for developing an understanding of client needs.

As a second-stage analysis technique, it is helpful to further break down each client segment into age-income subgroups. Then, for each subgroup, a more detailed demographic profile should be developed, including the number of households in that segment, the amount of household income in each segment, an estimate of the financial services revenues annually contributed by the segment, and both historical and projected growth in the composition of the segment.

A more specific characterization of the financial services products of each segment should then be specified, both qualitatively and quantitatively. The purchase profile of new and repeat customer behavior should be characterized, as well as the distribution preferences of the typical member of the subgroup. Finally, a product profile for each subgroup should be analyzed, including for each major product group the average annual payments made, the net revenue generated by the product group and, most important, the company's current position in supplying each product. Exhibit 22-2 is a sample of second-stage analysis that should help to clarify each client subgroup's needs. A consolidated look at all subgroups will additionally indicate where a company is strong and/or weak with respect to a specific customer group. Only by performing such a second-stage, or possibly even a third- or fourth-stage analysis, can a company gain a firm grasp of its strategic strengths and weaknesses and options for improvements, by customer segment. The strategic planning challenge is to go to that level of detail that is appropriate to develop a viable strategy, giving consideration to customer application and service requirements, distribution channel capabilities, competitive implications and so on.

The Deregulatory Environment

Another major difference facing the financial services industry is the state of the deregulatory environment. For the 40 years following the New Deal, the picture was clear. The lines separating financial services providers were sharp and distinct—banks were banks, brokers were brokers, and insurance companies were insurance companies. That situation has changed radically in the last decade both on a de jure and on a de facto basis.

Regulations began changing rapidly in 1975 when the SEC eliminated fixed broker commissions. It continued with the Depository Institutions Deregulation and Monetary Control Act of 1980, which included a phaseout of interest rate ceilings, and with the Garn-St. Germain Depository Institutions Act of 1982, which gave federal regulatory agencies greater flexibility to

EXHIBIT 22-2 Customer Segmentation Analysis

CUSTOMER SEGMENTATION ANALYSIS

GROUP 3

MAJOR MARKET: Individual
CLIENT SUBGROUP: Age of Household Head: 25-44 Years
Household Income: $35-50,000

Demographic Profile	Characteristics	Customer Needs	1981 Financial Services Product Profile				
			Percent Using	Average Annual Payments	Net FSI Revenue ($mm)	Percent of Total Net Revenue	Current Position
Number of Households: 3.9 m.	**Financial Services Priorities:**	Products Used:					
Percent of Total Households: 4.7%	Most members of this affluent, well educated group are married, have two children at home and will purchase two homes. Priorities vary greatly depending upon age. See groups 2a and 2b for differences. Building of household net worth becomes a significant priority as age increases.	**Lending**					
		Mortgage	78%	$3,984	$6,215	15.0%	Moderate
Total Household Income: $157.1 b.		Auto	29	495	644	10.3	
Percent of Total Household Income: 9.6%		Other Installment Credit	39	852	1,158	8.5	
	Purchase Profile:	Other Loans	10	1,338	1,838	24.5	
Average Annual 1981 Income: $40,300	**New** – Mortgages, auto loans, all insurance, mutual funds, CDs, education loans and trusts.	**Insurance**					
	Repeat – Savings and checking account, mortgages, auto loans, special insurance increments.	Life	81%	$1,173	$1,865	8.4%	Moderate
Average Household Financial Services Expenditures: $9,514		Health & Accident	87	118	201	5.7	
		Auto	80	630	992	7.5	Moderate
Total Financial Services Revenues: $17.7 b.	**Distribution Preferences:**	Homeowners	73	215	392	7.4	Strong
Percent of Total Financial Services Revenues: 9.3%	Savings banks dominate expenditures.	**Investment & Money Management**					
	Real estate brokers are important suppliers.	Savings Accounts	74%	$ 0	$1,033	2.8%	None
Annual Growth Rate	Commercial banks make inroads with increasing age and breadth of investment needs.	Securities	25	146	459	5.8	Moderate
1970-1980: 3.8%		Mutual Funds	4	9	36	5.8	
1980-1990: 3.0%		Money Market Mutual Funds	4	17	68	13.1	Strong
		Real Estate		416	1,623	15.0	None
		Transactions					
		Checking Accounts	87%	$ 24	$ 517	3.9%	None
		Travelers Cheques	25	4	41	10.6	Strong
		Payment Cards	28	13	130	11.6	Strong
		Credit Cards	50	27	279	10.8	None
		Advisory Services					
		Tax Advice/ Preparation		$ 13	$ 51	5.2%	None
		Travel Related Services		40	158	9.5	
		Total Financial Services		$9,514	$17,700	9.3%	

m. = millions
b. = billions

Source: American Express U.S. Financial Services Strategy Study, September 1982.

handle failing institutions, significantly expanded the powers of thrift institutions, and gave depository institutions a new deposit instrument to compete with money market funds (see Exhibit 22-3).

At the same time, de facto deregulation has had an even greater impact on the financial services marketplace. There are numerous examples of powerful structural shifts in the industry. Insurance companies like Prudential entered into the brokerage field through the acquisition of Bache. Investment firms like Merrill Lynch expanded into insurance. Sears acquired Dean Witter and Coldwell Banker, and American Express acquired Shearson and IDS. Even companies like Xerox, American Can, and Kroger are beginning to get into the financial services business.

The net result is a blurring of the boundaries that once separated banking, insurance, and brokerage. Furthermore, this trend is likely to continue, with changes in formal regulations continuing to ratify what is happening in the marketplace. There is no certainty that it will, however, because dissatisfaction with the current legal and regulatory situation is becoming increasingly

---

EXHIBIT 22-3   *Financial Services Legislation*

1975	*SEC Deregulation of Securities Industry's Commission Rates.* SEC eliminates fixed commission rates allowing for a new competitive strategy to be employed in offering retail brokerage services.
1978	*Financial Institution Regulatory and Interest Rate Control Act.* Broadens the prohibitions on management and director interlocks among financial institutions, extends banking antitrust laws to individuals seeking to buy banking institutions and provides for regulation governing the use of deposit accounts subject to electronic fund transfers. *International Banking Act.* Establishes treatment of foreign banks in the U.S. determining that foreign banks would be treated, as much as possible, the same as U.S. banks.
1980	*Depository Institutions Deregulation and Monetary Control Act.* Provides comprehensive regulatory reform including six-year phaseout of Regulation Q, reserve requirements at all banks and thrifts on transaction accounts, access to Federal Reserve Services and pricing of Fed services.
1981	*Economic Recovery Tax Act.* Includes a variety of measures to encourage retirement-related long term savings and specifically excludes favored tax treatment of capital gains on tangible assets.
1982	*Garn-St. Germain Depository Institutions Act.* Gives thrifts new lending powers and authorizes an account competitive with money market funds for all depository institutions. *SEC Rule 415.* Enables corporations to register for debt or equity offerings in advance, then sell the securities within two years after filing is accepted, in one or several sales.
1983	*FED Changes in Regulation Y.* Requires nonbank companies to divest banking operations or be classified as bank holding companies and engage only in "permissible" Fed activities by broadening the definition of commercial loans and demand deposits.

widespread. For example, there are conflicts among regulatory authorities over interpretations of statutes that occasionally give them overlapping jurisdiction; Congress is deeply divided on how to proceed; and intense lobbying by the banking, insurance, thrift, real estate, and securities industries tends to thwart the possibility of a consensus.

Given this confusion, it becomes increasingly important for FSIs to be knowledgeable about, and active in, what is happening in the governmental area. Unless a firm is willing to allocate some of its resources to monitor what is happening in Washington and the states, it could be in danger of finding itself the victim of some adverse laws and regulatory decisions. Thus the strategic planning challenge is to find what is appropriate for the individual firm to do in order to maximize its impact, whether it is to take action on its own or in concert with other organizations such as trade associations and consumer groups.

Technology

The other major factor that distinguishes planning in the financial services industry is technology. As the Hudson Institute points out, "The revolution in electronics, particularly in computers and telecommunications, has opened a vast potential for improvement in the efficiency of consumer financial services."[2] The implications of rapid technical progress in these areas are now competing heavily for senior management time and attention within the industry.

Exhibit 22-4 gives a glimpse of the major changes expected in the decade of the 1980s. Technical advances in communications, industry and regulatory changes in communications, developments in the processing and information management technology, and progress in electronic technologies are likely to have major consequences for the financial services industry. Each area should be investigated thoroughly for possible applications by financial services providers.

In the field of communications, for example, by 1990 a high percentage of the transmission and switching services offered in the United States will probably be digital, a process which offers higher quality, more reliability, and possibilities for immediate modification of service configuration according to customer needs. The concept of a "programmable network" may provide business planners with opportunities in electronic product delivery and systems planners with flexibility in building corporate communications infrastructures. Commercial videotex service represents the front line of the new consumer-oriented communications technology and of an electronic information business that has an estimated 1990 revenue potential of 9 billion dollars. For in-building business communications, local area networks (LANs) are becoming an accepted way to interconnect terminals, computers, word processing equipment, and the like. For mobile communications, cellular mobile telephone service is progressing rapidly, and may develop into an alternative to the copper wiring used for ordinary telephone service.

EXHIBIT 22-4   *Major Technological Changes Expected During the Eighties*

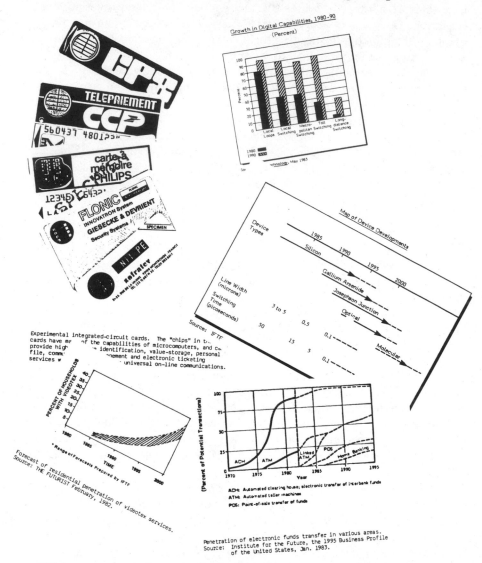

With respect to industry and regulatory changes, user demands have stimulated the emergence of new communications companies and the recent steps toward deregulation of the communications industry. A clear segmentation of the industry now exists: unregulated terminal equipment companies, "bypass" and "value-added service" suppliers, local exchange carriers, and interchange carriers. Significant competition exists in each segment, but the general trend in communications expense can be expected to be upward. Therefore, a major potential for cost savings and service improvements appears to exist in bypassing local exchange services, such as the use of PBX instead of Centrex service or the use of regional bypass facilities provided by a teleport, a cable company, or a microwave operator.

In the data processing and information management field, much is happening. Higher-speed mainframes may emerge, but the important hardware development will probably include building mainframe capabilities into much smaller machines. Personal computers are the hardware focus now and for the near future. By 1987 it is estimated that 49 million such units will be installed, and their growing acceptability will make them important elements in both office automation and home electronic service delivery.

Software developments will probably be even more significant than hardware changes. The combined "value-added services" market of software, professional DP services, and processing services could grow to 58 billion dollars by 1987. "Fourth-generation" computer languages, which are exceptionally easy to program, will have many important applications in management information systems. Artificial intelligence (AI) programs, which incorporate human expertise and judgment into software packages, promise to be useful as training devices for financial personnel and could even give financial advice directly to customers.

Supporting all of these technical and economic changes is the continuing phenomenal progress in electronics. Very Large Scale Integrated (VLSI) chips will substantially enhance the capabilities of information and communication systems for effective and low-cost servicing of operational and customer needs. The expectation of fundamental performance improvements and cost reductions in electronic technologies lends credibility to a strategy of steady migration to digital communication and electronic financial services support and delivery.

The strategic planning challenge for the financial services industry resulting from this rapidly changing technology is twofold. On the one hand, to be competitively successful, companies will have to be both major appliers of these new technologies and developers of technically based products and operations capabilities. A fascinating menu of specific technology-based financial services products will likely be available to customers, including such appealing possibilities as bill paying via payroll deduction, vending machines for five-dollar to fifty-dollar "investment tickets," cafeteria-style employee benefits programs, or "smart cards" as alternative forms of currency. Technical applications, particularly to improve the level of service quality, will increasingly be seen as strategic weapons in the competitive struggle. The availability of better and cheaper electronic access and processing, plus the growth of "computer consciousness" among both employee and customer populations, will make the transition to electronic financial services delivery much easier. Consumers will likely accept electronically delivered financial products and services whenever it clearly enhances their choice and convenience.

On the other hand, extreme care will be necessary to avoid expensive blind alleys that interesting technologies tend to encourage. While the application of technology is obviously basic to the design, servicing, and delivery of financial services, it must be done practically. Technology is a means to accomplish solid business objectives and should be applied when it contributes to the execution of a strategy at acceptable cost. Suffice it to say that the technological resources available to the financial services industry provide tremendous potential for developing and executing a variety of innovative, competitively effective business strategies. Care must be taken to pursue these technologies cost-effectively.

The Planning System

In addition to the external factors important for strategy development within the financial services industry, it is important to establish a planning system to support strategy developed. In their landmark article in the *Harvard Business Review* in 1980, Fred Gluck et al. described a four-phase model of evolution for formal strategic planning systems. Exhibit 22-5 depicts this model, and the article discusses the normal progression from Phase I—Basic Financial Planning—through Phase IV—Strategic Management. The authors are careful to point out that not all companies fit the pattern precisely, but that the generalizations are broadly applicable.

The financial services industry generally fits this mold. It usually takes at least five years to pass through the first two phases, that is, to build the infrastructure necessary to progress into the later phases where external orientation, team work, and flexiblity are so important. For those companies that were "lucky" enough to do a good job in establishing the foundation in the mid-to-late 1970s, the transition to the financial services revolution of the early 1980s must have been easier. For those companies that are still in the earlier stages, considerable effort should be devoted to establishing the basic system quickly. However, a thorough job should be done in setting up the fundamentals. Without them, the chances of success in Phases III and IV are not likely to be very great, particularly if competitors have done their planning homework well in the earlier stages.

Most of the major companies in the financial services marketplace are probably somewhere in Phase III–IV. Several senior level executives have said that they are trying to manage their companies strategically, but their organizations are firmly rooted in the realities of Phase III. This, by the way, is not a bad place to be, considering that many positive things are happening here—increasingly, external regulatory and technological events are being factored into strategic decision making; much more attention is paid to the strategies of the competition; and emphasis is being placed on what is happening in the marketplace.

As companies progress to Phases III and IV, however, much more attention is needed on how to tailor the planning system to support the needs of the later phases. What works systematically to "Meet budget" (Phase I) and "Predict the future" (Phase II), may or may not work for "Think strategically" (Phase III) and "Create the future" (Phase IV).

EXHIBIT 22-5   *Four Phases in the Evolution of Formal Strategic Planning*

	Phase I Basic financial planning	Phase II Forecast-based planning	Phase III Externally oriented planning	Phase IV Strategic management
Effectiveness of formal business planning				Orchestration of all resources to create com- petition advantage Strategically chosen plan- ning framework Creative, flexible planning processes Supportive value system and climate
			Increasing response to markets and competition Thorough situation anal- ysis and competitive assessment Evaluation of strategic alternatives Dynamic allocation of resources	
		More effective planning for growth Environmental analysis Multi-year forecasts Static allocation of resources		
	Operational control Annual budget Functional focus			
Value system	Meet budget	Predict the future	Think strategically	Create the future

Source: F. W. Gluck, S. P. Kaufman, and A. S. Walleck, "Strategic Management for Competitive Advantages," *Harvard Business Review,* July–August 1980.

22.13

Typically, corporations have developed calendar-oriented planning systems along the lines depicted in Exhibit 22-6. In the first half of the year the long-range planning efforts are undertaken, and in the second half of the year the annual business planning and budgeting is done. This approach fits well with the forecast-and-fact–based needs of Phases I and II and the internal finance and planning requirements of many organizations. It also permits corporate control of strategic objectives and resource priorities and the review of management capabilities on a regular basis.

Unfortunately, thinking and managing strategically does not always fit nicely into a neat calendar time frame. Competitors make strategic product/ service introductions when it best suits them, not according to the calendar; legislative developments in Washington or the states often come without much advance notice; and technological innovations in financial services delivery systems can be introduced at any time.

Given these realities, it becomes increasingly important to modify the existing planning systems and structures to meet the challenges of the times and the changing nature of the financial services industry. What is suggested is the introduction of a project-oriented planning system into the existing framework (see Exhibit 22-7). This will permit installation of the corporate

EXHIBIT 22-6   Calendar-Oriented Planning System

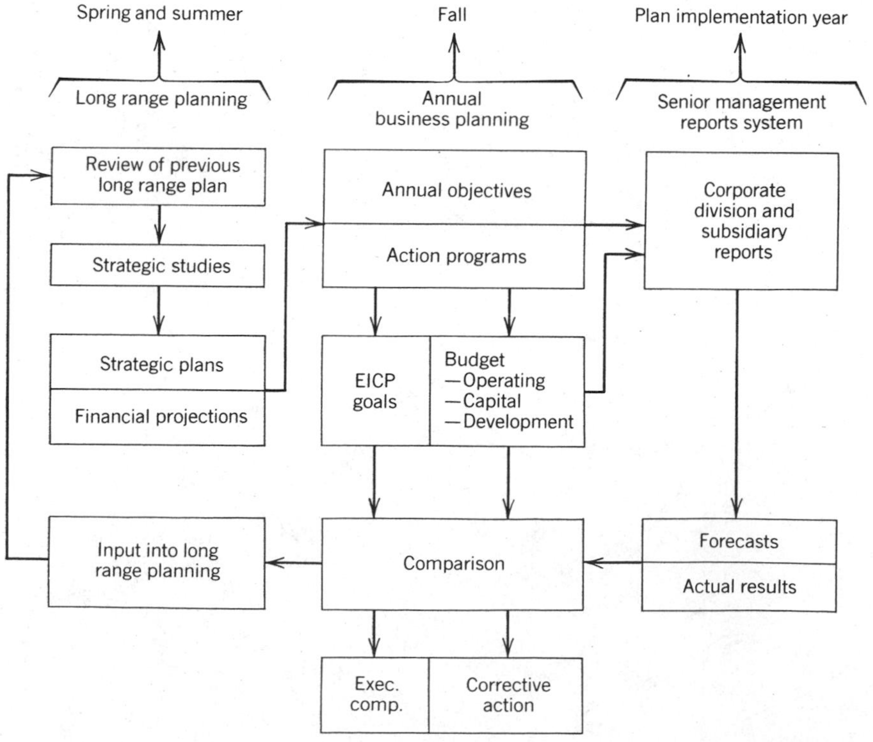

EXHIBIT 22-7 Project-Oriented Planning System

I OVERVIEW: THE NEW WAVE OF
STRATEGIC PLANNING ...

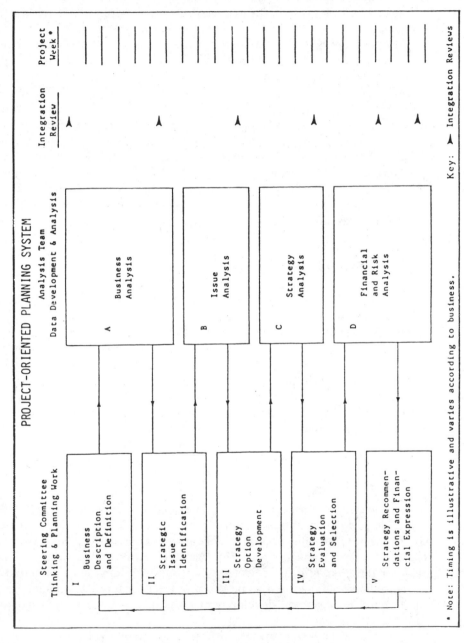

Source: The Michael Allen Company, 1984.

22.15

value-system elements discussed in Phase IV—themes such as "task-oriented organizational flexibility," "entrepreneurial drive," and "open communication." Such a strategic project planning system is particularly needed at the business unit level in order to permit updating or rethinking of strategy faster and more effectively than competitors. Furthermore, it must be designed to capture and integrate both business management experience and staff intelligence into the strategy development process.

The addition of a project-oriented planning approach will enhance the calendar-oriented system, if care is taken to integrate the output of these special projects into the existing process. Both the mid-year and end-of-year sessions can be used as focal points to ensure this happening. Time at each meeting should be set aside to discuss the status of important projects that are underway, if only to state that things are on track and the strategy recommendations will be forthcoming in *x* months. Special review sessions should be arranged to review these special strategy projects when completed, and subsequent formal planning documents should integrate the strategies developed as a result of the projects.

STRATEGY IMPLEMENTATION

In addition to designing the planning system to promote strategy development, it is necessary to develop the management system that aggressively supports strategy implementation. Overemphasizing the importance of strategic concepts and business analysis without providing the delivery mechanism can be disastrous. It is often said that strategic concepts and business analysis are only 40 percent of the task, and that the remaining 60 percent influence on strategy success is the impact of management. To help management in this task, considerable attention must be paid to compensation practices, functional support, management education, and, above all, management involvement.

Compensation

Clearly, one of the most important tools available to induce strategy implementation is compensation. To put it simply, if you want good strategies, pay for them. Quite often, executive incentive compensation plans have been structured to pay managers primarily for short-term results — the "bottom line" for the coming year. Selected "hot button" items may be added to induce some specific actions to be taken in the near term, often such items as EEO and management development programs that senior management wants accomplished.

Year-to-year, however, these critical priorities tend to change and are not necessarily linked to the strategic direction of the business. To overcome this problem of short-term orientation, it is suggested that the criteria used to measure executive performance be restructured to emphasize ongoing strategy implementation. More emphasis should be placed on the strategic thrust of the business, and premiums placed on resolving the two or three strategic issues identified as critical and implementing the strategy for the overall business or group of businesses.

In those financial services institutions that have several interrelated business groups, incentive compensation should also be included for achievement of interunit cooperative efforts. The subsidiary's CEO should be held accountable for achievement of the two or three most important intergroup initiatives each year. These efforts could include programs in areas such as cross-selling, joint new-product development, shared facilities or processing capacities, and cooperative technological or financial programs. The point is, unless you pay for strategy implementation, there can be no guarantee that it will happen.

Functional Support

Also important to the development of successful business strategies is the contribution made by functional support groups. This includes the human resource function, marketing, operations, systems and data processing, and finance. Without their active involvement, viable business strategies are not likely to be forthcoming.

As an example of what is needed in terms of functional support, consider the importance of the human resource planning function. In light of the comment made earlier about the importance of management in strategy success, perhaps this is the most important functional area to incorporate into the process. In parallel with the business strategy development process, the human resource planning process should show how people and programs will be concentrated to achieve competitive success in attractive markets in the future.

Specifically, let us consider the steps needed for business strategy development. The first step an analysis team would take would be to do a thorough business analysis (as outlined previously in Exhibit 22-7). This would include a business segmentation definition, an environmental position assessment, a competitive analysis, and a resource analysis.

Briefly, the business segmentation analysis aims at understanding how the business situation differs by product/market segment so that differential strategies can be developed to gain or defend market position effectively. The environmental position assessment aims at developing the distinctive characteristics of each segment in order to define the specific business challenges for each segment. The competitive assessment aims at identifying which competitors are key in which segment, and resource analysis is conducted to identify what resources are crucial, the degree of scarcity of those resources, and how they might be allocated in the future.

Exhibit 22-8 contains a sample worksheet that might be used to integrate

EXHIBIT 22-8 *Functional Analysis Worksheet-Sample*

FUNCTIONAL SAMPLE ANALYSIS WORKSHEET

BUSINESS ANALYSIS: HUMAN RESOURCE CONSIDERATIONS	PHASE 1: SEGMENTATION — END USER SEGMENT: "UPSCALE"	"MASS MARKET"	PHASE 2: POSITION ASSESSMENT — BUSINESS CHALLENGES: "UPSCALE" Custom Products	"UPSCALE" Pers. Svcs.	"MASS MKT" Dist. Syst.	"MASS MKT" Effic. Oper.	PHASE 3: COMPETITIVE ANALYSIS — STRENGTHS/WEAKNESSES: "UPSCALE" Comp A	"UPSCALE" Comp B	"MASS MKT" Comp C	"MASS MKT" Comp D	PHASE 4: RESOURCE ASSESSMENT — CRITICAL NEEDS: "UPSCALE" Leadership	"MASS MKT" Contain
ORGANIZATION		X				X	-	-	+	+	o Matrix	o Functional
RECRUITMENT		X		X			-	o	-	-	o Ability	o Experience
TRAINING AND EDUCATION	X			X			o	+	+	o	o Heavy Commitment	
FUNCTIONAL SKILLS	X		X			X	o	o	+	o	o Marketing o Product Development	o Operations o Financial Control
MANAGEMENT DEVELOPMENT	X		X				-	o	o	+	o Creativity o Innovation	o Analysis o Skills
MEASUREMENT AND CONTROL		X	X		X	X	+	o	o	-	o Output	o Input
COMPENSATION AND MOTIVATION	X		X				+	+	+	o	o Pay for Growth	o Pay for Profits
SUMMARY	Tailor human resource strategies by business segment		Specify the role of human resource development in meeting the key business challenges of each segment				Compare human resource capabilities with relevant competition by segment				Differentiate management approach by strategy thrust - leadership, penetration, hold or contain	

22.18

the human resource planning function with business strategy development. A similar worksheet could be designed for the other functional areas as well. It is important to note that the approach suggested is only a framework for analysis, for each cell within the matrix could require extensive, in-depth research and analysis in order to come to a judgment about what strategy to recommend for each cell. Again, the point is to do thorough functional analyses in support of business strategy development, and to do them in a formal way.

Management Education

It has been said that "no amount of planning will replace dumb luck." On occasion this is probably true. But who of us really wants to rely on luck to be a success? There can be little doubt that experienced managers— whether their style is intuitive, entrepreneurial, marketing, or financial control —can perform better with good strategic information and analysis. And even the most brilliant, conceptual strategist is limited if he or she lacks basic information and strategy analysis.

Many managers acknowledge, unfortunately, that there is a gap in their strategic planning skills. This is particularly true of line managers—those very individuals who run the business. How often we have heard such comments from senior group or division executives: "As Division Manager, I've been in the company 25 years without formal training in planning," "we need to refresh and challenge our managers—particularly with new strategic analysis concepts," and "there is absolutely a major need for planning education."

It seems clear, therefore, that a key leverage point in gaining what strategic planning has to offer is management education. Having an extensive planning training program along the lines of major companies such as GE and IBM would, of course, be desirable. But for most financial services institutions such a commitment of resources is not likely to be feasible. Still, much can be accomplished with the dedication of a few individuals. Get a key planner together with a key executive trainer, and have the backing of a key senior corporate executive, and you will be amazed at the results.

In designing a seminar the focus should be on helping line executives to gain deeper familiarity, skill, and experience with strategic thinking and strategy development. Specific objectives might be to help participants to understand the thrust of strategic planning within the company, to provide participants with a better understanding of the nature of corporate strategy and business strategy development, and to improve participants' skills in formulating and implementing strategies within their own business units.

A typical program might have an agenda along the lines depicted in Exhibit 22-9. The faculty should be selected carefully, using a mix of external experts who have both strategic planning and teaching experience and internal managers who have had hands-on experience of doing strategy development

EXHIBIT 22-9   Strategic Planning Seminar Agenda

```
                         STRATEGIC PLANNING SEMINAR AGENDA


    Sunday                   Introduction

      6:00 p.m.              Reception
      7:00 p.m.              Dinner
      8:30 p.m.              Orientation and Welcome


    Monday                   Macro-Strategic Thinking (Outside Faculty)

      8:30 a.m.              A Framework for Strategic Thinking
     10:30 a.m.              Competitive Analysis
      1:00 p.m.              Strategy Formulation: Case Study and Discussion
      4:00 p.m.              Strategy Implementation Issues
      8:30 p.m.              An Outsider's View of the Company


    Tuesday                  Micro-Strategic Thinking (Outside/Inside Faculty)

      8:30 a.m.              Business Strategy Development Framework for FSIs
     10:30 a.m.              FSI Strategy Development: Case Study & Discussion
      1:00 p.m.              Company Specific Issues: Case Study & Discussion
      8:30 p.m.              An Insider's View of the Company: CEO


    Wednesday                Company Strategic Thinking (Inside Faculty)

      8:30 a.m.              Corporate Strategies
      9:30 a.m.              Subsidiary Strategies
     10:30 a.m.              Functional Strategies
     12:00 p.m.              Summary Remarks and Evaluations
```

within the company. At one of the evening sessions, a senior officer (preferably the chairman) should be the speaker, with the majority of the time spent in a question-and-answer session.

By conducting three or four of these sessions annually, with 20 to 25 participants per seminar, it will not take much time to achieve the desired result. Furthermore, if the seminars are done well, there will probably be a strong follow-up effort by the participants to institute something similar in their own business units—all of which is good for stimulating better planning throughout the organization.

Management Involvement

Most important of all is the commitment to strategic planning at all management levels, accompanied by active participation in the planning process. All of the management systems changes, the compensation system moves, the functional support system improvements, and the management education actions will be useless without this commitment. This commitment must start at the top of the organization, for without that example of planning leadership, the rest will become a paper tiger.

That doesn't mean that planners are not an integral part of this involvement. Far from it. Planners must be intimately involved. They must monitor change and recognize the implications of those changes for the company. They must provide strategic options and ask stimulating questions—all of which should result in better decisions.

SUMMARY

Strategic planning for financial services companies is similar to, but not identical with, many other businesses. The objective is to position the company for competitive success in the future, but the delivery mechanisms must be adapted to the specific situations of the industry. The key strategic driving forces are the needs of the customer. The successful business strategies will be those that focus more heavily on product/market initiatives, emphasize innovative approaches to satisfy customer needs, and rely on market testing and research to insure the viability of proposed strategies.

The most important environmental factors that must be considered in the development of strategies are the demands of an increasingly sophisticated financial consumer, the rapidly changing deregulatory climate, and the revolution taking place in technology. The companies that do the best job of incorporating the effects of these environments into their business strategies will have the best chance of competitive success in the future.

Finally, to accomplish the objective, it is critical both to tailor the planning systems to support strategy development and to establish the management system that aggressively supports strategy implementation. A combination of calendar-oriented and project-oriented approaches should best serve strategy development. A combination of compensation practices, functional support, and management education should facilitate strategy implementation. Above all, there must be a commitment to strategic planning at all management levels.

NOTES

1. The Hudson Strategy Group, *Financial Services Innovation and the American Consumer: A Study Prepared for American Express Company,* 1983.
2. Ibid., p. 4.

CHAPTER *23*

Strategic Planning for Consumer Retail Businesses

FRANK WILLARD

FRANK WILLARD was Director of Planning and Research at JC Penney, Inc. During his earlier years with JC Penney, he held positions as Manager of International Development and Manager of Financial Planning. He held financial positions with Mobil Oil, Union Carbide, and the Manville Corporation. Mr. Willard was a graduate of Harvard College. He was President of the New York Chapter of the North American Society for Corporate Planning, member of the Retail Research Society, and visiting lecturer at Rutgers University. He also served as President of the Harvard Club of New Jersey and Vice-Chairman of the Citizens Budget Advisory Committee of Millburn Township, New Jersey.

OUTLINE

This chapter begins with an overview of retailing and of its strategic characteristics. There follows a discussion of strategic planning concepts in retailing, including the "target consumer," the "offering," financial and competitive considerations, growth strategies, "enterprise" strategies, and, finally, strategies for specific retailing sectors and a brief summary.

PROFILE OF RETAILING

Retailing is part of the distribution pipeline, the path which moves products from creation to consumption. It is the end of that pipeline, connecting directly with individual customers. It is a major component of general economic activity.

Retailing is an enormously large and diverse group of activities with some physical presence in even the smallest hamlets. It includes the supermarket, the drug store, and the cleaner around the corner. It is the discount store, the variety store, the appliance dealer in commercial areas or along major roadways. It is the fast-food restaurant and the gas station at the crossroad, the giant department store downtown or in the mall, the furniture showroom, the automobile dealer, and the antique shop. It is a multitude of specialty stores, down to boutique size, addressing family fashion needs. It is even the invisible store that offers merchandise via catalog or other media. And, finally, retailing is the door-to-door salesperson, the street peddler, the flea market, the country auction, and the garage sale.

A few measures of retailing's size appear in Exhibit 23-1. In 1983 total sales of retail establishments as reported by the U.S. Department of Commerce exceeded 1.1 trillion dollars or about one-third the magnitude of the gross national product (the most common measure of overall economic activity). Spending at retail establishments represented one-half of all expenditures by consumers. Retailing employed 15 million workers in 1983, or about 15 percent of total employment.

The scope of retailing activity is illustrated in Exhibit 23-2. Based on the most recent (1977) Census of Retail Trade, the table breaks down overall retailing activity into 17 broad categories. There are 1.9 million retail establishments, mostly privately owned. Concentration in each sector varies from very low, for bars, to high, in general merchandise (e.g., department stores),

EXHIBIT 23-1   Retailing and the Economy

	1983
Total retail sales	$1,171.4 billion
GNP	$3,310.5 billion
Retail sales as a percentage of GNP	35.4%
Consumer expenditures	$2,158.0 billion
Retail sales as a percentage of consumer expectations	54.3%
Employment in retailing	15,277 thousand

Sources: U.S. Department of Commerce, Bureau of Economic Analysis; U.S. Department of Commerce, Bureau of the Census; U.S. Department of Commerce, Bureau of Labor Statistics.

EXHIBIT 23-2 Scope of Retailing Activity

Category	Establishments (in thousands)	Individual Proprietorships (in thousands)	Percentage of Sales of Top 8 Firms	Largest Firms
Food stores	252	57	22.8	Safeway, Kroger
Motor vehicle dealers	31	13	1.7	
General merchandise	49	36	49.6	Sears, K-Mart
Gasoline service stations	176	65	8.3	
Eating places	274	48	7.3	McDonald's, Marriott
Apparel and accessories	140	36	13.5	Hartmarx, Petrie Stores
Drug stores	50	28	23.4	Jack Eckerd, Walgreen
Building material and supplies	41	31	10.9	Wickes, Lowe's
Furniture, furnishings and floor coverings	96	52	6.0	Levitz
Nonstore retailing	33	52	24.3	ARA Services, Avon
Auto and home supply	47	43	13.1	
Liquor stores	44	45	13.3	
Appliance, radio, and television	42	52	16.5	
Drinking places	94	61	0.8	
Hardware	26	54	8.7	
Jewelry	34	58	15.7	Zale, Kay
Miscellaneous	426	—	—	
Total retail	1855	54	9.2	

Source: 1977 Census of Retail Trade—Establishment and Firm Size.

EXHIBIT 23-3   *Estimated Sales of All Retail Stores by Kind of Business, as a Percentage of Total Retail Sales: 1983*

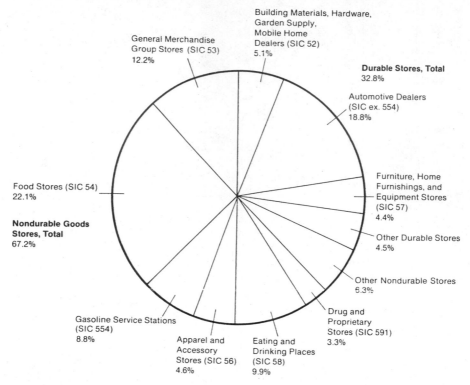

drug stores, food supermarkets, and nonstore retailing (e.g., door-to-door, catalog). Each area has its own character and competitive environment. However, overall, we can expect a continued trend toward concentration, with a rising share of retail sales being generated by chains.

The relationship of major subcategories to total retail sales is illustrated in Exhibit 23-3. Dollar volume breaks down into 70 percent in nondurables such as food, general merchandise, apparel, drugs, gas stations, and eating and drinking places versus 30 percent in durables such as automobiles, furniture, and building materials. The five largest retailing categories, accounting for 72 percent of sales, are food stores (22%), automotive dealers (19%), general merchandise stores (12%), gas stations (9%), and restaurants (10%).

Although retailing businesses vary widely in many respects, they have a unique set of characteristics that affects strategy development:

First—and most important—the market for retailers consists of individual consumers rather than other businesses, industries, or public and private institutions.

Retailing tends to be fragmented geographically to be close enough to its customers. The exception is nonstore retailing via catalog or other media.

The entry barrier is relatively low for most forms of retailing; almost anyone can participate on some scale.

It is highly competitive. Almost invariably a retail outlet faces a multitude of competitors that compete directly, or with a degree of overlap in the same markets.

Most forms of retailing offer relatively broad assortments of products. For example, the large department stores may sell hundreds of thousands of separate items, discount stores and major catalogs more than 50,000, supermarkets 10,000, and drug stores 5,000.

The life cycle of products offered ranges from very short—a few weeks—to several years.

Product/service/image differentiation is generally high; no two retailers are alike in their offerings.

Retailing, overall, is growing only moderately. Therefore, success in retailing increasingly depends on ability to increase market share.

STRATEGIC PLANNING CONCEPTS

The basic concepts in strategic planning have been discussed in prior chapters; they apply to all businesses—retailing no less than manufacturing, mining, or transportation:

A retailing business needs a statement of purpose or mission.

It needs a set of specific objectives consistent with its mission.

It needs strategies to achieve its objectives.

Strategic planning should establish a general direction, rather than a specific game plan, to follow.

Most important, strategy development is the responsibility of top management; it must reflect their vision, or it is little more than an exercise. Further, for effective implementation, a strategic plan must be understood by, must incorporate the input of, and must have the support of the entire organization.

The appendix to this chapter is a "statement of philosophy" by the Dayton-Hudson Corporation, an outstandingly successful major retailer with a strategic orientation. The statement illustrates how the elements of strategy can be articulated.

Some of the larger retailers have broad visions of their areas of activities that may extend beyond operating a certain type of store. Most of the giants in retailing—Sears, K-Mart, JCPenney, Federated, Dayton-Hudson—engage in various kinds of retailing, from high fashion to discount, catalogs, supermarkets, restaurants, financial services. It will be useful, therefore, in the discussion that follows, to distinguish between strategies for achieving success in a particular chosen mode of retailing and "enterprise" strategies that cover all the various activities—retail or other—that the enterprise chooses to pursue.

In a strategic sense, what distinguishes retail activity from other forms of enterprise is a focus on the consumer. The market of a retailer does not consist of other businesses, institutions, or industries. It does consist of individuals with money to spend for the fulfillment of their expectations.

What are these expectations? The consumer shops with the expectation that retail merchants will satisfy, even anticipate, his or her desire for goods and services under circumstances that meet his or her requirements of time, place, price, quality, store ambiance, and so on. To match this expectation and complete the sale, the retail merchant devises an appropriate and unique "offering." Since no retail merchant can expect (or indeed has the resources) to satisfy the expectations of all shoppers at all times, the "offering" has to be aimed at a segment of consumers—the "target consumer." These are the basics of retailing strategy.

Target Consumer

Before examining the considerations that enter into defining the target consumer, it will be useful to look at consumer spending in general from the merchant's point of view. The merchant derives revenues from the individual transactions of consumers with money to spend. The more consumers and the more money each has to spend, the greater is the potential for retail sales. On average, consumers spend about 80 percent of their total income. The other 20 percent consists of taxes, savings, and interest expenses (see Exhibit 23-4).

Somewhat more than 40 percent of total income is spent on purchases from retail stores. The other 40 percent goes for housing, health care, education, transportation, and other nonretail expenditures.

As retailers develop their strategies, they must concern themselves with the size and per capita income of the population they expect to serve. Obviously, the total retail potential for growth is greatest in areas where there is an influx of population with average income on the rise. However, it is necessary to look beyond totals and averages to the shopping behavior of various groups that make up the total population.

Among the principal factors determining the shopping needs of individual consumers are:

1. *Disposable Income.* What is available for purchases of goods and services. The level of disposable income can also serve as a clue to spending patterns. Low disposable income usually results in a spending pattern that focuses on basic necessities such as food; high disposable income permits more spending on intangibles such as fashion, ambiance, and personal service.

EXHIBIT 23-4 Breakdown of Consumer Spending

	1983			Compared to 1973	
	Dollars in Millions	Percentage of Income		Dollars in Millions	Percentage of Income
Personal income	$2742		Personal income	$1065	
Taxes	407	14.8	Taxes	151	14.2
Interest payments	63	2.3	Interest payments	23	2.2
Savings	114	4.2	Savings	79	7.4
Consumer spending	2158	78.7	Consumer spending	812	76.2
Retail sales	1169	42.6	Retail sales	510	47.9

2. *Age.*   Young singles tend to spend more for clothes, entertainment, and vacations; young marrieds tend to spend more on home and children; retirees tend to spend more on travel and health care.

3. *Family Status.*   Being single, married, or divorced, and having or not having children are conditions that influence purchases. In fact, a useful concept in analyzing consumer markets is the household. This concept recognizes that a group of people sharing their place of dwelling may pool their income, on the one hand, and incur common expenditures (e.g., rent, utilities), on the other hand.

4. *Employment Status.*   The type of work people do can influence the way they dress, travel, eat, and spend their leisure time. It certainly influences household income; two-career families tend to have more discretion on how to spend their money.

5. *Education.*   Level of education can have pervasive influence on where consumers work and live, how they furnish their homes, how they spend their leisure time, and so on.

6. *Values and Lifestyles.*   This is a broad label to signify what people believe in, what they like and dislike, and, therefore, how they live. Some people like to express themselves as being "in" with what they wear and do and with how their homes look. These tend to be "high spenders" in certain categories of merchandise. Others are into outdoor life or sports or the "simple" life, or are "conservative" when it comes to appearance, home, car. Obviously the conservative consumer is not the best prospect for, say, a Ferrari sports car or a mink bathrobe.

7. *Time.*   How much time is the target consumer willing or able to invest in shopping? How far is he or she willing to travel? Is time saving an important value in the shopper's mind, or is he or she willing to spend time to find the "best buy"?

These and other characteristics determine how people spend their money and therefore the size of the market for retailers. To be productive, retail merchants must be able to define the market for the "offering." They must be able to segment the totality of consumers into smaller groupings and to focus their efforts on these groupings that are most likely to buy what they have to offer: the target consumers.

To serve as a meaningful basis for strategic planning, the target consumer group must have three characteristics:

1. It must be distinguishable from other consumer groups (and measurable).

2. The shopping needs of a target group should be similar.

3. The target group must be of sufficient size to support a profitable retail business.

Management Horizons, Inc. of Columbus, Ohio, a well-known retailing research and consulting company, has developed a Consumer Matrix (see Exhibit 23-5) for use of retailers in developing their segmentations strategies.

The matrix shows five important "life stages," further divided into above- and below-average income groupings (down market/up market).

Each life stage has certain key consumer characteristics:

Younger singles (under 45) tend to be self-oriented, with few responsibilities or ties, and socially active.

Younger couples (under 45) in this category are childless and tend to be pair-oriented and socially active, with increasing responsibilities.

Young parents (under 45 with youngest child under 18) are characterized by a dramatic increase in responsibilities and ties; they are family- and child-oriented.

Midlife families (head of household over 45, working, with adult children) are pair-oriented, with fewer family responsibilities and with easing of financial and temporal constraints.

Older households (head of household over 45) This group comprises retirees, widows/widowers, and nonfamily households. They are more self-oriented, with more free time and more orientation to the present.

In cases where these consumer matrix segments are not adequate for defining the target consumer, Management Horizons has suggested a number of additional characteristics:

Nature of housing—owner- versus renter-occupied dwellings, single- versus multiple-family structures, and so on.

Socioeconomic status—a composite index based on the income, the educational level, and the occupation of the head of household, as well as the type of residence.

Major leisure-time interests—such as educational activities, spectator sports, active sports, gardening, television.

Fashion interests—such as leaders, early adopters, or conformists.

Physical characteristics—height, body type, or special problems, such as the need for corrective footwear.

Concept of value—whether responsive to lowest possible price, to special price sales of regular merchandise, to special offerings of seconds or irregular merchandise, or to quality appeals which are related to value in use through time.

A study by JCPenney, which appeared in the *Planning Review* in March 1983, illustrates the strategic implications of age/income segmentation. The study compared age/income mixes in 1981 with corresponding projections for 1991. For each age/income segment there is an estimate of population

EXHIBIT 23-5   *The Management Horizons Consumer Market Matrix: Distribution of U.S. Households by Life Stage, 1981*

Life Stage	Down Market		Up Market		Total	
	Number of Households	Percentage of All U.S. Households	Number of Households	Percentage of All U.S. Households	Total	
Younger singles	4,200,000	5.1%	4,200,000	5.1%	8,400,000	10.2%
Younger couples	3,200,000	3.9%	3,200,000	3.9%	6,400,000	7.8%
Younger parents	12,600,000	15.3%	12,600,000	15.3%	25,200,000	30.6%
Midlife families	9,100,000	11.0%	9,100,000	11.0%	18,200,000	22.0%
Older households	12,100,000	14.7%	12,100,000	14.7%	24,200,000	29.4%
Total	41,200,000	50.0%	41,200,000	50.0%	82,400,000	100.0%

Source: U.S. Bureau of the Census, *Current Population Reports*, Series P-20, Nos. 371 and 372, March 1981, and Management Horizons, Inc.

23.10

EXHIBIT 23-6 Age/Income GAF Sales Matrix (Income to $000)

	Under $10		$10–$30		$30–$50		Over $50		Totals	
	Number	Percentage of GAF	Number	Percentage of GAF	Number	Percentage of GAF	Number	Percentage of GAF	Number	Percentage of GAF
1981										
Under 25	2	1	4	5	1	1	0	0	7	7
25–44	6	3	22	23	10	17	3	7	41	50
45–64	6	2	14	11	8	12	4	8	32	33
Over 64	11	3	7	5	1	1	1	1	20	10
Totals	25	9	47	44	20	31	8	16	100	100
1991										
Under 25	2	1	4	3	1	1	0	0	7	5
25–44	6	3	22	20	13	21	5	12	46	56
45–64	4	1	11	8	7	10	5	11	27	30
Over 64	10	2	8	5	1	1	1	1	20	9
Totals	22	7	45	36	22	33	11	24	100	100

Source: JCPenney estimates.

23.11

and a percentage of GAF sales (general merchandise, apparel, and furnishings) consumed in 1981 dollars (see Exhibit 23-6). The comparison shows that as the post-World War II baby boomers enter their most productive years they account for a rising share of income and GAF sales.

In 1981, the 25–44 age group with an annual income of 10,000 dollars represented 35 percent of the population and 47 percent of GAF sales. In 1991, this group will be 40 percent of the population and will account for 53 percent of GAF sales. This is an affluent, rapidly growing market, which many retailers will be planning to serve. Here lies the reason why so many stores are "trading up."

The Offering

In response to their assessments of the expectations of their target consumers—expectations that constitute their business opportunities—retail merchants devise an offering designed to capitalize on this opportunity.

The offering consists of all the elements that must come together to trigger sales, such as:

1. Assortment of merchandise
   Categories of merchandise carried
   Breadth of selection (how many different items)
   Depth of inventory (how many of each)
   Price ranges
   Taste level
   Quality
2. Physical plant
   Location
   Size
   Layout
   Construction
   Decor
   Signing
3. Customer service
   Store hours
   Sales help
   Checkout method
   Change rooms
   Alterations
   Credit
   Product service
   Delivery

4. Promotion
    Advertising
    Price breaks
    Markdown policy
    Special events

Exhibit 23-7 is a visual representation of the offering and its role in retailing strategy development.

There is infinite variety in the way retailers can design their offerings. No two stores are ever alike. Each merchant seeks to develop a unique approach to meet the expectations of his or her target consumers. This offering is, in fact, his or her basic strategy.

The merchant adds value to the goods and services by making them available under conditions that satisfy customer expectations. The value added varies with the expectations, but might include the following considerations:

Convenient location and hours and one-stop shopping are obvious plusses where time and transportation constraints are important.

Price may be uppermost in the mind of some shoppers. In fact, they may invest time to find the lowest priced merchandise.

Wide selection can be important.

EXHIBIT 23-7   Summary Model of Retailing Marketing Strategy

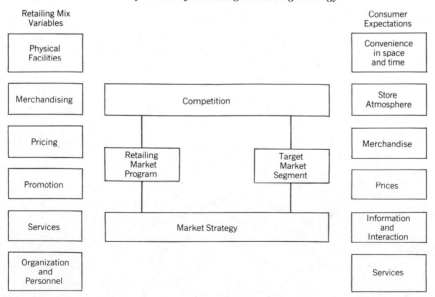

Source: W. R. Davidson, D. J. Sweeney, and R. W. Stampfl, *Retailing Management,* 5th ed. Wiley, New York, 1984.

Quality may outweigh price, or vice versa, in the shopper's mind.
Knowledgeable sales help may be the key in selling more technically complex products.
Store ambiance and family labels can be important.

A retailer's perception of the value added by conventional department stores was well articulated in the Federated Department Stores' 1983 Annual Report:

> Conventional department stores are validators of fashions, styles and tastes for a broad segment of the American population. Fashion in both apparel and home furnishings is a dynamic and potentially confusing phenomenon with which relatively few customers are really comfortable. They rely on buyers to edit the dizzying array of merchandise offerings for them and the presence of edited merchandise in our stores and windows and advertising validates its acceptability. No other form of retailing performs this essential function for upscale American shoppers across so many classifications of merchandise.[1]

Another useful visual that arrays different retailing concepts according to their degree of specialization and value added is given in Exhibit 23-8. Each retailer has to make a decision about where he or she must appear on this matrix in order to provide the appropriate response to the expectations of his or her target consumer.

An essential consideration in developing the "offering" is that of the life cycle. It is one of the characteristics of most forms of retailing that they deal with merchandise with relatively short life cycles. Furthermore, the retailing

EXHIBIT 23-8   *Retailers as Specialists and Value-Adding Institutions*

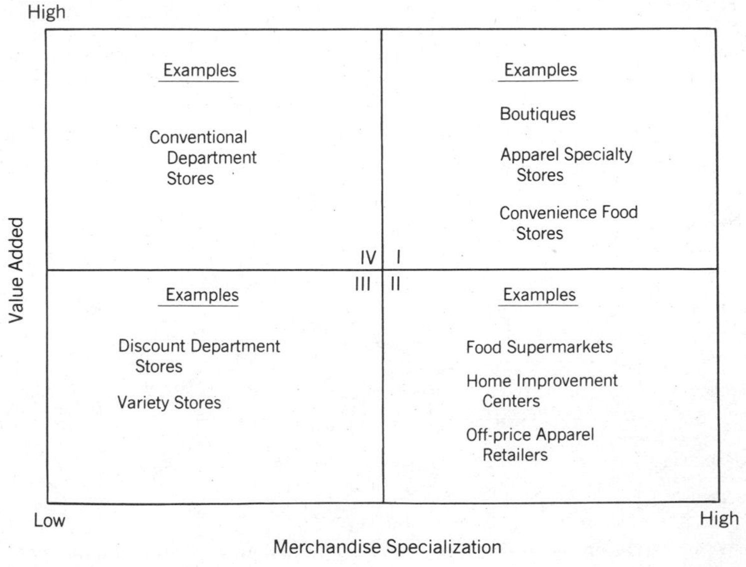

concept itself has its own life cycle from innovation to decline. Exhibit 23-9 is a strategic guide for the development of retailing strategies at various stages of the life cycle.

In most forms of retailing the offering requires frequent updating and, at times, drastic revision. This is so because of changes in target consumers' incomes and spending habits, as well as changes in the competitive environment. Today's success formula can easily turn into tomorrow's prescription for disaster. There have been many spectacular failures in retailing, such as those experienced by W.T. Grant, Korvette, and A&P. And there have been companies that have succeeded brilliantly over the years by redesigning their offerings. Bloomingdale's and Macy's are good examples of successful change.

EXHIBIT 23-9   *Management Activities in the Life Cycle*

	Area or Subject of Concern	1 Innovation	2 Accelerated Development	3 Maturity	4 Decline
Market Characteristics	Number of competitors	Very few	Moderate	Many direct competitors Moderate indirect competition	Moderate direct competition Many direct competitors
	Rate of sales growth	Very rapid	Rapid	Moderate	Slow or negative
	Level of profitability	Low to moderate	High	Moderate	Very low
	Duration of new innovations	3 to 5	5 to 6	Indefinite	Indefinite
Appropriate retailer actions	Investment/ growth/risk decisions	Investment minimization --high risks accepted	High levels of investment to sustain growth	Tightly controlled growth	Minimal capital expenditures and only when essential
	Central management concerns	Concept refinement through adjustment and experimentation	Establishing a pre-emptive market	Excess and "over-storing" Prolonging maturity and revising the retail concept	Engaging in a "run-out" strategy
	Use of management control techniques	Minimal	Moderate	Extensive	Moderate
	Most successful management style	Entrepreneurial	Centralized	"Professional"	Caretaker
Appropriate supplier actions	Channel strategy	Develop a premptive market	Hold market position	Maintain profitable sales	Avoid excessive costs
	Channel problems	Possible antagonism of other accounts	Possible antagonism of other accounts	Dealing with more scientific retailers	Servicing accounts at a profit
	Channel research	Identification of key innovations	Identification other retailers adopting the innovation	Initial screening of new innovation opportunities	Active search for new innovation opportunities
	Trade incentives	Direct concessions	Price concessions	New price incentives	None

(Column headers span under "Stage of Life Cycle Development")

Each aspect of the offering has implications regarding the costs of doing business and the required investment level. To be successful, a retailing strategy must pass three tests:

1. It must satisfy the expectations of target consumers.
2. It must be competitive.
3. It must generate sufficient profit to attract the necessary financial resources.

Financial Considerations

Like any other business, retailing can be viewed as a use of resources to achieve some benefit. The benefit is basically the efficient distribution of merchandise and services to consumers. One way of measuring benefits and resources required is in dollars. To prosper and grow, a business must be profitable: it must generate more dollars in income than it spends. Its level of profitability compared with those of all other businesses must be sufficient to attract the necessary investment capital.

There are many ways of measuring profitability. Among the most important to the investor is return on stockholder equity (ROE). In 1983, the average ROE of all businesses listed in *Forbes* was 12.6 percent. The ROE of retailing businesses ranges from far above the average to far below (see Exhibit 23-10).

The principal financial variables that determine ROE in retailing are the following:

Sales revenues (units sold × unit price)
Cost of goods sold (units sold × cost)
Overhead (fixed and variable expenses)
Fixed assets (buildings and fixtures)
Inventories (merchandise in stores/warehouse or transit)
Accounts receivable (purchases on credit)
Accounts payable (vendor bills for merchandise sold)

There are various successful strategies for achieving above-average financial results; they tend to fall somewhere between two extremes. At one extreme are high-margin, high-asset retailers (e.g., department stores and fashion specialty stores). There the emphasis is on value added to the product in the store by category dominance, stylishness, store ambiance, customer service, credit, and so on.

At the other extreme are low-margin, low-asset retailers such as food supermarkets. In this approach the offering tends to consist of frequently replenished, readily comparable items where price and close proximity to the

EXHIBIT 23-10   Return on Equity

Company	Latest 12 Months (ended 1983)	Five-Year Average
Limited	40.0	33.2
Wal-Mart	33.0	33.1
R.H. Macy	22.3	20.0
Long's Drug Stores	17.5	18.9
K-Mart	15.2	12.9
Safeway Stores	14.5	13.4
Sears, Roebuck	13.3	9.9
All-industry mediam	12.6	15.1
Carter Hawley Hale	8.0	9.3
Heck's	6.3	14.6
Zale	5.0	9.7
Industry Median		
Specialty Retailers		
Drug chains	18.6	19.8
Fast food chains	19.9	19.4
Other specialities	15.0	15.7
General Retailers		
Department stores	13.6	12.2
Discount and variety stores	14.1	12.9

Source: Forbes, January 2, 1984.
Note: The all-industry median ROE for the latest 12 months for all 1,008 companies is 12.6 percent—off slightly from 1982's 12.4 percent.

home are of paramount importance. Supermarkets tend to operate on very slim profit margins, but are capable of achieving above-average returns due to high asset turnover. High-asset turnover is achieved by stocking fast-selling items, offering no credit, and paying for merchandise after it is sold.

There are other important considerations that determine the financial strategies of retailers:

1.   Typically, a retail business requires physical plant, staff, and inventories before the first dollar of sales revenues is received. These front-end costs, which can be very large, shape capital requirements for expansion.
2.   Much retailing activity is affected by seasonal changes in weather (wearing apparel) and traditional holidays or gift events (e.g., Christ-

mas, Mother's Day). Other categories of retailing, particularly those dealing in highly discretionary spending (to satisfy wants, rather than needs), tend to rise and fall with the business cycle. Such volatility requires adequate capital reserves to sustain the business during periods of revenue decline.

3. Sustainable growth is the maximum sales or (asset) growth that a business can support using both internally generated funds and debt. It is particularly important for strategy development in the more volatile sectors of retailing.

4. Because of the front-end costs of expansion and the volatile environment in which they operate, most successful retailers find that in the long run they can better capitalize on their growth potential by taking their business public.

In the development of financial strategies, it is essential to understand the profit contribution made by each element of a retail business. This can be relatively simple in retail businesses such as gas stations or fast-food restaurants, where the offering is limited to a few important products. It can be complex in broad-assortment vehicles such as conventional department stores, discount department stores, and supermarkets, where the offering may consist of tens of thousands of individual stock-keeping units or services. However, even in broad-assortment retailing, it is possible to estimate the profit contribution of individual products/services.

Financial analysis reveals which elements of the offering produce above-average returns, which store locations, store types, and store sizes produce the most profit, and which marketing programs produce the best results. Financial analysis also can determine the return from various assets. The result of all this is that management can allocate its resources to the high-return activities and can divest itself of underperforming assets.

Competition

Development of retailing strategies, or selection of target consumers and development of an offering, must take account of the competitive environment. As a rule, competition will be intense. For each spending decision there are alternatives, which means that a new winter coat may have to yield to a much-needed refrigerator, the school tuition, or a hospital bill. More directly, there are other retailers offering the same or similar merchandise.

Direct competition may come from a similar retailing format (e.g., a shoe store competing with another shoe store) or from a different format. A women's wear specialty store may be in direct competition with another specialty store, with the women's wear department of a department store, with an off-price store, and with a catalog retailer. A drug store may be in direct competition with health-and-beauty-aid products offered by supermarkets and by discount stores, and so on.

As mentioned earlier, retailing has the following competitive characteristics:

It is heavily fragmented.

It involves relatively low entry cost.

It is in direct or indirect competition with numerous other suppliers of similar merchandise/services.

It usually involves carrying broad assortments of individual products with short life cycles.

Growth is only moderate overall.

It attracts a high degree of product/service/image differentiation (no two stores are alike in their offerings).

In this competitive environment there is a constant inflow of new formats designed to capitalize on some distinct competitive advantage and an outflow of retail businesses that are no longer viable. Much of this ebb and flow follows Professor Malcolm McNair's (Harvard University) "Wheel of Retailing" concept: A new format enters retailing as a bare-bones, low-cost operator. In time, competitive pressures force the new format to upgrade its offering, thus creating new opportunities for the next low-margin innovator.

Retailing competition also deals with a constantly changing consumer environment. As people age, marry, and increase their income, their needs change, as do their values and lifestyles. These changes require continuous adjustment of retail offerings, erecting opportunities for the nimble merchant. Because of this intensity of competition in most forms of retailing, failures to keep up with target consumer expectations can be costly and, at times, fatal.

In the urban markets, where 70 percent of all retailing activity takes place, competition tends to follow certain geographic patterns, reflecting consumer shopping patterns. Conforming to these geographic patterns can spell success or failure.

In examining retail competition in urban areas, it is useful to establish two concepts. The first of these is the distinction between convenience merchandise and comparison merchandise. Convenience merchandise consists primarily of consumables such as food, health-and beauty aids, stationery, and hardware, or frequently recurring services such as cleaners. Merchandise tends to be standardized and low-cost. The customer's risk of making a mistake due to insufficient opportunity for comparison is minimal. Comparison merchandise purchases require decisions based on perceptions of style, taste, and status. Clothes and home furnishings are the dominant categories. Important considerations here are fashion, quality, cost, and selection. The risk of making a mistake may be costly, and the effects of a mistake may be long-lasting. Under these circumstances the effort required to compare offerings within and among stores is considered worthwhile.

The difference between convenience and comparison shopping is such that each requires its own distinct shopping environment. The shopping environment, in turn, dictates location, size, merchandise, mix, decor, and just about everything else that describes a store.

The second concept distinguishes between three major shopping environments (see Exhibit 23-11):

1. Regional comparison
2. Intermediate convenience
3. Neighborhood convenience

Regional comparison areas are the downtown shopping districts in major cities and the large suburban malls. Tenancies consist mainly of major department and specialty stores. These areas can be viewed as one-stop shopping centers for high quality, fashionable apparel and home furnishings. Shoppers are willing to travel considerable distances for the benefit of choice and for the opportunity for leisurely, pleasant browsing among fine stores, restaurants, and places of entertainment. Fully two-thirds of all adult apparel and cosmetics, plus more than half of shoes, household linens, and fabrics are sold in this environment (see Exhibit 23-12).

Intermediate convenience areas include community shopping districts and strip centers, as well as freestanding discount department stores. This is where you can expect to find junior department stores, discounters, and supermarkets. Such areas are one-stop shopping centers for convenience goods in a full spectrum of merchandise categories, including food. Here is where one-third of children's clothes are sold and from 30–40 percent of

EXHIBIT 23-11   *Comparisons of Shopping Environments*

Regional Comparison	Intermediate Convenience	Neighborhood Convenience
	Retail Configuration	
Downtown of major cities	Community shopping districts and centers	Strip centers
Regional malls	Freestanding discount department stores	Freestanding supermarkets
	Major Tenants	
Department stores and chains such as Sears, JCPenney, Montgomery Ward	Junior department stores	Supermarkets
	Discount department	
	Supermarkets	

Source: JCPenney estimates, based on 1972 Retail Census.

EXHIBIT 23-12   *Market Share Percentage by Type of Environment*

	Regional Comparison	Intermediate Convenience	Neighborhood Convenience
Soft Lines	64%	21%	10%
Women's	71	19	8
Men's	70	20	7
Children's	47	34	15
Shoes	55	21	14
Jewelry	65	15	14
Household textiles	52	25	13
Fabrics, sewing acc.	50	20	20
Hard Lines	27%	31%	14%
Housewares	35	40	15
Appliances	20	20	10
Furniture, floor cov.	30	15	8
Toys, hi-fi equip., photo	20	30	25
Books, cards, stationery, records	30	30	35
Health-and-beauty aids	15	20	60
Hardware, garden, building materials	5	20	25
Automotive	3	10	7
Food, beverages, other	3	20	70

Source: JCPenney estimates, based on 1974 Retail Census. (There have been no significant changes since then.)

housewares, toys, stationery and records are sold. Customers are willing to travel some distance for the selection and price advantage of such centers.

Neighborhood convenience areas consist of centers with a strip of stores and freestanding supermarkets. Tenancies include supermarkets, drug stores, dry cleaners, and other retail outlets where proximity to the shoppers is an especially important consideration. These are one-stop shopping centers for food, health-and-beauty aids, cleaning services, and other frequently purchased essentials that people like to find close to home. Seventy percent of all groceries and sixty percent of health-and-beauty aids are sold here.

The shopping environments described above define the arenas in which retail merchants compete with one another. By locating in the appropriate shopping environment, retailers will benefit from customer traffic generated by the entire area. By locating away from the appropriate shopping environment, retailers put themselves at a serious competitive disadvantage. To survive in the wrong environment, they need an unusually strong competitive advantage that will cause customers to depart from their usual shopping routes.

Korvette's is an example of a company that failed, in large part, through faulty location strategy. The company started as one of the pioneers of discounting. Its stores were appropriately located in intermediate convenience shopping areas around New York. It expanded rapidly, acquiring sites in various other cities and in comparison-shopping areas such as Fifth Avenue and 34th Street, New York City. This "split personality" affected results adversely by confusing shoppers regarding Korvette's offering. Management, sensing this confusion, attempted to be both discounter and fashion merchant (using the slogan "The Other Korvette's"). The company was hurt in its choice comparison-shopping locations by its discounter image, while the fashion campaign lowered its credibility as a discounter in convenience areas.

It is important to understand that the evolution of retailing location patterns in urban markets is not the result of retailing strategies. It is the result of consumer shopping behavior, the clearly expressed preferences of consumers regarding the environment in which they wish to satisfy their shopping expectations. Successful retailers have adopted location strategies that conform to consumer expectations.

In general, each merchant deals with the competitive environment by, on the one hand, understanding the expectations of his or her target consumers and, on the other hand, finding a better way to meet these expectations. This better way is the merchant's competitive advantage.

In *Competitive Strategy,* Michael E. Porter refers to three generic strategies: overall cost leadership, differentiation, and focus.[2] These generic strategies can be adapted to the retailing environment—one that tends to be fragmented and highly competitive, and tends to have low entry barriers.

Cost leadership can be achieved by volume buying, opportunisitic buying of distress merchandise, backward integration, self-service, low-cost location, low-cost construction, standardized small store units managed centrally, and so on. In general, cost leadership can be achieved by the use of economies of scale, standardization, and strong incentives for efficient operation. An illustration of all of the above is Canadian Tire, an outstandingly successful Canadian retail chain offering primarily automotive supplies and services, plus other convenience lines such as hardware and kitchenware. They have established strong motivation toward efficiency by franchising all stores, and the stores are supplied by a central buying staff; hence economies of scale. Operating systems are highly standardized. Cost leadership is obviously most important in retailing formats that emphasize low price as their principal value. Most food supermarkets fall into this category.

Differentiation in retailing involves the two basic components of strategy: the selection of a target consumer and the design of an offering.

Finding a target consumer that has been overlooked by retailers can result in significant differential advantage. For example, many people have body dimensions that differ from the norm—they may be too tall or too small, too heavy or too skinny. A number of retailers have designed their offerings to serve consumers with unusual body dimensions.

The cost leader can use its position advantageously to compete on price. The whole "off-price" retailing phenomenon is an attempt to compete with conventional department and specialty stores on a price basis.

One-stop shopping is a form of differential advantage that leads to the department store and mall format, as well as to the jumbo-sized supermarket and discount department stores. Category dominance—wider selection in the lines carried—can also be a strong differentiator.

Store ambiance, customer service, exchange policy, credit, delivery service, the "personal touch," and community services (like Macy's annual Thanksgiving Day parade), are all differentiation strategies that establish a value edge over the competition.

Focus is really a way of differentiating one's market by putting particular emphasis on one consumer segment, one line of merchandise or services, one location, and so on. One hardware store may carry more cabinet fixtures than any other, thereby earning higher prices and a significant competitive advantage. The trendy, kicky specialty store with rock music and flashing lights focuses on the younger set. Gas stations on turnpikes focus on the transient consumer who is prepared to pay a price for the convenience of filling up en route, and who may occasionally require quick emergency service.

In the highly fragmented and competitive retailing environment, the success formula usually reflects clear differentiation and focus. In forms of retailing where price is a dominant consideration, cost leadership may have to be part of the winning strategy.

Growth Strategies

Retailing strategy begins with the design of an offering that will satisfy the demand of a target consumer while generating a return on investment appropriate to the risk. Once such an offering has been successfully implemented, the most obvious step is expansion, leveraging the success of the initial retailing concept.

There are many options for expanding a successful retail store: opening similar stores in new markets, broadening the offering and enlarging the store, franchising the successful format, and so on. All successful expansion strategies are based on the multipliable concept that an effective philosophy or system of management will work in more than one specific application.

The most common approach to growth is opening similar stores in new markets; the words "similar" and "new" require further definition in this context. "Similar" may mean, literally, that all stores are of the same size, with the same layout, the same lines of merchandise, and the same organization. This is the "cookie-cutter" concept used very successfully by Toys'R'Us. The reason it works for them is that they are dealing with nationally distributed and advertised products—toys—with relatively little local variations in demand. On the other end of the scale are units that are similar only in name and image, or perhaps only in the way they are managed. A long-established nationwide retail chain such as JCPenney has a wide variety of store sizes and configurations, with major differences in external appearance, assortment, and other factors. A "new" market may consist of another area in the same part of town, in a different part of town, in another town in the same region, or in another region.

The development of an effective growth strategy will generally have to deal with five major issues: centralized versus decentralized management, cluster versus scattered expansion, resources for growth, rate of growth, and other considerations.

Centralized Versus Decentralized Management

Toys'R'Us is a good example of the centralized concept, by which all merchandising decisions are made at headquarters and all merchandise is purchased centrally. The advantages to this approach include profitable economies of scale and tight control. Store personnel can focus on customer service and efficiency.

Most conventional department store chains are, essentially, federations of regional stores. Each of these regional "divisions" does its own buying and has a different approach to its market. The advantage here is the focus on a particular geographic area with ability to adjust rapidly to changing demand trends.

National chains such as JCPenney and Sears combine central buying with a fairly high degree of authority on the part of store managers to select from the merchandise purchased by the central office. This is an attempt to blend economies of scale with local market focus.

Cluster Versus Scattered Expansion

There are obvious advantages in having a cluster of stores in the same geographic market. Such a cluster reduces the time spent by management visiting stores. It may permit location of support functions such as receiving, labeling, alterations, product service, and credit near all the stores. It may enable the use of one newspaper, radio station, or television station to cover the entire cluster, resulting in economies of scale. It also increases customer awareness of the business and the perception of area coverage, or even of dominance.

Clustering is very frequently the most effective way to grow. The limitation to clustering is trading area, the minimum target customer population required to support a particular store concept. Large-volume retailing concepts such as major department stores, furniture warehouses such as Levitz, or warehouse outlets (Price Company) may require a trading area population of 300,000 or more people. Here the cluster concept can be applied in the larger metropolitan areas, but in smaller markets there may be room for only a single store.

Another type of retail operation for which clustering may not work is a specialty store targeted at the very affluent. A very large trading area may be required to bring in enough customers in the targeted income bracket. A store such as Saks Fifth Avenue tends to expand in clusters only in major metropolitan markets, while reserving single-store representation for smaller affluent communities such as Bal Harbor, Florida.

Resources for Growth

When a successful retail store decides on a strategy of growth, it is making a significant change in its requirements for financial and managerial resources. Any expansion, no matter how slow, requires the attention of managers who, until then, were entirely concerned with ongoing operations. A growth strategy of magnitude and speed may require significant commitments of personnel, inside or outside the company, to handle site selection, leasing, construction, procurement of store fixtures, supplier developments, training, and so on.

A growth strategy almost always means that money has to be spent up front to acquire and merchandise a new unit before it opens its doors. The faster the rate of growth, therefore, the greater will be the financial resources required. It also means that there is some maximum sustainable rate of growth that can be exceeded only at considerable risk.

Rate of Growth

Rate of growth is a key strategic decision for the successful retailer. There is no legal way in which he or she can protect the "concept." Any offering that works well will attract the attention of others retailers and is likely to be copied quickly, at least in part. So, in order to leverage a temporary competitive advantage, the retailer may want to expand as rapidly as possible.

There are management and financial constraints that will limit the rate of growth. However, these critical resources themselves might be leveraged in a number of ways. Financial strategies might include broadening the equity base by going public or issuing additional stock, carrying additional debt, leasing rather than owning fixed assets, acquiring or merging with other companies, and so forth. One approach to the management and financial constraints might be franchising. Fast food outlets such as McDonald's and Burger King are examples of how to use the franchising concept to accelerate growth and leverage management skills. These successful businesses incorporate another important strategic concept: they have designed their business for maximum simplicity and uniformity, thereby facilitating the management of growth.

Another common growth strategy is to expand the store offering and, with it, store size. Retailers may find that they can capitalize on their success in selling to their target consumers by broadening the offering of merchandise and services. Virtually all the major department stores started on a much more limited basis, often as specialty stores. Their favorable image with their target consumers and the expertise acquired in developing a successful retail business enabled them to expand their franchises. Although expanding in place has advantages, such as familiarity with the market, local franchising with consumers, and easier access by management, it does require added management and financial resources, much as geographic growth does.

Other Considerations

This is not intended to be a full discussion of planning for growth. We have tried to touch on the principal strategic considerations. Clearly, there are other factors that need to be considered, such as:

Size of targe consumer population
Intensity of competition
Availability and cost of desirable sites
Availability and cost of advertising media
Labor conditions
Proximity to suppliers
Legal restrictions
Political environment

Enterprise Strategies

The discussion so far has dealt primarily with strategy development for a particular retailing mode—how to develop a successful concept and make it grow. We now turn briefly to strategies for diversification. We refer to these as enterprise strategies because they may change the character of a business.

There are many reasons why retailers may choose to diversify—or why nonretailers may choose to enter retailing. However, the great majority of reasons for diversification can be grouped in seven major categories (see Exhibit 23-13).

1. One reason for diversification is the need of retailers to be able to *control sources of supply*. Large retailers such as JCPenney and Sears often do business with a multitude of small suppliers. In order to assure the required volumes of merchandise at the specified quality levels, such companies have, at times, provided technical and financial assistance, helping to develop the supplier. Under the circumstances, backward integration—acquisition of suppliers—is one way to assure adequate supply. Theoretically, at least, the captive could receive priority on orders, with independents used to cover demand peaks. In practice there has been relatively little backward integration, probably because the various supplier industries have done an effective job of supplying their retailer customers.

EXHIBIT 23-13 Major Reasons for Diversification

Objective	Strategy	Examples
Control sources of supply	o Retailer or wholesaler acquires supplies (manufacturer or wholesaler).	o Safeway manufactures dry pet food. o Sears stake in Kellwood. o Sears World Trade.
Control of Distribution	o Manufacturer or wholesaler acquires retail stores.	o Melville – which started as a shoe manufacturer still makes shoes but is now a specialty retailer. o Super Value, a food wholesaler, acquires Pantry Pride.
Disposal of surplus merchandise	o Non-retailers or large scale retailers open outlet stores.	o Sears, JCPenney outlet stores. o Factory Outlets
Control Store Sites	o 70's retailers acquire real estate, participate in malls. o Real estate developers acquire retail stores.	o In the 1960's & 1970's, Dayton Hudson, JCPenney, Sears and Federated start realty companies. o In 1984 Taubman Holdings acquires Woodward & Lothrop.
Enlarge total market future share – balance growth prospects which are different in different segments of retailing.	o Acquire other forms of retailing.	o Associated Dry Goods acquired Caldors, Loehmanns. o Dayton Hudson with department stores, discount stores, bookstores. o Allied Stores, a department store chain, acquires specialty chains: Garfinkel, Brooks Brothers, Miller & Rhodes. o Revco acquires Odd Lot Trading Co.
Reduce cyclical swings	o Acquire businesses with different cyclical characteristics.	o Sears – Allstate (financial services). o Federated – Ralph's (supermarkets).
Synergistic Businesses: Capitalize on existing know-how or buying leverage.	o International expansion; acquisition of independent stores; know-how agreements. o Retailer uses internal strengths such as buying power, credit card lists, communications network, systems, physical facilities, consumer image to provide new business with competitive edge.	o Direct mail/catalog businesses of Sears, JCPenney. o Arco develops gas stations/ convenience stores. o Allstate in Sears stores. o Sears World Trade. o JCPenney sells credit card communication system to oil companies. o International expansion.

2. A more frequent phenomenon is a manufacturer's or wholesaler's taking *control of the retail distribution channel.* The oil companies have felt it necessary to control their gas station networks, automobile companies their dealerships, and manufacturers of consumer goods their retail outlets. Control is sometimes achieved by ownership, but is more frequently achieved through franchising methods.

3. One aspect of control is *acquisition of "real estate,"* the land and/or building in which retail operations are conducted. It is not uncommon, therefore, for retailers to own real estate.

4. Another enterprise strategy is to increase total market share by *addressing additional target consumer groups.* This strategy can result in retail conglomerates such as Dayton-Hudson with its department store, promotional department store, and discount and specialty store divisions, or Melville Corporation with its various specialty and "off-price" divisions.

5. Some forms of retailing are highly cyclical, particularly those that sell high-ticket, relatively discretionary merchandise. One way to *reduce cyclical influence* on the entire enterprise is to add businesses with stable growth characteristics, such as grocery or drug stores.

6. Successful retailing concepts constitute "know-how" that has a value in the marketplace. The *value of know-how* can be realized by acquiring and turning around underperforming stores, by expansion abroad where competition may be weaker, or by know-how agreements with other retailers. Sears, Roebuck is an example of an enterprise that uses know-how in all the ways described.

7. Many retailers have *used some of their strengths to spawn new businesses.* K-Mart, Sears, and JCPenney are using their network of stores and their reputation to gain entry into financial services. JCPenney and Sears sell communications services using their extensive communications networks. Atlantic Richfield has used gas stations to offer convenience merchandise.

All diversification strategies have this in common: they are designed to improve performance, forestall a competitive threat, or both. Diversification invariably brings new management challenges and requires appropriate modifications in the organizational structure, if not in the corporate culture and management style. There are many success stories in retailing, including Sears with its financial services, Dayton-Hudson and Federated Department Stores with different forms of retailing, Melville Corporation and U.S. Shoe with a shoe manufacturing/specialty retailing mix, and Marriott with hotels, fast food, and catering. There are also many examples of diversified formats proving indigestible. The point is that diversification, the portfolio approach to business, requires a more sophisticated and versatile top management team than does the single-format retail business.

Category-Specific Strategies

The discussion so far has focused on concepts that are widely applicable in retailing, regardless of the particular market or store format. The material covered is particularly pertinent to the larger general merchandise retailing businesses that have successfully expanded and diversified. We will now touch briefly on some the strategic issues in retailing formats other than general merchandise. We will cover five of the largest retailing classifications (see Exhibit 23-14): food, motor vehicle dealers, gas stations, eating places, and drug stores.

Food is the largest retailing category, with 1983 sales of over 250 billion dollars. It is very largely a business of necessities that are highly standardized, highly comparable, rapidly consumed, and frequently replenished. Consumers generally look for a store close to where they live, with an assortment that enables one-stop shopping and prices that are competitive. The emphasis is on needs more than wants. Customers pay by cash or check.

The retailer (or wholesaler) in food deals with vendors from a position of strength; many vendors are in competition for limited shelf space.

These conditions result in the following elements of strategy:

Stringent cost control

Economies of scale on every level: buying, transportation, warehousing, and retailing facilities

Fast turnover to minimize working capital and carrying costs

Clustering of retail outlets

Trends to layer stores

Self-service

Battle for market share

Constant price promotion

To realize economies of scale, the great majority of food retailing aims at a broad segment of target consumers—virtually the entire population within reach of the store—hence the trend to larger stores.

Commonly used strategies to establish differential advantage or added value are:

Superior management of fresh foods (better looking vegetables and meats, fresher baked goods)

Added features such as deli, gourmet foods, and liquor, as well as higher margin lines such as apparel and home furnishings

Traffic generators such as banking and pharmacies

EXHIBIT 23-14 *Category-Specific Retailing Strategies*

SIC	Retailing Category	Format	Target Consumers	Offering	Differentiation Strategies	Competitive Assets
54	Food	Supermarket	All households in area.	One-stop shopping. Price Competitive. Close to home.	Fresh food management. Deli-gourmet food – pharmacy.	Other supermarkets. Restaurant
		Convenience Store	All households in area.	Limited selection of frequently needed items. Available around the clock. Close to home	Gas station Merchandise Mix	Round-the-clock supermarkets. Gas stations with convenience retailing assortments.
		Warehouse	Price shoppers	Economies of scale. Self-service. Limited selection of high volume items. Lowest prices in town.	Membership. Merchandise mix.	Other warehouse formats Supermarkets Discount stores
		Health Food	Health conscious consumers.	Headquarters for vitamins and natural foods. Prices of secondary importance.	Merchandise mix. Promotions.	Supermarkets Drugstores Discount stores
		Gourmet	Upscale consumers	Highest quality at a price.	Merchandise mix.	Other Gourmet stores. Supermarkets Restaurants
551	Vehicle Dealers		Each make and model targeted to specific consumer segment.	Combination sales/service. Price competitive on car sales. High prices on options, automotive supplies, service. Supplier determines marketing plan.	Service Follow-up	Other dealers
554	Gasoline Stations	High volume/ thruway	All motorists that pass. Non-repeat business.	Gas and oil at a price. Emergency service at a price. High traffic location.	Brand	Other gas stations Convenience stores with gas
		Neighborhood	Neighborhood traffic. High repeat ratio. Motorists who prefer the brand	Gas and oil at competitive. Service/sales	Brand Scope and quality of service	Other gas stations Convenience stores with gas.
		Discount	Price conscious wide area.	Gas and oil only. High traffic location.	Brand/location	Other gas stations and convenience stores with gas.
		Self-service	All motorists that pass.	Gas only No sales/service	Brand/location	Other gas stations and convenience stores with gas.

23.30

EXHIBIT 23-14 · *(continued)*

SIC	Retailing Category	Format	Target Consumers	Offering	Differentiation Strategies	Competitive Assets
53	General Merchandise	Conventional Department Store	A cluster of target consumers in large trading area.	One-stop shopping for apparel and home furnishings at a price. Emphasis on strong brands.	Infinite possibilities for varying the offering. Category dominance	All other stores or non-store formats (such as catalog) that offer similar merchandise.
		Mass Merchandiser	A cluster of target consumers in large trading area.	One-stop shopping for apparel and home furnishings at a price. Price competitive. Emphasis on house brands.	Infinite possibilities for varying the offering. Category dominance	All other stores or non-store formats (such as catalog) that offer similar merchandise.
		Discount Department Store	A cluster of target consumers in large trading area.	One-stop shopping for convenience items. Low prices. Emphasis on strong brands.	Limited possibilities for varying the offering. Management Category dominance	All other stores or non-store formats (such as catalog) that offer similar merchandise.
		Variety Store	A cluster of target consumers in large trading area including people who work nearby.	One-stop shopping for convenience items at a price.	Limited possibilities for varying the offering. Category dominance	Particularly discount department stores, drug stores, food supermarkets.
5812	Eating Places	Fast Food	Cluster of target consumers within easy driving distance.	Limited selection of simple, popular dishes. No table service. Low prices-fast-informed.	Menu Management Advertising	All other restaurants and food retailers.
		Cafeteria	Time and price conscious consumers within easy reach.	Selection of popular meals meals. No table service. Low price-fast-informed.	Menu Management Advertising	All other restaurants and food retailers.
		Lunch Counter	People who work or shop nearby.	Limited selection. No table service. Low price-fast-informed.	Menu Management	All other restaurants and food retailers.
		Service Restaurant	Carefully targeted to selected consumer groups from young families to upscale consumers.	Combination quality, service ambiance to fit the target customer.	Menu Service Ambiance Prices	All other restaurants and food retailers.
56	Apparel & Accessories	Specialty	Carefully targeted to selected consumer groups.	Ranges from category dominance to narrow focus, low price to upscale, etc.	Infinite possibilities for varying the offering.	All other stores and non-store formats (such as catalog) selling similar merchandise.
		Off-Price	Price shoppers in targeted consumer group - large trading area.	Fast moving items, opportunistic buys, in bare bones format.	Infinite possibilities for varying the offering.	All other stores and non-store formats (such as catalog) selling similar merchandise.

EXHIBIT 23-14 (continued)

SIC	Retailing Category	Format	Target Consumers	Offering	Differentiation Strategies	Competitive Assets
591	Drug Stores	Regular	All households in neighborhood.	Prescription, drugs, plus health and beauty aids. Price competitive	Added services such as photo processing, optical department catalog desk, equipment rental. Location.	Supermarkets and discount department stores with pharmacies, mail order drugs, drug dispensing, health plans.
		Expanded	Convenience shoppers in a large trading area.	Prescription drugs plus convenience merchandise mix. Price competitive	Same as for regular drug stores.	Supermarkets and discount department stores with pharmacies.
		Discount	Price shoppers in a large trading area.	Prescription drugs plus health and beauty aids at low prices. Focus on fast moving items.	Location Promotions	Mail-order drugs; drug dispensing health plans.

There is also room in food retailing for special niches, such as:

The convenience format geared to a broad, mainly geographic target consumer segment with an immediate need for certain necessities such as bread, milk, snacks, cigarettes. Such stores are in convenient locations, are open around the clock, and charge higher prices than supermarkets.

The rock-bottom price, warehouse, limited selection, and self-service formats for the price shoppers.

The purveyor of gourmet foods, ethnic foods, or health foods geared to narrow consumer segments.

Motor vehicle dealers are the next largest retailing category, with 1983 sales of over 150 billion dollars. This is a business in which the suppliers—the car manufacturers—tend to be dominant. One of the most important strategic issues is the dealer's affiliation and the dealer/supplier relationship. Since each type of car is aimed at a particular consumer segment, the choice of supplier largely determines the target consumer.

Selling vehicles is a cyclical business requiring considerable capital to maintain the necessary facilities and inventories. Competition among manufacturers tends to keep profit margins low on new cars. The opportunity for much greater profit lies in the sale of optional equipment and accessories, as well as in after-sale service. Sale of used cars is frequently a natural outgrowth of a dealership. Availability of customer credit is essential.

The typical dealership serves a broad, middle-income target consumer group. However, there are upscale formats that go along with the more expensive models, as well as low-margin, high-volume dealerships geared to the price-conscious shopper.

Differentiation begins with the choice of car types and models offered, each promoted by the car manufacturer. Differentiation among dealers with similar lines in the same trading area will often be reflected in the scope and quality of after-sale service, the promotional effort, and the effectiveness with which a dealer uses his or her customer data bank to stimulate sales or service.

Key strategic issues for automotive dealerships include vendor affiliation, single versus multiple brands, services provided, market share, and financing.

Gas stations' total more than 100 billion dollars in volume. This category of retailing, like motor vehicle dealers, is heavily dependent on the supplier. Here again, affiliation and supplier relationship are crucial, with the supplier frequently providing various support services. Gas stations deal with a broad consumer segment—people who drive cars. Location generally defines the specific market—drivers who pass by the station.

Common formats include:

The high-volume turnpike station that provides fuel and emergency services to consumers who have few, if any, alternatives. Prices tend to be high.

Neighborhood stations that rely primarily on repeat business and light repairs. Prices are competitive.

Discount gas stations that aim for high volume by attracting the price shopper.

Self-service stations that provide bare-bones, low-overhead gas and oil sales.

Differentiation among gas stations begins with the brands, which are generally promoted by the suppliers. Where interbrand competition is important, price, credit policy, personal service, and quality of service can be decisive.

A gas station frequently offers for sale lines of automotive supplies, including tires. Its location, on frequently traveled routes, provides it with the opportunity to become a convenience retail outlet for food, snacks, smoking supplies, and so on.

Strategic issues for gas stations include vendor affiliation, location, differentiation, market share, and add-on business.

Eating places, which constitute a 100 billion-dollar business, come in a multitude of formats, such as fast-food restaurants, cafeterias, lunch counters, and service restaurants. Successful restaurants tend to have well-defined target customer segments that range from fairly broad to narrow. Competition—not only from other restaurants, but also from food stores selling prepared, easy-to-eat dishes—is intense. Differentiation is everything.

At one extreme in this business is the fast-food format aimed at time- and price-conscious consumers, often families with small children. The basic format consists of prototype facilities designed to provide a certain selection of dishes in a uniform efficient way. Procedures are standardized to the point where the owner/operator need only learn to follow the manual. Success ingredients in this business are:

A menu that appeals to the target customer.

An operating package that assures good execution in accordance with required standards.

Specification buying.

A successful program for recruiting and supporting strong franchises.

Site selection.

A strong marketing program.

From the operator/owner's perspective, the principal strategic issue is selection of the franchises.

At another extreme is the high-value-added gourmet restaurant where superb food and wine, ambiance, and service are offered to those who can afford it. Such a restaurant, if located within reach of a large enough base of affluent consumers, may rely largely on media reviews and word-of-mouth references. The success ingredient is the quality of the offering.

Between the high-quality gourmet restaurant and the quintessential fast-food operator lie an almost infinite number of offerings, individuals or chains, that are aimed at some consumer segment: the mall shopper, the business lunch trade, singles, families, people with a taste for certain types of foods or cooking styles.

Effective strategies here develop an offering of food, service, ambiance, and location to meet the expectations of a target consumer group that is sufficiently large and affluent to provide an adequate return on the restaurateur's investment.

Drug stores are the final retailing format we will discuss in this chapter. They fall into the category of convenience retailing and are usually found close to residential areas.

The principal types of drug stores are:

Regular (Eastern) type—pharmacy plus health-and-beauty aids, and other (6,000–15,000 square feet)

Expanded (Western) type—pharmacy, health-and-beauty aides, liquor, snacks, variety, housewares, and other (15,000 square feet and up)

Discount drug stores

Pharmacy departments in supermarkets

Pharmacy departments in discount department stores

This business resembles food retailing in the sense that it deals largely with standard packages of readily comparable items—or with prescriptions of readily comparable drugs. Competition is keen, and price is important. The retailer deals with numerous suppliers competing for shelf space.

A major difference between the drug store and the food retailer, however, is the pharmacy operation, which requires a trained pharmacist and which is subject to stringent regulation. The target consumer is virtually the entire population of the trading area.

The key elements of strategy for the drug store resemble those for food retailing:

Careful cost control

Economies of scale in buying, transportation, warehousing, and store facilities

Fast turnover and quick replenishment

Clustering of stores

Self-service for nonpharmacy products

Battle for market share

Constant price promotion

Customer service assumes added importance in a pharmacy, where the ability, integrity, and helpfulness of the pharmacist, who sometimes deals with emergencies, become important parts of the store's image.

Differential advantage must be the result of managing better in a very competitive environment and of comparable assortments and prices. The advantage may lie in a better-looking, neater store, in friendlier, more knowledgeable personnel, in home delivery, in prompt filling of prescriptions, or in special promotions.

There are opportunities to enrich the offering by adding film processing, optical departments, rental of wheelchairs, and of other medical aids, exercise equipment, etc. In fact, the drug store may position itself as a local headquarters for helping customers feel better through both cures and preventions.

SUMMARY

We have seen that the basic principles of strategic planning apply to all businesses, including retailing. However, in retailing businesses the target consumers are individual customers, rather than other businesses or institutions.

The most important strategic decision retailers have to make is to select the target consumer group and to develop offerings that will enable them to meet profitably the expectations of this group. To be successful and to return an adequate profit, the offering also must be perceived by the target consumer as having some clear advantages in comparison with the offerings of the competition.

Once a successful retailing format has been established, strategy will focus almost inevitably on expansion—how to multiply a winning idea.

Retailing is dynamic business. As a result of changing customer expectations, environmental changes, and competitive action, yesterday's success formula may be tomorrow's road to failure. Self-renewal, therefore, must be a constant strategic concern. Diversification is one renewal strategy; repositioning the store is another.

No matter how large the business grows, the fundamental goal is the same: to develop offerings that meet target consumer expectations profitably and competitively. As the business grows, target consumer groups and their expectations tend to get larger and more diverse.

NOTES

1. Annual Report, Federated Department Stores, 1983.
2. M. E. Porter, *Competitive Strategy*, Free Press, New York, 1980.

APPENDIX: DAYTON-HUDSON CORPORATION'S STATEMENT OF PHILOSOPHY

Strategic Mission and Direction

Dayton-Hudson Corporation is a diversified retailing company whose business is to serve the American consumer through the retailing of fashion-oriented quality merchandise.

Serving the consumer over time requires skilled and motivated employees, healthy communities in which to operate and maximum long-range profit. We are committed to meaningful and comprehensive employee development; to serving the business, social, and cultural needs of our communities; and to achieving levels of profitability equivalent to those of the leading firms in industry.

Thus, Dayton-Hudson Corporation serves four major constituencies: consumers, employees, shareholders, and communities. The common denominator in serving these constituencies is profit—our reward for serving society well. Long-range profit is thus our major responsibility so that we can continue to serve our constituencies in the future.

Corporate Purposes

The corporation has specific purposes with regard to serving each of its four constituencies. These purposes and associated key objectives are as follows:

A. To serve as the consumers' purchasing agent in fulfilling their needs and expectations for merchandise and services.
    1. To offer dominant assortments of quality and fashion merchandise.
    2. To offer merchandise which represents true value to consumers.
    3. To support merchandising activities with appropriate levels of service, creative yet informative advertising, and well-maintained stores.
    4. To occupy pre-eminent competitive positions in each market we serve and in the merchandise lines we carry.
    5. To maintain the highest levels of honesty, integrity, and responsiveness in meeting merchandise and service needs of our customers.
B. To contribute to the personal and professional development of our employees.
    1. To provide the opportunity for all employees—regardless of age, race, color, sex, religion, or national origin—to develop their full potential through education, training, and work experience.
    2. To provide employees the opportunity to advance in position and in responsibility consistent with proven performance.
    3. To provide an atmosphere that encourages initiative and input and that fosters trust, creativity, and economic security.
    4. To support the concept of superior compensation for superior performance.
C. To provide an attractive financial return to our shareholders.
    1. To be a premier investment as measured against the best in the retail industry and industry in general.

2. To provide shareholders with consistent growth in dividends per share and current income.

3. To provide shareholders with growth in share value over time, consistent with growth in earnings—ranking in the industry's top quartile in terms of Price Earnings multiple, Return on Investment, and Return on Equity.

4. To achieve the following standards of financial performance.

D. To serve the communities in which we operate.

1. To demonstrate exemplary corporate citizenship in the conduct of our business and in the relationship of the corporation and its employees to all their constituencies.

2. To observe the highest legal, ethical, and moral standards.

3. To work cooperatively with business, civic, and governmental agencies to improve the environments in which we operate.

4. To contribute annually 5 percent of federally taxable income to improve the quality of life in communities of which we are part.

Corporate Objective

Our primary objective is to be premier in every facet of our business. We aspire to be recognized as premier in fulfilling our obligations to all four constituencies—customers, employees, shareholders, and communities. Furthermore, we strive to be innovative and at the forefront of the retail industry in its continuing evolution.

Achievement of this objective assumes attaining premier status as a retail investment. While profit is our reward for serving society well, it is also a requisite for continuing to serve society at all. Thus, the task is to manage the corporation so that it is recognized as a premier investment in the retail field.

Merchandising Philosophy

The aim of each of our operating companies is to serve its customers better than any comparable retailing organization in its markets. Each strives to achieve a specific customer orientation and a clear customer perception of its merchandise and service offering. Inherent in this philosophy are four key elements:

A. *Dominance* means both merchandise dominance and market pre-eminence. Specifically, we strive for a merchandise offer that assures consumers our stores have the best selection of the items they seek. Furthermore, we strive to be the leading retailer in those markets and merchandise lines in which we elect to compete. Implicit in a decision to enter a market is the long-term financial commitment to achieve pre-eminence in that market.

B.   *Quality* is the essence of all our operations. It is expressed most importantly in merchandise, but the concept of quality applies equally well to the corporation's management team, to its facilities, and to its locations. Our customer should perceive us as a quality business operated by quality people selling quality merchandise and providing quality services.

C.   *Fashion* is at the heart of our business. Fashion is change—change with direction. Newness and change can be predicted, however, through Trend Merchandising. Our aim is for each company to be the fashion leader within its markets. Regardless of the specific merchandise category, our companies will lead customers to that which is new and exciting in the marketplace.

D.   *Value* is more than price alone, it is giving the customer a favorable return on investment. For the merchandise itself, value means quality at a price. Our companies seek to provide maximum value to customers by acting aggressively as their buying agent—in purchasing quality goods and negotiating for the best possible price. Our companies seek to keep cost structures and operating expenses lean—recognizing that such costs are inevitably reflected in consumer prices. Furthermore, we are sensitive to the expanded meaning of the term value: customer time spent locating products or waiting for service, energy costs incurred in a shopping trip, serviceability of durable goods, and the psychic and emotional value of the shopping experience itself.

Real Estate Philosophy

The corporation recognizes that long-range success is as dependent on a sound real estate strategy as on a merchandising strategy. The hallmark of the corporation is the successful melding of the two. The concept of dominance, quality, and fashion applies as much to locations and facilities as to merchandise. We aim, therefore, to have quality stores that bespeak fashion and good taste. We seek premier locations, building our stores and our facilities for the future.

Management Philosophy

The management philosophy of the Dayton-Hudson Corporation is a balance of operating autonomy and flexibility on the one hand, and corporate input and direction on the other. To this end:

A.   The corporation will:
   1.   Set standards for ROI and earnings growth
   2.   Approve strategic plans
   3.   Allocate capital

4. Approve goals
5. Monitor, measure, and audit results
6. Reward performance
7. Allocate management resources

B. The operating companies will be accorded the freedom and responsibility:

1. To manage their own business
2. To develop strategic plans and goals which will optimize their growth
3. To develop an organization that can assure consistency of results and optimum growth
4. To operate their businesses consistent with the corporation's Statement of Philosophy

C. The corporate staff will provide only those services that:

1. Are essential to the protection of the corporation
2. Are needed for the growth of the corporation
3. Are wanted by operating companies and that provide a significant advantage in quality or cost

D. The corporation will insist on:

1. Uniform accounting practices by type of business
2. Prompt disclosure of operating results
3. A systematic approach of training and developing people
4. Adherence to appropriately high standards of business conduct and civic responsibility, in accordance with the corporation's Statement of Philosophy

Growth Philosophy

The stability and quality of the corporation's financial performance will be developed through the profitable execution of our existing businesses, as well as through the acquisition or the development of new businesses. Our growth priorities, in order, are as follows:

1. Development of the profitable market pre-eminence of existing companies in existing markets, through new store development or new strategies within existing stores.
2. Expansion of our companies in feasible new markets.
3. Acquisition of other retailing companies that are strategically and financially compatible with Dayton-Hudson.
4. Internal development of new retailing strategies. Capital allocations to fund the expansion of existing operating companies will be based each company's return on investment, in relationship to its ROI ob-

jective and its consistency in earnings growth, and on its management capability to perform up to forecasts contained in capital requests. Expansion via acquisition or new venture will occur when the opportunity promises an acceptable rate of long-term growth and profitablity, an acceptable degree of risk, and compatibility with the corporation's long-term strategy.

Ethical Standards and Business Conduct

The policy of the corporation is to maintain a consistently high standard of business conduct, ethics, and social responsibility. Individual employees are expected to demonstrate high levels of integrity and objectivity, unemcumbered by conflicting interests in all decisions and actions affecting the corporation.

Corporate policies governing the business conduct of employees will serve as a minimum standard of performance. Premier status requires exemplary behavior and attitudes—conduct befitting employees.

CHAPTER **24**

Strategic Planning for Small Businesses

RUSSELL A. PATTERSON

RUSSELL A. PATTERSON is a consultant, currently manager with Deloitte, Haskins & Sells Tax Engineering Valuation Group. He was formerly associated with staffs of Arthur Young and Arthur D. Little Valuation, Inc. He has over 15 years of experience in small business consulting in such areas as business planning, merger, acquisition and divestment analysis, fair market value studies, licensing, financial communications, and cash flow analysis. Mr. Patterson has served on numerous corporate staff and management positions at W.R. Grace & Co. He was a White House Executive Fellow, serving as assistant to the chairman/managing director of the Civil Aeronautics Board when deregulation of the airline industry was implemented. He earned an M.B.A. degree from New York University and a B.S. degree from The Citadel, The Military College of South Carolina.

OUTLINE

Small business strategic planning includes a scope of activities which, in essence, lead to more effective ways of doing business. Small businesses must deal with limited resources, both human and financial, and this makes the management of smaller enterprises more difficult than the management of huge multinational concerns. Therefore, it is imperative that the leader of the organization make full use of those resources—from the original targets or ideas through all the planning and construction—until the actions that have been set in motion are completed.

This chapter covers the underlying guidelines associated with strategic planning (SP) for small businesses, those with sales less than 50 million dollars. In addition, management tools, pitfalls to be avoided, and first steps toward strategic planning are discussed. This chapter provides business strategists with the practical knowledge and information necessary for them to contend with the complexity of society, the rapid change and cost of technology, and the increasing rate of service and product obsolescence. If the fundamentals are followed, then executives engaged in small business planning will not only provide direction for the firm but, will also be able to fulfill their roles effectively.

SCOPE AND VISION

Small business planners addressing long-term issues are like home builders—they have a vision of converting raw land into their reality. While the plot of land is specific to the end product, the ultimate completion, or success, cannot be limited to its boundaries. The actual construction requires that efforts be extended beyond the area defined by the plot plan. Instrumental in support of the project are such external considerations as environmental impacts, zoning conformance, or amenities and conveniences that must be added to satisfy the community needs. The business strategist, by definition, should be open to proposals for action that may not have been attempted previously. In other words, the boundaries of the business entity itself are defined, but from a planning point of view there are no limits to the activities in it that may be undertaken in order to achieve results. Correspondingly, to reach targets, strategists should not impose artificial and unnecessary contraints on tackling solutions to opportunities or problems.

The key contribution that business makes to society is to produce and distribute goods and services in an efficient way—on a sustained and long-term basis. The by-product of that—the social function—is to grow and earn a reasonable profit. The standards of good strategic planning, regardless of

EXHIBIT 24-1   The Strategic Planning Matrix

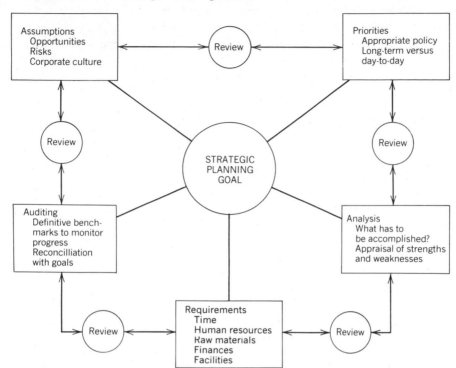

corporate size, are basic to the long-term interests of business. The compatible functions of earning a profit and the rational strategy to make it happen are both integrative and interactive experiences.

Planning is simply providing an orderly step-by-step transition from one situation to another by first recognizing the company's competitive position, and then by proceeding to define its position in five to ten years. How and when the projected growth increments are to be reached and the price one is willing to pay to achieve discernible results are the most logical variables to consider. Within the framework of planning are six processes that must be followed on a consistent basis to tailor the strategy to a predetermined set of circumstances (see Exhibit 24-1). These include:

1. Taking a look into the future, making *assumptions,* and developing an appraisal of the range of possible requirements. In order to do this, however, the chief planning executive must know the life and death factors of the business and how to turn problems into opportunities.

2. *Analyzing* the situation and defining in specific detail what has to be accomplished to reach the goal. Each step in the situational analysis must be a logical progression from the previous one.

3. Considering the *requirements* for time, human resources, physical plant capabilities, raw materials, and financial limitations.

4. Expressing *priorities* with appropriate policy statements as to availability and limitations to the requirements; any degree of safety margin should be explicitly stated.

5. Monitoring the progress of the planning cycle with the use of definitive benchmarks. Consideration to the time frame is set for each major goal's attainment. SP must be measurable over time, and the periodic *audit* is necessary to determine whether goals are being achieved and to respond to changes.

6. *Reviewing* all elements of the plan format to insure that assumptions are sound and priorities are clear before proceeding to the technical (implementation) phase.

SUCCESS BREEDS SUCCESS—THROUGH COMMITMENT

Strategic planning is a means to provide a proper and unified sense of direction for the overall activities of the business enterprise. It must be remembered, as others have stated, that we are dealing with long-term objectives. Time horizons exceed one year. It is, then, major policy issues that meet the needs of the business, as opposed to administrative/operational elements. The degree to which success breeds success, rather than failure, is a direct result of the *commitment* that top management places on the role of strategic planning. It is crucial that the lead decision makers instill a behavior pattern in the organization that is geared toward acceptance of a positive approach to problem solving and toward the survival of the business as a whole, by the full management support cadre.

Day-to-day performance and productivity are results of the strategic development function. Commitment to the function must be firm but flexible. It must also be a dedication to applying a proven set of principles and techniques that are in the best interests of achieving growth *and* strengthening the business. This means that SP must be practiced earnestly, and must not give way to panic-driven management pressures to stem the tide when temporary dislocations in performance occur. Long-term objectives, if sound, cannot be sacrificed at the expense of true short-term gains or crises.

There are certain myths and realities associated with the long-term decision-making mission. The central notion to SP application is not one of great complication; on the contrary, the subject essentials are based on simplicity. Within the purview of top management responsibility and stewardship is the primary task of seeking and exploiting growth opportunities. The complicated responsibilities of this task are the development of airtight analysis, the elaboration of that analysis, and the precise reading of results that support the policy to be implemented. Adaptation to changing economies and changing technologies is an even more complicated process, but it must be accomplished if the small business entity is to stay one step ahead in a competitive environment.

ENTREPRENEURIAL SPIRIT AND THE GOOD STRATEGIST

Before an organization can embark on a formal strategic planning path, it is critical to isolate the person responsible for identifying the respective goals and for setting the agenda. Typically, small businesses do not have built-up layers of management support. The most senior group of players consists of one, two, or, at most, three individuals on whose shoulders rests the job of setting the corporate course. This hierarchy of rugged individualists does not usually rely on a corps of professional researchers to create plans and offer suggestions on direction. The entrepreneur taps his or her functional knowledge of the business to create the strategy through total immersion in every facet of the operations. To this he or she combines the gut feeling of how to perform, given a set of circumstances.

There is no hard and fast prescription for becoming a good strategist. There are, however, a minimum of ingredients that should be possessed if one is to be classified as an expert in the field. First, the strategic planner must be fully aware of, and must accept the consequences of taking risks in proportion to the reward that the plan is expected to yield. Second, the strategist must have mental flexibility, the ability to solve problems logically, as opposed to emotionally, good common sense, the expertise to apply experience appropriately, and at least a modicum of imagination, creativity, and ingenuity. To these are added the proper balancing between strategic planning and everyday activities of the business. With total knowledge of the environment, coupled with a good memory, the astute planning executive knows the difference between problems that threaten disaster and those that may solve themselves.

BYPASSING ROAD BLOCKS FOR STRATEGIC DEVELOPMENT

In small businesses there are seven basic pitfalls that obstruct the optimal development and practice of strategic planning. These are:

1. Failure to manage with objectives
2. Crisis management
3. Lack of contingency, or alternative, planning
4. Reactive management versus proactive style
5. Not realizing SP is a means to an end
6. Not knowing the business
7. Failure to employ existing systems for decision-making applications

Objectives

Management *with* objectives, irrespective of business size, is synonymous with strategic planning. It is a topic that has been discussed on innumerable occasions. If it weren't so important, it wouldn't be discussed to the point of redundancy. Any business must have targets by areas of concentration. To plan strategy is to plan objectives. In this case, reference is made to where a particular company is going to be in a minimum of three to five years from point zero. Translation of objectives to the lowest level of the organization equals the direction the company is going, along with the disciplines it takes to get there.

At the top level of the organization, objective formulation requires setting general parameters tailored to the culture of the business. At lower levels, the generalities are refined to mirror, in varying degrees, the management style of the CEO, to insure that directives are carried to fruition.

The essential ingredients of management *with* objectives are:

1. The chief planner (CEO) explicitly states the policies to be followed. The tasks for developing the structures to implement them are delegated to subordinates.
2. Objectives must be suitable to the corporate culture.
3. Objectives must be measurable over time.
4. Confusion and ambiguity must be avoided.

AXIOM: An organization with appropriate objectives set in motion doesn't flounder because of lack of direction.

A successful Dallas-based commercial and residential developer, with astute management obsessed with objective setting, set a path 15 years ago to become one of the leading construction management companies in the East Texas area. By plotting specific long-range objectives, such as pioneering property end-line building plans, correctly targeting growth regions ahead of, or in line with, industrial development, and planning for consumer financing alternatives in advance of the competition, the company today has sales in excess of 30 million dollars. Granted, foresight played an important part in the company's growth, but setting the objective timetable in advance and adhering to it were equally important.

Crisis Management

Entrepreneurial leadership tends to be crisis-oriented because of the shotgun approach to solving problems. The delegation of responsibilities oftentimes remains in the domain of the top-tier circle. In the instance of a one-man show, for example, the founder, common to a great many small businesses, the CEO often manages the business like shooting buckshot.

For example, the president of a 10-million-dollar, New York-based meter control company maintains that he is indispensible when it comes to making decisions regarding production schedules, technical design, making sales calls to develop business, keeping track of the general ledger, and so on. He is all things to all departments, even though good salaries are being paid to people who administer the functions. To him the entire operation is the strategic plan. However, the company hasn't shown any real growth in sales for the past five years. Further, if pressed to state where the company would be if his two largest accounts—not necessarily the most loyal—deserted the fold, the president is at a loss to defend his past policies; not being able to keep pace with current change would undoubtedly spell bankruptcy.

Here, the SP function becomes clouded with the operational aspects of the business. It is a pitfall that dilutes the effectiveness of policy creation, and it is a chief reason why many strategists fail to attain optimal results.

A lesson to be learned from this is that the chief policymaker should not spread himself or herself, or the company resources (which are limited to begin with), too thin. The entity's survival is at stake when the sightest glitch occurs. In the above case, the CEO, given that he has the wisdom to surround himself with a compliment of capable professionals, must require that they provide him with precise and accurate information that is not to be summarily second-guessed. This frees him to make decisions, not to implement them. Without a procedural change of delegating operational/administrative responsiblity to those already hired to do so, there is bound to be a circuit overload. This in turn leads to decisions that later prove to be wrong or unproductive. For the differences between elements of strategic planning versus technical (downstream) planning, refer to Exhibit 24-2.

EXHIBIT 24-2   *Strategy versus Operational Aspects of Small Business Enterprises*

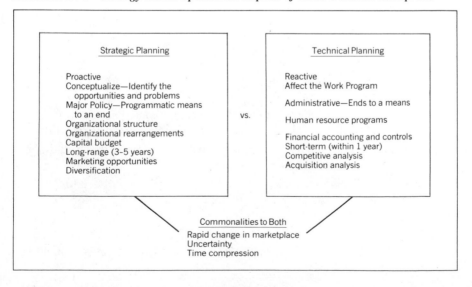

> *AXIOM: Small businesses succeed and avoid crises when their chief policymakers differentiate between developing strategy and implementing it.*

Anticipation

Small-business managers know that aside from death and taxes, there is another certainty to their environment—uncertainty. A fine-tuned organization must be prepared for, and be able to gear up to, the unexpected events that happen. An essential element of strategic planning is to be able to accommodate certain response mechanisms that can be effected when critical departure points from what has been forecast become evident.

A reason for NASA's technical successes in the space development program over the past 25 years is that the agency is an excellent manager of uncertainty. This is a result of contingency planning. This means having back-up systems for even the most refined back-up systems if disaster is to be averted. Small businesses aren't expected to bring total resources to bear, especially financial resources, when implementing a program as extensive as NASA's, but it is important to remember that the basic disciplines can be transposed, usually at a cost-effective rate, just by adhering to simple fundamentals. This can be translated into the equation

$$\text{what if } [x] = \text{opportunity } [y]$$

derived by:

    creative thinking
+ systematic execution
+ intuitive judgments
+ mission planning
+ situation adaptation
+ historical probability

The basics to alternative planning are:

1. Identify the factors of the business that are crucial to success and develop the fundamental strategy.
2. Indicate a degree of probability that events complementary or contrary to the key factors will either create an opportunity or spell disaster.
3. Isolate the controllable and uncontrollable conditions that could affect the complementary/contrary events.
4. Define critical departure points with appropriate feedback loops, i.e., error messages, that would indicate that corrective action needs to be taken.
5. Develop subplans that can be accessed if the what-if situation arises, and assign mechanisms that permit quick responses to potential upside/downside risks.

6. Reassess the original planned strategy when unexpected developments occur, and determine if response mechanisms can be tailored to the situation.

7. As a last resort, weigh the strengths of the original plan and, if a faulty base exists, then, and only then, determine if a full scale realignment of the plan is at issue.

AXIOM: An ounce of anticipatory planning is worth a pound of cure when factors outside the original policy affect its balance.

A case in point is that of a 25-million-dollar, Connecticut-based chemical company engaged in the manufacture of wood coatings that developed a technologically innovative product, a waterborne oil-based stain. The product, when cured, had the same superior properties of the company's original and well-known pure oil stain, but with the principal added attraction of easy water clean-up after use. The company was the only one to have this unique product in marketable form. If marketed according to plan, a significant share of the latex "stain" market would be garnered.

The company performed meaningful consumer testing, and the results yielded acceptance on a wide spectrum. The strategic plan called for replacement of the original formula with the introduction of the new product. All marketing efforts on the consumer-oriented side of the business were mere extensions of its existing successful campaign. It was assumed that contract (professional) painters, representing 40 percent of the company's revenue stream, would welcome the unique product with open arms, as the survey results showed the do-it-yourselfers (40 percent of sales) did. Hence, the strategy was effected and the old oil-based stains were removed from the product line.

One restriction of the new stain was that it couldn't be diluted, or thinned. Doing so altered the superior properties of the applied product.

Here a problem becomes evident. While the coverage factor of both old and new products is similar, a restriction is placed on the contractor's ability to make the stain last longer by thinning it, even if done marginally.

The end result was that a substantial base of the company's market bought rival brands. It was also learned that professional painters didn't care much about easy clean-up; they preferred to use solvent to clean the brushes, as they always did.

For some companies the move to eliminate a product line could have caused irreparable harm, but not in this case. The company had in place, as part of its original strategy, a what if scenario. Feedback information indicated a critical departure from what was expected. A proper response mechanism was instituted, and by the next outdoor painting season the tried-and-proved can of original stain was back on the shelves. The original customer base returned to using a superior product that met their needs. Sales advanced, and the healthy recovery is now history.

Proactive Planning

As was stated earlier, small business management entails crisis management. Another simple way to turn this form of activity into a direct benefit of the strategy function is to avoid decisionmaking on a *reactive* basis. The positive direction to follow is proactive planning. It is behavior that mandates, figuratively speaking, that you do fire first before the redcoats get close enough for you to see the whites of their eyes.

If the chief planner is to contend with change in the business environment, he or she must differentiate between which is more important: doing the right things, or doing things right. Oftentimes there is a convergence of these two principles in the corporation as it grows and matures. However, the common denominator of all small businesses—time compression—dictates that the former be stressed more than the latter. The demand for more prompt decisions today has grown geometrically from the demand that was present only 25 years ago. Doing things right, i.e., efficiently, is difficult to define, and it manifests itself in various ways. Carried to an excess, it can paralyze a business by not allowing it the time needed to institute fast decisions. Therefore, acting effectively enables one to accomplish more in a shorter period of time. Remember, the decision-making process should be flexible enough to leave room for actions that may not have been attempted in the past. So, who's to say that established procedures for achieving efficiency are best when translated into vision and strategic planning? The entrepreneurial climate wouldn't be what it is if all were managed by rote, except for the most mundane administrative activites. Excess standardization when it comes to planning dilutes the ingredients needed to be a good strategist.

> *AXIOM: By the time competitors have incorporated your original design and concept into theirs, the next planned creative step forward should be well on its way to implementation, not starting to be developed.*

Planning: A Means to an End

SP is not new to many small businesses. Some, in fact, are deft at developing and building on successes, as has been discussed. There are hard facts that prove, however, that planning can become an effort in futility. This is not because of lack of experience or intelligence, but because the *top decision makers* get so wrapped up in the methods to achieve the goals that the initial plan no longer bears resemblance to the stated program. If the original plan is allowed to run its course, the chances are good that a level of success will be attained. (That is, if the other pitfalls discussed here are avoided.) When operational (technical) aspects enter into implementing strategic policy, the result is that more power is put into it than is actually necessary. Small business planners should not try to kill a fly with a two-ton hammer.

An ensuing problem is created if planning is looked at as an end to a means. If one allocates the cost of all the corporate resources to the planning cycle, it becomes evident that the expense to create it is greater than the benefits that can be generated by truly productive areas of the business; hence, a road block to planning success develops.

> *AXIOM: Small business strategists succeed when they realize that the planning exercise is a means to accomplish an end (solving the opportunity/problem equation), rather than an end in and of itself.*

A 25-million-dollar fast-food organization nearly went bankrupt when the senior management/planners failed to keep the strategic plan simple. Every operational goal became an integral part of the policy to the point that error messages flagging severe problems went undetected. The net result was that the business direction went tangential to what was originally perceived to be a sound policy. It took some three years to get the company back on track and, oddly enough, the initial concept was deemed to be the best course to follow.

Know the Business

This is a straightforward comment that too often is ignored. Only by being informed about all the particulars, both internal and external, is the chief strategist able to use his or her experience and translate it into solutions that others might overlook.

The best chances for success are to stay within areas that are best known. For example, diversification of one's business is a natural subject for strategic planning consideration. However, the central theme should be based on moves that are synergistic with, or natural extensions of, the current operation. Careful preparation, when planning to expand the boundaries of the existing company, must be given to *long-term* fit versus short-term investment-type moves.

Looking at one's business as a whole can be linked to traditional product life-cycle analysis. In essence strategy should be geared to coincide with the company's progress through its own life-span curve. As with marketing the principal products or services, the corporate strategist must have full knowledge of the degree of the company's overall competitive advantage. This dictates the path taken when obsolescence factors enter the picture. The company's maturation point also dictates the resources that can be tapped in order to contend with developing new paths that lead to growth opportunities. Each stage of survivablity is a logical progression from the prior one.

In order to keep the life-span curve alive, efforts must be channelled into building and refining that which is the lifeblood of the organization. Unless the company is in the terminal illness mode, regeneration and redirection strategy is best targeted to what the entity can do best, what is known. A violation of this precept, especially when charting diversification decisions, can throw the organization into a tailspin. The time, effort, and gains that could perpetuate growth and reasonable profit will be for naught if the move is out of sync with the appropriate expertise level (See Exhibit 24-3).

AXIOM: The more knowledge of the specific business, the more the strategist can bring to bear in making long-term decisions.

Take, for instance, the classic case of an entrepreneur who founded and built a successful Long Island-based engineering concern. The president was a good manager of the firm, and he continued to build his small 8-million-dollar revenue organization according to plan for 10 years. Each year record sales and earnings were logged.

An opportunity presented itself whereby the president could expand his current business by buying a leisure-time company, a well-known roller skating operation. It was believed that he would be the white knight and the only one that could set the company back on its wheels. A considerable investment was made, and the roller skating company was merged into the engineering firm.

Because of the success he'd had with managing his core business, the president began to superimpose what worked in one unit to the other. However, the natures of the two businesses were totally incompatible. Controls for the engineering business were different. Marketing was aimed at an entirely different demographic group. The net results were that the amount of time that was consumed to manage an investment decision, at the expense of the core operation, proved disastrous to both sides. The strategy implementation of the engineering firm crumbled and the new business fell further

EXHIBIT 24-3   *The Corporate Life Span*

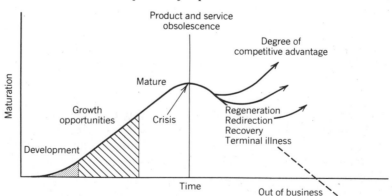

into the red. This case is the direct result of violating the axiomatic rule presented above.

Another look at the previously mentioned Connecticut-based chemical company shows how that situation differs from the above example. The original set strategy of the chief executive officer was to consider diversification options only if they fell within the extension of the existing business category, that is, if the diversification involved acquiring the sorts of businesses about which the CEO knew a great deal. During the company's growth span, two companies were acquired and merged into the parent as niche fillers to the exterior coating business. The market characteristics were the same. Existing distribution channels were integrated. Promotional campaigns were linked and, in certain cases the original trademark was transferred to one of the acquired company's products. This is a good example of the long-term profit interests of the company's being an interactive and integrative experience with strategic planning.

Expand Existing Systems

The ability to master new subjects quickly is a prerequisite for the strategist if he or she is to correctly identify opportunities and set goals. To this end, effectiveness is only as good as the information flow that is available. For accurate projections to be made, more precise analysis of the organization's productivity and optimum use of resources is needed.

As mentioned, the central notion to strategic planning is simple. The development and elaboration of the analysis are difficult tasks; reading the results of the analysis correctly is an equally difficult task. But, without good information, all plans are doomed to failure at the outset.

It behooves each small business strategist to uncover the opportunities within the organization that will yield more and better information. This will make the decision-making job easier. It will probably be done more expeditiously, too.

Enough cannot be said about this simple guideline. It is especially relevant in light of the widespread availability of computer-assisted management tools. For example, on the financial side of the business, a good hard look should be given to upgrading existing systems. The entire general ledger system most likely can be expanded for use in financial planning. Similarly, the accounts receivable and order entry setups are ideal for use in market analysis. These are just two examples; the list is endless.

AXIOM: The chief strategist who doesn't extract more information from the existing inventory of systems and procedures to make the decision-making process easier and more effective is dumb.

WHERE TO START AND HOW TO MEASURE THE RESULTS OF STRATEGIC PLANNING

Once the basic concepts have been assimilated and the roadblocks to effective strategic planning have been removed, the next steps—organizing and implementing a formal planning process—fall into place naturally. To initiate small business SP there are essentially three requisites needed by the good strategist: A data base around which the strengths and weaknesses of the business can be measured; precise qualitative and quantitative information extrapolated from the day-to-day realities of the business; and, most important, the fortitude to run with the planning disciplines during the growing pains stage.

A representative case study is the best means of portraying a small company with exceptional planning acumen. The company is an 18-million-dollar Huntsville, Texas food service organization that is successful in both the dinner-house and fast-food segments of the restaurant industry.

The company was formed some 20 years ago and started with one restaurant. Today, it operates more than 50 units. Earnings from one unit in Houston today exceed the first-year sales level of the original restaurant. Formal strategic planning has been a way of life around the company for the past six years. Each year the planning process becomes more sophisticated, as experience itself dictates.

The company's planning cycle commences each year at midsummer. At this time the two key planning officers (chairman and president) cloister themselves for one week away from the corporate headquarters. They begin with a broad-based interpretation of the corporate progress for the previous year. Each of the three proceeding plans is reviewed as it becomes interactive with the one to be formulated.

The starting point is always an explicit presentation of the end results of the three previous plans. Each of these formal policy statements contains no more than ten key elements that are reviewed by year, and their performance is charted, taking into consideration specific modifications that affected each target on a year-by-year basis.

The primary issues that are deemed to be strategically the most important for the three-year period could total 30, theoretically. However, in reality the most issues that the chief strategists address at any one session number 10 to 12. Most of the targets are extensions of themselves. For example, unit openings, customer-count goals, and comparable store performance are three cornerstone issues that are recurring items from one year to the next. Specific personnel/manpower needs are items that may drop from one formal planning policy statement, but may be added to another down the line.

The next step in the initial planning phase is to reconcile the variances in performance between what was expected to happen when the targets were first set and what actually transpired. The purpose of this exercise is not only to track results, but also to test the soundness of the reasoning that went into the ultimate formulation of the goals. How close to the mark the results were is a clear indication of how well the strategists know their business.

Both favorable and unfavorable variances are important to the planners; they show the degree of the planners' accuracy in analyzing a myriad of variables or situations, and of their being able to make current assumptions. It is as important for them to know and understand the reasons for marginal performance or failure as it is for them to learn of successes that exceeded expectations by an extraordinary amount. In the latter instance, particularly, variance ànalyses become relevant, for they reveal that possible significant factors affecting growth might well have been understated or overlooked. Given that resources could have been made available, they further indicate lost opportunities or less-than-optimal performance.

All formal strategic plans of the company are based on one-, three-, and five-year increments. It is realized at the outset that the farther out the forecasts are made, the less accurate they are expected to be. Nonetheless, the disciplines used in projecting a vision are the essential ingredients that add to the total honing process of strategic planning.

Still within the time frame of the initial planning session, the chairman and the president then proceed to measure the immediately preceding plan's key elements and to determine the viability for success in the future according to the stated yearly increments. Here one sees the weighing of the validity of assumptions. Are we right? Are we wrong? Are things still on track? What must be done given the current information available? This questioning is the first cut in a continuing refinement process. After numerous cuts, the planners come away with an abstract set of points that may or may not be incorporated into the new plan.

The stage is now set to proceed to the development of the strategic plan for the next five years. The executives return to the corporate headquarters and collectively discuss their initial findings with the top-tier operating, financial, and administrative staff. Total participatory involvement is expected, and received, during the two-day group meeting. Critical departure points, market indicators, the economy, historical financial data, and other areas are communicated in detail among the group. After all is said and done, the corporate performance vis-à-vis the strategic plan is judged to be: either at peak, or not at peak, level.

The by-product of the group interaction is the start of the information collection process that is to be added to the ever-expanding corporate data base of variables, which is the crux for defining the life and death factors of the company. For the next six weeks, in addition to their regular responsibilities, the respective management groups compile their forecasts, which are to be included in the plan. By mid-September, this phase is completed, and the senior strategists use the information to support the setting of the new goals. Before the first of October, the plan is locked in and disseminated.

From the new set of strategic targets emanates a subset of operational/ administrative directives that are to be accomplished (at given times) over the planning horizon by the respective managers. A continuing audit of these is performed as a matter of course during the regularly scheduled monthly performance meetings.

How successful has the company's SP process been? A few concrete examples are presented below:

A conclusion was reached during one planning cycle that corporate growth had outpaced the usefulness of the accounts reporting system. It was determined that a financial officer should be recruited to design and implement a state-of-the-art, computer-generated financial management information system. The goal was to have the person onboard within six months and the system on-line within 18 months. It was fully accomplished in less than 12 months.

The decision to begin franchising units was the result of another plan. The entire program was up and running a year ahead of schedule, with dramatic bottom-line results.

The decision to upgrade restaurant designs was the outgrowth of an early formal session. An architect was commissioned to do this; results were successful, and he was called in to join the staff and to manage a newly created division within the company.

Expansion into the dinner-house segment of the market was another target within a strategic plan. The company was able to capitalize on this two years ahead of the target date.

ARE YOUR PLANS ON TARGET?

One of the best measuring devices to indicate the success of the end results of strategic planning is the Waterfall Chart (see Exhibit 24-4). At a glance it can show whether the goals that have been formally established are reasonable.

Results of the Waterfall Chart variance analysis put a quantitative perspective on the strategic planning process. Good planning requires an appraisal and reconciliation of numerical performance with an organization's qualitative performance. To measure the latter aspect, the chief strategist should evaluate his or her successes by taking the test that appears at the end of this chapter. In summary, the correlation of both subsets of results brings us back to a total understanding of the circular relationships outlined in the Strategic Planning Matrix.

EXHIBIT 24-4. The Waterfall Chart: A Quantitative Measure of Strategic Planning Results
Any Variable That Is Measurable
Five-Year Variances in Performance
($ or units, as applicable)

	1980	1981	1982	1983	1984	1985	1986	1987	1988
Actual results	XXX	XXX	XXX	XXX	XXX				
Plan 1: 1980–84	XXX	XXX	XXX	XXX	XXX				
Plan 2: 1981–85		XXX	XXX	XXX	XXX	XXX			
Plan 3: 1982–86			XXX	XXX	XXX	XXX	XXX		
Plan 4: 1983–87				XXX	XXX	XXX	XXX	XXX	
Current forecast: 1984–88					XXX	XXX	XXX	XXX	XXX

Favorable/(unfavorable) variance between actual and:	1980	1981	1982	1983	1984
Plan 1	+	+	+	+	+
Plan 2		+	+	+	+
Plan 3			+	+	+
Plan 4				+	+
Current forecast					+

Favorable/(unfavorable) variance between plan 1 and:	1981	1982	1983	1984
Plan 2	−	−	−	−
Plan 3			−	−
Plan 4			−	−
Current forecast				−

and so on . . . to 1988.

24.17

*Evaluation: How Successful Is Your Strategic Planning?—A Qualitative
Approach*

(Ranked on Strong to Weak Basis, 10 Points to Zero)

Long-Range Elements in Strategic Plan	Your Company	Your Competitors
1. Assumptions vis-à-vis risks and opportunities.		
2. Ability to develop and prioritize major policy issues.		
3. Analysis and appraisal of strengths and weaknesses.		
4. Correlation of corporate requirements to items 2 and 3.		
5. Monitoring progress of plan. a. Definitive benchmarks. b. Goal reconciliation.		
6. Ability to review all planning elements to avoid confusion and ambiguity.		
7. Committment to planning. a. Deviations in good and bad times. b. Success to deal with short-term crises.		
8. Simplicity of plan in terms of setting agenda and subject essentials.		
9. Support documentation for the plan. a. Air-tight analysis. b. Precise reading of results. c. Adaptation to changing economy. d. Adaptation to changing technology.		
10. Delineation of who's responsible for identifying and setting goals.		
11. Management with objectives. a. Explicit. b. Measurable over time. c. Avoidance of confusion and ambiguities. d. Proper direction.		

Long-Range Elements in Strategic Plan	Your Company	Your Competitors
12. Leadership		
a. Avoids crises; applies rifleshot approach to solving problems.		
b. Sets proper direction.		
c. Able to keep pace with current changes.		
d. Avoids clouding operational aspects with strategic formulation.		
e. Effective management of time.		
f. Chief strategists surround themselves with capable professionals for informational feedback.		
g. Delegates responsibility to implement plan targets.		
13. Contingency planning.		
a. Ability to isolate conditions and unexpected developments.		
b. Probability assignments to 13a.		
c. Subplan development to what-if situations.		
d. Quality of response mechanisms to unexpected.		
14. Proactive environment.		
a. Effective planning formulas to do the right things.		
b. Intuitive fast decisions that are right.		
c. Flexible planning process that avoids excessive standardization.		
15. Plans are an end to means. Decision makers do not get too wrapped up in methods to achieve goals.		
16. Knowledge of business.		
a. Lifeblood of organization.		
b. Competitive advantage.		
c. Diversifications are a natural extension of business.		
d. Central planning theme is based on moves synergistic with current operations.		

Long-Range Elements in Strategic Plan	Your Company	Your Competitors
e. Can appropriate resources contend with developing new paths for growth opportunities.		
f. Understanding of corporate lifespan curve and position on it.		
17. Ability to identify and uncover better use of existing systems to aid decision making.		
18. Information data base is suitable for quality decision making.		
19. Precise qualitative and quantitative analysis can be extrapolated from day-to-day realities to aid in strategy development.		
Total Score		

If your score is: Maximum 430 = SP at its best.
                    Above 400 = Sophisticated, on way to the best.
                    350–400 = Good systems, needs some refining.
                    300–349 = Needs improvement.
                    Below 300 = Poor strategy developer.

BIBLIOGRAPHY

Brandt, S. C., *Strategic Planning for Emerging Companies,* Addison-Wesley, Reading, Mass., 1982.

Drucker, P. F., *Managing for Results,* Harper & Row, New York, 1964.

Lorange, P., *Implementation of Strategic Planning,* Prentice-Hall, Englewood Cliffs, N.J., 1982.

Lorange, P. and Vancil, R., *Strategic Planning Systems,* Prentice-Hall, Englewood Cliffs, 1977.

McNichols, T. J., *Executive Policy and Strategic Planning,* McGraw-Hill, New York, 1983.

Osborn, A. F., *Applied Imagination,* Scribner, New York, 1953.

Steiner, G. A., *Strategic Planning: What Every Manager Must Know,* Free Press, New York, 1979

Yavitz, B. and Newman, W. H., *Strategy in Action: The Execution, Politics and Payoff of Business Planning,* Free Press, New York 1982.

CHAPTER **25**

Strategic Planning in the Voluntary Sector

GEORGE W. WILKINSON

GEORGE W. WILKINSON is Vice President, Strategic Planning of United Way of America. At the nation's largest charitable organization, Dr. Wilkinson is responsible for corporate strategic planning and the development of consultation and technical assistance programs for the organization's 2200 local and autonmous United Way organizations. Dr. Wlkinson began his United Way career in 1972 at the United Way in Bridgeport, Connecticut. There he developed and directed numerous public–private partnership efforts in the fields of criminal justice, home health care, day care, and refugee resettlement. His work in pioneering long-range planning in the United Way system led to his joining United Way of America in 1980. He is the author of several articles and publications on environmental scanning and strategic planning. He holds three college degrees, including a doctorate in Educational Administration.

OUTLINE

A period of unprecedented change, economic uncertainty, federal reduction in funding, and heightened competition has made the planning and management of the voluntary not-for-profit sector all the more difficult, and all the more complex.

Like it or not, however, the years ahead will undoubtedly bring even greater change, increased uncertainty, and a more diverse field of competition. New technologies, new industries, and new market forces demand new approaches to the way voluntary agencies do business. Indeed, corporations, not-for-profit and for-profit alike, have begun to learn that their challenges will lie in the combination of strategic planning and strategic management.

Ralph Waldo Emerson said, "If you learn only methods, you will be forever tied to the methods. However, if you will learn principles, you can devise your own methods." Devising their own methods, voluntary organizations in the 1970s have developed a strategic planning process that is largely patterned after the basic strategic process in business, but is adapted to their own style, corporate character, and needs.

THE BASIC MODEL

The basic model used by many voluntary not-for-profit sectors is shown in Exhibit 25-1. It incorporates a six-step process that includes external environmental analysis, internal capability analysis, strategic direction setting, definition of base and contingency plans, policy/strategy/program implementation, and performance evaluation. All of these phases are tied together and are an annual activity.

Recognizing the need for the nonprofit voluntary organization to mold the principles inherent in this process to their own organizational culture, the first important step before launching a strategic planning process is the development activity known as preplanning/organization.

PREPLANNING/ORGANIZATION

The preplanning/organizational phase of the strategic process is extremely critical, for it is in this phase that the scope, the discrete activities of the

EXHIBIT 25-1   The Strategic Process

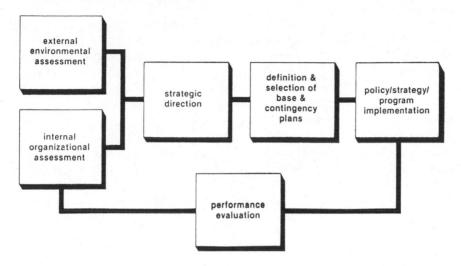

strategic process, and the resources needed are identified and planned. Here voluntary agencies ask such questions as:

Do I need a voluntary committee? If so, what should its composition be?

What staff resources are needed, and who should be assigned the responsibility?

What should the role of volunteers be, and what should be the role of professional staff?

What additional committees and/or task forces are needed?

Over what period of time will we undertake our process?

What means shall we use to conduct our environmental scanning, and is original research necessary?

How do we undertake the internal capability analysis, and what are the key areas to evaluate?

What kind of process or techniques do we need to identify the kind of organization we should be, and what issues are important for us to resolve?

These are just some of the questions that must be addressed in this preplanning stage.

Commitment

Commitment is the essential ingredient in the preplanning phase. Do the chief professional and volunteer officers of the organization really want to undertake the strategic process? These are the leaders of the voluntary organization. Without their visible and enthusiastic support, the process is doomed to fail.

Also key to the commitment concern are the functional area managers and their respective volunteer counterparts. The people who run and who are involved in the day-to-day business generally understand the organization better than anyone else. This practical knowledge is critical for the strategic planning process. It keeps planning "down to earth." In addition, these are the people who will carry out the strategy, and its success depends on their cooperation. They are far more likely to be enthusiastic over strategy when they have a hand in its development. Regarding the chief professional and volunteer officers, we must recognize that mere support is not enough. After all, by definition, strategy planning may change the thrust of the organization. Unless these people are deeply involved in making such plans, they are not likely to approve them. Besides, deciding the future directions of the organization is the job of these leaders. Anything less than full participation will lead to disappointment for everyone.

Make Time for Planning

The desire to wait until time is available is often used as an excuse for avoiding strategic planning. However, most observers will note, as well, that job pressures are not likely to diminish. Time requirements are another reason why the chief professional and volunteer officers must lead the planning effort. If this responsibility is delegated to someone else, it soon becomes evident to everyone how little these leaders rate its importance. Other top managers will not put their efforts into strategic planning, either. They will work on something that they feel the "president" or executive director views as most important.

Organization

Typically, the voluntary organization will form a strategic planning committee composed of 18 to 25 volunteers who represent the major constituent groups of the organization. This group would meet anywhere from four to ten times during the course of the process to review key findings and recommendations. In some voluntary organizations a steering committee will be formed to do the major work. This allows top community leaders to serve on the strategic planning committee which might meet three or four times.

The first meeting of the strategic planning committee is normally an orientation and would, at the minimum, contain the following items:

A review of the history of the organization, including its original, and subsequently modified, role and mission statements.
A review of the charge to the committee.
A review of the strategic process.

Often voluntary agencies use this opportunity to undertake a mini strategic process in which a facilitator leads the committee through an exercise designed to identify preliminary views on strengths and weaknesses of the organization and what it ought to be in an ideal circumstance.

Also at this first organizational meeting, the first two committees are named to initiate the process. These committees are an environmental scanning committee and an internal capability analysis committee.

EXTERNAL ENVIRONMENTAL ASSESSMENT

External environmental analysis is a process in which information is collected to help volunteers and staff identify changes in the organization's operating environment that could become either threats to its long-term viability or opportunities to fill new or unmet community needs and improve effectiveness. As such, it normally defines the major forces of change in the macroenvironment. This macroenvironment includes four major areas:

1. *Social.* Information that focuses on values, lifestyles, and demographic characteristics of the population.
2. *Economic.* Information that focuses on the monetary getting, spending, and trading behavior of the area's economic system.
3. *Political.* Information that focuses on policymaking, regulatory, and legislative behavior, as well as on public opinion and responses to public policy issues.
4. *Technological.* Information that focuses on the scientific and technological developments influencing the way people live, work, and interact among themselves and with their environment.

Additionally, the external environmental assessment identifies facts and trends in the industry in which the organization is operating. United Way organizations, for example, would study the history and scope of philanthropy, while YMCA organizations may study the industries of family and health services. As an organization defines its industry it also conducts a third level of external environmental analysis that involves identifying the primary competitors in the industry with whom the organization competes for resources and program services. Again, for a United Way organization this could involve other federated fund-raising efforts or major single-interest groups. For an organization like the YMCA it could be a diverse range of organizations, including proprietary health spas.

Macroenvironmental Analysis

The main environmental assessment activity engaged in by most voluntary organizations is definition of the macroenvironment. Many United Way organizations, like the United Way of the Capital Area in Austin, Texas and the United Way of the Capital Area in Hartford, Connecticut, are good examples. A few extracts from these assessment documents are shown below in Exhibits 25-2 and 25-3.

In addition to local and national United Way publications, information of this type is often available through Chambers of Commerce, governmental planning bodies, and universities.

EXHIBIT 25-2   *Austin Environmental Assessment*

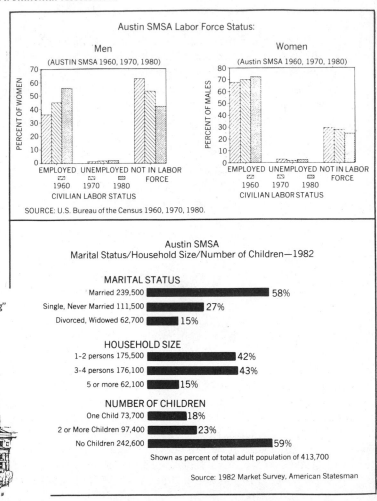

Austin SMSA Labor Force Status:

Men
(AUSTIN SMSA 1960, 1970, 1980)

Women
(AUSTIN SMSA 1960, 1970, 1980)

SOURCE: U.S. Bureau of the Census 1960, 1970, 1980.

Austin SMSA
Marital Status/Household Size/Number of Children—1982

MARITAL STATUS
Married 239,500 — 58%
Single, Never Married 111,500 — 27%
Divorced, Widowed 62,700 — 15%

HOUSEHOLD SIZE
1-2 persons 175,500 — 42%
3-4 persons 176,100 — 43%
5 or more 62,100 — 15%

NUMBER OF CHILDREN
One Child 73,700 — 18%
2 or More Children 97,400 — 23%
No Children 242,600 — 59%

Shown as percent of total adult population of 413,700

Source: 1982 Market Survey, American Statesman

AUSTIN in the 1990s
"A Practical Resource for Planning"

United Way/Capital Area
Austin, Texas
January, 1984

EXHIBIT 25-3   Connecticut's Economy

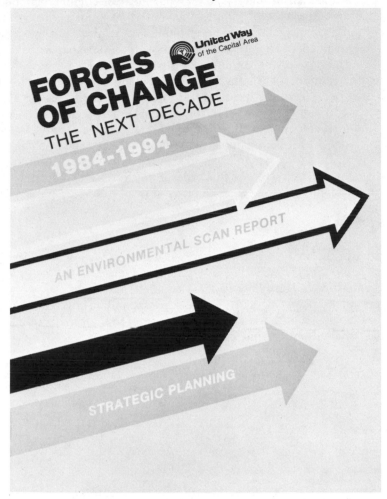

To produce an environmental scan such as this, voluntary organizations form committees composed of people in the community who have access to information. The effort is normally one of gathering secondary data and putting it together in a single report. Typically, a committee of this type would meet three to five times, in which it:

1. Identifies the sources of information available.
2. Reviews a draft report that puts together this secondary information.
3. Reaches conclusions regarding the diversity of data and identifies potential implications for the organization.

Preparation of drafts can be done by either the organization's professional staff or volunteers. In some cases, consultants may be hired.

Sources for information abound in all communities. It can be found in reports from the Census Bureau, the Department of Commerce, state and municipal governments, universities, business and industry, as well as in reports from regional planning bodies, voluntary organizations, and planning divisions or councils. In addition to this data, a local newspaper file can also serve as a useful repository of information.

If an organization, for whatever reason, does not seem to be able to find information or to have the inclination to undertake such a research effort, it may want to use national, state, or regional reports. It can review the trends identified in these reports and, through a committee process, determine whether or not the local community will follow these trends or deviate from them, and, if deviation occurs, can determine in what direction and with what magnitude. The results of this type of an exercise can become a base scenario for planning purposes. Exhibit 25-4 is an example.

Industry Analysis

Illustrative of the analysis of the industry is a United Way of America report entitled *Scope and Trends: Some Aspects of Philanthropy in the United States,* published in December of 1981. Exhibit 25-5 shows the segments of this report that define American philanthropy and public policy implications, as well as the scope of the sector. This is a useful tool for understanding the dynamics of charitable giving.

EXHIBIT 25-4   Consensor Meeting 1—Future Trends in Eastern Fairfield County

Trend   Scores

	OWN	WGHT	GRP	WGHT

• SOCIAL

1. The national trend shows a decline in the needs-oriented group.
   (RD 21a page 4)   0 1 2 3 4 5 6 7 8 9 10

   Compared with the national trend, what will be the rate of change in Eastern Fairfield County?

   Lesser rate of change   Same rate of change   Greater rate of change

2. Nationally, there will be an increase in the socially conscious subgroup.
   (RD 21a page 10)   0 1 2 3 4 5 6 7 8 9 10

   Compared with the national trend, what will be the rate of change in Eastern Fairfield County?

   Lesser rate of change   Same rate of change   Greater rate of change

Weighing: Studied Material-100; Read Material-75; Skimmed Material-50; Did Not Look at Material-25

EXHIBIT 25-5 Typical Industry Analysis

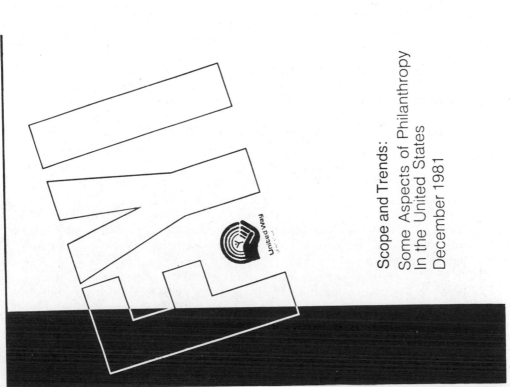

Scope and Trends:
Some Aspects of Philanthropy
In the United States
December 1981

CONTENTS

Conclusions

The importance of engaging in the external environmental assessment can be readily identified for nonprofit organizations as one looks at the changing patterns of governmental funding that have transpired over the last ten years, as well as the impact of the recent 1982–1983 recession.

From an economic standpoint, these changes in funding streams and economic conditions spawn more agencies with special interests. As a result, the 1980s will be a time of intense competition within the voluntary sector. This competition will not be for resources only, but for volunteers as well, since the demographics show that more and more women will enter the work force.

Other demographic changes such as the aging of the population, the decreasing percentage of youth, and the changing racial composition of our country will continue to create havoc for organizations that do not plan ahead.

From everything that we can see, the 1980s will be a continuing time of turbulence that will present a myriad of threats and opportunities for the nonprofit sector. To ignore that turbulence and plan business on an as-usual basis is unrealistic. The organizations that think they can get by with this strategy are merely waiting for their own demise, and they will go the way of the dinosaurs.

INTERNAL ORGANIZATIONAL ASSESSMENT

The internal organizational assessment parallels the activity used to identify the threats and opportunities of the external environment. This assessment identifies the organization's strengths and limitations through a diversity of process steps. Within this self-assessment is an evaluation of the organization's human, financial, technological, structural, and information capacities.

Nonprofit organizations often engage in this self-assessment through the process of testing perceptions of key constituency groups regarding their view of the organization. This may be done by conducting individual or focus group interviews or by survey instruments. The constituency groups are normally identified as those that are involved in some way with the organization, including internal staff and volunteers, funders, and other key community leaders who have interests in the general sphere of the organization's business. Not to be forgotten are the clients or beneficiaries of the organization's program and services.

In addition to perception testing, a review of the organization as it compares to similar organizations locally and nationally often provides benchmarks for coming to conclusions regarding success and/or limitations of operations. For example, United Way organizations often compare themselves to communities whose characteristics (size of population, size of work force,

EXHIBIT 25-6 Profile: 1983 Campaign Performance Series

United Way of America
Research Division

Leaderboard :
LOUISVILLE, KY

STATISTIC	METRO I STATISTICS				METRO I LEADERS		
	YOUR LUWO	MEDIAN	UPPER THIRD	RANKING	COMMUNITY – 1	COMMUNITY – 2	COMMUNITY – 3
PER CAPITA AMOUNT RAISED							
1983	$ 13.61	$ 13.78	$ 20.07	25 / 47	CLEVELAND, OH* $ 26.72	ROCHESTER, NY* $ 24.88	HARTFORD, CT* $ 24.72
1973	$ 6.45	$ 6.89	$ 10.01	28 / 47	ROCHESTER, NY* $ 17.27	WILMINGTON, DE* $ 12.21	CLEVELAND, OH* $ 12.17
PER 10,000 E.B.I.							
1983	$ 15.32	$ 14.78	$ 19.57	20 / 47	CLEVELAND, OH* $ 26.50	WILMINGTON, DE* $ 23.33	ROCHESTER, NY* $ 23.21
1973	$ 16.00	$ 17.31	$ 24.10	29 / 47	ROCHESTER, NY* $ 38.02	CLEVELAND, OH* $ 29.26	WILMINGTON, DE* $ 29.02
PER PERSON EMPLOYED--1983	$ 32.38	$ 32.38	$ 44.06	24 / 47	CLEVELAND, OH* $ 59.75	ROCHESTER, NY* $ 56.07	HARTFORD, CT* $ 53.72
PERCENT CHANGE IN DOLLARS RAISED							
1 YEAR 1982-1983	12.4 %	10.2 %	17.5 %	14 / 47	SAN DIEGO, CA* 32.9 %	SAN ANTONIO, TX* 29.3 %	NORFOLK, VA* 24.1 %
5 YEARS 1978-1983	70.3 %	58.7 %	89.5 %	14 / 47	ORANGE, CA* 141.2 %	SANTA CLARA, CA* 135.2 %	HARTFORD, CT* 119.5 %
1O YEARS 1973-1983	109.1 %	132.0 %	256.2 %	30 / 47	ORANGE, CA* 1138.4 %	SANTA CLARA, CA* 279.0 %	HARTFORD, CT* 252.5 %

NOTE: Statistics relating to 1983 amount raised represent total campaign results including all funds raised in the Combined Federal Campaign (CFC).

* Indicates CFC community

and effective buying income) are similar to their own. In this regard they compare national data on giving by trade groups, per capita of employment, and percentage of distribution of giving from employees, corporations, individuals, and foundations. Exhibit 25-6 demonstrates this type of comparison. Based on this analysis, local United Way organizations can judge whether they are doing as well as, better than or worse than similar organizations in similar communities.

Another means of self-evaluation is to look at accomplishments versus stated goals of the organization. An example of this is testing whether the stated goal in fund raising has been met over the last five years and looking for reasons for nonaccomplishment or for overaccomplishment. For human service providers this may also be a measure of the number of clients who have continued to use program services over the last five years versus the capacity of programs over those same years.

Another form of measurement is market penetration. In this regard, human service agencies determine the size of the potential client base and over time measure their share of that base to which they are providing services. The expansion or contraction of this market share is an evaluation of program success.

STRATEGIC DIRECTION SETTING

In this phase of the strategic process the external environment's threats and opportunities and the internal organizational assessment's identification of strengths and limitations are brought together to find the best organizational fit. By "fit," we mean the clear identification or ratification of the organization's purpose and vision of what it ought to be five years out. This process of strategic direction setting creates what is known as strategic vision. It identifies operational mission, goals, and objectives for the organization.

Organization's Mission

A major step in the process is the examination of the organization's evolution from its inception, as stated in corporate articles of incorporation or bylaws, and the record of how the organization has changed over time. An understanding of its current mission and activities is essential for positioning it in the future.

Often this process is hindered in the voluntary sector by attitudinal problems. These problems include such things as:

1. The notion that the organization's purpose is self-evident. Many volunteers and professionals alike believe that people associated with the organization have a clear picture of the reasons for the organization's existence and its purpose in the community. They believe

that its purpose is so obvious that examining it would be a waste of time.

2. The belief that an existing charter, a set of bylaws of mission statements, will automatically suffice for the future. This view is based on the belief that a sense of purpose, once it has been established, will serve the organization indefinitely. Therefore, where there is a mission statement, or a rough equivalent thereof, there is no reason to develop another one.

3. The sense that spending time on the task of constructing a mission statement is important, but that it takes time away from the main purpose of the process to develop strategies and construct action plans.

Each of these views can create significant problems in motivating volunteer committees to construct mission statements. If one or more of these views causes the committee to bypass the deliberation of the organizational mission, it can create significant problems later in the process.

It is for these reasons that the first meeting of the strategic planning committee must contain a review of the historical perspectives that we have mentioned.

A good example of the importance of role and mission can be seen when one reviews the history of the National Foundation for Infantile Paralysis. It was formed in 1938 to raise money through the March of Dimes to support research, education, and patient care in connection with the dreaded disease of infantile paralysis. It continued to do so until the discovery of the Salk vaccine in 1955. Within a short time the disease was virtually eliminated and so, too, was the need for the National Foundation of Infantile Paralysis.

When an organization loses its mission, it is on the road to extinction. The National Foundation for Infantile Paralysis, however, decided not to give up, believing that it could contribute to the value of society by using its volunteers to raise money for some other cause. The organization identified a number of health causes that needed financial support, and chose one, birth defects, that was consistent with its reputation for serving children who are victims of ill health. In 1958, it changed its name to the National Foundation and became a major charitable organization supporting research, education, and patient care for victims of birth defects. Trends and events thus affected the organization and its mission. It strategically viewed the future and repositioned itself with a new mission and continued forward.

In a similar vein, many United Way organizations that were originally formed to raise money for a select group of agencies have paused to reflect on changing times and have recast their purposes to a much broader mission. Many are now using this mission: To increase the organized capacity of people to care for one another.

With this mission statement, they have moved to develop a variety of programs beyond fund raising. Programs that encompass activities in the realms of government relations, year-round education, volunteer recruitment and training, management assistance to agencies, information and referral, community needs assessment, the use of donor option, endowment-deferred giving programs, venture, emergency, and transition funding are all examples of programs that go beyond the older, more traditional, once-a-year campaign.

Strategic Issues Identification

Once the mission is stated, it must be examined in light of environmental change and internal capabilities so that strategic issues can be identified and narrowed down to those that are most critical. In this process a critical issue is described as a forthcoming development, either inside or outside the organization, that affects the ability of the organization to carry out its mission. The issue may be a welcome opportunity in the environment to be grasped or an internal strength that can be exploited, or it may be an unwelcome external threat, or internal weakness that imperils the continuing success, or even the survival, of the enterprise.

When deciding whether strategic issues are important for the organization, a three-way test is often used regarding the issue. The test involves answering three questions:

1.   Will the issue impact the performance of the organization?
2.   Will it require allocation of organizational resources?
3.   Can the organization reasonably expect to control or exert significant influence on the issue?

If the answer to these questions is yes, then a strategic issue has been stated, and it should be considered for further study.

Issue Identification Techniques

A variety of techniques exists to help identify and examine strategic issues in order to determine their impact on the organization and to determine which are now the most critical for the organization to focus on in the strategic process. One useful technique for determining the implications of the issue is known as the futures wheel. This is a process that was developed by Joel Barker at the University of Massachusetts and has been incorporated into many nonprofit and proprietary organizations as a means to identify the effects or implications of the issue on the organization. The exercise begins with the placing of the issue in the center of a wheel (see Exhibit 25-7). Implications are spun out from this center until the study group runs out of ideas, which usually occurs in 20 or 30 minutes. In this process, no censoring is allowed, and every implication is considered, no matter how seemingly irrelevant. The group quickly builds implications from implications, some-

EXHIBIT 25-7   Futures Wheel Exercise

The above exercise was run by the Long Range Planning Committee of the United Way of Essex and West Hudson, Newark, New Jersey. Only partial results have shown.

25.15

EXHIBIT 25-8   Issues Probability Exercise

ISSUES PROBABILITY EXERCISE

■ What is the probability that this will develop into a major issue?

   (As measured by extent of, e.g., interest group activity, media attention, legislation, regulation, litigation, etc.)

0	1	2	3	4	5	6	7	8	9	10
highly improbable			unlikely		as likely as not		more likely than not			highly probable

■ In assessing probability consider:
  —Pressure of trends (net: reinforcing trends less inhibiting trends)
  —Pressure of interest groups/constituencies (net: support less opposition)

Issue:_____

0	1	2	3	4	5	6	7	8	9	10
highly Improbable		unlikely			as likely as not		more likely than not			highly probable

ISSUES IMPACT EXERCISE

■ Assuming that this does become a major issue, how great would its eventual impact be on the United Way?

   (As measured by extent of its effects on, e.g., costs, fund raising, allocations, management organization/policies/practices, "image"/reputation, etc.)

0	1	2	3	4	5	6	7	8	9	10
negligible Impact			incremental change			substantial change			major structural change	

■ In assessing impact consider:
  —Opportunities as well as threats/problems
  —Longer term as well as immediate impact

Issue:_____

0	1	2	3	4	5	6	7	8	9	10
negligible impact		incremental change			substantial change			major structural change	

ISSUES MATURITY EXERCISE

■ In what time-frame will the issue mature sufficiently to require significant resources for its analysis/management?
  —Near-term: this year-next year, e.g., 1980-81
  —Medium-term: the following three years, e.g., 1982-84
  —Long-term: the five years after, e.g., 1985-90

Issue:_____ 1980-81   1982-84   1985-90

25.16

times out to a third or fourth order. At the end of the session each implication is labeled as a threat or an opportunity for the organization.

Once the exercise is completed a narrative is written that describes this range of opportunities and threats. In this manner, the group begins to identify the level of significance that the issue poses for the organization. From the list of potential issues as developed in the future wheel exercise or from other such brainstorming exercises, a further refinement may be done in order to identify those issues that are most critical.

Issue Prioritization

A simple rank ordering exercise is probably the most frequently used vehicle. However, this one-dimensional approach to sorting is giving way to more sophisticated means of selection. One such means is to use the study group to assess (1) the probability of the issue's becoming a major issue for the organization, (2) the amount of impact that issue would have on the organization should it become a major issue, and (3) a potential time dimension in which the issue could surface. This three-way test can be adjudged on a zero to ten scale (see Exhibit 25-8) and then plotted in a series of three 9-cell matrixes (see Exhibit 25-9). In this manner the study group can see which issues have the highest probablity of occurrence and the heaviest impact on the organization, as well as the time dimension in which they should be considered.

After issues have been sorted in this manner, the strategic process can focus on those of highest critical nature that will affect the organization in the closest time dimension for possible development of immediate strategies, while being able to develop longer-term strategies for those that are in the medium- and long-term time frames.

Issue Framing

Once the critical issues (normally six to nine) have been determined, a detailed issue brief is prepared for each issue. This issue brief should contain several distinct segments. These segments should be (1) a title and definition of the issue, (2) identification of the strategic significance of the issue (its threats and opportunities), (3) a background and identification of driving influences—the key environmental forces now and in the future, as well as the organizational strengths and limitations that make this an issue, (4) prospects of the issue—potential outcomes under alternative scenarios, (5) effect on the organization—quantitative measures of the potential impact on the organization under each of the scenarios selected, and (6) planning challenges—a set of "need to" statements setting out the overall actions required of the organization to maximize the opportunities or minimize the threats.

An example of an issue brief, in outline form, follows.

Segments	Example
Title of issue	Mounting competition for access to workplace solicitation.
Strategic significance (challenges/opportunities)	Challenge: Multiple campaigns at the workplace would significantly erode United Way fund-raising capacity—foster popularity contests.
	Opportunity: United Way could capitalize on demand for access to become more inclusive and guarantee legitimacy of participants.
Background (driving influences)	High inflation Changing values Rise of special interest groups Reduction in government funding for social services Changing work environment
Prospects	Worst Case: Workplace solicitation becomes a popularity contest run by payroll departments. United Way fund-raising/allocations functions go defunct.
	Current Path: Continued inroads are made for multiple in-plant solicitations and/or designation campaigns.
	Best Case: United Way becomes "all inclusive," balances donor interest in selection with citizen review process.

Current Path	$ Raised (millions)	Market share	Health/ welfare
1981	1.5	60%	
1984	1.7	45%	
1990	1.9	30%	

Effect on United Way (quantitative measures over three time periods in $ campaign production and market position)

Segments	Example
Planning challenges ("need to" statements)	Need to develop new approaches to "inclusiveness" that will avoid "campaign popularity content."
	Need to introduce motivational techniques compatible with new work environment to build United Way acceptance.

Now that the most critical issues have been selected and issue briefs prepared, we now move to the next phase of the strategic process.

EXHIBIT 25-9   Issues Priority Matrix

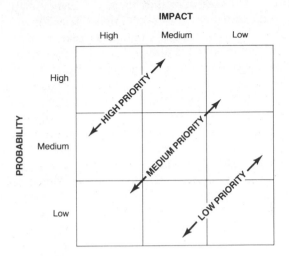

DEFINITION AND SELECTION OF BASE AND CONTINGENCY PLANS

In this phase of the strategic process the organization studies the critical issues and begins to develop strategies that will assist in issue resolution and insure that the organization is trying to carry out its mission and mission objectives. In most organizations the issues are identified and selected by the strategic planning committee. The committee then forms study groups around each of the issues or clusters of issues. These study groups normally are composed of volunteers and are staffed by the professional in the organization who has prime responsibility for the general area most affected by the issue.

Strategy Development Techniques

In seeking feasible strategies, the organization may employ several techniques to generate ideas that will form the basis of strategies. These techniques range from open discussion and brainstorming to structured activities that are designed to enumerate ideas that can further be refined to strategies. One such approach is called the nominal group process, another is known as synectics.

Using the nominal group process, a question is posed to the group, and each group member writes down his or her ideas without conversation. These ideas are then collected one at a time by a group leader who asks each member for one idea until all ideas have been put forth. These ideas are recorded in sequential fashion on blackboards or flip charts. Upon completion of the idea expansion, the group reviews each idea for clarification and linkage to other ideas that have been put forth. Ideas that are similar are then combined as a single premise. Upon completion of the clarification and compression, the group votes on those ideas that they see as being the most feasible. These ideas are then further explored in open discussion or in another round of the nominal process in order to identify the reasons why each of them is good and the advantages and disadvantages that they may pose for the organization. A series of alternatives is developed that can then be subject to analysis regarding its feasibility for the organization as it relates to the need for resources, the impact on structure, and potential resolution of the issue.

Another means of idea generation is the process of synectics. Synectics is a process designed by an organization of the same name in Cambridge, Massachusetts. It involves, generally, a small group of eight to ten participants who are led through the synectics process by a facilitator. In this process a member of the study team is selected as a client to pursue the issue. The client identifies why the issue is important and some of the things that have already been tried to deal with it. The facilitator then involves the group in a process known as "goal wishing," which is the suggesting of potential ideal ways that the organization may deal with the issue. If the idea is actionable, that is, if it can be translated into strategies, an activity is engaged in to identify the advantages, or what one likes about the idea, as well as to identify the areas of concern about idea implementation. The group goes to work on each of the concerns until satisfactory resolution has been reached, if possible, from the client's perspective.

If in the synectics process the ideas that has been suggested is not actionable and is more of a direction, the group potentially may go on an "excursion."This is a movement away from the direction itself to areas that may seem to be "far out." In this manner, word association and other such means are used to create thoughts that are then brought back to the problem and potential ideas generated. In this excursion process the group begins to replicate the type of process that great thinkers go through in linking seemingly irrelevant conditions or observations to problems they are considering. Examples of such connections are Newton and the falling apple and Archimedes and the tub of overflowing water.

In both processes, the list of alternative strategies is analyzed and preferred strategies are selected.

Strategy Contingencies

Once strategies have been selected, the group should begin to examine these strategies in light of alternative scenarios that may differ from the base condition or planning scenario that they have selected. Alternative scenarios provide the opportunity to consider what they would do if these scenarios occurred that would be different from the preferred strategy. If the answer is nothing, then the preferred strategy will hold up under most conditions. However, if in one of the scenarios something different should happen, then the group details what it would do in that instance and begins to build contingency strategies. These alternative courses then form the basis of contingency plans that should be part of the overall strategic plan.

The Strategic Plan

Both the preferred strategies and the contingencies are framed into a strategic plan. Typically, the strategic plan in a nonprofit organization is a written document that contains several major components. First is an introduction that identifies why the process was undertaken, identifies the methodologies used, and the time it has taken to accomplish the planning process. The second section normally identifies the people who were involved in the process. A third section identifies the selected or recommended organizational mission statement, together with organizational mission objectives. The fourth section identifies the issues that were studied and the conditions that were enumerated to make them critical issues. The fifth section lays out the strategies that were selected and sets forth a rationale for their selection, together with the resources needed, the time frame identified for accomplishment, and the responsible operating divisions within the organization to be charged with carrying out the strategies.

The strategic plan is presented to the board of directors for their acceptance and direction to the organization in building its annual budget and subsequent work programs.

POLICY/STRATEGY/PROGRAM IMPLEMENTATION

This phase of the strategic process brings the planning into reality and calls for adoption by the board of the strategic plan and formation of appropriate policies and programs. It involves the building of the organization's budget and divisional work programs.

Often in voluntary organizations the development of division work programs is a joint responsibility of professional staff and volunteer advisory committees. Staff and volunteers examine the strategies and develop the discrete steps that must be taken by them to implement the strategy. Often in this process a document is prepared that follows the general management by objectives (MBO) format as an organizational tool throughout the organization. Division, department, and individual work programs are tied in this manner to the strategic plan. The aggregation of these MBOs is moved forward for executive and board approval in the budgetary process.

PERFORMANCE EVALUATION

In this phase of the strategic process expected results and actual results are compared. Reasons for the magnitude of difference are enumerated and form a critical juncture in the strategic process becoming an ongoing management tool. It is critical because it is necessary to link the first year's activity and its subsequent efforts with activities that need to take place in subsequent years. If strategic planning is to be an ongoing function, then it must be renewed on a continual basis, and performance evaluation is the tool for this renewal.

Performance evaluation is not, and should never be a once-a-year activity. There should be periodic monitoring by department heads and divisions as well as periodic, quarterly, or semiannual evaluations of accomplishments versus expected results by the executive and/or strategic planning committee. Fine-tuning of implementation plans can then appropriately occur, and the organization can be alerted in early stages if strategies are running into difficulty.

To make the process come alive, recognition for accomplishment as well as rewards must be an intrinsic part of the process. Annual adjustments in salary and opportunities to participate in training programs and conferences ought to flow from the performance evaluation. The performance evaluation also frames the basis for human resource acquisition and termination.

Performance evaluation feeds the second year of the strategic process and all subsequent years thereafter as an ongoing mechanism for renewal. After the first year, most voluntary organizations find themselves fine-tuning their strategies and identifying new issues, to the point that 25 percent of their plan is adjusted annually. These adjustments are due in part to changes in the operating environment as well as to accomplishments of the organization.

CONCLUSIONS

As it has been enumerated the strategic process is both a process of planning and of management. It is the latest step in the evolutionary process of organizations' attempts to find a better way to manage themselves in times of turbulent environmental change. In very simple terms, it is the process of exploring the identification of where they want to go, by when, what they will need to get there, and what they expect to find when they get there. It is a great deal like planning a vacation trip.

The process should be tailored to meet the sophistication and the organizational culture of the organization and used as a device for guidance of both volunteers and professional staff.

The major end products of the strategic process are an identification of the areas requiring improvement or change, and thus the process forces decisions and actions, together with definitions of the resources required. Second, it begins to define the organizational structure and the climate that is needed to support the planning process. It embraces and builds responsbilities and commitment to a process and provides guidance for day-to-day operations.

Some of the common pitfalls that organizations find themselves in are (1) shelving the plan once it is completed; (2) failure to agree on the organization's objectives and strategies, (3) failure to build on "ownership" of the plan within the organization, (4) a tendency to be overly optimistic about goals and the ability to achieve them, (5) failure to plan for contingencies, (6) allowing the plan to become outdated, (7) a tendency to underestimate the time and the commitment required to make the planning process work, (8) lack of a commitment to the planning process by top professional and volunteers, (9) failure to integrate the strategic plans with the day-to-day operations, and (10) failure to define measurable goals for success.

The crucial aspect of the strategic process is to engage in it. Organizations sometimes continue to put it off because they say they don't have the time. This is a weak excuse and should be overcome by beginning the process, at least in a simple form. Work in subsequent years can refine the process and make it more sophisticated.

The major reason for engaging in the strategic process is to bring a culture of strategic thinking into the organization, to let it guide the everyday activities and to remind the organization that it lives in a broad environment that is changing, and that the organization must be attuned to that change and refine its programs and services as necessary.

CHAPTER *26*

Strategic Planning in the Military

JOHN H. CUSHMAN

JOHN H. CUSHMAN, Lieutenant General, U.S. Army, Retired, is a U.S. Military Academy graduate who in 1950 earned a Master of Science degree in Civil Engineering at the Massachusetts Institute of Technology. He has commanded the 101st Airborne Division and was in 1973–1976 Commandant of the U.S. Army's Command and General Staff College at Fort Leavenworth, Kansas. Before retiring from active service in 1978, he was for two years commander of the 200,000-man, 12-division, Korean-American force defending the western sector of Korea's Demilitarized Zone and the approaches to Seoul. Since leaving the Army, General Cushman has as a management consultant made use of his considerable experience as a military manager and has been a writer, teacher, and consultant on military command and control from the viewpoints of the operational user. He is a research affiliate of the Program on Information Resources Policy at Harvard University and has been a consultant to the Department of Defense Science Board, most recently as a member of a Task Force on the Military Application of New-Generation Computing Technologies. He is the author, for the Army War College, of the text *Organization and Operational Employment of Air/Land Forces*.

OUTLINE

The renowned nineteenth century philosopher of war Karl von Clausewitz wrote that "war does not belong in the realm of arts and sciences; rather it is part of man's social existence. . . . Rather than comparing [war] to an art, we could more accurately compare it to commerce. . . . the decision by arms is for all major and minor operations in war what cash payment is in commerce.[1]" Over the years (and consistent with these thoughts of Clausewitz), much of the language of war has been adopted by practitioners of commerce— the sales "campaign," the "battle" for market share, not to speak of "strategy" and "tactics." Such terms are not entirely inappropriate, even though the marketplace is not quite as unfriendly a place to operate as is the battlefield, and even though the costs of failure (though often high) are not quite as profound as are the consequences of losing a battle or war.

During the past few years, increasing interest has surfaced within the business community in military planning as a useful analog for corporate planners. Rather than just being *descriptive,* military terms (and their underlying concepts) have come to be viewed increasingly as of direct value to the process of strategic business planning.

One need not look far for signs of this interest in the military metaphor. Articles on the topic have appeared in business journals; the topic has been the focus of at least one recent book.[2] Most significantly, many of the leading management education firms have begun to offer seminars that promise to bring the lessons of the battlefield to the marketplace.

This chapter has been sparked by the existence of such interest. As such, it seeks both to explain the essence of "military strategic planning" and to demonstrate its commonalities with "corporate strategic planning."

A useful way to begin doing so, it would seem, would be by briefly outlining the organization of the Department of Defense.

THE BASIC STRUCTURE OF THE DEPARTMENT OF DEFENSE

Exhibit 26-1 shows the basic structure of the United States Department of Defense, the organization charged with responsibility for protecting and maintaining United States national security. More specifically, the figure outlines the relationships, the responsibilities, and the flow of authority within what is called the National Military Command Structure (NMCS).

It can be seen that within the U.S. Department of Defense and below the level of the Secretary of Defense and his immediate staff deputies and assistants, there are essentially two major groupings of organizations. First, on the right, are what we can call the *providers* of the military forces of the United States. These are the three military departments—the Departments of the Army, the Navy, and the Air Force. Within these departments are the military Services—the U.S. Army, the U.S. Air Force, and, in the single department of the Navy, both the U.S. Navy and the U.S. Marine Corps. We can call these the "providers" because their functions, as set forth in the statutes that govern the Department of Defense (the National Security Act of 1947, as amended), are the "preparation" of forces and those forces' "administration" and "support."

It should be emphasized that these "providers" are not responsible for the *employment* of the forces. Employment is the function of the second major grouping of organizations under the Secretary of Defense—the multiservice "combatant commands"—identified on the left in Exhibit 26-1 as "unified and specified commands."

These "provider" establishments are huge. Each has its military secretary, its service chief or chiefs, its departmental civilian and military staffs, and an immense substructure of commands and agencies, posts, camps, stations, air bases, arsenals, shipyards, hospitals, and so on. All of these are organized, coordinated, managed, and funded with public monies to accomplish the departmental task.

These headquarters staffs and their substructures do the research and development for new material; they develop and state the requirements for new weapons and equipment; and they produce the material or write contracts for its production. They store and issue the material, and they arrange for its repair parts and its maintenance. They organize units for combat and for the support of combat units, they write the doctrines for these units, and they train the units according to those doctrines. They bring men and women into the military service; they motivate these men and women, school them, promote them, pay them, keep their records, and reassign them.

And, in accordance with the directions of the Secretary of Defense and

EXHIBIT 26-1 The Structure of Defense Organization

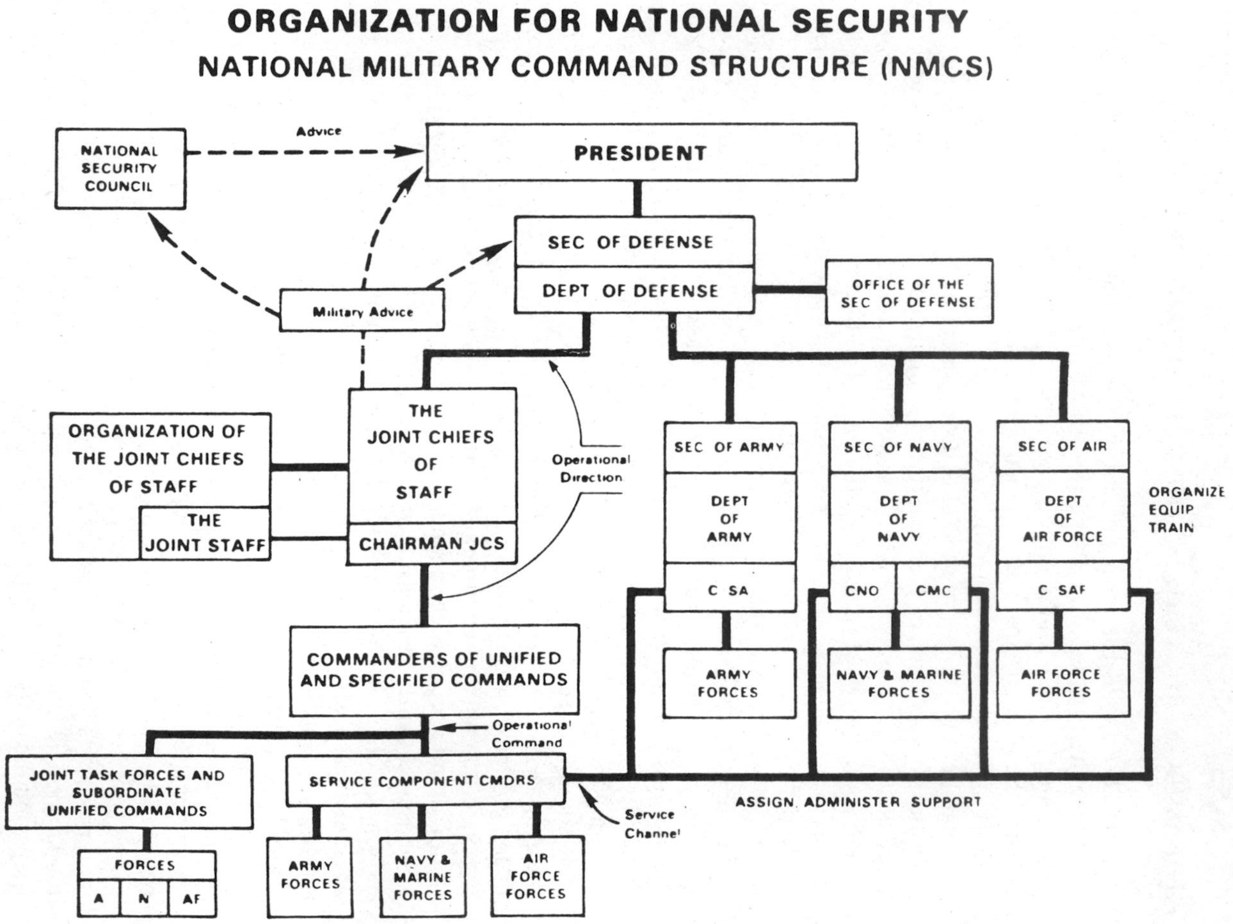

ORGANIZATION FOR NATIONAL SECURITY
NATIONAL MILITARY COMMAND STRUCTURE (NMCS)

his staff, and of the Joint Chiefs of Staff, these providers also assign the units (which they organize, train, and equip) to the combatant commands, for the latter to employ.

STRATEGIC PLANNING IN THE PROVIDER ESTABLISHMENT

Obviously, the major components of this provider establishment must engage in strategic planning. The military departments, the services within those departments, all the major subdivisions down in the subordinate structure— each must do what strategic planners always do. They must forecast the environment of the future. They must study the possibilities as to what they should do within that environment, so as to best accomplish their functions. They must decide what to do. And, they must make action plans to carry out those decisions.

Ben Tregoe (of Kepner-Tregoe in Princeton, New Jersey) has written both extensively and sensibly on "strategic planning." He says that many people confuse "strategic planning" with "long-range planning." He prefers to call this endeavor not "strategic *planning,*" but "strategic *thinking,*" in order to distinguish it from "long-range planning." Correctly thinking through an organization's "strategy" or "strategic approach" provides an objectively correct intellectual foundation for the long-range planning that stems there-from.[3]

The subject matter dealt with by the strategic planners (i.e., "top management doing strategic thinking," in Tregoe's formulation) in the provider establishments of the Department of Defense obviously differs from that of a major corporation engaged in strategic planning. But, the process—department by department and service by service—is not very different from that of corporate strategic planning/thinking.

However, this kind and level of strategic planning is not what most people seem to have in mind when they talk about "strategic planning in the military" or when they seek to define its relevance to corporate planning. Instead, their focus is more the operational employment of military forces and the planning related thereto.

WARFARE: THE SUBJECT MATTER OF THE OPERATIONAL MILITARY PLANNER

So, let us look instead at the planning requirements and methods of the *operational,* or employment, groups within the U.S. military, i.e., those shown on the left side of Exhibit 26-1.

This is *not* "strategic planning" or "strategic thinking" in the Ben Tregoe sense. What this chapter will describe, and what is done in the realm of military strategy and operations, we can call simply "military planning"—

or, to be more descriptively correct, "operational military planning on the grand scale." As such, it more closely resembles, in scope and general concerns, strategic business planning than does that done by the military's provider establishment.

The people who perform this type of planning are, by and large, in field commands. They are military officers, ranging from the most senior to the middle ranks, e.g., down to major or lieutenant commander. Most importantly, they are practicing a military craft.

These officers are, or should be, professionals. The methods that they use have evolved from decades, even centuries, of field experience and from countless hours of research, writing, and teaching at the staff colleges and war colleges of their profession. The methods have been proven to work, when properly applied, again and again. What is the subject matter of this (and here we no longer call it "strategic") planning? Its subject matter is *warfare*—the employment of force and military assets to achieve specified objectives.

DOMAINS OF WARFARE

We can look at warfare in three domains. There is "strategic warfare," and, here, "strategic" has an entirely different meaning from "strategy" as used above, a meaning more akin to "intercontinental." This is warfare fought by the long-range bombers and missiles of the U.S. Strategic Air Command and the Navy's Trident submarines with their Poseidon missiles at sea, and by the U.S. and Canadian forces of the North American Air Defense Command.

There is "maritime warfare," or warfare fought by the U.S. Navy and allied fleet operating forces, including their accompanying amphibious forces such as those of the U.S. Marine Corps. And, then, there is what we can call "theater warfare" (which can also be called "air/land" or "air/land/ sea" warfare), which takes place on the land, in the envelope of air above the land, and on or over the land's waters, either contained or adjacent. Theater warfare is usually a combination of "air warfare" and "air/land" warfare, and in many cases includes "sea warfare" or "maritime warfare."

The 1944 Normandy invasion and General Eisenhower's following campaigns into the heart of Hitler's Europe are an example of "theater warfare." The naval campaigns westward from Pearl Harbor toward the Philippines in 1942 and 1943 are examples of "maritime" or "sea" warfare. We have no historical examples of "strategic warfare," and we devoutly pray and ceaselessly work so that there will never be any.

LEVELS OF WARFARE

We can also think of war on three conceptual levels: strategy, operations, and tactics. Strategy was once defined as the process of bringing forces onto the battlefield. As such, it can be seen as the "where" and the "what" of war—deciding where the military forces are to be employed and what they are to do. It is, in essence, the determination and the setting forth of the basic goals of warfare.

Strategy is the province of decision makers and planners at the seat of government. It was the sort of thinking that the British and American military staffs did immediately after Pearl Harbor, when fundamental decisions were being made by President Roosevelt and Prime Minister Churchill about the relative priorities of the wars against Germany and Japan, and about where and how the major campaigns would be undertaken.

Strategy can also be the province of the top commander in a theater of war, as it was for MacArthur in the Pacific in World War II when he conceived his island-hopping campaigns. It was again his province in the Korean War, where in August 1950 with his back to the wall in the Pusan perimeter he made the strategic decision to land at Inchon in September.

The "operational level" of warfare, or "operations" in the military lexicon, encompasses the use of military means—land, sea, and air forces—to attain the goals of strategy within a theater of war. Essentially, this level involves the theory and the practice of planning and executing larger unit operations.

The operational level is the province of senior commanders in the theater, of tactical air forces in the air chain of command, and of the fleets in naval formations. These are generally senior officers of four-, three-, and two-star rank.

Operations and strategy, as defined above are closely linked. When well-conceived, each reinforces the other. The Inchon landing was a brilliant strategic decision, but it required an equally remarkable operations accomplishment to make it happen.

"Operations" then links with the third level, which is "tactics." Tactics is the province of the brigade, battalion, and company commanders in land warfare, of the wing, squadron, and flight leaders and individual airmen in air warfare, and of the battle group and lower formations (down to the individual ships) in naval warfare. And, as noted, if tactical competence is not there, any operational scheme is in jeopardy regardless of its conceptual excellence.

THE SCOPE OF MILITARY OPERATIONAL PLANNING

Military operational planning on the grand scale (for example, the planning for the 1944 invasion of Normandy) involves the setting of goals, the organizing of the forces, the ordering of campaigns, the development and perfection of operational and tactical concepts, and so on. It also involves what we can call "logistics" or, more accurately, "administration" (or, inaccurately, "administration and logistics").

Logistics encompasses all those supporting and sustaining activities through which the operating forces are supplied, maintained, moved, based, sheltered, and serviced; those through which their personnel strength and fitness are maintained; and those through which the personal needs of their people are taken care of.

In this one word—logistics—there is involved what to an outsider must seem a bewildering array of systems and activities. There is the resupply of everything from food and medicine to tank engines and radiator hoses, from diesel and aviation fuel, to aircraft engines for land- and sea-based air forces, to rifle, naval gun, and artillery ammunition, and on and on in endless number and detail. There are repair and maintenance needs, in equal detail and complexity. There is transportation by truck, rail, boat, ship, and air. There are housing and troop assembly, storage and transfer, sea and aerial port operation, hospitalization and medical evacuation. There is the pay, discipline, welfare, and personnel administration of each soldier, sailor, or airman, and the providing of replacement personnel and crews for those who may be killed or wounded. The planning and managed execution of this extraordinarily complex, vibrant, and dynamic array of logistics activity is an art and science of its own.

Military operational planning on the grand scale often also involves what is called "campaign planning." Campaign planning is the process of research, study, thought, and writing through which the commander of a major force (with his staff) produces the scheme of action for a campaign. A campaign is essentially a series of related military operations to be undertaken toward a specific military objective or outcome and to be conducted over a period of time (usually weeks or months) in a theater of operations or in part of a theater of operations.

Generally, a *war* can be looked at as comprising at least one (and usually several) *campaigns,* separated in time or space or in both time and space. These campaigns, collectively and in sequence, are undertaken toward the war's objective, with each campaign encompassing a number of *battles,* and the battles being made up of many battalion- and brigade-sized *engagements*.

Under contemporary conditions, engagements (and perhaps even some battles) can be visualized as pure "land combat" in which tactical air or naval forces are not involved. But, it is not possible in today's world to visualize in a theater of operations a purely "land campaign." Thus campaign planning must of necessity be "air/land" or "air/land/sea" campaign planning. Likewise, almost without exception, forces will engage in military operations alongside and in conjunction with forces of allied nations. Campaign planning is thus almost always done in a multiservice and multinational framework.

The content of a campaign plan generally follows the well-understood and accepted sequence of the "operations plan/order," the components of which are:

The situation (the enemy, our own forces, the area of operations, political/economic/social considerations, etc.)

The mission

The task organization (the subordinate command entities of the land, sea, air, or multiservice forces, and their organization for combat and support)

The concept of operations (the intent of the plan and the basic methods through which that intent and the plan's objectives are to be achieved)

Tasks for subordinate organizations

Administration and logistics

Command and control arrangements

TOOLS OF THE MILITARY PLANNING CRAFT

The format outlined above is one of the tools of the military professional's craft—the "operations order." Since time immemorial, military commanders have issued orders. But it was not until the beginning of the nineteenth century, when the Prussian General Staff with its school for staff officers began to take shape, that military men began to have practical statements concerning the theory of staff organization and duties, and of commander-staff relationships and responsibilities. At that time, there also began to evolve the logical sequence and standard format of the commander's orders. Along with that, there began development of the logical thought sequence that could assist a commander and staff in arriving at what should be the *content* of such orders.

In our own country, the late nineteenth century saw the emergence of a school system in both the Army and Navy for the professional education and training of staff officers and commanders. The military reforms within the Army and Navy following the experience of the Spanish-American War (with its poor staff work and confused operations) led to the establishment of the General Staff within the War Department and a Chief of Naval Operations with his operational staff within the Department of the Navy.

The American Expeditionary Force in France in 1917 and 1918 was well served by staff officers who had been trained at the Command and General Staff School, established by the Army in the early 1900s at Fort Leavenworth, Kansas. Then, in the two peacetime decades between World Wars I and II, the theory and practice of professional command and staff methods were perfected at Fort Leavenworth, the Army War College, and the Naval War College.

For the waging of World War II, the armed forces of the United States expanded from some quarter of a million men in the late 1930s to about 50 times that number at the war's end. They engaged in operations on a grand scale, from the campaigns in Europe and the Southwest Pacific to the Pacific Ocean's naval campaigns. They launched invasions from North Africa and Normandy to Leyte and Okinawa. That American armed forces were able to do all this so well was in large part because of the training American officers had received in the school systems developed between the wars, and because of the standardized methods that these schools had developed.

During the war and after, many of these concepts of military organization and procedure found their way into the business schools of America.

Since 1945, as warfare has become increasingly complex, the "tools of the military professional's craft" have been further developed and refined within the military services and at their staff and war colleges. An Armed Forces Staff College has been established; it has published a *Joint Staff Officers Guide*.

THE ESTIMATE OF THE SITUATION

In what we have called "military operational planning on the grand scale," the first and fundamental intellectual challenge posed to the commander and his staff is this: Given my mission, what do I do? Desirably, the commander will be provided with a clear-cut statement of his mission; but often, a commander will be forced to formulate his mission in his own words, based on both the implied and explicit instructions he has received.

The estimate of the situation (see Exhibit 26-2) is the established process of logical thought through which a commander and his staff officers proceed from the statement of the command mission to a decision as to how to accomplish that mission. As such, the estimate of the situation is simply a structured approach to the five-step problem-solving process that is so well-known to planners and decision makers:

Step 1: Recognition of the problem
Step 2: Collection of necessary information
Step 3: Development of possible solutions
Step 4: Analysis and comparison of these solutions
Step 5: Selection of the best solution

The titles of the paragraphs in the standardized estimate and the subject matter in each paragraph are shown in the flow chart in Exhibit 26-3, which is used in instruction at the Army's Command and General Staff College. This format has stood the test of time; it has been essentially unchanged since the 1920s.

The estimate is ubiquitous, and has been adapted for various staff purposes. For example, in the U.S. Army's 1984 edition of its Field Manual 101-5, *Staff Organization and Operations,* there are also examples of the estimates made by the G1 (Personnel), the G2 (Intelligence), the G4 (Logistics), and the G5 (Civil-Military Operations) staff officers—all of which contribute to the development of the commander's estimate. There are also formats for a "deception estimate," a "psychological operations estimate," and an "operations security estimate." But the key estimate—and the format of most interest to the strategic planner in any walk of life—is the "commander's estimate" just described.

EXHIBIT 26-2   Estimate of the Situation

MISSION	COURSES OF ACTION
● What must be done and when?	● What *general* ways are there to use these forces on this terrain to accomplish this mission?
SITUATION	**ANALYSIS OF COURSES OF ACTION**
● What enemy forces oppose and where are they?	● What can be gained and what may be lost in each of these ways?
● What is the terrain and how can it be used?	**COMPARISON OF COURSES OF ACTION**
	● Which of these ways is best in this situation?
● What forces are available?	**DECISION AND CONCEPT**
● What are other friendly forces doing?	● What must be the scheme of maneuver, organization, and plan for fire support to best accomplish this mission with least damage to the force?
● What are the effects of weather and visibility?	

THE STAFF STUDY

For administrative and management problems, rather than problems of an operations nature, the staff tool known as the "staff study" is often used. As described in the Armed Forces Staff College's *Joint Staff Officers Guide,* the staff study is flexible in content and in the range of problems to which it may be applied. It may be the work of one officer, done in a day or less, or of a group that takes a month or more. The staff study is not simply a dressed-up staff memorandum. Its correct use requires time, effort, and research. It should be reserved for complex or controversial questions. To use the staff study for each small problem that confronts the staff is to waste time and effort.

The first words of a staff study should be a concise, accurate *statement of the problem.* This is often the most difficult part of the staff study to write. It may require rephrasing as the study progresses. Correctly stated, this provides a foundation for all that follows.

The staff study's second part is *assumptions.* Although assumptions are dangerous in staff work, they may be needed in order to treat the problem logically. They are written down to set assumptions apart from what are known to be facts, and to insure that any assumptions are made known to the reader. Then come the facts bearing on the problem. To list every fact related to the study is too lengthy a process; but it is useful to cite those facts that need to be highlighted.

The *discussion* is the heart of the staff study. It is where two, three, or perhaps four workable alternative solutions to the problem are described, their advantages and disadvantages are discussed, and logical comparisons are made. The *conclusion* presents the solution to the problem. It follows logically from the discussion, essentially restating the superior solution.

Finally comes the *recommendation,* which described how the conclusion

EXHIBIT 26-3   Military Planning Process

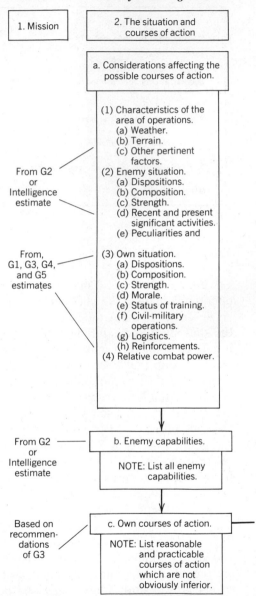

will be put into effect. Desirably, the recommendation will be in the form of a letter or decision memorandum that the commander or other authority will simply sign.

Once again, note the similarity of the staff study to the classic problem-solving process: recognition of the problem, collection of data, development of possible solutions, analysis and comparison, and selection of the best solution.

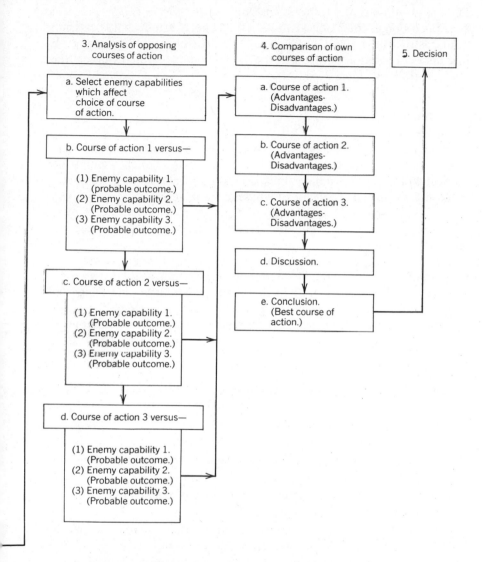

OTHER PLANNING TOOLS

There are other "tools of the craft" of the military staff officer that may be of interest to strategic business planners. There is, for example, the full process of "deliberate planning" in joint (i.e., more than one military service) commands, with its five steps: initiation, concept development, plan development, plan review, and, finally, supporting plans.

The full kit of these tools is described in two publications. One of these can be ordered from the U.S. Government Printing Office. It is Field Manual 101-5, 25 May 1984, Headquarters, Department of the Army, *Staff Organ-*

ization and Operations. The other is the *Joint Staff Officers Guide*, published by the Armed Forces Staff College as its AFSC Pub 1. Although it is classified as "For Instructional Use Only," it may be possible to obtain a copy by writing on a corporate letterhead to the Commandant, Armed Forces Staff College, Norfolk, Virginia 23511.

NOT BY TOOLS ALONE

In reading a recitation (such as that above) of the tools of the commander's and staff officer's craft, it is easy to lose sight of a fundamental point: not by intellectual tools and planning skills alone—important as these may be— does the soldier, airman, or sailor of whatever rank achieve success in war, but by such intangibles as tactical skill, determination, will, and the "fighting heart" (urge to dominate the enemy). Traits such as these are the decisive components of victory in war.

I cited Clausewitz earlier, noting his comparison of war to commerce. But, people of commerce would be better advised to look at this comparison the other way around. Especially in the highly competitive and dangerous business world of today, *commerce can and should be compared to war*.

It is useful to review the U.S. Army's summary of the "Principles of War" and, as one does, to think about how they can be translated to the world of commerce:

1. *Objective.*   Every military operation should be directed toward a clearly defined, decisive, and attainable objective.
2. *Offensive.*   Seize, retain, and exploit the initiative.
3. *Mass.*   Concentrate combat power at the decisive place and time.
4. *Economy of Force.*   Allocate minimum essential combat power to secondary efforts.
5. *Maneuver.*   Place the enemy in a position of disadvantage through the flexible application of combat power.
6. *Unity of Command.*   For every objective, there should be unity of effort under one responsible commander.
7. *Security.*   Never permit the enemy to acquire an unexpected advantage.
8. *Surprise.*   Strike the enemy at a time or place and in a manner for which he is unprepared.
9. *Simplicity.*   Prepare clear, uncomplicated plans and clear, concise orders to insure thorough understanding.

GEMS FROM GREAT MILITARY THINKERS

Similarly valuable, and stimulating, are some gems of thought from those who have either waged or studied war.

Clausewitz

The absolute, the mathematical as it is called, nowhere finds any sure basis in the calculations in the Art of War; . . . from the outset there is a play of possibilities, probabilities, good and bad luck, which spreads about with all the coarse and fine threads of its web, and makes War of all branches of human activity the most like a gambling game.

Great part of information obtained in War is contradictory, a still greater part is false, and by far the greater part is of doubtful character. What is required of an officer is a certain power of discrimination, which only knowledge of men and things and good judgment can give.[4]

Sun Tzu

Now the general who wins a battle makes many calculations in his temple ere the battle is fought. The general who loses a battle makes but a few calculations beforehand.

If you know the enemy and know yourself, you need not fear the result of a hundred battles.[5]

Pericles

What I fear is not the enemy's strategy, but our own mistakes.[6]

Frederick the Great

It is necessary to put oneself in the place of the enemy and say: What would I do? What project could I form? Then examine all these projects, and above all reflect on the means to avoid them.[7]

John Paul Jones

The sources of success are ever to be found in the fountains of quick resolve and swift stroke. . . . .He who will not risk cannot win.[8]

Napoleon

To keep your forces united, to be vulnerable at no point, to bear down with rapidity upon important points—these are the principles which insure victory.[9]

Henderson, on Stonewall Jackson

Not a single one of his maneuvers but was based on a close and judicial survey of the situation. Every risk was weighed. Nothing was left to chance. . . . His soldiers said that "he knew every hole and corner of the [Shenandoah] Valley as if he had made it himself."[10]

Douglas MacArthur, on Ghengis Khan

He devised an organization appropriate to conditions then existing; he raised the discipline and the morale of his troops to a level never known in any army, unless possibly that of Cromwell; he spent every available period of peace to develop subordinate leaders and to produce perfection of training throughout the army, and, finally, he insisted upon speed in action, a speed which in comparison with other forces of his day was almost unbelievable. . . . Over great distances his legions moved so rapidly and secretly as to astound his enemies and practically to paralyze their powers of resistance.[11]

Erwin Rommel

It is my experience that bold decisions give the best chance of success. . . . Even [when a commander's forces are so superior that victory is a foregone conclusion], I still think it is better to operate on the grand scale rather than to creep about the battlefield anxiously taking all possible security measures against every conceivable enemy move.

Normally, there is no ideal solution to military problems; every course has its advantages and disadvantages. One must select that which seems best from the most varied aspects and then pursue it resolutely and accept the consequences.[12]

George S. Patton, Jr.

In carrying out a mission, the promulgation of the order represents not over ten percent of your responsibility. The remaining ninety percent consists in assuring by means of personal supervision on the ground, by yourself and your staff, proper and vigorous execution. . . .

Plans must be simple and flexible. Actually they only form a datum plane from which you build as necessity directs or opportunity offers. They should be made by the people who are going to execute them. . . .

You can never have too much reconnaissance. Use every means available before, during, and after battle. Reports must be facts, not opinions, negative as well as positive. . . .

Information is like eggs: the fresher the better.[13]

THE STARTING POINT: UNDERSTANDING THE SITUATION

Let us tie together the essence of the preceding quotations with what was said earlier about the tools of the professional military craft.

It is no coincidence that in each of the tools—the operations plan/order, the estimate, the staff study—describing the situation is either the first or second step. It is also no coincidence that the most skilled of commanders have always sought, above all, to understand the situation. That process is illustrated by Exhibit 26-4.

In war, as in commerce, everything depends on correctly understanding

EXHIBIT 26-4   *Holistic Dynamics of Battle*

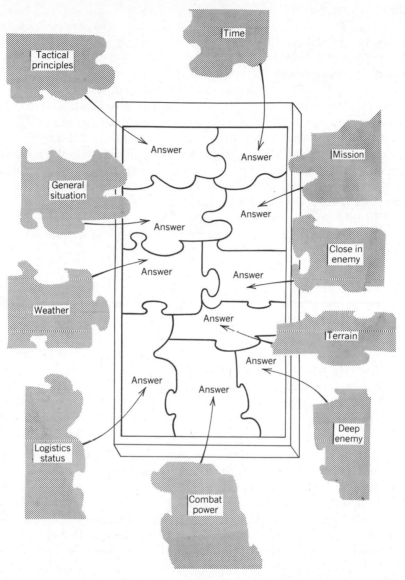

the situation. If you understand the situation, decisions are easy. If you do not understand the situation, whatever you decide to do will be right only by accident.

There are two components to understanding the situation: (1) gathering information—information that is accurate, timely, complete and germane to the situation at hand, and (2) interpreting that information with insight and judgment. To Sun Tsu, who wrote 2500 years ago, or to George S. Patton in 1944, the lesson was clear: *information is power.*

THE BUSINESS COMMUNITY'S INTEREST IN COMPETITOR INTELLIGENCE

Here is how intelligence works in war.

In war the real situation lies out there on the battlefield: the terrain, the weather, the population, the resources, our own forces, and, most particularly, the enemy—determined to thwart us or to do us in.

Commanders seek to know that situation and to understand it and its dynamics and direction. So, commanders and their staffs gather information, and they correlate what they gather, and they assemble all this into a picture in their minds. And, of all the minds, the most important is the mind of the commander, because he is the one who must decide what to do. Consider only the enemy. In war the real enemy lies out there in a situation which we can call The Truth—that which actually is. The commander in war fights to obtain that Truth with every means at his disposal. Here is how "The Truth" (or a perception of it) gets into the mind of the commander or his intelligence officer:

1. Pieces of The Truth—what is actually out there—are observed (sometimes inaccurately) by sensors (directed by someone) and by other sources (e.g., deep patrols), also directed by someone. So, skill in deploying and directing sensors and other sources is essential. The military man calls this "collection management"—developing and carrying out the "collection plan."

2. Through various communications, such as down-links from overhead collectors, and so on (any of which may be in war blocked by an enemy or by other actions), these pieces of information are reported. Thus, reliable and accurate communications are also essential.

3. The information is reported to commanders, to operations centers, and to intelligence assessment or "fusion" centers, where people assign credibility values and meanings to what is reported, combine it with other information already reported, think about it, draw conclusions, share their conclusions, and make necessary decisions. Here, insight and judgment enter the equation. The question is not simply, What is the situation? The question is also, What do we make of it?

The perception that the commander forms in this way becomes the basis for his actions. That perception begins to resemble The Truth, if and when:

The commander and his intelligence officer energetically and skillfully seek information, spurring on their sources and sensors to find the facts and report them quickly and accurately.

The sensors and sources do their jobs well.

Information is moved quickly and well.

Relevant information is recognized and properly correlated.

The assessment—that is, the analysis and judgments—is good.

And, if the resulting perception closely matches the Truth as to what is out there, the commander, as Sun Tzu said 2500 years ago, "in a hundred battles, will never be in peril."

Does that sound like a recipe for success in the world of business? The only real difference seems to be that in the military world there is only the enemy as a thinking "competitor," while in the world of commerce there are usually multiple competitors, all operating in the same real situation. Looking at competition this way makes it easy to understand the business community's natural interest in what is coming to be known as "business competitor intelligence."

ACTION IS THE NAME OF THE GAME

In business, as in war, the process of competitor intelligence is only the first step. If results are to flow from this effort, there must be *action*. It might be useful to conclude the final chapter in this collection on strategic planning, by trying to convey to those in the business world some current ideas of those in the military world on how to make successful *action* take place in the battlefield.

We say that the essence of the operational art is, first of all, a grasp of warfare as a duel; second, a thorough understanding of what goes on in the dynamics of the battlefield; third, the ability of the commander to think in terms of the harmonious orchestration of time, space, force, and logistics toward his ends; then gathering information and deciding what to do; and, finally, getting it done.

We say that to the seasoned and skilled operational commander with reasonably good information, deciding what to do is the easiest part. The difficult part is to get it done—especially to get done that "supereffort" which, if made to take place in the way visualized, will bring the enemy to his knees right there in the battlefield.

And so, we say that the operational art is, thus, more than just thinking. It is fighting for information. It is doing. Its most skilled practitioners are men of thought and at the same time men of action.

And we summarize by saying that skill in warfare if possessed by that commander who, having the combative instincts and urge to dominate the enemy that can be called the "fighting heart,":

Understands the situation

Can visualize "what will happen if . . .."

Grasps risks and opportunities in their true perspectives

Has that tactical insight that leads him unerringly to what to do

Has in his hands the means of control to make the right things happen
Drives on to make those things happen, motivating his force and keeping
track of the situation as it moves.

That may be one way for those who read this to keep "strategic planning
in the military" in its right perspective.

NOTES

1. *On War,* by Karl von Clausewitz. Edited and translated by Michael Howard and Peter
    Paret, pp. 97, 148–149.
2. E.g., P. Kotler and R. Singh, "Marketing Warfare in the 1980's," *Journal of Business
    Strategy,* Winter 1981, pp. 30–41; William Peacock, *Corporate Combat: The Application
    of Military Strategy and Tactics to Business Competition,* Facts on File, New York, 1984.
3. B. Tregoe and J. W. Zimmerman, *Top Management Strategy,* Simon & Schuster, New
    York, 1980.
4. Carl Von Clausewitz, *On War* (London: Pelican Books, 1968), pp. 117, 162.
5. Sun Tzu, *The Art of War,* cited in Thomas R. Phillips, *Roots of Strategy* (Harrisburg, PA:
    The Military Service Publishing Co., 1940), pp. 23, 28.
6. Thucydides, *History of the Peloponnesian War,* cited in B. H. Liddell Hart, *The Sword
    and the Pen,* Thomas Y. Crowell, New York, 1976, p. 24.
7. Frederick the Great, *Memoirs,* ibid., p. 114.
8. John Paul Jones, letter to Vice-Admiral Kersaint, 1791, ibid., p. 139.
9. Napoleon Bonaparte, 77 Maxim, cited in *Jomini, Clausewitz, and Schlieffen,* Department
    of Military Art and Engineering, U.S. Military Academy, West Point, N.Y., 1943, p. 91.
10. G. F. Henderson, *Stonewall Jackson,* cited in Liddell Hart, *The Sword and the Pen,* p.
    233.
11. Douglas MacArthur, *Annual Report of the Chief of Staff for the Fiscal Year June 30,
    1935,* cited in Liddell Hart (ibid.), p. 283.
12. B. H. Liddell Hart, *The Rommel Papers,* Harcourt, Brace, New York, 1953, p. 201.
13. George S. Patton, Jr., *War as I Knew It,* Houghton Mifflin, Boston, 1947, p. 397. The
    quotation is from a letter of instructions to his commanders before the invasion of Nor-
    mandy.

Index